Robert Franklin Williams Speaks

Robert Franklin Williams Speaks

A Documentary History

Edited with an Introduction
by Ronald J. Stephens

Anthem Press
An imprint of Wimbledon Publishing Company
www.anthempress.com

This edition first published in UK and USA 2024
by ANTHEM PRESS
75–76 Blackfriars Road, London SE1 8HA, UK
or PO Box 9779, London SW19 7ZG, UK
and
244 Madison Ave #116, New York, NY 10016, USA

© 2024 Ronald J. Stephens editorial matter and selection;
individual chapters © individual contributors

The moral right of the authors has been asserted.

All rights reserved. Without limiting the rights under copyright reserved above,
no part of this publication may be reproduced, stored or introduced into a retrieval
system, or transmitted, in any form or by any means (electronic, mechanical, photocopying,
recording or otherwise), without the prior written permission of both the copyright owner
and the above publisher of this book.

British Library Cataloguing-in-Publication Data
A catalogue record for this book is available from the British Library.

Library of Congress Cataloging-in-Publication Data: 2023948201
A catalog record for this book has been requested.

ISBN-13: 978-1-83998-457-0 (Hbk)
ISBN-10: 1-83998-457-0 (Hbk)

Cover Credit: Walter P. Reuther Library, Wayne State University

This title is also available as an e-book.

I pray Robert and Mabel Williams are smiling from above and resting in peace knowing my coverage of their legacy and experiences in the Black freedom struggle lives on. Their advocacy and activism to liberate America and save the world should never be forgotten. Robert F. Williams was a patriot, a flexible pragmatist, and a champion who agitated to preserve the human dignity and rights of African Americans. Rob's ethical convictions and moral stance were profound. Robert F. Williams, my hero, devoted his life unapologetically to the betterment of human civilization and future generations.

CONTENTS

Dedication	v
List of Photographs and Illustrations	xiii
Acknowledgments	xix
Prologue	xxi

PART I   1

Introduction   3

Roots, Racism, Routes, and Resistance: Robert and Mabel Williams's Take on Patrick Henry's "Give Me Liberty or Give Me Death"   3
- *Racism, Rights, and Resistance: Robert and Mabel Williams in the Newtown Community*   5
- *Sankofa vs Communism: Robert and Mabel Williams Navigating Castroism and Maoism*   12
- *Returning to the States, Resigning from the RNA, Navigating China and Racism in the United States, by Championing Civil and Human Rights in Lake County, Michigan*   22

PART II   31

Chapter 1   MONROE, NORTH CAROLINA, 1955–1961   37

Sermon Delivered at All Soul's Chapel Unitarian Fellowship, MONROE, NORTH CAROLINA, Sunday, March 25, 1956   41

NAACP Findings and Recommendations in Hearing on Robert Williams Before Committee on Branches, June 3 and 8, 1959   45
North Carolina State Conference of Branches   49
Letter to Gloster B. Current from Charles A. McLean, June 15, 1959   49
Crusaders for Freedom Press Release   51
The Monroe Program   52
Robert F. Williams, Letter-to-the-editor   53

John Schultz's Interview with Robert Williams in Chicago, February 1961   56

Testimonies of Robert and Mabel Williams   67
- *Testimony of Robert F. Williams in the Case, State of North Carolina versus Richard Crowder, Harold Reape, John Lowry, and Mae Mallory, August 27, 1961*   67
- *Testimony of Mabel R. Williams in the Case, State of North Carolina versus Richard Crowder, Harold Reape, John Lowry, and Mae Mallory, August 27, 1961*   69

Letters to Robert F. Williams 70
Roy Wilkins Writes to Robert Williams, May 8, 1959 70
Ray and Gilessa Write to Robert Williams, May 23, 1961 71
Letter to Mae Mallory from Robert and Mabel Williams, May 26, 1961 72

Chapter 2   HAVANA, CUBA, 1960–1966 73

- *Williams Hails Cuban Military Might, January 3, 1962* 77
- *Robert Williams Interviews a South African* 79

Robert Williams States Afro-American Struggle Is Bound to Triumph, September 27, 1963 80

Robert Williams Discusses First Trip to China During Radio Interview in Peking, October 22, 1963 82

- *Afro-American Internationalist Robert Williams Discusses U.S. Imperialism and Failures in Johnson's War Economy, November 17, 1964* 82
- *Williams Speaks about the Great Thought of Mao Tse-Tung Who He Characterizes as Transforming the Whole World, 1964* 83
- *Robert Williams Speaks at the International Conference for Solidarity with the People of Vietnam against U.S. Imperialist Aggression for the Defense of Peace, Hanoi, Democratic Republic of Vietnam, November 25–29, 1965* 84

Statements by Robert F. Williams 88

- *Robert Williams States "Let Us Bury the Yankee," October 30, 1962* 88
- *Robert Williams States "No Freedom in U.S. for Afro-American," November 17, 1962* 88
- *Williams Sends Protest Statement to Kennedy, September 27, 1963* 89
- *Williams Holds Press Conference in Peking to Discuss His Impressions of China and the Chinese People, November 13, 1963* 90
- *Williams Makes International Appeal to End Savage Brutality in Racist White America Against Black Humanity, March 15, 1965* 91
- *Williams Delivers Remarks to U.S. Afro-American Servicemen, March 17, 1965* 92
- *Williams Speaks on Freedom Now or Death, December 18, 1965* 93

Letters Exchanged between Richard Gibson and Robert Williams, and Letters by Gibson to His Marxist-Leninist Comrades Tore Hokason and Leon Leopoldo about Williams 94

- *Robert Williams Writes to Richard Gibson, September 7, 1965* 94
- *Richard Gibson Writes to Robert Williams, September 20, 1965* 94
- *Richard Gibson Writes to Robert Williams, October 14, 1965* 96
- *Robert Williams Writes to Richard Gibson, November 23, 1965* 97
- *Richard Gibson Writes to Robert Williams, December 8, 1965* 98
- *Richard Gibson Writes to Tore Hokason, December 8, 1965* 98
- *Richard Gibson Writes to Robert Williams, December 26, 1965* 99
- *Robert Williams Writes to Richard Gibson, January 14, 1966* 99
- *Richard Gibson Writes to Tore Hokason, February 1, 1966* 100

CONTENTS

- *Richard Gibson Writes to Robert Williams, February 1, 1966* — 100
- *Richard Gibson Writes to Robert Williams, May 2, 1966* — 101
- *Richard Gibson Writes to Leon Leopoldo, June 20, 1966* — 102
- *Richard Gibson Writes to Leon Leopoldo, July 18, 1966* — 103

FBI/CIA Memorandum Identifying Richard T. Gibson as an Informant, March 10, 1966 — 105

Chapter 3   PEKING, CHINA, 1963–1969 — 107

Letter to Fidel Castro from Robert F. Williams — 110

Letter to Fidel Castro from Robert F. Williams in Peking, China, August 28, 1966 — 110

- *To All Individuals, Parties, and Groups Concerned by Robert F. Williams, August 1, 1967* — 122

Speeches by Robert F. Williams — 123

- *Speech Deliverd at the International Conference for Solidarity with the People of Vietnam against U.S. Imperialist Aggression for the Defense of Peace, Hanoi, Democratic Republic of Vietnam, November 25–29, 1965* — 124
- *During Beijing (Peking) Demonstration Robert F. Williams Condemns Racial Discrimination in the U.S. and Encourages Support for Afro-Americans to Use Revolutionary Violence, August 8, 1966* — 127
- *Robert F. Williams Speaks on the Third Anniversary of Chairman Mao* — 133
- *Letter to Lawrence F. O'Brien, U.S. Postmaster General, September 21, 1967* — 140
- *Letter to North Carolina's Legal Counsel about the Kidnapping Case, December 2, 1967* — 140
- *Letter to Brindley Benn, May 18, 1969* — 141

FBI/CIA-RDP75 Memorandum about Richard Gibson and Robert F. Williams — 141

- *Richard Gibson Reports International News Report about Robert F. Williams Second Exile, October 15, 1966* — 141
- *Sugar's Alleged Involvement with the Revolutionary Action Movement, October 11, 1966* — 145

Letters between Richard T. Gibson and Robert F. Williams — 145

- *Richard Gibson Writes to Comrade, October 15, 1966* — 145
- *Robert Williams Writes to Richard Gibson, October 17, 1966* — 147
- *Richard Gibson Writes to Robert Williams, October 21, 1966* — 147
- *Richard Gibson Writes to Robert Williams, October 28, 1966* — 148
- *Richard Gibson Writes to Robert Williams, November 18, 1966* — 149
- *Robert Williams Writes to Richard Gibson, February 27, 1967* — 150
- *Richard Gibson Writes to Robert Williams, March 18, 1967* — 150
- *Robert Williams Writes to Richard Gibson, March 27, 1967* — 151
- *Robert Williams Writes to Richard Gibson, April 17, 1967* — 152
- *Robert Williams Writes to Richard Gibson, May 17, 1967* — 152
- *Robert Williams Writes to Richard Gibson, May 24, 1967* — 153
- *Richard Gibson Writes to Robert Williams, January 27, 1968* — 153

- *Richard Gibson Writes to Robert Williams, April 6, 1968* — 155
- *Richard Gibson Writes to Robert Williams, April 13, 1968* — 155
- *Robert Williams writes Richard Gibson, June 25, 1969* — 157
- *Richard Gibson Writes to Robert Williams, June 28, 1969* — 157

Statement by Afro-American Leader in Exile to American Servicemen in South Vietnam, February, 1966 — 160

Statement by Richard T. Gibson about King's Assassination and the Swedish Government's Banning of Williams Proposed Visit, April 6, 1968 — 161

Statement by Milton R. Henry about Williams' Return to Detroit, September 12, 1969 — 161

Letter from Brother Imari Obadele, RNA Minister of Information to Robert Williams, April 5, 1968 — 162

- *Robert Williams Is Interviewed by Viewpoint* — 163

Williams's Return Announcement Letter, May 18, 1969 — 168

Chapter 4   DETROIT AND ANN ARBOR, MICHIGAN, 1969–1972 — 171

Letters Between S. Abdullah Schleifer and Robert Williams
- *S. Abdullah Schleifer Writes to Robert F. Williams, February 1971* — 175
- *Robert Williams Writes to Marc Schleifer, August 11, 1971* — 176

Statement in Support of Robert F. Williams from 10,000 Japanese Citizens against North Carolina Extradition Charges, 1977 — 180

- *The Black Scholar Interviews: Robert F. Williams, Recorded on April 23, 1970, and Published May 1970* — 221
- *Robert F. Williams Interviewed by U.S. Students for the Marxist Leninist Quarterly, 1972* — 234

DOJ FBI Summary Report, November 12, 1969 — 246

Legacy of Resistance: Tributes to Robert and Mabel Williams, October 25, 1996 — 247
- *John C. Williams, Words Are Inadequate to Express My Love* — 247
- *Charles E. Simmons, Memorial: A Legacy of Resistance* — 247
- *Ron Scott* — 248
- *Yoriko NaKAJIMA* — 248
- *Grace Lee Boggs, the Crusader* — 248
- *Mary L. Trucks, Robert Williams, My Hero* — 248
- *Muhammad Ahmed, Rob Lives! Tribute to a Great African American* — 249
- *Internationalist Freedom Fighter* — 249
- *Gwendolyn Midlo Hall, Few Americans Understand* — 251
- *Luke Tripp, Ora Williams Sweeting* — 251

CONTENTS

Chapter 5 BALDWIN, MICHIGAN, AND THE NATION, 1973–2002	255
Letter between Robert F. Williams and Richard T. Gibson	262
• *Richard Gibson Writes to Robert Williams, June 15, 1976*	262
• *Richard Gibson Writes to Robert Williams, June 28, 1976*	262
• *Richard Gibson Writes to Robert Williams, August 5, 1976*	263
• *Robert Williams Writes to Richard Gibson, August 20, 1976*	263
Lake County Peoples Association for Human Rights Letters to Michigan Congressmen by Robert Williams	264
• *Robert F. Williams, President, Writes Congressman David Bonior, June 21, 1994*	264
• *Robert F. Williams, President, Writes Congressman John Conyers, June 21, 1994*	264
Lake County Star Protest Letters by Robert F. Williams	265
• *Robert F. Williams, Williams Questions Rotary's Choice for Award, June 8, 1978*	265
• *Robert F. Williams, Constitution More Than Words on Scrap of Paper, September 25, 1987*	265
Happy Hopeful New Year 1995 Join the Right to Live Movement, Buy Yourself a Gun	266
Letters between Robert F. Williams and Calvin C. Cunningham	270
• *Robert F. Williams Writes Calvin Cunningham, February 12, 1994*	270
• *Robert F. Williams Writes Calvin Cunningham, June 27, 1995*	270
• *Robert F. Williams Writes Calvin Cunningham, August 8, 1995*	270
Letters between Calvin C. Cunningham and Ronald J. Stephens	270
• *Calvin Cunningham Writes Ronald J. Stephens, January 1, 2015*	270
• *Calvin Cunningham Writes Ronald J. Stephens, March 28, 2015*	271
• *Ronald J. Stephens Writes Calvin Cunningham, April 3, 2015*	271
Dedication of the Robert F. Williams Community Development and Family Center, Published in *The Lake County Star*	272
• *Reverend Stanley U. Sims, Get the Facts Straight, May 22, 2000*	272
• *Audrey Kathryn Bullett, Robert Williams Is a Role Model, May 22, 2000*	272
• *Robert L. Watkins, Misinformation and Omissions, May 22, 2000*	273
• *Reverend John E. Simpson, May 22, 2000*	274
Letters about Robert Williams from Richard T. Gibson to Ronald J. Stephens	274
• *Richard Gibson Writes Ronald J. Stephens, November 19, 2001*	274
• *Richard Gibson Writes Ronald J. Stephens, February 18, 2002*	276
• *Richard Gibson Writes Ronald J. Stephens, February 28, 2002*	276
• *Richard Gibson Writes Ronald J. Stephens, April 8, 2002*	276
• *Richard Gibson Writes Ronald J. Stephens, April 9, 2002*	277
Epilogue	279

PART III	**283**
Selected Bibliography	285
PART IV	**293**
Appendices	295
Poems by Robert F. Williams	295
• *Pearly Teeth at the White House, April 1963*	295
• *Birmingham, USA, June 1963*	295
• *Black Madonna of Harlem Square, July 1967*	296
• *America the Bruteful, Summer 1969*	296
• *The Hangman*	297
• *Pusher Man, ca. 1970*	300
• *Tomorrow, Past*	301
• *The Freedom Man, 1980*	301
• *Re-Run, 1980*	302
• *A Cross of Cocaine, 1981*	302
• *Homeward Journey, 1981*	303
• *China: The Future Revisited, December 16, 1986*	303
• *A Spark of Reconciliation, December 1988*	303
• *A Poem of Comfort for Calvin Cunningham: S and L Blues, 1995*	304
Interview Transcripts with Two Lake County Associates and John Williams About Robert F. Williams	305
• *Interview with Jeffrey L. Davenport, August 11, 2014*	305
• *Interview with Mary L. Trucks, August 14, 2014*	319
• *Interview with John Chambers Williams, January 3, 2015*	333
Index	363

LIST OF PHOTOGRAPHS AND ILLUSTRATIONS

Monroe, North Carolina, 1955–1961

Map of Newton Monroe, NC, published in Truman Nelson's pamphlet *People with Strength: The Story of Monroe, N.C.* Nelson, a socialist worker's party and NAACP member, co-founded the Committee to Combat Racial Injustice. Courtesy of Robert F. Williams in the Robert F. Williams Papers at the Bentley Historical Library in Ann Arbor ... 37

Front Page of the *Journal and Guide* article with the headline, "Citizens Fire Back at Klan," October 12, 1957, page 1. ... 38

Rosa Parks at Rob's Burial. Rosa Parks says farewell at Rob's gravesite at the Hillcrest Cemetery, Monroe, North Carolina. Standing to the right of Mrs. Parks is her personal assistant and friend, Elaine Steele, and left of Mrs. Parks is an unidentified woman. There are two bodyguards standing behind Mrs. Parks and Ms. Steele, 1996. Photography courtesy of Aukram Burton, *RamImages.com* ... 38

Robert F. Williams Lying in Repose. Robert F. Williams draped with Pan African flag and the U.S.A. flag recognizing his dedication to his people and his service in the Marine Corps, Monroe, NC, 1996. Photography courtesy of Aukram Burton, *RamImages.com* ... 39

Rosa Parks at Rob's Homecoming, 1996. Rosa Parks is with John C. Williams (Mabel and Rob's son), Mabel R. Williams, and Rob's brothers, John and Edward, who are standing in front of Rob's casket. Photography courtesy of Aukram Burton, *RamImages.com* ... 39

Robert F. Williams Historic Marker Dedication unveiled in the Monroe Newtown community commemorating and honoring the contributions and legacy of Robert F. Williams on a Saturday afternoon of August 26, 2023. "A crowd gathered at the Battle Center on the campus of Wingate University" early that morning "to attend [a] program [organized] by A Few Good Men, Inc. to celebrate [the] Highway Historical Marker on the corner of Boyte street and Highway 74." ... 40

Franklin H. Williams (Robert F. Williams's surviving son is seen wearing black jeans and a long shelve blue or gray shirt) witnessing the unveiling of the Robert F. Williams Historical Marker. Franklin, who is contracted to publish Robert Williams's autobiography, *While God Lay Sleeping*, was quoted in Monroe's newspaper, *Enquirer Journal*, stating my "father would have been proud to see this and would want young people to know his story and be inspired by it. I know there is political turmoil and things going on, but my father had an optimistic spirit. He thought people could overcome problems; he believed in civic pride, being involved in the community, and looking out for people" (A4). Photographer: Patricia M. Poland. 40

Havana, Cuba, 1960–1966

Robert F. Williams Meets Fidel Castro. On the first trip to Cuba in 1960 through the Fair Play for Cuba Committee, (left to right) Robert F. Williams and Richard Gibson of the FPCC, Salvador Allende of Chile, Fidel Ruis Castro, Juan Marinello Vidaurreta, Cuban lawyer, professor, and writer, and [unidentified Latin American woman] ca. 1960. Courtesy of the Union County Library in Monroe, North Carolina. 73

Front Page of *The Crusader-in-Exile*, Robert and Mabel Williams traveling from Cuba to China are seen together on a trip to China where Mao Zedong greets them, 1964. Courtesy of Robert F. Williams in Box of the Robert F. Williams Papers at the Bentley Historical Library in Ann Arbor 74

May-June 1964 issue of *The Crusader-in-Exile*, exiled Robert F. Williams challenged racial oppression, African American human rights violations, and anticipated the rise of the Black Power Movement. While stationed in Cuba, Williams' reasoned that the causes for an Afro-American Revolt in the USA would rest on the potential for a minority revolution. This statement in the newsletter essentially helped to inspire the formation of the Revolutionary Action Movement, Student Nonviolent Coordinating Committee, Black Panther Party, the Republic of New Afrika, when he stated "the brutally oppressed Afro-American" would respond violently by resisting "to savage racial dehumanization." 75

During the Cultural Revolution, exiled Robert F. Williams traveled from Cuba to meet Mao in China for the first time, marking his first trip to China. Williams is seen shaking hands with and being welcomed by Chairman Mao Tse-Tung who is seen sharing a copy of The Little Red Book, 1963. Courtesy of Robert F. Williams in the Robert F. Williams Papers at the Bentley Historical Library in Ann Arbor, Michigan. 76

Front Cover of second edition of *Negroes with Guns* was published by Third World Press. 77

LIST OF PHOTOGRAPHS AND ILLUSTRATIONS

Peking, China, 1963–1969

Robert and Mabel Williams Overlooking Sites in Peking with three Chinese tour guides, 1966.   107

Front Page Forgery of *The Crusader-in-Exile*. This forgery bears a masthead with a drawing of a crusader warrior on a horse that Williams was no longer using. This scan of the front page of the April–May 1966 forgery is numbered volume 8, number 4—and is stamped "Counterfeit" at the top. This is the first of two forgeries that were mailed out to ML members in Europe and France, according to Williams, under the auspices of Cuban G-2 (secret police). It was found online through the CIA's FOIA Reading Room. After leaving Cuba for China the spring of 1966, the masthead Williams used to publish *The Crusader-in-Exile* was the "Torch" and the "Machine Gun." "Now, soured by his personal experiences in Havana, Williams says: At this stage of betrayal of oppressed peoples by the American-Soviet Cuban axis, we are beginning to wonder if the junior partner is specializing in documentary forgery." Courtesy of and approved for Release by the CIA, June 17, 1967. See CIA-RDP75-00149R000800070010-9.pdf   108

Front Page of *The Crusader-in-Exile*, November 1968. Courtesy of Robert F. Williams in the Robert F. Williams Papers at the Bentley Historical Library in Ann Arbor.   109

Robert F. Williams in Tanzania. RNA president-in-exile, Robert F. Williams in Tanzania with Mae Mallory, second left David Maphumzana Sibeko, Chief Representative of the PAC to the United Nations, Milton Henry, fifth left Jacob, PAC Secretary, Peter Nkutsoeu, PAC Secretary of Education and Publicity, Abednigo Bekabantu Ngcobo, PAC Secretary for Finance. ca. 1968. Courtesy of Robert F. Williams in Box 14 under Africa and Cuba in the Robert F. Williams Papers at the Bentley Historical Library in Ann Arbor.   110

Detroit and Ann Arbor, Michigan, 1969–1972

Robert F. Williams Exiting TWA Plane. Robert F. Williams TWA Flight Landing in Detroit. From top to bottom: Brother Gaidi A. Obadele (aka Milton Henry), unnamed State Department official, Robert F. Williams at the bottom exiting the plane as a second State Department official meets him, ca. 1969. Courtesy of the Detroit Public Library.   171

Robert F. and Mabel R. Williams are photographed during a Republic of New Afrika Press Conference in Detroit. In view are Robert F. Williams Sr. sitting at the microphone, Mabel Robinson Williams, Audley "Queen Mother" Moore, Milton Henry (aka Gaidi Abiodum Obadele) and Richard B. Henry (aka Imari Abubakari Obadele), ca. 1969. From the Detroit News Collection # 27980. Courtesy of Walter P. Reuther Library, Wayne State University.   172

Robert F. Williams Speaks. While on a one-year Ford Foundation fellowship at the University of Michigan-Ann Arbor campus, Robert F. Williams speaks with *Detroit Free Press* staff writer, Julie Morris, in his office at the Center for Chinese Studies, September 19, 1971. Courtesy of Union County Library in Monroe, North Carolina. 173

Baldwin, Michigan, and the Nation, 1973–2002

Rosa Parks Visits Baldwin Elementary School. Mabel Williams, Al Nichols (a 1961 Bug Reds graduate, former basketball all-state Detroit Free Press 1960 selection, and Baldwin Elementary School Principal from 1972 to 1998), Rosa Parks, and Elaine Steele, longtime friend of Mrs. Parks and co-founder of the Rosa and Raymond Parks Institute for Self-Development, ca. 1978. Photographer Eugene Harmon. Courtesy of Al Nichols. 255

One Man Protest. Williams stages One-Man Protest of *The Lake County Star* over its refusal to publish a protest letter. When the editor refused to accept a paid advertisement, Williams staged a one-man demonstration, filed a lawsuit against the paper, and won the suit. He was awarded $1500 dollars, funds he used to organize the Lake County Peoples Association of Human Rights. Protesting as the Town Crier, Williams with the help of Mabel and a local artist constructed the poster and created a sandwich of a poster that he marched back and forth down M-37 with a battery pack, cassette player, and flashing star and strikes forever lighted helmet as he paraded back and forth the office of *The Lake County Star,* playing the song, John Brown's Body. Courtesy of *The Lake County Star/Pioneering Press.* 256

Poster about *The Lake County Star* refusal to publish news of Robert Carew's case. The poster was designed and erected by Robert Williams. Courtesy of the Lake County Historical Society. 257

Gwendolyn Midlo Hall and Robert F. Williams in 1976 in Monroe, NC, at the home of Mabel Williams's sister's house the evening before Rob's extradition hearing was dropped. Photographer John Williams. Courtesy of Gwendolyn Midlo Hall. 258

Robert F. Williams Speaking. Robert F. Williams points finger during speech at the Black Solidarity Conference at Tuffs University, Medford, MA. November 14–17, 1976. Photography courtesy of Aukram Burton, *RamImages.com* 258

Robert F. Williams and Queen Mother Moore. Robert F. Williams and Queen Mother (Audley) Moore at the Black Solidarity Conference at Tuffs University, Medford, MA, November 14–17, 1976. Photography courtesy of Aukram Burton, *RamImages.com* 259

LIST OF PHOTOGRAPHS AND ILLUSTRATIONS xvii

Rear view of Robert F. Williams being introduced before speaking about U.S.-China Relations at the headquarters of the Chinese Progressive Association Northeastern University. Courtesy of Northeastern University Library, Archives and Special Collections, (M163) Box 12, Folder 38. 1978.   259

Front Page of *The Crusader* Editorial Letter, volume XIII, number 1, Winter 1983. In the image, Williams writes "As Family Physician, I Advise War as A Cure," as commentary about unemployment and the U.S. economy with a picture of Adolph Hitler, the KKK, and the John Birch Society in the background.   260

Robert and Mabel Williams on September 2, 1996. The Williams couple, who were married for over forty-nine years, are seen sitting outside their cottage in Pleasant Plains Township of Lake County, Michigan. This photographs was taken approximately forty-three days before Robert Williams passed. He died at the age of 71 from Hodgkin's Lymphoma on October 15, 1996. Courtesy of John Herman Williams.   261

ACKNOWLEDGMENTS

This work would not have been possible without the support of Robert F. and Mabel R. Williams, and their son, John Chambers Williams, who believed in its promise. I would also like to thank John Herman Williams, Rob's brother and photographer for sharing rare photographs, family stories, and granting permission to reproduce images. I thank Signe Swanson at the University of Nebraska-Lincoln's Love Library University of Nebraska-Lincoln, various librarians at Grand Valley State University, Metropolitan State University of Denver, and Ohio University, and the College of Liberal Arts ASPIRE Program at Purdue University. I thank Caitlin Moriarty and Diana Bachman of the Bentley Historical Library at the University of Michigan's Bentley Historical Library for assisting me in retrieving important items from the Robert F. Williams Papers; Pat Bartkowski and Margaret Raucher of the Walter P. Reuther Library at Wayne State University; the manuscript division staff at the Wisconsin Historical Society;; the librarians of the History Department and Burton Historical Library at the main branch of the Detroit Public Library; Susan Dooley of the former Yates Township Public Library in Idlewild, Michigan; Howard Dodson and two archivist staff members of the Manuscript division of the Schomburg Center for Research on Black Culture; Diana J. Franckowiak of the Hackley Public Library's Local History and Genealogy Department in Muskegon, and Gypsy Houston of the Union County Library Genealogy and Local History as well as Elvia Paloma Manjarrez, former Genealogy and Local History Assistant of the Union County library in Monroe, North Carolina. To Mary Trucks of FiveCAP, Inc. thanks for sharing the special report detailing Robert F. Williams's efforts as a grassroots activist in Idlewild, Baldwin, and Muskegon, Michigan. I am humbly indebted to Paul Lee, General Baker, John Bracey, Muhammad Ahmad, Gwendolyn Midlo Hall, Richard T. Gibson, Gaidi A, Obadele (aka Milton Henry), Grace Lee Boggs, Aukram Burton, Abdul Alkalimat, John C. Williams, Attorney Melissa El, S. Abdallah Schleifer (aka Marc Schleifer), Charles E. Simmons, Luke Tripp, Tony Van Der Meer, Paula Marie Seniors, Woodrow Wilson III, Huey P. Newton, Molefi K. Asante, and Miron Clay-Gilmore, Marvin R. Ponder, for planting seeds. My reading and interacting with scholars and their scholarship such as Timothy B. Tyson, Reiland Rabaka, Errol A. Henderson, Judson L. Jeffries, Carlos Moore, Pero G. Dagbovie, Walter Rucker, Thomas J. Sugrue, Robin D.G. Kelley, Kellie Carter Jackson, Robeson Taj Frazier, Karin Stanford, Carol Ann Dennis, Bill V. Mullen, Van Gosse, Stephen M. Ward, Jefferson Morley, Denise Hill, Barbara Cheshier, and Jeanne Theoharris, was also critically important. Working over the years with graduate and undergraduate students at the different institutions where I have taught also deserves mentioning. This list includes Tosha Sampson-Choma and Patricia Ruiz, Benjamin Braddock, Rikako Arima, Yawen Yang, Jeremiah Johnson, Martasia Monay Ann Carter, and Erin L. Brock. A special thanks goes to Kathy R. Middleton for proofreading and retyping lost documents, and to David Rollock and Joseph C. Dorsey of Purdue University for critiquing early drafts of my introduction. I also want to thank the people of Lake County, Michigan, including Alfred and Kenneth Nichols, Mary Trucks, Melissa El Johnson, Jeffrey L. Davenport, Ann Waters, Bruce Micinski, Eugene Harmon, Audrey K. Bullett, Momma Helen Curry, Ethel A. Johnson, John Meeks, Sr., and of course, Robert F. and Mabel R. Williams, who helped over the years, I thank you deeply for your assistance, beliefs, and support over the year in having faith in the promise of this project.

PROLOGUE

I remember my first encounter with Robert Williams as if it happened yesterday. I was briefly introduced to Robert Williams by Mabel Williams, whom I had met three weeks earlier in Baldwin, Michigan at St. Ann's Lake County Senior Meals Program. Mabel worked as program director "for many years, sitting on the church's finance board and serving as Lector and Minister of the Eucharist."[1] During my second or third week at the center to meet with and interview Idlewild elders, Mabel invited me to a senior citizen's party at the Henrietta Summers Senior Citizens apartment reception room in Idlewild. As I entered the building that evening, Mabel introduced me to Robert. We shook hands, greeted one another, and briefly chatted. I was impressed by the humble and welcoming demeanor he displayed. I was in awe. I was teaching at West Shore Community College in Scottsville, Michigan, as an associate professor of Communication during fall 1992 and spring and summer 1993 semesters. It was in February of 1993, when I met him a second time. Robert Williams was invited to give an African American History Month presentation at West Shore. David McCullough, a former colleague and professor, who taught sociology courses, extended an invitation to join his class during what was one of Rob's annual presentations in the area. I sat in the front row of the classroom with a notepad and pen in hand eager to actively listen and take notes. I was thoroughly impressed. Rob blew my socks off as he shared stories about his family's travels, his civil rights activism, calls for armed self-defense, NAACP leadership agenda in Monroe, North Carolina, and being exiled in Cuba and China from 1961 to 1969. He also talked briefly about his return to the United States in September 1969. The details were attention getting to say the least. The national impact and international appeal that Robert and Mabel planted left a permanent footprint in American and worldwide history in shaping Black political thought during the turbulent decade of the 1960s and beyond. Hearing Rob's firsthand account of the experiences he and his family encountered was exciting. As he concluded the WSCC presentation, I approached him and asked if I could interview him sometime in the near future. He agreed to an interview and asked, after sharing his telephone number, for me to leave a message if he did not answer. I was excited about the Williams project being added to my list of research projects. I visited the Bentley Historical Library first to see the finding aid for the Robert F. Williams papers, an enormous collection that would take lots of time to get through. I felt blessed at the time that Williams had given me written permission to use and publish from the collection. I shared the story with a childhood friend (whose mother was my family doctor and had saved my life when I was a child), Paul Lee, who reminded me that Williams was a neglected important

Black figure in twentieth-century American and world history. Lee's response widely opened my eyes and cultural awareness. He shared copies of *The Crusader* that he let me borrow from his private collection and a copy of Robert C. Cohen's *Black Crusader*. Returning to Ludington, where I lived at the time, I found myself calling Rob daily to find out when we could meet for the interview. I must have called six times with no replies or returned calls. I left multiple messages on the answering machine. One day, after teaching a summer course at WSCC, a former African American female student who lived in Baldwin approached me and asked for assistance. She had car problems and needed a ride to Baldwin. I gave her a ride. To my surprise, she directed me to Mabel and Robert's cottage in Pleasant Plains Township. Williams must have planned this outcome for us to meet because he had my number but had been traveling and he was still under FBI surveillance through its Michigan division. His phone had been wiretapped and he was constantly being watched. Entering the couple's cottage, Mabel and Rob warmly welcomed me, and we talked for about an hour in the comfort of their living room. Rob talked, and Mabel and I listened, and every now and then, I asked open-ended questions while Mabel was washing dishes and listening. As I sat there, I noticed the famous rifle hanging over the desk that Timothy Tyson described in *Radio Free Dixie*. At one point during the informal interview, I remember Robert saying to Mabel that he did not want her to listen to part of the interview. Mabel replied, "Why not? I was involved." Mabel later indicated that she was retiring for the evening since she had to work the next day. Rob and I talked for hours. I learned so much that evening and into the early morning hours. He shared lots even as a local citizen and community activist in rural Lake County, Michigan. He was a celebrated civil rights movement elder, veteran of two wars, the Army during World War II and the Marine Corp during the Korean War. He was a veteran, community activist, and internationalist living in a northern rural Michigan African American resort community. As we conversed in the privacy and comfort of his space, I learned about the couple's partnership in resistance to the Black liberation struggle. It was around two o'clock in the morning by the time our interview ended. I was determined and motivated after interviewing and meeting Williams to write about him. As I left their cottage with signed permissions on an index from Robert to share with the archivists at the Bentley, I was going to write about the life and times of Robert Franklin and Mabel Ola Robinson Williams because I was going to allow Robert Williams to speak for himself as opposed to presenting a scholarly framing about him from a particular theoretical lens, critical perspective, and worldview. To that end, this volume begins with an introductory chapter about Robert Williams, followed by a presentation of important documents that are arranged in a chronological and topical format, which focuses on the geographical spaces where the family lived and stayed in order to provide readers with details about their travels experiences domestically and abroad. To arrange these documents, I examined a set of common procedures used by historians and literary scholars with backgrounds in producing edited volumes about notable African American men and women and introductory essays. The papers and/or correspondences of Frederick Douglass, Booker T. Washington, W.E.B. DuBois, Shirley Graham DuBois, Marcus Garvey, Malcolm X, Martin Luther King, Jr., Paul Robeson, and Huey P. Newton were considered.[2] I selected *Paul Robeson Speaks: Writings, Speeches, Interviews, 1918-1976*, edited with introductory notes by historian Philip S. Foner, as my model to arrange *Robert Franklin Williams Speaks: A Documentary History*.

Notes

1 MNA Staff. Lake County community leader dies, *State News*, April 23, 2014. See https://www.manisteenews.com/state-news/article/Lake-County-community-leader-dies-14217480.php
2 *The Frederick Douglass Papers*, edited by John McKivigan; *The Booker T. Washington Papers*, edited Louis R. Harlan; *W.E.B. DuBois Speaks: Speeches and Addresses, 1890-1919*, edited by Phillip Foner; *Race Woman: The Lives of Shirley Graham DuBois*, edited by Gerald Horne; *The Marcus Garvey and Universal Negro Improvement Association Papers*, edited by Robert Hill; *Malcolm X Speaks: Selected Speeches and Statements*, edited by George Breitman; *The Papers of Martin Luther King, Jr.*, edited by Stanford University, *Paul Robeson Speaks: Writings, Speeches, Interviews, 1918-1974*, edited with an introduction by Phillip Foner; and *The New Huey P. Newton Reader*, by Huey P. Newton, edited by David Hilliard and Donald Weise with an introduction by Elaine Brown.

Part I

Robert Franklin Williams Speaks: A Documentary History is organized into four parts. Part I explores in chronological order the Williams story and the geographical spaces where the family lived, worked, and resided while Robert and Mabel Williams worked in partnership advocating for the civil and human rights of African Americans. It reveals how Williams is and remains a central yet complex figure in the United States. It provides the historical substance and analytical clarity that is necessary for readers to discover for themselves how Williams's messages of resistance, advocacy for armed self-defense, and protests against racial injustice resonate today through "new civil rights movement" causes, efforts, grievances, and protests spearheaded by Black Lives Matter movement activists, proponents, and supporters who continue to dominate the twenty-first-century social justice agenda with renewed liberation demands and themes. In Part II, which follows, the documents illustrate how the Williams couple's activism, travels across continents, and exiled experiences in Cuba and China were flexible and pragmatic. Williams is presented as a defender of African American human rights, fundamental principles and meanings of American democracy, patriotism, armed self-defense, and social justice.

INTRODUCTION

Roots, Racism, Routes, and Resistance: Robert and Mabel Williams's Take on Patrick Henry's "Give Me Liberty or Give Me Death"

"Self-Defense is not a love for violence. It is a love for justice. We must defend ourselves. We must fight back."

Robert F. Williams, c. 1961

In the American tradition, Patrick Henry's rousing 1775 speech during the Second Virginia Convention "fired up America's fight for independence." Henry's meaning of self-defense in the battle for independence internalized a love for freedom and humanity against tyranny. Robert and Mabel Williams's meaning of self-defense expressed the same kind of love for freedom, justice, and independence. Robert Williams's meaning was offensive, not on the defensive despite what some imagine. Williams was a pragmatist and he believed, to borrow from Malcolm X, that armed self-defense meant to embrace a "by any means necessary" approach if required to defend oneself and to achieve freedom. Williams's mandate was a rallying call for self-love but open to guerrilla tactics to achieve self-preservation, human dignity, and community objectives. The philosophy of Robert F. Williams as president and Dr. Albert Perry as vice president of the Union County Branch of the National Association for the Advancement of Colored People (NAACP) believed "self-defense prevents bloodshed," "forces protection," is "born of our plight," and is "an American tradition."[1] Self-defense, from Williams's perspective and Afrocentric worldview, guarantees humanity and that every African American individual, family, and community receive equal protection and support from the three branches of the federal government. Williams insisted on and petitioned for these native-born American rights. However, when studying him, scholars tend to under-appreciate important aspects of his political philosophy, identity, and family history. As such, multidimensional figures such as Robert F. and Mabel R. Williams—and by extension their most vocal supporters: Mae Mallory, Rosa Parks, and Gwendolyn Midlo Hall—"are often ignored [and/or misinterpreted] because they cannot be captured by singular analytical constructs nor reduced to single dimensions of Black political activism for social justice. Extant treatments of complex figures such as Robert F. Williams are often framed by scholars as homogenized or reduced to characters that fit one of the diverse dimensions of their makeup." Exiting the Monroe, North Carolina, scene in the early afternoon on August 18, 1961, Robert Williams was adamant about "Black lives mattering for [current and future generations of] activists, including leaders and followers of the nexus that intersects domestic and global Black liberation struggles." Rob's advocacy for armed self-defense influenced generations of leftist activists who embraced in some way, shaped, or formed aspects of his philosophy and advocacy for armed self-defense. Recognizing the intersection of historical and contemporary black nationalism and activism, Thomas Surge reminds us how some "observers of the [period] painted black nationalism and black power as a key departure from the past, a new historical moment,"[2] where "so many of the key figures in Black power, including Williams and Malcolm X, were actually products of the previous generation of activism."[3] This volume illustrates how Williams worked with but "was not a Black nationalist or a union leader," even though he was "inspired by the labor movement."[4] Rob "was not a Communist or Socialist, but he supported the anti-imperialism of Fidel Castro's Marxist regime as an expatriate revolutionary from the US. The contradictions about him do not end there either. After leaving Cuba in 1966, and arriving safely in China with his entire family, Rob became a critic of Castro." The Robert F. Williams story deserves revisiting since Americans and the rest of the world are witnessing mass killings and a resurgent civil rights movement with the Black Lives Matter Movement dominating the narrative. *Robert Franklin Williams Speaks: A Documentary History* is timely in terms of contextualizing ongoing debates surrounding the first and second amendment rights of African Americans, black female and male subjectivity and agency, and an increase in police shootings. It brings to the forefront the activism and political philosophy of a complex figure such as Robert Franklin Williams for at least three important reasons: (1) Because the Black Power Movement (BPM) members, leaders, and organizations of the period were activist offspring of Robert F. Williams, meaning William's actions, along with Malcolm X, gave rise to the BPM. Consequently, Williams remains the second most important Black figure behind Malcolm X in articulating a framework and understanding for the rise of the BPM; (2) Because the Robert and Mabel Williams husband and wife team, alongside Marcus and Amy Jacques Garvey, and W. E. B. and Shirley Graham Du Bois, serve as the template for the study of any militant activist couple locally, nationally, and internationally, then and now; and (3) Because Robert Williams can speak for himself on his own terms as opposed to scholarly conceptualizations and ideological perspectives about him. Robert and Mabel Williams are recognized for championing "anti-Black violence in the U.S.,"[5] anti-racism in Cuba, and anti-imperialism in China, as well as for shaping the consciousness of future generations of activists, citizens, and scholars domestically and abroad.[6] Although Rob and Mabel were not the first Black activist couple to internationalize the Black freedom struggle during what Mary L. Dudziak defined as the Cold War Civil Rights Movement era,[7] they were the first to successfully navigate Castroism, Maoism, and racism in the United States in practical ways. As transformative figures, the couple fought unapologetically for the right to bear arms and to defend oneself against racial terror, violence, and discrimination in the United States.[8] As Tommy Curry and Max Kelleher observed the radical integrationist stance Williams embraced in Monroe are directly linked to "the continuation, not the birth, of" the radical tradition and "militant civil rights strategies introduced with T. Thomas Fortune's agitationist philosophy, which was developed earlier by" Frederick Douglass, Harriet Tubman, and Ida B. Wells-Barnett.[9] Despite claims advanced by some scholars, the agenda of Robert and Mabel Williams was not imagined but rather pragmatic, even after they returned to the U.S. This chapter offers preliminary insights surrounding the philosophy of Robert Williams and by extension Mabel Williams' support for armed self-defense in the U.S. and Black rights abroad. It explores the couple's activism and resistance history in the Newtown community from 1955 to 1961, challenges they encountered as exiles from 1961 to 1969 in Cuba and China during the Cold War/Civil Rights era, and the legacy they left behind as a couple in Black resistance history who settled in what Erik McDuffie[10] defines as the "Black Diaspora of the Midwest." As returning American citizens in 1969, Robert and Mabel Williams were not only successfully navigating Castroism and Maoism, but were also outsmarting some aspects of racial discrimination and victimization in the Black Diaspora of the Midwest in Western Michigan.

Racism, Rights, and Resistance: Robert and Mabel Williams in the Newtown Community

At first, the Robert and Mabel Williams team during the mid-1950s was feeling optimistic about a degree of progress being made in southern America amidst challenges to systematic racism in North Monroe and elsewhere in other regions of the country.[11] This measure of thought came alongside major ongoing campaigns for, notwithstanding the counterprotest campaign against, the Montgomery Bus Boycotters, and the U.S. Supreme Court's ruling in the 1954 *Brown v. Board of Education* decision which supposedly claimed to reverse the court's earlier 1896 *Homer Plessy v. Ferguson* decision and to desegregate public schools. Before becoming the newly elected Union County NAACP chapter president in 1955, discharged U.S. Marine Corps Private First-Class E2 Robert F. Williams knew he wanted to join the NAACP,[12] before returning to his southern hometown and state. "In the Marines I had a taste of discrimination and had run-ins that got me in the guardhouse. When I joined the local chapter of the NAACP it was going down in membership, and when it was down to six, the leadership proposed dissolving it. When I objected, I was elected president and they withdrew, except for Dr. [Albert] Perry,"[13] a World War II veteran, like Robert Williams who was destined to become an effective leader in waging local battles against the thrones of racial discrimination in Monroe. Williams fought against Monroe's local government, police, and county sheriff departments by challenging its misguided racist segregationist policies. Williams and six other members of the chapter, which included veterans and stay-at-home wives and moms mostly, led an extensive recruitment campaign to increase the chapter's membership, recruiting potential members in pool halls, barbershops, beauty parlors, and other areas where working-class Newtown community members shopped, ran errands, and celebrated themselves. Williams built a larger chapter than the previous middle-class leadership, whose members at the time had been under pressure from the racist white establishment. "We ended up with a chapter that was unique in the whole NAACP because of a working-class composition and leadership that was not middle class."[14] Six months into his term as president, Robert and Mabel read an article together about the arrest of Mrs. Rosa Parks on December 1, 1955. Parks was tired after a long day at work, even though historians discovered the event and incident were planned, that she would refuse and be arrested for not giving up her seat in the colored section of the bus so that a white man could sit down. Arrested, jailed, and released on bond, Parks was eventually found guilty of the charges filed against her by the close of the business day on December 5.[15] The Reverend, Dr. Martin Luther King Jr., then a young pastor at Dexter Avenue Memorial Baptist Church and the newly elected president of the Montgomery Improvement Association, was under pressure by the community. At the advice of his inner circle of civil rights activists and intellectuals, King organized and led the Montgomery Bus Boycott. Jeanne Theoharris, who reminds us that King benefited the most from the event nationally and internationally, even though it was Parks's efforts and sacrifices that should be credited and recognized.[16] Reverend King's notoriety as a rising civil rights leader and young minister helped to recruit the cooks, maids, and janitors who refused to ride on the bus because they rejected the city's existing policy. They demanded an end to racial discrimination on the bus. Although King persuaded and supported the workers' boycott, it was the demonstrators who were the movers and shakers to demand from the local government to enforce improvements and changes in the southern city's transportation policies and regulations. The 382 days of boycotting inspired the demonstrators to walk miles and/or join carpools to get to work paid off. The NAACP Monroe Program of Robert and Mabel Williams, like the Montgomery Bus Boycott, had pledged to fight for civil rights causes and laws to end racial discrimination in housing, transportation, policing, education, and, as Mabel explains, against other evil forces and practices that invoked racial tensions in Newtown, and elsewhere in the United States. Robert, Mabel, their neighbor, Ethel A. Johnson, Dr. Perry, and women and veterans, including Mrs. Crowder and Woodrow Wilson, intensified their efforts to improve socioeconomic conditions of people living in the Newtown community. The chapter Williams built acquired a National Rifle Association (NRA) charter, established and trained armed guardsmen and women, and raised money to purchase rifles and ammunition. This represented a significant undertaking considering the NRA was widely recognized as a major political force and defender of Second Amendment rights. Battle-ready commander Rob Williams and his guard dug fox holes and established battle stations on the property of Dr. Perry's brick-framed ranch home after repeated death threats and phone calls made by James "Catfish" Cole who had been promising to bring an armed motorcade of Klansmen to kill Williams and destroy Dr. Perry's house. Tyson explains that with the closing of a textile mill nearby and a backlash against some minor measure of racial progress that followed World War II, the Ku Klux Klan (KKK) was becoming "a powerful resurgence in the area."[17] On October 5, 1957, after a large KKK rally ended in Monroe, a group of white men leaped in their cars and trucks armed with shotguns in hand were "ready to have a little fun" in the Newtown neighborhood. Armed and fully prepared to fend them off, battle-ready Robert Williams "strapped a pistol to his belt and took a stand,"[18] and was backed by "a small group of veterans who had dug the trenches for fixed foxhole positions stationed within rifle range." Williams and "the armed guards" were determined to go up against the KKK despite "the NAACP's philosophy and position on non-violence."[19] As the motorcade approached loud and unruly, Williams and his armed guards fired shots right back at them when fired upon by the racist intruders. The next day of the event the story was published in the *Norfolk Journal and Guide*, a Virginia newspaper, about the Klan's retreat, and not in the Monroe press. The Norfolk newspapers blamed the KKK for inciting the incident and the city council thereafter immediately passed an ordinance banning KKK motorcades. Dr. Perry "was arrested on the charge of performing a criminal abortion on a white woman, an allegation he vehemently denied the next day."[20] A philosophy the Williamses and their Newtown neighbors shared with Rosa Parks was the belief that self-defense meant "self-protection."[21] The strategic actions of the Newtown community were to protect families, which was the philosophy that inspired members of the Socialist Worker Party, the Progress Labor Party, and Black nationalist advocates to support armed self-defense and to participate in the struggle for equal rights. In the urban wastelands of America, Revolutionary Action Movement (RAM) members were among the first to dedicate themselves to organizing and protecting Black people against racist practices in unamiable ways in cities, neighborhoods, and communities. Rob's grand proclamation that "there is no Fourteenth Amendment in this social jungle called Dixie" and his philosophy of armed self-defense influenced RAM, the Black Panther Party (BPP), and the Republic of New Afrika (RNA) years later. Before then, Rob and Mabel Williams, Dr. Perry, Woodrow Wilson, and Ethel Azalea Johnson organized a Negroes with Guns Campaign, and its members worked shifts of armed neighborhood patrols. He called the Monroe Chapter of the NRA the Black Armed Guard. Williams relied most on the military veterans from the Newtown community, as well as financial support from across the country. Williams, a loving husband, dedicated father, grandson of former enslaved grandparents, U.S. Army and Marine Corps veteran, and civil rights leader, "was inspired to change the trajectory of relations and resistance" in Monroe by shaping 1950s meanings of "white-black relations in America."[22] His activism as a militant civil rights activist, leader, and neighborhood patrolman escalated and shifted into a combat leader and solider prepared to engage in armed self-defense for the safety and security of himself, his family, and community. Frowned upon and always discouraged by old-guard middle-class members of Monroe's NAACP leadership who were not in charge or living under the same racist conditions as members of the Newtown community characterized Williams's efforts and actions as detrimental to the local organization's causes. In contextualizing the historical moment, African American historian Brenda Gayle Plummer explains how "many [in the civil rights movement] who expressed a commitment to nonviolence at home were," according to Williams, "too weak-kneed to protest the warmongering of the atom-crazed politicians of Washington."[23] She continues noting, "Ever since the American Revolution, it had been commonplace to support black civil rights by referring to African Americans participation in the country's wars—where they had borne arms—and thus their entitlement to equitable citizenship and belonging. Defending oneself at home was an important part of the Williams story. Were Williams's remarks designed to challenge tactical assumptions about the civil rights movement's aims and being an American patriot? If so, was the purpose to achieve full citizenship only allowed for Black people to participate in U.S. imperialist ventures?"[24] Daniel Rasmussen, author of *American Uprising: The Untold Story of America's Largest Slave Revolt*, details how Black people "have had to fight every step of the way for their civil [and human] rights—from the right to eat in the same restaurant as whites to their right to not be sold into slavery," to exercising their second amendment and voting rights. "Coming to terms with American history means addressing the 1811 uprising led by a group of between 200 and 500 enslaved men dressed in military uniforms and armed with guns, cans, knives, and axes"[25] in a rural town near New Orleans, and the grievances that Robert F. Williams presented—"and [by] not brushing these events under the rug because they upset safe understandings about who we are as a nation."[26] African Americans "assumed arms against" those intending to do them great bodily harm or even to kill them." They fought against U.S. government agents, they supported the overthrow of legally sanctioned racism, and they were exiled or executed for their actions."[27] Also documenting early slave revolts against chattel slavery, Kellie Carter Jackson's *Force and Freedom* examines Frederick Douglass's insistence that African American Civil War troops should be "in uniforms when they killed Confederates,"[28] and Ida B. Wells-Barnette's decision to arm herself with a pistol for self-defense and self-preservation purposes after her life was threatened during Reconstruction. Jackson adds, "African Americans have never been afraid to use violence to defend themselves, to obtain their freedom, and to fight against injustice."

Although the Klan discontinued riding through the Newtown neighborhood and threatening families, the mission of the community to fight back continued and Williams received support from the Progressive Labor Party (PLP) and other outside groups. Almost one year later an innocent incident between Black and white children evolved and became "the famous Kissing Case," which made national and international newspaper headlines, due to Williams's efforts. The detailing surrounding the emergence of the case began almost a year after a federally funded public swimming pool in Monroe proved that racial tensions in the town needed addressing. Setting the stage involving a series of events that led up to the case, Rasmussen states, "The problem was simple: the only pool in the area was barred to blacks, and several Black children had drowned swimming in unsafe swimming holes."[29] Williams's solution was to integrate the use of the pool in accordance with the U.S. Supreme Court's ruling in *Brown v. Board of Education*. But city officials refused to responsibly abide by the federal law. After a series of public swimming pool protests, Williams, who wrote letters to the editors of the local press and the federal government about the segregated pool, was confident that real changes would result from the protest. "Mabel thought the plan was preposterous. White folks do not want you to sit beside them on the bus, Rob, she said. You really think they are going to let you jump in the water with them half-naked. Williams insisted that he was going to try."[30] Williams showed up at the entrance to the pool with a group of eight youth with bathing suits and towels. "Turned away, they returned the next day, and the day after that, standing outside the area in protest of an injustice that was both humiliating and life-threatening to the area's Black children. But most white residents of Monroe did not see the situation the same way." Following Robert Williams's leadership, a small group of neighborhood men and women supported the pool demonstrations. In October of 1958, months after the city's public pool integrated, the story about the two Black boys, eight-year-old David "Fuzzy" Simpson and ten-year-old James Hanover Thompson, who were joined by a small group of white boys to play cowboys and Indians, came out.

Sissy Sutton, an eight-year-old white girl, and her girlfriends were observing the boys as they were playing. As Tyson explains, "it was not uncommon for young Black and white children to play together,"[31] although they lived in the racially segregated town of Monroe. At the conclusion of playing cowboys and Indians, "a kissing game ensued" between James and Sissy, who were happy to see one another. As the story goes, Sissy kissed James on the cheek. Later that day, Sissy idly shared the story about the game with her mother and father, and they became furious. Sissy's father armed himself and searched for the boys, whom the Monroe police had found, questioned, placed under arrest, and put in an adult jail cell without notifying their mothers. Six days later, the mothers of the two boys contacted and informed the city's mayor about the two missing youth being charged "with assault and [if found guilty would be] sentenced to serve time in a juvenile reformatory." None of this was imagined as Monroe mayor Fred Wilson contacted Robert F. Williams and asked if he would intervene on behalf of the boys after their mothers had contacted him and asked for his assistance. Denied entry into the juvenile courtroom by the court's security, Williams waited patiently. Judge Hampton Price had already met with Sissy and her parents, and claimed it was best not to mix the races and to hold separate but equal hearings. In response to this blatant racist act of injustice, Robert Williams contacted NAACP officials in New York, who responded and declined on behalf of the organization to not get involved in any case involving sexual politics, "especially cases involving the volatile issue of miscegenation."[32] Deviating from the NAACP's policy position, Robert Williams, who was known for operating independently of the national office, took the lead since the typically cautious approach and insufficient method of the NAACP would not have any meaningful "affect [or] change in Monroe."[33] Robert F. Williams, whose viewpoints were considered militant and radical, contacted Conrad Lynn, a New York-based civil rights attorney and social justice activist, who contacted George Weissman, a founding Socialist Workers Party member and writer to get involved as the kissing case began making front-page news nationally and internationally. Due to Williams's insistence, an article with the headline "A Story of Two Little Boys in Carolina" was published in *The New York Post* by journalist Ted Poston, who became aware of the case after one of the boys' aunts had written to him. Although the NAACP continued to maintain its distance, Williams and his allies, Attorney Lynn and socialist Weissman, organized the Committee to Combat Racial Injustice (CCRI) with the objective of freeing the young boys from incarceration.[34] Weeks later, on November 13, Williams composed a telegram to President Dwight Eisenhower pointing out the disparities in Black and white cases in Union County courts and requested that the U.S. Department of Justice get involved and introduce the fourteenth amendment of the U.S. Constitution "to ensure justice in this" social jungle called Dixie. Two and a half weeks later, in December, Robert Williams and others drove reporter Joyce Egginton, which included Dr. Perry and the boys' mothers on a two-hour trip to Morrison Training School where the boys were serving time. Determined Williams smuggled a camera into the visiting room and took photographs of the boys and their mothers and shared them with Egginton. Around the same time the CCRI launched a public relations campaign that piqued the interest of a New York-based reporter writing for the *London News Chronicle* who expressed an interest in further interviewing the boys. Once the newspaper published the story resulting from that interview, "other overseas newspapers" covered what had become known as "the kissing case." This, in return, inspired the NAACP's leadership to "reverse its position and offer legal assistance and financial support to the boys' mothers, and to implement some public relations tactics." Alongside the media coverage, the NAACP, and the grassroots efforts of the CCRI, forwarded "hundreds of letters, telegrams, and petitions [that] flooded North Carolina Governor Luther Hodges's office" which as a response produced a counter "public relations campaign to justify the boys' incarceration." Although the kissing case was resolved by February 13, 1959, Williams and his armed guard continued to defend the rights of the Newtown families and community. There were other terrifying incidents to follow that motivated Robert and Mabel Williams and other community activist members that sparked further protest during the summer of 1959 and took a different attitude toward white racists and their treatment of law-abiding citizens of Black ancestry. The first of these events occurred after a Black mother of five children, Georgia Davis White, who worked as a maid, was kicked down a flight of stairs and into a hotel lobby by Brodus Shaw, a railway engineer, because she was making too much noise as she was mopping the hall floors while he was sleeping. The second incident happened after a married Black woman, Mrs. Mary Ruth Reed, who was eight months pregnant, became the victim of an attempted rape by a white perpetrator, Lewis Medlin, who chased her from her home and beat her during an attempted rape. Arrested and charged with assault and attempted rape, Medlin was later freed because "he was just drinking and having fun." After the acquittal of Medlin, twenty-five-year-old Mary Reed and other Black women stood outside the courthouse and told Williams why they did not feel safe in the community where they lived and worked. Mabel describes the reaction of every Black woman in the courtroom, angry and in tears, when the court took the accuser out the back door, and they met Williams. One of the women said, "these people have declared open season on Black women what are we going do now." When confronted by three reporters, the president of the Union County branch of the NAACP Robert Williams issued a statement in the defense of Black women that set the stage for the showdown between himself, the NAACP, and misinformed racist white America. Williams's unapologetic protest statement on the courthouse steps said, "This demonstration today shows that the Negro in the South cannot expect justice in the courts. He must convict his attackers on the spot. He must meet violence with violence, lynching with lynching," which was printed and reprinted in most newspapers throughout the United States and abroad. In an interview that followed the incident the next day, Williams repeated the point about flaws in the judicial system. This led to Williams' suspension as head of the local chapter. During the suspension, Mabel and Ethel Johnson "founded the Crusader Association for Relief and Enlightenment, known by the Monroe community as CARE,"[35] which served as "a mutual aid society run" with the help of eight volunteers who provided many needed services to the poor such as "clothing and canned-goods drives,"[36] food banks through the support of local farmers, and sewing and history classes for women and children. Mabel was active in other ways too since. She, Ethel Johnson and Robert founded *The Crusader* in 1959. Robert authored the articles published in the *Monroe Enquirer* and *The Crusader,* challenging segregation and racial violence against Black people. Mabel typed, proofread drafts, and edited final versions of the articles before sending "the galleys to the printers."[37] Robert Jr. and John Chambers and their friends circulated issues of the community newsletter throughout the Newtown neighborhood. As the readership of the newsletter grew through word-of-mouth and an extensive mailing list, the boys helped with mailing copies to subscribers. *The Crusader* had become the vehicle for "readers everywhere to protest" [vilify and objectify] the U.S. government and the Justice Department; because the 14th Amendment did not exist in Monroe and city officials, the FBI in Charlotte, and the Governor of North Carolina "were in a conspiracy to deny Monroe Negroes their constitutional rights."[38] By the early spring of 1961, approximately six months before he was temporary suspended and stripped from his NAACP leadership position, CORE dispatched a group of Freedom Riders who traveled to Monroe to test nonviolence. While staying at the Freedom House in Newtown, Willams advised and encouraged the civil rights student group to not plan their public integration demonstration over the weekend. Against this advice, the group proceeded and was surprised when forced to comply to restraints defined by the Monroe police to stand 15 feet from the courthouse door and confronted by an angry mass reactionary counterprotest and violence. After learning that the guard would not be involved in the demonstration, KKK members and their racist police officer allies and supporters attacked and savagely beat certain members of the pacifist demonstrators, who had been arrested and jailed, including James Foreman and Constance Fever. Other demonstrators retreated to Newtown, before a racist elderly white couple, Bruce and Mabel Stegall, drove through the neighborhood amid the escalating violence, and were dragged from their automobile by angry protesters who were community members. The mob marched the couple down Boyte street in front of the Williams home, where the frightened elderly white couple was provided shelter by Williams. While engaged in a series of telephone conversations with others and the Chief of Police of Monroe who had threatened to capture, apprehend, and hang Robert Williams in front of the Monroe Courthouse town square on the back side of the buildings where a confederate display stood, Williams and his family fled the state by way of a funeral hearse at the urging of his supporters, who believed that he was the main target. The family traveled to New York and split up. Charged with kidnapping and fleeing the State of North Carolina, the FBI now hunted Williams. Hearing about the hunt through allies, Williams and his family left New York and headed to Canada, where he thought they were safe. Before learning about the Canadian Mounted Police being on the alert to apprehend him, Williams migrated to California and then to Mexico, and from there to Cuba. Mabel and the boys arrived separately and a bit later. Williams and his family were granted political asylum from Fidel Castro. Reflecting on Williams before his exile in Cuba, Harold Cruse described him as an "avowed integrationist" whose advocacy for Black armed self-defense and citizenship rights was on to something. While in Cuba, his Black Power advocacy of armed self-defense influenced the formation of the Deacons for Defense and Justice in Jonesboro, Louisiana by 1964.

Yet, a set of prevailing views in the literature suggests that he sought to lead a mass movement. What could be false—Williams was neither a communist, Black nationalist, or pawn and/or tool of propaganda in the way that scholars of global politics suggest. Cruse's observations about Williams as an uncompromising radical integrationist, who advocated for the armed self-defense ends by 1967, years before his internationalist reputation grew as an exiled Cuban public figure. Complex and multidimensional, Robert Williams was a leading advocate for armed self-defense even as he was a member of the NAACP—hardly an institution noted for advocating armed self-defense. In exile, he embraced black nationalist precepts that would influence Malcolm X, Max Stanford (aka Muhammad Ahmad) as well as John Bracey of RAM; Huey P. Newton, Bobby Seale, Stokely Carmichael (aka Kwame Ture), Assata Shakur, Angela Davis, and H. Rap Brown of the BPP; Milton (aka Gaida Obadele) and his brother Richard Bullock Henry (aka Imari Abubakari Obadele) of the RNA, and selected members of the FPCC who "supported Castro and the Cuban Revolution." Newton and Seale, co-founders of the Black Panther Party for Self-Defense, both praised and critiqued Williams's philosophy. Newton adamantly disagreed with one aspect of Williams's philosophy. In *Revolutionary Suicide*, Newton states he did not appreciate the dependency and/or insistence "on federal government assistance; we [the BPP] viewed the government as an enemy, the agency of a ruling clique that controls the country."[39] Later, in *To Die for the People*, Newton defines the relevance of "the party's name change. For Self-defense is dropped. The organization became the Black Panther Party (BPP)." Favoring Malcolm's spirit, Newton states, "The Party's outlook was broadened. It was now a more effective weapon for self-defense because it sought a line of offensive activities that could, if consistently pursued, put an end to police terror. It now began to use the historical necessity to remove the racist from the seats of power in the economic and political life of the country. That Party had taken a leap forward in its theoretical outlook but by no means had it mastered the science it espoused."[40] Then, in reply to an article written by Communist Party USA member William Patterson, "The Black Panther Party: A Force Against U.S. Imperialism," Newton explains "a program of self-defense, no matter how militant in and of itself, gets an oppressed people nowhere. The police of the oppressor use force and violence under the direction of business and political leaders who label it law and order. It is a method of political relationship of the administrative branch of the government with minority groups. It is to the great credit of the Black Panther leadership that it quickly recognized this structural set-up."[41] Unlike the BPP, a centralizing aspect of Robert Williams's advocacy for and philosophy of armed self-defense was linked to the specific grievances he advanced that directly targeted the irresponsibility of the political establishment in Monroe and Washington, D.C.

Sankofa vs Communism: Robert and Mabel Williams Inside Cuba and Castroism and China and Maoism

By mid-1961, as an exile in Communist Cuba following the Cuban Revolution, Williams felt assured the Cubans would not challenge or attempt to silence or prevent him from achieving his objective in the telling of the story of Monroe. This perspective was broadened to embrace a national and global perspective "in forming a transnational black freedom struggle to end racial injustice," discrimination and practice of racial violence in the United States. Despite the shift in the political climate during the Cold War as exiled in Cuba, the grievances Williams espoused and the overtures he expressed through articulations of Black nationalism were revealed in *The Crusader-in-Exile,* the first edition of *Negroes with Guns,* and *Radio Free Dixie* broadcasts. Williams was known for making the case that "oppressed Black People are becoming more militant [...]" And while "it is difficult at this stage to say what organization will have the proper line to lead the Afro-American to freedom."[42] Because in the final analysis, "America is not God." "The Afro-American masses will have the final say."[43] Williams's grievances against the United States became problematic for certain Cuban communist and government officials because of his calls they imagined could give rise to a wave of Black and white men and women activists in the United States and Cuba to adamantly agree with him. In refusing to disagree with the concerns and fears of Cuban officials, Williams would explain his issue with exploitation and racism of any form. "We know of exploitation. We know that racism sprang from exploitation itself. Racism is an outgrowth of a need to justify racial exploitation. We must concentrate on the people who suffer most. The Black People are the lowest strata, the lowest class, economically, politically."[44] Although Cuban communists and government officials disagreed with and challenged him, Williams continued to petition and demand civil and human rights (i.e., the equivalent of BLM), for African Americans not only for them to exercise their freedom of speech rights but also to adhere to his calls for armed self-defense for self-preservation, racial justice, and survival. The federal government was not implementing any meaningful changes or reforms to address the American crisis. Williams's calls to African Americans in Monroe were to demand their rights, and if not honored and if required necessary, to use an armed self-defense philosophy "by any means necessary" approach to bring about radical social change. As far back as the summer of 1959 and summer of 1960, Williams's criticisms of the federal government were consistent in demanding of the federal government to allow him to tour Cuba. Traveling to the country in June of 1960 during a weeklong tour around the island from Pinar del Rio Santiago de Cuba, Williams and other FPCC members perceived that racial equality and social justice in Cuba came positively as a result of the Cuban Revolution.[45] Williams, who had previously been in contact with Fidel Castro when he was in New York for the United Nations meeting, was one of Cuba's staunchest allies among African American civil rights leaders at the time and had gone on record in support of Castro openly during "mass rallies organized by FPCC. He even assisted in to turning Washington into a laughingstock internationally by sending a telegram to Raul Ro and the United Nations, requesting the immediate landing of Cuban troops in the U. S. South to liberate American negroes from the Ku Klux Klan."[46] "Adding to that, historian Timothy Tyson explains, how Castro's Cuba [had secured] the services of Rowe-Louis-Fisher-Lockhart, Inc., a New York advertising agency, during the spring of 1960 in which former Heavyweight champion Joe Louis was a partner" and seen sitting at the head of a table with Castro while celebrating with his wife at the Havana Hilton on New Year Eve. As a partner, Louis was charged with promoting Cuba as a playground for African Americans. Unlike the Brown Bomber, Williams boldly declared a desire to visit Cuba. Williams also visited Cuba twice before ultimately the Caribbean Island and nation he thought would become a neutral country where he and Mabel could discuss and speak freely about from their perspective the injustices, racist policies, and common practices in American courts and law enforcement agencies.[47] In Cuba, Williams imagined that he had established and fostered a mutual and genuine interaction with Castro, Afro-Cubans, and a few white Cuban communists. Castro assigned Comandante Manuel Pinero Losada, who served as assistant minister of foreign relations to assist him and his family in their transition. Soon the sentiments appeared to diminish. Having fought alongside Castro in the Sierra Maestra Mountains, Pinero first "impressed Williams as a sincere and well-meaning"[48] official, who would go to great lengths to help so long as the only things Williams requested were for personal use. However, when Pinero's attitude toward him changed, reality soon set in. Ruth Reitan explained three major reasons why an alliance with Cuba appealed to Williams before his exile there. First, she explains "a revolutionary Cuba under Fidel Castro offered solidarity and support to civil rights leaders and urban revolutionaries alike, publicized throughout the world the plight of oppressed African Americans and exemplified a successful eradication of yanqui imperialist control from their nation." Second, Cuba represented a safe haven for militant Black leaders, because "Cubans fought against colonialism in Africa, promised to train U.S. militants in insurrectional tactics and weaponry and provided a haven for exiles." Finally, she contends "the Castro regime claimed to have purged racism from Cuban society."[49] It stands to reason then that Williams would envision "significantly more freedom in Communist Cuba than he would ever enjoy at home."[50] Though welcomed and supported by Castro, whose inner circle was framing a different agenda in support of Cuba, Williams would ultimately reject Cuba's emphasis on classism and maintain his on racism as the central focus of his propaganda and critiques of structural racial issues and policies in the United States. Pinero insisted from his perspective that Williams should support a "worker's revolution" as opposed to a "separate Black revolt."[51] Considering this viewpoint, Williams understood that Cuba actually failed to solve its persistent problems of racism. Although the first two to three years of the Williams family residency in the small Caribbean country involved a readjustment, family members, including Robert, Mabel, and their sons, Robert Jr. and John Chambers Williams, were learning some Spanish. Their adjustment and adoption to the new environment, cultural landscape, language, meeting, employing, and conversing with Afro-Cubans proved for Williams to focus on obtaining support from certain Cuban officials representing the Cuban government, and Cuban people. Robert (and Mabel) observed that few Afro-Cubans were in leadership positions within the Cuban government, and though they often wondered about Cuban politics they were sincerely appreciative of Castro, the Cuban government, and Cuban people for opening Cuba's doors to their family. Two years later, on August 8, 1963, during Williams's first trip to China from Cuba,[52] he met with Chinese supreme commander, Chairman Mao Zedong, who had issued a statement in support of African Americans in their struggle for civil liberty. Following this trip to China, the couple traveled there together with their sons as they continued to condemn racist practices in the United States and calls for Black rights and uprisings in urban America. Comandante Manuel Pinero Losada, assistant minister of foreign relations, insisted that the Williams couple lend their support for a "worker's revolution" as opposed to responding to the "separate Black revolt that was occurring and happening in North America."[53] He wanted Williams to focus on problems among Black and white workers. Williams disagreed and argued that the U.S. Constitution needed to be enforced and applied equally to all "Americans."[54] According to Cuban historian Osvaldo Cardenas, the different perspective may have been there because Cuba and the United States have a long history that is rooted in the transatlantic slave trade and slavery. In both countries, there have been complex issues that are linked to the abolition of slavery, although in the United States chattel slavery dictates the terms. Peoples of African descent in the United States were treated as less than second-class citizens and as "part of a minority population, but in Cuba, Afro-Cubans make up most of the Cuban population, although that comes as a result of a complex and complicated history in terms of race relations. Cuban scholars believe that the Cuban Revolution made this come into reality, and that the revolution introduced the possibility, but did not solve the issue of race and prejudices in Cuba."[55] This all became apparent to the Williams couple midway into their stay in Havana and residency at the Hotel Capri, where they communicated their activism through Radio Havana airwaves and print media. Robert found himself "caught up in the web of insinuations." In *Cuba, Cold War America, and the Making of a New Left*, Van Gosse offers yet another conceptualization about the early relationship between Williams and Richard Gibson in Cuba and China. Gibson,[56] a pro-Cuban journalist and activist back in 1959, was a FPCC member and the acting secretary for a brief period in 1962 after CBS reporter Robert Taber left for Cuba. Before and after the Cuban tours, Gibson served as "a bridge to people like Robert Williams, Leroi Jones (aka Amiri Baraka), journalist William Worthy, historian John Henrik Clarke and other Black activists and intellectuals such as Harold Cruse in making the equation between African American militance and solidarity with Castro and Cuba's Black population." Taber as did others, according to Gibson, "viewed revolutionary Cuba as a valuable ally in the struggle of African Americans against American racism and the remnants of white racist imperialism clinging to power around the world."[57] Castro's victory had transformed the thinking of the new left and throughout the political landscape of Latin America. Salvador Allende of Chile was one of the first to visit the small Caribbean country in 1959, "shortly after the insurgents" had "gained control, to meet with the Cuban leadership." Allende's visit was made to recognize the Cuban people's "spiritually and materially mobilized and fully interpreted government." During a photographed moment, Williams, Gibson, Castro, and two others joined Allende during the summer of 1960. By July 1962, around the time of Gibson's resignation as FPCC's Acting Secretary, angry Gibson Marxist-Leninist comrades accused him of being a CIA informant for proposing to spy on certain members. In federal documents reported to J. Edgar Hoover, FBI agents branded Gibson with the codename SUGAR, while the CIA used the codename ORPHONE1 in the Department of Justice surveillance files. This was happening after the Cuban tours and during Williams's exile in Cuba. The evidence suggests that during and after the Cuban revolution, the Bay of Pigs, the Cuban missile crisis in 1962, and a year before the assassination of President John F. Kennedy, Gibson served as acting FPCC secretary, and he was aware of Lee Harvey Oswald membership with the FPCC. Writing about Gibson's connection to Oswald and Williams, Jeffrey Morley, an antiwar activist in the San Francisco Bay Area, reported in an article that Gibson was a CIA informant. The story had broken in *Newsweek* and *The Washington Post* on April 26, 2018, after the National Archives released thousands of documents pertaining to the November 22, 1963, assassination of Kennedy, that the records "included three fat CIA files on Gibson." The CIA had questioned Gibson about Oswald, and he told them, "What little he knew and indicated he wanted to maintain contact with the U.S. government." Other documents in the files indicate that Gibson "served U.S. intelligence from 1965 until at least 1977." In one set of letters to and from, and about Williams, at least two of Gibson's Marxist-Leninist comrades violently accused and denounced him as a CIA informant. Gibson denied the charges. In a follow-up article published on May 15, 2018, about Gibson, Morley writes what the larger context of the Gibson story "tells us [...] about the CIA's surveillance of Lee Oswald in 1963." The Gibson angle to the Oswald story illustrates the extent to which the CIA, FBI, and State Department agents went to successfully penetrate, manipulate, disrupt, and control the narrative mindset of American sympathizers who supported the Cuban revolution and independence. Williams and Gibson maintained contact after Gibson returned to London due to low wages for his services as FPCC secretary while exiled in Cuba and China, and even after he returned to the states. One question posed by Charisse Burden-Stelly deserves our attention: Why were Gibson's nefarious affiliations blatantly obvious to some, but inconceivable to others? Three considerations need to be factored in answer to Burden-Stelly's burning question: 1) Gibson was in fact a CIA informant, but to what extent did he provide the CIA with discrediting information about Williams? 2) Why did the CIA release Gibson's name when he was still alive? 3) Was it a CIA retaliation against Gibson because he was not forthright with them when it came to providing information about Williams and other targeted subjects? Before leaving Cuba for China in 1966, Williams had given Gibson written authority to organize speaking engagements and to promote *Negroes with Guns* in England, France, Italy, Germany, and Sweden. As far back as 1965, "Williams suspected and accused the CIA and Cuban intelligence of trying to ruin him politically,"[58] and assigned his attention to the struggles of Afro-Americans in the United States using *Radio Free Dixie* broadcasts and *The Crusader-in-Exile*. *Radio Free Dixie* broadcasts aired Mondays, Wednesdays, and Fridays. Williams wrote the editorials, defended the liberation struggles of African Americans, and boldly spoke out against white supremacy and racial discrimination and violence in the South (a pattern of unjustified acts, attacks, and killings in America), which were not occurring in the states where Cubans or Cuban Americans resided and/or were treated differently. Afro-Cuban workers volunteered, Mabel explains, to help print *The Crusader-in-Exile* out the same way "we did in Monroe." At the center of Williams's criticism of the federal government was its refusal and mishandling to protect the equal rights guaranteed to Americans of African descents. Carlos Moore, an Afro-Cuban born in Jamaica, worked with the Williamses as a translator and one of their volunteers. Mabel always read news clippings sent to her and Robert presented disturbing reports on race which irritated certain Cuban officials, Cuban Communist Party leaders, and Communist Party USA members who in return defined, labeled, and tagged him a Black nationalist, simply because he refused to tone down his grievance rhetoric against the United States and to focus on redefining the class dynamics as a possible solution. This determination to disseminate and communicate the race problem provoked hostility with a lobbyist of pre-revolutionary communists who gained influence and power in the new regime and through ICAP did everything to thwart his militant agenda. Frazier points out how Afro-Cuban musicians were encouraged "to not play jazz, rhythm and blues, and gospel music—musical genres celebrated by Cuba's Afro-Cuban population. These restrictive elements of Cuban life gave credence to the Williamses' beliefs that the Cuban Communist Party was opposed to black nationalism and any movements or organizations advocating for black consciousness in Cuba."[59] Carlos Moore also acknowledged that his association with the Williamses "placed me on a collision course with ICAP officials." The celebrity status Williams once enjoyed during the early years of the Williamses residency was "gone with the wind." The "Big name in Cuba [and celebrity status disappeared], [...] [even though the Williamses] lived in a sort of golden exile," and was admired among Afro-Cubans and Castro who saw America's racial dilemma as Washington's Achilles' heel and so he considered Williams a huge asset in the war against the United States. Williams's weekly incendiary broadcasts, urging African Americans to revolt, continued to fuel an act of retaliation by certain Cuban officials toward his aggression. He later learned certain officials "reduced the transmission power of his broadcasts, part of what he believed was an effort by Cuban Intelligence Chief Pinero to limit his emissions." Between hours of interviewing that had been conducted and recorded in Cuba by journalist Robert Carl Cohen back in 1962 and 1963, for the documentary film *The Violet Crusader,* and Gibson whose ability to travel and promote the first edition of *Negroes with Guns,* Williams and the Monroe story was gaining lots of traction. Gibson labored to get the book published in several countries and languages as Williams spoke favorably about the case against the Monroe Defendants. For a short time, Ethel Johnson worked with CARE through the Freedom House. Mae Mallory was serving a prison sentence in Cleveland, Ohio, and Clarence Senior led the Monroe Defense Committee in support of Mallory. Williams privately suspected and accused Mallory of being a spy and/or FBI informant.[60] What led to the accusation came from a statement Mabel Stegall made during her interview with reporters when she blamed Mallory in a clip in *The Violet Crusader* documentary and from Tyson's research in *Radio Free Dixie.* On the day of the event leading up to the trumped-up kidnapping charges, Mallory had apparently taken "the terrified couple into a front bedroom, where they were perched on the side of the bed. John Lowery had noticed the couple's automobile sitting in the middle of the street and moved it to the curb, an act that later netted him a three- to five-year prison sentence for kidnapping. While Williams was on the telephone, talking to his informants around the county and allies around the country, Mallory took charge of the white couple. Mabel Williams confirmed this story and acknowledged that Mallory was a bitter woman. Robert Williams and others had to confront her several times about her rash temper." Days earlier, Woodrow Wilson reported, "Mallory had declared that she had a machine gun and said somebody was going to get killed since she was in Monroe. I told her we did not want to kill anyone," Wilson recalled and then said, "That was the stupidest thing I ever heard of, and I talked to her good." Williams kept a close eye on her, and at one point, Mallory recalled, "he chased me back in the house, and came back into the kitchen to reprimand me when I had seemed bent on violence." Although her story changed after the documentary was aired, each time Mabel Stegall was interviewed, she said, "this Mae Mallory was one of the main leaders she was giving out orders and she held a gun on me." Then she said, "We did not have anything, and we could not do anything but beg, which I did, and she told me that she did not want to hear my sob story. All the nasty remarks she made," Stegall concluded. "Mae Mallory ought to be strung up, and if she ever come up to Union County, she might get just that."[61] Even though they continued to write one another while Robert and Mabel were exiled in Cuba and China, Robert Williams suspected Mallory of being a spy and/or informant. Mallory wrote Robert and Mabel while in and out of prison, and they wrote to her too. In a letter dated March 29, 1967, however, Mallory discusses her true feelings about her interactions with Robert Williams and her traveling plans to Tanzania, stating, "He even accused me of being a spy for the man. Never in my life had I been so insulted. Rob should be the last person to accuse me of such a thing" and "I called Rob three times when he was in Africa. Never did he so much as write me a line until about three weeks ago. In fact, I think I will have the letter xeroxed so that you may have a copy and see for yourself that now he wants me to bring him up to date which means that the Henry [brother]s has not been writing him." Further complicating the conflict between Mallory and Williams,[62] the issue of Blacks in Cuba, and the racial struggles of African Americans in the United States, continued to surface. Andy Petit explains how those "with a long enough memory can recall their article on Robert F. Williams which claimed he had a falling out with Castro and had turned against the Revolution. This is a bold lie—Williams, who was chased out of the United States by the FBI, also had problems in Cuba with Soviet-oriented middle management, with the Soviets themselves, and with the FBI-dominated US Communist Party. Williams was on incredibly good terms with Che Guevara." After a *Time*'s article went public, he explains, "he was banned from ever returning to Cuba, as I discovered in the early nineties when one of his friends asked me to discuss a return visit with a Cuban consular official. When I did, the response was an immediate, tense but diplomatic "no en ese momento," which when translated in English means "not at that time." "Other evidence presented reveals that there were a series of efforts orchestrated by Robert and Mabel Williams while in Cuba with a distinct set of strategies that brought international and national attention to the racial crisis in the United States. His intentions were not to engage or lead a revolutionary nationalist movement as critics and scholars appear to suggest. However, there is no question the challenges and obstacles encountered during the latter years of Robert and Mabel's stay in Cuba were due to retaliation and shifting agendas by external forces working against him and other leftist activists' efforts. These disruptions did not prevent him from forging forward to advance his advocacy and to encourage Black cultural awareness and consciousness before, during, and after the Cuban Revolution. Once the entire family settled in China in July 1966 during the last decade of the Chinese Cultural Revolution (CPR),[63] Gerry Tannenbaum, a longtime foreign resident, recalls, Williams "was treated as one of the heads of state in Africa and elsewhere." Robert and Mabel continued to publish *The Crusader-in-Exile*, and Robert accepted invitations to give reports during radio interviews over Beijing airwaves about politicians in Washington, D.C. Months after Stokely Carmichael (aka Kwame Toure) began popularizing the Black Power slogan, rumors and accusations from abroad suggested that Williams was responsible for the riots in urban cities in America. Williams responded refuting the claims stating, "he was not responsible for the many riots in the urban wastelands of America. Washington, D. C. was responsible for doing nothing to prevent the mood from occurring, and for escalating the mood in the first place."[64] Going beyond its claims that Williams was a CIA informant, the most pressing concern he had in communist China came when Cuban communist officials charged with ruthless efficiency and released tens of thousands of two forged copies of *The Crusader-in-Exile*, a forgery of the April–May 1966 and May 1967 issues of the news magazine, carrying a metered postmarking from Havana, and mailed to the United States, Africa, and throughout the Caribbean, documenting a vicious smear attack against the People's Republic of China (PRC) and its leader, Chairman Mao. Bearing Williams's signature and masthead, the two forgeries denounced Mao and called him an arrogant, power-mad underlings and thugs for having betrayed the Cuban Revolution. The racist chauvinism and ethnocentric fanaticism charged in the fake copies of *The Crusader* inspired Williams to issue indignant press releases from Peking that denounced the forgeries and where they came from, stating beyond the "shadow of a doubt under the auspices of Cuban G2 [...] [and by] a high official of the Cuban Commission of the Tricontinental Organization."[65] The rumor and accusation that Williams was a CIA informant resulted in his association with China, and represented a failed attempt to discredit him and disrupt the alliance built between Williams and certain Chinese officials. The long campaign waged against Williams "by his enemies, presumably in Moscow or Havana," or Washington through the CIA, may have been involved, even though the evidence points toward Cuba. There is no doubt Williams encountered a "series of tricks and snares" during his last year in Havana. The case he presented through *Radio Free Dixie* and *The Crusader-in-Exile* remained his agency, and the messages he conveyed about lived experiences in the United States and Vietnam through the "social media" of the day exemplified his grievances with the United States and inspired a wide range of domestic and international activists and intellectuals in parts of the states, Cuba, and elsewhere to agitate and protest. Williams's interrogating voice heard over radio excited thousands of Black and white activists representing different ideological positions from southern and midwestern distances in the states by appealing to their ethics, sensibilities, and moral values. As this was occurring, "the Sino-Soviet conflict was raging, and Cuba sided with the Russians against Maoism."[66] As an international peace conference convened in Vietnam in 1965, Williams attended and made a few eye-opening remarks before U.S. Servicemen. Days after the speech, Williams interviewed Everett Alvarey, a U.S. Navy pilot who was shot down during an August bombing raid on Hanoi and Haiphang in South Vietnam. Williams, then the elected president-in-exile of the RAM, had also spoken about the United States' involvement in the Vietnam War, which made no sense to him, especially since thousands of drafted African American troops were fighting for democracy abroad while their families were being forced to fight for equality and civil rights in their home country. In Chairman Mao Tse-tung's China, during the split and after Williams's first trip there Williams had made a request for international support of the Afro-American struggle in the United States from world leaders, Mao's response came first on August 8, 1963, with his Statement in Support of the Afro-American Struggle against U.S. Imperialism. This helped to elevate Williams's status and case against the federal government. However, as Cohen reminds us, it also "triggered a new rash of attacks in the U. S. press, and [among] the anti-Peking Bourgeois Communist" [in Cuba, which] began to refer to him [Williams] as a "Chinese-controlled Black Nationalist."[67] Before all this, during autumn of 1964, Robert, Mabel, and their sons visited China (Robert Williams' second trip) and were treated as special guest of the 15th Anniversary of the PRC. On September 30, Mao "welcomed Williams in the Great Hall of the People, and October 1st during a celebration commemorating the birth of the PRC, Williams joined a roster with other Chinese officials to speak in Peking Square." A parade followed with a Chinese drama, "The East is Red," as the family admired the sparkling colorful scene. By November 28, Mao issued a statement in support of the people of the Congo and Leopoldville in objection to U.S. aggression there. As the second visit to China was ending, a departing banquet was hosted by the vice chairperson as part of a Chinese World Peace toast. Analytically, in my framing and contextualizing of "the Williamses' relationship and collaborations with the PRC," including "the benefits and the limitations of" the international interaction, I remain neutral. Reading Robeson Taj P. Frazier's research, which "unpack[s] how China's projects of socialism, anticolonialism, and support for African American liberation affected the internationalist politics of the radical couple,"[68] was instructive. Frazier's analysis and Erik McDuffie's review of Frazier's book, *The East is Black*, is based on a recasting of historian Robin D. G. Kelly's "radical black imagination" to explain how "this history demonstrates successful moments of international interchange and interconnections, as well as the various disconnects, omissions, and miscommunications within"[69] the Black liberation movements efforts. Rather than addressing Robert and Mabel Williams's agency, Frazier links Williams's agenda to the liberation movements occurring in the states in ways that may not necessarily be accurate. What is accurate, though, is Frazier's coverage of the two long months the couple traveled throughout northern China and experienced "a sense of recognition and nationality they had never encountered before" is on target considering an observation he made about Mabel's acknowledgment, "we had to go overseas to be recognized as Americans."[70] Capitalizing on the Chinese sights and tours for public relations purposes, a crew of three Chinese cameramen—Chen Kai-chu, Chin Ching-yi, and Chen Chin-ti—filmed scenes from the Chinese celebration and snapshots of the Williams family as they were seen visiting an automobile factory and a train shop factory in Northeastern China, and commuting by train to sightsee a ranch with deer and goat, as a narrator mentioned "agricultural experimental centers being opened and the nation's increasing numbers of Chinese scientists."[71] As the family continued the arranged tours, the three Chinese cameramen and/or filmmakers recorded other scenic scenes, including a visit to Tientsin University "where water jar dance" performed a traditional Chinese dance to the flow of Chinese music as a backdrop while the narrator spoke about Williams presenting "flowers to [the lead female] actress," along with "informational tidbits on China's economy and society."[72] They toured other parts of the Asian country, visiting sites in Peking, Mongolia, Shanghai, and Guangdong, which began in Peking, and they showed the couple visiting steel city, "open faced coal mine" and Williams dressed in overalls, safety hat and glasses looking inside the pit. Other sites they visited included an oil refinery, heavy machinery building plant, wire and cable factory, and industrial exhibition hall. Robert, Mabel, and their sons, Robert and John Chambers, who stayed in China, were also able to admire the National Arts Gallery and Peking Cultural Palace.[73] Williams believed in less than a year later that he had finally arrived in a neutral country, though communist, where he and Mabel could engage his propaganda without any interference, just as Mao's China planned for its production of the documentary film and its version of "a masterpiece of propaganda."[74] In three articles published in *The Crusader-in-Exile*, Williams praised Chairman Mao on the pages of the magazine and continued to present evidence against U.S. practices of racial discrimination, white supremacy, and imperialism. During the same visit in China, Ho Chi Minh had invited Robert and Mabel Williams in 1965, to attend a peace conference where Williams was able to deliver a rousing address that designated the United States as an aggressive bully seeking to control the world. Anti-imperialist Williams had urged those involved in South Vietnam National Front for Liberation to join forces with the North to defeat U.S. imperialist. In the March 1965 issue of *The Crusader-in-Exile*, Williams criticized the Johnson administration for using drafted African American troops in the war because it was convenient. In condemning Johnson's actions and the Vietnam War in Listen Brother, Williams praised Muhammad Ali for refusing to be inducted in the U.S. armed forces as well as criticized Johnson for being extremely slow in doing something about the treatment of full class Black citizens in the states. "Brothers of Vietnam patriots of the world, and lovers of peace and freedom, I greet you in the name of those of my fellow countrymen who are civilized enough to oppose U.S. aggression, I specifically greet you in the name of Afro-American freedom fighters who are waging a liberation struggle against American colonialism. As chairman-in-exile of the Revolutionary Action Movement, an American based united liberation front, comprising many groups and organizations, I resolutely offer support in our gallant brothers of Vietnam and to this international Conference for Solidarity with the People of Vietnam Against U.S. Imperialist Aggression for the Defense of Peace."[75] Speaking to Black troops on the scene at the time while denouncing both the Kennedy and Johnson administrations, Williams presented a case, stating: "God damn Bro! If we live under democracy in America, ain't no need to try to save nobody who lives under tyranny. If the oppression is worse than Mississippi, they're already dead."[76] Williams continued a month after Malcolm X's assassination in February of 1965, "We are opposed to the barbaric acts of the hyprocritical Johnson administration, at home and abroad. Our human decency will not allow us to prettify and serve as spineless apologists for savage Yankeeism. Not only do we condemn, protest and raise our fists in indignation at these brutal crimes perpetrated against noble patriots of this gallant land, but we promise, our brothers, and let the whole world bear witness, that we shall intensify our struggle for liberation in the so-called free world of the racist USA."[77] Three years later, after King was assassinated in 1968, Williams was not only recognized as the new voice of Black America but also considered and desired by many to be the symbolic leader for the African American revolutionary movements in the states. Williams's admirations and respect for China's efforts to build the country into something great was also a topic communicated in the pages of *The Crusader* as he explained, "The Chinese people are hard at work to accomplish the difficult today and the impossible tomorrow. An example of Chinese initiative and drive is the fact that when I visited there in 1963 many suburban busses and trucks carried rubber vats, inflated with natural gas, strapped on them. Chinese engineers had produced converters that enabled these vehicles to operate on natural gas instead of gasoline that was no longer obtainable abroad. When I turned the following year, China had already eliminated the necessity of using natural gas for motor vehicles. There was also a notable increase in road traffic."[78] From readers in the states, this all sounded impressive. Gibson recalls in an email insight he acquired at the time about Williams's trusting of and the support he [Gibson] was receiving from Marxist-Leninist activists. "I must confess that reading these files after so many years has reminded me of many events and people long forgotten. I also fear that, considering the complexity of the ideological, political, and personal struggles, you may have some difficulty understanding just what was going on. Remember that I was in very wide contact with Marxist-Leninist groups throughout Western Europe and many African liberation movements. Strong support for Rob came from the Pan Africanist Congress of Azania (South Africa) and, in Peking, Rob met several of their leading cadres, such as Gora Ebrahim and Lionel Morrison." I was authoring[79] a book on the liberation movements, published in 1972 by OUP to the consternation of the naïve and gullible and the dishonest. That book has stood up well to the test of time, although OUP was pressured into refusing me permission to do a second, revised edition. "Throughout my active political life, I have been under attack and have managed to cope with it, but Rob was clearly distressed at times, I admit, by my close relationship—without party membership—with many ML groups, and he clearly did not want, nor did I, to identify the African American struggle with the Marxist-Leninist, pro-Chinese Left in the international movement. But they were the ones who were trying to help him by translating and publishing locally *Negroes with Guns* and other materials, and it was they who tried to force the Swedish government to grant him a visit." This revelation from Gibson revealed also the transformation as an ideological and political shift since Williams had the Chinese connection, coming from other sources with imagined agendas and motivations who were desiring the same opportunities and privileges, including ML (Marxist Leninist) and an intensify in the states that influenced young African American radical leaders such Max Stanford of RAM, Huey P. Newton, and Elaine Brown of the BPP; Maulana Karenga of the Black Cultural Nationalist group, US, and Gaidi and Imari Obadele of the RNA, to lean more toward Maoism in China rather than Castro's unresolved racism and classism in Cuba which was backed by Moscow. Robin D. G. Kelly, Robeson Taj Frazier, and Erik McDuffie's interpretation of Frazier's scholarship about imagination serving as the "catalyst for political engagement and social transformation" "among African-descended activists, writers, and artists [...] [who] dreamed of a new world different from the status quo," and "not racism, oppression, and exploitation,"[80] is not applicable when it comes to the struggles of Robert and Mabel Williams. There is no doubt that Robert Williams's agenda, actions, and intentions were different. They were not imagined; they were consistent and praxis.

Returning to the states, resigning from the RNA, navigating China and racism in the United States, by championing civil and human rights in Lake County, Michigan

Back in 1969, "there was no US Embassy in Peking." There were no American officials that Robert Williams could approach for assistance as he and Mabel planned a return flight to the United States to face the pending kidnapping charges. Williams did "possess a valid US passport but while residing in Tanzania was unable to renew the Visa for his return trip home."[81] Leaving the East Africa country before Robert, Mabel and the boys' flight to Detroit, and before Williams would board his flight, Gibson suspected "somebody in the U.S. Government was unhappy about the decision to allow Rob to return home." An arrangement had been made for Williams to return and to be immediately released on bail for the kidnapping charges by the Federal Commissioner in Detroit. The evidence suggests that the CIA had taken an interest in Williams, and, according to Gibson, "it would have had the assets on the ground to arrange such a curious if provident accident." Delayed by the British authorities as he was enroute to Detroit, "the US Embassy [in London] had maliciously informed the British government that Williams was not wanted in the States and should be deported from the UK to Egypt," where his Egyptian Air flight had stopped from Dar es Salaam en route to London. "Rob knew no one in Cairo. There were demonstrations in London against Rob's imprisonment in the Pentonville Detention Center by British Black activists [BPP members] and much attention in the British press that was embarrassing to the British government." Locked up in detention, [which at first, he thought when advised he would be staying overnight, Williams imagined it would be in a hotel but it turned out to be a jail], he went on a four-day hunger strike in protest. Bill Sutherland, one of his associates who was in contact with him while imprisoned, is alleged to have contacted Mabel who was upset, and who contacted Attorney Milton Henry. Sutherland, "who was married to the Ghanaian dramatist and actress Efua Sutherland," also contacted Tony Smythe, who worked for the British Civil Liberties Union. Writing the author in an April 9, 2001, email message, Gibson then explains, "The last time I saw Rob was on 15 September 1969 when he was flown back to the USA on a special Trans World Airline (TWA) flight from the Heathrow Airport in London to Detroit. With him was his lawyer and associate Milton Henry, who stayed [...] at my home in West London during the struggle to get the US Government to permit Rob to return to the States." Gibson and friends from the Pan Africanist Congress of South Africa in London and others "assisted Milton Henry in organizing [a] press conference at the London Hilton to publicize this scandalous double-cross of an agreement made between Henry and the Department of Justice for Rob to return and appear before a Federal Commissioner on the North Carolina Kidnapping charges."[82] Henry had made the details of Williams's return clear and safe as previously agreed upon with the Department of Justice. Another press conference held at Williams's request thanked hundreds of supporters in the London area. Eventually, according to Gibson, the "US gave way." The U.S. State Department granted Williams a one-way passport [and visa] for the return trip, although four airlines in succession, two of them American, had refused to carry him on the ground that he was a safety hazard. "They considered him too dangerous to be allowed to take a regular flight, so a Black TWA vice president named Jimmy Plinton piloted a special flight" for Williams from the Heathrow Airport on flight TWA 707 to Detroit along with Attorney Milton Henry, and two federal marshals. The action, according to TWA airline officials, was taken in response to a request from the U.S. government, which paid the 20,000 dollar bill for the private flight, despite hundreds of letters complaining to the president and the State Department criticizing them for bringing "a traitor" back to the United States with tax dollars. Letters contained passages such as "Brother Williams should be shot on entering the U.S.A." when he "spent eight years in Communist countries spouting communist doctrine and defiling the United States," he should "be tried for treason." In another letter dated November 26, 1969, an anonymous writer addressed his letter to Congressman Laurence J. Burton of the House of Representatives in Washington, D.C., stating, "Several times recently while listening to the radio, we have been told of the radical views and activities of one Williams, a Negro who left this country (self-banishment), to take up residence in Cuba and Red China. There he was thoroughly schooled in revolutionary propaganda and activities. He was rejected as an undesirable citizen when he sought to enter Great Britain but was provided with a chartered plane to come to the United States to promulgate his doctrines. How can this country open its doors and put out the welcome mat to such an individual, and at the same time send our troops to Asia to try and contain the spread of communism? We listened to President Nixon's address last month and support him in his efforts to achieve an honorable peace. But how can we condone within our own boundaries that activities of persons who are known to be working for the subversion and overthrow of this government? Surely all the laws that would restrain such a person in these acts of sedition have not gone down the drain. We believe that many others of the silent majority are like us in expecting our representatives in Washington to take immediate and effective action to safeguard this commonwealth. P.S. Cannot something be done through government channels for the Prisoners of War in North Vietnam?" In yet another pressure letter objecting to Williams's return and release on personal bond, except this time written to Senator Stuart Symington indicating, "Will you please use your influence to see that this man is placed behind bars on charges of sedition, kidnapping, and treason (Article III, Section 3, [of the] U. S. Constitution: or in adhering to their enemies, giving them aid and comfort." His writing in his paper, "The Crusader," leaves no doubt as to which side he is on. Will you please also answer three questions for us? (1) Who is responsible for bringing him back to the United States? (2) Who paid for that plane flight by TWA? (3) Why is he free now on bail? Immediately upon arrival to Detroit, Williams was arrested by FBI agents for an outstanding Federal fugitive warrant (under the authority of the Fugitive Felon Act, 18 U.S.C. 1073), where Williams would be charged in the U.S. District Court in Detroit and released on a personal 10,000 dollar bond. Once released on the federal charge, Williams was apprehended by Wayne County authorities and appeared before another judge for an extradition hearing. The State of North Carolina had requested extradition from the State of Michigan. Williams did not waive extradition. An extradition hearing date was set for November 12, 1969, and Williams was released again on a 10,000 dollar personal bond. By early October, Robert, Mabel, and one of their sons, John Williams, were joined by Detroit attorneys Milton Henry, Kenneth Cochran, and Shelton Helpurn who arranged a meeting at the Capital Building in Lansing with Michigan governor William Milliken's legal advisor Joseph Thibodeau to present their case on why Robert Williams should not be extradited to North Carolina. Weeks later, Williams resigned from the RNA. Gwendolyn Midlo Hall organized the Committee to Aid in the Defense of Robert F.

Williams. While serving as a Ford Foundation Fellow in the Center for Chinese Studies at the University of Michigan, Williams cooperation and collaborated with political scientist Allen Whitling in the Center for Chinese Studies, who served as a consultant to Secretary of State Henry Kissinger on behalf of President Richard Nixion's administration regarding its international agenda and plans to discuss opening diplomatic relations with Communist China. The grievance rhetoric of Robert Williams, despite the contradictions surrounding him, reveals that while "he vacillated back-and-forth in terms of his flirtations with Black Power,"[83] he was relevant then and remains so in contemporary America. Rob no longer served as RNA president after December of 1969,[84] so that he could fight against the North Carolina extradition charges.[85] Nor did he join the BPP, although Newton offered Party support. Two years before the charges were dismissed in 1973, Robert and Mabel Williams relocated to Western Michigan where they worked effectively and tirelessly in Baldwin and Idlewild, Michigan, promoting cultural awareness, spreading Black political consciousness, and raising critical questions about enforcing justice and practices of democracy in Congress, the White House, the courts, and law enforcement agencies in Baldwin and Muskegon, Michigan. Rob fought against power inequities in Lake County (LC), Michigan, particularly incidents involving injustices and wrongs inflicted among African American citizens in the area. Police-community interactions and relations with the press needed addressing. For example, few scholars know that Williams challenged free speech rights when he staged a one-man protest against the editor of the *Lake County Star* in 1985 for refusing to publish a letter about the Ruby Chatman Nelson case as a paid advertisement. Williams also took the newspaper to court, won the case, and was awarded a Civil Rights complaint in 1989. The award from the case was used to organize the Lake County People's Association for Human Rights. Williams's activism was successful locally although contested by the editors of the newspaper and different county sheriffs as he petitioned to end prostitution during deer hunting season, police brutality, and political corruption in LC government within the Sheriff's Department.[86] Rob Williams, as he was known by colleagues and friends, championed human rights and principles and practices of civil rights, from the standpoint of what it means to be an American citizen of African descent. Timothy Tyson and Richard Mares correctly documented how Williams was "catching hell" during his and Mabel's last year in Cuba but incorrectly suggested that he was singularly used as a tool of propaganda by the Cuban and Chinese leadership during the Cold War Civil Rights era. This observation denies, dismisses, and/or ignores the power of Williams's agency. Although Williams was challenged, restricted, and prohibited in Cuba from spreading his political philosophy, in China he established a transnational collaboration with Mao's Chinese government "which sought to cultivate political alliance with the African American left in a meticulous, targeted, and effective"[87] way in an attempt to define racism as second to classism. As these activities were occurring abroad, Black Power organization leaders and activists in the states, according to Robin D. G. Kelly and Besty Esch, "took Mao quite literally, advocating for armed insurrection and drawing inspiration and ideas directly from Williams's theory of guerrilla warfare in the urban United States. RAM leaders believed such a war was not only possible but could be won in ninety days."[88]

Notes

1 These definitions are expressed throughout Robert F. Williams, *Negroes with Guns*. Foreword by Gloria House. Introduction by Timothy Tyson. Detroit: Wayne State University Press, 1998, which is the third reprint of *Negroes with Guns*. The original copy was published in 1962 by Marzani & Munsell, Inc., while Robert Williams and his family were exiled in Cuba. In a letter written to Marc Schleifer (aka S. Abdullah Schleifer) on August 11, 1971, Williams raised questions about the publication of the book, writing "I got your letter. Marzani still has not come through with any money. He has sold the rights of the book to Floyd McKissick who claims that he cannot get it printed. Marzani claims that he only owes me $300. Because the book did not sell very well. A lot of B. S. has gone down."
2 Thomas J. Surge, author of *Sweet Land of Liberty: The Forgotten Struggle for Civil Rights in the North*. New York: Random House, 2009, 316–18.
3 Ibid., 317.
4 Ibid., 318.
5 Walter Rucker, "Crusader in Exile: Robert F. Williams and the International Struggle for Black Freedom in America," *The Black Scholar*, 36 (2006): 2–3, 20.
6 Abayomi Azikiwe's tributes to Mabel Williams were published in three articles: (April 26, 2014). "The Legacy of Mabel Robinson Williams," *Pan African News Wire*, 1–4; (April 30, 2014). "Mabel Williams: A Legacy of Struggle and Community Service." *Workers World* https://www.workers.org/2014/04/174/ and (May 28, 2014). "Tribute to Mabel Robinson Williams (1931-2014)," Mabel and Robert Williams led a campaign for self-defense that shaped the 1960s. https://sbayview.com/2014/05/tribute-to-mabel-robinson-williams-1931-2014-mabel-androbert-f-williams-led-a-campaign-for-self--shaped.
7 Mary L. Dudziak, *Cold War Civil Rights: Race and the Image of American Democracy*. With a new preface by the author. Princeton: Princeton University Press, 2000. Dudziak reveals how "American racism became a major concern of U. S. allies, a chief Soviet propaganda theme, and an obstacle to American Cold War goals throughout Africa, Asia, and Latin America …" She argues "the Cold War helped facilitate key reforms, including desegregation, as the U. S. government sought to polish its international image."
8 See Harold Cruse, *The Crisis of the Negro Intellectual: A Historical Analysis of the Failure of Black Leadership*. New York: Quill, 1967; Robert Carl Cohen. *Black Crusader: A Biography of Robert Franklin Williams*. Secaucus: Lyle Stuart, 1972; James Foreman, *The Making of Black Revolutionaries*. Seattle: University of Washington Press, 1972, 1985; Marcellus Barksdale, "Robert F. Williams and the Indigenous Civil Rights Movement in Monroe, North Carolina," *The Journal of Negro History*, 69 (1984): 73–89; and the first edition of Timothy B. Tyson's *Radio Free Dixie: Robert F. Williams and the Roots of Black Power*. Chapel Hill: The University of North Carolina Press, 1999.
9 Tommy J. Curry and Max Kelleher, "Robert F. Williams and Militant Civil Rights: The Legacy and Philosophy of Pre-emptive Self-Defense," *Radical Philosophy Review*, 18, 1 (2015): 45–68.
10 Erik McDuffie's framework on the Black Diaspora of the Midwest identifies both the boundaries and scope of the Midwestern states. See Erik S. McDuffie, "The Second Battle for Africa Has Begun" Rev. Clarence W. Harding, Jr., Garveyism, Liberia, and the Diasporic Midwest, 1966–1978, in *Global Garveyism*, edited by Ronald J. Stephens and Adam Ewing, Gainesville: University Press of Florida, 2019, 89; "'A New Day Has Dawned for the UNIA': Garveyism, the Diasporic Midwest, and West Africa, 1920–80," *Journal of West African History*, 2, 1 (Spring 2016), 73–114; and "The Diasporic Journeys of Louise Little: Grassroots Garveyism, the Midwest, and Community Feminism," *Women, Gender, and Families of Color*, 4, 2 (Fall 2016), 146–170.
11 In my next book, *Robert and Mabel Williams: Matrimonial Partnership in Black Resistance History*, I detail how Mabel worked behind the scenes and on the ground in the communities where they lived. Mabel assisted Rob, who functioned as chief spokesperson advocating for the constitutional rights of African Americans.
12 FBI surveillance files report that Williams received an honorable discharge from the U.S. Army in 1946. Agents also report that his army record indicates that he was a subject of considerable controversy for failure to obey orders, disrespect toward an officer, and because

he went absent without leave on several occasions. In the Marine Corps, he was dishonorably discharged for disobeying an officer and other charges due to racism. Williams scored high on an officer candidate test to be assigned in the intelligence division but was denied entry into the program. This incident further fueled Williams's determination to fight against racism.

13 Williams, *Negroes with Guns*, 26.
14 Ibid., xxv.
15 In Jeanne Theoharis, *The Rebellious Life of Mrs. Rosa* Parks. With a new introduction. Boston: Beacon Press, 2013, she writes this outraged Mabel Williams and "many felt that while King was being promoted as the great leader, Mrs. Parks was not getting her due." Mabel was not making this observation as a feminist but as an Africana womanist, when she states, "I don't think she was too concerned about that. But people who were concerned about history were. [...] A lot of the male chauvinism that went on, we talked about that. But she was not bitter. [...] She wasn't fighting anyway for credit," 162.
16 Ibid., 162.
17 Ibid.
18 Ibid.
19 Robert F. Williams, *Negroes with Guns*.
20 Denise Hill, "Public Relations, Racial Injustice, and the 1958 North Carolina Kissing Case." Dissertation. University of North Carolina, Chapel Hill, 2016, 3.
21 Ibid., 212.
22 Rucker, "Crusader in Exile," 19.
23 Brenda Gayle Plummer, *In Search of Power: African Americans in the Era of Decolonization, 1956–1974* (New York: Cambridge University Press), 70.
24 Ibid.
25 Daniel Rasmussen, *American Uprising: The Untold Story of America's Largest Slave Revolt*. New York: Harper Perennial, 216.
26 Jackson explains during a virtual panel discussion she participated in a panel organized at Purdue University, through the African American Studies and Research Center.
27 Rasmussen, *American Uprising*, 215–16.
28 Kellie Carter Jackson, *Force and Freedom: Black Abolitionists and the Politics of Violence*. University of Philadelphia: Pennsylvania Press, 2019.
29 Rasmussen, *American Uprising*, 211.
30 Ibid., 211–12.
31 Ibid., 3.
32 Ibid., 3.
33 Robert Carl Cohen, *Black Crusader*, 112 and Lynn, 143.
34 Hill, "Public Relations, Racial Injustice, and the 1958 North Carolina Kissing Case," 3.
35 Pero Gagio Dagbovie, "God Has Spared Me to Tell My Story," *The Black Scholar*, 43, no. 5 (Spring 2013): 75.
36 Ibid., 75.
37 Ibid., 80
38 Tyson, *Radio Free Dixie*, 1999.
39 Huey P. Newton, *Revolutionary Suicide*, with the assistance of J. Herman Blake. Introduction by Fredrika Newton. New York: Penguin Books, 1973, 117.
40 "Reply to William Patterson," in *To Die for the People*, edited by Toni Morrison with a foreword by Elaine Brown. San Fransico: City Lights Books, 2009, 168. This reply was reprinted in the July 4, 1970, issue of *The Black Panther Party* newsletter.
41 Ibid., 168.
42 Williams made these statements during an exclusive interview, while he was exiled in Cuba during the summer of 1963. The interview was published in *Marxist-Leninist Quarterly*, II, 1. Transcription, Editing and Markup by Paul Saba on Encyclopedia of Anti-Revisionism On-Line.
43 Ibid.
44 Ibid.
45 Ronald J. Stephens, "Praise the Lord and Pass the Ammunition: Robert F. Williams' Crusade for Justice on Behalf of 22 million African Americans as a Cuban Exile," *Black Diaspora Review*, 2 (2011): 18.
46 Timothy Tyson, *Radio Free Dixie*. page 241.

47 Ibid., 1.
48 Cohen, *Black Crusader*, 207.
49 Ruth Reitan, *The Rise and Decline of an Alliance: Cuba and African American Leaders in the 1960s*. East Lansing: Michigan State University Press, 1999, 1.
50 Rucker, "Crusader in Exile," 1.
51 Carl Cohen, *Black Crusader*, 208.
52 Robert Jr. and John Chambers traveled to China with their parents. They wanted to stay and attend school there which they did, according to John during an interview I had with him. They learned the language and worked in the fields with other children.
53 Cohen, *Black Crusader*, 208.
54 *Testimony of Robert F. Williams. United States Committee on the Judiciary United States Senate*. Washington, DC: US Government Printing Office, 1971, 11–12, in the NAACP Papers at the Library of Congress.
55 Two-hour telephone interview with Cuban Historian Osvaldo Cardenas, March 30, 2023.
56 Richard Gibson was born in 1931 in Los Angeles, and he grew up in Philadelphia, and attended Kenyon College in Gambier, Ohio. He enlisted and did a short stint in the U.S. Army and stationed in Europe, which gave him an admiration for a European life. He lived in Rome and soon thereafter in Paris, where he wrote a detective novel entitled *A Mirro for Magistrates*. Gibson was an associate of Richard Wright and at some point "fell in and out with Wright and other expatriate intellectuals [such as E. Franklin Frazer, and Julian Mayfield]" who "raised suspicion about Gibson's affiliations as early as 1959," according to Charisse Burden-Stella. Sometime in 1957, Gibson left Paris for employment with CBS Radio News as a radio reporter.
57 Richard Gibson sent an email message to the author, November 19, 2001, as part of a series of interviews.
58 Carl Cohen, *Black Crusader*, 282.
59 Robeson Taj P. Frazier, "Thunder in the East: China, Exiled Crusaders, and the Unevenness of Black Internationalism," *American Quarterly*, 63, no. 4 (December 2011): 938–39.
60 In Paula Marie Seniors' *Mae Mallory, the Monroe Defense Committee, and World Revolutions: African American Women Radical Activists*. University of Georgia Press, 2024, she discusses domestic and international conflicts between Mallory and Williams.
61 Tyson, *Radio Free Dixie*, 279–80.
62 Floyd Bixler Missick of the Congress of Racial Equality (CORE) apparently had the pamphlet published through World View Publishers of New York, under the title *Listen, Brother!* which is based on an address Williams gave in 1965 during the Vietnam conference. Mae Mallory authored the foreword indicating she was a guest in the couple's home that eventful weekend in August 1961, when the Rob saved the Stegall's lives and he was later charged with kidnaping (obviously at the instigation of the police and Klan). As a result of my presence, she explains, I was tried and convicted of kidnapping and sentenced to 16 to 20 years. Three others along with Rob faced the same charge," Williams, *Listen, Brother!*, 6.
63 Robert and Mabel Williams's discreet exit from Cuba was indicated in the letter to Castro stating that the only official in the Cuban government who showed any genuine interest in the struggle he waged was Che Guevara, and even then, there were some serious limitations. This marked a snowball effect as other Black leaders, including Kwame Toure, who was at the height of popularity, would distance themselves from the Caribbean nation, according to Moore.
64 Williams is quoted in an interview with Cohen in Dar Es Salaam, Tanzania, in East Africa, ca. 1968. It was recorded, aired, and released on Cohen's documentary entitled *Let It Burn: The Coming Destruction of the USA*.
65 Carlos Moore, *Castro, the Blacks, and Africa*. Los Angeles: Center for Afro-American Studies, University of California, 265–6. According to Moore, "Williams accused them all of being nothing less than a gang of unscrupulous vipers who openly engaged in counter-revolutionary activity, graft, piracy and all manner of subversion" (265).
66 Dagbovie, *The Black Scholar*, 82.
67 Cohen, *Black Crusader*, 266.
68 Frazier, "Thunder in the East," 932.
69 Ibid., 932.

70 Ibid., 935.
71 Ibid., 937.
72 Ibid., 937.
73 The Bentley Historical Library in Ann Arbor owns the Robert F. Williams Papers. As part of the collection there are three video tapes on ¾ inch U-Matic, entitled "Robert [and Mabel] Williams in China 1964." My observations and notes I took during my two visits to the library in 1993 and 1994 to view the film footage and document some of the scenes from the Chinese documentary film.
74 Frazier, "Thunder in the East," 937.
75 Robert F. Williams, *The Crusader-in-Exile,* monthly newsletter, March 1965, 6, 8, 1.
76 Williams, *Listen! Brother,* a pamphlet composed, printed and bound entirely by voluntary labor, which was sold for 30 cents, April 1968, 14.
77 Williams, *The Crusader-in-Exile,* 5.
78 Ibid., 6.
79 Word suggested changing the "word" writing, which appears in Gibson's email message to me to "authoring."
80 Erik S. McDuffie. Review of Robeson Taj Frazier, *The East is Black: Cold War China in the Black Radical Imagination.* Durham: Duke University Press, 2014, *Left History,* 135.
81 Gibson explains in an email message to the author, on April 9, 2002, detailing incidents and the circumstances surrounding Williams's return to the states.
82 Detailing the incident in a small book published in French, Gibson wrote the introductory chapter in *Robert F. Williams, Rivoluzioone in Minoranza,* a cura di (introduction by) Richard Gibson. Tutti I Diritti Riservati: Tindalo, 1970, 5–30, in which he discusses the British government and TWA issues and responses in greater detail.
83 This comes from one of the external reviewers who reviewed my book proposal for *Robert Franklin Williams Speaks.*
84 "Resigns as President of New Africa," staff writer, *Detroit News,* December 4, 1969, 1, 14.
85 Gwendolyn Midlo Hall, *Haunted by Slavery: A Southern White Woman in the Freedom Struggle.* Chicago: Haymarket Books, 2021.
86 For more details surrounding Robert Williams's activism in Lake County, see Ronald J. Stephens, "Narrating Acts of Resistance: Explorations of Untold Heroic and horrific Battle Stories Surrounding Robert Franklin Williams's Residence in Lake County, Michigan," *Journal of Black Studies,* 33, no. 5 (May 2003): 675–703.
87 Ruodi Duan, "Black Power in China: Mao's Support for African American Racial Struggle as Class Struggle," March 8, 2017, 5. https://medium.com/fairbank-center/black-power-in-china-maos-support-for-african-american-racial-struggle-as-class-struggle-767312a66abb.
88 Robin DG Kelly and Betsy Esch, "Black Like Mao: Red China and Black Revolution," *Soul* (Fall 1999): 17. See also Errol A. Henderson's *The Revolution Will Not Be Theorized: Cultural Revolution in the Black Power Era.* New York: SUNY Press, 2019, 238–39. Henderson explains how "RAM endorsed armed struggle as a means for the colonized black nation to free itself from the bonds of imperial rule, just like anticolonial struggles throughout the world" (238). RAM argued that a major part of guerilla warfare in the U.S.A., will take place in the cities, which they viewed as the pockets of power and heart of the economy. RAM's black liberation army would be tasked to take over cities, cause complete social dislocation of communications, etc." (239). "Maoism died when Mao did in 1976." See Kelly and Esch, "Black Like Mao," 37.

Part II

The documents selected for the prefatory notes for Robert Franklin Williams Speaks provide a summarized account of Williams's life and activism across various geographical locations, offering insight into the broader content of the civil rights movement, racial tensions in the U.S., and international solidarity during the mid-20th century. Each section of document serves a specific purpose in illuminating Williams's journey and the political and social environment he and Mabel navigated.

In Chapter 1, from 1956 to 1961, the family of Robert Sr. and Mabel Williams, which included their sons, Robert Jr. and John Chambers Williams, lived on Boyte Street in the Newtown neighborhood of Monroe. After returning home from the Marine Corps in 1955 and being elected as president of the Union County chapter of the NAACP, my detailed account of his efforts to combat racial injustice, his involvement in the Negroes with Guns campaign, and his early activism are revealed. This section underscores the genesis of Robert Williams's approach to civil rights, emphasizing his philosophy of armed self-defense and direct action against systemic racism. It sets the stage for understanding his evolution from a local activist to an international figure in the Black liberation movement. Four months after the August 28, 1955, Mississippi kidnapping, brutal beating, lynching, and murder of fourteen-year-old Emmitt Till, and three months after the arrest of Mrs. Rosa Parks and the beginning of the Montgomery Bus Boycott, Robert Williams escalated his resistance against the policies of the Monroe government, its local police and sheriff's department, and the white racist and terrorists threats from citizens over Jim Crow beliefs and politics. A map drawing of Monroe illustrates the racial divisions in Monroe through the railroad track marking. Because Williams, a veteran of two wars, believed the Constitution guaranteed African Americans full citizenship rights, he made efforts to address white America's refusal in Monroe and elsewhere to abide by its federal laws. Williams delivers a rousing sermon on March 25, 1956, entitled, "Col. Jim Crow's Last Stand" at All Soul's Chapel Unitarian Fellowship Church, calling out "the hypocrisy of a democracy with Jim Crow policies."[1] During the sermon, he predicted worsening racial tensions in Monroe, and elsewhere in the South. Williams and other Newtown community members patrolled the neighborhood and organized a *Negro with Guns* Campaign raising concerns about a series of racial injustices from 1957 to 1959 that he and others witnessed. As Union County's NAACP president, Williams was consumed by demonstrations to integrate Monroe's public library and swimming pool, the famous kissing case and arrest of two Black youths, the acquitted of two white men for the brutal assaults of two Black women, and NAACP hearing and letters regarding his suspension as president. Days after Williams issued that statement if we cannot get justice in the courts, "we must convict perpetrators on the scene, meeting violence with violence, and lynchings with lynchings," NAACP Secretary Roy Wilkins's letter announcing the suspension, and as a result the development of the Monroe Defense Committee in support of the defendants in the Monroe kidnapping case, as well as the transcripts of Robert and Mabel Williams's testimony in defense of Harold Reape, John Lowry, and Mae Mallory, who were the Monroe defendants. In February 1961 during an interview with John Schultz in Chicago, a few months before Williams, the radical integrationist, and his family went in exile in Cuba, Schultz raised questions about civil rights causes, and then about Williams's use of "we" and a "collective" Blackness, and other topics pertaining to militancy and Black resistance.

Cuba, 1962–1966

Documents detailing Williams's exile in Cuba, his interactions with Fidel Castro, and his efforts to navigate the complexities of living as a Black internationalist in a communist country illustrate the global dimensions of the African American freedom struggle for civil rights. These selections highlight the ideological shifts and challenges Robert and Mabel Williams faced, showing Rob's adaptability and unwavering commitment to racial justice, even when it led to conflicts with Cuban officials over race and class issues.

In Chapter 2, where Robert Williams had traveled twice before being granted political asylum from Fidel Castro, he was considered an exiled celebrity as he gave Havana Radio interviews and traveled to China twice (in 1963 and 1964). Williams frequently delivered statements condemning the U.S. government, and continued to publish his transnational newsletter, *The Crusader-in-Exile*. Robert and Mabel Williams also produced weekly broadcasts of *Radio Free Dixie*. Additionally, Williams's relationship with Gibson continued, although it was reported that he was a CIA informant. Rob exchanged letters with Richard Gibson about the publication of *Negroes with Guns* and other topics about life in Cuba as a Black internationalist. Writing about the publication of the first edition of *Negroes with Guns*, Gibson tried to have the book published in English and translated in Italian, French, German, and Swedish. In one letter, for example, Williams explains to Gibson he was "catching hell" from certain Cuban officials who were sabotaging his work.

Letters about certain Communist Cuban officials who were getting in the way and sabotaging his efforts are also revealed in letters to and from Gibson. Gibson worked with him on the possibility of getting the book translated and published in English, Italian, French, German, and Swedish. But, as the rumors surfaced about Gibson's identity as a CIA informant continue to circulate while he was in Algeria, Gibson was on record asking, "for money to denounce the FPCC" and for the federal government "to grant fugitive Robert Williams immunity from protection if he returned from Cuba." Gibson defended Williams's safe return to the States based on reports from the intelligence community reports which were provided to FBI Director, J. Edgar Hoover, and shared with Attorney General Robert F. Kennedy, the CIA and State Department whose recommendations were that "Gibson was untrustworthy" and that they "were not initiating any more communication with him."

Although Gibson denied the charges advanced by his ML comrades when questioned about Lee Oswald's membership with the Fair Play for Cuba Committee he willingly cooperated and further offered to share information about other members for money and if the federal government would grant "fugitive Robert Williams immunity and protection if he returned from Cuba. Documented in the RAM Papers are reports revealed by the U.S. intelligence community under the direction of FBI Director, J. Edgar Hoover about Gibson that were shared with the CIA, the State Department, and Attorney General Robert F. Kennedy, which stated, "Gibson was untrustworthy," and that they "were not initiating any more communication with him." In addition, Gibson stated in a September 1965 letter that he was not allowed to travel to Cuba to participate in the Tricontinental Conference. Gibson further reported that when the conference was held, not one Black American was permitted in—no Black newsmen—although the old revisionist hacks from the U.S. was there. An effort was even made to keep Rob out, and he would have been kept out if it had not been for Jariretundu Kozonguzi and Dr. Ana Kiva Cordero, who threatened to make a scene if he were not admitted. Gibson turned his attention to the whereabouts of Williams Worthy who had gone missing, a subject he and Williams raised concerns about. After Fidel Castro had declared that racism no longer existed in Cuba, Robert Williams found his political philosophy about race in defense of the civil and human rights of African Americans was in opposition to Castro's Communist philosophy and policy about race in Cuba. Castro wanted to create a class structure as opposed to addressing the race concerns raise by Williams.

China, 1966–1969

Chapter 3 on the Williams family's time in China provides insight into his broadening perspective on global anti-imperialist struggles and the role of African Americans within them. By including his broadcasts to U.S., soldiers in Vietnam, and the letters Williams exchanged with Gibson, these documents reveal his expanding influence and efforts to link the civil rights movement in the U.S. with anti-colonial struggles abroad. This selection also underscores the personal sacrifices Robert Williams and his family made, including their immersion in Chinese culture and the impact of political exile on their lives. he letters exchanged between Williams and Gibson are revealing too.

When and wherever the couple lived they worked independently, and while visiting China from Cuba, Robert, Mabel, and their sons traveled there and toured the country, the boys stayed in 1964 as they learned Mandarin and English. Robert, Jr., and John embraced what they were learning about Chinese culture. Increasingly, however, Williams's advocacy and opposition to U.S. imperialist policies toward North Vietnam, enabled him to meet with Ho Chi Minh and to deliver and broadcast antiwar themes to U.S. Black soldiers fighting in South Vietnam, while remaining silent about the treatment of his loved ones. Silent but against Cuba's agenda and Castro's Communist Party policies to create a class structure as opposed to addressing its race problem,

Robert Williams, after settling in China, wrote Castro to explain his reasons for leaving Communist Cuba. It remains unclear whether Castro was ever received a copy of the letter. Despite continuing with the publication of *The Crusader-in-Exile*, Cuban officials produced and released two forgeries of the newsletter, which he believed were under the auspices of Cuban-G-2 secret police and the CIA. Williams, who believed that these efforts were spurred on by the Cubans, was soured by this gesture of betrayal of oppression peoples by the American-Soviet Cuban axis. These international engagements become important in terms of contextualizing efforts aimed against Robert Williams by Cuban, Soviet, and U.S. intelligence agents and officials, including the CIA and FBI agents and their operations to escalate spy campaigns before and after his return to the United States.

Detroit, 1969–1996

Upon returning to the United States, Chapter 4 explores Williams's involvement in academia and community activism in the Midwest, as well as his continued influence in international politics, is showcased through his association with the University of Michigan and local communities in Detroit and eventually in Baldwin, Michigan The documents from this period reflect on Williams's legacy, demonstrating his ongoing commitment to justice and equality, his influence on future generations, and the recognition of his contributions to the civil rights movement and beyond. Two to three months after returning to Detroit, Robert Williams resigned from the RNA as its president and was awarded a one-year Ford Foundation Fellowship to work with the Center for Chinese Studies at the University of Michigan. Drawing from his extensive travels and stay in China, Williams advised political scientist Allen Whiting, who in turn served as a consultant to Henry Kissinger, who at that time served as Nixion's national security advisor, shortly before Nixion's 1972 trip to China. Williams used his knowledge of Mao's Chinese government for his safe passage home and willingness to assist the U.S.-Chinese governments. A petition from ten thousand Japanese citizens who were against Williams extradition to North Carolina, and a 1970 interview with Nathan Hare that was published in *The Black Scholar*. For the next twenty-six years, the Williams couple lived in Lake County, Michigan, and on November 1, 1996, *A Legacy of Resistance: Tributes to Robert and Mabel Williams* was organized in Detroit at Wayne State University, to honor the legacy of Robert and Mabel Williams during the celebration.[2]

Baldwin, Michigan and the Nation, 1972–2002

During the early 1970s, support for Robert and Mabel's decision, after Robert resigned from the RNA, to focus exclusively on the North Carolina case. Chapter 5 reveals the support first came from Gwendolyn Midlo Hall, who led the Robert F. Williams Defense Committee, and from Yoriko Nakajima who assisted with the mobilizing of signatures from Japanese citizens, along with the signatures of two governors, nine mayors, and seven national dietmen, to send a signed scroll and petition to the Nixon administration to drop the charges. Before the case was dismissed in 1973, a pamphlet was printed and had been circulated. After leaving Detroit and relocating to Pleasant Plains Township near Idlewild, Michigan the fall of 1971, Robert toured the country from 1971 to the early 1990s. Early in 1970, Nathan Hare on behalf of *The Black Scholar* interviewed Williams, who at the time had been sporadically touring around the country and speaking about U.S.-China relations, Afro-Americans and China, and Afro-American conditions in the United States. Ethel A. Johnson relocated from Monroe to Detroit, and by 1974 to the Idlewild community, where she worked with Robert and Mabel Williams and cared for one of her sisters.[3] Johnson was active in the Idlewild community, having served as a member of Williams's Lake County People's Association for Human Rights, NAACP, and Yates Township Planning Commission. Johnson was also a member of the Tabernacle AME Church. Mabel worked as director of St Ann's Meals Program, served as a board member of the Lake County Merry Makers, the Lake County Enterprise Committee, and FiveCAP, Inc. on various projects for the development of the Idlewild Historic Cultural Center and its photographic exhibitions. Whenever Rob was in town, he served as an active member of community-based organizations and as a leading protester against racial discrimination, police brutality, sex-crazed deer hunters. Williams worked on various committees to petition against unaddressed civil and human rights causes, issues, and violations in Lake County. As president of the Lake County Peoples Association for Human Rights which developed after the Ruby Nelson Chatman case in Idlewild and Baldwin, Michigan.[4] He petitioned the county government to change its policies of police-community relations based on evidence he collected for a report that was published in 1985 as an official document shared with county officials, the FBI, and for the governor's office to review the history of racial incidents and tensions in Lake. A year before Robert Williams passed on October 15, 1996, he and Mabel published a "Happy Hopeful New Year 1995" seven-page newsletter, where he stated, "Join the Right to Live Movement, Buy Yourself a Gun." Three years later in September of 1999, FiveCAP's Board of Directors voted to dedicate its new Head Start building in memory of Robert Williams. *Lake County Star* editor, Buck VandelMeer, published a story about the center and a vote to name a day in May, Robert F. Williams Day. These two community events were questioned and mocked by VandelMeer, who attempted to mobilize the white power structure in Baldwin against the dedication ceremony. Then, on December 23, 1999, VandelMeer published another article with a headline that read, "Bucky's list of top twenty outrages of the year," which amidst a host of other issues, designated "The Robert F. Williams Center," outrage number three. Naming a daycare after him, he indicated, "is an insult to American soldiers who gave their lives in Vietnam, black or white."[44] In this section, there is also an exchange of letters between Robert Williams and Calvin Cunningham, a North Carolina inmate who was originally sentenced to the death penalty, whose conviction was overturned, and who is now serving a life sentence. The kangaroo court system in North Carolina had denied Cunningham competent legal representation from Detroit attorney, Melissa El, who Robert Williams recruited to manage the case. Letters are also exchanged between Cunningham and me, as well as letters Williams wrote to the editors of *the Lake County Star* involving mental health issues and legal representation in the Ruby Nelson case and the Robert Carew case.[5]

The chosen documents for this edited volume collectively portray a nuanced picture of Robert Franklin Williams as a dynamic leader whose activism transcended national boundaries and racial lines. They highlight his pivotal role in advocating for armed self-defense among African Americans, his contributions to international discussions on race and class during the Cold War, and his enduring impact on civil and human rights, and Black liberation globally. These notes are intended to provide readers with a summarized understanding of that documents that follow about Williams's life, the evolution of his political thought and the diverse settings in which he and Mabel operated, from the Jim Crow South to communist Cuba and China, and beyond in the urban and rural landscapes of the North.

Notes

1 Mabel and Robert were active members of Unitarian Fellowship, which was led by a white woman who was a Socialist by ideology. Box 3, Folder 3, Robert F. Williams Papers, Bentley Historical Library.
2 Box 11 of the Robert F. Williams Papers at the Bentley Historical Library in Ann Arbor, Michigan.
3 An obituary of Ethel Azalea Johnson was published in *the Lake County Star*. She was born on January 31, 1916, and died on June 26, 1985, at the age of 69 in Reed City at the Reed City Hospital. Johnson lived in Idlewild in Paradise Gardens on Sincerity Street. She had two sisters, Mrs. Ruth George of Idlewild, and Mrs. Sara Elizabeth Young of Baldwin Michigan.
4 See State of Michigan Circuit Court for the County of Lake, The People of the State of Michigan vs. Ruby Nelson (aka Ruby Nelson Chatman aka Ruby Chatman Fuller, and the eleven-page transcript of the court's opinion following a non-jury trial, which was filed on June 5 and 7, 1978. The former Ruby Nelson Legal Defense Committee became the People's Association for Human Rights, which Williams served as its founding president. For more information about the case and other civil and human rights activities Williams championed the last twenty-seven-years of his life in Lake County, Michigan, see my essay, "Narrating Acts of Resistance: Explorations of Untold Heroic and Horrific Battle Stories Surrounding Robert Franklin Williams's Residence in Lake County, Michigan," *Journal of Black Studies*, 13, 5, May 2003, 675-703.
5 Department of Mental Health, Center for Forensic Psychiatry Summary Report, addressed to the Honorable Judge Charles A. Wickens, Lake County Circuit Court, July 17, 1978, Filed July 21, 1978, pp. 1 and 2. See also Donna L. Karasienski. Nelson to appear in Circuit Court: New information surfaces in prelim. *Lake County Star*, January 5, 1978, 1. The Lake County Report is in Box 11 of the Robert F. Williams Papers at the Bentley Historical Library in Ann Arbor, Michigan. The report was produced by Robert Williams as a board member of FiveCAP, Inc.

Chapter 1

MONROE, NORTH CAROLINA, 1955–1961

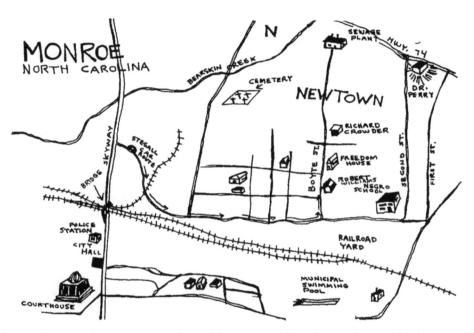

Map of Newton Monroe, NC, published in Truman Nelson's pamphlet *People with Strength: The Story of Monroe, N.C.* Nelson, a socialist worker's party and NAACP member, co-founded the Committee to Combat Racial Injustice. Courtesy of Robert F. Williams in the Robert F. Williams Papers at the Bentley Historical Library in Ann Arbor

Front Page of the *Journal and Guide* article with the headline, "Citizens Fire Back at Klan," October 12, 1957, page 1.

Rosa Parks at Rob's Burial. Rosa Parks says farewell at Rob's gravesite at the Hillcrest Cemetery, Monroe, North Carolina. Standing to the right of Mrs. Parks is her personal assistant and friend, Elaine Steele, and left of Mrs. Parks is an unidentified woman. There are two bodyguards standing behind Mrs. Parks and Ms. Steele, 1996. Photography courtesy of Aukram Burton, *RamImages.com*

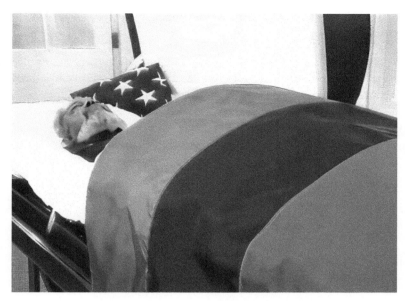

Robert F. Williams Lying in Repose. Robert F. Williams draped with Pan African flag and the U.S.A. flag recognizing his dedication to his people and his service in the Marine Corps, Monroe, NC, 1996. Photography courtesy of Aukram Burton, *RamImages.com*

Rosa Parks at Rob's Homecoming, 1996. Rosa Parks is with John C. Williams (Mabel and Rob's son), Mabel R. Williams, and Rob's brothers, John and Edward, who are standing in front of Rob's casket. Photography courtesy of Aukram Burton, *RamImages.com*

As a final tribute to Robert F. Williams a historic dedication and marker was unveiled in the Monroe Newtown community commemorating and honoring the contributions and legacy of Robert F. Williams on a Saturday afternoon of August 26, 2023. "A crowd gathered at the Battle Center on the campus of Wingate University" early that morning "to attend [a] program [organized] by A Few Good Men, Inc. to celebrate [the] Highway Historical Marker on the corner of Boyte street and Highway 74."[1]

Franklin H. Williams (Robert F. Williams's surviving son is seen wearing black jeans and a long shelve blue or gray shirt) witnessing the unveiling of the Robert F. Williams Historical Marker. Franklin, who is contracted to publish Robert Williams's autobiography, *While God Lay Sleeping*, was quoted in Monroe's newspaper, *Enquirer Journal*, stating my "father would have been proud to see this and would want young people to know his story and be inspired by it. I know there is political turmoil and things going on, but my father had an optimistic spirit. He thought people could overcome problems; he believed in civic pride, being involved in the community, and looking out for people" (A4). Photographer: Patricia M. Poland

SERMON DELIVERED AT ALL SOULS' CHAPEL UNITARIAN FELLOWSHIP, MONROE, NORTH CAROLINA, SUNDAY, MARCH 25, 1956[2]

COL. J. C.'S LAST STAND BY ROBERT WILLIAMS

Col. J. C. calls himself American. He claims Maryland as his place of birth, but it matters not where the stigma of his birth is placed; for today he dwells in many places throughout this republic. He has many aliases, such as John and Mary Christian, Lord and Lady Blueblood, Sam Tradition, and Capt. Race. There are others, many others, but we know him best as Jim Crow, Col. Commandant of other Reactionary Forces, United States of America. He claims his longevity will rival that of Methuselah, but it is too bad that he cannot read the signs of times, for they pronounce his doom. Yes, he calls himself American, a STATES' WRIGHTER WITH A DEMOCRATIC HEART. Strangely enough, he is an American, for he, too, stood at Concord Lexington, and Valley Forge to bequeath this nation the right to be free and democratic. Old Col. Jim Crow is stubborn. He is opinionated. He was too opinionated to absorb and practice the tenets inherited in the democratic doctrines that he fought so gallantly to wrest from the imperialists who were oppressing and stifling the progress of the new world. Col. Commandant Jim Crow's prejudiced forces have won many battles in their incessant war against righteousness, liberty, and justice. He was John Brown's captor at Harper's Ferry. He held fast at Richmond. He shook the very foundation of this republic by the fury of his aggressiveness at Gettysburg. Jim Crow is a wily and rugged warrior. His legions number among them ignorance, reactionary tradition, do nothing conservatism, fear, and downright indifference. His evil forces have long prevailed against God and country, but his ranks are being slowly depleted. The populace is becoming more democratic minded. Democracy and Jim Crow are incompatible; therefore, the forces of reaction are faltering in their efforts to enlist unlimited recruits from the new generation. The young students at Georgia Tech, Wake Forest, the University of North Carolina, and A&T are snubbing their noses at him. The liberals and true Christians are turning him from their doors. He has turned to his allies, the Citizens Councils and the KKK, and together they have vowed to stand, and together they shall perish, for they had elected to obstruct the path of justice. Deep down in his heart, Col. Jim Crow knows that he's fighting a rear-guard action for a hopeless cause. He petitions a God whom he would lead us to believe favors his cause. He distorts scripture. And spreads his venom of hate. In the unadulterated analysis, the old Colonel's war is just a spiteful delaying tactic that worsens a bad situation. Jim Crow and segregation are longer a regional stigma. It is a stigma on the whole of America. World opinion is pointing its finger scornfully at an America that claims to be a world champion of human rights. How can a nation, with a tenth of its people still in bondage and oppressed, profess to believe in democracy? Ask Col. Jim Crow; he's well-versed in answering critics. No doubt, he'll say to heck with the foreigners, or that we'll do as we darn, please, and if they don't agree that we've got a right not to practice what we preach, remind them of our deadly bomb. Old jingoistic Col. Jim Crow would rather destroy the world and all the wonders in here, than be co-beneficiary rather than lord and master. The young generation has heard enough of him, the liberals are tired of him, and the true Christians are ashamed of him, and Col. Jim Crow's days are numbered. In Atlanta, in Birmingham, in Vicksburg, and Richmond, whoops his rebel yell, but the people are growing weary of rebel yells and flags, for the liberty bell peals once more and the stars and stripes shall wave forever. Col. Jim Crow arrays his forces for a desperate stand. He blames the NAACP, white liberals, and our beloved Supreme Court for his social woes. In his self-conceived way of evaluating facts, everyone who differs from his ideology is communistic. His forces are making a feeble stab at psychological warfare. In this element of social struggle, time and enlightenment are his chief adversaries. His Citizen Councils are active. Who are these dupes and gullible hate-mongers? Time's News Time Magazine says that they are solid southern citizens. It states further that they had a recent meeting in Jackson, Mississippi, (population 117, 000) in the city auditorium with an attendance of two thousand planters and small businessmen, 40 state legislators, Congressman John Bell Williams, and Governor Hugh White. They were well-dressed people of the sort found in Rotary meetings or dancing at the country club. This was the first statewide meeting of the Mississippi Association of Citizen's Councils; U.S. Senator James Oliver Eastland addressed them. His subject: SCHOOL DESEGREGATION. Said he: "We in the South cannot stay longer on the defensive. We must take the offensive. We must carry the message to every section of the U.S." The senator urged a southern regional commission, financed by state tax money, to publicize the fight against desegregation, which he called a monstrous crime: dictated by political pressure groups vent upon the destruction of American system of government and the mongrelization of the white race. The pressure groups, he said, run from the blood red of the communist party to the almost equally red of the National Council of the Churches Christ in the U.S.A. The drive for racial amalgamation is both illegal and immoral, and those who would mix little children of both races in our schools are following an illegal, immoral and simple doctrine.

Senator Eastland, whose message was soberly applauded sixty-eight times and whose tax supposed commission proposal was unanimously endorsed, also paid tribute to his listeners: "No one knows better than the National Association for the Advancement of Colored Peoples how effective the Citizens Council have been. No one is more aware: how highly contagious your organized efforts have been." "Contagious" might seem an odd word for Eastland to have chosen, but there was no doubt that the Citizens Council had caught on throughout the deep South, especially in Mississippi. Manning the Ramparts against any form of racial equality are 260 new Citizens Councils in towns across the state, with about 60,000 dues-paying members who claim alliance with similar groups in other southern states, including Teas, Arkansas, South Carolina, Alabama, and Tennessee. The first S.C. was organized in Indianola, Mississippi, two months after the Supreme Court's segregation decision in May 1954, numbered among its 14 charter members one of the town's bank presidents. He is typical of C.C. members-churchgoing leading citizens who believe that the cause of the unhappy days upon them is the NAACP whose local members and leaders they are determined to expel from their midst. C.C. tactics are far from the crude, violent visitations of the now discredited K.K.K. for the C.C. shuns blood-letting and blunt instruments. It prefers the sharp, sophisticated weapons of economic and political pressures to change the minds of Negroes who work for school integration (or whites who aid them). Are these militant organizations organized to fight the red menace and to make the world safe for democracy? I think not; let's see what enemy they have avowed to fight. Example: Gus Courts, 68, a Negro American grocer in Belzoni, declined to move his name from the Negro voter's registration lists. Courts landlord refused to continue renting him his store, forcing him into a smaller one. Wholesalers denied his service; a bank refused credit; whites warned Negro employees not to trade with him, and his average monthly gross went down from $2,000.00 to $800.00. Courts' resistance to these cold war tactics led to a hot one. Someone shot and seriously wounded him. The Belzoni C.C., stressing its reputation for being law-abiding, promptly posted a $205,00 reward to catch assailants (who have not been caught). W. R. Wright, a successful Negro plumber in Yazoo City and active NAACP member, had his credit and supplies cut off, lost jobs, and finally moved to Detroit. T. V. Johnson, a prosperous Negro undertaker in Belzoni, was treated to the arrival of a C.C. imported rival funeral home, which tried to slash his business. The most vocal spokesman for the C.C. is well-tailored Tom Brady, a Circuit Court Judge, whose reiterated premise is that slavery brought the Negro "The greatest benefit one man ever conferred upon another: a moral standard was presented to him: which he does not now appreciate." Judge Brady is the author of *Black Monday*, a book titled for the day desegregation was announced. Wright He: "The social, political, economic and religious preferences of the Negro remain close to the caterpillar and the cockroach: proper food for a chimpanzee." Franz Boas, a German American anthropologist, wrote: "FREEDOM OF JUDGMENT CAN BE OBTAINED ONLY WHEN WE LEARN TO ESTIMATE AN INDIVIDUAL ACCORDING TO HIS OWN ABILITY AND CHARACTER. THEN WE SHALL FIND, IF WE WERE TO SELECT THE BEST OF MANKIND, THAT ALL THE VARIETY OF FORMS THAT HUMAN THOUGHT AND ACTIVITY HAVE TAKEN, AND ABHOR, AS LEADING TO COMPLETE STAGNATION, ALL ATTEMPTS TO IMPRESS ONE PATTERN OF THOUGHT UPON WHOLE NATIONS OR EVEN UPON THE WHOLE WORLD." Judge Brady is a circuit court judge, and judges are supposed to be honorable men. No doubt Judge Brady, too, is an honorable man and perhaps a well-rounded, solid American citizen with an affliction peculiar to southerners. Judge Brady's affliction is tantamount to a severe case of monomania. Racial monomania is so widespread throughout the south today that it has reached epidemic proportions. Judge Brady is sick, the south is sick, and the government is sick that will allow such a man Tom Brady to sit in judgment on a people whose culture he considers not yet evolved to the human level. All this ranting by the old Colonel is no more than a premature death rattle, for the white citizens' councils are eleventh-hour choruses organized to sing Jim Crow's swan song. He is running a clear feel field unopposed. There are forces of goodness counteracting his plays. A short while ago, a white girl risked her live to rescue a Negro child from the river in which Emmett Til's body was found. A Mississippi town raided $2,000 dollars (both races) to send a Negro high school band to New York, the only band invited from the State of Mississippi to participate in the Negro Elks Parade. A second Negro Staff Physician was appointed to the State Mental Hospital. A Negro is an active staff member of the Jackson (MISS.) News. Zin the wake of the mass meeting in

Mississippi's Homes County, at which Dr. D. R. Minter and F. A. Fox were told to leave the county because of their liberality toward Negroes, a score of the citizens admitted that they were ashamed. The very fact of my speaking to you today is itself a paradox uniquely American. I dare say that no place else in the world can an individual so denied democratic citizenship mount a speaker's rostrum and denounce the unconstitutional laws inactive by local governments. This is an American right purchased and paid for in full by the Republic's gallant sons who fought and died in the grip of battle. It is ironic that this subject of civil rights is so explosive so long after our glorious revolution of which this nation was to give liberty and social justice to all its people. Crispus Attucks, a Negro, was the first to die in the war for American Independence and Civil Liberties, and yet, today it is necessary for the Supreme Court of the United States to rule against shameful social inequalities. The Supreme Court has proposed to make America democratic. Col. Jim Crow has proposed to make the Supreme Court passe, but it is Col. Jim Crow whose days are numbered. Col. Jim Crow's South today is poverty-stricken and undernourished due to a lack of heavy industry. The force of necessity will also aid in the fight against Jim Crow. Northern industrialists are inclined to run away from the scene of labor and capitalist turmoil, they want to locate in communities devoid of class conflict. Forward-looking southerners know the industry is not willing to exchange one scene of turmoil for another. They know that the sooner a solution to the southern race problem is honestly attempted the sooner more industry will look toward the sunny south for possible location. Time is against Col. Jim Crow's many legions. He is a long-suffering and wily fighter, but enlightenment is the master of the battlefield of social revolution.

Enlightenment is his archenemy. He is dishonoring the republic and the republic cannot long afford to keep him in its midst. The NAACP believes that by 1963 there will be very little need for an organization in its nature; that is quite a contrast when compared to an organization that speaks in terms of its activities a hundred years henceforth. The Axis nations of the Second World War claimed that their armies would march for a thousand years. We all know their fate. We of the South know the perplexity of the problem that must be solved. It is a difficult problem, but Americans are noted for being able to solve difficult problems. Is the problem of one American's relationship to another so baffling? It is a simple problem that prejudice has complexed or caused to seem complex. Prejudice is Col. Jim Crow's staying power. It has made him distort scripture and adulterate scientific facts. It has made mountains out of molehills, brothers' enemies, and Christian's hypocrites. In Montgomery, Alabama, it has erupted into racial animosity. At the University of Alabama, it has made a simple American citizen a world symbol of American bigotry. It has returned the seldom used and repulsive word "Interposition" back into widespread American usage. Prejudice is ungodly. Prejudice is hell, it is damnation to the Christian and a curse on the nation. Col. Jim Crow, unwittingly, has aroused the moral forces of the world. The world is waiting, the democratic-minded Americans and the liberty-less Negroes are acting. No doubt Col. Jim Crow remembers the persistent voice of the downtrodden Indian that filled the royal jails of the British Empire with the patriots of the passive revolution. Passive Resistance is a commodity that high tariffs cannot embargo. Passive Resistance has been implored and Montgomery, Alabama, United States, is the consignee. Running true to the form of oppressive governments, the governments of the city and state of Montgomery, Alabama, have acted. They have not acted to right a wrong or to promulgate justice. They have acted to quell a boycott that is depriving the city of 60 percent of its bus receipts. Has an American no right to walk when to ride would degrade his dignity? Has our beloved Republic reached the stage that the jails have no room for criminals because they are filled with liberty-loving citizens whose only crime is that their voices cry out for freedom? Col. Jim Crow's zeal for preserving the status quo is a snare that he cannot escape. The world wants to know if America is to be a democracy or is it not? The conduct of the South is shaming the nation. Tantrums are seizing the South tantamount to a spoiled brat. The heart of the world cannot be moved by histrionics. The race problem of the South is no longer regional. This problem cannot be deferred longer. It must be solved now. We of the South know the perplexity of the problem that must be solved. Its solution must be worked out mutually between the two factions of humanity considered. Social reaction, dogmatic tradition, and personal prejudices must be overcome. Education and objective honesty must be diligently implored. With the world situation as it is today, the brains and resources of this nation need to be freed from the burden of internal strife, for at this psychological moment, the freedom of the world is at stake. This Republic must choose between the appeasement of Col. Jim Crow's beleaguered and hell-bent forces or the friendship of almost four-fifths of the population of the entire earth. Jim Crow travels along an avenue that leads to an inescapable dead end. Democracy has marked it for doom and the communist can see no value in it other than as a wedging tool to divide and conquer. The bugler has sounded the charge. Col. Jim Crow is ready to lead his forces to the attack. This attack is not offensive. It is a defensive action of the stubborn doomed. Col. Jim Crow knows that he is doomed. He is making his last stand as Col. Commandant, reactionary forces, United States of America. Robert F. Williams

NAACP FINDINGS AND RECOMMENDATIONS IN HEARING ON ROBERT F. WILLIAMS BEF0RE COMMITTEE ON BRANCHES, JUNE 3 AND 8, 1959

1. On May 5, 1959, after two white men had been acquitted in a trial for brutal assaults on two Negro women, and a Negro, of limited intelligence, had been convicted and sentenced to two years' imprisonment for a far less offense, Mr. Williams made the following statements: We cannot take these people who do us injustice to court and it becomes necessary to punish them ourselves. In the future we are going to have to try and convict these people on the spot. We cannot rely on the law. We can get no justice under the present system. If we feel that injustice is done, we must right then and there on the spot be prepared to inflict punishment on these people. "Since the Federal government will not bring a halt to lynching in the South and since the so-called courts lynch our people legally, if it's necessary to stop lynching with lynching, then we must be Willing to resort to that method."
2. This statement was released to UP and received wide publication.

3. On June 3, Mr. Williams testified that on the morning of May 6, he had explained to the *Carolina Times*, a Negro weekly, that the following was a more accurate reflection of what he had meant: "These court decisions open the way to violence. I do not mean that Negroes should go out and attempt to get revenge for mistreatments or injustice. But it is apparent that there is no Fourteenth Amendment nor court protection of Negroes rights here, and Negroes have to defend themselves on the spot whenever they are attracted by whites."
4. He and his counsel allege that what this statement was intended to convey was that Negroes should exercise the right of self-defense.
5. Mr. Wilkins talked on the telephone to Mr. Williams on May 6. According to Mr. Williams's testimony, this was after the explanatory statement had been issued to the *Carolina Times*. At no time during that telephone conversation did he advise Mr. Wilkins that he had backed down from his original statement and, indeed, left Mr. Wilkins with the impression that he was planning to repeat the May 5th statement on a nationwide television broadcast.
6. Mr. Williams received appropriate notice of charges filed against him in a letter from Mr. Wilkins dated May 8th. He was subsequently given notice of the time, place, and nature of the hearing on the charges before the Committee on Branches which had been authorized by the board of directors to examine the facts and report to the Board on June 8. Mr. Williams was advised of his right to be represented by counsel and introduce testimony on his own behalf.

Mr. Williams availed himself of the rights, filed an answer and brief, prepared by his counsel Conrad Lynn and Helen Minken and appeared at the next board meeting to these attorneys and Pauli Murray. He testified on his own behalf.

REPORT AND LETTERS TO AND BY ROBERT F. WILLIAMS

NORTH CAROLINA STATE CONFERENCE OF BRANCHES
NATIONAL ASSOCIATION FOR THE ADVANCEMENT OF COLORED PEOPLE
TO: MR. ROY WILKINS, EXECUTIVE SECRETARY AND THE COMMITTEE ON
BRANCHES,
NATIONAL ASSOCIATION FOR THE ADVANCEMENT OF COLORED PEOPLE
SUBJECT: AN OFFICIAL REQUEST THAT THE SUSPENSION OF THE PRESIDENT OF
THE MONROE, UNION COUNTY, NORTH CAROLINA BRANCH, MR. ROBERT
WILLIAMS, BY THE EXECU
TIVE SECRETARY BE MADE PERMANENT AND THAT THE OFFICE OF PRESIDENT

BE DECLARED VACANT AND THE BRANCH ORDERED TO HOLD A NEW ELECTION.
FROM: NORTH CAROLINA STATE CONFERENCE OF BRANCHES, NATIONAL ASSOCIATION FOR THE ADVANCEMENT OF COLORED PEOPLE KELLY M. ALEXANDER, PRESIDENT

INTRODUCTION

DATE: MAY 15, 1959

This is an official request from the North Carolina State Conference of Branches that the suspension of the president of the Monroe, Union County, North Carolina Branch, Mr. Robert Williams, by the executive secretary of the NAACP, Mr. Roy Wilkins, be made permanent and that the office of the president be declared vacant, and the Branch ordered to hold a new election. The North Carolina State Conference of Branches is an effective and efficient organized unit of the National Association for the Advancement of Colored People. It has always followed the established policy and procedure of the association and there has always existed an excellent cooperative relationship between the branches, state conference, and national office. In fact, each year the state conference sponsors a branch officials and state officers meeting to explain the national and state programs of the NAACP and how they are to be implemented on the community level. Notice of these meetings is sent to every branch in the state. The attendance is always representative of the NAACP in North Carolina. (Group picture of 1959 Meeting is attached.) We have always asked for Negroes to receive only that to which they are morally, legally, and rationally entitled. We have approached our task in North Carolina with reasonableness and calmness but never compromised on principle or statements of Mr. Williams, but it is common knowledge that Mr. Williams acknowledged the correctness of the quotations credited to him and asserted that he would repeat them on radio and television. (Attached are newspaper reports of his statements). After Mr. Williams postponed his appearance before the national board on Monday, May II, on the advice of his attorney, Mr. Conrad Lynn, it was reported in the Raleigh News and Observer, an outstanding North Carolina Newspaper, and other state newspapers by UPI that his attorney, Mr. Conrad Lynn, said, "Mr. Williams makes no apologies for his stand, which is simply that Negroes in any part of the South where the law has broken down for them, have the common law right to defend themselves with arms." It is also reported that Attorney Lynn said that Williams also believed that Negroes should make "Citizens arrests" of any white person committing an offense against them. He said that the NAACP board would be asked to disqualify Kelly Alexander, state president of the *NAACP* in North Carolina, from sitting on the board when it considers the charges against Williams. Attorney Lynn charged that Alexander was prejudiced against Williams and would not be an impartial judge. (Attached are newspaper articles concerning the above statements.)

SPECIFICATION OF CHARGE

In the judgment of the state conference, Mr. Robert Williams is guilty of such conduct which is inimical to the best interest and welfare of the NAACP. Statements made by him are jeopardizing the entire program of the NAACP in North Carolina. The North Carolina State Conference of Branches, since its organization, has followed a course of action in line—with our American constitutional system and always worked cooperatively with the policy and procedure of the national office. Noteworthy gains have been made, such as:

1. Negroes being admitted to the State supported Universities and Colleges.
2. Some Negro school children attending public elementary, and secondary schools in major cities on a nonsegregated basis.
3. Elimination of segregation in recreational programs and facilities in major cities.
4. An expanded Voter Registration Program has resulted in the increase of Negro participation in nonpartisan political action and the election of qualified Negroes to public office. North Carolina has more Negroes elected to public office than any other state in the south.
5. An effective race relations program which has decreased opposition to the NAACP as a recognized civil rights organization on the community level.
6. Progress in the field of employment. In industry and government, Negroes are now in positions of employment they have never held before.

The above are only some of the gains made by the North Carolina State Conference of Branches and they were not made by advancing the policy of Mr. Robert Williams, meeting "Violence with violence" and stopping "lynching with lynching."

The NAACP would not be any better than the White Citizens Councils and other hate groups if it would embark on a course as advanced by Mr. Williams. Since Mr. Williams has been president of the Monroe, Union County, N. C. Branch, (elected in 1957), he has not acted in good faith and has been most difficult to work with. He is noncooperative with the state conference program. In fact, the state conference doubts very seriously that Mr. Williams is a member of the NAACP in good standing, and we request this fact be verified. His branch does not pay assessments to support the NAACP in North Carolina. This act of nonsupport is certainly in violation of Article 5, Section 6 of the Constitution and By-Laws for Branches of the Association. It is our opinion that Mr. Williams is not basically interested in the NAACP because of his gross neglect of duty as President of the Monroe, Union County, N.C. Branch. His interest and loyalty are questioned because of his reported leadership in a rival organization known as the Committee to Combat Racial Injustice. This organization is in direct competition with the NAACP, and, by Mr. Williams being chairman, it places the NAACP in North Carolina in a most embarrassing position. The very fact that Mr. Williams is president of one of our Branches, each time a statement is made, and it is reported by the press the article states very clearly first that he is President of the Union County Branch of the NAACP and not the chairman of the Committee to Combat Racial Injustice. It is not fair to the branches of the North Carolina State Conference for one individual, because of his personal views, to impede the progress of such an important organization as the NAACP in a state where progress in the field of civil rights is making such great advances. These advances were being made long before Mr. Williams ever became interested in the leadership of an NAACP Branch. The state conference takes the position, Mr. Williams is not an asset to the NAACP but a liability. The best thing that could happen to improve race relations in Union County and the NAACP is for Mr. Williams to be permanently suspended as president of the branch. There are many people in Union County who are very capable of leadership and would be willing to participate in the NAACP program. They will never support Mr. Williams and it is very necessary that the office of president be declared vacant, and the branch ordered to hold a new election. We urge the Committee on Branches to realize how important it is to the NAACP in North Carolina and the nation to permanently suspend Mr. Williams so he can give full time to the Committee to Combat Racial Injustice and be free to say whatever he pleases and not on behalf of the NAACP in any way to advance his personal ideas.

Respectfully submitted,

NORTH CAROLINA STATE CONFERENCE OF BRANCHES

Kelly M. Alexander, President
KMA/man
Enclosures
TO: Mr. Gloster B. Current
FROM: Chas. A. McLean
North Carolina
Field Secretary
DATE: June 15, 1959
Report of facts in answer to directions given to me by phone and letter, June 12, 1959, as pertains to the Monroe, N.C. Branch.

BRANCH OFFICERS

President,	Robert F. Williams, (Suspended)
1. 1st Vice. Pres:	Dr. A.E. Perry (Resigned in March office 405 N. Church St., Res. 1008 1st Street
2. 2nd Vice. Pres:	Mrs. E.A. Johnson 503 N Boyte St. Insurance Agent, Continental Ins. Co.
3. Secretary	Mrs. Mabel Williams 410 N Boyte St.
4. Treasure	Mr. J.W. McDow 819 2nd St.

196 Members
20 memberships expire in August 1959
Members of the Executive Committee of Monroe, N.C. Branch, NAACP.

1. Mr. Benjamin Winfield, (recently fired), Route 3,
2. Mr. Woodrow Wilson, 808 1st Street,
3. Mrs. Marie Richardson, 602 English Street,
4. Mr. David Covington, Telleyrand Avenue,
5. Mr. Elbergus Mills, 424 English Street,
6. Mr. George Rushing, 1st Street,
7. Mrs. Lena Smith, 903 John Street,
8. Mr. J. W. McDow, 819 2nd Street,

THE MONROE DEFENSE COMMITTEE has already begun a campaign to tell the story of Monroe to the world. An important part of that story is the criminal negligence displayed by Attorney General Robert Kennedy, who turned a deaf ear on repeated pleas from Mr. Williams and others for Federal protection after the complete failure of local and state police to defend Afro-Americans from racist mobs. He (Kennedy) did, however, move w\swiftly when North Carolina authorities called him for help in catching Williams. THE MONROE COMMITTEE will also direct its efforts to inform the public of how Afro-Americans in Monroe are forced to endure the constant betrayal of their rights in the courts, denial of welfare assistance, and systematic exclusion in employment, housing, and recreational facilities.

THE MONROE DEFENSE COMMITTEE will bring its message to as broad a national and international audience as possible. However, it will pay particular attention to Afro-American communities across the nation to achieve mass solidarity behind the fighting spirit of Monroe citizens and Robert F. Williams. Apart from the educational job the committee intends to perform, there is the extremely urgent situation concerning the four Freedom Fighters locked up in the Monroe, N.C., jail on kidnapping and similar charges. One of them is only 17 years old.

The legal expense for these valiant people is most assuredly going to be astronomical. Mr. Williams is a free man, but his friends in jail desperately need financial support. WHAT Can You do? For THE MONROE DEFENSE COMMITTEE to be truly effective in accomplishing its desire to aid the people of Monroe, to aid those in jail and to aid those who are still being terrorized by the racists, we must have the active and generous support of all progressive and freedom-loving people.

We urge all interested people to send their contributions too.

Calvin Hicks, Exec. Secy.	**Enclosed please find contribution of $_____.**
MONROE DEFENSE COMMITTEE	**I would like to know more about the Committee.**
53 West 125th St.	Name _____
New York 27, N.Y.	Address_____
Phone: LE 4-8411	City_____
	State_____Zone_____

C R U S A D E R S F O R F R E E D O M

Mae Mallory, Secretary   Gerald Quinn, Press Relations
212 West 129th St.
New York, N.Y.
For Immediate Release: Harlem, NYC, May 17, 1961

MLITANT MASS PROTEST CAUSES NAACP TO ABANDON RALLY AND TURN IT OVER TO ROBERT WILLIAMS

Mass resentment against the NAACP leadership reached an all-time high in the Harlem community when the NAACP leadership was unable to go through with what they thought would be a giant rally in support of their policies. So strong was the militant opposition from the masses, that the leadership lost control of the meeting. For the first time in the memory of Harlem political leaders, the NAACP was forced to abandon a meeting—but not without first turning it over to Robert Williams, one of the principal opponents of their policies. A leaflet signed by the COMMITTEE FOR THE RIGHT TO HEAR ROBERT WILIAMS SPEAK was distributed prior to the meeting. It called for Harlem to come and demand that Robert Williams of the Monroe, N. C. Branch of the NAACP, be allowed to speak. The leaflet went on to say, "Today a rally is scheduled to take place, arranged by the NAACP. But one leader (Robert Williams) of Black America—who has boldly and courageously raised the banner of meeting violence with violence—has not been scheduled to speak at this rally. Why not? "Is it because he has denounced the cheek-turning policy of the Uncle Toms and refused to knuckle under to the agents of the oppressor within our own ranks? "Demand that Robert Williams be allowed to speak. Demand that the Uncle Tom leaders stop their attack upon the militant black people—the Nationalists and Muslims. Demand they attack instead the real enemy, the white supremacists." Just before the rally began, about 50 young men carrying picture placards of Patrice Lumumba and signs denouncing the leadership of the NAACP joined the crowd of about 3,000 persons attending the rally. From the very outset of the rally, the large majority of those present hissed and booed down speaker after speaker. Not even two renditions of the National Anthem, the invocation, or the benediction could quiet this demonstration of the Black masses of Harlem. An incessant chant of "We want Williams—We want Williams—"arose from the crowd. And the NAACP bigwigs on the platform, which included Roy Wilkins, Percy Sutton, Daisy Bates, and others were forced to concede to the wishes of the audience. Taking the microphone, Williams denounced Uncle Toms for telling the Afro-Americans "to continue turning the cheek which has been slapped now for more than 400 years." He then called on all Afro-Americans to defend themselves, and their women and children. "If the Uncle Toms want to teach Pacifism," he said, "let them teach it to the Ku Klux Klan and the White Citizens Council." There was a thunderous ovation as Williams left the platform. The crowd surged forward, lifting him to their shoulders, and carried him through a cheering crowd. Although the NAACP leadership had spent an inordinate amount of time with an extraordinary amount of publicity to obtain mass support for the rally, the amount of support garnered was the smallest in many years, and what little there was, was totally ineffective in the face of the mass opposition. To end the meeting, the only attention paid to the minister saying the benediction was a lone egg that splattered on his lapel.

THE MONROE PROGRAM

On August 15, 1961, on behalf of the Union County chapter of the NAACP, Robert Williams presented to the Monroe Board of Aldermen a ten-point program that read as follows:

Petition

We, the undersigned citizens of Monroe, petition the City Board of Aldermen to use its influence on:

1. Induce factories in this county to hire without discrimination.
2. Induce the local employment agency that non-whites have the same privileges given to whites.
3. Instruct the Welfare Agency that non-whites are entitled to the same privileges, courtesies and consideration given to whites.
4. Construct a swimming pool in the Winchester Avenue area of Monroe.
5. Remove all signs in the City of Monroe designating one area for color and another for whites.
6. Instruct the Superintendent of Schools that he must prepare to desegregate the city schools no later than 1962.

7. Provide adequate transportation for all school children.
8. Formally request the State Medical Board to permit Dr. Albert E. Perry, Jr., to practice medicine in Monroe and Union County.
9. Employ Negroes in skilled or supervisory capacities in the City Government.
10. ACT IMMEDIATELY on all these proposals and inform the committee and the public of your actions.[3] (signed)

Robert F. Williams
Albert E. Perry, Jr., M.D.
John W. McDow
New York, N.Y.
To the Editor:

On Saturday, August 26, 1961, violence was unleashed on a group of non-violent Freedom Riders in Monroe, N.C. These Freedom Riders had been invited to this racist community to aid in the Negro struggle for human rights and liberation. They, along with other Negroes, were attacked because they had established a peaceful picket line around the Union County Courthouse and Mayor Fred W. Wilson's office. The police refused to make any arrests of the people who attacked Negroes and Freedom Riders. As president of the Union County branch of the National Association for the Advancement of Colored People, I had repeatedly appealed to the Federal and State governments to accord Negroes and White Freedom Riders equal protection under the law. These appeals were in vain. On Saturday night August 26, 1961, I talked to one Hugh P. Cannon, an aide of the governor of North Carolina (by telephone). I appealed for protection under law. The governor's aide said that he didn't give a damn who was being beaten, that I was getting just what I deserved. He said that I had asked for violence and now I was getting it. The U.S. Justice Department also refused to intervene. On Sunday, August 27, 1961, the Monroe Non-Violent Action Committee, consisting of Freedom Riders and local Negro youth staged a picket line around the Union County courthouse protesting the absence of police protection for Negroes and all forms of racial injustice. A mob of almost 5,000 racists gathered at the square and started attacking the nonviolent pickets unmercifully. The local police joined in the attack on the peaceful pickets. Police held fourteen- and fifteen-year-old pickets while the mob beat them. Negroes from other communities tried to rescue the pickets but the police attached them and armed the white thugs. While all this was going on I was home where I had remained all through the picketing. Carloads of white KKK invaded our community and started attacking Negroes. A group of Negroes gathered on the street where I lived to form collective guards to fight the KKK. They started returning the fire against the Klan. A car was stopped and the driver, a white man and a woman were captured, disarmed, and placed under citizen's arrest by a group of Negroes. I was not part of this group. However, the group said this was done to prevent killing the couple who had been recognized as part of the Klan group that had attacked them in town on Saturday. The pair of whites were brought up the block to my yard. I asked the colored group to let them go and they did. I told the whites they could go; however, they would have to leave through the angry crowd. The woman said she did not want to go through the crowd. I turned to go into the house, and she followed. I was called out into the back to set up a rear defense of the house. I was informed by others, escaping from the riot scene, that Negroes who needed medical attention were being locked in jail by police. I called the police station and asked for a possible bond for the injured, it was denied. I could hear a lot of gunfire in from of my house. I received a telephone call from a voice I identified as that of the Chief of Police. He said that I had caused a lot of race trouble, and that state troopers were coming, and that in 30 minutes I would be hanging on the courthouse square. I saw police cars blocking off the block in which we lived. I remembered that I had filed charges against the Chief of Police with the Federal government because he had refused to protect Negroes. He had also threatened to kill me. I told my wife that we had to leave with the children right away and that we didn't have time to get any clothing or anything. The white couple had disappeared long before this time. We slipped through an alley and past police cars to a highway. I wanted to leave so that I would be able to tell the world of the brutal racist oppression in Monroe, N.C. Some Negroes who passed the highway drove us to Greensboro, N.C., and from there we caught a bus to New York. We arrived on August 28, 1961. We tried to telephone a number in Monroe to see if anyone was at our house. The operator informed us that all circuits to Monroe were busy. We learned later in the evening that warrants had been issued for my arrest. This is indeed strange because four attempts have been made on my life and local, State and Federal officials refused to issue warrants. I had saved the lives of people who were now accusing me of kidnapping. I am not guilty. My only crime is that I am a Negro who has loudly and militantly protested America's ruthless oppression of Negroes. The U.S. government sought my arrest at the request of Union County Klansmen because my newsletter "The Crusader" was in opposition to Kennedy's censorship plan. In conjunction with the KKK, the U.S. government is seeking to lynch me for political reasons. The U.S. government's interest is based solely upon the fact that I refuse to be an Uncle Tom apologist for the State Department and because I have openly supported Revolutionary Cuba. The U.S. government knows that I am innocent of any crime. It seeks to take over where the KKK failed. It intends to lynch me to silence my international newsletter, which represented unbridled opposition to imperialism and racism.

ROBERT F. WILLIAMS

NATIONAL GUARDIAN SEPTEMBER 25, 1961

MONROE, NORTH CAROLINA, VICTIMS OF RACIAL INJUSTICE NEED HELP

Why Do Afro-American Citizens in Monroe Need Your Help?

For many years in Monroe, North Carolina, Afro-Americans could not walk the streets without fear of attack. They were constantly beaten, shot, and raped by racist mobs, including elements of law enforcement agencies. On many occasions, the mobs, robed in the garb of the KKK (Monroe is KKK Southeastern headquarters), would visit the Black community to fetch some "nigra" who hadn't "stayed in his place" or simply to shoot up the area as an after-church, Sunday afternoon recreational. Because the constituted judicial and civil authorities allowed such conditions to go unchallenged and failed to extend equal protection under the law to all citizens, Afro-Americans in Monroe, under the dynamic leadership of Robert F. Williams, were obliged to meet force with force in defense of their homes and families.

No longer did the Klan terrorize the community. But the concept of self-defense raised a terrifying maelstrom of hatred from racist elements against Robert F. Williams, and the Black community in general. Monroe became a racial tinderbox, needing only a tiny spark to set off a major conflagration. On August 27—following a series of peaceful picket lines conducted by Williams and his followers in front of the segregated swimming pool (during which three attempts were made up Mr. Williams's life in full view of local and state police who stood and laughed)—the Klan did cause combustion along racial lines. Apparently dissatisfied with their heretofore haphazard terrorist tactics, the Klan launched an armed attack against Black citizens with, one must presume, every intention of wiping out that community.

What Does the Monroe Defense Committee Plan to Do?

THE MONROE DEFENSE COMMITTEE has already begun a campaign to tell the story of Monroe to the world. An important part of that story is the criminal negligence displayed by Attorney General Robert Kennedy, who turned a deaf ear on repeated pleas from Mr. Williams and others for Federal protection after the complete failure of local and state police to defend Afro-Americans from racist mobs. He (Kennedy) did, however, move w\swiftly when North Carolina authorities called him for help in catching Williams.

THE MONROE COMMITTEE will also direct its efforts to inform the public of how Afro-Americans in Monroe are forced to endure the constant betrayal of their rights in the courts, denial of welfare assistance, and systematic exclusion in employment, housing, and recreational facilities.

THE MONROE DEFENSE COMMITTEE will bring its message to as broad a national 8105789153526961759915352and international audience as possible. However, it will pay particular attention to Afro-American communities across the nation in an effort to achieve mass solidarity behind the fighting spirit of Monroe citizens and Robert F. Williams.

Apart from the educational job the committee intends to perform, there is the extremely urgent situation concerning the four Freedom Fighters locked up in the Monroe, N.C., jail on kidnapping and similar charges. One of them is only 17 years old.

The legal expense for these valiant people is most assuredly going to be astronomical. Mr. Williams is a free man, but his friends in jail desperately need financial support.

WHAT Can You do?

In order for THE MONROE DEFENSE COMMITTEE to be truly effective in accomplishing its desire to aid the people of Monroe, to aid those in jail and to aid those who are still being terrorized by the racists, we must have the active and generous support of all progressive and freedom-loving people.

We urge all interested persons to send their contributions to:

Calvin Hicks, Exec. Secy.	**Enclosed please find contribution of $_____.**
MONROE DEFENSE COMMITTEE	**I would like to know more about the Committee.**
53 West 125th St.	Name _____
New York 27, N.Y.	Address_____
Phone: LE 4-8411	City_____
	State_____Zone_____

JOHN SCHULTZ'S INTERVIEW WITH ROBERT WILLIAMS,
February 1961

John Schultz has published stories in *Evergreen Review, Big Table #5*, and *Chicago Review*. In April 1962, Grove Press will publish a novella by Mr. Schultz in a collection titled *Three by Three*. In the fall, Grove Press will publish a collection of his stories and novellas.

The following interview took place in Chicago, in February 1961. Readers may remember Mr. Williams as the president of the Monroe, North Carolina, branchy of the NAACP, who challenged the policy of nonresistance set down by both the Association's national leadership and by the Reverend Martin Luther King. At present Mr. Williams is living in Cuba, a fugitive from the Monroe police and the Federal Bureau of Investigation, as the result of an alleged kidnapping during a period of racial strife in Monroe.

Q. I noticed that you used the word "Afro-American" several times tonight, as did a good many people at the meeting. Could you give us an idea of what meaning this word has for what you are trying to do?

A. The reason I prefer the word "Afro-America" is that this identifies the so-called "Negro" in this country with the African people and the African struggle. We are descendants of the African people. There is a psychological effect in using the word Afro-American: when an Afro-American is lynched, it means that his lynching involves the African people as well. The international question makes this carry weight. There's a struggle underway now in the world, a struggle for the minds of the Africans and of the Asian people. In days gone by, when a Negro was lynched, the people in Africa, in most cases, looked upon us as a different people altogether. But now they can see that this lynching happens in the same country that claims it is trying to introduce "democracy" and the "democratic way of life" in Africa. They can see that Afro-American babies are being starved for no other reason than that they were born Black. In this way, the people in Africa will identify Afro-Americans with their struggle. We believe that the African people will learn that we represent their brothers, and that if this country is willing to treat their brothers that way, then there's no reason to believe this country is interested in giving them justice. This also helps us in our struggle here. We believe this is one way to take advantage of the world situation today.

Q. Using this word, then, strengthens your identification with the current revolutions and with those that have been successful in Africa,—thereby arousing a greater sense of power in the American or Afro-American.

A. Yes. There was a time when we were told by the movies, by the comic books, and even by television, that the African people were a barbaric, savage people. We were told that they were people who lived in the jungle and that they had no culture. We were told they were below the level of the other nations of the world. But with the emergence of the new African nations, with the coming of the new African representatives to the United Nations, we saw dignified men, educated men, coming from Africa to represent their new countries in the United Nations. We could no longer consider them as the savages portrayed by the American racists. Now we feel proud to identify ourselves with the Africans. They are proud and cultured people. WE feel now that we belong more to them than we do to the racists of the United States. You see, we've always been rejected here as citizens. We fought and we've tried to become citizens, but we've always been rejected. WE find that the Africans are anxious to call us brothers. They are anxious to accept us. And that is why we like to identify ourselves with the African struggle.

Q. Who is the "we" in the United States that you are referring to?

A. Well, there are a lot of movements. There's a trend now towards nationalism among the Afro-American people. There are some exceptions among us. The Black bourgeoisie would deny this rising Afro-American nationalism. They do everything possible to make the white Americans think that it is not true. But when I speak of "we," I speak of the masses, the masses of the Afro-Americans that I know. The masses that I have visited in Jacksonville, Florida; in Atlanta, Georgia; in Greenville, South Carolina. The masses I know at home in Monroe, North Carolina. The masses that I've met on the streets of Harlem, on the streets of Detroit, and in Chicago. And when I say we I mean these people who feel the same way I feel about this.

Q. You spoke before of the inhibiting effect of the presence of white people upon the Negroes in the audience. Would you describe a meeting in Harlem or Detroit, or in Atlanta, where there was no such inhibiting factor? What was the response to what you had to say?

A. Well, I've had audiences in Atlanta and in Harlem, all Afro-American audiences; I find that the response is much greater when I speak to a solely Afro-American audience. I've noticed that in some places, with mixed audiences, there seems to be an attitude or an atmosphere where the Negroes are inhibited. They just don't feel free to let themselves go. They just don't feel free to let the white people know how they feel. Now this is misleading, and some misconceptions have been formed about the whole thing. This is one criticism that I have of the white liberals and of some of the radicals on the left. They think they understand us. They think they understand our feelings and our problems because they know a few inhibited Afro-Americans, the Negroes who never let the whites truly know their sincere feelings. In speaking to mixed audiences, I've seen people become very uneasy. They are sensitive to talk about the race problem. I find that when Negroes are alone, the spirit is much more intense. There is much greater interest in the race problem, and greater interest in the idea that we must become more militant.

Q. You mean that if a man from The New York Times or from The Reporter talks to the Negro, he's going to get a considerably watered-down response compared to what he would get if he talked to the same man in private or in a group in which there were only Negroes?

A. Yes, sure he would. The first thing is that there's a tendency in this country to penalize or punish outspoken, militant Negroes. This is a matter of security. It is also a matter of tradition. As a result of our past as an oppressed group, we realize that it is dangerous to really let our true feelings be known. There is a possibility of reprisals. This is true in the South and in some sections of the North. When an Afro-American speaks out, he becomes a target of the white supremacists. It is a different matter with the liberals. They think they know our problems, so, in many cases, they refuse to listen to us. Instead of listening to our feelings and our problems, instead of trying to determine whether we know what we are doing, or if we know the best way to solve these problems—they usually end up by telling us what we should do, and by advising us. This is paternal. And you'll find that most Afro-Americans are growing tired of this paternalism.

Q. Whom do you include among such liberals who act in a paternal manner no matter how well-intentioned they think they are?

A. Well, this would even include a lot of the socialists with whom I've come in contact. It would include liberals that I personally know, such as Harry Golden of Charlotte, North Carolina—of *The Carolina Israelite*. Incidentally, dear old Harry lives about twenty-four miles from my hometown. I knew Harry before he became as wealthy as he is today. And he was much more militant in the days when he wasn't so wealthy. This is another quality that we are beginning to see in liberals. Harry Golden hired a friend of mine, a girl from my hometown, an Afro-American girl. She served as his secretary. She learned all of his business. So, what happened? Harry became famous after *Only in America*, and more and more of the Southern people started visiting Harry. He was considered a cultured man, so they came to his home. But he had this Afro-American girl as his receptionist. And these Southern gentlemen, these Christina ladies and gentlemen, didn't like the idea. So, Harry eventually decided to promote her: he made her head of his subscription department and put her upstairs in the back room. He hired a Southern white Christian girl as his receptionist and secretary. It happened that the Southern white Christian girl didn't know all about Harry's business, and she was embarrassed about having to ask a Negro who was inferior to her. So, a lot of friction arose between them. Harry always took the side of the white Christian girl, and eventually he got rid of the Afro-American girl.

Now this is the liberal spirit we see in the South: we know that these liberals won't hold up under pressure. We know that they will go along with us as long as it is profitable, but, in many cases, we are seeing them become turncoats.

Q. In other words, their paternalism is only another expression of their feeling of superiority toward the Afro-Americans. And when the chips are down…

A. That's right. And that's the feeling I find among a lot of ex-progressive Negroes and Ex socialist Negroes. I see many of them in the industrial centers. They all say that we have been betrayed by the white liberals and by the socialist, that we must determine our own destiny. WE must lead our own struggle. The white people just can't understand what our struggle is and how we feel about it. We followed these liberals and these socialist for many years—they always made our struggle secondary. Our Struggle was just a by-product of what they considered the real struggle. After all those years, we never got any place. In a lot of instances, we feel betrayed. Now we feel that we must strike out on our own, that we must determine our methods and the extent to which we will go. A good example of this is the recent demonstration in the United Nations over the Lumumba lynching. When we were trying to determine what kind of demonstration we would have, there were some white socialists who said that we should demonstrate by carrying picket signs, and that these placards should be on the sidewalk, a block or two from the United Nations. But I said, "Two blacks and picket lines, hell. The man's been lynched, and this is what you propose?" So, we went right into the United Nations. But you see these white socialists didn't want to make a sacrifice. They wanted to play it safe; they wanted to appear respectable. But we know that we are in a struggle. We're in a struggle for existence, for liberation: you cannot afford to be respectable in any liberation struggle. Respectability is a luxury that is reserved for the oppressor class only. The mere fact that we are oppressed, the mere fact that we are considered inferior, the mere fact that we're denied justice, means that we can't afford to be respectable. For if we had been respected in the past, we wouldn't be in this predicament now.

Q. Not being respectable means taking action. Is that right?

A. Yes. Taking militant action.

Q. This is a good place for you to say something about your trouble with the National Association for the Advancement of Colored People—about the time when you said that violence might well be necessary in the coming struggle for desegregation.

A. Yes, I personally believe this. A lot of people say that we should turn the other cheek; if we have the right jawbone broken, we should turn the left one. If we lose the left yes, we should turn the right. But I don't see why this struggle for liberation an endurance contest must be. No, we don't subscribe to this. There are many liberals and many organizations in the North that are dumping hundreds of thousands of dollars into our struggle in the South. This money is sent into the South to convert us to nonviolence, to make us pacifists. But you see the thing is that we've always been too submissive. We've served in slavery; we were submissive then. We've gone through a period of lynching, of all types of brutal exploitation. And our children have been denied the right to grow up, to develop as total human beings. Our women have been raped and our men deprived of the right to stand up as men. And now they ask us to be nonviolent. Why do they ask us to be nonviolent? You see we are not the aggressors. We're the ones who've been subjected to all of this aggressive oppression, all of this tyranny, all of this brutality, for over three hundred years. Nobody spends money to go into the South and ask the racists to be martyrs or pacifists. But they always come to the downtrodden Negro who's already oppressed, who's already too submissive, and they ask him not to fight back. Now let's take a look at the past.

When we were enslaved, nobody came to us and told us not to fight. We've been subjected to lynching and all types of brutality through the years, and nobody tried to convert us to nonviolence. But now—why now?—All of a sudden all of these forces with all of this money start moving into the South trying to convert us to nonviolence. The reason is that they know we are becoming more militant. They know that we are becoming a real threat, and that now there is a possibility that we will fight back. Out of fear they come and pump hundreds of thousands of dollars into the South to convert us to nonviolence. But nobody ever spends a cent to convert the white supremacist. Now, there are many Uncle Toms, and Judases, and Quislings in the South who profit from the struggle. They live the lives of luxury while the masses of the people live the way they always did. And these Uncle Toms are the most outspoken exponents of nonviolence. If these Afro-American ministers are true pacifists, if they are pure pacifists, why is it that they never speak out against the war preparations of this country? Why is it they never speak out against the bomb? Why is it they never speak out against the violence of Negro against Negro in the Negro community? It is because they try to stop violence against white people only. Their one interest is that we do not fight white people. They constantly tell us that if we resort to violent self-defense, we will be exterminated. But, with the world situation it is today, only a fool would believe that a nation could exterminate twenty million people inside its boundaries. We know there's a great power struggle going on in the world today. We know we control the true balance of power. We also know, from the statistics of the Detroit race riots that production in this country fell to nothing during the peak of the riot. If there was an outright massive campaign to eliminate us, we know that this country would fall in a period of forty-eight hours. People everywhere in this world would be ready to support our struggle. Now, we've been loyal to this government. But the question is: do they hate us so much that they would rather see this nation destroyed than see us have justice? If that's their choice, then I have no compunction about seeing this country destroyed. There are a lot of people who feel this way. The government should be for the protection of the rights of its citizens. A government should stand up for the rights of man. A government should see to it that all of the people are fed, that all of the people are given a chance for medical attention. A government should see to it that all of the people fare well. When a government fails to do these things, it forfeits its right to exist.

Q. Let's go back to your case against passive resistance. A while ago I mentioned that passive resistance could work only as long as it inspired shame and restraint in the white men involved. Would you say something about what was achieved by passive resistance in the Montgomery situation, and what might have been achieved in some other way?

A. The Montgomery bus boycott was a good example of passive resistance. But we must remember that passive resistance is not the total solution. We must remember that even the people in my group, who are not pacifist, recommend nonviolent action. However, we also believe in self-defense. But we must also consider that in Montgomery, where Negroes are riding in the front of buses, there are also Negroes who are starving. The Montgomery bus boycott was a minor victory. It did not raise the standard of living of the masses of people. The Montgomery bus boycott does not mean that more people or more children are being educated. It does not mean that we are making any economic advances. Now I recommend the type of action that appeared in Montgomery, but I also recommend self-defense. You must also consider the fact that they found firearms in some of the churches in Montgomery. So, all of those ministers were not pacifists. We must also remember that the idea of nonviolence is only fed to the Negro.

I'll give you an example. In my hometown, Monroe, North Carolina, we had it out with the Ku Klux Klan in 1957. Before this clash our community had been invaded on two occasions. Once, a colored woman was caught on the street, and she was forced to dance at pistol point by the KKK. Pacifist ministers from our community protested before the City Council and asked that the Klan people be barred from our community. But the city officials said, "Well, you know that these Klansmen have the constitutional right to organize. Much right to exist as your NAACP, and there's nothing that we can do about it." So, we put up sandbags and dug foxholes and armed ourselves. We clashed with the Klan and rove them out. Afterwards, the local papers said that this was a dangerous incident and that it must not be allowed to happen again. Therefore, the city fathers outlawed Klan motorcades in the town. In the past, police cars escorted the Klan motorcades. Now I say this in order to point out something about the sit-ins. I am now under seven hundred fifty dollars bond for sit-ins at lunch counters; my case is on the way to the United States Supreme Court. But there was less violence in the Monroe sit-ins than any other sit-ins in the United States. And why was this? It was because we showed the willingness to fight and defend ourselves. We didn't appear on the streets of Monroe as beggars depending upon the charity and the generosity of white supremacists. We appeared as people with strength. And it was to the mutual advantage of all parties concerned that peaceful relations be maintained. For that reason, we had less violence. But this is the sort of thing that the support of nonviolence never tells. In other communities there were Negroes who had their skulls fractured. But not even one even had his face spat upon during our demonstrations. No, a single impolite word was passed. This all means that we've had less violence because we've shown willingness and the readiness to fight. Because of this fact we've not had to fight; there's been no cause to fight. And we believe that this is a deterrent against violence.

Q. Would you explain who the Muslims are and what they are trying to do? What is their program? What do you think they have to offer? What criticisms do you have of them?

A. I don't know much about the Muslims. I'm not affiliated with them, although I have had contact with them. They have helped me in the way of contributions. The Muslim Temple in New York contributed on my behalf when I was having a very hard time remaining in the South. I also received a telephone call from home the night before last, and I understand that the treasurer of my branch of the NAACP has become a Muslim. Now the only reason that I am not interested in the movement is because I think we have got too much religion. I think religion is a handicap. It has handicapped us in the past. It was a weapon used by the white supremacists to hold us in check. I believe that if this were not a religious organization, it would catch on faster and win many more converts. But you also must remember that all Black Nationalist groups are not Muslims. There are different degrees of nationalism. We have some sense of Black Nationalism sweeping through the race. I know that in the South the Muslim group is doing some good. For one thing, it's instilling pride. It's giving the people a rallying point. It's beginning to inspire the people to stand up and to fight. They are beginning to develop their backbone. That means a great deal to me. When an individual is determined to stand up, he makes a very poor subject for the oppressors.

Q. Don't the Muslims want to set up a separate Black Republic?

A. Yes, the Muslims say that we need some land, and that we need to set up our own Black Republic. Now this may be true, but I don't see how we can set up a Black Republic in this country under the domination of Wall Street; Wall Street is white. Unless Wall Street considers it to its best advantage. When there's so much friction, so much trouble, when the Afro-Americans refuse to be docile any long, then the time may come that the whites may see fit to let us separate and set up our own Black Republic. But I believe that our freedom will come from the world situation. I believe that the power struggle going on in the world and internal difficulties will force our government more and more to the left. It will be a matter of survival. It will have to go left or perish. Under those circumstances we may have some true integration. But as things stand now, I don't believe that these people would ever allow us to set up our own Black Republic. This is the thing that got Lumumba killed. He wanted a free Congo; a Congo that would be ruled by a Black people and that would be independent.

Q. You were saying earlier that you foresaw much violence in the coming struggle here in the United States. Do you want to say more about that?

A. Social change is violence itself. You cannot have progress without friction and upheaval. For social change, two systems must clash. This must be a violent clash, because it's a struggle for survival for one and a struggle for liberation for the other. And always the powers in command are ruthless and unmerciful in defending their position and their privileges. Afro-Americans are becoming more determined to be free. The racists and exploiters regard them as becoming more dangerous every day. The more we demand, the more they consider us an enemy, and feel that we should be eliminated or intimidated. But we've reached the state now where we are just about immune to intimidation. We've lived under intimidation so long that we are no longer afraid. So, what will happen? The socialists have long said that we should have working-class unity between the whites and the Black in the South. This is impossible with the present attitude of white southerners. You see, you can appeal to the conscience of a civilized man. But these white southerners are monomaniacs about eh race questions. They are not civilized about this question.

They have no conscience, so we can't appeal to it. The only way to unite and live in harmony with them is to impress upon them that it is in the best interest of both parties that we have peaceful relations, co-existence and harmony. But this can only come about after we've had great upheaval and much violence. The white supremacist will never relinquish their position; they will never share the good things, without this sort of struggle. The Negro will retaliate against his oppressor. And only after the struggle will we have the foundation and the basis for harmony. Now the white liberals, radicals, and socialists in the North are dumping much money into the South. They're placing all their eggs in one basket. They're betting on this Martin Luther King campaign of nonviolence. They're betting that he can convert the Negro people to nonviolence.

But they're on dangerous ground because violence is sure to come out of the South. And when the violence comes, these liberals and socialists who backed Martin Luther King are going to be out on a limb. And Martin Luther King is going to be out on a limb. He's going to have to make a choice: to publicly denounce his own people who defended themselves against the barbaric attack of the prejudiced whites in the South, or to go against the barbaric attack of the prejudiced whites in the South, or to go along with them. Now if he denounces them, he will be destroyed. He will no longer be useful to the white liberals. The white liberals' cause of showing their friendship to the Negroes will be lost, while the Negroes, showing their friendship to the Negroes will be lost, while the Negroes, on a mass scale, will lose confidence in these so-called liberal movements.

Q. Do you see no significant aid whatsoever coming from white people in this struggle?

A. There are a few white people who will help. I don't know whether they have political views. But our branch of the NAACP in Monroe is integrated. We have some white members, and these white members are pacifists. When I was suspended for saying that we should be ready to defend ourselves, these white people protested my suspension to the National Office and said that they knew the conditions under which I had made these statements. Also, I wouldn't have been able to remain in the South if it had not been for the support that I got from some white people in the North. These people are willing to give aid without strings attached. They are willing to let us direct our own struggle. But you see, in this nonviolent movement, the Negroes have become captives of these so-called white liberals who want to convert the Negroes in the South. I feel that some help will come from a minority of whites, those who will be genuinely interested in the liberation of the Negroes. They will give aid; they will be willing to help for the sake of justice, for the sake of human decency. Yes, I feel that a lot of help will come from these whites.

Q. Do you expect much help from the presently constituted liberal or leftist groups in the North?

A. No. The organized groups are too dogmatic; they're not flexible enough. In my hometown, where we fought the Klan, we are being penalized. There are children there who are growing up without education. Children without shoes, children without food. Old people without medical attention. But from all the money raised in the North, no one will send a penny to North Carolina, because the white liberals who raised this money consider us outlaws and thugs. They would rather let us suffer than identify themselves with our stand. But they're making a mistake. These liberals collect hundreds of thousands of dollars. They send truck convoys into other places in the South. They penalized us because we took a militant stand. Yet our militant stand proved right, because we've had less violence. But they're not interested in less violence.

They're just interested in no violence against white people.

Q. Do you foresee any sort of real racial war?

A. No. But I see skirmishes in many different places. Not a race war, no. There's a possibility, but I don't see such a war, unless the white supremacists feel that we are making too many gains and demanding too much, and then become fools enough and hysterical enough to attack us on a broad scale. But I don't believe that the government and the army could afford to stand idly by and allow this thing to develop into a national conflict. Because, you see, this would be certain death to the United States.

Q. In other words you think that the militant stand, the willingness to fight, will hasten positive results?

A. Yes, I'm sure of it. They always talk about Montgomery. What they don't understand is that Montgomery is in the past. This is a constant struggle, and it's never the same all the time. This struggle is continuing, but all the liberals use Montgomery as an example. They keep referring back to Montgomery. But Montgomery is in the past. It was just one milestone along the way.

We're not looking back to Montgomery. We're looking ahead; only the liberals are exalting Montgomery and the power of nonviolence and love. If the power of nonviolence and love is so great and so powerful, why do we build all of these missiles? Why do we continue to turn out hydrogen bombs? Why don't we adopt the policy of nonviolence and love? Why don't we try loving the Russians to death?

Q. What you're saying, then, is that Montgomery was a very minor success. When you get down to something really important, such as a struggle for equal opportunity in jobs, schools, living side-by-side, it's going to arouse much stronger feelings among the segregationists. These strong feelings are going to express themselves in violence, and you're going to have to defend yourselves.

A. That's right. You must remember that in Montgomery most of the white Americans now have automobiles. It's just like in my hometown when we integrated the library. I first called the Chairman of the Board in my county. It told him that I represented the NAACP, that we wanted to integrate the library, and that our own library had burned down. And he said, "Well, I don't see any reason why you can't use the same library that our people use. It won't make any difference. And after all, I don't read anyway." This was his attitude. It is the attitude of a lot of people about the bus boycott. A lot of the city officials and the white people who control the city didn't ride the buses anyway; they had their own private cars, so it didn't make any difference to them. But when you get into the struggle for the right to live as a human being and the right to earn the same amount of money, then you'll meet the greatest amount of resistance, and out of it will come violence. To say that we are pacifists, turn the other cheek, is an invitation to violence. It is asking to become the subject of brutality. In a civilized society, the law is meant to be a deterrent. It is meant to be a protective force. But where there is no law, and in the South, there is no Fourteenth Amendment to the United States Constitution, there is no collective deterrent. In that case, we must create our own deterrent. We must revert to the law of self-preservation and the survival of the fittest. The South is a social jungle, so we must create our own deterrent. We must serve notice that no man can attack us, our children, or our homes, with immunity. He must be made to realize that in attacking us he risks his own life. After all, his life is a white life, and he considers the white life to be superior so why should he risk a superior life to take an inferior one?

Q. Do you think the Communist Party will offer any significant leadership in this struggle?

A. No, no. This is the tragedy of the Communist Party. They may intend to, they may mean to help us, but they don't understand what our problem is. They don't understand that we have a struggle going on for liberation. And they always put our struggle in the background. I've seen communists, progressive white people, and socialists, and I've been surprised and sometimes shocked to find that they would never listen to me when I tried to tell them about this new militant trend. They would always tell me what Marx said, and that this is the symbol of certain things that are supposed to take place. But they never listen. They never want to learn. But they're always ready to dictate to us.

When I first made the statement that we should meet violence with violence, the first people who criticized me were the socialists. The Communists and the Trotskyites criticized me; in fact, they even said that I was a fool. But a lot of Negro papers started supporting my side, backing me up, and then these socialists started trying to reverse themselves. They should have known enough about revolutions to know that the stranglehold of an oppressor cannot be loosened by a plea to conscience. They should know that from the Russian revolution and the Chinese revolution. It would seem that they would be the first ones to agree that you must break the stranglehold of this brutal master with force. But what do they suggest? They suggest that we be meek and submissive, and they are way behind the trend of the people.

Q. Do you think that at this moment the Communists would suggest going along with passive resistance simply because it is an easy way to keep the struggle before the public eyes, and that they might be waiting to advocate force later—one which they consider dogmatically opportune?

A. They may be waiting to do that. They may be waiting. They may be trying to keep it before the public eyes. But we're just not interested in the publicity, in being in the spotlight. We're interested in becoming free. We want to be liberated. To me, oppression is harmful. It is painful. I wake up in the morning as a Nero who is oppressed. At lunchtime, I eat as a Negro who is oppressed. At night, I go to bed as a Negro who is oppressed. And if I could be free thirty seconds from now, it wouldn't be too soon. Now, maybe the Communists are in a position where they can afford this luxury of waiting. But I can ill afford it.

Q. Do you think there might be an analogy here to the Cuban Revolution where the Communist Party didn't know where the revolution could begin?

A. I see the same thing taking place here as happened in Cuba. The Communist Party didn't wholeheartedly support the Cuban Revolution. They wouldn't call strikes. They wouldn't come to support the Revolution. And when they showed an interest in the Revolution, it was after the Revolution had been won. It seems now that they're trying to gauge the Negro struggle; they're trying to determine which way it's going. They're not with the struggle, but if we ever reach a stage where it appears that we're going to be successful, I imagine they will jump on our bandwagon—whether we have a violent approach or a pacifist approach. But it should be remembered that nothing is ever gained without sacrifice. It seems to me that the liberals and communists are trying to eat their cake and have it too. They'll have to either believe in the struggle and be willing to make sacrifices, or they'll have to get out of the picture. That is the choice. This thing is moving so fast that we're going to leave all of these liberals and so-called radical groups behind. And the next thing they know we'll be too far ahead of them. You see, then they won't have anything to contribute to our struggle at all. *Q. Then what is your program?*

A. Well, we believe that we've been too prone to try to prove that we are loyal to this system. People who are oppressed should not be expected to remain loyal to oppression and to the system that oppresses them. We know that this is really a world struggle. We believe that we hold the balance of power. This is the time when we must speak out. This is the most opportune time that we've ever had in history. So, our program is that we will continue with the sit-ins, and we will continue with pressure, pressure, pressure. But all the time we will identify ourselves with the African struggle, with the struggle of Latin Americans, with the struggle of Asians. We know that this country cannot afford a lot of internal dissension. This is the time to demand our rights. This is the time for demonstrations like the demonstrations we had in the United Nations. In no uncertain terms, we must speak out. We must display the type of courage that will embarrass this nation before the world. In that way, we will force them to consider our case. We realize also that we must not rely anymore on the Uncle Toms and the Judases and the Quislings of the Black bourgeoisie who are the apologists for the very people who oppress us. We realize that there must also be a struggle within our own ranks to take the leadership away from the Black bourgeoisie who betray us. We believe that when the Black bourgeoisie can no longer show that they control us, the white liberals and the white supremacists will have no further use for them. Then the unity of our people will come, and then, through united militant effort, we can force this country further to the left. And the strange thing about this, the curious thing is, that it seems that the further to the left the country goes, the more justice you find. Now, as an individual, I'm not inclined toward politics. The only thing I care about is justice and liberation. I don't belong to any political party. I'm registered as a Democrat. I switched from a Republican. I first registered as a Republican because I wanted to protest the one-part South. I don't belong to any of the socialist parties. But I do see, as an individual, that the only hope for us seems to be socialism. I don't know what form; I don't know what kind. But I believe, and a lot of other Negroes do too, that we must create a Black let of our own. We must direct our own struggle, achieve our own destiny. We must also realize that many Afro-Americans are becoming skeptical and suspicious of white people, and especially of the so-called white liberals. They feel that we've been betrayed. And they just feel that no white person can understand what it's like to be a suppressed Negro. And since we know our case better than any individual on earth, we must be one together and be willing to state our case to the world. We must be willing to state it without compromise. And this is the new spirit that is beginning to develop among our people, in this country, now.

Q. You see an increasing pressure in the year ahead. Where will it go next?

A. My primary interest now is in liberation in this country. But there's only one place it can possibly go. It's already been every place else it could possibly be. And the only place that it didn't go yet was socialism. And with conditions as they are now, the intensifying economic problems, it's only logical that this country must turn to socialism.

Q. I remember reading The Saturday Review just recently that there are over nineteen hundred segregated school districts in the South, and that nineteen of them were desegregated last year. The Saturday Review seemed to regard this as wonderfully hopeful progress. But it takes only a little figuring to see that, at this rate, with present means and efforts, the desegregation process in the schools alone would take a hundred years. You're saying that the prejudice-system is so embedded in our social, economic, and political life that only a profound, thoroughgoing change will solve the problems of race in this country?

A. I'm convinced we will never have that kind of desegregation so long as this government stands as it is now. This is a Jim Crow government. This government, if it wanted, could eliminate racial discrimination overnight. It's just that powerful. But it represents Jim Crow. And if this government stands, I don't think that we're going to be integrated into American society.

There will have to be great political changes before that can come about.

TESTIMONIES OF ROBERT AND MABEL WILLIAMS

State of North Carolina
Versus
Richard Crowder, Harold Reape, John Lowry, and Mae Mallory, Defendants
RE: Testimony of Robert F. Williams

On Sunday, August 27, 1961, late in the afternoon, I was at my home at 410 N. Boyte Street, Monroe, North Carolina, engaging in a telephone conversation. Since many persons were disturbed by the violence that was taking place as the outgrowth of an anti-segregation picket line at the Union County Courthouse, my telephone had been ringing incessantly for more than an hour. During my occupation with the telephone, I heard a loud commotion that seemed to be located about half a block from my home. Within moments the angry voices grew louder as I ascertained that a crowd of people were converging on my home.

Inasmuch as my telephone was located about halfway down the hallway of my home, I could see some of the crowd milling about in my front yard. Unknown voices summoned me angrily out of my house. I responded to the call and was surprised to see a middle-aged white man and woman surrounded by the group. My yard and the street were filled with people. There must have been around 300 people present. When I stepped onto the ground the white woman spoke indignantly to me. She exclaimed in an angry tone that she and her husband had been kidnapped. The anger of the huge crowd intensified. Many of the enraged voices shouted for the couple to be turned over to them. The huge throng of people who had come from the street was unknown to me. They were strange faces that I had never seen before. There were about 30 persons whom I knew at my house who had come to aid me against a threatened KKK attack, and they had been moved to my backyard after a highway patrolman had ordered the street cleared earlier. Fearing that some harm might be done to the white couple, I entered the ever-narrowing circle in which the white people stood and with decisive motions of my hands forced the group out of the reach of the couple. In an indignant tone, the woman exclaimed again that they had been kidnapped. I told her that I didn't have anything to do with the street, but that they were not kidnapped in my yard. I told them that they could leave my yard anytime they wanted to. The white woman then demanded that I escort them out of the Black. She stated, "You take us out of this block! You can protect us and kept them from bothering us!" I explained to the woman that I was preparing to defend my home from the threats of the KKK, and that I didn't have anything to do with their being in the block and that I was not going to have anything to do with their going out. I told her that I was not half as brutal as her people, because if I had been in her community her people would have lynched me and I was protecting them. She admitted that I was right and thanked me for helping them. I was called to the telephone and when I started up my front steps, the white woman followed me and pressed tight against my back. The white man followed closely behind her. The crowd yelled that I should not let the white couple into my house, but the white couple forced their way into my home without being invited. I didn't turn them back because I feared for their well-being, and I felt that I was doing a humanitarian deed. Inside the house, the woman thanked me again for being so nice to them. My wife, Mabel, met them in the hallway and offered them seats.

During this time, I had seen John Lowery, whom I later learned had been indicted only once during the time the couple was there and he was sitting on the porch of a house next door (408 Boyte Street) away from the crowd. Mae Mallory was in the kitchen of my home preparing food for the Freedom Riders, she was not involved with the white couple at all. Richard Crowder and Harold Reape had been absent from the community all day Sunday, August 27th, 1961. Their absence was conspicuously obvious because they had been daily active in the Monroe Nonviolent Coordinating Committee, and they had avoided mustering to take their places on the picket line that was to be staged at the Courthouse. Before departing for the picketing, the Committee had sent youths in search of them, but it was reported that they were out of the community. When I answered the telephone, it was first nightfall, and in contrast to the many previous calls I had received all afternoon, the voice on the telephone identified itself as Chief of Police, A. A. Mauney. He said, "Robert, you have caused a lot of race trouble in this town, now state troopers are coming and in 30 minutes you'll be hanging in the Court House Square!" I took this threat seriously because four attempts had been made on my life within the two-month period before Chief Mauney's call. The Monroe Police force had sided and abetted two of those attempts. I told my wife to gather our two children and to tell Mae Mallory that we were leaving. I told her that we didn't have time to take anything. I didn't tell anyone else because I was afraid that the news got out that I had left and that the white couple may have been harmed. We left them sitting in our house at around 8 p.m. The next day in New York, I learned that I had been indicted and charged with kidnapping a couple named Mr. And Mrs. Bruce Stegall. Being fully aware of the fact that the formal accusation was a racist way of using the courts for vengeance against colored people who fight for constitutional rights and whites who believe in justice for all Americans, I knew that I could not receive justice in such an atmosphere, so I left the country rather than face lynch justice.

State of North Carolina
Versus
Richard Crowder, Harold Reape, John Lowry and Mae Mallory, Defendants
RE: Testimony of Mabel R. Williams

On Sunday evening, August 27, 1961, I, Mabel Williams was in the kitchen of my home at 410 N. Boyte Street, Monroe, North Carolina preparing food for the Freedom Riders along with Mrs. Mae Mallory and other women volunteers. We heard angry screaming voices in the front. I went to see what was happening. When I reached the front porch of my home, I met my husband, Robert F. Williams, and a white man and woman following closely behind him, coming up the front steps. A large crowd of people were milling around in our yard and the street in front of our house. My husband continued down the hall and I stood in the hall and talked with the white people. The crowd outside kept yelling and screaming about killing the white people and killing my husband. I asked the white man and woman if they wanted to sit down, and the woman said yes. They sat in chairs in my front bedroom, and I sat on the bed and talked with them. The woman thanked me for allowing them to remain in my home and praised my husband for saving their lives and protecting them from the angry crowd. Some of the people in the crowd were screaming and yelling for us to make the white people come out of our house. Some of the women were crying and saying that the white people who were in our house had helped to beat up some little colored children uptown. The woman asked me to try to get my husband to take them out of the Black through the crowd outside. I told them that my husband was busy preparing to defend our home and that she would have to take that up with him. I was called outside the bedroom several times to answer the phone or to talk with Mrs. Mallory and the others who were preparing the food. The bedroom door remained open, and we would hear the crowd in the street outside. I was the only other person to enter my bedroom besides the two white people. After a while, my husband called me and told me to get the children and tell Mrs. Mallory that we had to leave because he had just received a call from Chief Mauney that the State Troopers were coming, and they were going to hang him in the square. I got my two children and told Mrs. Mallory to get ready to leave. We left the white people sitting in a bedroom. The crowd outside had begun to scatter, but some of them were still raging.

Neither Harold Reape, Richard Crowder, nor John Lowry was in or around my home during any of the time that the white people sought refuge on our property. Neither Richard Crowder nor Harold Reape was even in the community because other students had been looking for them all day but found they were not around.

LETTERS TO ROBERT F. WILLIAMS

May 8, 1959
Dear Mr. Williams:

I have your telegram of May 7 indicating your intentions to appear before the National Board of Directors at its meeting May 11, and to be accompanied by counsel to discuss the matter of your suspension as president of our Union County Branch. Our action resulted from your statements of May 5, which you acknowledged to be correct in a telephone conversation with me on May 6. My subsequent telegram of the same day directed you to suspend your activities as president pending consideration by the Board. This is to notify you that in accordance with Article IX, Section 2 of the Constitution and By-Laws for Branches, I prefer charges against you alleging that statements attributed to you as president of the Union County, N.C. Branch, by radio and press May 6, 1959, are inimical to the best interest of the Association, to wit:

> We cannot take these people who do us injustice to the court and it becomes necessary to punish them ourselves. In the future we are going to have to try and convict these people on the spot. We cannot rely on the law. We can get no justice under the present system. If we feel that injustice is done, we must right then and there on the spot be prepared to inflict punishment on these people. Since the Federal government will not bring a halt to lynching in the South and since the so-called courts lynch our people legally, if it's necessary to stop lynching with lynching, then we must be willing to resort to that method.

This advocacy of "meeting violence with violence" is in direct violation of the national policy of the NAACP as set forth in its Articles of Incorporation, Constitution and By-Laws, and the policy resolutions of its annual conventions. Thus, your statements compromise the position and the effective functioning of the Association. The Constitution and By-Laws for Branches, governing the removal of officers, provide as follows (Article IX, Section 2): "The National Board of Directors upon satisfactory evidence that the officer is guilty of gross neglect of his official duties, or of such conduct as would be inimical to the best interest of the National Association for the Advancement of Colored People or of the Branch, shall instruct the Executive Committee to declare such office vacant and hold a new election by the Branch for said office within thirty days. If the said Executive Committee fails or neglects to remove said officers within thirty days, the National Board of Directors may declare such an office vacant and conduct a new election.

> The charges against the officer must be preferred in writing and signed by the person or persons making the same and forwarded to the National Office. Immediately on receipt of

the same, the Secretary of the National Association shall forward a copy of the charges by registered mail to the officer at his last address on file in the National Office. No action shall be taken on the charges until fifteen days after the copy should have reached the officer by ordinary course of post. He shall be entitled within fifteen days to file with the National Office his answer in writing to the charges. The National Board of Directors reserves the right to hear and act on the charges and defense of written judgment justifies may require. Notice of the findings and action of the Board shall be sent to the officer by registered mail at his last address on file in the National

Office and at the discretion of the Board of Directors, published in the official organ of the National Association. Immediately upon the entry of the National Office into the matter, the officer shall perform no official act and shall hold all records and monies of the Branch subject to the disposition of the National Office.

In accordance with the above, you have fifteen (15) days after receipt of these charges to file in writing your answer thereto. If you choose to answer in writing or verbally before the board on May 11, you are free to do so. The meeting is scheduled for 2 p.m. at the National Office, 20 West 40th Street.

Very sincerely yours, Roy Wilkins, Executive Secretary

May 23, 1961
Dear Robert,

Regarding Sat. night telephone conversation, this is what happened. After talking to you, I finally got A. J. Lewis on Sunday a.m. to get Richard Gibson's phone number. A. J. gave me the wrong number, but I finally got the right one from the N. Y. operator. Richard was on the road traveling. He was to be in Chicago that day. He, according to Bertha Green, was to call them that day from Chicago. Bertha asked me to tell her what I wanted. I told her "No, I would just rather speak to Richard" and left my number for him to call me. She promises to tell him. I haven't heard from him nor her since. I said this to point up one thing, the Black man's freedom fight has to be in the hands of Black men at all times and those that are supposed to be fighting for our freedom must be in a position where they can be reached without going through the white man.

Now, I was in Cuba with Richard Gibson and to this day he hasn't met, nor have I met him. He was always busy taking care of white folk business. He through The Fair Play for Cuba Committee, ask me to sign the "Declaration of Conscience." Now, it's time for another declaration and Richard should use the same energy, if not more, to see that it's put on the floor of the U.N. Otherwise, he's just as big an Uncle Tom as Ray Wilkerson. They will just have different bosses. Now that I've said all that, let's get down to business. At 12 o'clock on Sunday, I started calling people. By six, I had 25 people in my home. We discussed this Alabama situation considering all the things that have been happening to us for three hundred years. We organized ourselves and called ourselves the Freedom Now Committee. We want the 26 Afro-Americans who signed the Declaration along with the organization you spoke to me about on the phone to join us in placing this question on the agenda of the United Nations. We also think we could send out a call to a conference to map this whole thing out. In the meantime, we are getting the resolution in shape. We are contacting the Guinea delegation asking them to get this on the agenda for us. We are also sending these resolutions to all the nations in the United Nations whom we feel would help us in this undertaking. In the meantime, I am still waiting for Richard to call me, but could you either write or call these 26 signori' and tell them what we are doing and ask them to support it since you do have their address or phone numbers. Or you may be in New York where you can contact them. Thanks, Bob, for listening. Please let me hear from you presently.

Ray & Gilessa Cox

LETTER TO MAE MALLORY FROM ROBERT AND MABEL WILLIAMS

May 26, 1961
Mae,

As a result of a telephone call and the enclosed letter from L.A., we are sending out copies of the enclosed letter signed by Rob. We feel it is most important that you contact these people immediately. They are our opinions, obviously. We told them they would hear from you right away. Please send in the names of the Crusaders (who want their names included.) Also, any group of Nationalists or any other Afro-American that you can get. Looking forward to moving fast together.

Mabel and Rob
PS Did you get the money yet?

Notes

1 Ed Cottingham, "Panelist Discuss Robert F. Williams' Contribution before the Historical Marker Unveiled," *Enquirer Journal,* August 30, 2023, 1.
2 Sermon, Col. J.C's Last Stand, March 1956, Box 3, Folder , in the Robert F. Williams Papers, Bentley Historical Library, University of Michigan
3 On August 15, 1961, on behalf of the Union County, Williams presented to the Monroe Board of Alderman the 10- point program; see Robert R. Williams, *Negroes with Guns.* Foreword by Gloria House. Introduction by Timothy B. Tyson. Detroit: Wayne State University Press, 1998, 39.

Chapter 2

HAVANA, CUBA, 1960–1966

Robert F. Williams Meets Fidel Castro. On the first trip to Cuba in 1960 through the Fair Play for Cuba Committee, (left to right) Robert F. Williams and Richard Gibson of the FPCC, Salvador Allende of Chile, Fidel Ruis Castro, Juan Marinello Vidaurreta, Cuban lawyer, professor, and writer, and [unidentified Latin American woman] ca. 1960. Courtesy of the Union County Library in Monroe, North Carolina

Front Page of The Crusader-in-Exile, Robert and Mabel Williams traveling from Cuba to China. The image was taken during the Second Meeting, during the 15th Anniversary. Courtesy of Robert F. Williams in Box of the Robert F. Williams Papers at the Bentley Historical Library in Ann Arbor

In the May-June 1964 issue of The Crusader-in-Exile, exiled Robert F. Williams challenged racial oppression, African American human rights violations, and anticipated the rise of the Black Power Movement. While stationed in Cuba, Williams' reasoned that the causes for an Afro-American Revolt in the USA would rest on the potential for a minority revolution. This statement in the newsletter essentially helped to inspire the formation of the Revolutionary Action Movement, Student Nonviolent Coordinating Committee, Black Panther Party, the Republic of New Afrika, when he stated "the brutally oppressed Afro-American" would respond violently by resisting "to savage racial dehumanization."

During the Cultural Revolution, exiled Robert F. Williams traveled from Cuba to meet Mao in China for the first time, marking his first trip to China. Williams is seen shaking hands with and being welcomed by Chairman Mao Tse-Tung who is seen sharing a copy of The Little Red Book, 1963. Courtesy of Robert F. Williams in the Robert F. Williams Papers at the Bentley Historical Library in Ann Arbor, Michigan.

This is the cover of the second printing of *Negroes with Guns* which was published by Third World Press.

WILLIAMS HAILS CUBAN MILITARY MIGHT[1]

Havana English School of the Air in English January 3, 1962–F

(A Special Broadcast: Robert Williams Tells His Impressions of the Third Anniversary Rally and Military Parade on the Plaza de la Revolucion)[2]

Question: Tell me, Bob, are you an American citizen? **Answer**: Yes, I was born in the United States as an Afro-American. An Afro-American in the United States is a second-class citizen.

Question: Were you invited here as a member of the delegations to the anniversary of the revolution? **Answer**: Well, I am a foreigner here. I am a guest of the Cuban people.

I was invited indirectly by John F. Kennedy and the Federal Bureau of Investigation on a trumped-up charge of kidnapping in the United States. **Question**: Have you seen any Americans here among the guests who were invited from all over the world? **Answer**: No, I have not seen any American with the exception of the ones who are already here. It is very difficult for Americans to come to Cuba. In fact, such displays as we witnessed today are meant to be kept away from the American people. The U.S. government is determined not to let the truth be known about Cuba. Therefore, they have decided not to let Americans travel here, and the strong thing about this is that the United States claims to be a democracy. Yet I tried to come here for the 26 July and asked permission to do so from the U.S. State Department. The U.S. State Department said that I could not be allowed to travel to Cuba, because they had broken off diplomatic relations with Cuba and that they could not guarantee my safety here. The strange thing about this is that in another two weeks the U.S. government attempted to kill me. It happened that I ended up in Cuba and that is the only place that I could be safe. **Question**: Are you a veteran? **Answer**: Yes, I am a veteran of the U.S. Army and the U.S. Marine Corps of my State. **Question**: I suppose then that you have seen a great many military parades in your life? **Answer:** Yes, I have participated in military parades in the United States in the Army and in the Marine Corps. **Question**: What do you think of the equipment that you say today in the parade? **Answer**: Well, after seeing the parade today, I am certainly glad that I am on this side and that I am not on the other side. I think much of the equipment as a soldier and as a marine. I wish that all the American people and particularly the invaders of Cuba could have seen the equipment today, because then they would realize that it would be suicide to attempt an invasion of Cuba. I think that, if they could see the modern equipment here, they would realize that Cuba is here to stay. This equipment is superb. What I like about it is that it is the equipment of the people. This equipment is to defend true democracy—the only democracy in this hemisphere. **Question**: Did you get a chance to talk with the militiamen and the rebel soldiers today and, if you did, how does their morale compare with that of your fellow servicemen when you were in the Army? **Answer:** Well, it is quite a contrast. In fact, I hear that the Pentagon in the United States wishes that they could encourage the military personnel of the United States to have such a high morale. You know that in the United States the method is to conscript people to serve in the armed forces. But the Cuban people are volunteers. There is no draft here. The Cuban people believe in the Cuban way of life and in the democracy of Cuba. Therefore, morale is very, very high. I remember as a serviceman in the United States, we used to do everything to avoid duty. I notice here that people like their equipment and are proud of it. **Answer:** It gave me a greater feeling of security because in the United States I heard so much talk of Cuba being invaded and about mercenary training. In fact, not far from where I live, at Fort Jackson, South Carolina, I learned that they were training Cuban mercenaries to come back and invade. In the beginning this made me wonder whether I would be safe in Cuba, because I realize that I am still wanted and I feel hunted by the U.S. government. But after today I am quite sure that I would be much safer in Cuba than in the United States, and that it would not pay anybody to commit aggression against Cuba. To me it was the first time in my life that I Truly felt that I belonged to a people. I realize that this is truly a government of the people, for the people, and by the people.

ROBERT WILLIAM INTERVIEWS A SOUTH AFRICAN

Havana English School of the Air in English January 9, 1962
(Robert Williams interview with South African Negro leader (Mac Kawanna)
(Summary) **Question:** What is the attitude of the African people toward the Negro struggle in the United States? **Answer:** The African people in South Africa regard the United States of America and South Africa as the chief fortresses of barbarous servitude and racial discrimination. We regard the struggle of the Negro people in the United States as we regard the struggle of the African people in South Africa. **Question:** Last year, a Negro from my native state of North Carolina, a man named Dr. (Peeler?), visited South Africa. This trip was sponsored by the U.S. State Department. When he returned to the United States, he said that South Africa was making progress and that most of the struggle was caused by (word indistinct) on both sides. What is your opinion on this matter? **Answer:** First I must say that Africans in South Africa have little or no regard for Negroes who come to South Africa sponsored by the State Department. The (Afrikaners?) invited them to disturb peace in South Africa.

Question: Mr. (Mac Kawanna?), do you feel that the Americans in South Africa (apply?) democracy to South Africans? **Answer**: The United States is not a democracy, in that the Negro people are discriminated against and in that the United States monopolizes capitalism, and not only in South Africa. **Question:** Have the colored people in South Africa begun to feel that the American Negroes are united with them in their struggle and that we have a common enemy?

Answer: Yes, the people of South Africa regard the struggle of the American Negroes as their struggle. There is a feeling of kinship. **Question:** Mr. (Mac Kawanna?), coming from a racist and capitalist country like South Africa, what contrast do you find between a country like socialist Cuba and South Africa? **Answer:** The people of South Africa greatly admire the struggle of the Cuban people, and what I have seen justifies their admiration. What is remarkable about the Cuban revolution is that it has passed within a short time from a democratic to a socialist revolution. Cuba is an example not only for Latin America but for all peoples who are fighting for national liberation and who are oppressed by monopolistic capitalism.

Question: What do you think of Dr. Fidel Castro as a revolutionary leader? **Answer:** Dr. Fidel Castro is a man who really inspires the people. The enthusiasm of the people during the anniversary celebration showed that the people know that he is a man who really represents them. **Question:** What is the purpose of your visit to Cuba? **Answer:** "The purpose of my visit to Cuba is to set up an information office that will enable us to present our case throughout Latin America and North America." We have come to Cuba because we feel that we can propagate our cause without interference, and we will be able to propagate our ideas without fear that we might offend others. **Question:** As a Nero from the United States, I know that the U.S. press conceals evidence and facts from the North American people, and that many times news stories are distorted or outright lies. I would like to know whether information on brutal racist incidents such as the murders of Emmet Till and (Parker?) reaches Africa. Till was a 14-year-old Negro who was murdered. The people who murdered him have gained great wealth and fame from well-known magazines in the United States for articles written on how they murdered him. What is the reaction in Africa when people hear about these cases? **Answer:** Some information does seep into Africa about the brutality, but it is not reported (accurately?). However, the people of Africa, particularly those in South Africa, know about these brutal acts perpetrated by the fascist police. The United States has all its friends publicize what is referred to as desegregation. Unfortunately, even some Negro people (were misled?). But in South Africa, we know the truth. We regard desegregation as (words indistinct) like the Ku Klux Klan to murder the Negro people in the United States. **Question:** Are you aware of the fact that when violence broke out in South Africa, when Negro mothers in South Africa had babies murdered in their arms, when Negroes had to resort to fighting tanks with stones, that the racist states Georgia and Mississippi sent notes of congratulations and support to the South African government, and that the racist Ku Klux Klan also sent a note of support to the South African government? **Answer:** I was not aware of these facts, but they do not surprise me at all, because we have always regarded the Ku Klux Klan and the racist states as the same as those who are in power in South Africa You must remember that the fascists who are ruling South Africa were open admirers of Hitler during the war. **Williams:** Thank you for appearing here today and for talking with me. I am sure that we will be able, in the future, to show the connection between racism and imperialism all over the world. I would also like to say to you that as an Afro-American I realize that our struggle is the same, that we have a common enemy, and that we must unite in our struggle against this enemy. I am sure that in the end we will triumph.

ROBERT WILLIAMS STATES AFRO-AMERICAN STRUGGLE IS BOUND TO TRIUMPH.

Peking NCNA in English to Asia and Europe 1805 GMT September 27, 1963.

He took the initiative, Williams said, in writing to Chairman Mao Tse-tung who "has a greater understanding of the oppressive nature of the United States than most of the world leaders and because China has at heart the sincere interest of all the brutally exploited, brutally oppressed people of the world." The struggle of the U.S. Negroes for justice is significant to the worldwide struggle for liberation, he declared. "The United States is the most powerful enemy of the progressive people of the world. When the people throughout the world struggle against U.S. imperialist domination, they weaken it and make our struggle for liberation easier," he said. "When the United States speaks of democracy around the world," Williams went on, "the people of Africa and Asia must remember what democracy means to the colored people in the United States." Robert Williams has taken refuge in Cuba. The Kennedy administration, in pressing a framed-up charge against him, used hundreds of FBI agents to try to arrest him.

But the people helped save him from almost certain death at the hands of the racists. "I haven't violated the law or committed any crime. I advocate that all Americans have human rights and be treated as human beings. This is what Kennedy swore to do. Be he fails to do it. Kennedy has the power as president to protect the rights of the Negroes. He has refused to." The Kennedy administration, Williams said, "claims that it is establishing democracy around the world. But how can this be, when our people are fighting and dying in U.S. streets for democracy?" He cited the experience of the Negro people in Birmingham, Ala. While repression and murder of Negroes are taking place when Negro children are being brutally attacked, the Kennedy administration refuses to lift a finger, Williams pointed out. "But as soon as the Negroes rose in violence to defend themselves," he said, Kennedy sent in troops "to protect the white racists, to stop the demonstrations of the Negroes for freedom. After Kennedy sent the troops to Birmingham, not a single racist or policeman who participated in the slaughter of Negroes was arrested," he said. "I am more convinced than ever that the U.S. government is a government of savages, and it is the greatest threat to peace and the happiness of the people of the world."

Giving many instances of oppression of the Negroes, he said: "Their only crime was being born black in the United States." "Many people outside the United States are led to believe that racial segregation and brutality only exist in the southern United States. That is not true. Even in the north, the black workers constitute four to everyone white worker unemployed." As to foreign policy, Williams continued, the true nature of Kennedy is shown "in his open defense of the racist South Africans and Portuguese in the United Nations. In defending their racist crimes, he is defending his cause." He said: "Now the revolution is beginning to sweep Latin America and Africa. The struggle of the Negro people in the United States is fast becoming part of the worldwide struggle against exploitation and oppression. Our struggle is bound to be successful, because it is part of the worldwide struggle for liberation of all oppressed people. The struggle will be more violent and more brutal, but it is bound to triumph, because the oppressors, the U.S. imperialists, exploitation, and racism will be destroyed." "The more brutal the struggle becomes, the more the masses of our people will realize that our greatest hope is the unity, the solidarity of our cause with the struggle of all the people for freedom." Despite suppression and maneuvers of the Kennedy administration, he said, the movement for Negro liberation is mounting. He pointed to the movement in his hometown of Monroe, N.C. "We organized the first Negro guard of the people's militia in the first collective defense in the freedom struggle of the U.S. Negroes. We have been able to defend ourselves for many years against KKK attacks. The guards for self-defense have now become part of the assistance of Negroes in many places," Williams said. The reason the U.S. government is "so determined to destroy my people," Williams declared that "is because I advocate that Negroes meet violence with violence to defend themselves." He has wanted to come to China ever since the triumph of the Chinese revolution, the American Negro leader said. The U.S. government made great efforts to distort the Chinese revolution. During his short stay, Williams said he has found the Chinese people very friendly. "The Chinese people cannot be intimidated by the United States. Only a nation which cannot be intimidated by the United States can give sincere support to the peoples who are fighting for civil rights," he declared. "I hope that my visit here shall serve to bring about a better unity between the Chinese people and the American Negroes," he said.

ROBERT WILLIAMS IS INTERVIEWED BY HSIUHUA IN PEKING, October 22, 1963

The visiting American Negro leader Robert Williams said, "As an Afro-American freedom fighter, I feel more confident of victory in our struggle, more secure in our resistance to the white supremacy plan of genocide because China, a champion of the oppressed people of the world, has exploded a bomb of freedom." He went on: "I rejoice over the explosion of the Chinese bomb because that is not a bomb of those who advocate racial and imperialist oppression. China's bomb is a freedom bomb. It offers hope to all who struggle against tyranny and oppression and in the shadow of nuclear intimidation."

AFRO-AMERICAN INTERNATIONALIST ROBERT WILLIAMS DISCUSSES U.S. IMPERIALISM AND FAILURES IN PRESIDENT LYNDON JOHNSON'S WAR ECONOMY, November 17, 1964

Peking NCNA International Service in English 1547 GMT 17 November 1964 -- W (Text) Peking, 17 November -- People cannot expect anything from Lyndon Johnson though he made many promises during the presidential election, the American Negro leader, Robert Williams, said here on Monday in an interview with NCNA. "This is because the U.S. Government is based on racism and imperialism. Its economy is a war economy," he said.

Robert Williams called upon Afro-Americans to continue their struggle. He stressed that the only alternative for the Afro-Americans is to bring their protests to the streets and use violence against violence. While claiming to be a champion of peace, Lyndon Johnson is discussing with White House specialists how to extend the war in South Vietnam, he added. The struggle of the Afro-Americans is part of the worldwide struggle against imperialism and for human dignity, he said. The outlook of Afro-Americans is becoming increasingly internationalist. Their struggle is drawing inspiration more and more from the teachings of Chairman Mao Tse-tung Robert Williams expressed confidence that the combined struggle of the world's anti-imperialist force and the anti-racist force within the United States will hasten the fall of U.S. imperialism.

Turning to his impression of his second visit to China, Robert Williams mentioned the greater variety of improved consumer goods in the ships, more transport, and more construction projects underway. Robert Williams and his wife, we have been in China more than six weeks, have visited the Inner Mongolia Autonomous Region, northeast industrial centers, revolutionary bases, and big cities. "I am highly impressed by the great patriotism of the Chinese people and their great capacity for constructing their motherland. The people of all nationalities in China have the same devotion for their motherland and work as one for their common cause," he said. He said that he drew this conclusion from his many contacts with Tibetans, Mongolians, Koreans, and other Chinese minority people. The people of all nationalities in China know about the struggle waged by the Afro-Americans and support Chairman Mao Tse-tung's statement calling upon the people of the world to unite against racial discrimination by U.S. imperialism, he said. The American Negro leader described the entry of a U.S. nuclear submarine into Japanese ports as "a show of force perpetrated to intimidate the people of the Orient who promote their national independence in the best interests of the people of Asia and who refuse to accept the Yankee as the new god of the Orient. It was meant to intimidate all of the people of Asia but was specifically aimed at the CPR and independent-minded and anti-imperialist Indonesia. It was a contemptuous act, designed to emasculate the ever-growing spirit of self-determination and national pride of the anti-colonialist Japanese people. It is also an attempt to separate the Japanese people from their sisters and brothers of Asia and to force Japan to serve as the base area of the Yankee military conspiracy to conquer and subdue the Orient." Robert Williams said that the Yankees could best serve the cause of peace and freedom by limiting their bases to their own soil.

WILLIAMS SPEAKS ABOUT THE GREAT THOUGHT OF MAO TSE-TUNG WHO HE CHARACTERIZES AS TRANSFORMING THE WHOLE WORLD, 1964.

Comrades, Revolutionaries, and Friends:

In the name of all the revolutionary American people, and especially in the name of the brutally oppressed a victimized Afro-American freedom fighter, I salute our glorious Chinese brothers and the mighty Chinese People's Republic on this historical 17th anniversary. To salute our glorious Chinese brothers and the mighty Chinese People's Republic is to pay tribute to its great architect, liberator, helmsman, and universal leader and teacher, whose thought is transforming the whole world. On this great National Day, revolutionaries throughout the world realize more than ever how much we are indebted to the architect of people's warfare, the immortal leader and teacher, Chairman Mao Tse-tung. This mighty assemblage here today is a vivid testimony of the people's determination to make and sustain the revolution. It is symbolic of the growing unity and solidarity of the struggling peoples of the world. It reflects the fraternal ties of we who labor and struggle in a common front against a common enemy, U.S. imperialism. On this glorious 17th anniversary, I am convinced that from People's China shall flow the spirit and inspiration that shall inspire patriots everywhere to resolutely struggle to build a people's world. Only in a people's republic would a refugee from racist "free world" tyranny, grandson of chattel slaves robbed from Africa, one imprisoned on his own native soil for sitting on a public seat reserved for "white people only," one fanatically and violently pursued by the fascist U.S. government for demanding human rights, social justice and stressing the right of armed self-defense, be extended the honor representing his oppressed people as I am accorded here today. We brutally oppressed Afro-Americans, the nearly exterminated American Indians, Puerto Ricans, Mexican

Americans, and other oppressed U.S. minorities know the true nature of the savage Yankee. We know what he truly means when he so piously and hypocritically proposes to bring peace and democracy to Vietnam and the world. He is a jingoist, a cold-blooded murderer and plunderer who respects the rights of colored peoples less than those of common street dogs. We revolutionary Afro-Americans know the true nature of the peace she offers and we prefer the rigors and sacrifices of redemptive people's struggle. We call upon our oppressed people to further intensify the battle and to coordinate their revolutionary activity with the liberation forces of Asia, Latin America, Africa and the justice and peace-loving peoples of all races throughout the world. We do not seek peace and fraternity with the devil and a favored lackey status in his hell. Instead, we seek his resolute and total destruction and the glorious heritage of a people's world. Contrary to what some cynics would have us believe our vicious enemy is not invincible. Chairman Mao has said he is "a paper tiger" and our people have come to realize this incontrovertible truth. And the thunder of BLACK POWER echoes throughout the land while U.S. imperialist tyrants armed with horrible death weapons tremble from the terrifying shock of a confrontation with wretched an angry mass armed with a common household match and a bottle of gasoline. On this glorious 17th anniversary of the Chinese People's Republic, a reliable base area of the world's peoples' struggle, we take great pride in the technical and scientific achievements of the glorious Chinese people, which explode the U.S. imperialist (unreadable) racist myth of the inferiority of non-Anglo-Saxon peoples. We are more confident than ever of the final triumph of our cause. In this mighty year of the Great Chinese Proletarian Cultural Revolution, racist and imperialist America sees her last big hope for world domination slipping fast away. We revolutionaries of the whole world shall intensify our revolutionary struggles, confident that our Chinese brothers and sisters in the Red Guard, armed with Mao Tse-tung's thoughts are at their battle stations in a mighty base area of world revolution, being waged for the heritage of a people's world.

Long live the People's Republic of China!
Long live Mao Tse-tung's thought!
Long live Chairman Mao Tse-tung!
Long live the solidarity of the revolutionaries of the world!

ROBERT WILLIAMS SPEAKS AT THE INTERNATIONAL CONFERENCE FOR SOLIDARITY WITH THE PEOPLE OF VIETNAM AGAINST U.S. IMPERIALIST AGGRESSION FOR THE DEFENSE OF PEACE, HANOI, DEMOCRATIC REPUBLIC OF VIETNAM, November 25–29, 1965.

Brothers of Vietnam, patriots of the world, and lovers of peace and freedom: I greet you in the name of those of my fellow countrymen who are civilized enough to oppose U.S. aggression; I specifically greet you in the name of Afro-American freedom fighters who are waging a determined liberation struggle against mainland American colonialism. As chairman-in-exile of the Revolutionary Action Movement, an American-based united liberation front, comprising many groups and organization, I resolutely offer support to our gallant brothers of Vietnam and this International Conference for Solidarity with the People of Vietnam Against U.S. Imperialist Aggression for the Defense of Peace. Not only do we support the right of our brothers of Vietnam to defend themselves against the armed aggression, repression and tyranny of U.S. imperialism and its running dogs, but we wish to thank our brothers for the splendid examples they are giving us. Our people are being inspired by the effectiveness and the great successes scored by the Vietnamese people in their armed struggle for self-defense and liberation. After almost 200 years of inhuman bondage and shameful dehumanization under the present U.S. government, our meek and passive people, like our brothers of Vietnam, Cuba, the Congo, Mozambique, and throughout Asia, Africa, and Latin America, are beginning to cast off the imperialist inspired curse of turn—the other cheekism. Yes, on the very mainland of Neocolonialism our oppressed people are turning the streets of racist and imperialist America into battlegrounds of resistance. More than any other people in the world, our people understand the savage and beastly nature of barbaric Yankeeism. We know the hypocrisy and inhumanity of the evil government of our beloved country. Perhaps you may wonder why I, an oppressed descendant of African slaves, would refer to America as our beloved country. It is because the blood, sweat, and tears of our African people have drenched the mountains, hallowed the valleys and swelled the rivers of America. It is because the first patriot to fall in the American Revolution was a Black man named Crispus Attucks. Yes, almost 200 years ago a Black man fell first in the struggle for liberation, in the struggle for American freedom and independence. Yet today our people are still suffering and dying in their quest for freedom in the so-called "free world" of racist America. There has never been a revolution so grossly betrayed in the history of the world. There never was such a cruel hoax so brutally perpetrated on a noble people. We, the captive people of the free world of racist America, support the right of all oppressed people to meet violence with violence. We resolutely support the right of all people to self-determination. We are resolutely opposed to the fate of oppressed people being decided in any international body where the racist United States holds sway. We are opposed to so-called "justice" being meted out to the victims of U.S. racism and imperialism by running dog lackeys, hired thugs, and agents of Yankeeism. We want to remind those who cherish freedom and justice that the Yankee honors his treaties, agreements, and legal writs only to the extent that they promote his sinister cause of world conquest. Yankee imperialism is a racist imperialism. It is a threat to the peace and security of the entire world. The American Indian, the first American, is a perfect example of those who trust in the promises of the Yankee plunderers. The proud and once great American Indian sought to honorably and peacefully share his native land with the conniving intruder who came preaching a new doctrine of so-called "Christian brotherhood." More than a one hundred treaties signed with the American Indians have been violated and shamelessly discarded by the U.S. government. The American Indian was the first victim of the U.S. government's strategic hamlet, the so-called "Indian Reservation." Today, he too, is a prisoner on his own soil, and he has all but been exterminated. What is a treat, what is an agreement, and what is a constitution to the racist, imperialist administration? The

Johnson administration is a racist, imperialist administration desperately trying to conceal its inherent dishonor in a deceptive cloak of so-called "representative democracy." Wherever it can, it thrusts its imperialism deceptively upon the deceived through phony Alliances for Progress, Peace Corps, Aid Programs, Military pacts, phony democratic slogans, Yankee dollars, and chewing gum. Wherever it can, it hides its brutal and evil racist face behind the clever façade of mercenary Negroes. It stages a repulsive parade of handpicked Negro puppets, Judases, and apologist-for-the-system before the world to extol the virtues of fabled representative democracy for a government that respects the human rights of colored people less than those of common street dogs. The so-called "U.S. Civil Rights Bill" allegedly guaranteeing rights to colored people is a farce of the first magnitude. The Constitution of our country guarantees all people equal rights. It has never been enforced and honored by the U.S. government. A Civil Rights Bill similar to Johnson's was enacted in 1875. It has never been enforced. The racist United States, like racist South Africa, is a member of the United Nations and they both stand in contempt of its human rights charter. It is ironic that the very body, which is asked to condemn racialism in Portuguese, Angola, and South Africa maintain their seat within the borders of the racist United States. The non-white delegates to this very body, themselves, do not enjoy immunity from the brutality and violence of U.S. racism. Delegates themselves have been made victims of ruthless police brutality and humiliating racial discrimination. Yes, like all people who struggle for human dignity and liberty, we Afro-Americans have traitors and mercenaries in our ranks. The chief apologist for its corrupt, decadent, racist, and imperialist system is the head of the U.S. Information Services. This man, Carl Rowan, is a running dog for the racist and imperialist Johnson Administration. A Negro was especially designated for this highly sophisticated system of deception because more and more the U.S. imperialists are smarting from the embarrassment their racist policies are causing them abroad. It is the height of cynicism, the cruelest of hoaxes, for a government to practice genocide against a minority while sending one of its own members to help bait the trap for other potential victims. This Negro spokesman for white supremacy democracy, Mr. Rowan, visited his home in Tennessee and was not allowed to dine nor use the public toilet in the U.S. government subsidized airport because his skin is black. Yes, the U.S. government has sunken to the level of the devil of the world. The same racist savages whose bombs blow the heads off black babies in Birmingham, United States, who viciously club pregnant Afro-American women into insensibility on the streets of America are the same best who murder, torture, and maim the patriots of Vietnam. It is the height of man's inhumanity to man when a slave is sent to extend his master's brutal slavery to his brothers. Afro-American soldiers themselves are being slaughtered like wild beasts on the streets of the so-called "free world" of racist America, yet they are being sent as aggressors against the anti-racist, anti-imperialist, peace-loving people of Vietnam in a fraudulent crusade of containing communism. Corporal Roman Duckworth, an Afro-American soldier, who had obtained leave from his post in Mississippi to visit his seriously hospitalized wife, was viciously gunned down by a racist sheriff because he refused to submit to the racist demands that he, a Negro soldier, restrict himself to the rear of the bus. Was Cpl Duckworth killed because the United

States wanted to contain communism in Mississippi? No! Lt. Colonel Lemuel Penn, one of the very few high-ranking Afro-American officers in the Army reserves, while returning to his family had his head blown off at the very gates of Ft. Benning, Georgia, United States. His brutal and savage murderers readily identified themselves as members of a Ku Klux Klan terrorist group and boasted that they killed him because he was Black. As in the case of Cpl. Duckworth and countless other lynched Afro-Americans, the savage criminals have been acquitted and acclaimed honored heroes in their racist communities. Was Col. Penn killed because the U.S. government wanted to contain communism in Georgia? No! These loyal servants of U.S. imperialism were killed simply because their skins were Black. The racist U.S. government cynically pleads no jurisdiction over America's southern soil, yet it brazenly proclaims the right to act as policeman, judge, and executioner in Vietnam and throughout the world. Throughout racist America, our people are being terrorized, murdered, maimed, bombed, lynched, raped, starved, sterilized by the states, and imprisoned. Besides conducting a campaign of genocide against our people, the fascist organizations are also attempting to intimidate our white allies by subjecting them to all forms of violence, terror and murder. These fascist forces are arming themselves with weapons from the U.S. Military arsenals. They are openly training for their publicly proposed policy of exterminating our people. We warn the racists of America that they are not living in the fascist era of Hitler's Germany and that our brothers of all races throughout the world are not going to passively submit to genocide. Let them remember that the anti-racist, anti-imperialist forces of the socialist camp are growing more powerful every single day. We are learning from the people of Vietnam. We are learning from the people of Cuba. We are learning from the people of Algeria, Angola, and the Congo. We believe in the right of armed struggle. We believe in the people's right to defend themselves in Vietnam as well as in Harlem, New York or Jackson, Mississippi, United States. We proudly hail the nuclear achievements of the staunch defenders of the oppressed, our Chinese brothers, in developing weapons for self-defense against nuclear intimidation by the racist United States. Our people, who have for many generations been defenseless victims of monopolized white supremacy terror, consider the Chinese bomb, a people's bomb, a freedom bomb of the oppressed. Our principles and our love for humanity demand that we place ourselves on the side of the Vietnamese people. As a representative of the Revolutionary Action Movement, I am here to give support to the Vietnamese people in their struggle against U.S. imperialist aggression. We are opposed to the barbaric acts of the hypocritical Johnson administration, at home and abroad. Our human decency will not allow us to be pretty and serve as spineless apologists for savage Yankeeism. Not only do we condemn, protest and raise our fists in indignation at these brutal crimes perpetrated against the noble patriots of this gallant land, but we promise our brothers, and let the whole world bear witness, that we shall intensify, our struggle for liberation in the so-called "free world" of the racist United States. We shall take the torch of freedom and justice into the streets of America, and we shall set the last great stronghold of Yankee imperialism ablaze with our battle cry of freedom! Freedom! Freedom nor or death! For our people, for our country and for our compatriots throughout the world, we shall reclaim the nobility of the American Revolution. We shall raise our flag in honor, true peace, and brotherhood to all the world.

Thank you,
Robert F. Williams—United States

STATEMENT BY ROBERT F. WILLIAMS, "LET US BURY THE YANKEE," October 30, 1962

Havana CMQ Television Network in Spanish 0030 GMT October 30, 1962—F

(Text) Robert Williams, who was persecuted on several occasions in his native land, that is, the United States, is now a political refugee in Cuba. Robert Williams is being persecuted in his country simply because he wants an end to the brutal racial discrimination prevailing in his native country. In our socialist fatherland, there are no race classifications. We are all equal here and Robert Williams, a progressive leader who loves our people, is surprised by the Mimar cameraman in Havana Central Park when, together with the U.S. citizens residing in Cuba, he had just laid a wreath at the foot of Jose Marti's statue. Robert Williams had this to say: "Revolutionary patriots of Cuba and the world. I am proud to have the opportunity of speaking to you today in Camilo's spirit. I am proud to speak to you in this moment of grave crisis for Cuba. I am proud to be in Cuba; I am proud to be with you and against the Yankee oppressors. The racists who want to come to invade Cuba are the oppressors of 20 million Americans."

> "It is not necessary for us to refute the brutality of the Yankee imperialists for the whole world knows now of the lives, the oppression, and the brutality of racist Yankees. I will not talk to you long about the Yankees. This is not the time to talk. It is the time to mobilize to defend free Cuba from Yankee imperialism and the racists. The U.S. citizens living in Cuba--citizens who support the Cuban revolution--say that they will not pass. We have spoken in the past and we have spoken enough. Now let us sharpen our machetes. If the Yankee dogs come here, let us prepare not to (praise?) them but to bury them. : Cuba has many friends in the world. The real friends of Cuba will be with Cuba to the death. We swear as long as we live that we shall never surrender to racism and imperialism. As an oppressed refuge from John F. Kennedy's so-called free world, instead of bringing his hypocrisy to Cuba, we invite him to take his free world and go to hell."

WILLIAMS STATES "NO FREEDOM IN U.S. FOR AFRO-AMERICANS"

Havana Radio Progreso in English 0400 GMT November 17, 1962—F
(Radio Free Dixie program—Robert F. Williams Commentary)

(Excerpts) Greeting my friends: The (o-fay) in the United States are showing their true colors now. While they are talking loud and long about maintaining democracy around the world as defendants of the so-called "free world," they are treating Afro-Americans like dogs. In fact, they are treating Afro-Americans worse than dogs. Dogs have the protection of the law. The Society for the Prevention of Cruelty to Animals really gets hot under the collar when "old hound dog Bozo" is abused and mistreated. Yes, the animal society offers shelter for homeless dogs while dark children go begging. The crux of the matter is that the (o-fay?) (Phonetic—meaning unknown—Eco*) Yankee thinks he is God. He thinks the turn of the very universe should be governed by his control. The racist (o-fay?) thinks that the Black man should be happy and content just to catch the crumbs that fall from his table He thinks the Black man should be more than happy in his phony crusade for racist democracy just for the sake of proving his loyalty to his master. Yes, this is the way of dogs. Is it not true that if a dog is abused and kicked, he will tuck in his tail and lick the very foot that kicked him? No! A thousand times, no! This must never be said to be the nature of a Negro. It is a first-magnitude tragedy that so-called liberal (o-fays?) and their "Uncle Tom flossiest" they call "good negroes" are broadcasting from the top of the earth about how much progress the race is making in the racist United States. Yes, they are telling the whole wide world about Joe Louis, Jackie Robinson, Lena Horne, Ralph Bunche, and other Black stars of fame in the land of racist shame. Our people are not so stupid as to think they have arrived at the promised land because of this token (world indistinct). We know that the lips of most of these favorite sons will be just as sealed as a corpse when it comes to speaking out against oppression. But militancy is spreading among many of our race. We are fortunate also to have a growing number of militant whites joining our struggle—not the phony liberals. The Afro-Americans must wake up now. This is not the time for foot-dragging. The racist United States is the greatest hypocrite and lying nation in the whole world. The Afro-Americans have no freedom to defend themselves in the United States. The government does not believe in freedom. Freedom, like charity, begins at home and spreads abroad. Colored people are tired of being treated worse than dogs in the United States. Four hundred years of brutal oppression and inhuman Jim Crow have worn thin our patience. The racist white man is the Afro-American's only enemy and if his security means defense of a Jim Crow system then he is taking a hell of a risk to arm young Afro-Americans to defend an oppressive way of life. Afro-Americans demand freedom now. The cry goes out: liberty or death!

WILLIAMS SENDS PROTEST STATEMENT TO KENNEDY,
September 27, 1963

American Negro Leader Robert Williams, now visiting China, today sent a message to the U.S. President Kennedy protesting against the savage persecution of American Negroes by U.S. racialists enjoying Kennedy's aid and comfort. The message reads:

> From the liberated CPR, staunch supporter of the Negro struggle for freedom, as a former official of the National Association for the Advancement of Colored People again I add my voice to the many peoples of the world who are protesting the savage persecution, murder, and unjust imprisonment of Afro-Americans. The barbaric conduct of U.S. racists enjoying the aid and comfort of your government exposes your pious-sounding speeches as the vilest

sort of hypocrisy. Is Birmingham indicative of the democracy the United States would like to export to Latin America, Asia, and Africa? Let me remind you that these heathen racist crimes against Black humanity shall be avenged.

WILLIAMS HOLDS PRESS CONFERENCE IN PEKING TO DISCUSS HIS IMPRESSIONS OF CHINA AND THE CHINESE PEOPLE

Peking in English to Western North America 0400 GMT November 13, 1963—W

(Summary) We now bring you a recording of the American Negro leader, Robert Williams speaking of his impressions of China at a recent press conference in Peking.

Since coming to China, I have visited (Yenan?), Shanghai, Hangchou, Wuhan, Tsinan (as heard), and in these places, I have met and talked with people from many walks of life in China. I have visited the homes of the people of communes, farmers; I have visited factories, workshops, universities, schools, and some resort places. I am very much impressed by the Chinese people, and I am convinced beyond a shadow of a doubt that the interest of the Chinese in the Negro race problem and the support of the Chinese for our struggle is sincere, that it reaches even down to the small children, children as young as eight and nine years old. I have never felt more welcome in a place than here or been welcomed by so many people. I have been impressed most of all by my visit to Wuhan--my visit to the heavy tool (building?) industry. In the West we have been told by U.S. propaganda media that the Chinese economy is on the verge of collapse, that there are no consumer goods being produced in China, and that the Chinese are incapable of building or creating a heavy industry. I must admit that I have been rather taken aback by the success that I have noticed in the factories, especially in heavy industry. I have also been told, or I have heard from the United States directly, that there is no food in China in the marketplaces, but I have visited marketplaces and even in rural communities I have found that they are well stocked. I have also heard that Chinese-manufactured products are very shoddy. This is not true; I find that the quality of Chinese products is very high. In many instances I have noticed that the quality is higher than that of products made in the United States. I have been told that China is a warlike nation, that the people of China are belligerent and hostile. I find this not true—the people of China are among the friendliest people (anywhere?). I find also that in China the people are not full of hatred toward anyone. I have also been led to believe that China is a police state that the people are being forced to do forced labor at bayonet point. I have been surprised not to see anyone being forced to work at bayonet point in China. In fact, more people are being prodded by bayonets in the United States today—I would say a hundred or a thousand times more people. I find that there are more bayonets in the so-called free world, and if China is what they call a police state of terror, then a lot of people in the United States must be praying for such a police state to be introduced there soon. That was Robert Williams speaking of his impressions of China.

WILLIAMS MAKES INTERNATIONAL APPEAL TO END SAVAGE BRUTALITY IN RACIST WHITE AMERICA AGAINST BLACK HUMANITY, March 15, 1965

Havana Radio Free Dixie in English 0500 GMT March 15, 1965—F

The following international appeal was released to the press on March 11 by Robert F. Williams, and I quote: The savage brutality being released against Black humanity in the free world of Alabama and throughout racist America is symbolic of the type of democracy it is endeavoring to practice on the non-Anglo-Saxon and non-Aryan peoples of the world. In Alabama, the savagery of the American social system, the conscience of its jungle society, and its concept of law, order, justice, morality, and human life stand bare and naked before the entire world. Persons with normally human sensibilities can only react with horror and bitter indignation at the sight of U.S. storm troopers indiscriminately clubbing defenseless men, women, and children in insensibility. In the free world of the much-boasted-about representative democracy of self-righteous American, Black humanities being jabbed, gunned down, and dragged through the streets like slaughtered cattle simply because (world indistinct) for human life. The civilized world cannot afford to look with indifference at this barbaric concept of a beastly nation which has set itself up as a policeman, judge, and executioner of law and order throughout the world.

American justice, now on display at Selma, Alabama, is the type of justice that racist America aspires to extend to the non-Anglo-Saxon and non-Aryan peoples of the world. The Johnson administration piously and hypocritically proclaims to be defending democracy in far-away Indochina and the Congo while supporting fascist terror and genocide against colored humanity in the very confines of its own borders. It is a ruse and a farce in the most sinister spirit of barbarity that the United States pretends to be moved to the defense of democracy abroad while following a policy of tyranny by terror at home. The new brand of fascist Americanism is embarked on a ruthless course of world conquest and domination. It is out to add the entire colored population of the world to its stockyard of human bondage. While murdering and maiming the peace-loving women and children of Vietnam in the name of democracy, it has unleashed unmitigated terror against the Black women and children of American to the glory of white supremacy. Alabama is as much American as Washington. It represents the true nature of American (world indistinct). Not only is the Johnson administration in league with the racist terrorists, but it is manipulating Negro puppet leaders and Fabian-minded white Negroes to dilute and curb the revolutionary spirit of the dehumanized Black masses. Agents of the Johnson administration have infiltrated the militant mass liberation movement in order to tidy up, and whitewash racist America's beastly and brutish image before the world. Americanism is a degenerate beast which constitutes a menace to the peace and well-being of the entire world. Universal Americanism is wiped from the face of the earth. Passive resistance and peaceful coexistence (several words indistinct) to all who suffer from the illusion of the power of nonviolence. The struggle of the Afro-American in his unending quest for justice and freedom in racist and fascist America warrants a common cause of action by all the civilized peoples of the world. Revolutionary freedom fighters of the social jungle of the United States beseech our brothers and fellow humans throughout the world to vigorously condemn and violently protest the outrageous savagery and terror which has been unleashed against colored humanity and its civilized white allies in the blood-stained social jungle of the racist United States.

Signed: Robert F. Williams, Exile Chairman of the Revolutionary Action Movement. The preceding appeal was issued from Havana, Cuba on March 11.

WILLIAMS DELIVERS REMARKS TO U.S. AFRO-AMERICAN SERVICEMEN

Hanoi in English to American Servicemen in South Vietnam 1330 GMT March 17, 1965

Four months ago, one of your mates, a former U.S. Marine officer, Robert F. Williams, the president of the American Revolutionary Movement of the American Negroes, came here as our brother on a visit to this country with a number of other Americans. In connection with your government's recent dispatch of the U.S. Ninth Marine Brigade to South Vietnam to intensify its war there at a time when your Negro compatriots are being brutally suppressed by the racists in the state of Alabama, we would like to recall to you, especially to those 3,500 U.S. Marines, the ideas expressed by Robert F. Williams when he visited us. Williams said: (Voice in English, presumably Williams, is heard ed.) And this is a tragedy that our troops would be in a place like Vietnam on the wrong side, on the wrong side of the fence on the wrong side of the people, at the time when our people are being brutally oppressed in the racist United States. There is also a growing spirit of resistance, a growing spirit of solidarity on the part of the American people in support of the people of Vietnam. Demonstrations have taken place inside the United States. Many petitions are being circulated. The people are asking that the American troops be brought home from Vietnam. The people are asking that the American troops be spared from death and destruction 10,000 kilometers away from home. Many people are signing petitions, are petitioning Congress. They are petitioning the Senate, they are asking that the boys be allowed to come home, and that the senseless slaughter that has taken place in Vietnam be discontinued. We must also consider the fact that the American people who live up to the American tradition are bound, are duty bound, to support the liberation struggle and the reunification struggle of the people of Vietnam. Because it is written in the Declaration of Independence of the United States that the American people have a right to bear arms at home in the United States, that the American people when they are faced with a government of oppression and tyranny, that they have a natural right, that they have a God-given right to abolish such a government even by force when necessary. So, this is the tradition of the United States, and this is also the spirit of the people of Vietnam. We must also remember that in the United States a great war was fought—a Civil War—and in the Civil War many Americans died for the reunification of the country. We must remember this. We should also remember that the American Revolution in the beginning was an example for many countries to follow, for many people. We should also remember that in the American Revolution the first American to fall, the first American to die, was a Black

American by the name of Crispus Attucks and yet 200, almost 200 years since the death of Crispus Attucks, Black Americans are still being murdered because they beg for freedom, because they petition for freedom, because they pray in the streets for freedom in racist America. We should also bear in mind that almost 200 years after the death of Crispus Attucks in defense of American independence, in defense of American liberty, in the defense of justice, that almost 200 years hence we find American troops 10,000 kilometers from home oppressing the liberation struggle of people who want to be free, of people who are living in the tradition and the spirit of the American Revolution. I wonder if the American troops—who are so far away from home, who can expect death at any moment, who may never live to see their loved ones and their homeland again—I wonder if deep in their hearts they can understand the brutal crime that they are committing against innocent people, innocent and freedom-loving people. I wonder if the American troops know the history of the Nazi troops under Hitler. Oh, Hitler had words to justify his brutal acts of conquest. German soldiers believed that Hitler was right. They thought they were fighting for a noble cause. But only through defeat where they made to realize that their cause was evil, their cause was vain. No American can say before any just-minded person, and can give any justification, can give any rational reason why American boys are fighting for so-called "freedom in Vietnam." What freedom? How can the government of the United State be so interested in freedom in Vietnam when there is no freedom in the racist United States? If the United States believes in freedom, if the United States is a country that would like to see freedom brought to the world, it is a matter of fact that freedom would first start at home and like charity then would spread abroad (end of statement, presumably by Williams).

WILLIAMS SPEAKS ON FREEDOM NOW OR DEATH!

Havana Radio Free Dixie in English 0400 GMT December 18, 1965
(Robert F. Williams Commentary)

(Text) Greetings, my brothers and sisters; once again we witness another sickening inscription of injustice in the book of time wherein is recorded the endless malfeasances of kangaroo justice. yes, once again we see cold-blooded and savage butchers of defenseless Black and white humanists go free to maim and kill again in the faltering cause of white supremacy. The mad-dog racists of the social jungle of Alabama slap themselves on the back and toast themselves with blood-stained nectar in homage to a brutal deed well done. Yes, they rejoice and drink to another masterwork of distorted justice. They bask in the victory of savage fools. Their warped minds see further hope that in the name of white supremacy they may main and kill with impunity forever. Yes, in racist America, their sadistical hearts are fired with the conviction that the Black man and the white humanist have no rights that the white racists are bound to respect. Yes, it is common knowledge that the human rights of Afro-Americans are less respected than those of common street dogs. But time marches on. The very heavens roll with anger. The winds of retribution rise in all quarters of the earth, and judgment day looms on the horizon. For it is written that their sins shall surely find them out.

LETTERS EXCHANGED BETWEEN RICHARD GIBSON AND ROBERT WILLIAMS, AND LETTERS BY GIBSON TO HIS MARXIST - LENINIST COMRADES, TORE HOKASON AND LEON LEOPOLDO ABOUT WILLIAMS

September 7, 1965, La Habana, Cuba[3,4]

Dear Richard:

This is just a fast note to let you know that I received your letter and the cable. Is Worthy supposed to be here? I was told quite some time ago that he had requested permission to come here. That's been so long ago that I thought he had given up the idea. If he is here, I don't know anything about it. Of course, such things have happened before. I am sorry to have to say it, but I recommend you, you will never be admitted to Cuba. Every Afro, including Charles P. Howard (UNC-News service), whom I have interceded for has been denied a visa here. Some got as far as Mexico and didn't make it. However, I object to what Carlos is doing and saying he's got too much truth mixed in with his exaggerations for comfort. A lot of things I have tried to conceal, but the case looks hopeless. It seems that a certain group here is trying to compete with Mississippi. I agree with you concerning the projects. We'll have to try to work something concrete out. There is a lot of red tape involved in sending photographs through the mail from here. If at all, they never arrive in time. You may do better by trying the New China News Agency. If possible, I plan to move from Cuba in the very near future. I asked for an exit visa more than two months ago. I'm still waiting. They are so tied up with the white Americans here. I can't get them to do a thing unless it's in praise of Rev. M. King and the glorious white working class. Their attitude is if you are not an Uncle Tom then you're a Black racist. I am sure that things would have been much better here if I had had a white American to speak for me. You know it's like being down home all over again. Mr. Charlie's word goes farther. The people in power here insist that we can never expect anything unless we are led and supported by the good white folks. Our friend Finlay didn't help the situation a bit. Worthy trusted in him to get materials to me. All the last of it went astray. The old cat turned out to be the real Mr. Charlie. The whole set looks to white Americans to advise them on the Afro-American struggle and their word is gospel.

Rob

September 20, 1965, London[5]

Dear Rob,

I received yours of the 7th of Sept., and was horrified, to say the least. We are very disturbed about your personal situation, and, moreover, we cannot fathom what has happened to Worthy. Lionel Morrison of the Afro-Asian Journalists' Association in Djakarta told us here in London last July that Worthy had left Djakarta by Garuda Airways for Prague, where he was supposed to pick up a Cubana plane for Havana. Worthy talked of returning to the States, despite warnings from friends that the gringos were preparing a very warm welcome for him. He must have a bit of a martyr complex. But, in any case, he wanted to see you first in Havana and he had received assurances that the Cubans would give him a ticket. I fail to understand how he could just disappear. We can be certain he did not return to the States. You would have heard of that, especially if the FBI picked him up for all these illegal travels abroad. Let this be a great lesson for us all. Don't move anywhere unless you're sure of your communications all along the route. Bill Worthy was very sloppy on that point. So was Malcolm X, with the serious consequences we all know. The French essayist Albert Camus used to say that "politics is murder" and he meant it literally. We must remember that we are playing for bug stakes and no longer in the Boy Scout leagues of our youth. I'm sure you will take every precaution, but, above all, keep your cool. Don't fall for provocations. Our basic problem is one of communications and it is, as you will have noted from my previous letters, a problem that has obsessed me. The mail is not to be trusted anywhere. One thing that I think that I can help you with in the future is to provide a turning point for communications via Europe. Moreover, if the *Crusader* is halted elsewhere, it can even be printed somewhere in Europe by my comrades and distributed in numerous ways. We must meet somewhere discreetly to discuss this and many other matters. Where and how remain to be discussed. I fear, however, that you won't get that exit permit unless some big friends in Asia speak up loudly on your behalf. But perhaps they can solve our communication problem temporarily. They could contact me directly here in London or through my friend, Grippa in Brussels (they know him, don't worry) or through Nils Anderson in Switzerland. I am in constant touch with Grippa and Anderson and may be moving back to Switzerland after the Afro-Asian Conference in Algiers in November. I had hoped desperately that you would be able to get to the conference to speak out on behalf of our struggle. I realize our enemies everywhere do not want that. Try to understand the nature of our enemies, realizing that some white men—not all, fortunately—waving red flags are even more reactionary where we are concerned than LBJ. Carlos is wrong because he does fall straight into Black racism and fails to understand the fight against imperialism. Carlos is not helping Afro-Cubans nor himself by becoming a counterrevolutionary. But you must know what the real revolutionary position is, and not accept just any peaceful coexistence line. I am sure you understand better than I do. The main thing is to get to work, to push forward the struggle on every front, to obtain the materials and the funds we need, to establish lines of safe communications, to "organize." You are the undisputed leader and you have shown yourself to be worthy of our support. Now we must all work harder than ever to be effective and to win! Try to send me that film about you, if possible. Two or three copies can be used and will (1) make you better known; (2) get moral, political, and material support for our struggle; (3) fight the calumnies of our enemies who want to pass you off as a wild man. We can raise cash for you here in Europe—A. Manchanda of the Afro-Asian-Caribbean Organization in the United Kingdom, whom you met in Hanoi, has pledged to work for us, but I need a letter from you designating me as a representative of yours and qualified to transmit your message and collect funds on your behalf. Send me such a typed and carefully phrased letter as soon as possible and I'll get to work. Tell me also what you want me to do with the funds. And try to reach me through your friends, as I have explained above. I'm now not expecting that Pablo can do anything for me, but that doesn't matter. The main thing is for us to keep in touch. There is so damned much to consult with you about that I hardly know where to begin. We are working against time, but I think my personal position—after a terrible attack on me by Verges and other enemies—is secure for the moment, thanks mainly to Comrade Grippa and Comrade Anderson. I have discussed your problem with them, and you can rest assured that they want to help. Sarah joins me in wishing you and your family well. If there is anything at all that we can do here for you, do not hesitate to let us know. And don't worry about anything at present but getting along the road to a more friendly place. We all must learn in time who our real friends are. I hope that you remember me as one of yours. (Speaking of friends, I got a letter recently from Julian. He seems a bit unhappy down there. He, too, apparently has serious problems, but you have some idea what Africa can be like!). Waiting to hear from you.

Richard

October 14, 1965, London[6]

Dear Rob,

I have just got some clarification for the mystery of Bill Worthy's movement. Apparently, he has been in Indonesia all the time and in Czechoslovakia. Perhaps, he never got his vias for Cuba either. Did Pablo tell you about my wire and letter? I've never received any answer from him or through the Cuba Embassy in London. Now back to Worthy, my information comes from Mr. Soekarno, Press Attaché at the Indonesian Embassy here and from Tom McGrath, features editor of the English Weekly Peace News. Worthy reportedly left Djakarta after the September 30 coup, which has yet to be explained sufficiently. In any case, nothing happened to him, and he went to Prague. On Monday, October 4th, Worthy wrote McGrath from Prague that he intended to fly to Toronto, Canada, on an Air India flight, passing through London early in the morning of Friday, October 8th. Worthy said he was going to participate in a teach-in at Toronto University on October 9th and then he was going to New York for a few days before going to Ghana for the October 21st meeting of the Organization of African Unity in Accra. How the hell can he fly around the world without a valid U.S. passport, in fact without any passport, I don't understand. And I am correctly baffled as to how he can go back to the States and get out again after being in North Vietnam and elsewhere without U.S. permission. Personally, even today, I'm not too keen about returning to the States because of my activities in 1960–1962. How can he get away with it? Anyway, I am very pleased to learn that no harm has come to him. I learned from Hsinhua that you were still in Havana on October 1. Not having heard from you again, I wondered if you had received my latest letters. Speaking of your problems, I wrote Julian Mayfield in Ghana and asked him to do what he could down there. He has never even replied. Mrs. Edwards went to see him, but he seemed frightened to make a move. She thinks he is in too weak a position to risk anything for anybody. And I'm afraid there isn't much that she can do. But I realize you did not have any exaggerated hopes for assistance from Africa. And

I, frankly, think it will be the same in every aspect of our struggle. There is still no certainty that the Afro-Asian Conference will be held as scheduled in Algiers. I am leaving here on the 17th and will visit my friends in Belgium and Switzerland. If it seems that there will be a conference, I'll go straight to Algeria. Otherwise, I'll return to London. I hope by that time your problems will have been solved. But in any case, please do write and let me know the situation and let me know what you want me to do. Sarah joins me in sending you and your wife our love and hopes for success in the struggle.

November 23, 1965, La Habana, Cuba[7]

Dear Richard,

I received your letters. I am deeply sorry that I cannot offer you any encouraging news. As far as my activity in the struggle from here, things are at a standstill. As far as the Afro-American struggle is concerned, things are at a standstill. The Cubans won't lift a finger to assist in our cause. They are all out for Martin Luther King. The line is the same as Russia's. The anti-China sentiment is running very high here and anyone who is pro-Chinese is looked upon as counterrevolutionary, and I'm no exception. For the first time since I started the struggle, I feel that I am wasting my time. The Cubans have done what the Yankees could never do, that is to make me feel that there is no place in the communist camp for the Negro. The Chinese are solid but the white communists are not going to allow them to help us. If we cannot fight for our own people and our own cause, there is no reason to fight at all. I am catching hell from the Trotskies and the communists.

Both are sabotaging the struggle and it is extremely dangerous to oppose them on their territory. I don't think I'll get to Africa, China or anyplace else. It seems that the only channel left open leads to the States. The racist devils in the states are much cleverer about the race issue than the racist communists. I don't know what Worthy's role is. I haven't heard from him since he's been abroad. However, he showed up in Montreal, Canada, and contacted the lawyer who was handling my Chinese film, which I had already committed to ABC-TV, and told him it would be better to let him personally deliver it to CBS. Worthy was supposed to be hot and should have expected to be picked up at the border, yet he tried to confidence the lawyer to let him take the film across the border. There was a mix-up, confusion, and so on resulting in a serious delay after the Canadians refused to release the film to ABC's contact man. How Worthy got mixed up in a confidential film deal is a mystery. I can very well understand Julian's predicament and sympathize with him. The Yankees are wheeling and dealing everywhere, and the white communists are solidly in their corner. I hope you can get *Negroes with Guns* published in Europe with an up-to-date chapter or two. Tore' Hokason is trying to get a Swedish version published. You may want to contact him. He also arranged some speaking engagements in Sweden for me, but I doubt very seriously if my friends will let me fill them.

Sincerely,
Rob

December 8, 1965, London[8]

Dear Rob,

Your letter of the 23rd of November arrived this morning, and you can imagine how aghast Sarah and I were at your situation. I know what you are saying is true, all too damn true. But you are too big a person now to be destroyed by anyone but yourself, so don't panic. Just continue to take care. You know how difficult it would be for you to return to the North. However, I don't say impossible. I would rather that you were able to carry on the struggle elsewhere and I think that you should make all efforts possible to do so before making any drastic revision of your plans. In any case, try to hang around until after the Three Continents Conference in Havana, even if you can play a role in it. By rights, of course, you should be the spokesman there for our people! What you had to say about Worthy has prompted some doubts on my part as well. What I don't understand is how he learned of your "confidential" deal. A leak from a friendly source? And did CBS use the film? Remember, I asked you to get me 16mm copies, if possible, for distribution here and elsewhere in Europe, but I never heard any more from you about it. I can perhaps sell a copy to the BBC or the commercial ITV television here, not to mention the use of it for fundraising and propaganda on your behalf, so do try to get your friends to send me a copy or two. Even a big print would be better than nothing. I was also surprised that Hokason was working for you. Schleifer said Hokason had been very much a King man at one point. Perhaps he learned better? Anyway, I'm going to try to get your book reprinted over here, so please keep me informed of your whereabouts. There is really so much that can be done over here, so much that is possible to do, so don't give up hope. Hokason's idea about speaking engagements sounds splendid, if your security could be protected. If there is any chance of the deal going through, let me know and I can check out the plans on the spot. I can get to Sweden in two and a half hours from here so there won't be any "slipups" which you may regret. I'll write more later if I can. This is being written in hast so that it can go off to you right away. Enclosed is a copy of my report, which I send out regularly to some newspapers in the States, Africa, and Europe. I have to be very careful about politics, which explains its mildness, as I have been warned I may be thrown out of England. That wouldn't be so bad if I knew a better refuge, where I could continue the work and the struggle. Sarah joins me in sending you and your wife our love.

Richard

December 8, 1965, London[9]

Dear Tore,

Greetings after a long, long, silence! I would have thought that you had settled in tropical warmth if had not been for a message from Rob Williams suggesting that I contact you. I am pleased to hear that you were examining the possibilities of Scandinavian publication of *Negroes with Guns*. Have you made any progress? On my part, I have been trying to get the book translated into Italian, French, and German, and to arrive for its reprinting in England. I must confess the going has been slow, but I do believe that it will be possible. I am very excited about the possibility of a speaking tour for Bob in Scandinavia. Of course, this must be handled very delicately. After all, Rob is still considered a "wanted criminal" by the U.S. Justice Department and there is a possibility that they might demand Williams's extradition at all friendly to the United States. On the other hand, the chance of breaking his present physical (and political) isolation is well worth some risk, but that risk must be kept slight. Rob asks that, if you arrange anything, I come over to give the arrangements a last-minute on-the-spot check. Anyway, let me know how you are progressing or if the project is not feasible. Since I left the States in September 1962, I have been in Algeria, Switzerland, France, and now England. There has been some much happening that I can't hope to tell you all until we somehow get together again in the future. At present, I am doing freelance journalism and running a very modest feature service, mainly for American Negro papers and papers in Africa. Here is a sample copy of the feature service. I'd like very much to visit Scandinavia one of these days. And not merely because of your celebrated beauties! If Bob is coming, I'll certainly be over to see you. And if you get to London, please don't feel like visiting us. Moreover, we could even put you up, if you don't mind sleeping in the living room. It is warm and comfortable, however. Sarah joins me in sending you our love.

Richard Gibson

December 26, 1965, London[10]

Dear Rob,

Just a note, being brought personally by a very good and reliable friend whom you can trust. I had hoped to see you myself, but it seems I am down on somebody's blacklist, along with Charlie Howard and other Afro Newsmen. Our friend will explain the situation to you. Keep cool and keep in touch with me at all costs. You can always wire me to collect at the above address (you might add my telephone number so that I can get a message even quicker). The situation here in Europe is not impossible for you. I think there are several interesting possibilities, and you have some real friends here! But please keep cool and work as hard as you can on that trip to Scandinavia but hold off on any trips North without letting me know first. Darah joins me in sending you and your wife our love and admiration.

Yours in the struggle
Richard

January 14, 1966, La Habana, Cuba[11]

Dear Richard,

I saw and talked to our mutual friend here. Things have gone from bad to worse. I am sure he will explain things to you. You didn't miss anything by not making it to the conference. I have asked Tore' to work for an invitation from that end. If you can do anything in any country about getting a visa for me, I hope you will do it right away.

Even if it is just for 30 days. That will be ample time. Try Britain, France, or any other place you may have contact. The situation is most urgent.

Rob

February 1, 1966, London[12]

Dear Tore,

I was away on the continent for a few days and had hoped to find a letter from you when I return to London. Can you please let me know what the situation is in Sweden concerning the invitation to Rob? Swift action now is extremely vital. Have you been able to obtain the official invitations and secure formal (but naturally discreet) guarantees from Swedish officials that Rob will be given full protection from extradition while he is in your country? How will the invitation be forwarded to Rob? Can it be sent by Swedish diplomatic channels? As for Rob's immediate financial needs, I am sure that comrades of mine will be able to assist in this matter.

As soon as you indicate the concrete steps you are taking, I will fly to Sweden to see you and to examine the situation on the spot. But it is essential that you keep me informed of your progress now. After a month or less in Sweden, there are numerous possibilities for Rob, as you surely understand. The important thing is that he be given time to breathe and reflect after the enormous pressure he has been put under by the Cubans. I hope that we will be able to arrange for Rob's arrival in Sweden provided we obtain his release from Cuba—in either March or April. Every day he remains in Cuba, he runs a greater risk of never leaving there alive. The situation, as you know, is very serious, so please do make every possible hast and do let me hear from you.

Very best wishes,
Richard

February 1, 1966, London[13]

Dear Rob,

This is being written in hast. Our African friend brought me your message and I am in touch with Tore', hoping that he can plan quickly and get solid guarantees about your safety. I have also discussed the matter with very good comrades and admirers of ours and they all agreed to get all the material support necessary. So, keep up your spirits and hold on, calmly, watching and wary of provocateurs. Now this is what I want you to do immediately. I have been discussing your book with French, Belgian, and Swiss comrades, and with an Italian publisher. If you send me a cable concerning that I am fully authorized to negotiate the sale and translation of *Negroes with Guns* in Europe, I will be able to finalize arrangements with Le Livre International in Brussels and Editions La Cite in Lausanne. I am also negotiating with Boppani in Rome. The terms for the French translations are very good, as you will see. I've not got that far with the Italians, but I think they are very interested. Be sure to sign your name in full at the end of the cable. As soon as Tore' gets his invitation, I will go over there to check on the security arrangements. I will wire you immediately as soon as I have looked over the situation. In any case, just keep in mind that you have many friends and admirers throughout the world, and we are all concerned that you remain a free man and a leader in the struggle.

Yours in the struggle,
Richard

May 2, 1966, London[14]

Dear Rob,

I have just returned to London from the trip to Italy that I wrote you about and I have both good and bad news for you. Concerning the French edition of *Negroes with Guns*, I am in failure to keep his bargain with you. However, I am informed by my friends in Switzerland that the French left-wing publisher Francois Maspero is bringing out the book in French within the month, in the translation that Verges had made, but was unable to use because of his virtual bankruptcy. Unfortunately, Maspero has made his deal with Marzani and perhaps with Schleifer, but I am not certain about Schleifer. I'm told that he has a legally binding contract with Marzani and that there is nothing that can be done with his edition, regardless of Marzani's failure to keep his bargain with you. However, I am writing to Maspero in Paris advising him of the situation and asking that he hold any money that might be owed to you. Unfortunately, there is nothing legal that can be done to force him to do so in the present circumstances. You might write directly to Francois Maspero and tell him your side of the story with Marzani. What I really fear is that he already knows the story. Moreover, he is a friend of Verges and may have paid Verges for the translation, and I can assure Verges and Strelkoff are no friends of yours. What is most disturbing is that you will not be able to revise the text of the book and bring it up to date. On the other hand, Maspero is a very well-known publisher in France and the book as it will get wide publicity. Perhaps Maspero might be urged to invite you to France to launch the book. He has many important connections, despite his left-wing politics. However, he is a convinced and fanatical revisionist, and you know what that means. As for the Italian translations, I had a most fruitful talk in Milan with Signora Maria Regis, director of Edizioni Oriente. She is going to Peking for a month but seems quite eager to bring out your book. As far as I can tell, Marzani is not in touch with any Italian publishers yet. I suggest you drop a note to Signora Regis at Edizioni Oriente and tell her that I have informed you of their interest in your book and that you would be pleased if a speedy agreement could be reached. At long last, Tore' Hokanson writes. He says that he will get more publicity for you in Sweden and says that if you can have someone buy Iberia tickets for you and Mabel from Havana to Madrid to Stockholm, he thinks you will be permitted to fly and that he can assure your entry into Sweden. Can you get your friends to pay for the plane tickets or do you want me to try to raise the funds here? The main thing here is that you don't have any travel documents, provided we know well in advance when you are coming. I am certain your anonymous informer could not fail to know him. Comrade Manchanda has been a Marxist-Leninist for more than twenty years. He is also convenor of the committee of

Afro-Asian-Caribbean organizations in Britain and editor of the West Indian Gazette and Afro-Asian Caribbean News. He was most recently a delegate at the Emergency Meeting in Peking of the Afro-Asian Writers Organization. I feel sure that Comrade Manchanda can evaluate the merits of your anonymous friend's story. If there were grave doubts raised, Comrade Manchanda would not be one to remain silent. However, if this fraternal and frank means of resolving this problem is rejected, then I and other comrades are more than willing to come to Milan to hear and refute the actualization made against me. Would you be afraid of that? I am certain that Comrade Nils Anderson would be most interested in what you have to say about me. Failing to find agreement on such a means of getting to the bottom of this matter, I would be forced to take other measures against the slanderer and to warn others of the potential dangers of association in any way with alleged progressives who persisted in indulging in malicious gossip.

Fraternally Yours,
Richard Gibson

June 20, 1966, London[15]

Comrade Leon,

I was indeed astounded and saddened by your letter of June 16th, in which you stated that the Centro Franz Fanon wished to cease any "collaboration" with me because of my "present political affiliations." You should be informed that I have no present political affiliations and am not a member of any political party or group, although I do consider myself an Afro-militant and have written authorization from Robert F. Williams, leader of the Revolutionary Action Movement in the United States, to act on his behalf here in Europe. On the other hand, I also consider myself a Marxist-Leninist and I do maintain fraternal contacts with various Marxist-Leninist organizations and national liberation movements in numerous countries. It is, hence, a matter of grave importance to me that I clarify the attitude of the Centro Franz Fanon towards me, and as quickly as possible and in as comradely a fashion as possible. It is not my desire to out any public polemic, but I hope you will reluctantly recognize that your behavior toward me is strongly reminiscent of McCarthyite behavior in the United States. You merely mention my "present political affiliations" in your letter without once stating what you believe or have been told they are, and you claim this "information" comes from an unidentified source which you dare not reveal to me. I have seen witch hunts before and I know the quickest way to stop them and arrive at the truth is to find out what the charges are, and who the accusers are, then all can be discussed and resolved in a civilized fashion. I am sure you will agree. I suggest that you, therefore, state by return mail what "information" you have against me and who is my anonymous accuser. I will reply as best as I can by mail and will make a trip to Milan at my own expense to discuss this matter with you and other comrades in a frank and cordial manner. I would be most interested and personally confronting the anonymous and cowardly source of your "information" and believe it would not be difficult to expose him as a lying tool of imperialism or a silly dupe of ruses.

July 18, 1966, London[16]

Comrade Leon,

Forgive my delay in replying to your letter of June 25. During the time that has passed, I have been able to make some investigations of my own and to discuss this possibility with comrades. On this point, I would like again to stress that I have no desire to enter any public polemic with you and others at the Centro Franz Fanon, but if it proves impossible to obtain greater clarification of the unspecified slander against me from an itinerant and anonymous "British professor," I shall have to take more strenuous measures. Bourgeois slander is the cause of bourgeois law. At present, I am still attempting to resolve this matter in a comradely fashion. This is because I believe you have been misinformed, and perhaps deliberately by an unscrupulous adventurer. In any case, the truth will come out in due course. And nothing can protect this culprit from exposure. What your ingenious defense of McCarthyism overlooks is that McCarthyism is not very successful "peaceful measures in self-defense," as you put it, but a particularly stupid and vicious way of attacking someone with insinuations, hast-truth and complete lies. The most important thing about McCarthyism is that it failed entirely. I, for one, do not believe as you do, that this is "one of the unpleasantness of the socialist posture." Slander is slander, and it is a favorite instrument of revisionist Trotskyites and adventurers as well as their masters, the imperialists. The Great Cultural Revolution now being achieved in China does not deign to use slander. Marxist-Leninist groups that have any principles left do not sink in this pig-sky. Your facetiousness about the "King of Prussia" was particularly uncalled for. If you have accusations worthy of the name to make against me, then you must bring them out. When M. Masson was exposed as a Belgian police and CIA agent by the comrades of the Marxist-Leninist Communist Party of Belgium, they did not whisper this fact about, in the fashion of aging gossips. They exposed this criminal. Moreover, it should be your duty as conscious revolutionaries to warn others, but, if you attempt to imitate the tactics of the adventurer Jacques Verges, you will end in the same discredit as he, driven out of France, politically and financially bankrupt. In any case, I am appalled that you honestly believe that your behavior is worthy of socialists and revolutionaries. If you reexamine your position, I am sure you will find that it is unworthy of you personally and of Centro Franz Fanon. Otherwise, who will be next? Did I not myself hear one of your comrades describing the valiant armed struggle of the freedom fighters of the Zimbabwe African National Union as a "false guerrilla"? And why should another of your comrades in Milan mock the courageous stand of the militant Pan-Africanist Congress of South Africa, while praising the revisionist-dominated African National Congress of South Africa? On the other hand, when I asked you for information about Italian neocolonialism and the liberation struggles in the former Italian colonies. I was told that the Centro Franz Fanon did not have that sort of material which was of "lesser importance" in comparison to your interest in Latin America and Asia. It seems to me that a little humility is called for on your part. Surely, as an Italian progressive organization, you could give some attention to the misdeeds of your own capitalists at the behest of U.S. imperialism. Finally, let me repeat once again that I never sought any political collaboration with the Centro Franz

Fanon. When I attempted to discuss the struggle of the Afro-American people in the first line of battle against U.S. imperialism, I was told you did not interest yourselves in that struggle. I did think, nevertheless, that you might be willing to offer an invitation to Robert F. Williams, capitalized chairman in exile of the Revolutionary Action Movement of Black North Americans, but you never even replied to my request. You asked for "credentials from unquestionable Marxist-Leninist organization." I would like to know what you call "unquestionable." As you know, I have written authorization to represent Robert F. Williams in Europe. I am enclosing a letter of introduction from the editor in chief of the *Liberator*, Black America's most militant monthly, of which I am the editor for Africa, Asia, and Europe. Personally, I am a Marxist-Leninist, but I am a foreigner in Britain, and I cannot participate fully in British political life, as you well know. However, I am known to the real Marxist-Leninist here and elsewhere, but I do not abuse their confidence, as does your anonymous informer whose anonymity is fading swiftly. As for practical matters, I shall be away from London for nearly three weeks. During my absence, your informer can call at his leisure to discuss his fantasies about me with comrade A. Manchanda, Convenor of the Britain-Vietnam Solidarity Front, which I am pleased to note that the Centro Franz Fanon "unreservedly support." As you know, comrade Manchanda's address is against the Ku Klux Klan and other white racist. Williams's heroic stand has been described in his book, *Negroes with Guns*, which I am told a Swedish progressive publisher may translate into Swedish sometime soon. Since 1961, Williams had been living in exile in Cuba, publishing his newsletter, *The Crusader-in-Exile*, and broadcasting over radio Havana to the Afro-American people, but recent events in Cuba forced Williams to move to Peking where he could find a surer haven from U.S. imperialism and its revisionist lackeys. His visit to Sweden will have considerable international importance and it is hoped that he will have possibilities of speaking to Marxist-Leninist and other progressive people in your country. There is also a problem of assuring his security from imperialist agents. All of these things require contact and discussion. Until now, all arrangements have been made by Mr. Tore' Hokanson, whom you may know as a progressive person. I am an Afro-American journalist who has been living in Europe for a number of years and a supporter of Robert F. Williams's struggle for many years. He has asked me to represent him in Europe and investigate arrangements for his visit to Sweden. I hope to be able to come to Scandinavia sometime before Williams's arrival to check all arrangements and discuss security problems. It would be especially useful if I could speak with a reliable lawyer who could advise me on all aspects of the law that might affect his stay, estimated at two or three weeks. When I do visit, I hope that I may call upon you to talk over this matter and other questions of mutual interest. The Afro-American people are carrying forward a bitter struggle within the heartland of U.S. imperialism and they need the solidarity and active support of all the world's revolutionaries and progressive people. Hoping to hear from you soon, I am fraternally yours.

Richard Gibson

FEDERAL BUREAU OF INVESTIGATION/ CENTRAL INTELLIGENCE AGENCY MEMORANDUM IDENTIFYING RICHARD T. GIBSON AS AN INFORMANT

March 10, 1966
Memorandum for Chief, CI/QA
Subject: Derogatory on QREBONY

Richard Gibson, while employed by the Columbia Broadcasting System, and a fellow colleague Robert Taber established the Fair Play for Cuba Committee (FPCC) in April 1960. The subject was fired from his job with CBS because of his activities with the FPCC. The parent organization of FPCC is the institution for the improvement of inter-American relations. The subject was president of the New York chapter of the FPCC and became acting national executive secretary of FPCC when Robert Taber went to Cuba in January 1961. Subject in his role as acting executive secretary was in contact with many personalities from such organizations as Socialist Workers Party, CPUSA, Monroe Defense Committee, the Committee to Aid the Monroe Defendants, and so on. The subject was also accredited to the United Nations as a correspondent covering UN affairs for the Cuban newspapers, *El Mundo* and *Revolucion*. While a member of the FPCC, he traveled in 1960 and 1961 to Cuba and met Fidel Castro, Ernesto Guevara, and various other Cuban officials. The subject was involved with the Monroe Defense Committee which is made up of Negro nationals and members of the Communist Party. He is well acquainted with Robert Williams, the American Negro from Monroe, North Carolina, who emigrated to Cuba. The subject resigned from the FPCC in the fall of 1962 because his income was inadequate for his services. In late 1962, the subject was recommended by the Algerian Ambassador to the United Nations to be on the staff of *Revolution Africaine* in Algiers, a paper which was then edited by Jacques Verges, a well-known Communist. When Verges was ousted by the Algerians because of a dispute with Ben Bella in May 1963, the subject remained loyal to Verges and eet up headquarters in Lausanne for the publication of Africa, Latin America, and Asia revolution, more commonly known as *Revolution*, and served as editor of its English Language version. This publication was characterized as being transparently a vehicle for spreading Chinese Communist opinions on international and world Communist problems. Gibson while in Lausanne worked with Freddy Gilbert Nils Anderson, Swedish citizen, editor-publisher, who printed the *Revolution*. Anderson has been known to have numerous contacts in international leftist circles of all shades including FLN-Algerians, Congolese, Angolese, other African politicians, Spanish emigres, French "refractairs Anti-Colonialist," and so on. Despite all these contacts Anderson cannot definitely be labeled as a Communist. The subject on November 1963 spoke to Workgroup Informatic Cuba and the democratic-socialist student organization Politeia in Amsterdam. This speech was reported to be more anti-American rather than pro-Cuba. It was also reported in November 1963 (the source of this information is considered unreliable) that the Soviet Ambassador to the Netherlands Ivan Ovich Tugarinov recommended a Gibson to the Cuban Ambassador Maristany as one who could help them in their propaganda effort. Tugarinov said that Gibson was in Amsterdam at this time. In December 1963 subject's

Swiss resident permit was not renewed and the subject went to Paris where he was still editor of the English-language version of the *Revolution*. Subject split with Verges in July 1964, because he was accused of misusing his office as former executive secretary of FPCC in order to penetrate the rank of the international revolutionary movement. He was accused of being an agent of the FBI and CIA. Gibson, unable to find employment in Paris, went to England in October 1964.[17]

Notes

1. Robert Williams spoke in English and his words were translated into Spanish, one sentence at the time, by a translator the cameraman brought along with him.
2. Williams spoke in English and his words were translated into Spanish, one sentence at the time, by a translator the cameraman brought along with him.
3. Robert Williams' ideas proved quite correct, considering Malcolm X was assassinated on February 21, 1965, while addressing African Americans during a rally in Harlem at the Audubon Auditorium. The Reverend J. Reeb, a white minister who supported the Black Liberation struggle, was brutally murdered in Selma. A dispatch of 3,500 U.S. Marines sent to South Vietnam were ordered to repeatedly bomb North Vietnam in an attempt to intensify and expand the U.S.'s aggressive war.
4. Richard Gibson Papers, Box 13, Folder 5.
5. Richard Gibson Papers, Box 13, Folder 5.
6. Richard Gibson Papers, Box 13, Folder 5.
7. Richard Gibson Papers, Box 13, Folder 5.
8. Richard Gibson Papers, Box 13, Folder 5.
9. Richard Gibson Papers, Box 13, Folder 5.
10. Richard Gibson Papers, Box 13, Folder 5.
11. Richard Gibson Papers, Box 13, Folder 5.
12. Richard Gibson Papers, Box 13, Folder 5.
13. Richard Gibson Papers, Box 13, Folder 5.
14. Richard Gibson Papers, Box 13, Folder 5.
15. Richard Gibson Papers, Box 13, Folder 5.
16. Richard Gibson Papers, Box 13, Folder 5.
17. Clarity is important. It is well documented that Richard Gibson served as an informant for the FBI and CIA, and not as an FBI/CIA agent.

Chapter 3
PEKING, CHINA, 1963–1969

Robert and Mabel Williams Overlooking Sites in Peking with three Chinese tour guides, 1966.

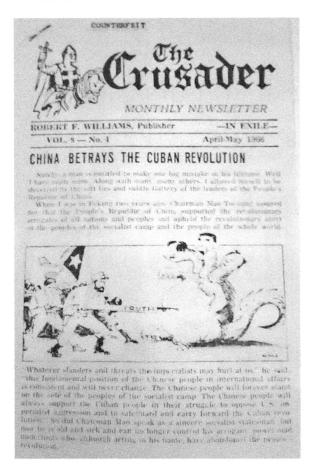

Front Page Forgery of *The Crusader-in-Exile*. This forgery bears a masthead with the drawing of a crusader warrior on a horse that Williams was no longer using. This scan of the April-May 1966 forgery is numbered volume 8, number 4---and stamped "Counterfeit" at the top. It is the first of two forgeries that were mailed out to ML members in Europe and France, according to Williams, under the auspices of Cuban G-2 (secret police). It was found online through the CIA's FOIA Reading Room. It was released after Robert and Mabel Williams left Cuba for China the spring of 1966.The masthead Williams used to publish *The Crusader-in-Exile* was the "Torch" and the "Machine Gun." In an article published in the *Carolinian*, explaining the forgery, it is revealed and Williams is quoted saying, "Now, soured by his personal experiences in Havana, Williams says: At this stage of betrayal of oppressed peoples by the American-Soviet Cuban axis, we are beginning to wonder if the junior partner is specializing in documentary forgery." Courtesy of and approved for Release by the CIA, June 17, 1967. See CIA-RDP75-00149R000800070010-9.pdf

Front-Page image of *The Crusader-in-Exile*, November 1968. Courtesy of Robert F. Williams in the Robert F. Williams Papers at the Bentley Historical Library in Ann Arbor.

Robert F. Williams in Tanzania. RNA president-in-exile, Robert F. Williams in Tanzania gathers with Mae Mallory, 2nd right to Williams, and David Maphumzana Sibeko, Chief Representative of the PAC to the United Nations, and unknown male. To Williams's left is an unknown official, Milton Henry, and to the left of him is Jacob, PAC Secretary, Peter Nkutsoeu, PAC Secretary of Education and Publicity, and Abednigo Bekabantu Ngcobo, PAC Secretary for Finance. ca. 1968. Courtesy of Robert F. Williams. Photo located in Box 14 under Africa and Cuba in the Robert F. Williams Papers at the Bentley Historical Library in Ann Arbor.

LETTER TO FIDEL CASTRO FROM ROBERT F. WILLIAMS

August 28, 1966, Peking, China

Dear Fidel:

First of all, I want to thank you and the Cuban people for assisting me when I was escaping from the United States. I will always be grateful to the Cuban people, and I will always be a friend of the Cuban Revolution. In fact, this is the very reason that I take the liberty to write you this letter from my second exile. The reason that I bother to bring these matters to your attention, or later to the attention of the public, if necessary, is because I find it impossible to believe that Commandante Vallejo, Peniero, and others close around you have fully, truthfully, and faithfully informed you of these ignominious experiences that I encountered while living in Cuba.

    Shortly after my arrival in Cuba, I requested support for the Afro-American struggle in the United States. I first requested an information office with the purpose of acquainting the peoples of Latin America, Asia and Africa with the revolutionary potential of the Afro-American struggle and the brutal nature of U.S. racism and its relation to U.S. imperialism. This revolutionary request was never granted. I also requested permission and facilities to broadcast both long and short wave, especially to the Afro-American people in the United States. After much bickering and red tape, I was finally allowed to proceed with the broadcast from Radio Progresso, however, the facilities of Radio Havana, which was to be the short-wave broadcast in the name of Radio Free Dixie, were completely denied. I was told that this was because Radio Havana is the official voice of the Cuban government and that the Cuban government could not be identified in this way with the Afro-American struggle. I was never allowed the use of the shortwave facilities which would have enabled me to reach the great masses of our people all over the United States and especially on the West Coast where there is a heavy concentration of my fellow workers and followers. We would have also been able to reach the people of Africa, Latin America, and other places where the people manifested great interest in the letters that we received. Also, I made a request from the government and the Party for a certain amount of dollars that would have enabled me to subscribe to the newspapers, magazines and other publications that were necessary for me to maintain a close relationship with our struggle. Finally, the Party had allocated $200 dollars a month. I was told this by Comandante Peniero's office, and that this $200 dollars was to allow me to subscribe to papers, magazines, and to buy phonograph records so that I would have the latest music from the United States to use on Radio Free Dixie to increase our listening audience. The $200 dollars a month was to be used by somebody who was working at the United Nations and the things would be sent to me often in the pouch from the United Nations. However, I never received any of the $200 dollars a month or the publications. Later I was able to get donations and contributions from supporters inside the United States for publications, records and materials that I needed for my work. Also, many of the listeners of Radio Free Dixie donated musical recordings currently popular among the Afro-American masses to be used on Radio Free Dixie. However, these publications and records when sent were taken from the mail, taken from the Post Office and sometimes when things were sent by boat they were taken from the boat. And there were instances when even personal things purchased by persons in our movement in the States and sent to me were deliberately taken. They were taken from the pouch and taken from the Foreign Ministry. When I went to the Foreign Ministry to complain, I was always given the excuse that they did not know who was responsible for this and that they did not know who was taking these things out of the pouch. So, this handicapped our struggle very much. Later, I discovered that some of the newspapers and recordings were showing up in other places and they were showing up more and more in the Foreign Ministry. The Foreign Ministry, and the officials there, were allowing mercenaries, thieves, and pirates to practice piracy against our struggle and against the property of our struggle and the things we needed to work with. Also, this was a way to cripple our broadcasts and weaken our publication and keep us behind so that we could not keep up with the news. I even complained to the Party about these dishonorable practices being carried out. There were many other Americans living in Cuba and they were able to use the pouch. The Amigos de Cuba, an organization of Americans living there, was able to receive things from the pouch. Many of them and their representatives were able to travel in and out of Cuba to make purchases in the United States and Canada and to have these things sent back by ship and they were able to receive all kinds of things that did not have anything to do with the struggle. Even after I found it impossible to rely on the Foreign Ministry, the pouch and the Mambisa shipping lines, I requested through Commandante Paniero's office that my wife be allowed to go to Canada so that she could contact our friends and purchase the records and pick up the magazines and books and all the things pertaining to our struggle that we needed. I was repeatedly told that this would be impossible because there were so many repatriates returning to Cuba that there was no room on the ship for her to travel. I found out later that this was untrue because other Americans were traveling from Havana to Canada and into the United States and back to Cuba at will and as much as they wanted to. I later discovered that this was just a plot to try to wreck our struggle and crush our organization and was done in conjunction with forces inside the United States, including the U.S. Communist Party which was opposed to our method of struggle, and which advocated a policy of nonviolence in support of Rev. Martin Luther King. After our program, Radio Free Dixie became very successful, and it was noted throughout the world that it was a successful broadcast that had a great impact on the Afro-American masses in the United States, after many international publications in the United States, Latin America, Asia, and Africa had written a great deal about the impact of our program the power was reduced so low that our listeners inside the United States could not hear the broadcast. Some who could hear Radio Free Dixie heard it coming through the station at Santa Clara. The Havana transmission was so weak that sometimes they could not even hear it in Florida. This was direct and deliberate sabotage committed to protect U.S. racism and imperialism from being exposed for its brutal racist crimes against the Afro-American people. It was also done at the instigation of Americans living in Cuba. They were the first to advise that this radio program should be abolished. In order to maintain a false image as supporters of our cause, while at the same time dealing it a crippling blow, Radio Difusion reduced the power of the facilities over which we were broadcasting. Our publication, The Crusader, had become popular throughout the world and was being used as a manual on armed self-defense by freedom fighters throughout the United States, however, the more popular it became the more difficulty we experienced in getting it printed in Cuba. There was always some excuse about, paper, or we had to go through a lot of red tape which would make it impossible to publish some issues while others came out extremely late. We found it impossible to continue publishing under these conditions. We also had the case where some copies of *The Crusader* were forged and distributed throughout the world. This forged copy was an attack on the Soviet Union and surreptitiously anti-China and was designed to make my exile in Cuba difficult. I reported this to the Party and had hoped that I would get some cooperation to help facilitate my making a public announcement on it or a statement that the October 1965 Special Edition of *The Crusader* was not published by me and that it was a forged copy not published by friendly forces, but I was unable to get any cooperation from the Party as far as making this public announcement. In many instances also our mail was held up. It was on some occasions sent back to the United States but the people in the States continued to contact me. Some sent the letters back by people traveling to Cuba to show that the Havana post office had stamped them returned to sender address unknown. On some occasions, long-distance telephone callers were informed that I was unavailable. This completely severed the lines of communication between my coworkers and me. After the request for my wife to go to Canada and take care of the business there was denied I asked that some members of our organization and Negro journalists be allowed to visit Cuba. This was also denied. All Negro journalists who applied for visas to enter Cuba were denied visas while white reactionary journalists from the capitalist press were being admitted from all over the world. The Foreign Ministry systematically barred all Negroes, who were coming to confer with me in relation to our struggle, out of Cuba. Some Negro members of our organization traveling on our money got as far as Prague and were barred from Cuba and were forced to return to the United States after their funds were exhausted. This caused us to spend a lot of dollars, dissipating our funds. There were other cases wherein many of our people went to Mexico hoping to come to Cuba to confer with me about the struggle and set up communication lines so that we could coordinate our efforts, but all of this was sabotaged, and all of the plans frustrated by officials and functionaries of the Cuban government, especially those in the Foreign Ministry and Comandante Peniero's office. Comandante Peniero's office was one of the main factors in bringing about the frustrating conditions of our struggle, the very man that had been assigned by you to take care of me. The only official in the Cuban government who showed any genuine interest in our struggle and who had really promised to help was Comandante Che Guevara. Comandante Guevara called me into his office and told me that he believed that my policy of self-defense was correct, and he showed me an editorial in the newspaper Hoy, an editorial in support and praise of Rev. Martin Luther King. He told me that he disagreed with that view that he had some disagreement with some of the officials of the government and that he was going to help me all that he could. He told me he was going to the interior of Cuba and promised he would return in one month and telephone me as soon as he arrived in the city. However, he stated that while he was gone it would not be necessary to wait the full thirty days for a solution of some of the minor problems I had. He said that Captain Arrogones would take care of my problems while he was away. Later, I discovered that Captain Arrogones was unavailable. After thirty days Comandante Che Guevara failed to return to Havana. So, I did not get any help from the Cuban government, and I did not receive attention as far as the problems of my struggle were concerned. My interview with Comandante Che Guevara was one day before the letter that you read from him over the radio and television was dated. On the day before that letter was dated, he gave me the understanding that he was going into the interior and that he was not leaving the country again, but that he would return to Havana, contact me and give me the needed assistance when he returned. Even though I had seen Comandante Guevara the day before the letter was dated to you, in which you said that he had gone and joined another revolution, I find this hard to believe after he told me that he was coming back in thirty days and that he had me waiting for him and relying on him to give assistance to our struggle. The reason that I bring this up at this time is because I wonder if "Che" did not meet with foul play in the interior and that maybe the same people who contrived his disappearance may be planning to do away with you in the same manner. During the time of the Tri-Continental Conference, Afro-American journalists tried to come to Cuba to cover the conference. These journalists also had been to Cairo; they had been accepted there as journalists and were given cooperation there and were able to write about the Afro-Asian Conference and to bring the information back to the Afro-American people. When they tried to enter Cuba, they were denied the right to come, and they were told that they could not come because they were American journalists. However, representatives from The Worker (the official organ of the C.P. United States) from a Jewish publication and other white Americans were allowed to come to Cuba as guests of the government and they were admitted to the Tri-Continental Conference. Also, I was living in Havana at the time and as a representative of the Afro-American people and I was not given an invitation to attend the Tri-Continental Conference. I was barred from the conference and was only admitted after the question had been raised by some of the delegates from Africa, and only after they had asked why I lived in Havana and I was not inside the conference halls and that there were others there who did not have as much in common with the peoples of the conference as I did. Later they were told in the conference by Captain Osmany Cienfuegos that I had been invited to the Conference but that I had refused to pick up my invitation, that I was refusing to attend and that I was boycotting the Conference. So, the Africans came back and told me this and told me that I should come to the Conference and that they had been told that I had an invitation and wouldn't accept it. I told them that this was not true. They then said that they could not see why a man in a high position like Osmany would tell a lie about a little thing like that. I told them if they were so sure I would go with them to see. We went to the Conference headquarters and no credentials had been made out and there was no invitation there for me, but this was a scheme to keep all Afro-American revolutionaries and other true revolutionaries out of the conference. The conference was being manipulated specially to keep Afro-Americans out and this was being done by officials of the Cuban government and not by the conference as a whole. I found this to be incompatible with your policy, the policy that you had always advocated. I know that you have always advocated a policy of racial equality and brotherhood and I do not see how this could have been done with your knowledge. While in Cuba all of my work for the Afro-American struggle was sabotaged. Some of it was sabotaged by Cuban functionaries who unwittingly were led to carry out sabotage against our struggle and my work in Cuba were Americans who had been brought there as so-called "technicians and advisers" who spread all kinds of vicious lies and misled some honest Cuban officials who really thought that these American members of the U.S. Communist Party were beyond reproach. Some of these people are highly suspect as agents of the U.S. government and the CIA yet they were able to do a very effective job. They were able to completely sabotage and derail our struggle. They were able to do what the racist and imperialist government of the United States was never able to do while I was there and that was to demoralize me and frustrate my efforts to the point that they were all but ineffective. Also, during the Tri-continental Conference, one of the persons who was invited there was a fellow who came from Tanzania, Africa named D. H. Mansur. Mansur was invited and was supposed to be a newspaperman working for "Uhuru." He had been to Cuba the previous year. At that time, he was traveling in the company of a military delegation, and someone introduced to me as the vice-minister of defense, all from Tanzania. He was housed along with the vice-minister and the military delegates in the Cuban protocol house. I did not know him previously but during that visit, he was brought to my house by representatives of ICAP along with two men, the vice-minister and one of the military officials. Mansur told me at that time that there was a possibility that Tanzania would establish diplomatic relations with Cuba the following year and that he was going to be appointed the ambassador to Havana. On his second visit, during the Tri-Continental Conference, Mansur stayed at the Hotel Capri and was given special privileges and was able to summon Osmany to the hotel whenever he saw fit. He was also seen, and I personally saw him with Comandante Peniero. He told me that since I was having difficulty in Cuba if I wanted to see anybody in the government, other than Fidel Castro, he could arrange it for me. He said that Fidel Castro was the only official in the Cuban government that he could not arrange an interview with for me. He also told me that officials of the Cuban government were soliciting people to try to smear me and make me look bad, and that they were deliberately working against me, and that he would advise as a friend that I try to leave Cuba. When I had met Mansur the previous year when he was visiting with the military delegation and the vice-minister of Defense of Tanzania, he appeared to be a revolutionary person and was supposed to have been working with Cuban officials. D. H. Mansur told me that he expected to go through New York for some business that he had to take care of in the United Nations soon. I asked how soon, and he replied he was not sure when but wanted to know why I had asked. I told him that I had something that I wanted to send to the States. He replied that if I had anything to send, I could send it by the "Chief of Secret Police" of Tanzania who was in Cuba on a secret mission and was supposed to leave within a couple of days. He told me that this chief of the secret police was in Cuba attending the Tri-Continental Conference but that the Cuban government did not know his true identity but that whatever I wanted to send would be alright to send by him because he would be traveling with diplomatic immunity to the United Nations. I then told him that I may want to send some money to the Negroes in the United States; a personal contribution that I was making to them. He said that he thought that this minister would take it but that he would talk to him first. He later returned and said that the minister would leave in two days and that if I had whatever I wanted to send ready on the night before he left there would be no problem. He said that the man was alright, he had diplomatic immunity and that he was there in Cuba on a secret mission. The night before the "minister" was supposed to leave I brought $3.550 dollars and a letter written in code and gave it to Mansur to be sent to some Afro-American people working in the struggle to help them out. I took the envelope containing the message and the money to the lobby of the Hotel Habana Libre. I gave Mansur the envelope and the money and he went upstairs while I waited in the lobby for his return. He stayed upstairs for about 15 minutes and returned in the company of the Comandante Peniero and the man he had pointed out to me as the Chief of the Secret Police of Tanzania. Mansur and Peiero walked to a deserted side of the hotel that led to the cafeteria and talked for three or four minutes, then the two of them passed back through the lobby and went out of the hotel through the door leading to the Polynesia Dining room. Even though he knew I was there waiting for him he did not return that night. The next day when I saw him, I asked him why he did not return. He said for me not to worry and voluntarily injected that he had not discussed my business with Comandante Peniero because "I know these people don't like you and are working against you, but 'the red beard' is a friend of mine and I went out to talk to him." He said that his friend "red beard was the head of the Cuban Secret Police. He told me later, after the Tri-continental Conference that he served as a guide and translator for Osmany and other Cubans who were visiting and working in Africa. He also told me that the Cuban government, in conjunction with the Soviet government was trying to break relations and wreck the union between Tnanyike and Zanzibar, because the Cubans, Soviets and East Germans wanted to use Zanzibar as a base to operate in Africa to try to subvert the African governments. He said that there were two factions in the government in Dar es Sallaam and that one faction, backed by Cuba and the Soviets, was working against President Nyerere and they wanted to break up the union because they felt that Zanzibar would be more useful to them as an independent country. Mansur also stated to me that the Cuban government was responsible for a lot of trouble in Congo, Leopoldville. That they had sent many Black Cuban troops there disguised as Congolese and that these Black troops fought in the Congo and had a base in Tanzania where they received their food and supplies and often came for rest. He went on to say that the Cuban government was using these Black troops in Africa to engender political influence on behalf of the Soviet Union and that most of these troops discovered their presence. He claimed that the Cubans and Russians were giving pro-Moscow African leaders weapons to fight against the nationalists, and that instead of fighting against the imperialists they were fighting against the revolutionary nationalists in the Congo in order to prevent a nationalist in the Congo in order to prevent a nationalist revolution that would not have been under the influence and domination of the Soviet Union. I asked Mansur why he had turned against the Cubans since his last visit, and he said it was because he found out that the Cubans were no good after working with them directly through the Embassy of Cuba in Dar es Salaam. He claimed that Cuba had a Black Cuban there as an ambassador who had to take orders from a white Cuban who was the first secretary and that this proved the Cubans to be racists who did not believe in the equality of the Black man but were using Black puppets to further their own political interests and those of the Soviet Union. I asked him why he had come to Cuba, and he said that the Party had brought him there to work as an adviser on African affairs and to set up broadcasts to Africa in Swahili over Radio Havana. He started the broadcasts and often laughed about it afterwards because none in Radio Havana understood what he was broadcasting in Swahili. I discovered him to be very reactionary and laughed about the bad conditions he created in Radio Havana and how he alienated and antagonized a lot of the workers there. He told me that the director of Radio Havana asked him what Cuba could do to counteract the Chinese influence in Africa and that he should work for them in trying to do so. Mansur, while living in the Hotel Capri, created a lot of friction between himself and the Cuban workers. He struck a Cuban waiter with his fist in the Capri dining room because the waiter did not serve him "fast enough" and then had the Party make the victim apologize to him! He was extremely rude to the workers. He demanded that the director of the Hotel Capri secure a prostitute for him. When he was informed that prostitution had been abolished in Cuba by the Revolutionary government, he told the director that was a lie and that most any Cuban woman on the street would sleep with him for money. He then called officials of the party and told them that he wanted the tone of the chorus girls working in the show at the Club in the Capri. The officials of the

Party forced an unwilling showgirl to submit to his demands for a prostitute in order to pacify him. I told Mansur that I had never known a guest of Cuba to come there before and get away with such shameful conduct and abuse and I asked him how he could get away with such action. He replied that he had information on officials of the Cuban government and subversive activity that they were carrying on in Africa and that they dared not bother him. He ostentatiously went into the hotel bar and invited many people to drink with him and told them to drink all they wanted because it was free and being paid for by the Cuban government. While Mansur was using these threats to divulge this so-called "secret information" to intimidate high officials of the Cuban Party, he boasted that this information had already been sold to Finnish television men who were then visiting Cuba and that in the future it was going to be published under a pseudonym. After one week of observing Mansur's reactionary conduct, I became apprehensive of his trustworthiness and called New York and discovered that neither the money nor the letter had arrived there. I went back to D. H. Mansur to ask him about the "Chief of Secret Police" who was supposed to have taken the money and communique to New York. He said that if the message and money had not arrived yet, maybe the man did not go directly to New York, and that maybe he went first to some other place, or maybe stopped over in Mexico. I said well maybe that was possible. I waited another week and called New York again to find out that no such person had come to the Tanzanian Mission to the United Nations, so I went back again to D. H. Mansur. He then said that he had to personally go to Tanzania himself to get the money because he did not want anyone to think he was a thief. In the meantime, becoming more suspicious of Mansur, I sent cables of two Minister "Babu," with whom I was acquainted and to President Nyerere. Minister "Babu" responded immediately replying that Mansur did not represent the government of Tanzania and that he had no official position in the government of Tanzania. When I went to Mansur and faced him again, he broke down and started crying, begging me to please shoot him. He promised that he would get the money back and that he would even get the Cuban Party to pay it back. He begged me not to involve his government and his president in this matter because the government of Tanzania may kill his family or put them all in prison and kill him or put him in prison. I told him that all I wanted was the money and the message back, that his money was supposed to go to our people in New York and that we had sent a secret coded message and I wanted to know what he had done with the communique. He then said that it was possible that he gave the money and the communique to a Cuban official. I then said to him that in that case there would be no problem because if he gave it to a Cuban official we would be able to get it back because I thought they would cooperate with me. He then stated that he did not think we could get it back because the Cuban official that he gave it to may have been working with the CIA. I kept insisting that I wanted the money back and the message and he continued crying and then suggested that I go together with him to the British Reuters news service and the Associated Press office in Havana and that he would write a confession in the presence of the agents there saying that he had received the money from me and that the money had been lost and that he would be responsible for making restitution. I asked him why he wanted to go to the British and Americans who were our enemies and the enemies of his country, especially since his president had denounced the activity of the A.P. there in Tanzania as a subversive counter-revolutionary agency working against the government. He said that President Nyerere only denounced one correspondent of the A.P. and that the reason he wanted to go there and get them involved was that he was working with the two news services and that this would be a form of collateral or assurance for the money. I then asked how he could be a loyal supporter of his government and his president while working for the British and American news agencies. His sinister maneuver was obvious. The fact was that the coded message, sent along with the money, was signed by a code name. Legally there was no evidence to connect Afro-American freedom fighters with Cuba or with me. It was obvious that Mansur and other agents had devised a conspiracy to create a state of hysteria and journalistic sensationalism by attempting to link U.S. civil rights forces with foreign interests and portray me as an intermediary of foreign intrigue and subversion. Mansur had told me that Cuban government officials were plotting to get rid of me and that I should not rule out the possibility that they would readily murder me and that, though I may doubt that they were capable of this, he could assure me that they were capable of this because he worked for and had close contact with them. He said that they were soliciting others, including himself, in their malicious campaign to discredit and silence me. Obviously, he assumed after telling me all this that I was sufficiently against the Cuban Revolution to the extent that he could afford to admit to me that he was working for the British and Americans. When the African students studying in Havana, who were also friends of Mansur, were informed that Mansur had stolen money entrusted to him for the Afro-American movement, they confronted him as a delegation to investigate the veracity of the charges. Mansur confessed to them that he had had the money but not being aware of its source of origin he became frightened at the amount and turned it over to the Cuban authorities.

An African woman freedom fighter, wife of a diplomat, reported to me that Mansur had approached her and some of her Cuban friends and tried to bribe them into taking him to places where he claimed he had heard from foreign sources that Lesbian women frequented. She said he told them that he had plenty of money, ostentatiously flaunted Cuban bills in 50-peso denominations, and said he would pay them if they would take him where he could take pictures showing this type of life in Cuba. These women were shocked and became highly suspicious of his mission in Cuba. Mansur had told me that he had forced African freedom fighters from Angola out of Dar es Salaam by publishing photographs he had taken of them in undesirable places enjoying nightlife. It was more than obvious that he was seeking pictures of African freedom fighters that he could use to compromise and blackmail them on the continent.

After I began to question Mansur more about the money and the coded message and discovered all of these things about him, I found that he had suddenly requested permission to leave the country even though he was supposed to remain there another month to set up the Swahili broadcasts and to await the arrival of two other Tanzanians to take over from him. Despite the fact that his services were supposedly indispensable to Radio Havana, he was hurriedly sent on a trip to the interior of Cuba by party officials. When

I discovered that he was back and planning to leave right away, I called Comandante Vallejo. During the interim, I had talked to a Congolese woman freedom fighter who was in search of Mansur, whom she thought to be a true African brother and revolutionary, to give him confidential information and organizational communiques to be taken by him to Dar es Salaam to be sent to revolutionary forces inside the Congo. In order to prevent her from becoming another victim of D. H. Mansur, I related to her what he had done about our message and money that were sent to our friends in the United States and disclosed to her the secrets that Manusur was openly telling about the Congo. She became horrified, and after a long discussion on the matter the Congolese revolutionary stated that they had been trying to ascertain how the imperialist forces obtained information about their movement and the arrival of Black Cuban soldiers in the Congo. She said that Mansur represented the missing link that they had been searching for, and that it was now obvious to them that he was the man who had caused many revolutionaries to be massacred and their campaign to be frustrated. I immediately called Comandante Vallejo again and asked for an urgent emergency conference. Comandante Vallejo came to my house, and I told him that I had talked with the Congolese freedom fighter and that we were both convinced that Mansur was an agent of the imperialists and was the one responsible for the massacre of Congolese and Cuban revolutionaries in the Congo by revealing secrets to the imperialists. I showed him the cable from Minister Babu of the Tanzanian government. I discussed all of the aforementioned facts, at length, and asked him to report this directly to you, Fidel. I also asked Comandante Vallejo to prevent Mansur from leaving Cuba until he could be questioned more by me and the Cuban officials about the theft of the money, my missing communique and his direct connections with the A.P., Reuters, officials of the Cuban Communist Party, and the circle of Finnish television men, whose woman informer claimed to be an intimate girlfriend of yours, Fidel. Comandante Vallejo informed me that the matter would be investigated and that he would take it directly to Fidel. He left hurriedly. The following night at 12:30 a.m. two men from G-2 came to my house. In a belligerent manner, they demanded that I tell them what I had told Comandante Vallejo. I inquired as to what office they were from, and they said Comandante Peniero's office. I told them to tell Comandante Peniero that I did not deal with crooks and that anything I had to say I would tell Fidel. One of the men stated that they did not have to stay there and listen to my insults and that Mansur was a "good revolutionary friend of Cuba" who only "talked too much." As the two security men left my house, one was heard to say that Williams had better "watch out." It was obvious that Vallejo, who had been appointed by you personally to aid me with my problems was not reporting my problems and informing you but instead was turning my complaints over to the same man that I was complaining against for sabotaging our struggle or allowing it to be sabotaged by his subordinates. After I revealed that I had become convinced that Comandante Peniero and Captain Osmany were working with subversive elements and shielding agents of the U.S. and British imperialists I was unable to contact Comandante Vallejo again. He refused to see me and refused to relay my messages to you. I was unable to see any responsible official in the Cuban government and D. H. Mansur was sped out of the country by official representatives of the Cuban government. I continuously sent telegrams and made telephone calls requests to talk to you Fidel. I also called President Dorticos's office and the office of Dr. Celia Sanchez seeking an audience that I was never granted. I could only see the same people from Peniero's office who had all along been instrumental in helping to sabotage my work in Cuba. I was only granted audiences with petty functionaries from Peniero's office who displayed an attitude of indifference and laughed at the whole affair as if it were some comedy, but this was a serious matter to our struggle and it should have been a serious matter to Cuba, because I could not understand how a government or an official of a government like Vallejo, Peniero, or Osmany could see Cuban soldiers, even if they were Black, wiped out, slaughtered and massacred in the Congo and here was the man who was responsible for it right there in Cuba and they refused to apprehend him or to even take him into custody and question him. Here was a man whose pretentious masquerade as a representative of his government had been officially unmasked and they refused to do anything about it. Here was a man who had stolen $1,550 dollars from a struggle that Cuba claimed to be supporting and they refused to bring this thief in, even for questioning, which meant that he, as well as other pirates, as well as Cuban pirates, had the right to practice piracy against our liberation struggle. He had impunity granted him under the power and authority of the Cuban government. So, the fact was that even though this man was a thief, it made no difference, he was an honored guest who among other things had stolen from the Afro-American struggle which these officials of Cuba were opposed and to which they had been in opposition all along and had done everything they could to sabotage. One of the main characters in this sabotage was Comandante Peniero. We expected more consideration from Comandante Vallejo, but we found him to be working hand in glove with Comandante Peniero and Captain Osmany. I think it also important to note that much of the secret organizational information that I had filed with Comandante Peniero's office was later cynically cited to me by an official of one of the so-called "free world embassies" in Havana. It was also positively obvious that through Comandante Peniero and Comandante Vallejo a flippantly promiscuous North American woman was transmitting all confidential matters related to her by them pertaining to my activities to this same so-called free world embassy. I had much more difficulty before then. I had been invited to Sweden on a speaking tour and I had asked for permission to leave Cuba, but permission was never granted, and no cooperation was given to me whatsoever. Finally, the people working with the Party had begun to do all manner of things to handicap and hinder our struggle and their actions were beginning to become antagonistic whenever I had contact with them. During my last months in Cuba, hostility toward me by members of the Party became very intense. They displayed much resentment toward the fact that I was receiving a small stipend in pesos as the government's support of me and my activities on behalf of the Afro-American struggle. Due to the fact that this stipend was used to make me appear a part of the new class of those enjoying the dulce Vida in Cuba, while at the same time, piratical Party officials were robbing us of the direct material support received from the revolutionary people of the United States and deliberately and viciously sabotaging all our efforts in our struggle, I refused to continue accepting this stipend from the Party. Despite the fact that I had evidence that D. H. Mansur was a thief, a charlatan, an unprincipled counterrevolutionary, and an admitted agent of the imperialist forces, and I had personally found him to be unscrupulous, anti-socialist, anti-Nyerere and an outright bandit of the worst sort, functionaries of the Party and Comandante Peniero's office insisted that he was an "honest man," a "revolutionary," and a guest of the Cuban government who just "talked too much." From Mansur's point of view, he felt safe and secure in the fact that he had connections with officials high in the Cuban government. He suggested to me that if I wanted aid, any special favor or permission to leave Cuba that I had better direct my efforts more toward Captain Osmany Cienfuegos because his power was on the rise and Fidel's was on the decline and it would be only matter of time before Fidel would be completely powerless. I can't believe that Osmany, Peniero, and Vallejo, I do not believe that they have accurately, truly and faithfully informed you of what was and is transpiring because I cannot conceive of your being aware of this matter and of all these things that were going on, not only against our struggle but also against the Cuban Revolution, and the Cuban people and remain indifferent. I write you this correspondence now because of my support of the Cuban people and the Cuban Revolution. As desperately as the $1,550 dollars are needed by impoverished Afro-American freedom fighters, I know that it is now an irretrievable loss and that those racist officials of the Cuban government, who so effectively sabotaged our struggle were glad that we lost the money, and they deem it a great victory for whatever because they serve. The only ones who could possibly profit from this are those who work for the CIA and U.S. imperialism. I deem it my revolutionary duty to bring these facts to your attention. I want to be sure that you know this because I also see in this a conspiracy against the Cuban Revolution and yourself and I am convinced that if you are, and remain, unaware of these corrupt and sinister machinations taking place around you, you will soon be in the same predicament as Nkrumah, Ben Bella, or Sukarno and the Cuban Revolution will be subverted and destroyed from within. I think that you owe it to the cause of the Cuban Revolution to revolutionaries throughout the world and especially to the revolutionaries in Latin America and the western hemisphere to let us know if these reactionary scoundrels of your government were acting in accordance with your concept of revolutionary conduct as a part of your ruling clique or whether they were usurpers engaged in unscrupulous subversive activities contrary to your beliefs and ideas. Again, I say that I support the Cuban Revolution and I am grateful for the hospitality and friendship that the Cuban people have shown me. I hope that these demoralizing and agonizing experiences do not indicate a new fascist tendency on the part of the Cuban Revolution. The only complaint that I make to you is on behalf of my people, the Afro-American people who are engaged in a struggle for survival, liberation, equality and freedom inside the United States. I make this complaint to you because of the fact that your government has allowed saboteurs to sabotage our struggle and have set us back for a number of years and have allowed them to frustrate and demoralize our people in our struggle against our oppressive enemy. I also make this complaint as a revolutionary obligation to the Cuban people themselves who have sacrificed their lives, their blood and their loved ones and gone to great lengths to promote the Cuban Revolution and to make it a living reality. I think that I owe it to them that I bring this matter to your attention so that you may deal personally with it or place it into the hands of the people so that they may know about the characters and personalities of those persons who are supposed to be leaders of the Cuban Revolution; people like Comandante Vallejo, Peniero, and Osmany. They should know the caliber of three men who represent them before the world, these men who are either outright thieves and crooks themselves or who keep company with and give aid and comfort to crooks who are enemies of the Cuban people and revolutionaries throughout the world. Personally, my stay in Cuba turned out quite well and my stay in Cuba, as far as my relationship with the Cuban people, was quite enjoyable, but I deeply resent the fact that a revolutionary government that came to power through revolution would sink to the level that it would give aid and comfort to imperialist agents, thieves and pirates who practice piracy against freedom movements, freedom fighters and those struggling for liberty and equality. There are many other things that I feel should be brought out, things I should say to you but I am not sure that this correspondence will reach you, but if it is impossible to reach you this way, I feel that it is my revolutionary duty to reach you in whatever manner I possibly can, even if it must be through the mass media of the world. I am doing this completely on my own initiative. I have not discussed this with any other official or individual nor with members or officials of my organization inside the United States. This is a personal matter that I am taking upon myself, and I assume full responsibility. I feel that this is my duty because I feel a personal obligation, a personal duty and a personal loyalty to the Cuban Revolution and the Cuban people and I hope that I will be more fortunate in reaching you than I was in the more than four years that I resided in Cuba. I hope at least this time you will feel that what I have to say is important enough for a personal response and I hope you will not commit this very important and serious matter to the hands of the same racist, degenerate, counterrevolutionary agents of U.S. imperialism who are responsible for frustrating and subverting that part of the Afro-American freedom struggle that was being conducted from the revolutionary territory of Cuba. Revolutionarily yours.[1]

Robert F. Williams

TO ALL INDIVIDUALS, PARTIES, AND GROUPS CONCERNED,
August 1, 1967, Peking, China

This is to certify that Richard Gibson is authorized to make all arrangements necessary regarding my projected lecture tour to Europe for October 1967. Mr. Gibson is further authorized to handle the arrangements for the publication and distribution of the revised edition of *Negroes with Guns*, tentatively entitled, *America is the Black Man's Battleground*.

Respectfully submitted,
Robert F. Williams

SPEECHES BY ROBERT F. WILLIAMS

THE GREAT THOUGHT OF MAO TSE-TUNG IS TRANSFORMING THE WHOLE WORLD

Comrades, Revolutionaries, and Friends:

In the name of all the revolutionary American people, and especially in the name of the brutally oppressed a victimized Afro-American freedom fighter, I salute our glorious Chinese brothers and the mighty Chinese People's Republic on this historical 17th anniversary. To salute our glorious Chinese brothers and the mighty Chinese People's Republic is to pay tribute to its great architect, liberator, helmsman, and universal leader and teacher, whose thought is transforming the whole world. On this great National Day, revolutionaries throughout the world realize more than ever how much we are indebted to the architect of people's warfare, the immortal leader and teacher, Chairman Mao Tse-tung. This mighty assemblage here today is a vivid testimony of the people's determination to make and sustain the revolution. It is symbolic of the growing unity and solidarity of the struggling peoples of the world. It reflects the fraternal ties of we who labor and struggle in a common front against a common enemy, U.S. imperialism. On this glorious 17th anniversary, I am convinced that from People's China shall flow the spirit and inspiration that shall inspire patriots everywhere to resolutely struggle to build a people's world. Only in a people's republic would a refugee from racist "free world" tyranny, grandson of chattel slaves robbed from Africa, one imprisoned on his own native soil for sitting on a public seat reserved for "white people only," one fanatically and violently pursued by the fascist U.S. government for demanding human rights, social justice and stressing the right of armed self-defense, be extended the honor representing his oppressed people as I am accorded here today. We brutally oppressed Afro-Americans, the nearly exterminated American Indians, Puerto Ricans, Mexican Americans, and other oppressed U.S. minorities know the true nature of the savage Yankee. We know what he truly means when he so piously and hypocritically proposes to bring peace and democracy to Vietnam and the world. He is a jingoist, a cold-blooded murderer and plunderer who respects the rights of colored peoples less than those of common street dogs. We revolutionary Afro-Americans know the true nature of the peace her she offers and we prefer the rigors and sacrifices of redemptive people's struggle. We call upon our oppressed people to further intensify the battle and to coordinate their revolutionary activity with the liberation forces of Asia, Latin America, Africa and the justice and peace loving peoples of all races throughout the world. We do not seek peace and fraternity with the devil and a favored lackey status in his hell. Instead, we seek his resolute and total destruction and the glorious heritage of a people's world. Contrary to what some cynics would have us believe our vicious enemy is not invincible. Chairman Mao has said he is "a paper tiger" and our people have come to realize this incontrovertible truth. And the thunder of BLACK POWER echoes throughout the land while U.S. imperialist tyrants armed with horrible death weapons tremble from the terrifying shock of a confrontation with wretched an angry mass armed with a common household match and a bottle of gasoline. On this glorious 17th anniversary of the Chinese People's Republic, a reliable base area of the world's peoples' struggle, we take great pride in the technical and scientific achievements of the glorious Chinese people, which explode the U.S. imperialist (unreadable) racist myth of the inferiority of non-Anglo-Saxon peoples. We are more confident than ever of the final triumph of our cause. In this mighty year of the Great Chinese Proletarian Cultural Revolution, racist and imperialist America sees her last big hope for world domination slipping fast away. We revolutionaries of the whole world shall intensify our revolutionary struggles, confident that our Chinese brothers and sisters in the Red Guard, armed with Mao Tse-tung's thoughts are at their battle stations in a mighty base area of world revolution, being waged for the heritage of a people's world.

Long live the People's Republic of China!
Long live Mao Tse-tung's thought!
Long live Chairman Mao Tse-tung!
Long live the solidarity of the revolutionaries of the world!

SPEECH DELIVERED AT THE INTERNATIONAL CONFERENCE FOR SOLIDARITY WITH THE PEOPLE OF VIETNAM AGAINST U.S. IMPERIALIST AGGRESSION FOR THE DEFENSE OF PEACE, HANOI, DEMOCRATIC REPUBLIC OF VIETNAM, NOVEMBER 25–29, 1965

Brothers of Vietnam, patriots of the world, and lovers of peace and freedom: I greet you in the name of those of my fellow countrymen who are civilized enough to oppose U.S. aggression; I specifically greet you in the name of Afro-American freedom fighters who are waging a determined liberation struggle against mainland American colonialism. As chairman-in-exile of the Revolutionary Action Movement, an American- based united liberation front, comprising many groups and organization, I resolutely offer support to our gallant brothers of Vietnam and to this International Conference for Solidarity with the People of Vietnam Against U.S. Imperialist Aggression for the Defense of Peace. Not only do we support the right of our brothers of Vietnam to defend themselves against the armed aggression, repression and tyranny of U.S. imperialism and its running dogs, but we wish to thank our brothers for the splendid examples they are giving us. Our people are being inspired by the effectiveness and the great successes scored by the Vietnamese people in their armed struggle for self-defense and liberation. After almost 200 years of inhuman bondage and shameful dehumanization under the present U.S. government, our meek and passive people, like our brothers of Vietnam, Cuba, the Congo, Mozambique, and throughout Asia, African, and Latin America, we are beginning to cast off the imperialist inspired curse of turn—the other cheekism. Yes, on the very mainland of neocolonialism our oppressed people are turning the streets of racist and imperialist America into battlegrounds of resistance. More than any other people in the world, our people understand the savage and beastly nature of barbaric Yankeeism. We know the hypocrisy and inhumanity of the evil government of our beloved country. Perhaps you may wonder why I, an oppressed descendant of African slaves, would refer to America as our beloved country. It is because the blood, sweat, and tears of our African people have drenched the mountains, hallowed the valleys and swelled the rivers of America. It is because the first patriot to fall in the American Revolution was a Black man named Crispus Attucks. Yes, almost 200 years ago a Black man fell first in the struggle for liberation, in the struggle for American freedom and independence. Yet today our people are still suffering and dying in their quest for freedom in the so-called "free world" of racist America. There has never been a revolution so grossly betrayed in the history of the world. There never was such a cruel hoax so brutally perpetrated on a noble people. We, the captive people of the free world of racist America, support the right of all oppressed people to meet violence with violence. We resolutely support the right of all people to self-determination. We are resolutely opposed to the fate of oppressed people being decided in any international body where the racist United States holds sway. We are opposed to so-called "justice" being meted out to the victims of U.S. racism and imperialism by running dog lackeys, hired thugs, and agents of Yankeeism. We want to remind those who cherish freedom and justice that the Yankee honors his treaties, agreements, and legal writs only to the extent that they promote his sinister cause of world conquest. Yankee imperialism is a racist imperialism. It is a threat to the peace and security of the entire world. The American Indian, the first American, is a perfect example of those who trust in the promises of the Yankee plunderers. The proud and once great American Indian sought to honorably and peacefully share his native land with the conniving intruder who came preaching a new doctrine of so-called "Christian brotherhood." More than 100 treaties signed with the American Indians have been violated and shamelessly discarded by the U.S. government. The American Indian was the first victim of the U.S. government's strategic hamlet, the so-called "Indian Reservation." Today, he too, is a prisoner on his own soil, and he has all but been exterminated. What is a treat, what is an agreement, and what is a constitution to the racist, imperialist administration? The Johnson administration is a racist, imperialist administration desperately trying to conceal its inherent dishonor in a deceptive cloak of so-called "representative democracy." Wherever it can, it thrusts its imperialism deceptively upon the deceived through phony Alliances for Progress, Peace Corps, Aid Programs, Military pacts, phony democratic slogans, Yankee dollars, and chewing gum. Wherever it can, it hides its brutal and evil racist face behind the clever façade of mercenary Negroes. It stages a repulsive parade of handpicked Negro puppets, Judases, and apologist-for-the-system before the world to extol the virtues of fabled representative democracy for a government that respects the human rights of colored people less than those of common street dogs. The so-called "U.S. Civil Rights Bill," allegedly guaranteeing rights to colored people is a farce of the first magnitude. The Constitution of our country guarantees all people equal rights. It has never been enforced and honored by the U.S. government. A Civil Rights Bill similar to Johnson' s was enacted in 1875. It has never been enforced. The racist United States, like racist South Africa, is a member of the United Nations and they both stand in contempt of its human rights charter. It is ironic that the very body, which is asked to condemn racialism in Portuguese. Angola and South Africa maintains their seat within the borders of the racist United States. The non-white delegates to this very body, themselves, do not enjoy immunity from the brutality and violence of U.S. racism. Delegates themselves, have been made victims of ruthless police brutality and humiliating racial discrimination. Yes, like all people who struggle for human dignity and liberty, we Afro-Americans have traitors and mercenaries in our ranks. The chief apologist for its corrupts, decadent, racist, and imperialist system is the head of the U.S. Information Services. This man, Carl Rowan, is a running dog for the racist and imperialist Johnson Administration. A Negro was especially designated for this highly sophisticated system of deception because more and more the U.S. imperialists are smarting from the embarrassment their racist policies are causing them abroad. It is the height of cynicism, the cruelest of hoaxes, for a government to practice genocide against a minority, while sending one of its own members to help bait the trap for other potential victims. This Negro spokesman for white supremacy democracy, Mr. Rowan, visited his home in Tennessee and was not allowed to dine nor use the public toilet in the U.S. government subsidized airport because his skin is black. Yes, the U.S. government has sunken to the level of the devil of the world. The same racist savages whose bombs blow the heads off black babies in Birmingham, United States, who viciously club pregnant Afro-American women into insensibility on the streets of America are the same best who murder, torture, and maim the patriots of Vietnam. It is the height of man's inhumanity to man when a slave is sent to extend his master's brutal slavery to his brothers. Afro-American soldiers themselves are being slaughtered like wild beasts on the streets of the so-called "free world" of racist America, yet they are being sent as aggressors against the anti-racist, anti-imperialist, peace-loving people of Vietnam in a fraudulent crusade of containing communism. Corporal Roman Duckworth, an Afro-American soldier, who had obtained leave from his post in Mississippi to visit his seriously hospitalized wife, was viciously gunned down by a racist sheriff, because he refused to submit to the racist demands that he, a Negro soldier, restrict himself to the rear of the bus. Was Cpl Duckworth killed because the United States wanted to contain communism in Mississippi? No! Lt. Colonel Lemuel Penn, one of the very few high-ranking Afro-American officers in the Army reserves, while returning to his family had his head blown off at the very gates of Ft. Benning, Georgia, United States. His brutal and savage murderers readily identified themselves as members of a Ku Klux Klan terrorist group and boasted that they killed him because he was Black. As in the case of Cpl. Duckworth and countless other lynched Afro-Americans, the savage criminals have been acquitted and acclaimed honored heroes in their racist communities. Was Col. Penn killed because the U.S. government wanted to contain communism in Georgia? No! These loyal servants of U.S. imperialism were killed simply because their skins were Black. The racist U.S. government cynically pleads no jurisdiction over America's southern soil, yet it brazenly proclaims the right to act as policeman, judge, and executioner in Vietnam and throughout the world. Throughout racist America, our people are being terrorized, murdered, maimed, bombed, lynched, raped, starved, sterilized by the states, and imprisoned. Besides conducting a campaign of genocide against our people, the fascist organizations are also attempting to intimidate our white allies by subjecting them to all forms of violence, terror and murder. These fascist forces are arming themselves with weapons from the U.S. Military arsenals. They are openly training for their publicly proposed policy of exterminating our people. We warn the racists of America that they are not living in the fascist era of Hitler's Germany and that our brothers of all races throughout the world are not going to passively submit to genocide. Let them remember that the anti-racist, anti-imperialist forces of the socialist camp are growing more powerful every single day. We are learning from the people of Vietnam. We are learning from the people of Cuba. We are learning from the people of Algeria, Angola, and the Congo. We believe in the right of armed struggle. We believe in the people's right to defend themselves in Vietnam as well as in Harlem, New York or Jackson, Mississippi, United States. We proudly hail the nuclear achievements of the staunch defenders of the oppressed, our Chinese brothers, in developing weapons for self-defense against nuclear intimidation by the racist United States. Our people, who have for many generations been defenseless victims of monopolized white supremacy terror, consider the Chinese bomb, a people's bomb, a freedom bomb of the oppressed. Our principles and our love for humanity demands that we place ourselves on the side of the Vietnamese people. As a representative of the Revolutionary Action Movement, I am here to give support to the Vietnamese people in their struggle against U.S. imperialist aggression. We are opposed to the barbaric acts of the hypocritical Johnson administration, at home and abroad. Our human decency will not allow us to be pretty and serve as spineless apologists for savage Yankeeism. Not only do we condemn, protest and raise our fists in indignation at these brutal crimes perpetrated against the noble patriots of this gallant land, but we promise our brothers, and let the whole world bear witness, that we shall intensify, our struggle for liberation in the so-called "free world" of the racist United States. We shall take the torch of freedom and justice into the streets of America, and we shall set the last great stronghold of Yankee imperialism ablaze with our battle cry of freedom! Freedom! Freedom nor or death! For our people, for our country and for our compatriots throughout the world, we shall reclaim the nobility of the American Revolution. We shall raise our flag in honor, true peace, and brotherhood to all the world.

Thank you.
Robert F. Williams—United States

DURING THE DEMONSTRATION IN PEKING ROBERT F. WILLIAMS CONDEMNS RACIAL DISCRIMINATION IN THE U.S. AND ENCOURAGES SUPPORT FOR AFRO-AMERICAN RIGHTS TO USE REVOLUTIONARY VIOLENCE, August 8, 1966

The following speech was delivered by Robert F. Williams during a demonstration in Peking on August 8, 1966, to condemn racial discrimination in the United States against Afro-Americans, and to encourage support for their rights to use revolutionary violence in response to the counter-revolutionary violence of the U.S. government and local governments in the United States and other racist reactionaries against them.[2] Brothers, Sisters, Patriots, Revolutionaries. Once again, I want to thank Chairman Mao Tse-tung and our brothers, the great Chinese people for the support of our struggle. Commemorating the third anniversary of Chairman Mao Tse-tung's statement calling upon the people of the world to unite against racial discrimination by U.S. imperialism and support the American Negroes in their struggle against racial discrimination, the greatest tribute that can be paid to the correctness of his immortal words lie in current analysis and assessment of this present development of struggle being waged by the Afro-American people. Chairman Mao Tse-tung's statement of August 8, 1963, gave inspiration to a people long and brutally oppressed and dehumanized, then laboring under the masochist-like philosophy of neo-Gandhism. His words gave impetus to a floundering and feeble movement of armed self-defense. And today all of the reactionary world is shocked and terrified by the turbulent winds of ever-increasing armed resistance now sweeping the mighty fortress of savage imperialism and beastly racism. In racist America's mighty northern cities, in the small towns, in the countryside, in the dark and deep jungle wilderness of the southland, from coast to coast, oppressed and dehumanized Black people are meeting oppressive racist terrorist violence with revolutionary violence. The thunder of BLACK POWER echoes throughout the land. A mighty firestorm sweeps through the ghettoes rife with rebellion. In their paradise of stolen wealth, ringed by massive arsenals of horrible death weapons, the tyrannical kings of imperialism tremble from the terrifying shock of a confrontation with wretched and angry slaves, armed with a common household match and a bottle of gasoline. What is the meaning of this cry BLACK POWER in a land dominated by the unmerciful power of white intruders who murdered and all but exterminated the rightful owners, the American Indians? Black power means that Black men want to have some control over their own lives, and to have a respected voice in public affairs that affect them. We resent being a colonial people, treated as third-class citizens in our native land. We resent being forbidden to speak for ourselves, even in Black belts where we constitute as much as 85 percent of the population. We resent being deformed by a white man's mold in a degenerate white supremacy society that derides and belittles our African heritage and makes us ashamed of our ethnic characteristics. Black power is the vehicle of an apology for our non-Anglo-Saxon features. The dominant society in racist America is reactionary, imperialist, racist, and decadent, and we wish to disassociate ourselves from it. Black power is a descendant force challenging the racist white power structure that is so heinously exterminating the people of Vietnam and threatening the world with nuclear destruction. We have been victims of white racism for 400 years in the new world. We have been victims of racist barbarism for almost 200 years under the present form of government. Our people are slaughtered like swine on the main streets of racist America. Our churches and homes have been bombed. Our women raped with impunity. Our men have been emasculated. We are hated and murdered for no other reason than being born Black and because we refuse to commend and love our savage oppressors, we are called racists. We are oppressed people. Our objective is to destroy the hurtful stranglehold of our enemy oppressors. An opponent without the courage to designate his enemy by his true characteristics cannot expect to confront and defeat him. We propose to call our enemies what they are. We propose to rally our people and fight on this basis. We do not propose to mince our words for the sake of peaceful coexistence. It is a natural law that a humble lamp cannot peacefully coexist with a rabid wolf in close proximity. Yes, we have some white Americans with us in our struggle. They are our true brothers. These revolutionaries understand and share our anger. They know it is justified. Their spirit is an extension of the glorious spirit of the great and noble antislavery fighter, John

Brown. Yes, they too are a hated and persecuted minority people in Johnson's majority mob rule Hitlerite jungle society. Yes, and like all other people we have enemies in our ranks. We have Black traitors who practice treason for 30 pieces of silver. We have Black Judases, insensate running dogs for the Johnson administration, and its racist white power structure. Like their puppet masters, these Black puppets too have days that are numbered. Our wrath is as intense against the Black lackeys of our white oppressors as it is against the white supremacy oppressors themselves. These mercenary Uncle Toms are the most vocal nonviolent peace peddlers in the storm centers of racist America today. The ghettoes are ablaze, but they advocate peaceful submission to continued tyranny and oppression. Johnson, the great civil rights advocate, the former senator from the racist state of Texas, who as a senator voted against every civil rights bill that came before the U.S. Senate, claimed to be a modern-day Moses to Black Americans so long as they passively allowed themselves to be mauled and maimed by white supremacy brutes and thugs. But now, with brutal white supremacy Federal Power, he threatens those who defend themselves, their homes, and their women and children. Mr. Johnson, the big daddy white supremacist, would remind our people that we are a minority, and the brutal racist white savages are a majority. Like his fellow-traveling Ku Klux Klansmen, he endeavors to frighten and intimidate us by the mere numbers of our eternal oppressors. In the same fashions that Mr. Johnson would like to intimidate the Chinese people with a massive arsenal of nuclear weapons, he is endeavoring to intimidate the Black Americans by alluding to great hordes of white supremacists who are ready and willing to exterminate our people. We say to Mr. Johnson that intimidation, violence, and brutality will not stop the raging fires in the people's liberation struggle. The only force on earth powerful enough to halt the flames engulfing ghettoes and main streets of racist America consists of fair play, brotherhood, equality, and justice. We serve notice on big daddy Texas Lyndon B. Johnson that he can no more intimidate the Afro-American people with his threat of unleashing his great hordes of mad-dog racists than he can intimidate the Chinese people with the threat of unleashing a nuclear attack. The day when brutal white racist oppressors and imperialists can frighten colored peoples into submission by threats of savage violence is gone forever! We revolutionary Afro-Americans respond to Mr. Johnson and his KKK fraternity of white supremacy with the city of BLACK POWER, FREEDOM NOW! JUSTICE! We proclaim our inalienable right to live as human beings and we shall implement our demand with blood and fire. Yes, Mr. Johnson, we are a minority but more than that we are an oppressed minority determined at all costs to be free, and we are resolved to pay any price, to perform any task, and to go to any length for our freedom. Yes, we are a minority, but we are a minority with the power of a righteous cause and justice on our side. We are a minority marching in the endless files of the great multiracial masses of the invincible anti-imperialist and anti-racist forces of the world. For the benefit of Mr. Johnson, who puts so much stock in numbers, we remind him once again, in the words of a great people's leader a liberator whose words, thoughts, and teachings stand as impeccable in the turbulent winds of time as the mighty Rock of Gibraltar, yes we remind him once again that our great leader and teacher, Chairman Mao Tse-tung has said:

We are in the majority and they are in the minority. At most, they make up less than ten percent of the three thousand million percent of the people of the world, the American Negroes will be victorious in their just struggle. The evil system of colonialism and imperialism arose and throve with the enslavement of Negroes and the trade in Negroes, and it will surely come to its end with the complete emancipation of the Black people.

Today, in the social jungle of racist America the rights of colored people are less respected than those of common street dogs. The law and the kangaroo courts of the so-called "free world" of "Christian" democracy protect the rights of common street dogs and other dumb animals but there is not a single court of law that dispenses even-handed justice and unbiased constitutional and human rights to colored Americans. The long, brutal, and miserable plight of our people throughout the history of barbaric America encompasses one of the most shameful and savage chapters in the history of slavery and man's injustice to man. The dominant class in racist America is one of the most hypocritical the world has ever seen. It captured the African in Africa, enslaved him, ripped his culture from him, raped him, reproduced from him, completely dehumanized him, and reduced him to the level of the beast of burden and stamped him with the name Negro as a tribute to the white man's creation and invention of a new implement of agriculture and an instrument of labor. And all the while, he promoted this brutal slavery, he proclaimed himself the architect of democracy and a Christian society. All the while, he brutally and savagely exterminated the American Indian and piously proclaimed Thanksgiving to his white god for being so generous in blessing him with the bounty of the Indian's rich land and paradise. He built a brutal imperialist prison wall around the peoples of Latin America and piously named it the protective Monroe Doctrine. He stretched his bloody hand to Asia and arrogantly called it an "Open Door Policy." The Open Door Policy was the policy of an armed bandit at the door of a peaceful man. Today, the same bandit rapes and plunders the land Vietnam, murders defenseless women and children, and exterminates the people in the name of "free world Christian democracy." The same bandit who exterminated and starved the American Indian on his own native soil now piously proclaims to practice charity to the nation of India in a hypocritical effort to use them in his campaign to subdue and enslave the peoples of Asia. What is the nature of his democracy? What does such a beastly, imperialist, racist savage know about democracy? Should not democracy, like charity, start first at home, and then spread abroad? What is the democracy of the Black American captives in the miserable ghettoes, in the Cottom fields of Mississippi, battered by the savage policeman's club in Washington, D.C.? What is the democracy of the Puerto Ricans, of the Mexicans, and of the American Indians in racist America? Only the most naïve can believe the empty words and promise of such a morally bankrupt charlatan. Deceptive American white supremacy is personified by hypocrites like Bobby Kennedy, a sophisticated huckster and charlatan of the first magnitude who struts and sways into the hotbed of African white supremacy and colonialism, hugging and kissing Black babies and masquerading as a great white father and savior of the Black Africans. Mr. Kennedy's action in racist Americas are quite a contrast to his deceitful conduct in Africa. When Mr. Kennedy served as the attorney general of the

United States, he was sworn to uphold the right of equal protection under the law, yet he collaborated with the most barbaric racists in the nation. He entered into a "white gentleman's agreement" with the notorious racist governor of Mississippi, Ross Barnett, defenseless and helpless Black women and children were bombed, gassed, clubbed, raped, and murdered on the main streets of racist America and Mr. Kennedy is yet to punish a single white supremacist heathen transgressor. As attorney general, he did nothing about the fact that Africans were being beaten in the United States, even the diplomats assigned to the United States. It is strange indeed how Mr. Kennedy can perform in the racist chorus of those who chant slogans of hatred, vilification, and dehumanization for Black people in America while proclaiming his pretended great love for Black humanity in Africa. Such is the nature of a deceptive and barbaric Yankee. In America, Mr. Kennedy publicly proclaimed himself to be opposed to Black nationalism. In his white supremacy logic, he calls it racism in reverse. Black nationalism is a survival reaction to white nationalism. White nationalism transcends religious, class, social, and political lines. The reason that no massive Black-white unity on a national scale exists today is that the white supremacy ruling class has poisoned the minds of white workers. Most white workers identify with their white imperialist rulers. White liberals insist on paternalism. Even bourgeois-minded so-called "socialists" are more and more identifying and grouping on a racial basis rather than on a class basis. We Afro-American revolutionaries have discovered that some so-called "socialists," we thought to be our comrades and class brothers have joined the international Ku Klux Klan fraternity for white supremacy and world domination. To our consternation, we have discovered that the bourgeois-orientated power structure of some socialist states, even one with a Black and white population, would prefer to preserve the white reactionary anti-communist power structure in racist America, their natural national enemy, than to see a just, democratic, fraternal socialist interests of all peoples and races. Like their Yankee counterparts that they love to ape so well, even to the point of emulating their racism, they are moving might and main to frustrate and defeat the revolutionary movements of the oppressed peoples throughout the world. We of the Afro-American liberation movement resolutely condemn and oppose all counterrevolutionaries and purveyors of white supremacy whether they cloak their treachery in the grab of Marxist-Leninist phraseology or the hideous bed sheets of the KKK and its phony Christian doctrine. We who are engaged in the struggle for liberation and survival vehemently condemn the use of Black dehumanized troops as cannon folder in a white man's war of imperialism in Vietnam. We oppose Johnson's vicious crusade to dehumanize, emasculate, and enslave the great Vietnamese people. Black Boys from the slum housing of Black ghettoes, ill-educated in segregated schools, emasculated and dehumanized by police brutality and a savage white power structure. Yes, Black boys who cannot find employment, Black boys who are victims of white racists who hate them because of the color of their skin. Black boys whose mothers, sisters, and loved ones are being savagely clubbed, gassed, raped, maimed, lynched, and railroaded to prison in racist kangaroo courts simply for begging and praying for elementary justice are forced to share foxholes and shed their blood alongside racist Negro haters in Vietnam, who like in racist America refuse to fraternize with them in places of amusement in Tokyo and Saigon. Even out of proportion to the self-styled master race, vast numbers of Black soldiers are forced to suffer and die in that vain effort to prolong and extend the brutal racist white man's imperialism. They are forced to suffer and die in the cause of a racist power structure that is as much the enemy of Black people in America as it is the people of peace and freedom-loving Vietnam. And why do we call the massive KKK type action in Vietnam a racist white man's war of imperialism while many Black men are fighting there? It is because in racist America no Black man is part of Johnson's policy-making clique. The United States is governed by white power. The Pentagon is a white-dominated repressive arm of a ruthless elite white power structure. Wall Street is an exclusive club of the great white chiefs of business and industry. Black Americans are resisting the racist and imperialist lily-white power structure. How can a people who are fighting and dying simply to wrest the most basic of human rights from an intransigent and tyrannical power structure be said to be partners of that power structure and willing participants in its racist and imperialist ventures and crimes against humanity? The United States today is a fascist society more brutal than any the world has ever known. It has all but exterminated a whole people. It has robbed and raped an entire continent with impunity. It has divided the peoples of the world into national factions and set them against themselves and their brothers. With no more authority than the wave of its bloody imperialist hand, it has abrogated the right of self-determination of small nations. It has appointed and crowned itself both king and armored knight of the whole universe. It threatens the globe with annihilation. It is a super colonial power that is colonializing the colonials. The world famed and brilliant philosopher, Lord Bertrand Russell has justifiably stated that racist America has exterminated more Black people than Hitler exterminated Jews in Nazi Germany. Lord Russell and many other fair-minded humanists throughout the world have justifiably stated that the U.S. military aggression in Vietnam is executed in a more cruel and barbarous manner than even the horrible campaigns of aggression, genocide, and conquest carried out by Hitler's fascist Germany. Yet, there is a mighty tendency, promoted by the sinner American devil himself, to engender more sympathy and fraternalism for the so-called "good reasonable American" than for the wretched victims of vicious and brutal U.S. imperialism. The U.S. constitutes one of the greatest fascist threats ever to cast its ugly shadow across the face of the earth. When the butchers of Nazi Germany were on the plunder, the world cry was "Crush the Fascist Power Structure!" Crush Germany!" Total war was unleashed without deference to any who may be considered "good Germans" inside Nazi Germany. No sane person opposed to fascism pleaded for a soft policy toward Nazi Germany or pleaded for victims to wait for deliverance through the benevolence of "good German workers and liberals." Racist America didn't give a damn about sparing the good Japanese people when they dropped their horrible and devastating atom bombs. What is the motive of those who plead for the exemption of liberal Americans, whose feigned liberation merely serves as a cloak and shield around the naked power of savage and racial U.S. imperialism? The time is fast approaching when the so-called "good reasonable American" must make a decision either to overly side with American chauvinism and jingoism or to make a resolute anti-imperialist and anti-racist stand that will be a firm basis for a just and lasting world peace. We who are brutally oppressed and victimized cannot forever afford to spare the fortress of social reaction and tranny because there are allegedly silent dissenters within its gates. Those who are without righteous cause of the oppressed must be prepared to suffer the consequences of the gathering storm of the violent and turbulent winds of retribution. A good man who is silent and inactive in times of great injustice and oppression is no good man at all. He is no ally to freedom and justice but is a silent partner to tyranny and condemnation. He does not deserve exemption from the condemnation and the vengeance of those whom his silence allows to be victimized. The myth of the good reasonable American who is yet to be heard is a ruse perpetrated by the psychological arm of the imperialist forces of tyranny. It is one minute to zero in racist America. Four hundred bloody and gruesome years have passed. For 400 years, our good silent partners have remained silent and inactive. Time is running out and they stand at the diving liner still beseeching patience, still beseeching the slave to leave his fate to his silent fiends ever infected with inertia. They plead for deference on behalf of the good people who yet stand at one camp. We call to them to separate themselves from the devil's legions. We inform them that they have not 400 years more years to decide but one minute before the hour of zero, before the Armageddon between the slave master and the slave. Once again, in closing, let me thank our great leader and teacher, the architect of people's welfare, Chairman Mao Tse-tung, for his great and inspiring statement in support of our struggle. And to our great Chinese brothers and true revolutionaries throughout the world, we revolutionary Afro-Americans vow that we shall take the torch of freedom and justice into the streets of racist America, and we shall set the last great stronghold of Yankee imperialism ablaze with our battle cry of Black Power! FREEDOM! FREEDOM! FREEDOM! FREEDOM! NOW OR DEATH! For our people, for our country, and for our compatriots throughout the world, we shall reclaim the nobility of the American Revolution. We shall raise our flag in honor, true peace, and brotherhood in all the world! Long live the People's Republic of China! Long live Chairman Mao Tse-tung! Long live the people's resistance to imperialism, racism, and tyranny! Long live the militant friendship between the Chinese and revolutionary American people!

Robert F. Williams Speaks on the Third Anniversary of Chairman Mao

Brothers, Sisters, Patriots, Revolutionaries:

Once again, I want to thank Chairman Mao Tse-tung and our brothers, the great Chinese people for their support of our struggle. Commemorating the third anniversary of Chairman Mao Tse-tung's statement calling upon the people of the world to unite against racial discrimination by U.S. imperialism and support the American Negroes in their struggle against racial discrimination, the greatest tribute that can be paid to the correctness of his immortal words lies in a current analysis and assessment of the present development of struggle being waged by the Afro-American people.

Chairman Mao Tse-tung's statement of August 8, 1963, gave inspiration to a people long and brutally oppressed and dehumanized, then laboring under the masochist-like philosophy of neo-Gandhism. His words gave impetus to a floundering and feeble movement of armed self-defense. And today all of the reactionary world is shocked and terrified by the turbulent winds of ever-increasing armed resistance now sweeping the mighty fortress of savage imperialism and beastly racism. In racist America's mighty northern cities, in the small towns, in the countryside, in the dark and deep jungle wilderness of the southland, from coast to coast, oppressed and dehumanized Black people are meeting oppressive racist terrorist's violence with revolutionary violence. The thunder of BLACK POWER echoes throughout the land. A mighty firestorm sweeps through the ghettoes rife with rebellion. In their paradise of stolen wealth, ringed by massive arsenals of horrible death weapons, the tyrannical kings of imperialism tremble from the terrifying shock of a confrontation with wretched and angry slaves, armed with a common household match and a bottle of gasoline.

What is the meaning of this cry BLACK POWER in a land dominated by the unmerciful power of white intruders who murdered and all but exterminated the rightful owners, the American Indians? Black Power means that Black men want to have some control over their own lives, to have a respected voice in public affairs that affect them. We resent being a colonial people, treated as third-class citizens in our native land. We resent being forbidden to speak for ourselves, even in Black belts where we constitute as much as 85 percent of the population. We resent being deformed by a white man's mold in a degenerate white supremacy society that derides and belittles our African heritage and make us ashamed of our ethnic characteristics. Black Power is the vehicle by which we hope to reach a stage wherein we can be proud Black people without the necessity of an apology for our non-Anglo-Saxon features. The dominant society in racist America is reactionary, imperialist, racist, and decadent and we wish to disassociate ourselves from it. Black Power is a dissident force challenging the racist white power structure that is so heinously exterminating the people of Vietnam and threatening the world with nuclear destruction.

We have been victims of white racism for 400 years in the New World. We have been victims of racist barbarism for almost 200 years under the present form of government. Our people are slaughtered like swine on the main streets of racist America. Our churches and homes have been bombed. Our women raped with impunity. Our men have been emasculated. We are hated and murdered for no other reason than being born Black, and because we refuse to commend and love our savage oppressors, we are called racists.

We are oppressed people. Our objective is to destroy the hurtful stranglehold of our enemy oppressors. An opponent without the courage to designate his enemy by his true characteristics cannot expect to confront and defeat him. We propose to call our enemies what they are. We propose to rally our people and fight on this basis. We do not propose to mince our words for the sake of peaceful coexistence. It is a natural law that a humble lamb cannot peacefully coexist with a rabid wolf in close proximity.

Yes, we have some white Americans with us in our struggle. They are our true brothers. These revolutionaries understand and share our anger. They know it is justified. Their spirit is an extension of the glorious spirit of the great and noble antislavery fighter, John Brown. Yes, they too are a hated and persecuted minority people in Johnson's majority mob rule in Hitlerite jungle society. Yes, and like all other peoples, we have enemies in our ranks. We have Black traitors who practice treason for 30 pieces of silver. We have Black Judases, insensate running dogs for the Johnson administration and its racist white power structure. Like their white puppet masters, these Black puppets too have days that are numbered.

Our wrath is as intense against the Black lackeys of our white oppressors as it is against the white supremacy oppressors themselves. These mercenary Uncle Toms are the most vocal nonviolent peace peddlers in the storm centers of racist America today. The ghettoes are ablaze but they advocate peaceful submission to continued tyranny and oppression.

Johnson, the great civil rights advocate, the former senator from the racist state of Texas, who as senator voted against every civil rights bill that came before the U.S. Senate, claimed to be a modern-day Moses to Black Americans so long as they passively allowed themselves to be mauled and maimed by white supremacy brutes and thugs. But now, with brutal white supremacy Federal Power, he threatens those who defend themselves, their homes, and their women and children. Mr. Johnson, the big daddy white supremacist, would remind our people that we are a minority and the brutal racist white savages are a majority. Like his fellow-traveling Ku Klux Klansmen, he endeavors to frighten and intimidate us by the mere numbers of our eternal oppressors. In the same fashion that Mr. Johnson would like to intimidate the Chinese people with a massive arsenal of nuclear weapons, he is endeavoring to intimidate the Black American by alluding to great hordes of white supremacists who are ready and willing to exterminate our people. We say to Mr. Johnson that intimidation, violence, and brutality will not stop the raging fires in the people's liberation struggle. The only force on earth powerful enough to halt the flames engulfing ghettoes and main streets of racist America consists of fair play, brotherhood, equality, and justice.

We serve notice on big daddy Texas' Lyndon B. Johnson that he can no more intimidate the Afro-American people with his threat of unleashing his great hordes of maddog racists than he can intimidate the Chinese people with the threat of unleashing a nuclear attack. The day when brutal white racist oppressors and imperialists can frighten colored peoples into submission by threats of savage violence is gone forever!

We revolutionary Afro-Americans respond to Mr. Johnson and his Ku Klux Klan fraternity of white supremacy with the cry of BLACK POWER, FREEDOM NOW! JUSTICE! We proclaim our inalienable right to live as human beings and we shall implement our demand with blood and fire. Yes, Mr. Johnson, we are a minority but more than that we are an oppressed minority determined at all costs to be free, and we are resolved to pay any price, to perform any task, and to go to any length for our freedom.

Yes, we are a minority but we are a minority with the power of a righteous cause and justice on our side. We are a minority marching in the endless files of the great multiracial masses of the invincible anti-imperialist and antiracist forces of the world. For the benefit of Mr. Johnson, who puts so much stock in numbers, we remind him once again, in the words of a great people's leader a liberator whose words, thought, and teachings stand as impeccable in the turbulent winds of time as the mighty Rock of Gibraltar, yes, we remind him once again that our great leader and teacher Chairman Mao Tse-tung has said:

We are in the majority and they are in the minority. At most, they make up less than 10 percent of the three thousand million population of the world. I am firmly convinced that, with the support of more than 90 percent of the people of the world, the American Negroes will be victorious in their just struggle. The evil system of colonialism and imperialism arose and throve with the enslavement of Negroes and the trade in Negroes, and it will surely come to its end with the complete emancipation of the Black people.

Today, in the social jungle of racist America the rights of colored people are less respected than those of common street dogs. The law and the kangaroo courts of the so-called free world of "Christian" democracy protect the rights of common street dogs and other dumb animals, but there is not a single court of law that dispenses even-handed justice and unbiased constitutional and human rights to colored Americans. The long, brutal, and miserable plight of our people throughout the history of barbaric America encompasses one of the most shameful and savage chapters in the history of slavery and man's injustice to man.

The dominant class in racist America is one of the most hypocritical the world has ever seen. It captured the African in Africa, enslaved him, ripped his culture from him, raped him, reproduced from him, completely dehumanized him, and reduced him to the level of beast of burden and stamped him with the name Negro as a tribute to the white man's creation and invention of a new implement of agriculture and an instrument of labor. And, all the while, he promoted this brutal slavery, he proclaimed himself the architect of democracy and a Christian society. All the while, he brutally and savagely exterminated the American Indian and piously proclaimed Thanksgiving to his white god for being so generous in blessing him with the bounty of the Indian's rich land and paradise. He built a brutal imperialist prison wall around the peoples of Latin America and piously named it the protective Monroe Doctrine. He stretched his bloody hand to Asia and arrogantly called it an "Open Door Policy."

The Open Door Policy was the policy of an armed bandit at the door of a peaceful man. Today, the same bandit rapes and plunders the land in the Vietnam, murders defenseless women and children, and exterminates the people in the name of "free world Christian democracy."

The same bandit who exterminated and starved the American Indian on his own native soil now piously proclaims to practice charity to the nation of India in a hypocritical effort to use them in his campaign to subdue and enslave the peoples of Asia. What is the nature of his democracy? What does such a beastly, imperialist, racist savage know about democracy? Should not democracy, like charity, start first at home, and then spread abroad? What is the democracy of the Black American captives in the miserable ghettoes, in the cotton fields of Mississippi, battered by the savage policeman's club in Washington, D.C.? What is the democracy of the Puerto Ricans, of the Mexicans, and of the American Indians in racist America? Only the naivest can believe the empty words and promise of such a morally bankrupt charlatan.

Deceptive American white supremacy is personified by hypocrites like Bobby Kennedy, a sophisticated huckster and charlatan of the first magnitude who struts and sways into the hotbed of African white supremacy and colonialism, hugging and kissing

Black babies and masquerading as a great white father and savior of the Black Africans. Mr. Kennedy's actions in racist America are quite a contrast to his deceitful conduct in Africa. When Mr. Kennedy served as the attorney general of the USA, he was sworn to uphold the right of equal protection under law, yet he collaborated with the most barbaric racists in the nation. He entered into a "white gentleman's agreement" with the notorious racist governor of Mississippi, Ross Barnett. Defenseless and helpless Black women and children were bombed, gassed, clubbed, raped, and murdered on the main streets of racist America, and Mr. Kennedy is yet to punish a single white supremacist heathen transgressor. As attorney general, he did nothing about the fact that Africans were being beaten in the United States, even the diplomats assigned to the United Nations.

It is strange indeed how Mr. Kennedy can perform in the racist chorus of those who chant slogans of hatred, vilification, and dehumanization for Black people in America while proclaiming his pretended great love for Black humanity in Africa. Such is the nature of a deceptive and barbaric Yankee.

In America, Mr. Kennedy publicly proclaims himself to be opposed to Black nationalism. In his white supremacy logic, he calls it racism in reverse. Black nationalism is a survival reaction to white nationalism. White nationalism transcends religious, class, social, and political lines. The reason that no massive Black-white unity on a national scale exists today is that the white supremacy ruling class has poisoned the minds of white workers. Most white workers identify with their white imperialist rulers. White liberals insist on paternalism. Even bourgeois-minded so-called socialists are more and more identifying and grouping on a racial basis rather than on a class basis. We Afro-American revolutionaries have discovered that some so-called socialists we thought to be our comrades and class brothers have joined the international Ku Klux Klan fraternity for white supremacy and world domination. To our consternation, we have discovered that the bourgeois-orientated power structure of some socialist states, even one with a Black and white population, would prefer to preserve the white reactionary anticommunist power structure in racist America, their natural national enemy, then to see a just, democratic, fraternal socialist state brought about by the revolutionary action of oppressed blacks that would serve the best interests of all peoples and races. Like their Yankee counterparts that they love to ape so well, even to the point of emulating their racism, they are moving might and main to frustrate and defeat the revolutionary movements of the oppressed peoples throughout the world.

We of the Afro-American liberation movement resolutely condemn and oppose all counterrevolutionaries and purveyors of white supremacy, whether they cloak their treachery in the garb of Marxist-Leninist phraseology or the hideous bedsheets of the Ku Klux Klan and its phony Christian doctrine.

We who are engaged in the struggle for liberation and survival vehemently condemn the use of Black dehumanized troops as cannon fodder in a white man's war of imperialism in Vietnam. We oppose Johnson's vicious crusade to dehumanize, emasculate, and enslave the great Vietnamese people.

Black boys—from the slum housing of Black ghettoes, ill-educated in segregated schools, emasculated and dehumanized by police brutality and a savage white power structure—yes, Black boys who cannot find employment, Black boys who are victims of white racists who hate them because of the color of their skin—Black boys whose mothers, sisters, and loved ones are being savagely clubbed, gassed, raped, maimed, lynched, and railroaded to prison in racist kangaroo courts simply for begging and praying for elementary justice are forced to share foxholes and shed their blood alongside racist Negro haters in Vietnam, who like in racist America refuse to fraternize with them in places of amusement in Tokyo and Saigon. Even out of proportion to the self-styled master race, vast numbers of Black soldiers are forced to suffer and die in that vain effort to prolong and extend the brutal racist white man's imperialism. They are forced to suffer and die in the cause of a racist power structure that is as much the enemy of Black people in America as it is the people of peace and freedom-loving Vietnam.

And why do we call the massive Ku Klux Klan type action in Vietnam a racist white man's war of imperialism while many Black men are fighting there? It is because in racist America no Black man is part of Johnson's policy-making clique. The United State is governed by white power. The Pentagon is a white-dominated repressive arm of a ruthless elite white power structure. Wall Street is an exclusive club of the great white chiefs of business and industry. Black Americans are resisting the racist and imperialist lily-white power structure. How can a people who are fighting and dying simply to wrest the most basic of human rights from an intransigent and tyrannical power structure be said to be partners of that power structure and willing participants in its racist and imperialist ventures and crimes against humanity?

The United States today is a fascist society more brutal than any the world has ever known. It has all but exterminated a whole people. It has robbed and raped an entire continent with impunity. It has divided the peoples of the world into national factions and set them against themselves and their brothers. With no more authority than the wave of its bloody imperialist hand, it has abrogated the right of self-determination of small nations. It has appointed and crowned itself both king and armored knight of the whole universe. It threatens the globe with annihilation. It is a supercolonial power that is colonializing the colonials.

The world-famed and brilliant philosopher Lord Bertrand Russell has justifiably stated that racist America has exterminated more Black people than Hitler exterminated Jews in Nazi Germany. Lord Russell and many other fair-minded humanists throughout the world have justifiably stated that the U.S. military aggression in Vietnam is executed in a more cruel and barbarous manner than even the horrible campaigns of aggression, genocide, and conquest carried out by Hitler's fascist Germany.

Yet, there is a mighty tendency, promoted by the sinister American devil himself, to engender more sympathy and fraternalism for the so-called "good reasonable Americans" than for the wretched victims of vicious and brutal U.S. imperialism. The U.S. constitutes one of the greatest fascist threats ever to cast its ugly shadow across the face of the earth. When the butchers of Nazi Germany were on the plunder, the world cry was "Crush Nazism!" "Crush the Fascist Power Structure!" "Crush Germany!" Total war was unleashed without deference to any who may be considered "good Germans" inside Nazi Germany. No sane person opposed to fascism pleaded for a soft policy toward Nazi Germany or pleaded for victims to wait for deliverance through the benevolence of "good German workers and liberals." Racist America didn't give a damn about sparing the good Japanese people when they dropped their horrible and devastating atom bombs.

What is the motive of those who plead for the exemption of liberal Americans, whose feigned liberalism merely serves as a cloak and shield around the naked power of savage and racist U.S. imperialism? The time is fast approaching when the so-called good reasonable American must make a decision either to overtly side with American chauvinism and jingoism or to take a resolute anti-imperialist and antiracist stand that will be a firm basis for a just and lasting world peace.

We who are brutally oppressed and victimized cannot forever afford to spare the fortress of social reaction and tyranny because there are allegedly silent dissenters within its gates. Those who are without righteous cause of the oppressed must be prepared to suffer the consequences of the gathering storm of the violent and turbulent winds of retribution. A good man who is silent and inactive in times of great injustice and oppression is no good man at all. He is no ally to freedom and justice but is a silent partner to tyranny and condemnation. He does not deserve exemption from the condemnation and the vengeance of those whom his silence allows to be victimized. The myth of the good reasonable American who is yet to be heard is a ruse perpetrated by the psychological arm of the imperialist forces of tyranny. It is one minute to zero in on racist America. Four hundred bloody and gruesome years have passed. For 400 years, our good silent partners have remained silent and inactive. Time is running out and they stand at the dividing line still beseeching patience, still beseeching the slave to leave his fate to his silent friends ever infected with inertia. They plead for deference on behalf of the good people who have yet to stand at one camp. We call to them to separate themselves from the devil's legions. We inform them that they have not 400 more years to decide but one minute before the hour of zero, before the Armageddon between the slave master and the slave.

Once again, in closing, let me thank our great leader and teacher, the architect of people's warfare, Chairman Mao Tse-tung, for his great and inspiring statement in support of our struggle. And to our great Chinese brothers and true revolutionaries throughout the world, we revolutionary Afro-Americans vow that we shall take the torch of freedom and justice into the streets of racist America and we shall set the last great stronghold of Yankee imperialism ablaze with our battle cry of Black Power! FREEDOM! FREEDOM! FREEDOM! NOW OR DEATH! For our people, for our country, and for our compatriots throughout the world, we shall reclaim the nobility of the American Revolution. We shall raise our flag in honor, true peace, and brotherhood to all the world!

Long live the People's Republic of China!

Long live Chairman Mao Tse-tung!

Long live the people's resistance to imperialism, racism, and tyranny!

Long live the militant friendship between the Chinese and revolutionary American people!

LETTERS TO U.S. OFFICIALS ABOUT THE BANNING OF THE CRUSADER,

September 21, 1967, Peking, China[3]

Mr. Lawrence F. O'Brien, U.S. Postmaster General
Dear Sir:

According to international press reports your department has banned my newsletter, *The Crusader*, from the U.S. mails and has ordered Hong Kong puppet authorities to do likewise. If this is correct, will you please be so civil as to inform me specifically, formally and directly why such repressive, undemocratic, unconstitutional, vindictive, and punitive action is being taken against such a small personal journal that uncompromisingly advocates the abolition of brutal racism, defense against terror, resistance of imperialism, violent resistance to tyranny, and struggle for a more just and peaceful world society? If, in Washington, there is still some feigned official belief in freedom of speech and of the press, then even America's consistency of hypocrisy dictates that your office clearly delineates the nature and extent of such ban and specify its charges and the reasons for this fascist-like action that is so inimical to freedom of the press. I, at least, expect to be formally informed as to what laws, codes, rules and regulations, both national and international, you have so summarily and arbitrarily acted under.

Yours for Freedom of Press and Speech
Robert F. Williams

LETTER TO NORTH CAROLINA'S LEGAL COUNSEL ABOUT THE KIDNAPPING CASE

December 2, 1967, Peking, China[4]

Dear Mr. Boyette:

Mr. Ragsdale, legal Counsel to Governor Dan K. Moore, has been kind and considerate enough to suggest that I direct legal questions pertaining to my case to you. Subsequent to Mr. Ragsdale's advice, I feel compelled to inconvenience you by making the following requests:

1. Please inform me of the specific statutes of North Carolina that I was charged with violating and under which I was indicted in Monroe on August 26, 1961.
2. Please inform me of all charges and specific statutes that I am presently charged with violating.
3. Please inform me if any new or additional warrants have been issued against me since the original one was issued in August 1961.
4. Inasmuch as I expect to return on my own volition and feel that it is imperative that I make preparations now to assure the realization of bond: I sincerely request that you assist me in getting a bond set in order that I may raise the money before my return. I have no contacts in Union County wherein I may feel certain of meeting

bond requirements. Consequently, it is necessary for me to make an immediate appeal for bond pledges and legal defense funds.

I feel that it will be in the best interest of all parties concerned to execute an early as possible disposition of this racial and politically inspired case of vengeance and harassment. It is in this light that I trust to find you as kind, considerate and cooperative as Mr. Ragsdale's letter indicates Governor Moore to be.

Yours in justice,
Robert F. Williams

ROBERT WILLIAMS SENDS A LETTER TO AN ASSOCIATE, May 18, 1969, Peking, China[5]

Dear Brother Benn:

Both your letters have been received. Sorry, that time only permits this brief note. The brothers over there who should have been host to the Black Unit Conference pleaded four of the men. They got cold feet. But we cannot afford to give up on the idea of uniting and educating our people universally. We must keep working toward this end. We are leaving for the Black man's hell, United States. Mabel and the boys will no doubt make it there before I will keep in touch and contact you from there. Give my regards to all the brothers and sisters and tell them to keep on pushing. Mabel and the boys will write as soon as they have established a new address. They send their best regards to all. Best wishes for freedom,

Robert F. Williams

FEDERAL BUREAU OF INVESTIGATION CENTRAL INTELLIGENCE AGENCY MEMORANDUMS TO THE STATE DEPARTMENT DOCUMENTING A RICHARD GIBSON INTERNATIONAL NEWS REPORT ABOUT ROBERT WILLIAMS AS PRESIDENT-IN-EXILE OF THE REVOLUTIONARY ACTION MOVEMENT (RAM)[6]

October 15, 1966

Richard Gibson Reports International News, Robert F. Williams Second Exile. Afro-American Leader in Exile Leaves Cuba for China. Robert F. Williams, chairman-in-exile of the militant all-Black Revolutionary Action Movement in the United States, has left Fidel Castro's Cuba for what he calls the "Second Exile" in China. Former president of the Union County, North Carolina branch of the National Association for the Advancement of Colored People (NAACP), Williams, who is now 41 years old, fled to Cuba in 1961 when local police and the Federal Bureau of Investigation sought to arrest him on charges of kidnapping a white couple during a racial clash in Williams's hometown of Monroe, N.C. In those days, one of the proudest boasts of Cuba's revolutionary leaders was that they had wiped out racial discrimination on the island, and it certainly seemed to be true. Although few Black Cubans were among the leaders of the revolution, the revolution quickly gained support from the country's large Black population. And in the United States, it was no accident that Fidel Castro received an enthusiastic welcome from the Blacks of Harlem in 1960, while anti-Communist whites picketed everywhere else, he went to New York City. It was no accident that Robert F. Williams fled to Cuba to continue his struggle. He had been one of the founders of the now-defunct Fair Play for Cuba Committee in the United States. Eight of whose original 30 founding members were Negroes, including such well-known writers as James Baldwin, Julian Mayfield, and John Killens. Such Negro participation in a movement not directly related to the civil rights struggle was virtually unprecedented. After his arrival in Havana, where he was joined shortly thereafter by his wife, Mabel and their two young sons, Williams resumed publication of his monthly newsletter, The Crusader, in April 1962 and at length persuaded the Cuban government to allow him to broadcast to the United States several times weekly over Cuba's Radio Progreso. He called his program "Radio Free Dixie" and its tone was set in Williams's first broadcast on July 27, 1962, the day after grandiose celebrations of the ninth anniversary of the beginning of the Cuban revolutionary struggle against the Batista regime. "The spirit of the 26th of July is no longer just a spirit for Cuba or the Cuban people," Williams declared. "It is a spirit for all of Latin America, for Asia, for Africa. Yes, and for the downtrodden and oppressed black people of the U.S.A. whose lives are valued less than common street dogs." But on August 8, 1966, Williams remarked bittered at a rally in Peking:

> Some so-called Socialist, we thought to be comrades and class brothers, have joined the international Ku Klux Klan fraternity for white supremacy world domination. To our consternation, we have discovered that the bourgeois-oriented power structure of some socialist states, even one with a black and white population, would prefer to preserve the white reactionary anti-communist power structure in racist America, their natural national enemy, than to see a just, democratic, fraternal socialist state brought about by the revolutionary action of oppressed blacks that would serve the best interests of all people of all races. Like their Yankee counterparts that they love to ape so well, even to the point of emulating their racism, there are moving might and main to frustrate and defeat the revolutionary movements of the oppressed peoples throughout the world.

The rally had been called to celebrate the third anniversary of Mao Tse-tung's "Statement Calling on the People of the World to Unite to Oppose Racial Discrimination by U.S. Imperialism and Support the American Negroes in Their Struggle Against Racial Discrimination," made on August 12, 1963, in reply to a request by Williams. Although given extensive coverage in the international press, The Worker and other publications of the U.S. Communist Party ignored Mao's statement. Williams had never been close to the CPUSA, and the party's leaders made no secret of their fear that the Black militancy that Williams and the late Malcolm X were advocating might destroy forever the party's lingering hopes for a "Negro Labor Alliance" that might eventually dominate the American political scene. In the years between 1962, when Williams arrived in Havana, and 1966, when he left for China, there had been occasional signs of persisting racial antagonism in Cuba. There remains open social prejudice against mixed marriages. Black lower-ranking Cuban army officers said to be sympathetic to the militant Chinese position in the Sino-Soviet dispute reportedly had serious difficulties with the regime in 1964. Carlos Moore, a young Afro-Cuban of Jamaican origin, violently attacked the Cuban government in an article in the Paris-based French-speaking African review, *Presence Africaine*, charging that "there has been no revolution-which explains the total absence or proletarians and Afro-Cubans in the affairs of the dictatorship of the proletarians and the government of the people." By this, the openly anti-Communist Moore alleged that the

> revolution was merely another attempt by white Cubans to maintain their tradition hegemony over the blacks on the island. In a letter to me on September 7, 1965, Williams categorically rejected Moore's extremist views, but Williams added that Moore had "got too much truth mixed in with his exaggerations for comfort.

Williams added: "a lot of things I have tried to conceal, but the case looks hopeless. It seems that a certain group here is trying to compete with Mississippi." Williams visited China twice before deciding to move there. His sons were sent to a Chinese school before then. When he did ask for permission to leave Cuba, he was prevented from doing so for many months. And his Cuban host suggested that he ought to return to the United States, despite the warrant for his arrest on kidnapping charges. Reaching China at last, Williams set down some of his reasons for leaving Cuba in an anguished 16-page, 8,550-word letter to Fidel Castro on August 28, 1966. But the Cuban Embassy in Peking refused to accept the letter for transmission to Havana and it was sent by ordinary airmail. In October, receiving no reply from Havana, Williams released the text of the letter. Declaring that he would "always be grateful to the Cuban people" for assisting him to escape from the United States, Williams told the Cuban Premier he was writing because he could not believe that those around Castro had informed him truly of the "ignominious experiences that I encountered while living in Cuba." Outlining in detail more than a dozen specific grievances, Williams declared that he hoped "these demoralizing and agonizing experiences do not indicate a new fascist tendency on the part of the Cuban Revolution. The only complaint that I make to you is on behalf of my people, the Afro-American people who are engaged in a struggle for survival, liberation, equality and freedom inside the U.S.A. I make this complaint because your government has allowed saboteurs to sabotage our struggle and have set us back for a number of years and have allowed them to frustrate and demoralize our people in our struggle against our oppressive enemy." Williams said that many promises made to him by Cuban officials had not been kept and many of his legitimate requests had been refused. He was never allowed to open an information office in Havana to tell the world of "the revolutionary potential of the Afro-American struggle." He was restricted to using only the progressively weaker long-wave facilities of Radio Progresso and never permitted to broadcast over a short wave on Radio Havana, the official government station. Even the promise $200 a month to purchase records and publications for use on the program was not kept. And when listeners began to donate records and other materials, much of this was stolen in the Cuban Post Office and even from the pouches of the Cuban Foreign Ministry, Williams charges. Unlike other Americans living in Cuba, Mrs. Williams was never authorized to visit Canada on business for her husband. Williams remarks:

> I later discovered that this was just a plot to try to wreck our struggle and to crush our organization and was done in conjunction with forces inside the U.S., including the U.S. Communist Party which was opposed to our method of struggle, and which advocated a policy of non-violence and support of Reverend Martin Luther King."

There were increasing difficulties in getting *The Crusader* published. "There was always some excuse about paper, or we had to go through a lot of red tape which would make it impossible to publish some issues while others came out extremely late," Williams writes. He asks that, when a so-called "October 1965 Special Edition" of The Crusader was forged and distributed, containing "an attack on the Soviet Union and surreptitiously anti-China and designed to make my exile in Cuba difficult," he had no cooperation from the Cuban Communist Party in making a public announcement about the forgery. Moreover, mail was held up or even returned to senders. Long-distance telephone callers were sometimes told that Williams was unavailable. When Williams requested permission for some members of his Revolutionary Action Movement and Negro journalist to visit Cuba for talks with him, the request was refused, although some of these persons had already traveled as far as Mexico City and Prague en route to Cuba. When the Tricontinental Conference was held in Havana in January 1966, not a single American Negro newsman was permitted to attend and Williams himself would not have been allowed into the conference if some friendly African delegates and a Puerto Rican delegate had not protested against his exclusion. White American journalists were present, however. "The conference was being manipulated specially to keep Afro-Americans out and this was being done by officials of the Cuban government and not by the conference as a hold," Williams charges. Williams tells at length how Cuban officials refused to investigate his charges that a Tanzanian newsman, D.H. Mansur, had received $1,335 and a coded message from him to be sent to some Afro-American people working in the struggle to help them out. Neither the money nor the message ever reached New York, Williams maintains. He also claims that "secret organizational information" that he had filed with a high-ranking Cuban official, Comandante Pineiro, "was later cynically cited to me by an official of one of the so-called free world embassies in Havana." When he was asked to make a speaking tour in Sweden, the Cuban government refused to allow him to travel there. And he says he was so criticized for receiving a small stipend in Pesos as the government's support of me and my activities on behalf of the Afro-American people, that he refused to continue accepting the stipend. The only Cuban official who "showed any genuine interest in our struggle and who had really promised to help was Comandante Che Guevara," Williams writes. He recalls how Guevara had told him that he would be returning to Havana from a trip to the interior of Cuba in 30 days and would help Williams then. Guevara said he was not leaving the country. "My interview with Comandante Che Guevara was one day before the letter that you read from him over the radio and television was dated," Williams tells Castro. Williams adds: "I find this hard to believe ... The reason that I bring this up at this time is because I wondered if Che did not meet foul play in the interior and that may be the same people who contrived his disappearance maybe planning to do away with you in the same manner." In conclusion, Williams explains he is writing to Fidel Castro because of his personal obligation and loyalty to the Cuban Revolution "and I hope that I will be more fortunate in reaching you than I was in the more than four years that I resided in Cuba. I hope at least this time you will feel that what I have to say is important enough for a personal response and I hope you will not commit this very important and serious matter to the hands of the same racist, degenerate, counterrevolutionary agents of U.S. imperialism who are responsible for frustrating and subverting that part of the Afro-American freedom struggle that was being conducted from the revolutionary territory of Cuba." Robert Williams still waits in Peking from an answer from Fidel Castro or any other official of the Cuban government. That silence itself marks a turning point in the Cuban revolution and certainly the end of the special relationship of Cuba's present leaders with Black militants in their neighbor to the North.

October 11, 1966

Sugar's Alleged Involvement with the Revolutionary Action Movement

Information has been received from a confidential source of insufficient contact to determine reliability that Max Stanford, Field Chairman of the Revolutionary Action Movement, had recently made several statements indicating the involvement of Sugar with the Revolutionary Action Movement. The Revolutionary Action Movement is an all-Negro, Marxist-Leninist-oriented organization which follows the Chinese Communist line and leadership of Robert F. Williams, a Negro fugitive from justice in voluntary exile in Cuba, who advocates achieving Negro rights by violence if necessary, including guerrilla warfare. According to the source, Stanford stated that the contact man between the Revolutionary Action Movement in the United States and Williams is Sugar in Paris, France. Stanford reportedly stated Sugar passed on messages from Williams and would be the man contacted by whoever is designated as a courier by Stanford to go to Communist China. The purpose of this trip is to obtain one million dollars that Williams allegedly has available for use by the Revolutionary Action Movement.

LETTERS BY RICHARD T. GIBSON AND ROBERT F. WILLIAMS, AND BY GIBSON TO HIS MARXIST LENINIST COMRADES ABOUT ROBERT F. WILLIAMS

October 15, 1966, London[7]

Dear Comrade,

Sometime ago I asked comrade A. Manchamde, secretary of the Britain-Vietnam Solidarity Front, to send you the bulletin of that organization which seeks to broaden its international relations. Any assistance is something like-minded comrades in Sweden and elsewhere in Scandinavia would be greatly appreciated. The Marxist-Leninist comrades who formed the RVSP did so when it proved impossible to collaborate on a principled basis with the Trotskyites-led Bertrand Russell Peace Foundation here in London. The bulletin explains in detail the events that caused both British and foreign Marxist-Leninists to walk out of the Trotskyites "Vietnam Solidarity Conference" on June 4–5th. It has saddened us to see that these same unprincipled rogues still seek to misuse world sympathy for the Vietnamese people in their struggle against U.S. imperialism for their own purposes. They now propose to bring their Vietnam War Crimes Tribunal to Sweden, having already lost the initial sympathy of the French government because of their crude publicity and improper behavior in France. The BVSF still hopes that, despite these scoundrels, the Tribunal will be a success wherever it is held. We hope that aware and conscientious comrades such as you will be able to oblige these people to follow a more correct path in the future, serving the cause of the freedom fighters of Vietnam. If you have any information concerning the activities of these people in Sweden, we would greatly appreciate hearing from you. Comrade Franz Strohl in Vienna recently gave me your address and I pasted it on to comrade Manohanda here because of the urgency of the situation vis-a-vis the Russell Foundation. But I also hope in time to meet with you and other Swedish comrades on behalf of Robert F. Williams, the African-American leader now in exile in China. Williams's hopes to be able to visit Sweden for speaking engagements later this year, despite the fact that he is wanted as a "fugitive from justice" by the U.S. government. Any assistance you can give him would be greatly appreciated. I hope that perhaps you already know of Williams and his courageous stand in leading Black people in North America in an armed struggle. I hope you are working on the revision and updating of *Negroes with Guns* for Tore's Swedish Publisher. The same revised manuscript could be translated into Italian and German. The important thing about a revision of that book is that Marzani could not claim any rights whatsoever. Speaking of Marzani, Frances Kelly, the Monthly Review representative here, wants to look at the manuscript of Radio Free Dixie for possible publication by their firm. They are certainly better than Marzani, and they are honest, which he is not; she thinks that Marc Schleifer who has dropped everybody new that he has turned Muslim and lives in Jordan—made a deal with Marzani about the unauthorized French translation by Maspero in Paris. Too late now to cry over spilled milk, but it is most strange that Maspero could go to Habana for the Tri-Continental and sit in the same hall with you without coming over to tell you that he was about to publish the French translation of *Negroes with Guns*. I hope that, eventually, the Chinese comrades will bring out a new addition to that book in a cheap pocket edition designed for distribution in Africa. That would be most helpful. Please let me hear from you soon about the P.O. Box even if you don't need the address immediately. Remember, there is no problem with using this address. And do let me hear from you about the trip, yours and the one I proposed. Sarah joins me in sending you and Mabel our very best wishes.

Yours in the struggle,
Richard

LETTERS EXCHANGED BETWEEN RICHARD GIBSON AND ROBERT WILLIAMS

October 17, 1966, Peking, China[8]

Dear Richard,

I have decided to hold up on P.O. Box for a while until something can be straightened out on this end and in the States. For the first few months, *The Crusader* will have limited circulation. At this time mail is coming through quite well. However, it is going to be very difficult to operate so fall from the struggle. The man is making some splitting moves over there and I want to study them for a while before I put all of my cards on the table. I am sending the introduction to Radio Free Dixie and a biographical sketch for information that you can draw from. I did not like Marzani's at all. If a publisher decides to publish, I would like to include some of the newspaper comments from the United States about the broadcasts and especially from the Los Angeles Herald Examiner 1964 which carried the Red Banner headline; "CUBA RADIOS U.S. NEGROES KILL." I had hoped to have a complete program format by now, but my things did not arrive via ship from Havana as yet. The format is for an hour-long program with music (jazz and protest), items read from the U.S. press, news as compiled, and edited by me, and so on. These things should arrive soon; however, you should not wait. Push the project as much as possible. If we can get the book out, I am sure it will sell. You know the struggle is a long way from being over. Push the Italian publisher. Use the enclosed letter to hold them to their request. Such a book will also be very important to the struggle at this time. It will be important to get it published in Europe first. This publisher also has a United States branch. Don't let politics stand in the way. It is important to get it out. Signed yours for Black Power!

Rob

October 21, 1966, London[9]

Dear Rob

This note is to confirm receipt of your letter of the 17th and its enclosures. I was really flabbergasted by the Mondadori letter. A friend spoke with them in Rome long ago and they showed no interest, but they probably knew nothing about your contact with Maria Servo of their New York office. I will do everything possible to push this. They are very big firms, and I don't expect any political problems. Unfortunately, I did not know of this before talking with Mrs. Maria Regis of Edizioni Oriente in Milan. Since she was very cagey about committing herself, and as she does not run a big publishing house at all, it is far more in your interests to have Mondadori publish the book, so, if you see her in Peking use your discretion in dealing with her. I will try to get a speedy answer from the other and bigger Italian firm. Tell Mrs. Regis that you understand another publisher has expressed interest in the book and that she should keep in touch with me. This will permit us to give the book to Edizioni Oriente, should the more attractive Mondadori deal fall through. With publishers, one can never tell what they'll do until the book is actually in your hands. And not even then, I'm quite convinced that Marzani sabotaged the sale of *Negroes with Guns* to please his revisionist buddies, for example. I'll see to it that the open letter to Fidel gets the attention it deserves. So, the Cuban Embassy wouldn't even transmit it to Havana! They certainly have gone down in the world. Your idea about the press clippings is very good, so please do collect and copy them for distribution to potential publishers. The biographical sketch was just what was needed. Now, if only you can get some good pictures of yourself to me. Sorry always to keep asking you things, but these things are essential to mount a good press campaign, as you know. Whenever you are ready to start up The Crusader, you can use this address. I don't know what you mean by the man "making splitting moves" in the States but holding an organization together in that pigsty is no easy job. Jacques thought it might be a good idea for us to discuss this and other problems before your proposed trip up North. He can make most of the arrangements on this end for me once he has a note from you that you would like to see me there. And it would be a wise thing for me to case the scene up North before your trip or before we meet so any information would be helpful or should I just work everything out with Tore'? Are you sure he agrees with your political position, especially now that you are where you are? I have no reason to doubt him, but I would like to be sure. Anyway, I can manage to get to see him as soon as you give me the necessary details. Concerning my Austrian friend, although he doesn't expect to see me, I can arrange to see him whenever necessary, especially if you have anything of a natural that he ought to carry for me. I am doing some more work for Jacques Grippa and he will certainly make it possible for me to get to that friend, so if there is anything, please give it to him and write to me when I should pick it up at his place. Now, about the program, if there is anything I can do here to assist, please let me know. We are not rich here, but funds and other material assistance can be found, provided we have a bit of time. By the way, your FOREWORD to the book is excellent. I would hate to see it cut by anyone. Keep up the great work! Give my regards to Lionel when you see him next. I am sending the stuff he asked for in his last letter. Sarah joins me in sending love to you and Mabel.

With you in the Struggle
Richard

October 28, 1966, London[10]

Dear Rob,

Enclosed is a letter from the British Post Office concerning my request for a P.O. Box for *The Crusader*, plus a circular explaining the curious British idea of just what such a box is. They gave me quite a runaround, and made me finally write a formal letter of application and this is the result. I am not out any money yet, but I want to know if you want me to get the box or not. I do hope, in any case, that you will start up *The Crusader* again soon. There is, of course, no need to get involved in organizational feuds, and I admit a lot of feuding is going on in the States among our people but stick at present to your really important message—the necessity of fighting U.S. imperialism. Building the fighting organization to carry out that task is another matter and perhaps it's best done discreetly, but your voice is needed! You can be the key spokesman for Black freedom fighters. You virtually are already, but the plots of the revisionists in Cuba kept you quiet for too long. Your August 8th speech was a good new beginning and the letter to Fidel was an excellent continuation, but the brothers need to hear more of your views on topical issues of the struggle and you should be recognized more generally in Africa and Asia as the leading spokesman for our people. That means publicity and plenty of it, as you well know. I have already contacted Mondadori and am continuing other contacts on the book project. Much more remains to be done. I am certain there must be exciting times in Havana, but I am hoping that you will try to remain calm and out of the fray. There are possibilities for you to visit Belgium, Holland, and France, as well as some African countries, after your speaking tour in Sweden. It grieves me that we have to move so slowly at this end, but I am dependent on Hokanson and he is not very efficient or dynamic. Alas! Sweden, nonetheless, remains the very best country, a neutral, non-NATO country for you to visit first. I know it is not easy, but you must make every effort to keep in touch with me. If you think that some publicity might help the prospects for your tour, please cable me immediately and I will take care of it. Otherwise, I will be discreet. But you have only said in the cable that you give full approval or are completely in agreement with my proposed itinerary and plans for me to go ahead. Sara joins me in sending you and Mabel our love. Taker care and be of good cheer.

Your friend,
Richard

November 18, 1966, London[11]

Dear Rob,

I am worried about whether you have been getting all of my letters. Please write immediately upon receipt of this note. I have the chance to get to Sweden, and also to Denmark, and Norway, at the beginning of December and need to hear from you quickly. Jacques Grippa is also back in Brussels, and I will be going over there to take him the translations that I have been working on for him. Tore' writes that he is leaving Sweden on a trip to the Canary Islands with his Cuban girlfriend, who was finally allowed to leave Havana, but will be back in Sweden at the beginning of December, ready to receive me. I am in touch with a number of individuals and organizations and hope to get "absolute" assurance concerning your security while there. We must take no chances. The Yankees will stop at nothing to destroy their enemies and there is no use pretending to ourselves that they are only tea-drinking liberals. One question you must answer is: Are you willing to visit Norway and Denmark to speak, if that is possible? They are NATO countries, and I am not sure it is possible, but I will check out the possibility if you are interested. Would you be willing to spend three weeks to a month in Scandinavia? I will need your letter to make arrangements by visiting to discuss this trip and the situation in the States with you before you set off for Sweden, so write soon. Tore suggests January or February as the best months for the speaking tour. That seems right to me but get yourself some very warm clothing ready as it is damned cold in those parts.

With you in the struggle,
Richard

February 27, 1967, Peking[12]

Dear Richard,

I hope things are going o.k. on that end at this time. We are doing o.k. here. The Cultural Revolution is still on the move, but it is more penetrating and better organized. I am sure that after this first stage is over many changes will come about that will be very helpful to the international revolutionary forces. I received the tape from Watts. Thanks a million. I hope you have received my earlier letter informing you that the idea of combining Radio Free Dixie and Negroes with Guns is a good one and that I hope it will be carried through soon. If it is done in English, we can get many people in the States to push it. We can also get some ads in the Afro & left press. It should be done as soon as possible because I am sure this is going to be a very hot year in the U.S. The modern revolutionist, liberals, and some other leftist groups have started a campaign to undermine my influence in the ghettoes and on the international scene. Soon you should receive a money order for about $130 or $140. American dollars (or equivalent in British currency). Will you please try to send the records listed herein? If you cannot get these same titles get the latest available by the same artists. If you know of any social content or protest, send them. If you have to order them through the stores there, it will be o.k. because I can wait for them (not too long though). Is it possible to send them air expressed collect from there/ If so, send them that way. Sincerely, Rob

P.S. Could you please also send 2 cans of dental adhesive powder (FASTEETH) for dental plates? Mabel sends best regards to Sarah and the children.

March 18, 1967, London[13]

Dear Rob,

This is a hasty note to let you and Mabel know that the Bank of China has sent me the money for the records. I will start hunting down what you want next week and will send off the first batch to you soon thereafter. I will ensure the parcels and send them air parcel post. By the way, I received 54-19-2 from the bank. Rest assured; I will give you a strict accounting of the amount spent. Please, please me hear from you concerning the Swedish trip. Our friends must know now if anything is to be planned. Tore Hokanson writes to me very anxiously and I know the other comrades and friends are also very concerned. If the time is not ripe the visit can be postponed, but again please try to pick a tentative date now, say in the early Fall. June or July might be possible, but I don't think the students will be around then. And remember this will be a good opportunity for brothers from the States over for some serious discussions, so they must be informed as well and tickets provided. As Sweden is neutral ground and we do have some substantial friends, the Americans won't be able to do much to stop anybody. And the security problem will not be too difficult. The main problem will be the reliability of some of our own brothers, who-alas!-are not known for their silence. Speaking of noise, you probably heard of the fuss caused by James Baldwin and Ossie Davis, quitting *Liberator* and accusing the mag of "anti-Semitism" because of two articles published a year ago. I thought the pieces were very tactless, to say the least, but I know the reality that they were attempting to describe. However, unless one tries Marxist terms, one always falls into the net of seeming anti-Jewish when talking about petty shopkeepers in the Black ghettoes. The disgusting thing is that *Freedomways*, a publication wholly financed and edited by the CPUSA, should have published Baldwin's and Davis's letters in a general attack on *Liberator*. (Esther Jackson, editor of *Freedomways*, is the wife of James Jackson, the Black revisionist stooge editor of *The Worker* and a leading anti-China figure). In any case, please remember that *Freedomways* does not represent the Black liberation movement but is just another loudspeaker (for Black dupes) of the American revolutionist. They are certainly no friends of our, and certainly not of you as the leading Black militant spokesman. Did the parcel of denture powder reach you safely? Please remember to confirm receipt of parcels. A postcard will do. Finally, remember that I can use photos of you in China. For instance, the story about your Peoples' Daily interview could have well been accompanied by photo, when I sent out my report. I can make copies of any good glossy photos here. I need photos of you alone and of Mabel and perhaps a good family shot with the boys, to show people you don't eat babies for breakfast and dine on white folk's innards! Seriously, a photo can often make a story travel twice as far and your interview was great ammunition in the battle against our enemies, especially those who claim they are Marxist-Leninist. With you in the struggle, Richard

March 27, 1967, Peking, China[14]

Dear Richard,

I received your letter and the adhesive powder. Thanks a million for sending it. I am just sending off a note because I forgot to ask you to send me four or five (4 or 5) copies of Ralph Ginzburg's, *100 Years of Lynching* I am still working on the addition to the book. It should be finished in a few days. Once it is out it should sell quite well. I have just heard from RAM that the USCP, PL, SWP, National Guard Group, and the white left in general have mounted a campaign to try to destroy my image in the states and to sabotage all of my work. This makes me feel that perhaps I am having some effect which I have not realized until now. It is good that the masses in the Ghetto are the first ones to realize what is going on. If they expect me to roll over and play dead because I live in a socialist country, they are sadly mistaken. If you cannot send the recordings collect, and the air cargo is too expensive, then it will be o.k. to send them by sea. Please also see if you can get some anti-static cleaner, a silicone formula for stereo and hi-fi records. The one that we have been using carries the brand name of RECOTON and is manufactured by Recoton Corp., Long Island, New York. If you cannot get that particular brand, please try to get a substitute. It is a liquid cleaner in a small plastic bottle with sponge. Thanks in advance. Respectfully, Rob

April 17, 1967, Peking, China[15]

Dear Richard,

I received your telegram. I have not received any reply from Hans. I don't know if he received my letter or not. Anyway, since I don't have any assurance of security, we had better cancel it again for the time being. I am sure the Fall of the year will be better and by that time things should be very hot in the U.S. I am sure that after the long hot upcoming summer, there will be heightened interest in the U.S. race issue. I am working on the final draft of *Negroes with Guns*.

I hope it will turn out o.k. Aside from the other books I mentioned, I need a copy of *The Wretched of the Earth*. I haven't been able to secure a copy of it. Have you been able to get any accurate information from Cuba? What really happened to Raul Castro? It appears that the Cuban Revolution is going from bad to worse. I expect to hear very bad news from there most any time despite the fact that the U.S. left is trying to snow everybody about what is going on there. *Monthly Review* claims that Cuba is moving left. What a joke? They must be covering for the U.S. State Dept. Best wishes to all. Sincerely, Rob

May 17, 1967, Peking, China[16]

Dear Richard,

At last, I am enclosing the addition to *Negroes with Guns*. Perhaps Grippa should seriously consider changing the title of the entire book. However, it depends on what he thinks may be Marzani's reaction. After constantly writing and telegraphing him (Marzani) since 1963, and having Conrad to threaten legal action, the bit about him in the last *Crusader* brought a response. He avoided legal action by insisting that I appear in court to testify. Now he is crying the blues because he says I am smearing him. His statement for royalties amounts to $142.00. Can you imagine this? For a new title I would suggest:
    AMERICA IS THE BLACK MAN'S BATTLEGROUND
    AFRO-AMERICANS WITH GUNS
    Or ARMED BLACK POWER

He can suit himself. I hope he will be able to use this new material and is successful in publishing the book as soon as possible. Photographs will be sent at a later date under separate cover. I have requested them from Hsinhua. Sincerely, Robert F. Williams

    P. S. Mabel received the package you sent. Thanks a million. If you can possibly locate a record on the Elektra label by Josh White ELK 158-A called Chain Gang Songs, please send it to me. Elektra Records, 2 Dean St. London W1

May 24, 1967, Peking, China[17]

Dear Richard,

Your letter and the recordings have been received. I also received a letter from Tore. I am not in contact with the people from Albania here. However, one of the Americans who made it to their last congress wrote me a letter explaining their great interest in our struggle. He gave them quite a bit of information on it. He seems to be very close to them, so I have asked him to sound them out on the idea. I haven't heard anything from him yet. I won't say anything to them on this end until I hear from him. He sent the paper he submitted to them on the U.S. race problem and asked for my opinion. I'll write Conrad again about the information that should be sent to Sweden. He is on the Tribunal and has recently been to Vietnam. Have you received the manuscript (*Negroes with Guns*) yet? It has already been forwarded to you registered mail. Be sure and let me know when you receive it. Tore asked for the addition for a Swedish publisher. Did you talk to him about that? Under separate cover, I also mailed you a photocopy of the forged *Crusader* that is currently being mailed from Cuba. The Cuban Revolution is really sinking to very low depths. Those guys are really not to be trusted. I am going to start working on the trip to Sweden for September. Things are moving very fast on the world scene and even faster here. It appears that revolutionaries are facing some very hard days ahead. Sincerely, Rob

January 27, 1968, London[18]

Dear Rob,

Perhaps even by the time this letter reaches you we may have been able to get a reversal of the Swedish Aliens Board decision concerning your visa. I and Tore are working for that end and we both feel fairly confident. In order to let you understand the situation in Sweden, you must recall that in the last several months Sweden has given political asylum to large numbers of U.S. servicemen who have deserted rather than fight the dirty war of Vietnam. Many of these men are Black, as you will discover when you get to Sweden. Sweden has been even better than France in sheltering and nourishing these young men, and the Swedish Social Democratic government is under intense pressure from the U.S. Government to change this policy of hospitality. So do go easy on the Swedish officials you meet. Above all, avoid any attacks on Sweden at this juncture. You can rest assured that Uncle Sam is ultimately responsible for any inconvenience. Tore will be returning to Sweden around the 7th of February and will be on the spot. If nothing has happened, I will go up on the 15th of February. I have already contacted the lawyer, Hans Goran Franck, who has been handling the cases of the deserters, and this morning I received a wire from Olof G. Tandberg that the Verdandi is using all its influence to get the government to issue the visa. The organizations, both radical and liberal, that have given assistance to the deserters can also be of use, especially since they know of you and I have met them. By the way the first deserter to find asylum in Sweden was Ray Jones III, a Black GI, whose German girlfriend was determined not to let him go to Vietnam. He's alright and he and other Afros in Sweden would be delighted to meet privately with you. As for the brothers from the States, most of them claim to have no bread. If you want to arrange airfares for really important people, I am certain the Chinese comrades would help. I or someone else can simply inform them that air tickets NYC to Stockholm are available, asking them to raise $200 or less, if necessary, for their personal expenses while in Sweden. They would have no problem in entering Sweden and need no visa, provided they have valid passports, which are easy enough to get nowadays. (See enclosed clipping latest U.S. court of appeals ruling). As for your contacts with the Swedish Embassy, pleas insist that you are only going to Sweden for a short visit and DO Not Want to Stay in Sweden---You are not another deserter! Make them understand that you are invited by reputable student organizations and in no way are seeking to provoke anti-American demonstrations, etc. or interfere in Swedish domestic politics. If necessary, agree to speak only in private to the students and others---once you are in Sweden, you cannot help if links get to the press, etc. The main thing is to get there. Tore thinks, and I agree with him, that six months ago you would not have been turned down, but since then, the number of U.S. deserters arriving in the country has been spectacular. Many of them are Black. Jobs, housing and often scholarships and pocket money are being provided to them. This is happening all over Europe, but the only countries that grant asylum are Sweden and France, with Holland being the center for recruiting deserters. Dutch Marxist-Leninists and other progressives have played a very important role in this work, but now the revisionists, after initially opposing this activity, are trying to muscle in, probably to sabotage the works. In Sweden, you will meet Black people and white deserters and the best of the people helping them, but such meetings must be strictly private and unannounced to avoid embarrassment to the Swedish Government. On the other hand, the deserters have powerful backers in all spheres of life, in Sweden and elsewhere, and many of these people could also provide valuable assistance to you and other Afro-Americans in the bitter, bloody years ahead. I would think your trip even more of a success if you were to make useful contacts with these progressive people in the groups supporting the deserters. Perhaps Swedish people in China can give you some advice and information? I have received and distributed the latest *Crusader*. Of course, you can count on international support for your return, but I must tell you that the prevailing opinion in Western Europe is very much against your return, unless you are prepared to be a martyr. You must show these people the political significance of your return, even granting that the worse does happen, how your return can further the struggle in the U.S. One point that some people have pointed: you speak of returning during the forthcoming electoral campaign. This is fell to be overly dangerous as it seems that both LBJ and whoever the Republican candidate is will both be taking a hard line on the Blacks. To return in such a climate of repressive opinion would mean that your arrest, trial and conviction, if not worse, would be used by the Government, Washington and North Carolina, to demonstrate that the democrats were taking no nonsense from Black people. You could be made a visual symbol of repression, which is much desired by the frightened white middle-class and skilled workers. The French newspaper, *LeMonde*, recently has indicated that it believes a big wave of arrests of Black militants will be timed for the party conventions and electoral period, in the hope of terrorizing the Black population into submission during the summer. This is only a guess, but everybody sees this as a bloody summer, hardly the right moment for you to go home. Anyway, we can discuss this in Stockholm. By the way, Edizioni Oriente, will do an Italian translation of your book. Signora Regis is seriously ill, having been taken ill in Peking, but she has given her agreement. Please send as quickly as possible a copy of the new chapter about your move to China to Edizioni Oriente. Yours, Richard

April 6, 1968, London[19]

Dear Rob,

The enclosed press statement, sent to the major Stockholm newspapers, was prompted by the sickening declarations of Swedish leaders about King's murder. I deliberately avoided, however, attacking Tage Erlander, the Swedish Prime Minister, by name so as to avoid creating personal animosity, and I am still hopeful that we might be able to shame the bastards into revising their decision to keep you out of the country. I did not mention the SNCC man, Sherman Adams, up there, but have heard that he claims that your trip is all part of "an imperialist plot to destroy the unity of the Swedish Left on the verge of the September elections," attack the Cuban Revolution and to permit you to "defect" from China to the United States. This fellow is being pushed by the so-called "Left Party-Communist," the revisionist party in Sweden, and I suspect they may have received a handout from the Cubans but am not at all sure of that. In any case, their hostility is certain. And I fear that our lawyer, Hans Göran Franck, may have double-crossed us. He does not answer my letters and seems to be doing nothing. I have asked Tore Hokansson and Nils Holberg to suggest other lawyers who might help. The trouble is Franck is the leading civil liberties lawyer in Sweden, and naturally is very close to the Moscow crowd, although he is not a member of that wretched party! As for the consternation caused by the King's murder, I can only say that this death, coming when it did, may push forward the cause of Black liberation faster than anyone ever thought. The age of nonviolence, in any case, is over. Did you get the large batch of clippings, the Report on Civil Disorders, and so on that I airmailed you?

Sincerely,
R. Gibson

April 13, 1968, London[20]

Dear Rob,

his is to confirm receipt today of the March *CRUSADER*. The bundle was opened, and some copies were apparently removed, but the rest arrived in good shape, nevertheless. Holmberg's wife, Marika, has written me, suggesting that a comrade in Uppsala, Bo Gustafsson, may be able to get a new lawyer to fight your case, since it seems that Hans Göran Franck has double-crossed us. The real proof of that came when Franck let the leader of the revisionist party—the so-called "Left Party Communist"—raise your case before the Swedish (Partisans?). This man, H. C. Hermansson, according to what I hear from Marika Holmberg, mixed your case up with that of the Trotskyite Ralph Schoenman, who ran the Russell Tribunal and went very easy on the Swedish government. I was shocked to hear this about Hermansson, as I had the agreement of the Centre Party people to raise the case in Parliament, as I wrote you, knowing full well that Hermansson speaking on your behalf is like letting a wolf guard the chickens. Hermansson and his corrupt party are up tight with the Social Democratic Party that runs Sweden and are pure Moscow-liners, not to mention pseudo-friends of the Cuban Revolution. Of course, Franck has never written to me since I left Stockholm, nor have I heard from Tore Hokansson. I have no illusions left about Franck, who undoubtedly has been pressured into sabotaging your case by his connections in the revisionist and Social Democratic Party. There is a chance that I might be wrong about him, and I have made no step that might antagonize him, but I am going ahead with plans for legal action against the Social Democratic newspaper, AFTONBLADET, that libeled me. Holmberg has given me some good advice about what action to take. What is surprising, however, is Tore's lengthy silence. I understand that the pseudo-Left in Sweden is claiming that you would cause serious trouble for them if you got to Sweden before the September general elections. They fear that you might sharply criticize Moscow and the corrupt elements in Havana and thus "endanger the unity of the Left." This phony unity is essential for the Social Democrats, if they are not to be defeated like Social Democrats were recently in Denmark and Norway. I am delighted that you did get some of the material I sent, but I do not understand why everything has not reached you yet. I hear practically nothing from the States these days, following the assassination of Martin Luther King. I am afraid his death may only be the first of a wave of terror killings, intended to terrorize Black leadership in the crucial election months. Although it is still too early to predict accurately, it would seem that Bobby Kennedy will make it to the White House, if the Democratic Party does not split badly at the Convention this summer. If it did, Nixon would be a sure winner. A lot depends on the prospects for peace in Vietnam, but I do not foresee any serious negotiations until after January 1969, when the new president is installed. Dan Watts told me long ago that Bobby Kennedy spread a lot of bread in the Black communities and cultivated the hustling pseudo-tough leadership, which many explain how Kennedy can waltz through Watts without so much as a boo. I wonder even if Adam Clayton Powell hasn't made a deal for the Harlem vote with Bobby? As for the Left scene, I can't figure out just what PL is about, but I know they remain extremely hostile to any form of Black nationalism, despite some slogans that might fool the naïve. Sarah joins me in sending our greetings to you and Mabel. Give my greetings to Gora and tell him that Manchanda is fighting the battle of his life against Reg Birch these days, after being Birch's man. Now, Ash of PL has moved in.

Yours,
Richard

Dar es Salaam, Tanzania

June 25, 1969

Dear Richard:

As you no doubt know by now, I am again in Dar es Salaam. Things are not much different here. Everything is extremely overpriced as far as lodgings are concerned and I am passing a lot of dead time waiting to return to America. I will pass through London on my way but I don't know whether or not they will let me stop. At any rate, I will call you when I come. I will be here a least another month. Mabel and the boys will probably leave here in the next two or three weeks. When the Crusaders arrive there (Special summer issue) please hold for me all that you cannot use because I can use them later in the States. You can contact me at: R.F. Williams c/o Sutherland, P.O. Box 822 Dar es Salaam, Tanzania Telephone 67812. Best wishes to all,

Sincerely,
Rob

June 28, 1969, London

Dear Rob,

Your letter of the 25th arrived this morning and I hasten to reply. Four packages of Crusaders have reached me now—three at the office address and one here at home. I will be ready to forward them when you want but will be making an extra wide distribution throughout Europe in view of your need for international support. Despite the many discouraging aspects of the situation, don't abandon ever the effort to widen your support as far as possible. Get as many supporters in as many places as possible, although don't have illusions about what that support can do if it is not steadily and continually cultivated with propaganda and personal contacts. When you return to the States, I still will make every effort to do what I can. The situation here in Britain on the race front is very tense. The British authorities are scared shitless of angry black people and it is extremely doubtful if they will let you enter the country if they know who you are and when you are coming. As soon as you get your reservations to fly this way, let me know, but not at this address. Send me a note c/o American Express, London, S.W.1 and I will get it. You must do this as early as possible and please don't alert anyone else up here, if you can help it. We might be able to get you in the country this way and you could spend up to three months, if you wanted. But if questioned, especially by immigration, do not indicate that you might be giving any public meetings or holding political talks, etc., in Britain. You should say that you want to visit an old personal friend and can stay at my home, etc. Now, the only problem is that I and the family are scheduled to leave here around the last week of July for Italy for our vacation. I was planning to be in Rome on the 28th of July and to remain there for about five days, before going to a small island in the South. I can meet you at Rome Airport or can put you up in Rome, if you can stop over. It should be far less difficult to get you into Italy than into Britain. (I myself would not be allowed to stay here one day if Sarah weren't a British citizen, and even with that, I am the only American correspondent in London to whom the police refuse to issue a press pass. Even the Tass correspondents have passes. But not your truly. The cops have been asked on my behalf by both the Foreign Press Association and the Association of American Correspondents, but without any results and even without the police giving any explanation except that a pass is not a right but a privilege and that "it is not possible to grant one to Gibson." And I assure you I have not been dabbling in British politics and hardly even public meetings of any kind, but of course the cops know I am on good terms with people like Manchanda and others and that alone annoys them.) If I don't hear from you again soon at American Express with your exact travel plans, I will write before we leave for Rome, giving you an address and phone number where you can contact me. Even if you are just passing through, I can come to the airport to chat with you, but I do hope you may be able to stay a few days with us in the Eternal City, which is a very pleasant place. For me, far more pleasant than gris and dreary London! You may recall, I lived in Rome in 1951 and 1952 and liked the city very much. Enclosed is a clipping from the *NY Times* concerning the Black Panthers' troubles with the Cuban racists. Once again, history is proving you right. It almost makes Carlos Moore seem perfectly justified. I wonder when the white radicals in the States and other places will start denouncing the Panthers, not the Cubans, in their usual cone-sided manner. Speaking of white phony radicals, the Swedish Press Council Has condemned the Stockholm newspaper Aftonbladet for its dirty insinuations against me over that deserter. It took long enough, but I was determined to press on with the case till victory. Personally, I am delighted and I understand that the lawyer Hans Horan Franck was hit hard by the decision. Not to mention the Moscow-Havana crowd. I sent a copy of the decision to our friend P. K. Leballo of the Pan Africanist Congress of Azania. I trust that you work out some sort of international ties between your movement and the PAC, who represent the closest thing to a Black Power grouping in Africa. The Pro-West mob inside the PAC—Mahomo, Nogobo, and Morrison— have been defeated decisively, I think. Morrison has been acting as a paid informer for the most reactionary and racist paper in London, *The Daily Telegraph*. From AAJA to that! Now, he has been uncovered and is in big trouble with all black embassies and groups. When he arrived here, I tried to be a friend and to warn him from that anti-China line, but he would not listen. See you very soon, I hope. And best wishes to the family. Richard

A Black Panther Assails Cuba; Hints Cleaver Is Discontented

HAVANA, June 25 (AP)—An American active in the Black Panther movement said today that he and other members of his party had been "isolated and imprisoned" in Cuba and wanted to leave. He implied that the Black Panthers' fugitive leader, Eldridge Cleaver, was among the discontented here.

Raymond Johnson, 22 years old, of Alexandria, La., told a newsman he had been instructed by a high-ranking Black Panther in Cuba to report this feeling.

Johnson, who described himself as a lieutenant in the Black Panther movement and an airliner hijacker, said: "The Panthers have not been received in a revolutionary fashion. We have been condemned to live in Cuba."

He added that members of the black militant organization had been imprisoned, isolated, banned from Havana and told they could not organize their party in Cuba.

"These imprisonments amount to more than just being confined for a period of investigation," Johnson said.

"Some have been imprisoned a second time. They have been sent to completely isolated sections of the island and forced to work in labor camps."

He Expects to Be Jailed

Johnson said he expected to be arrested at any time, adding: "It is possible some of the Panthers will be arrested today." He declared arrests "always come when they [the Panthers] become disenchanted and after they protest conditions and express a desire to leave the country."

"We would like this information to reach the Black Panther party in the United States so the party will know the unrevolutionary way we are being treated," he said. "We want them to protest at Cuban missions everywhere."

The only Cuban mission in the United States is at the United Nations.

Johnson said he had been jailed for 21 days after he hijacked a National Airlines jet from New Orleans to Havana Nov. 4, 1968.

"We think there's racial discrimination in Cuba," he continued.

"It's a peculiar kind of racial discrimination. In some ways it's comparable to attitudes in the United States. White Cubans have a subconscious conspiracy to maintain control of the island.

"We feel the Cubans have a misunderstanding of the political, cultural and revolutionary thinking of black Americans, but primarily of the cultural aspect of the black revolution.

"We are talking about a social and cultural revolution.

And in our experience, we have seen people here lagging in the revolution of the mind."

Johnson, a former student at Southern University in Baton Rouge, La., said the Black Panthers had been discouraged from talking to black Cubans about black awareness and the wearing of Afro hair styles. More than 30 per cent of Cuba's eight million people are black.

Called Counterrevolutionary

Johnson contended that some Black Panthers who had talked about a black culture to Cubans had been branded counterrevolutionary. He said that most of the Panthers would like to go to Africa, but that they had been told not to make contact with African embassies in Havana.

He reported that Omar Talif, a party member from New York, and his American wife and child had "disappeared" after having been told by Cuban officials that they were "black racists."

Johnson said he did not know how many Black Panthers were currently in Cuba but he identified four: Byron Muese Booth of Los Angeles, deputy minister of defense; Earl Farrow of Denver, deputy minister of information; Charles Rhaim Smith of Los Angeles, and Lieut. James Akili and his wife of New York.

Johnson said all the Black Panthers he knew had requested permission to leave Cuba. He turned aside on security grounds questions about Cleaver, wanted in California since he disappeared late last year when his parole on a 13-year assault sentence was revoked after a gun battle, but added:

"An exceedingly high-ranking Black Panther officer doesn't like the treatment of black revolutionaries and the Black Panthers here at all."

F.B.I. Terms Him Vicious

MIAMI, June 25 (AP) — The Federal Bureau of Investigation said today that Johnson was one of the more "vicious" of the hijackers.

"He called the passengers 'economic devils' and stood over the captain throughout the flight, continually hitting him over the head with a cocked .38 revolver," an F.B.I. agent declared. "He knocked the co-pilot's glasses off and ground them under his heel."

Johnson was a fugitive from an arson charge at Baton Rouge when he hijacked the plane. Earlier, he had been charged there with criminal mischief and criminal trespass. On the latter charge he was given a one-year suspended sentence.

Johnson was recently indicted in New Orleans on charges of aerial piracy and kidnapping. He used the name H. Jackson when he purchased his ticket.

STATEMENT BY AFRO-AMERICAN LEADER IN EXILE TO AMERICAN SERVICEMEN IN SOUTH VIETNAM, FEBRUARY, 1966

Hanoi in English to American Servicemen in South Vietnam 1300 GMT 18

Sent to Vietnam for what? Mr. Johnson says, "to defend the free world and democracy." If he is concerned with democracy, why is it that he does not see to it to send armed forces to protect the lives of Negro women and children who are being bombed, raped, murdered, and dehumanized for seeking human rights in racist America? Yes, for even seeking the right to vote in a so-called "representative democracy!" Boss Charlie is not sending troops to Vietnam to defend democracy. How can he pretend to defend democracy in the jungles of Vietnam and trample it underfoot in the streets of Washington, Harlem, Birmingham, and throughout the Black ghettoes of the racist United States? The United States cannot win in Vietnam. American soldiers are dying in vain there. Four-fifths of the country is already liberated. All the Vietnamese people are determined to fight to the end. Your only salvation for the deceased American troops there is for you to promote friendship with the people of Vietnam, to aid them, and to guide them in their struggle for true emancipation. A government that so brutally oppresses its own colored people is not sincere when it purports to defend the freedom of a colored people 10,000 miles away while ignoring it at home. The peace issue in Vietnam is like the civil rights issue in the United States. The more Johnson talked about peace, the more troops he dispatched to make war on the defenseless colored people of Vietnam. What is the nature of a soldier who will allow (word indistinct) to fight the liberation struggle while he allows himself to be led to a foreign land to help crush the freedom struggle of other people? When man sheds the responsibility of manhood, when soldiers fear to stand for liberation and justice, and when oppressed soldiers prefer to (?oppose) their own mothers, rather than honorably stand in the ranks of those who love justice more than life itself, then it is time for babies—yes, even young girls, six years old, to face their brutal oppressor in a manner wherein their noble little souls become synonymous with freedom. Yes, if our courage fails us, then let little children pick up the cry of (words indistinct) about Black soldiers crouched like robots (words indistinct) the heart of a true friend in Vietnam.

Announcer: You are told your presence in South Vietnam is required to help defend the freedom and democracy of the South Vietnamese people. Do these fine words conform with what you are doing in the southern part of our country? No! You are killing the Vietnamese with all kinds of weapons, including napalm bombs, (words indistinct) bullets, and toxic gases. To help you see the truth, here is a recording made by Mr. Robert Williams, an American Negro leader in exile. (Recorded statement follows—ed.) Racist America proposes to make the world safe for democracy. The racist and hypocritical Johnson administration has committed the U.S. Armed Forces to the defense of so-called "democracy" throughout the world. What is this democracy that racist U.S. imperialism boasts so much about? It is a democracy where the rights of colored people are less respected than those of common (word indistinct). It is a democracy where the homes and churches of Black people are being viciously bombed, where Black women and children are being gassed, whipped, and jailed simply for begging and praying for human rights in the so-called free world. Our oppressed Afro-American people in racist America are undergoing a current phase of terror. (Word indistinct) and violence flares in Jackson and all over the Mississippi Delta and Greensboro, Selma, and throughout the Black belt of Alabama and (Crawfordville–phonetic) and America's Georgia, in Philadelphia, New York, Chicago, and throughout the nation. It is the height of hypocrisy that President Johnson has announced to the world that many thousands more of American troops will be sent to Vietnam. Robert F. Williams exposes Johnson Administration's ban on freedom of speech.

STATEMENT BY RICHARD T. GIBSON ABOUT KING'S ASSASINATION AND THE SWEDISH GOVERNMENT'S BANNING OF ROBERT F. WILLIAMS PROPOSED VISIT (April 6, 1968)

Protests Continuing Ban on Sweden Visit by Robert F. Williams

LONDON—Learning of statements from certain quarters in Stockholm after the murder of Dr. Martin Luther King, Mr. Richard Gibson, personal representative in Europe of the Afro-American leader Robert F. Williams, issued the following comment: "The words of Swedish leaders following the killing of Dr. Martin Luther King are a pious sham and an insult to Black people everywhere so long as the Swedish government continues to appease international white racism by banning the proposed visit to Sweden by the militant Afro-American leader Robert F. Williams." He was recently elected unanimously by a national convention of Afro-Americans in Detroit to lead the all-Black State that will surely be formed one day on the North American continent. "Invited to address Swedish students in Uppsala and Lund, Williams, who lives at present in exile in China, has been denied entry to Sweden, and a certain pseudo-Left Party and its minions now insinuate, aping their Moscow masters, that Williams is a 'black troublemaker' who might disturb the comfortable tranquility and self-righteousness of a certain Swedish 'Left' and even that Williams' personal representative in Europe—the Afro-American journalist Richard Gibson—is an 'imperialist' and/or 'Maoist' agent." "This ludicrous attitude is in itself proof enough that, even in Sweden, there are two weights and two measures when black militants are involved."

STATEMENT BY MILTON R. HENRY ABOUT WILLIAMS' RETURN TO DETROIT, SEPTEMBER 12, 1969

In the absence of Robert Williams, and at his specific request, I wish to thank, for him, all of the many Black persons in the London Area who over the past week have so steadfastly carried on and supported the struggle of Mr. Williams for liberation from detention, and his transfer to the United States. It was a Herculean effort against at least two powerful governments and a powerful United States corporation; and, because of the pressure of our sincere protests combined with that of others throughout the world, we have all won a magnificent victory. It is not possible for me to name all of those whose efforts have led to Mr. Williams's release, but I would particularly like to express our deep gratitude to the Tanzanian government, both in New York and London; the West Indian Standing Conference; the Pan Africanist Congress; and to the Black nationalist community in London, for their extension to Mr. Williams of their prompt, effective, unstinting, persistent, and unrelenting support. I would like also to add a personal note of thanks to Messers Jeff Crawford, David Sibeko, and Richard Gibson, for their advice, counsel, and assistance in helping me make the most expeditious use of my time while here on this mission. It is hardly necessary for me to state that it was the total cooperation of each of the above-named persons and groups which contributed so importantly and vitally to the ultimate victory achieved. What happened here has no known counterpart in Black contemporary history; and the events have now become a permanent part of the remarkable struggle of Black men everywhere, throughout the entire pan-African family, for liberation from white oppression.

The lessons to be learned here were valuable for us all. First, the nature of the injustice being perpetrated was accurately assessed. Second, the reaction to that injustice was at once immediate, forceful and properly directed. Third, brothers on three continents, separated by thousands of miles of ocean, but united by thousands of years of history, cooperated together as one against a grouping of forces which likewise spread across thousands of miles of ocean and thousands of years of history. Our response was fully equal to the assault made on us. We acted as one people—and we prevailed. It is our intent and desire to strengthen those bonds which exist between our groups and peoples. This closer cooperation must be put into effect. In any event, I am writing these words for Robert, at his specific request, to thank those here in London who have worked so hard on his behalf. If he is not permitted to thank you personally at this time, you must understand that it is not because he does not wish to do so, but rather because the officials here have not permitted him to do so. You must rest assured that what you have done on his behalf will always remain in his heart. And for myself personally, and the Republic of New Africa officially, let me convey to you our deepest gratitude and sense of obligation for a job so well done, Again, let us continue the cooperation we have begun here. Our doors in America will ever be open to you.

Most gratefully yours,
Milton R. Henry, First Vice President of the Republic of New Africa

LETTER FROM BROTHER IMARI OBADELE, RNA MINISTER OF INFORMATION TO ROBERT F. WILLIAMS, APRIL 5, 1968

Dear Brother Rob,

Pursuant to your cable of tentative acceptance I have enclosed a set of the Convention working papers, marked up by pen to indicate the changes that occurred, together with copies of the Declaration of Independence, the Resolutions, and the post-convention news release. I think that these should provide a good general background. I might add some additional specifics. Mr. Howard (Charles P. Howard, Minister of State and Foreign Affairs) was being operated on in a Baltimore Hospital as we held the convention; I spoke to him beforehand but not since, yet and, except for the operation and his rather serious condition, he said he would have been with us. Because of his illness, which we know to be long term, the delegates elected a deputy minister: Stokely Carmichael. Stokely did not come to the convention, and he asked me to send him details, which I did just after the convention. Jim Forman is taking details to Rap Brown, who is still in jail. We should from both brothers affirmatively, I expect in a few days. I wish I could convey to you the sense of dedication and commitment that the delegates (nearly 200, from all sections of the country, although the North was predominant) displayed. Their passion for work and their determination to arrive at meaningful decisions within the two-day timeframe was something rare for any convention. Both days we began early and worked late, with little time for breaks. There was vigorous debate without rancor or animosity. The cabinet meets in New York on Easter; the National Council of Representatives meets in Chicago on May 30th. We, of course, will work for the aims of the revolution set forth in the Declaration and will undertake to set up the small commercial-industrial complex on a suitable base in Mississippi, on the gulf if at all possible. (I hope you received the copies of my book, War in America.) We hope that it will be possible for Milton and Betty, at the least to confirm with you, somewhere in the immediate future. Prior to the convention, in anticipation of its results, the Malcolm X Society approached one government with a request that they consider ceding us an island for a temporary capital, as indicated in the working papers; we indicated that our government would be anxious to discuss the details of this request at their convenience. I feel confident the cabinet at the Eastern meeting will authorize an approach to an African government for some land, over which we are sovereign. I assured everyone that you would be an active president, and president in fact. I hope our initiatives so far accord with your thinking. We feel the land and diplomatic recognition together with certain acts of nationhood in the United States, are essential now to aid our success. We look forward to early consultation on these and other matters. Very best regards.

We sincerely hope Mabel's health has improved and that you are well. Yours for the success of the Revolution

Brother Imari

WILLIAMS HAS INTERVIEWS WITH VIEWPOINT WHILE IN AFRICA

Robert Franklin Williams is a 43-year-old Negro from Monroe, North Carolina. He was active in the civil rights movement ten years ago, but struck off on his own path, by arming his Negro neighbors during racial tension in his home state; he was the first Negro leader to preach and practice armed resistance against the white terrorist organization, the KKK, and other white racist groups. He fled the United States in 1961 after local police tried to arrest him on a kidnapping charge—a trumped-up charge, according to Williams. After years of exile in Cuba and China, Williams arrived in Dar es Salaam two months ago. He has now been joined by his wife, Mabel. He is trying to get a U.S. passport to return home to America, where Black Power leaders this year elected him President of the Republic of New Africa—the Negro-controlled State, which they hope to carve out of the southern U.S. Williams talks with Viewpoint about how he hopes to achieve Negro Independence. **VIEWPOINT**: Is the gap between Negroes and whites in the United States growing so wide that it cannot be mended without considerable violence?

WILLIAMS: Well, it could be, but I don't think it's going to be. It could be because it's just a matter of justice being done, that consideration should be given to the most depressed and dehumanized of Americans. This will cost money, and I'm sorry to say that the capitalist system is not willing to spend money, sometimes not even to save itself. It appears the authorities are not going to do anything. They could avoid the coming showdown, but they will have to show a strong desire to avoid it. I don't think the desire and understanding are strong enough yet.

VIEWPOINT: Do you consider the present Negro campaign, with its emphasis on non-violence, the way to achieve civil rights? **WILLIAMS:** No. Nonviolence is no way to achieve civil rights, because if it was, we would already have civil rights, because we have had a lot of nonviolence. And we didn't accomplish anything. Most of the concessions that have been given have come more from violence or the threat of violence. Most Americans are motivated more by the threat of violence than by humanitarianism. So, I can't see where non-violence would do any good because the people, we're dealing with are not good-natured people. These are brutal people, and it requires force to meet this kind of force. **VIEWPOINT**: How would you conduct the civil rights campaign? **WILLIAMS**: As such, the civil rights campaign is a dead issue now. This era has already passed, and America let it pass. It wasn't necessary to let it pass. America could have avoided even the present state. But they may as well now forget about civil rights, because the issue is much greater. The civil rights movement could have worked. It didn't fall because it was impossible. It failed because not enough people worked to hit hard enough. The masses of the Black people of America have developed beyond this stage. Now they have developed a different outlook. At one time we all hoped, and we saw hope, in the Supreme Court decision of 1954. We believed that the United States was on the threshold of a great social change. We believed that the American people would be decent enough, the vast majority, to bring out this change, to integrate us into the mainstream of society, and to share equally as human beings. And this is what we wanted to do; we only wanted to be human beings, to be treated as human beings, with respect, with dignity, to have the same police protection, to have the same rights for education, the same security and government. The people of the United States have failed us, the society failed us. And now we have come to realize that the whites in America doesn't intend to give us human rights any more than the whites in South Africa intend to give the Black in South Africa, or the Rhodesian whites intend to give the Black in Rhodesia civil rights. We are faced with the problem, of where to go and how far to go. The vast majority of our people know that we are not going to be integrated into the society, and we know that we are not going to be integrated into the society, and we know that the whites don't want us to integrate with them. It is also a matter of our racial pride. We have decided that if they don't want us to integrate with them, we don't want to integrate. Now we look at the American society and we see how corrupt it is. And we see that it is foolish even to want to integrate with such a corrupt and degenerate society. We have the case of President Kennedy. Assassinated in that American society. Martin Luther King. Now, the second Kennedy, the Senator, is aspiring to be President. If this society cannot protect men of that caliber, what can we expect from such a society? Can the masses expect anything? **VIEWPOINT**: This is the background, in effect, to the decision to establish the Republic of New Africa. **WILLIAMS:** Yes, some people will say this is the work of extremists. Some will sneer at us, and they will portray us in many unfavorable ways. I was the first Negro leader to advocate armed self-defense. Then I was branded as an untouchable, as a great extremist who should be destroyed. But I was only trying to warn America of what was to come, and I hoped that they would see the light, that they would change. Now I know they are not going to change. I tell them once again, that the world situation has changed, and we know we are not going to attain equal rights. We have only one alternative, an alternative not just for us but for America. It has been proven that we are not going to be able to live peacefully together, because we are no longer slaves, we have no longer the submissive mentality. We are becoming more and more militant, and you can't expect militant people to be submissive. This means that an explosion is bound to come, a racial explosion, because the whites are not going to grant integration, and the Blacks no longer want integration. We are developing pride in ourselves, in race, and we don't see why we should fight to be in a society or community in which we are not wanted. We want the same as others, to have our own society. We have decided to strike out on this new road. This is the third stage of the rocket. Now we are going to go into orbit.

VIEWPOINT: Many people will say that carving a state out of the United States is pie in the sky, a dream. Practically, how do you propose to achieve this? **WILLIAMS:** I wouldn't say it's a dream. I would say it's a nightmare if they don't carve it. Now the idea is to do it peacefully, to do it with the aid and support of the sensible, peace-loving American people, of all races, even with the assistance of the government, if they will be sane enough to assist. I realize the intransigence of the government and the racist of the United States. So, if they don't want to save America by doing what is right, if they don't want to save America by giving us our target, it's all right with me. If they want to destroy America, they must be prepared to destroy America. My first choice is the peaceful way, but we also must be prepared to use any means necessary, to go to any length to pay any sacrifice, and this is what we intend to do. If it has reached the stage that requires bloodshed, then the burden of bloodshed is not on us. We cannot be condemned because we are the oppressed people asking for self-determination, asking for the right to have our own faith and destiny in our own hands. This right is recognized even in the UN Charter. We are an oppressed people, a colonial people, a colony within the United States and we are asking for the right to live as free people, for the right to self-determination. We are asking for the right to live among ourselves. We are already segregated from the mainstream of American life. The difference now is that we don't have any self-government; we don't even have adequate representation. So, this can, ultimately, lead to the destruction of the United States. But the present conditions under which we live, the present racism, is destroying us anyway. **VIEWPOINT**: When you talk of war, people must assume that the armed might of America would be used against them. You would be virtually people without arms, or people with side arms against tanks. How can you hope to win a war like this? **WILLIAMS**: Most people think this is impossible because they think of a war from a conventional point of view, tanks against tanks, cannons against cannons, planes against planes. We speak of developing a new concept of warfare, an urban guerrilla type of warfare. Speaking of numbers and power, we can also consider that in Vietnam there are 14,000,000 people. In the United States there are 200,000,000 people. The United States is the greatest military power on earth. But they're not doing so well against those peasants in Vietnam. In the traditional concept of war, we wouldn't have a chance. We live in the United States. We constitute at least 22,000,000 people, and a nation cannot destroy 22,000,000 fighting people who exist within its boundaries without destroying itself. Even though we are segregated from that society, we still constitute a part of America. Look at the uprising in the wake of the assassination of Martin Luther King. That was just a small thing, not an organized thing. It didn't really have any objective; it was more of a protest. Suppose you had an uprising of people determined to be free, all over the country, people who were willing to give their lives, what do you think would happen to America? It would be devastated. The more industrialized a nation becomes, the more dependent the people become on industry and machinery. The day this machinery cannot function, then the whole society disintegrates. The American society is built on automation, and this is where the power of such a conflict would come, not from military power. I don't buy the argument that we cannot win. If we cannot win, America cannot win either, because we are part of it. **VIEWPOINT**: What about the area of the Republic of New Africa? You hope for help from the US government. Have you considered where you want to establish your republic? **WILLIAMS**: Yes. We have decided that it should be in the States of Louisiana, Mississippi, Alabama, Georgia and South Carolina. These states are called the Black Belt. There is a heavy concentration of Black people there and these States benefited most from slavery. No reparations were ever paid, and we think that because slave labor primarily but these States, we are entitled to them, to live in peace. **VIEWPOINT**: You consider then that you have a moral, if not legal right to the territory? **WILLIAMS:** Yes, we have a moral and legal right. We have a moral and religious right even to America, but we are willing to settle for this. You must also consider the history of India and Pakistan. Some people thought partition was crazy. Actually, it has been a sensible solution. Any businessman knows it is better to give up some of his profit than to lose it all. **VIEWPOINT**: Is there any time limit to the project? Do you give the United States any certain period in which to make up its mind? **WILLIAMS**: No, and I don't think we should issue ultimatums. But if they are sensible, they will pursue this with the utmost urgency, for it is a very urgent matter. The Black people are becoming impatient and restless. The solutions the U.S. government has presented are not sufficient. They may be so stupid not to see it, and if they are, well I can assure them that it will not be long; it will not be many more years before they will reap the whirlwind. We advocate that all of the whites of that area, who do not want to live under a Black government—and incidentally it is stated in our Declaration of Independence that we will not tolerate racial or religious discrimination—be paid for their property, that the government give the proper compensation. **VIEWPOINT**: The partition of India and Pakistan entailed great migration. Do you envisage this kind of swapping of population? Negroes south from north, and whites north from south? **WILLIAMS**: Yes, if it is done peacefully. But not only will whites in the south have the opportunity to go north, but they will also have the opportunity to remain in other Southern States. They will have Florida, Virginia, Texas, North Carolina, Arkansas. **VIEWPOINT**: Do you expect all the Negroes of the northern cities to come to your southern state? **WILLIAMS**: Yes, the ones who are suffering and the ones who have human dignity. Many people are tired of living in an environment wherein they are humiliated. I expect that after an educational program, which would extend over a period of time, more people than is now expected would go to such a settlement. Of course, this would not be mandatory. **VIEWPOINT**: White people living in the southern states you want, if they wish to remain there can they do so and maintain their present properties? **WILLIAMS**: Yes, and they can maintain their properties with the exception of industry, because in such a society as ours, we will have collective ownership. We wouldn't want any exploitation of man by man. We don't want Blacks to be exploited by Blacks any more than we want them exploited by whites.

VIEWPOINT: Would you expect the United States to give your republic foreign aid? **WILLIAMS**: We will seek reparations from the U.S. government for slavery, and also compensation for people who move from property. But the biggest thing would be reparations. We would also seek foreign aid from any country willing to give it. **VIEWPOINT**: Would your republic be a one-party state? be thrashed out in a constitutional committee. It would depend on what the masses of the people would want. **VIEWPOINT**: You are living in Tanzania which is a one-party setup. Have you studied it to see if it might be suitable for your republic? **WILLIAMS**: In any country trying to develop it is more convenient to have a one-party system, provided that the one-party system is a just system, and the people have a voice and control. I think the one-party system need not be oppressive. I think it is a liberal system and I don't think they could do any better because when you are striving to raise your standards and to industrialize you have many problems. You won't help the situation to having all kinds of politicians running around creating friction and factions. We have had a two-party system in America—yet we have never had democracy. This is why we are asking for separation. **VIEWPOINT**: Do you look forward with any confidence in being recognized in the world as a newly independent state? **WILLIAMS**: We haven't asked that yet. The main thing is to get our machinery set up and functioning efficiently. Once we are functioning, we will ask all countries, with the exception of South Africa and Rhodesia and some others that may be racist, to recognize us. Of course, we don't expect all countries to do that. **VIEWPOINT**: Do you think then that eh U.S. authorities will admit your return? **WILLIAMS**: Well, I hope they will, but I don't know. I don't think they understand the situation well enough. I think they are going to be stupid about it. But I will return anyway, sooner or later, as soon as it is organized. I hope they will make it possible for me to return peacefully, as a normal citizen. I'm not a criminal. I've not committed any criminal offense. I have been out of the United States for seven years, and nobody has charged me with anything. **VIEWPOINT**: Have you tried in Dar es Salaam, through the U.S. Embassy, to get travel documents? **WILLIAMS**: No, I applied in Cuba, before I left Cuba, through the Swiss Embassy. I filed all the forms. They issued my wife with a travel document, but back more forms and questions for me to answer. It was just a dodge. They didn't intend to give me a passport. The U.S. government intervened in some way with progress in France, with a French lawyer, and the same thing in Sweden. The United States blocked things to prevent my return.

VIEWPOINT: So, the U.S. government is concerned about your power and your appeal to the Negro people? **WILLIAMS**: Well, as we can see now, this is how we are considering it. One party. But maybe in the future—we don't know. All of this would have to be discussed and determined. **WILLIAMS:** It is a political thing. I don't think it's my power they are afraid of, but my arguments. The ideas that are starting now are ideas I was advocating years ago. The government knows that it is not just theory with me—it is also practice. And they are greatly confused. They have created a Frankenstein, and they don't quite understand it themselves. **VIEWPOINT**: Are you getting support from such people as the Reverend Abernathy? **WILLIAMS**: I am not on the scene, but I doubt it, for he is a pacifist, and we're not pacifist. I don't suppose that at this point he could publicly come out in support of us, because he raises his money on the basis of peaceful solute-ions that are not going to take place. The case of Martin Luther King is a demonstration of this.

WILLIAMS 'S RETURN ANNOUNCEMENT LETTER, May 18, 1969

Dear Brother Benn:

Both your letters have been received. Sorry, that time only permits this brief note. The brothers over there who should have been host to the Black Unit Conference pleaded four of the men. They got cold feet. But we cannot afford to give up on the idea of uniting and educating our people universally. We must keep working toward this end. We are leaving for the Black man's hell, United States. Mabel and the boys will no doubt make it there before I will keep in touch and contact you from there. Give my regards to all the brothers and sisters and tell them to keep on pushing. Mabel and the boys will write as soon as they have established a new address. They send their best regards to all. Best wishes for freedom,

Robert F. Williams

Notes

1 This letter, which was not written to denounce Fidel Castro, but rather Williams intent was to offer a sincere observation, communication, and respectful suggestion to Castro from and in his voice. The letter was first presented in September of 1966 to the Cuban Embassy after he and Mabel's safe arrival in Peking. The letter was released for immediate transmittal to Fidel Castro, according to Williams, after the Cuban Embassy refused to accept it. A copy of the letter was also mailed by Robert F. Williams to go directly to Fidel Castro, but there is no concrete evidence to indicate that Castro ever received the letter. Under the circumstances Robert Williams decided to release the letter as a public document to set the record straight for those seeking to learn the truth about the outcome, circumstances, events, relationship, and speculations that led up to leaving Cuba and his relationship with Castro. Williams believed he had established a sincere intercultural relationship and arrangement with Castro.
2 Reprinted in the *Peking Review* on August 12, 1966, Volume 9, Number 33, pages 24–27. The speech was delivered during a rally in Peking on the third anniversary of Mao's Statement Supporting the American Negroes in Their Just Struggle Against Racial Discrimination by U.S. Imperialism.

3 See Robert F. Williams Papers, Bentely Historical Library, in Box, Folder
4 Ibid, Box, Folder
5 Ibid, Box, Folder
6 See JFK Assassination System Identification Form, FBI Record Number 124-901146-10111, Memo from Cregar to Brennan, February 24, 1966, regarding RAM and Richard Thomas Gibson
7 Gibson writes Williams, October 15, 1966, in the Richard Gibson Papers, Box 13, Folder 5.
8 Williams writes Gibson, October 17, 1966, in the Richard Gibson Papers, Box 13, Folder 5.
9 Gibson writes Williams, October 21, 1966, in the Richard Gibson Papers, Box 13, Folder 5.
10 Gibson writes Williams, October 28, 1966, in the Richard Gibson Papers, Box 13, Folder 5.
11 Gibson writes Williams, November 18, 1966, in the Richard Gibson Papers, Box 13, Folder 5.
12 Williams writes Gibson, February 27, 1967, in Richard Gibson Papers, Box 13, Folder 6.
13 Gibson writes Williams, March 18, 1967, in the Richard Gibson Papers, Box 13, Folder 6.
14 Williams writes Gibson, March 27, 1967, in the Richard Gibson Papers, Box 13, Folder 6.
15 Ibid, April 17, 1967
16 Ibid, May 17, 1967.
17 Ibid, May 24, 1967
18 Gibson writes Williams, January 27, 1968, in the Richard Gibson Papers, Box 13, Folder 6
19 Gibson writes Williams, April 6, 1968, in the Richard Gibson Papers, Box 13, Folder 5.
20 Gibson writes Williams, April 13, 1968, in the Richard Gibson Papers, Box 13, Folder 5.

Chapter 4

DETROIT AND ANN ARBOR, MICHIGAN, 1969–1972

Robert F. Williams Exiting TWA Plane. Robert F. Williams TWA Flight Landing in Detroit. From top to bottom: Brother Gaidi A. Obadele (aka Milton Henry), unnamed State Department official, Robert F. Williams at the bottom exiting the plane as a second State Department official meets him, ca. 1969. Upon the flight's landing at the Detroit International Metropolitan Air Port, Williams was cheered on by twenty to thirty supporters. Courtesy of the Detroit Public Library.

Robert F. and Mabel R. Williams are photographed during a Republic of New Afrika Press Conference in Detroit. In view are Robert F. Williams Sr. sitting center at the microphone, Mabel Robinson Williams to his right, standing behind them Audley "Queen Mother" Moore, and to his left sitting, Gaidi Abiodum Obadele (aka Milton Henry) and also standing next to unknown individual is Imari Abubakari Obadele (aka Richard B. Henry), ca. 1969. From the Detroit News Collection # 27980. Courtesy of Walter P. Reuther Library, Wayne State University.

Robert F. Williams Speaks. While on a one-year Ford Foundation fellowship at the University of Michigan-Ann Arbor campus, Robert F. Williams speaks with *Detroit Free Press* staff writer, Julie Morris, in his office at the Center for Chinese Studies, September 19, 1971. Courtesy of Union County Library in Monroe, North Carolina.

ROBERT WILLIAMS RESPONDS TO SENATE INTERNAL COMMITTEE'S SUBPOENA

Senate Internal Committee[1]

Upon my return to this country on the 12th of September 1969, while in custody of and being fingerprinted by the FBI, I was issued a subpoena. The internal security on the Judiciary Committee's subpoena commanded me to appear before its September 30, 1969, session in Washington. I was commanded to bring the following personal belongings: "Any and all wire or tape recordings, photographs, photographic or motion picture film, correspondence or copies thereof, notebooks, diaries, address books or lists, telephone books or lists, membership rosters or lists, or any other documents or papers now in your custody or under your control, the property of Robert Williams or Mabel Williams, having to do with the following subjects or any of them":

"1. Plans for revolutionary activity against the Government of the United States either in furtherance of a so-called 'Republic of New Africa' or in any other connection.

"2. The so-called 'Republic of New Africa' or 'New African Republic' and any officers, representatives, or agents thereof.
"3. Financing of a proposed Negro republic within the present boundaries of the United States of America.
"4. The activities of the revolutionary organization known as RAM or any member or members thereof as such."

The above-mentioned material was not available for me to take to Washington because the Committee had already had it stolen from U.S. Customs before I could take possession of it. Attorney Conrad J. Lynn of New York was only able to obtain a promised return of it after it had been photographed and the photos were presented for my identification during the first Washington session. The whole session was an invasion of privacy. Not a single senator showed up and the session was heavily based on notations from my diary, which had been stolen by the committee. Even though I was conscious of the fact that the whole affair was a brazen and sinister violation of my Constitutional and human rights, I answered all questions to the best of my ability in a vain effort to prove that I had nothing to conceal. On November 18, 1969, I appeared a second time in response to a subpoena. Sen. Strom Thurman arrived late and questioned me for a short time. He was the only Senator to appear. An aide of Sen. Birch Byer appeared to inform me that the senator had not been formally notified of the hearing and that he (Sen. Byer) thought the whole thing was unconstitutional. It was more than obvious to me that the whole affair was not a legitimate inquiry but a session of harassment and degradation. These sessions were conducted more by U.S. intelligence agents than by a duly constituted committee of the U.S. Senate. Though members of the U.S. State Department had invited me for a China discussion, Attorney Sourwine of the Committee tried to influence me not to go on grounds that I had "better be careful of those State Dept. people because of security leaks from there." He brought out a directory to show that those who had invited me were former journalist who had been assigned to Hong Kong and therefore were untrustworthy. I didn't care to be involved in a Washington feud. As a result of my appearance before the committee and as a result of the fact that a plot originated there to discredit me in the Black and liberal communities, I suffered vicious attacks upon my character. I was slandered and discredited as a result of the committee's insistence that I had cooperated by voluntarily turning my personal diaries over to them when they had stolen them. The committee used the power of the subpoena not for the purpose of legitimate inquiry but as a sinister punitive instrument. Even though I was under court order to remain in the State of Michigan because of an extradition proceeding, it insisted that I entail the danger of a trip to Washington, without the benefit of immunity. This placed me in great jeopardy. On July 8, 1971, I was again subpoenaed by the same committee even though I had been told that it had finished with me. For that reason, I didn't think I had to go back again in response to a conspiracy of character assassination, racial persecution, or personal vendetta and the nature of the subpoena was vague and placed a confusing and difficult burden on me. The committee was in telephone contact with my lawyers, and I assumed that the matter was being settled through them.

Robert F. Williams

LETTERS EXCHANGED BETWEEN S. ABDULLAH (MARC) SCHELEIFER AND ROBERT F. WILLIAMS

Dear Rob[2]:

The other day someone in the States sent me another clipping from the *New York Times* and there you were pumping Chairman Mao's hand. The piece you wrote read well and I was pleased to find an address of sorts at the end of the article. During the years that we have been away from the States. I have been kept in erratic touch with what was happening to you whenever Dick Gibson would periodically surface in Cairo, then a few years later in Amman and then in Beirut. During one of those Gibson appearances, I signed a release turning over whatever rights I had in *Negroes with Gun* to you for European editions. I do hope you received that release from Gibson and that something came of it. So much has happened to me since I last saw you in Havana. When I returned to the States in 1964, I married and converted to Islam. A year later, my wife and I had our children (from her previous marriage) left for North Africa. After a summer in Algeria, we made our way to Jordan and settled in Arab Jerusalem where I became the managing editor of Jordan's English-language daily., which was known in its last manifestation before the June 1967 War as The Palestine News. The War and the Israeli occupation finished off the paper, so I became a foreign correspondent working as a stringer first for the *New York Times* and now for NBC News (I broadcast under my old first name Marc). Among the magazines I was contributing articles to as a freelancer for *Jeune Afrique*, and in 1969 I became their Middle East correspondent based first in Amman and now in Beirut. I've written a book about the June 1967 War and the Palestinians, called *The Fall of Jerusalem*. It comes out in Arabic translation here in a week or two, but I am still trying to find a publisher in New York and London for it. The first couple of years out here were rough financially; now we are doing very well reaching a point of diminishing intellectual returns I have reached the point where journalism is now bringing in diminishing intellectual returns. I have become very familiar with the region, its people, their values and their language, but I think we should get away for a while and I should be sharpening my own sensibility, which too many articles and radio spots have begun to dull. So, I have thought about graduate study within some sort of teaching fellowship structure and I would very much appreciate your impressions of the University of Michigan and its atmosphere—as environment, as the degree of intellectual freedom and the quality of community life that would be available there for an interracial family (these words sound so weird sounding after all these years in the Muslim world), which is what, by American standards, we are. I already know that the University has a highly rated Muslim East studies program which is where my competence and interest (within the discipline of modern history) lies. Anyway, I'd very much appreciate whatever advice and observations you could extend. My regards to Mabel and the children.

S. Abdullah Schleifer

Dear Marc[3]:

Just a brief note to let you know that I received your letter. It was good to hear from you again. I had caught your newscast from time to time before I got your letter. Marzani still has not come through with any money. He has sold the rights to the book by Floyd McKissick who claims that he cannot get it printed. Marzani claims that he only owes me $300. Because the book did not sell very well. A lot of B. S. has gone down. The racist dogs are still after my scalp. I am fighting extradition to North Carolina. I have lost one appeal and the case is now before the Michigan Supreme Court. I was given a fellowship here by the Ford Foundation for one year to write a book on China. I do not have any information on the Middle East Studies Center here. If you plan to come to the States, it will be good if you can swing something here. The university community here seems very liberal about interracial marriages. There are quite a few here. Most people here are pretty much detached from the rest of the world. The Black population is also very small. I doubt you would have any trouble from the marriage angle. I will only be here through September; however, I will leave my forwarding address with the Center. Mabel sends best wishes to you and your family.

Rob

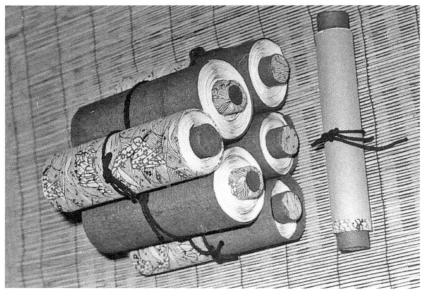

STATEMENT IN SUPPORT OF ROBERT F. WILLIAMS FROM 10,000 JAPANESE AGAINST NORTH CAROLINA EXTRADITION CHARGES

The Final Chapter: The Japanese and African Americans: Thirteen Thousand Japanese saved Robert F. Williams

I. The Ceaseless Movement for the Civil Rights, for Racial Equality, and for Peace (1977).

On the evening of August 10, 1976, one tall African American couple exchanged a firm handshake with a group of Japanese at Haneda Airport in Tokyo. The husband of the couple was Robert F. Williams who asserted the right of self-defense of the African American in the 1950s American South. Living in Monroe, NC, where the harsh white violence on Blacks was common, he was nearly assassinated by the local police on three occasions. Moreover, being falsely charged with the abduction of a white couple; he was forced to seek an asylum in Cuba and China for eight years. (See the Introduction, Sec. 2 & 4) In 1969, he finally returned to the United States and brought the case to court to prove his innocence. This story will remind many readers of the article about the signature-collecting campaign: "Justice for Williams, an African American" seven years ago. *The Asahi Journal* reported this issue several times in 1970, as well as *The Asahi News Paper* did in its readers' column (June 18, 1971). (Material: III) After fifteen years of arduous struggle, Williams finally cleared himself of the charge on January 16, 1976—the appeal was withdrawn! This time, he was visiting Japan to express his appreciation to more than 13,000 Japanese who signed their names to support him. In Japan, a number of civic movements occurred to support civil rights all over the world. Recent examples are one against the deportation of Vietnamese students who cried against war, and another to protect the human rights of Kim Dae Jung, and the growing movement of Amnesty International. One reason for the rise of those movements comes from the geographic location of Japan—the center of East Asia. However, many hold doubt about the effects related to these human rights movements. For instance, some questioned how much those signatures from Japan could exert an influence in the United States. Some said, "Having for the political authority our enemy, our effort will weigh no more than a piece of paper," while others were concerned about the direction of the support group. Fortunately, we had the opportunity to hear from the people who participated in the campaign for Williams during his visit. I would like to begin with the chronology of the campaign, and then the report from the hearing will follow.

1. The Isolation, Conspiracy, and Oppression

In the fall of 1969, on his return to the United States after eight years in exile, Williams said, "I was treated equally as a human; however, that would be a very unusual case in the U.S. I am going to return to the 'normal' life as an African American, which means a life fighting against the discrimination." It had been a year and a half from the assassination of Martin Luther King Jr., and the African American movement was in its transition—they had lost the core members and many of the members were at a loss, distrusting, and terrified about the movement. For instance, Stokely Carmichael a.k.a. "Black Power," once appeared to take on the leadership, but abruptly left for Africa, while H. Rap Brown was thrown into prison. At the same time, the government side had beefed up their suppression against the movement, with the strong power of President Nixon, and the new National Advisory Commission on Civil Disorders. In addition, the CIA and the FBI gained their influence in politics by their sophisticated conspiracies. J. Edgar Hoover, FBI director, successfully led to dissolve the Black Crusaders; several leaders of the Black Panthers were shot, and 385 members were imprisoned. So, Williams's return was about the only hope among the members of African American movement in its critical moment.[4] Despite the CIA's conspiracy to block his return, Williams arrived in Detroit to see a number of people packed into the airport to welcome him as a new leader; however, he needed to clear the frame-up charge of kidnapping before taking the role.[5] In Detroit, a support group for Williams was organized by African American groups, civil rights groups, the Caucasian liberals and churches. This support group, the Committee for Williams in Detroit, distributed several thousands of signature forms in town. I even heard that they had some from Quebec to participate in the support activity. The Committee wrote a petition to ask the governor of Michigan to stop the extradition of Williams to the South and let him face the court in Detroit. (Material III) For a while, everything seemed working in a favorable and smooth way for Williams. A new mayor of Detroit was elected by supporting this civic movement, while an African American Congressman from Illinois, John Conyers loaned one of his offices for the headquarters of the committee for Williams. However, in half a year, Williams and his support group faced enormous hardships which were severe enough to take their hope away. For instance, some unidentified African Americans committed violence all over the town, claiming that they belonged to the Committee for Williams in Detroit—this made the people in town furious, and terrified. Consequently, all the blame came to Williams. Moreover, the opposition among the support group became obvious, while the support of the citizens rapidly went down. A famous columnist criticized Williams in the editorial, and readers of major local newspapers in the United States read the article. Like this, without a chance to explain the situation, Williams became misunderstood, avoided, and regarded the hazardous by both the citizens and the press. The officials did not proceed with Williams' case promptly because it no longer had the citizens' support behind it. Even there was even a time when his attorney disappeared when the trial was about to start. What was worse, Williams was summoned three times by the Senate Committee on the Judiciary where James Eastland, a famous Republican Senator from Mississippi, worked as the chairperson. If ever he had rejected to appear for the third time, they would have charged him with contempt of the House of Senate; of course, they would require the fourth time if Williams had shown up the third time.[6] The phone line was tapped, the mail was opened, and telegraphs were often not delivered or altered in the contents.[7] There was no way to find employment. So, he had to earn a living by lecturing; however, more and more lecture schedules started being cancelled. The permission to travel over states was not necessarily granted on time for the schedule, which made it more difficult for him. Williams was constantly threatened with death at the same time—no one knew when and where someone would shoot him. At that time, many Black Panthers were thrown into prison for carrying a gun with them, even though the right of self-protection was granted by the Constitution. Moreover, Fred Hampton, the Black Panther leader in Chicago, was shot to death in bed late at night by the police force. The police arrested a number of Black activists by setting them up with some kind of false charges, such as carrying a gun, while they shot those who "resisted" the police. It would have not been surprising if Williams would have been slaughtered by machinegun fire from a running car. He constantly felt this kind of threat around him. The intent of the government was obvious—they tried to manipulate Williams to ruin himself through the steps as follows:

First, make Williams isolated from the masses by generating their distrust with him, in other words, make him ignored in society. Second, burden him constantly with extraordinary stress for a long time in various ways, so he goes the way of self-destruction, such as depression, alcoholism, and suicide. Lead him to self-destruction mentally and physically. This was the government's new strategy against the African American leaders to "kill [oppress]" them. In order to oppress African-American leaders, the government manipulated the confrontation inside the left wings, as well as utilizing both federal and local political authorities—which was the unique characteristic of the oppression. For Williams, who did not belong to any school of political ideology originating from Caucasian culture, had the most difficult time gaining support at that time. Unlike Williams, Professor Angela Davis had gained the support of the Communist Party, and the support movement spread out internationally. Since the party required those who needed assistance to join the party to get their support, Williams got no support from them. So, he became isolated and disrupted constantly. Moreover, he was reported as a "betrayer who sold the civil rights movement to the CIA" in the left-wing publications. For instance, the letter by Carl Yoneda was even read by the Japanese Committee for Williams. In short, the oppression was well crafted by the government to utilize any parties that were not happy with Williams, such as the KKK, and the Communist Party, to legally "throw Williams into a grave" by secretly cooperating with them. Williams started writing his autobiography as the last method to prove his good; however, the source of oppression arranged for another writer to publish William's biography before his real autobiography was done.[8] The conspiracy and the oppression by the government were about to suffocate Williams—a citizen of the nation.

2. The Effect of Signatures from Japan

One day when Williams was suffering from high blood pressure, insomnia, and migraine, a number of signatures in rolls arrived there one after another. These rolls were made of *shoji* paper and navy-blue *washi* [traditional Japanese paper], and one twelve-meter roll held 700 signatures. The signature collecting movement was started in April 1970. In the same year, 2,800 signatures were collected, and the number of signatures counted more than 10,000 by the end of the next year. They were sent to the governor of Michigan, the attorney general, and President Nixon during his visit to China. (Material IV) Fifty founders initiated the signature collecting by themselves, and it happened to be introduced by the mass media. Through the articles in *The Asahi Journal* and *The Asahi Newspaper*, the group gained the participation of the readers in forty-seven prefectures. We had wonderful supporters, such as students who collected signatures in their school festivals; teachers who did so through lecturing about Williams in American Studies class; a patient who led the whole hospital to participate in the signature petitions; doctors who did so by putting the appeal up in the waiting room of the hospital; and homemakers who did while working as saleswomen of dry goods. It spread as a really unknown "grassroots" movement, which had encouraged Williams and the uncertain support movement in America, more than we imagined. The other influence was that the signatures interested the mass media in the United States. The signatures from Japan brought the forgotten incident about Williams up to the public interest. The press must have had to report the issue that made a number of people sign petitions. In fact, "52 Diet men from Tokyo and Osaka, 161 politicians including the mayors of Yokohama, Yokosuka, and Machida, 429 Christian teachers and monks, 429 university professors, 1053 teachers, and 408 doctors and nurses" signed.[9] Once the press reported the case, citizens, especially the people in William's hometown Monroe were deeply moved. It woke their conscience and thoughtfulness up—because the movement made them realize the world was watching what was going on, the racial discrimination and oppression against African Americans. Over 2,500 Japanese high school students, over 2,000 college students, about 300 homemakers, and others in different occupations were watching the reality, with their trust in America's conscience and thoughtfulness. The following is what Aunt Azeri, an African American from Monroe, wrote in a mini newspaper, *"Did You Know?"*

> While Japanese people far away from here have done so much to support Williams, we Americans, including the people in Monroe, have not been able to prove his innocence. Thinking of this, I feel so little of myself.

Let us see the influence of the political authorities. They did not expect that simply these signatures could change their decision. However, once the press reported the case, they could no longer hide the fact of receiving the signatures and became conscious of the eye of the world. One day, a prosecutor from Monroe told Williams, "You must have Japanese friends who are very good at making up a propaganda."

3. The Comeback in Court

Williams lost the case regarding extradition to the South. After the repeated extensions of the trial by the governor of Michigan by not showing up in court with his privilege as a public servant, the Michigan Supreme Court decided the extradition of Williams's. On February 16, 1975, officials forcefully took him to North Carolina. At the same time, the court of Monroe demanded him 20,000 dollars for bail, which Williams refused to pay. "I am not going to pay for bail. I know that you all know that this charge is in fact a frame-up," he said to the officials. After their discussion in the recess, the judges decided to reduce the amount to ten thousand dollars, but Williams adamantly refused to pay for bail. Finally, a Monroe citizen offered to pay for his bail—so he was released without bending his policy of not paying for bail.

On January 19, 1976, the trial on Williams's charge of kidnapping was set out, and various support groups from different states gathered together for the group protest scheduled a day before the trial. Groups like National Association for Advancement of Colored People (NAACP), Committee of African People (COAP), Student Nonviolent Coordinating Committee (SNCC), National Lawyers Guild (NLG), Southern Committee of Educational Fund (SCEF), Northern Alberta Alliance on Race Relations (NAARR), and the Unitarian Church, assembled in the place as well as radical African American activists LeRoy Jones (a.k.a. Amiri Bakara). In addition, local groups such as African-American church groups, the Committee for the Wilmington Ten, and the North Carolina Committee of Protection of the Human Rights of Political Criminals, came together to the hall of West Charlotte High School.[10] Williams's return and the trial stimulated the African American movement in North Carolina.[11] A press conference was arranged on April 17, two days before the trial. While I was leaving Atlanta for Monroe, I heard that major presses like *the New York Times* and *the Washington Post* were to send correspondents for this occasion. It was seen in the local newspaper at that time that most of the citizens of Monroe were opposed to the extradition of Williams. The Caucasians opposed to "save their face by not revealing the old wound [the race issue] to the public."[12] The government officials kept their silence about this matter, while the prosecutor was eager to "let Williams have it this time." Despite the prosecutor's attitude a day before the trial, this very person suddenly declared the "withdrawal of the appeal" on the case—this surprised everyone.[13] It was reported that the withdrawal was made by the consideration of Williams's health. However, something else should have been the true reason because a few years before they did not accept Williams's request to drop the case for health reasons. The prosecutor told reporters, "Williams has sent the wrong message to African Americans and grew the hate and distrust against Caucasians. We should not regard him as a hero."[14] Now, let us consider why the prosecutor of Monroe suddenly withdrew the case. One of the factors was the superior strategy by Williams. As he talked in the press conference on December 10, 1975, he had substantial evidence about conspiracies in the FBI and the CIA, and other federal agencies. He said, "In the coming trial, I am going to disclose the political conspiracies among federal agencies including the CIA and the FBI, which ruined my life for over the last ten years. My attorney and I will try to have those responsible sits in the witness box."[15] He added,

Anyway, they will not keep me in prison for a long time because knowing my intention, they will try to hinder my effort to reveal the truth. They will either make the prosecutor of Monroe to drop the case or kill me in prison to keep my mouth shut.

In addition, before going to Monroe Williams had prepared to sue the following five in North Carolina for violation of the basic human rights, demanding one million dollars for compensation. The five were the former governor of North Carolina, Senator Morgan, the former head of the judiciary, the former director of Monroe city police, and the district attorney. He said, "They realized that the court they set up for me turned out to be the court that will judge them. This is my purpose of facing the trial—because I have never heard them explaining about their fault; however, they still expect me to explain [what I did not do]."[16] Even if he can reveal the truth in court, nothing can compensate for the fifteen years of damage and struggle he received by the false charge.[17] There had been no need for white men to apologize for their faults, while Blacks were always called cowards and were to apologize for something. If it were not being called discrimination against Blacks, what else it would be?

Chart 1: The number of the undersigned sorted by occupation.

Occupation	Number of People
* Politics: including Diet men (52), Governor of Tokyo and Osaka, Mayors (10), and Prefectural congressmen (34)	161
*Religion: monk, minister, YMCA, YWCA	429
*University President and Professor	419
*Teachers	1,053
*Attorney	21
*Commentator, Writer, Journalist	265
*Medical Doctor	128
*Nurse	280
*CEO	51
*Librarian	81
*Pre-school Teachers	105
*College Student	2,052
*High School Student	2,554
*Worker, Public, Commercial	2,893
*Farmer	171
*Homemaker	1,228
*Artist	67
*NPO	140
*Union	55
*Other	243
*Unemployed	291
*Patient	355
*Non-response	102
Total	13,144

Chart 2: The number of the undersigned in prefectures—as of the time the committee collected 10,000.

	Pref.	Number of Sig.		Pref.	Number of Sig.		Pref.	Number of Sig.		Pref.	Number of Sig.
1	Tokyo	2,463	13	Fukui	151	25	Shiga	32	37	Wakayama	7
2	Nagano	1,067	14	Nigata	127	26	Fukushima	29	38	Toyama	7
3	Kanagawa	942	15	Okayama	121	27	Iwate	27	39	Ishikawa	5
4	Kyoto	753	16	Miyagi	113	28	Yamagata	23	40	Gifu	5
5	Hokkaido	732	17	Aomori	88	29	Miyazaki	20	41	Tottori	5
6	Aichi	692	18	Ehime	63	30	Mie	19	42	Kumamoto	4
7	Hyogo	589	19	Nara	62	31	Kagoshima	16	43	Okinawa	2
8	Osaka	406	20	Shizuoka	61	32	Ibaragi	16	44	Akita	2
9	Chiba	400	21	Hiroshima	60	33	Shimane	16	45	Nagasaki	1
10	Saitama	339	22	Tochigi	53	34	Tokushima	14	46	Kagawa	1
11	Fukuoka	192	23	Kouchi	37	35	Gunma	13		Unknown	3
12	Yamanashi	178	24	Yamaguchi	32	36	Saga	10		Total 46 Pref.	10,000*

* 3,144 more signatures were collected, which included one from Oita Prefecture, the total of 13,144 signatures consisted of those from 47 prefectures in Japan.

4. Connection between the Abolition of Discrimination and the Abolition of Nuclear Bombs

What would have been the result if Williams put up the same strategy a few years before? He would not have had the following factors that led him to the victory. For instance, the crowd for the group protest would have been small, and only locals would have been there. Moreover, the media would not have paid attention to the case. Considering the unfairness in the Southern court, without the support from the society, Williams might have been killed before the trial, for seeing conspiracies against Blacks from 1961. Bearing that in mind, another factor of Williams's victory was the change in public opinion after Watergate—the rise of criticism of the government, the CIA, and the FBI, as well as the demand for citizens' right to be informed. Let us take some examples. Once public opinion changed in this way, the media suddenly became eager to uncover the conspiracies in the government.[18] Groups of humanistic liberals, including the Communist Party, unconditionally participated in the support activity and gathered together for the group protest. The Black mobs realized the size and the system of oppression and saw them being trapped in it. To the day of his victory, I admire Williams for surviving the long difficult time. In retrospect about the signature-collecting campaign, the signatures and postcards from Japan encouraged him while being isolated in the United States and being depressed. I believe the support we provided with him worked well, because it was from outside of the United States. This experience reassured me of the importance of international cooperation for the protection of human rights.

5. Toward the Cooperation with the Japanese

On August 13, 1976, the welcome meeting was held at Sendagaya Civic Hall in Tokyo. On that occasion, Williams said, "Despite of the high speech by President Carter, the minority groups, including African Americans, have not obtained the equality and justice. Racial discrimination is still deeply rooted in the American life." For instance, many African American civil rights activists, such as the Wilmington Ten, were thrown in prison for false charges. They were charged because of the discrimination. So, even after Williams had cleared his charge, he was determined to continue his fight against the injustice in and out of the United States. Williams was also eager to put his effort into abolishing nuclear bombs, neutron bombs, and nuclear power, which "threaten the whole human species." As a practice for the protection of human rights, he considers these two agendas: the abolition of racial discrimination and the peace movement. It is interesting how these two connect in his mind. "The basic human rights mean the right of survival," said Williams. He was going to fight against those that threatened the survival. This showed that he realized the similarity between the purpose of the fight against racial discrimination and the strife for peace. The following is the summary of his speech:

"Did you know that America's policies for Japan are made based upon their racial discrimination? How much do you know about the history of Japanese Americans during the World War II? Although they were citizens, the government took their property away, and threw them in camps. On the other hand, German captives were allowed to visit their families, and were treated as guests. In addition, the atomic bombs were dropped in Japan, but never in Germany. Taking the present example, the government attributes the rise of prices and the unemployment rate to the advancement of Japanese economy and tries to agitate Americans to hate Japan. This was never done against Germany. Now, I would like to cooperate with Japanese people to work for world peace—which was the message of Hiroshima and Nagasaki." The audience was overwhelmed by his speech. It made me believe that we Japanese were the ones who should feel the need for the cooperation from African Americans to promote world peace.

II. Perspectives for the Support Movement:

1. For Leaders of the Movement

Dr. Richard Kagan commented on the difficulty he had in understanding the long-lasting strong support movement in Japan for the unknown African American—while the case was not known widely even in the United States. In June 1972, Dr. Kagan, one of the organizers of the support group of the University of Michigan, had meetings with the group of the committee of Japan. At the party, lectures, and personal interviews, he talked about the reasons for the strong support activity in Japan. The following is the summary.

> First, most of the members of this support activity were very interested in the minority problems, such as about Koreans, the Ainus, and Burakumin [the outcast]. For this reason, learning the problem in the U.S. was very useful for them to compare the issues of the same nature. Second, the many in the group sensed some kind of racism by Americans whom they met in places like the U.S. bases, as well as business and academic arenas. Through their experience, they realized that the issue of race was the critical and fundamental issue of the U.S. Thus, they were extremely interested in the result of Williams' case. Third, they knew the importance to experience what they had learned in books. Fourth, some of them, like the two organizers, had personally met Williams. One had stayed in the Williams' while studying race issues, and another had met him at Asia-Africa Writers Conference in Beijing. Some of the founders of Japanese Committee have personally met Williams in the same manner. Remember that their writings made the opportunities for the case to be introduced in papers and journals. Of course, above all, the most urgent and concrete motive came from the letter of appeal by the African American movement in the U.S. In fact, Williams' cases unfortunately did not draw attention in his home country, but it did in Japan – and this was why the weak support activity in the U.S. needed the cooperation of that in Japan.[19]

As far as I know, there have been three support groups founded at different times, but all of them stopped their activity in short order. Likewise, Dr. Kagan stopped his correspondence with us after moving to another state for his new office. It should have been extremely tough for them to continue the activity in the middle of oppression.

Reaction from the Readers

Although we had to set up the system from scratch after receiving the appeal from the Detroit committee, the support movement widely spread in Japan, unlike that in the United States. I remember that I was at a loss, overwhelmed by the difficulties in making the signature-collecting movement successful. For one thing, we had no organizational structure to begin with; in addition, we had to convey the complicated nature of the false charge caused by discrimination that Williams was facing. Because of the complexity of the issue, we could not simply stand at the corners to ask pedestrians for signatures. In order to make the signatures influential in the international arena we had to collect them throughout the society, beyond the everyday social situation. Also, the volume of the collection was critical. Despite our concern, the group collected more than 10,000 signatures from all the forty-seven prefectures in two years. This volume and the range of the undersigned became one of the strengths of this movement. Despite my concern, reports by the press enabled the group to collect signatures from the various groups of the society. Generally speaking, it was very rare that the media reported this kind of civic movement; in fact, we had a difficult time drawing the media's attention. For instance, they decided not to report our movement "because nothing relevant is happening in the U.S." When Williams finally cleared his charge, they denied reporting his victory saying, "The happy ending never makes good news." Paradoxically, newspapers were likely to put letters from readers as a response to their articles. In this way, our letter of appeal appeared on *The Asahi Newspaper* on June 18, 1971. The following was the situation. Furious, two African-American students commented on the discrimination they received from the Japanese. Surprised, a few readers replied, "Sorry, we did not really mean it," while the other said, " Discrimination [against Black people] rarely happens." After letters and phone calls as above, those students felt offended further.[20] That was the time we sent the letter to introduce the support group for Williams and to ask for readers' cooperation in the movement. Soon, the letter appeared on the paper, which received a number of reactions. Over one hundred letters arrived at the committee, asking for more information and interest in participating in the signature collection. Considering the readers' interest, the editorial department decided to put more detailed articles with pictures about Williams and the support group in Japan, titled "Letter from Readers—Continued."[21] Before this newspaper article, our letter of "appeal" appeared for two pages in *The Asahi Journal* on October 4, 1970. Likewise, this received an enormous reaction from readers, and more than 3,000 signatures were collected among them. Having more reaction than they had expected, the editorial department started the series "America with Terrorism and Guerrilla." In the series, they reported guerrilla activities in Quebec, Chile, and Argentina. At the same time, they wrote about the United States—the introduction about the radicals such as Angela Davis and Weatherman, as well as the special contribution by Williams "Racism at Stake." In both cases, the interest of the readers led the editorial department to run these articles.[22] In practice, when they receive over a hundred reactions from readers, it shows that over a thousand readers are *highly* interested, and over ten thousand readers are *fairly* interested in the topic. Thus, the editorial department cannot go without following the topic. Once our letter appeared on the paper, we were able to make a series of articles about Williams's case. It was composed of the follow-up report, a letter of appreciation from Williams, questions from readers and responses from the support group, and the report of Williams's victory. Moreover, the paper allowed us to put the information of our lectures in the column "weekly schedule" to promote the tie between readers and the support group. Overall, we managed tactfully to use the media for our promotion. The participation of the readers not only increased the volume of the signatures, it also changed their character and the nature of the movement. Originally, the support group was started by fifty founders (Material II) collecting signatures. By the time one article was made in *The Asahi Journal*, more than 2,000 were gathered. The article made the ripple effect that the original undersigned led others to participate in the activity at their organization and meetings. In addition, we received enormous reactions from readers of *The Asahi Newspaper* and *The Asahi Journal* in half a year period. In both groups, people were highly interested in, and learning about the protection of human rights, the abolition of discrimination, and international cooperation. The former group was mostly composed of groups from universities, churches, and academic meetings. In this case, the group kept correspondence with the founders to collect signatures. The latter the readers, however, individually exchanged questions and answers with the organizers. The complex issue required the readers first to learn about the issue of discrimination before they got to actually sign their name. Common questions were if we could send more detailed information, the history of the racial discrimination in the United States, the reason why the Japanese support Williams, and the influence of the signatures. Unless being familiar with these points, it would have been difficult to collect signatures from others. In other words, the supporters were required to educate themselves about the issue in order to tell them about it. And finally, they can collect signatures from others, and make a substantial contribution to the rescue activity. This process was commonly done among readers. A good example was senior high school teachers. The following is a letter from a senior high school teacher interested in talking about Williams in his class. It shows what kind of meaning this movement has to teachers like him.

For Teachers

> I am teaching at a senior high school in Osaka. After reading the letter of appeal asking for the fair trial of Williams in *Asahi Newspaper*, I became interested in participating in the support movement for the African American leader. Even though I have tried to introduce the African American movement in classroom, it seems still difficult for students to understand what has been going on, and more difficult for them to do something for the movement. About Williams, I had the students read an introduction in a book "Black Movement Shaking the World." Through collecting signatures, I hope that the students get interested in, and start acting for issues like this. For this purpose, I would like to continue activities of this kind. Is it possible for me, or my student to correspond with activists in the U.S.? Could you give me your advice? (Shingo Iwasa, Osaka)

Several senior high schools shared time to learn about Williams. It conveyed to students that "through his life, Williams has harshly learned how one can be treated being an

African American in the U.S.—the reality of the racial discrimination." And then, signatures were collected and sent to the Japanese Committee. Teachers organized signatures: 330 from Kitami High School in Hokkaido, 210 from Ichihara in Chiba,[23] 322 from Nagano City, 179 from Yamanashi, and 86 from Tuyama High School.[24] A total of 13,144 signatures were collected from high school teachers (1,053) and students (2,554), which made as high as 27.4 percent of the total; compared to university professors (419) and students (2,052), which made 18.8 percent of the total. It is noteworthy that the newspaper articles motivated most of the undersigned from high schools, while many of the undersigned from universities were founders of the committee. For instance, in the column of the reaction to the article about Williams, letters from three high school students were reported in *The Asahi Journal*—each of them collected 100 to 180 signatures.[25] In addition, reading *The Asahi Newspaper*, a number of high school students collected more than 100 signatures from each prefecture, such as Fukui, Kyoto, Ueda, Sendai, Urawa, Tokyo, and Kamakura.[26] We organized them into five rolls and sent them to the United States.[27] Let me quote a letter from one high school student.

For High-school Students

> Please find 100 signatures we collected in our school festival. We collected them by making a sign and distributed 400 pamphlets about Williams. We made them all from a scratch. While collecting signatures, my friend and I had an argument. He said, "These papers can easily be tossed or burned! Don't you think our effort will never make any difference in America?" I answered, "If these signatures are ignored, America's conscience is gone." By the way, most of the signatures are by males, not because women ignored me, but because my school is just for boys. (Hiroshi Hiramatsu, Saitama)

While receiving scorns and denial from a friend about the signature-collecting activity and learning about African American problems to answer questions from those friends, he started understanding the problems surrounding Williams.

For the Youths

> I am 18 years old, preparing for college entrance exams. I am very interested in learning about the issue of prejudice and discrimination. Those problems seem very complicated and make me think if I have any bias and discriminate toward someone without knowing it. Since I was unsure if I was qualified to sign for Williams, it took me a long time to actually do it. I would like to share what else I thought about the discrimination issues. "Discrimination is too deeply rooted, and too widely spread, and a small movement like this cannot resolve." Seeing the huge issues of discrimination, I could not make sense in saving only handful individuals. I realized that I was wrong about this and was very impatient. I learned that it is more important to take an action, like collecting signatures, than only mulling over the problem. I started to get the true meaning to participate in the movement of discrimination abolition. In order to abolish any kind of discrimination, especially racial discrimination, takes a long time. Patience is the most needed thing. I keenly hope that this movement works as a boost to Mr. Williams, and more people get interested in support movements for equality. This particular movement may not only save one individual

directly, but also may expedite the whole process of racial equality through enlightening people. So, the world will become a wonderful place in this way. Actually, this movement enlightened me, and changed my view of life. Thank you, and I wish the best for all the members of this movement.

Here, I would like to share that the appeal reached the heart of hospital patients.

For Patients
(The 1st correspondence)

> I am a patient staying in a national hospice. Fighting against tuberculosis, I would not help thinking that the source of all the problems, such as race issues, the Vietnam War, *brakumin* [the outcast in Japan] issue, Koreans in Japan, environmental pollution, militarism, and traffic accidents, comes from the same place. In this process of thoughts, I feel that issues surrounding African American leaders became the problem of ours, the patients. At the same time, to me, the movement for racial equality seems possible to be the source of power to protest against the unreasonable policies on healthcare issues by the government. What I mean here is that the cooperation in the grassroots level is critical to solve these problems. If you decide that my support can make a difference, I would like to help this movement. Could you please send me the information about this case and forms for signatures? Thank you for your time and considerations in the busy schedule.

(The 2nd correspondence)

> My first letter to respond your appeal was intended only to let my close friends understand all the problems, including racial discrimination. However, my letter received much more reaction than I thought. More and more people in the hospital, including the nurses, became interested in Williams' case, and most of the patients (479 out of 650) signed to support him. Additionally, the organization of patients, which I belong to, recently agreed to talk about the signature-collecting campaign in a council. I am so glad to have the wider support to the movement for which I took action by myself.
>
> *(Isamu Hattori, Dazaifu Chubu Hospital, Aichi)*

In addition to the signatures from the hospital where Mr. Hattori is, we sent the officials in the United States the eighth roll of signature petitions. It consisted of 99 signatures from Nakano Sanatorium, 91 from Fukui Prefectural Hospital, 300 from Amakasu Hospital in Kamakura, and some more from Baptist hospitals in Kyoto and Kita-Kyushu. Even though *The Asahi Journal* has more than 8,000 readers, in addition to 8 million readers of *The Asahi Newspaper*, it is rare to see readers' responses to the letter from other readers. I suspect that even readers were deeply moved, more than 90 percent might not have gotten to write a letter because of the time restraint and other inconveniences. For example, some might not have found a piece of paper handy when trying to write, while others might have put off writing until later and forgotten to do so. Thus, the people who responded to the letters and collected signatures must have been extremely active people. Through these responses to our letter of appeal, thousands of signatures were sent. I was deeply inspired by the energy of the grassroots movement coming from each individual. I believe that this inspiration has supported the whole movement to the end. Next, I would like to write about how one homemaker felt about the support activity. She collected signatures while working as a saleswoman of dry goods.

For Homemakers

> In some points, Mr. Williams' article on *Asashi Journal* was too complicated for a homemaker like me to comprehend, but my intuition tells me that this movement to protect human rights is the right thing to do. I would like other people to participate in the signature-collecting campaign and feel the reality of the human rights movement. Even though I can only understand simple things, and do a little, I would like to continue collecting signatures so that someone in the undersigned can lead the movement, and as a group, we can grow, and make a change. (Chiyo Fujimoto, Osaka)

Likewise, the signature-collecting activities that were fostered through the founders increased the grassroots characteristics, which made the original two merge together. In both, more citizens started individually to proactively participate in different support activities. Examples were numerous. A group of daily workers sent me a handmade form filled with signatures; these ladies brought our letter of "appeal" to their workplace and collected signatures there. Also, there was a college student who appeared in a local newspaper in Hokkaido to collect signatures during the spring break. Many organizers of churches, YMCA, and YWCA, also helped the support group by holding lectures, contributing signatures, and raising funds. I cannot forget a mother of three who sent the kids to bed and helped me make signature forms every night. We were fortunate to have had magazine editors and newspaper correspondents who shared their time off for our *"News"* publications. Everyone started tackling the supporting movement in their own way. In the end, we saw a big circle of international cooperation among citizens from different classes and occupations. I would like to note that the circle also included politicians.

Politics by Citizens
Some say that only citizens must belong to civic movements, excluding politicians or any political interests. Otherwise, to them, movements appear corrupted. Unlike their standard, to me, the uniqueness of civic movements is that citizens are the core part of the activities. I see no problem for the citizens to ask politicians to participate in the civic movement. It does mean that the movement yields to the political authority; it is the same deal as they ask for help from students, ministers, and doctors. Regardless of the individual's occupation, each signature is equally valuable for the movement to succeed; the diversity of the undersigned can have a unique influence on the diverse American society. Who can perceive that signatures by politicians weigh more than that by over 2,500 senior high school students sincerely believing in America's conscience, or that by nearly 1,000 inpatients praying for justice? As participation of the other groups in the society, that of politicians, of course, has its unique influence; the larger number of their participation boosts the strength of the movement. On this point, since our organizers did not have connections with political groups, it was very fortunate of us

to have Senator Kan-ichi Nishimura as a part of the group. I knew that he used to be a Christian teacher in Otsu City, Shiga, and he had a successful experience of saving a Japanese American charged with espionage and sentenced to death. It was just after the last war when he launched the supra-party signature-petition movement in the Diet, for the life and human rights of the accused. After many difficulties, the petition received the signature of amnesty from President Kennedy in Dallas. Senator Nishimura readily consented to our rescue movement for Williams. Since then, he has been one of the best supporters of the movement. Even when I was unable to help him due to illness, he voluntarily collected signatures all through his office. He was the one who made a connection to the governor of Tokyo, Osaka, as well as to the mayors of Yokohama, Yokosuka, and Kamakura—where many Americans were found. In addition to his effort, another nine mayors of Machida, Kunitachi, Kokubunji, Chofu, Tanashi, and Koganei, participated in the signature petition at the citizens' request. The total participation of politicians counted one hundred sixty-one, including fifty-two members of the Diet, prefectural assembly, and city assembly. Talking of the relationship between Williams and the two organizers of the group, as Dr. R. Kagan pointed out, both Takahashi and Nakajima have had friendship with Williams. I was one of few witnesses to know his innocence, as written in the introduction. Since he fled to Cuba in 1961, I had determined to take the responsibility for being a witness, which meant taking on the role of organizer for the support group. The more signatures we collected, the more I felt responsible to the undersigned for the result of this movement. To make the movement successful, these signature lists needed to be seen by the citizens of the United States, avoiding suppression by the government. I was trying to draw the media's attention to this movement so that we could ensure to have these lists sent safely to the United States. All of the signature lists were organized into rolls, beautifully wrapped with *washi* paper—with a touch of Japanese culture. It was so beautifully made that it would make the most reluctant recipient, like the prosecutor of Monroe, intrigued to open them. In these roles, we typed names, addresses, and occupations of the undersigned beside all the signatures. In addition, we organized each roll in a way that the whole picture of the signature-petition movement could easily be understood. For example, every roll began with the petition, followed by the list of 700 undersigned sorted by their occupations, as well as the list of the total undersigned. Sometimes, we included a map of Japan to show where these supporters come from. Once new rolls were completed, we sent Williams a copy and kept the original, so that we could avoid the loss in mail or the disruption by interest groups including the government. After having a disruption in correspondence and the phone being tapped, we could not be too careful. In 1972, the committee was planning to ask Chinese Premier Chou En-lai to hand the lists of signatures to President Nixon during his visit to China. It seemed a much better plan than to send them to the White House where they would be hidden and ignored. We also knew that a firm friendship was established between Williams and Chou during his stay for three years of exile. Concerned with the reaction from the Chinese side, the opposition was made by the group of pro-China in the committee. This was when Professor Iku Yasui clearly showed the direction of the support group to proceed. In the conference among founders, he emphasized that the support activity had to make decisions based on considering the best for the supported, not for the position or interests of the supporters. Moved by his words, all at the table decided to take action for "politics by the citizens." For a side note, Williams also successfully utilized international relations to advance the African American movement in 1950s. So, he asked us to do it the same manner this time also. In this way, the Japanese Committee for the Defense of the Life and Fundamental Human Rights of Robert F. Williams sent the petition with 10,000 signatures to Nixon through Chou En-lai. At the same time, the committee sent this information to the press in Beijing, such as *The New York Times*, to draw their attention. By the way, it was later revealed by Williams that this successful plan was recorded in one of the files of the CIA.

Monroe Revisited

In 1972, the most difficult time for the Williams family, I visited them on my summer vacation, as an organizer of the support group. My purpose of the visit was to introduce American people to the characteristics of the support movement in Japan: the non-violent movement that includes a wide range of citizens, and the union of the citizens for protection of the life and the human rights of one American citizen beyond their political ideology and belief. Considering the secularism and distrust within the African American movement, it was especially critical to have our activities be understood by leaders of these movements. At that time, a number of leaders had mushroomed in the African American communities, though the communities were filled with confrontation over different interests, distrust among groups, and dissatisfaction as a whole. For example, on one hand, someone like Angela Davis had the states wide rescue movement because the Communist Party was behind her; on the other hand, others like Williams were ignored and left under the oppression. In this turmoil, I wanted these leaders to realize the importance of unity in the movement, by showing the example of Japan. Since it was the year of the Presidential Election, the major African American leaders were gathering in Miami where the Democratic Party Convention was to be held in July.[28] Carrying a large suitcase, everyone could tell that I was a foreign traveler. On my way to lodgings from Miami Airport, I was involved in a traffic accident [disrupted by the government, a part of their conspiracy].[29] Fortunately, I was not killed there, and was able to tour through Atlanta, Monroe, Washington D.C., and arrived in Detroit where Williams awaited. I managed to meet local African American leaders, to appear on TV, and to hold press conference. In Detroit, I met the mayor, the chairman of the city assembly, and the African American congressman John Conyers. On that occasion, I not only appealed to them on the hardship Williams was going through, but also requested them to launch the human rights movement throughout the city as they had done before. This visit was reported in *The Detroit Free Press*, the largest newspaper in the city, with a large picture showing Williams and his wife looking at the signature lists with me. It also reported detailed information about the Japanese Committee for Williams. In Monroe, where I used to be passed off, I visited the mayor in passing. When I entered the drugstore that he managed on the side, he was doing some accounting of the sale. I said, "You must be the mayor!" and immediately opened the signature list to read him the petition. I also showed him the statistics of the undersigned, saying,

"We are not a group of communists." Caught off guard, the mayor repeatedly told me, "All of you are nice people like us." I quickly took a picture of him holding the signature list and said, "You should report *that* in the next city assembly." Sharing Interest with Peace Movement

In the last seven years, strangers gathered together to make a union where everyone cared about an African American whom they had not met yet. The members pondered about what they could do for him, why he had been oppressed, why the American public kept quiet on this issue, how African-American leaders felt about it, and what the oppression was all about. While the governor refused to attend the trial, as well as the attorney for Williams, we felt the necessity of learning about the complex U.S. judiciary system, and the relationship between the system and the African American issues. The people gathered at Sendagaya Civil Hall to find these answers. From when we collected over 10,000 signatures to the day of Williams's victory in January 1976, the grassroots movement energetically continued. In the four years, the members continued on the "Postcard Project," while learning about the issues surrounding Williams. Twelve lectures on various topics started in January 1972 for two years. The following topics were discussed: *American Politics and Judiciary System, African American Literature, African American Issues and the Vietnam War, The Minorities: the Native Americans and African Americans, The Amnesty International, Discrimination in Japan*, and *The False Charges and the Rescue Movements*. At the same time, group readings and summer camps were organized. On the "Workday," the members typed the signature lists and did the statistics of the undersigned. On these occasions, college professors, students, homemakers, and other workers, worked together, and then held discussions at the civic hall. It was very fortunate to have many knowledgeable scholars in these lectures and group readings. This was another strength of this support movement. As shown in the list of founders, we had scholars of American Studies who not only gave lectures but also actually participated in the activities to support the movement. Having experts on African American Literature, African American Studies, Human Rights, and Peace Movement, made these meetings especially fruitful, and enlightening interactions. In retrospect, it was a great idea of the founders to establish the committee as a group that was to protect the life and the human rights of a citizen of the United States, rather than a group that was to protest against racial discrimination in the United States. Led by the brilliant and experienced founders, the directions and strategies of the rescue movement were decided from then on. For a side note, the year 1970, when this rescue movement was started, was a time of despair among Japanese citizens; the government decided the extension of the Japan-U.S. Security Treaty (JUST), despite their opposition. Many Japanese citizens had given up changing rules through the government; rather, they felt that it was necessary to appeal to the U.S. citizens for their help to change the relationship between the two nations. That was the exact time when the request for help in support for Williams arrived from America. I suspect that the timing was one of the significant reasons that many throughout Japan quickly reacted to the appeal. So, I cannot help thinking that their cooperation in Williams's case originated from the antiwar spirits and the earnest desire for peace among the Japanese that were deeply rooted in society after the last war. The connection between the human rights movement, antidiscrimination movement, and peace movement was also seen in the United States. One example was African-American congressman John Conyers who was so earnest to contribute to the support group that he allowed us to use his office. When I visited him in the summer 1972, he talked about his college life involvement in peace movement. He told me the difficult time he had to invite a prominent peace activist from Japan. A series of protests and petitions made the government accept the visit. Conyers fondly talked about the activist, and said, "I wish that the professor has been happy and healthy." He was talking about Professor Iku Yasui. I replied, "In fact, the professor is one of the founders of our support group, and actively leading our activities." Hearing this, his eyes sparkled with joy. He was one of those who knew the connection between the human rights movement, anti-discrimination movement, and the movement for world peace.

2. Our Response to a Criticism—Our Counterargument to Mr. Carl Yoneda

A disturbingly bizarre letter was found in "From Readers" in *The Asahi Journal*, November 5, 1971. The letter was from Mr. Carl Yoneda in San Francisco. The following is the summary of his letter:

> I recently heard from African-American activists that they regard Williams a "betrayer," or they "never heard of Williams." The reasons are as follows:
>
> 1. Williams gave evidence about the African American movement when being summoned by the Senate Committee on the Judiciary.
> 2. Since he did not want to take responsibility for the followers, Williams resigned as president of Republic of Afrika, which advocates African Americanism. Presently, twenty-seven Black activists in the same group were thrown in jail with the charge of civil disturbance.
> 3. The budget for the Center of Chinese Studies at the University of Michigan where Williams works as a consultant, is reportedly sponsored by the CIA for the last several years. The CIA has not denied the report.
> 4. Williams was receiving an enormous amount of money from the Ford Foundation to write his biography. Since the foundation is not supposed to fund activists, there should be a special relation between him and the foundation.

What was more, Yoneda added that Williams "are no more looked up to by any of African American activists, groups of the liberal, or the New Left," and concluded, "[Comparing to the proactive support movement for Williams,] I regret that there is no significant support for the release of Ms. Angela Davis in Japan." We were bewildered by his criticism about the support movement because his points were not applicable to the reality of the movement. In addition, we lost our trust in journalism, because while they had been reporting our movement for Williams with assent, they gave an account to Yoneda without confirming the source. The editor of the journal, Mr. Kurokawa expressed his sincere apology in response to our letter of appeal, and our counterargument was reported in the journal December 3, 1971.

Counterargument to Mr. Yoneda

By the Japanese Committee for the Defense of the Life and Fundamental Human Rights of Robert F. Williams

In his letter on November 5, Mr. Carl Yoneda proved our appeal that the agents of American government, including the CIA, have maliciously spread the false rumor about Williams. In our article "For Williams—Revisited," we made it clear that the government alleged that Williams traded himself to the government side, while not giving him any access to say his piece. His article shocked us because Mr. Yoneda was known as a Japanese American with the Communist Party, not as a conservative racist. As we repeatedly explained, unlike Mr. Yoneda's comment, our signature collecting movement is not favoritism for Williams that unfairly excludes the other African Americans to be protected. Instead, our true intention is to protect human rights beyond borders; our support for Williams is an example of our rescue activities. We deeply regret that Mr. Yoneda, who is supposed to foster U.S.-Japan friendship, wrote that hostile letter, without trying to understand the true intention of Japanese people. If Mr. Yoneda had seen our activity from the perspective of an American citizen, he would have had a different impression of the support group—the union longing to protect a citizen of his own country. For example, reading about our movement, Ms. Azeri Johnson in Monroe, realized our intention. The African American homemaker wrote in her handmade mini newspaper, "While Japanese people living at distance have done so much for Williams, we Monroe citizens have not proven his innocence. Thinking about this, I feel so ashamed." We accept Mr. Yoneda's appeal for Angela Davis who belongs to the Communist Party as he does; however, it is unbearable to us that he called Williams a betrayer, distorting the fact in the same context. His attitude not only split the unity of the human rights movement, but also his contempt for the goodwill of over 10,000 Japanese people. In the following context, we responded to Mr. Yoneda's argument based upon various references. To examine his claims, we used objective and detailed research about Williams, as well as testimonies from those who know him, from the United States, Cuba, and China.

(1) Williams attended hearings of the Senate Committee on the Judiciary, in order to avoid the charge of contempt of the House (a federal crime). Otherwise, he would have been accused of this charge also in a trial. Unlike some distorting the facts, accusing him of betraying the African American movement through his testimony, Williams took the Fifth Amendment in these hearings. In fact, the oppression against Williams became more prominent the following two years, while he lost his case in Michigan's Intermediary Court this April. On November 4 of the same year, we heard from him on the phone that Michigan's Supreme Court rejected his appeal. They decided to extradite him to the South in two months. This meant that they sent him to the unfair Southern court where the anti-Black emotion radically arose in the last ten years. Michigan's state law prohibits the extradition of political criminals like Williams; however, the governor and the judge did not follow it and decided to extradite him with the kidnapping charge.

(2) Contradictory, the same governor refused the extradition of three escapees charged with rape and murder, because "sending them to the Southern court would deprive them of the fair trial and their human rights." Comparing the two cases, it is obvious that the political authorities had a malicious intention to send him to an unfair court. This incident made it so clear about the series of disruptions vexing Williams and his support groups in the struggle. How could one accuse Williams who is suffering under this oppression for trading himself into the authority's side, and betraying the African American movement? These should be the best examples of the opposite to Mr. Yoneda's claims.

(3) Just after his return from exile, Williams resigned as president of the Republic of New Afrika, which contradicts Mr. Yoneda's claim that his resignation was this year. Mr. Yoneda claimed that the resignation was done because of Williams' incompetence in fostering and educating the young followers. However, it was actually because Williams had to concentrate on his trial over his extradition. He was never "irresponsible to the followers," as Mr. Yoneda mentioned. In addition, he had resigned long before those twenty-seven African-American activists from the same organization were thrown in jail in Mississippi. As reported in Japan, it was an incident this summer, not last year. Mr. Yoneda's letter sent the wrong message, Williams as a betrayer, to the readers.

(4) As we reported, Williams has been writing about his experience in China under the contract with the Center of Chinese Studies at the University of Michigan. Thus, he has been paid as a researcher by the university. Unlike Mr. Yoneda said, there is no proof that the Ford Foundation has funded particular individuals like Williams, while it has made some contribution to the university. In addition, the CIA stopped funding educational and research institutions after receiving public criticism in 1967. According to Rinjiro Sodei, Williams assured these facts before accepting the contract with the Center. Mr. Yoneda's claim, which implied bribery between Williams and the government, contradicts the fact.

(5) Mr. Yoneda claimed the support movement for Williams was done only in Japan, in contrast to the support movement beyond borders for Angela Davis. This claim is wrong again. We have received many signatures from other countries, such as China and Cuba, where Williams fostered friendship in his exile. This is an international movement, and Japan is a part of it. In any case, we strongly wish that both rescue movements should spread beyond borders.

(6) According to Mr. Yoneda, some young African-American leaders do not even acknowledge Williams's importance in the movement. Despite his argument, it would be impossible to ignore Williams if one knew the history of the movement.

We have no intention, nor time to single out an individual to insult or criticize him/her; however, we are determined to confront an argument that makes the victims of discrimination and bias suffer even more. In this dispute, we learned the importance of providing the correct information of the movement in order to make it stronger. We are going to correct the false information, scrutinizing this kind of argument, so that we will not be confused by rumors. Finally, we would like to ask your continuous cooperation in our signature-collecting movement. (*"News,"* 2nd Ed.)

III. "A Monument Stands Here"—the Evaluation of the Rescue Activity (1976)

The "Meeting to Celebrate William's Victory" was a long-awaited day for all of us. In the meeting, cheer and applause echoed to express our joy free from any concern about William's case. The discussion to finish off the support movement was held at Sendagaya Civic Hall on April 3, 1976. The topics were: What kinds of people supported the group? How each individual approached the movement? What kind of beliefs the member held to continue the movement? What the member learned through the participation? How their perspectives of life were changed through the activities? About the group as an organization, we discussed how the people's power gathered together to influence society and the possible direction of the support group in the future. The following is the summary of the discussion in the meeting.

Another Reason for the Victory
Yasui, Iku, University Professor

I know tremendous effort by several people supported the activities of the Japanese Committee for the Defense of the Life and Fundamental Human Rights of Robert F. Williams. So, today, I would like to consider the direction of the group in a face-to-face discussion with the members. This year, there are two times I considered the meaning of the victory in a movement to protect human rights. The first time was when Tatsuo Takano won his case against Mitsubishi Resin, Inc. Takano was fired for the reason that he had participated in the campaign against the Japan-U.S. Security Treaty (JUST) when he was a college student. He strived in court to return to his office for thirteen years. From time to time, he fell into adverse circumstances like when the decision was made against his favor; however, the resolution was made between him and Mitsubishi Resin, Inc., and his appeal to return the position was finally accepted. Through the experience of supporting Takano, I keenly realized that it is critical to be able to keep up this kind of movement. At the same time, I learned the hidden sacrifice behind the victory of the case. For instance, young Takano's hair had turned gray during the struggle. This was a symbol to express how harsh the thirteen-year strife worked on someone unfairly oppressed. His dark brown hair never comes back, while he won to return to the company. Although Takano said, "Thanks to the support movement, we attained an absolute victory in court," the victory was brought by a tremendous sacrifice. I believe that the right decisions should be made always by looking at one incident from different perspectives. This induction has been true when considering the meaning of a victory in the human rights movement. The true meaning of the victory of these movements, like in Williams's case, should not be judged by looking at only one aspect. Once the appeal was withdrawn, Mr. Williams sent a telegraph filled with his sincere appreciation to the people, especially Japanese friends, who supported him. At the same time, as Yoko Nakajima reported, he told us about the conspiracy among the government officials behind the withdrawal. Of course, it is no less significant that our movement contributed to this victory, but we must pay attention to this dark side of the withdrawal and watch our back in the future. As seen in correspondence from Williams, he might have been assassinated. So, avoiding that through our support movement can be called one aspect of the victory. When President Kennedy was assassinated, I was in the United States for a peace lecture tour. Arriving in Washington D.C., I watched as Oswald, a frame-up assassin, was shot on TV. I keenly realized how well governmental conspiracies were made in America. While celebrating William's victory after the fourteen-year struggle against oppression, we must watch for such a conspiracy, and further our movement for human rights. It is one thing to have laws for protection of human rights, such as UN Charter and the law of nations, but keeping them in the real world is another. To minimize the gap between the laws and the reality, it is crucial for support movements to tackle problems like the incidents that happened to Takano and Williams. In retrospect, the support movement for Williams was not a piece of cake. For example, it was beyond words how disappointed we were when some countries never responded to our request for help, while a setback in William's case was reported. If we had given up there, nothing could have been accomplished. However, we learned that "the long-lasting movement can witness a change in its favor." This was true in Williams's case, as well as in Takano's. Again, we should recognize the importance of endurance in the movement. This morning, I composed a *haiku* for today's meeting:

A Monument of the Strife, for Human Rights, Stands Here—

The monument we built might seem to have little significance; however, only through activities "to build a small monument" like this, humans can advance themselves. After the experience through the movement for Williams, I strongly hope that we can continue building this kind of monument for human life and human rights with our cooperation.

Proactive response against oppression
Saishiro Amakasu, Medical Doctor

During the '70s Japan–U.S. Security Treaty (JUST) Talks, I experienced oppression by the government: my son in college was arrested by the riot police, while I was upset with the government's decision to continue the JUST despite people's opposition. Right after that, I found out about this movement in *The Asahi Newspaper*, and spontaneously called Ms. Nakajima to participate. Since I was a medical doctor, I aimed to collect 500 to 600 signatures. In the waiting room of my hospital, I put up my long letter of appeal, and asked patients if they read it and if they signed it. In this way, we counted the number of signatures growing every day after work. I would like to express my sincere appreciation to those 300 patients who supported us. The great news, the withdrawal of the appeal, showed us the victory of the conscience and humanism of William's supporters. I even feel that we made a sort of revolution in terms of the conscience and humanism of common people in Japan to an American citizen defeated the oppression.

Tsutomu Yamasaki
When I heard that Tohoru Takahashi founded this movement, my intuition told me that something wonderful had started. I have been thinking that, unlike economists who pass off the sacrifice of one in order to save ninety-nine, those who study literature like us will fight for the one with their faith. Once I started the study of literature, I became interested

in African American and Biblical literature. In Japanese literature, what we learned was the literature produced at the summit of society, such as *The Tale of Genji*; however, I started to realize the importance of reading works by the people who support the society. That was about the time I got to know Mr. Takahashi and join this civic movement, which reminded me that it was critical to gather together to save the oppressed. I think that this kind of movement is vital, and the experience and knowledge that each individual gained in the activities should be brought to respond proactively against any kind of oppression in the future. From now on, I would like to see that happening in all over the world. To tell the truth, unlike Ms. Nakajima and Mr. Takahashi, I became impatient and sometimes felt disparate about Williams's case, thinking, "This is not going to work,"—I was not mature enough. However, now I strongly realize the importance of the perseverance of the movement, as Mr. Yasui said above. In fact, I was puzzled to hear the withdrawal of the appeal, feeling that it might be a part of conspiracies by the government. Ms. Nagajima's report proved me right. She added that Williams was determined to continue the strife to reveal the truth about the case. I really respect his perseverance.

Perseverance is Power
Kameo Yokoi, Superintendent of Maruki Art Museum

I joined this movement when supporters came to collect signatures at our museum which is famous for *Genbaku no Zu*, the painting of the site of the atom bomb. Today, I realized that many people are participating in this movement with all their family and some have been with us for a long time. This makes me feel encouraged and warm inside. Individual activities in the movement have not necessarily given the people a great sense of achievement, but there has always been a good rapport between members. In addition, I am glad to have learned about racial discrimination in the United States. By the way, we must try hard to make up the deficit of 700,000 yen from this movement.

Sotonari Arashi, Graduate Student

Although I knew the fact of racial discrimination, I trusted in the conscience of America. When the great news came, I was feeling helpless after six years of strife. I was so glad, but at the same time felt some reason I should not be completely satisfied. I have not figured out the reason, but it may be because discrimination still exists in Japan and in America. On this occasion, I would like to continue thinking about this kind of problem.

Hideomi Ota, Medical Doctor

I joined this movement with Mr. Arashi in college. Since I presently work as a pediatrician and have less time to spare, it is more difficult for me to contribute to the support group. In the last six years of participation, I got to know a lot of sincere people and learned so much through the activities of the support group. Is it just my optimism to make me believe that the world will be a better place if we all keep trying to abolish social evils?

Etsuko Imamura, Speech Therapist

I learned about this movement when I was taking an African American Literature course in the English Literature Department at Tokyo Women's University. At that time, the world witnessed the problems of discrimination around the world. So, I wanted to utilize what I learned at the desk by participating in a civic movement as a citizen. I remember attending Ms. Nakajima's lecture about African American movement at Friends Center in Mita [in Tokyo]—it was one of the lecture series about "Nonviolence of the Quakers." In the lecture hall, I felt so happy to be a part of the support group. After that, I collected signatures from friends and professors from my college and asked them to participate in the mass postcard mailing. I feel so fortunate that our effort contributed to William's victory. I would like to use my experience and knowledge in other cases, such as discrimination in South Korea, and Kakeaki Hayashi's case about his nationality in Taiwan.

Yoshimi Tagami, Director of Supplemental School
I joined the movement when I was a freshman in college. After graduating and working for a company for a year, I opened a supplemental school this April. My heart is filled with deep emotion thinking how long we have been fighting together. I am so glad that our effort has made an accomplishment. I was reassured of the strength of the peoples' ties through this support movement, even though Japan and America are geographically separated by the Pacific Ocean. Through this civic movement, I became confident about my life. In other words, I learned that if people try hard together, they could accomplish something significant in the end.

Kazutomo Kimura, Student
My sister studying in the United States three years ago introduced me to this support group. I remember reading interesting books about discrimination in the Group Readings [organized by the Japanese Committee to Support Williams]. I am delighted that our effort accomplished results in the end.

Tetsuo Iwashita, Salaryman (White-collar Worker)
I entered Chuo University six years ago when the university dispute was at its peak. One seminar about African American Literature made me decide to join the support group. After graduation, I was involved in *Hei-ren* [another equality advocate group] and was not active in this group. After *Hei-ren* discontinued the activity, I restarted my activity here.

I would like to utilize what I learned in this group when I supervise newcomers. In addition, with the experience and knowledge I gained through this movement, I would like to continue fighting against discrimination and oppression of human rights.

Joy of finding the people supporting grassroots movement
Ei-ichi Miyasaka, Editor of *Shinshu Shirakaba*
About the same time, we started *Sinshu Shirakaba*, the Japanese Committee to Support Williams was founded, and I accepted to become the organizer in the Nagoya-Tokai area. In retrospect, in the last several years, these two things have been growing at the same time. I feel so good to be able to attend this meeting today. I am especially moved by the speech by the youth. Gaining opportunities to think philosophically through

their participation must be a very valuable thing for them, and I believe the young people like them are the ones who are going to support the culture of our country. I do not want to appear conceited, but I learned the spirit of *Shirakaba-ha* [Shirakaba School] sixty-five years ago and have been determined to spread out the thoughts. Listening to the members' stories, I am deeply moved and glad to know people with grassroots spirit still exist. By the way, William's victory seemed to be a surprise to everyone, but it was no surprise to me—because I had seen the same kind of case before. When a fire broke out in a school in Nagano, the person on duty, a teacher of *Shirakaba-ha*, was accused of arson. They raised motives like, "He had debt with bookstores," "He was suffering from a broken heart after writing a love-letter,"—but there was no legal evidence to prove him guilty. A few people including myself trusted him and continued appealing his innocence. In the end, they caught the arsonist, and the teacher cleared his charge. From the beginning, my intuition told me that Williams would win the case, because I trusted him and respected his decision to return to the United States—even though he could have been treated well in China, he returned in order to fight against the oppression. At that time, I was sure about his victory.

Hiroshi Kudo, Salaryman (White-collar Worker)
When this committee was started, I wrote about Henry David Thoreau for my graduation paper, enlightened by Ms. Nakajima's Political Science course. At the same time, I was the leader of the Nonviolence Study Committee. So, I was thrilled to join in the movement, because it let me see the real case in the real world about what I learned in books. I met Mr. Takahashi for the first time at a café in Shinjuku while doing an errand for Ms. Nakajima. I fondly remember that we both slammed a large glass of beer and made plans for the support group. I presently work for an oil company, and it is rare for me to relate to the peace study I was involved in on campus. So, by trying not to do business related to the Defense Agency, I felt some sense of accomplishment in terms of contributing to the peace.

Yoko Nakajima, Organizer
I would like to fill you in with the chronology of this committee. In March 1970, the letter of appeal, asking for support from Japan, arrived from the Committee for Williams in Detroit. When I was at a loss, Mr. Tohoru Takahashi took on the responsibility of being an organizer of the Committee in Japan. It has been very fortunate to have a mature, enthusiastic, and laid-back leader for this organization. By the end of April, we welcomed many African-American Study scholars, as well as Iku Yashi and Katsuichi Honda to our committee. The committee reached a unanimous decision to do our best to support Williams. In this process, we assured to regard the activity as one to protect the human rights of a citizen of the United States, not as one to protest against discrimination against African Americans. Approximately fifty people in and out of Japan accepted to be founders of the group;—they actually were the ones who mainly collected more than 2,000 signatures in the first few months. After this, the media, like *Asahi Newspaper* and *Asahi Journal,* found out about the movement, and these articles on

the paper led readers; grassroots signature-collecting campaign by which more than 10,000 signatures were collected in two years. Mr. Kudo's speech reminded me of the strong support by the founders, and students like him that enabled this unknown rescue movement for an African American to grow into the present condition.

Chiyo Fujimoto, Homemaker—by Yoriko Nakajima
(Nakajima) I would like to introduce Ms. Fujimoto from Osaka. Unfortunately, she just left. She had been collecting signatures for us for six years from the day this movement was introduced in *The Asahi Journal* in the fall of 1970. I clearly remember the day I saw Ms. Fujimoto—on the day, I was lecturing about Martin Luther King Jr. at the YMCA in Osaka. While planning to ask for them from the audience I was hesitant to ask for signatures right after the lecture. That was when I saw Ms. Fujimoto stand up and appeal for the cooperation of the audience. Even though she was losing her voice from the cold, she did it for us with her courage. I was deeply moved and pleased by her enthusiasm and courage, as well as her thoughtfulness. She also collected signatures while working as a dry goods saleswoman. She asked customers for their signatures even when nothing was sold. Additionally, she sent me a letter of encouragement when Mr. Carl Yoneda's letter appeared in *The Asahi Journal*. "I can only understand simple things, but I know that protecting the human rights is the right thing to do. Let us continue doing the right thing to the last," she said in the letter. We should remember that the support from many wonderful people like Ms. Chiyo made this organization continue the movement until today. I take this occasion to say that she brought the *Bunraku* rice crackers and the *Uji* green tea before you from Osaka for the meeting today.

Sadao Nobuoka, University Professor
As one of the undersigned in the early days of the support movement, I have been watching this movement, hoping that Williams's innocence should be proven. Many world issues today are founded through the history of the Western invasion and its supremacy over the natives around the world. In my view, it is critical to preserve those cultures and autonomy among the natives and resist such kind of supremacy. For this purpose, the tie and cooperation between citizens is critical. I will do my bit to make a difference for societal peace, where the issue of African American appears especially critical for the purpose. On this glorious day in history, I would like to wish you the best in the future.

Aiko Yajima, Homemaker
I just heard Mr. Chimoto from *The Asahi Journal* call Mrs. Takahashi and Ms. Nakajima "two persistent women," which made me realize that the persistence of women is something else—something great. This characteristic of women should be utilized in this kind of occasion. Living close to the Takahashi family, from time to time I saw Mrs. Takahashi work in the backstage of her husband. For example, I knew she was the one who made some ten thousand mimeograph copies of postcards. Thank you so very much for all you did.

Shigeo Takahashi, Homemaker [Wife of Tohoru Takahashi]
In fact, I am the one who owes Mrs. Yajima an appreciation. She took on so many day-by-day tasks to help this organization keep going. When the committee had a meal together, she always made wonderful dishes for us. Especially, the meal she supervised for the meeting with Dr. Kagan from America was splendid. All of over 70 people in the party were delighted with the wonderful dishes. This is one of the unforgettable memories I have of the support movement. As a wife of the organizer of this support group, I always worked with husband—which sometimes made me feel all the pressure and stress my husband was feeling as an organizer. The pressure and stress came from the responsibility of being a representative of all the 14,000 undersigned who reacted to his appeal, and from the fact that he had to continue leading the support movement to the end. I started doing my bit, helping him with the clerical and operational part so that he can dedicate himself to the real job as an organizer. Frankly, I was not always enthusiastic about doing clerical tasks and other odd jobs and often felt depressed and isolated, not being able to connect what I was doing with the enormous goal of the civic movement and the Civil Rights Movement in America. On such an occasion, the spirit of the dedicated people whom I met in this kind of meeting encouraged me and enabled me to continue on. In addition, while many people started helping this movement, I saw them do their best without any hesitation. This taught me that any tasks supporting the core group activities were equally important to keep things going smoothly. I remember many, including Ms. Yajima, did their best in various tasks in different places, such as signatures and donations collecting, selling post-cards, and making lunch boxes. They went to ask for support of their neighbors, school meetings, and churches. Some even contributed the wage they earned by preparing mass mailing, while others spread this movement to the place they moved. Although the setting of "international" movement often overwhelms individuals because of the technical and academic complexity, I am grateful to have had learning opportunities.

Yoriko Nakajima, Organizer
Mrs. Takahashi not only took on clerical tasks, but also added a warm and homey atmosphere with her demeanor. Whenever we got together for the "Workday" to organize paperwork, and publishing *News*, she brought lunchboxes for everyone. The youths, especially ones living away from home, were excited about these lunchboxes.

Kenichiro Chimoto, Journalist
I entirely agree with Ms. Nakajima—the people like Mrs. Takahashi and Ms. Yajima have enabled this movement to grow up to the condition as we see today. Those everyday activities they did are difficult to be recognized but have been so critical for a successful civic movement.

While visiting the United States at the end of 1970s, I was introduced to Mr. Williams by Ms. Nakajima. Since then, I have done what I could do for the support movement. In fact, the only thing I could do was to help with the "*News*" publications, which was nothing compared to the everyday work other people have done for this organization. I was very intrigued by the consciousness and goodwill of the people who were concerned about worldwide issues. It appeared to be so valuable that common people were eager to learn about the relations between these complicated problems and their life. The year this committee was founded was the very time that various grassroots movements, such as the environment movement, arose.

Regarding the sustenance of these movements, although it seems fairly easy to get one started, it is very difficult to keep it running. It is also hard to keep the original aim that the movement was founded for. Unlike this movement, in fact, having these difficulties many movements have disappeared, or quit their activities. I highly respect the people who have supported the lasting movement like this. Recently, I realized that the governments have become slier when accused by the civic movement of their faults. In these social and political issues, including Williams' case, they try to appear to be negotiators; however, they in fact are plotting to weaken the tie among these citizen groups by showing them a carrot. For instance, there should be a conspiracy behind the withdrawal of Williams's case. When they seem to compromise like this, we citizens must be careful not to be wrapped up the crafty plot by the government. While having a certain amount of doubt about the "happy ending," I would like to extend my sincere respect to all the supporters who made the victory happen. Being merely an unknown journalist, I will continue the little contribution I can make to this citizens' union.

Hiro-o Ashizawa, University Professor

In studying political science, I was introduced to this support group by Professor Egawa from Chuo University. I believe that all those civic movements are somehow connected to one another. So, any kind of movement you join should be related to other movements. So, we must feel the tie whenever we participate in these movements. Personally speaking, schism in a civic movement is a critical problem. At this point, I am very interested in issues, such as African American movement, African nations after their independence, and human rights in the Soviet Union. This organization also helped me learn about them.

Tohoru Takahashi, Organizer

While listening to the stories about the last six years, I remembered the entire incident as if it just happened yesterday. The text above is the summary of the address to the meeting. On this occasion, I would like to extend my sincere appreciation to the supporters who could not attend this meeting and who moved away. I am afraid we missed their stories; however, we would love to hear from them. I hope that they see many thanks from the organizers and founders, as well as the Williams's. After this meeting, the members discussed the direction of the support group in the future. The following is the summary of the addresses:

- Although the group finished the signature-collecting campaign, it will not be broken up so it will be able to provide Williams with applicable support.
- Find a way to pay back the deficit of 700,000 yen with the members' cooperation.
- Preserve the record of the Japanese Committee for the Defense of the Life and Fundamental Human Rights of Robert F. Williams.

- Hold occasional meetings and lectures.
- As in the telegraph from Williams, he would like to visit Japan to personally to thank all the supporters. Let us find a way to invite him.

These are secondary goals generated in the process of the enormous goal, the victory of Williams.

Budget Report (JPY)	From February 15, 1970, to August 1, 1976
Revenue	1,067,501: from contribution, membership fee, and postcard sales
Expense	1,792,797: including the expense for *News* (1 – 6 ed.) publication and distribution (120,000)
Deficit	725,296

Finally, if we keep compassion for the oppressed and the sturdy activity among the members, this committee will grow further in unity—the source of civic activity. (From *News* by the Japanese Committee for Williams, 6th edition)

Letters of Celebration
Kan-ichi Nishimura
I am so glad that Williams finally won the case. I regret that I cannot attend the meeting due to illness that I have been suffering from last fall. Again, it is a great news. I am so grateful.

Yoshio Shiojima
God made no inequality between men. We are all brothers, and do not allow racial discrimination to happen.

Tamaki Uemura
I felt so grateful to hear the great news. I will pray for the abolition of all the inhumane discrimination in the world.

Iseko Kase
I am truly happy that the truth was revealed by the support from many people. I keenly realize that we still need to fight against oppression against human rights.

Takashi Wakasugi
The world eyed the tie between citizens who defeated racial discrimination and the overwhelming power politics in the United States. Yet, in social and political contexts, the lives and rights of humans are constantly threatened. So, we should unite to clear the threat one by one.

Noriko Yokoyama
I gladly received the telegraph of victory. I would like to send my sincere applause to the supporters for their constant effort that made this happen.

Mitsuo Akamatsu
The long-lasting support was not in vain. Congratulations!

Shichiro Hoseki
I would like to thank everyone who supported the movement and congratulate Williams.

Hisashi Iwasaki
I am glad that your efforts proved fruitful, especially after the long hardship. Congratulations.

Isamu Tanaka
Cheers! I realized that "International Cooperation [Tie?]" was not just a phrase.

Teikou Ishii
I would like to congratulate the victory you all earned through the effort. I reported the news to my colleagues and celebrate the victory together.

Nobutaka Kiuchi
The African American movement in the United States seems quieter these days, but to me, the condition surrounding them does not seem to improve as Mr. James Farmer was saying...

Aiji Takeuchi
I joined the signature-collecting movement to appeal the innocence of an African American charged with kidnapping. The public pollution does refer not only the toxic fume and illness like Subacute Myelo Optico Neuropathy (SMON), but also the racial discrimination and oppression. Since all the public pollution is artificially generated, every one of us is responsible for its abolition.

Mieko Okumiya
I remember an early day of the movement; the day Ms. Nakajima was composing the letter of "Appeal" next to the copying machine in our office. As soon as it was made, everyone in the office read copies of the letter. After seven years from that day, finally we have our victory. I will share the great news and the joy with my colleagues.

Yoko Kijima
What a wonderful news! When I joined the movement, I was fresh out of college and started a job at a newspaper company. After that, I got married and opened a supplemental school for students. At work, I often recognize the issue of discrimination and realize that what I learned through the support activities is supporting my confidence and leading my direction.

Akiko Izu

Thank you for letting me know the great news. Now I remember the long-lasting efforts of the supporters including Mr. Takahashi—from the lectures, group reading, and the tasks on the "Workday" at the room in the civic hall—typing, mass-mailing, organizing signatures, and so on.

Keiko Ueda

Given that it is a rarity to see the right thing happen in the real world, this result made me very happy.

Kaname Saruya

While I am so pleased to hear the news that Williams cleared his charge by the withdrawal of appeal, I have my heart full of emotions comparing my present feeling and one in the gloomy, suffocating atmosphere in the South fifteen years ago.

Hiromi Furukawa

Having seen that most African-American leaders were gone in the last ten years, I am interested in what kind of field Williams is going to lead in the future.

Material I

Chronology—surrounding the support activity in Japan.

(The mark * indicates things happened in the United States)

1961	October	• In Monroe, NC, Williams was accused of false charge with kidnapping Caucasian couple. He was exiled to Cuba with his family.
1969	September	• Williams returned to United States and resided in Detroit. The State of Michigan decided to extradite him to the South.
		• The Committee to Aid the Defense of Robert F. Williams in Detroit [the Committee for Williams in Detroit] was found to protest against the court decision.
1970	February March	• Nakajima received a letter of request to collect signatures from the Committee in Detroit.
	August September October	• The persons concerned about the African American issues decided to set up the founders of a Japanese committee to protect human rights across borders.
	December	• (24th) 1st' founders' orientation, set out "the Japanese Committee for the Defense of the Life and Fundamental Human Rights of Robert F. Williams [the Japanese Committee for Williams]." Informed the start to United States Attorney General Mr. William G. Milliken, Governor of the State of Michigan, and Williams.
		• Arranged meeting with the American ambassador in Japan.
		• Sent the 1st roll of petitions (700 signatures) to the Governor of Michigan and Williams.

(Continued)

(Continued)

		* Received letter of appreciation from Williams. (Reported by the Associated Press)
		• Sent letter of request to *The Asahi Journal*. Large reaction from readers.
		• In response to readers' interest, *The Asahi Journal* put special contribution by Williams, "Racial Discrimination in Crises." (December 27)
		• Twenty-nine signatures of the Dietmen were collected through Kan-ichi Nishimura.
		• Sent the 2nd, 3rd, and 4th roll of petitions (total 2,800 signatures) to the Governor of Michigan and Williams.
1971	February	• Received letter of receipt from Governor of Michigan.
	April	• Found organizers in Nagoya and Kyoto.
	May	
	June	* Williams lost case in Michigan.
	August	• Governor of Tokyo and Osaka participated in signature campaign.
	September	• Pamphlet, "Petition," (16 page) printed with an effort by Ei-ichi Miyasaka.
	October	• 1st edition of "News" published.
	November	• Sent the 5th (by high school students) and 6th roll of petitions to the Governor of Michigan and Williams.
	December	
		• (18th) 1st lecture about Williams and the civil rights movement in the last ten years by Yukiyama, Sodei, Takahashi, Oya, Chimoto, Nakajima, and others. In Chidage-dani Civic Hall. Number of audience is approximately eighty.
		• Sent the 10th roll of petitions (total 72,00 signatures) to the Governor of Michigan and Williams.
		• 2nd edition of "News" published.
		* Williams's petition was rejected in Michigan, and he appealed to the Federal Court.
		• Monthly group reading. African-American problem study group started by university students.
		• Lecture by Tomohisa, Shimizu, "The American Indians' Perspective on the African American Movement"
		• Response to article by Carl Yoneda, in *The Asahi Journal*
		* Williams faced an accusation of contempt of Congress (five years in prison).
		• (20th) Sent telegraph of petition to drop the charge to President, Chairman of Senator and Congress, asked Primer Chou En-Lai for cooperation.
		* (26th) Japanese signature-petition movement introduced in a local newspaper in Monroe, NC.
1972	January	• (14th) Sent a letter of request to Chou En-lai, asking for cooperation in the support movement for Williams.
	February	
	April	• Number of signatures reached 10,000.
	June	• (1st) Sent 10,000 Signature petitions to Nixon visiting China, in the care of Chou En-lai.
	July	
	August	• (5th) 3rd lecture. Jun Egawa, "Politics, Court System and the issues of African Americans in the U.S."
	September	
	November	• (6th) Received telegraph from the Chinese Committee of Friendship. They promised their cooperation after understanding the situation in the United States.
	December	

(*Continued*)

(Continued)

		• (20th) Provided information to reporters, (e.g., *the New York Times*) in Beijing.
		• (7th) Sent telegraph to Robert F. Williams Legal Defense Fund in the University of Michigan [the support group of the University of Michigan]. It was not sent by disruption in mail.
		• (22nd) 4th lecture. Tohoru Takahashi, "The History of African American Literature—from Harlem Renaissance to the present."
		• Published "News," 3rd edition.
		• Dr. Richard Kagan, Organizer of Robert F. Williams Legal Defense Fund at the University of Michigan, came to Japan.
		• (17th) 5th lecture. Dr. Richard Kagan, "The Status of anti-war, protests in the U.S."
		• Nakajima, Organizer, with 10,000 signature petitions, visited the United States, created an English version of the pamphlet.
		• (27th) Japanese signature-petition campaign, reported in *the Detroit Free Press*.
		• (23rd) 6th lecture. Yoriko Nakajima, "Visiting Williams in the U.S."
		• Williams's letter of appreciation on *The Asahi Newspaper* and *The Asahi Journal*.
		• (25th) 7th lecture. Iku Yasui, and Kaneyoshi Morikawa, "Peace in Vietnam and the Declaration of Human Rights."
		• (20th) 1st "Workday." In Sendagaya Civic Hall. (Typing signatures in English, Creating lists, preparing mass mailing)
1973	January March May June July September	• (20th) 8th lecture. Katsuhiko Nomoto, "Buraku [the outcast] Problem in Japan."
		• (17th) 9th lecture. Kei Ohara, "False Charges in Japan and international joint cooperation."
		• (26th) 10th lecture. Hisashi Iwasaki, "Racial Discrimination in American Movies."
		• Mass postcard mailing: (1) to appeal internationally; (2) to expand movement domestically)
		• (16th) 2nd "Workday," (mass postcard mailing, typing signatures in English)
		• (30th) 11th lecture. Yoriko Nakajima, "African American, a latent political power in the U.S."
		• Summer Study Group Trip (thirty participated for four days, three nights, in Izu)
		• (29th) 12th lecture. Kaname Saruya, "African American in racism in the U.S."
1974	February April June July August September	• (1st) 13th lecture. Sadafumi, Hirafuku, "The Record of American Indian."
		• (24th) 1st Consultation Group meeting
		• (7th) Letter from the Williams asking for continuous support activity.
		• Additional 2,600 signatures were collected. (G.T. 12,600 signature)
		• (2nd) Orientation of core members, appointed additional organizer to prepare Nakajima's study abroad for a year)
		• Published "News," 4th edition.
		• 3rd "Workday." Sending "News"

(*Continued*)

(Continued)

1975	February	• (23rd) 2nd Consultation Group meeting. (Yearly work schedule, learning plan)
	April	
	July	• (19th) Group Reading. Takahashi, Organizer. (Introduction to African American Literature)
	October	
	November	• Published "News," 5th edition. (G.T. 13,144 signatures collected)
	December	• (18th) 3rd Consultation Group meeting. (Preparation for next lecture)
		• (22nd) 14th lecture. Ruiko Yoshida, "Race Problems in today's U.S.A."
		* Michigan Supreme Court decided to extradite Williams to the South.
		* Williams held press conference in Detroit.
		* (16th) Williams was extradited to Monroe, NC.
1976	January	* (16th) Public Prosecutor of Monroe announced the withdrawal of an appeal on Williams for the charge of kidnapping.
	April	
		• (23rd) Received telegraph of victory from Williams.
		• (31st) Orientation of core members. (Detail report of William's victory)
		• Planning of next "News" publication.
		• (3rd) The "Meeting to Celebrate Williams' Victory."
		• Published "News," 6th edition.
1977	August	• (10th–14th) Williams and his wife visited Japan.
		• (12th) Press conference in Maru-Building, Yuraku-cho, Tokyo.
		• NHK [Japan's National Television] reported William's visit to "9 o'clock News Center."
		• (13th) Lecture to welcome Robert & Maybell Williams, and friendly meeting in Sendagaya Civic Hall.
		• (15th) Williams and his wife leave for the United States.

Material II
The Founder of the Committee for the Defense of the Life and Fundamental Human Rights of Robert F. Williams (September 15, 1970; No special order is observed.)

Name	Occupation/Status
Yasui, Iku	Professor of International Law, Housei University; former Director of Committee Against Atomic and Hydrogen Bombs of Japan
Nishimura, Kan-ichi	Senator (Social Democratic Party of Japan, SDP), minister of the United Church of Christ in Japan
Oonishi, Yoshinori	Superintendent of the Kiyomizu Temple in Kyoto; Chairman of the Committee of Religious World for Peace
Shimizutani, Yasunori	Bonze of Asakusa-Ji in Tokyo
Rikui, Saburo	Director of American Study
Honta, Katuichi	Journalist
Matukawa, Hiroshi	Honorary Chancellor of Ritsume-kan University
Sumitani, Etsuji	Chancellor of Doshisha University
Kitazawa, Shinjiro	Former President of Tokyo Keizai University; Honorary Professor of Waseda University
Matsuoka, Yoko	Commentator

(Continued)

Name	Occupation/Status
Watabe, Akira	Former Professor, Meiji University
Matsumura, Kazuto	Professor of Philosophy, Hose University
Okamoto, Sei-ichi	Professor of Political Science, & President of Kyoto Shoka Junior College
Nagano, Kunihiro	Attorney; Honorary President of the Committee for the Defense of the Human Rights of Japan
Morikawa, Kaneyoshi	Trustee of the Committee for Freedom and Human Rights
Inomata, Kozo	Attorney; former Diet member; member of the Committee for the Defense of Political Refugees of Japan
Hoseki, Shichiro	Former member of the House of Representatives (SDP)
Hirayama, Teruji	Minister of Yamate Christian Church; member of the Committee of Religious World for Peace
Takeshi, Naokuni	Acting President of Ryukoku University
Sakamoto, Norimatsu	President of Asia-Africa People's Association of Japan
Matsunaga, Yoshiichi	Attorney; Secretary of the Russell Society of Japan
Makinouchi, Takehito	Attorney
Tomura, Marahiro	Minister of the United Church of Christ in Japan
Hiratsuka, Raicho	Member of the Committee of Seven for World Peace; Honorary President of the Women's Association of Japan
Uemura, Tamaki	Member of the Committee of Seven for World Peace; Honorary President of Young Men's Christian Association (YMCA) of Japan
Nomiya, Hatsue	President of Kyoufu-kai (Christian group)
Inoue, Kiyoshi	Professor of History, Kyoto University
Kondo, Yuko	Secretary of Women's Democratic Party
Inoue, Yoshio	Professor of Tokyo University of Divinity
Oya, Chikusan	Commentator
Shinohara, Masahide	Commentator
Tomomatsu, En-tei	Bonze of Kanda-ji, Tokyo
Muto, Kazuya	Commentator
Nagata, Mamoru	Commentator
Nishikawa, Shigenori	Member of the Committee of Christian Journalists
Hamamoto, Takeo	Professor of American Literature, Meiji University
Kijima, Hajime	Poet; Professor of American Literature, Hose University
Kitamura, Takero	Lecturer of African-American Literature, Chuo University
Kanna, Yoshitaka	Professor of American Literature & American Culture, Kanda University of Foreign Languages
Ito, Kenji	Professor of American Literature, Ritsumeikan University
Akamatsu, Mitsuo	Professor of American Literature, Kanda University of Foreign Languages
Furukawa, Hiromi	Professor of American Literature, Osaka Kogyo University [Osaka University of Industry]
Saruya, Kaname Organizer	Professor of American History, Tokyo University
Takahashi, Tohoru	Professor of American Literature, Tokyo Keizai University [Tokyo University of Economics]
Nakajima, Yoriko	Professor of American Literature, Oubirin University

Material III
Call for Signatures to support Williams in Japan

1. A letter to the column: "From Readers" in Asahi Journal "Call for your support."

Robert F. Williams, an African-American leader from the American South, was falsely charged with kidnapping a Caucasian couple and was forced to seek an asylum in Cuba and China for eight years. Last fall, he finally returned to the United States, which has been reported in papers in Japan.

Staying in Detroit, Mr. Williams is going to bring the case into court to prove his innocence as soon as possible. Since it would give him a better chance to have a fair trial with less exposure to life-threatening danger, he chose to face a trial in Detroit (North) over in his hometown (Monroe, NC) in the South. However, those who made up the false charge for kidnapping against Williams urged the Governor of North Carolina to request the Governor of Michigan extradite Williams. So, the request was approved, and the warrant of extradition was signed off. Imagine the court in the South where racial discrimination is deeply rooted. Once Williams is taken back to the South as in the warrant, a fair trial for an African American is not a hope. Moreover, as many precedents, like Martin Luther King, Jr., showed us, his life may face the danger of being assassinated or being killed in jail. The signature-collecting movement began among the U.S. citizens. They required John Mitchell [United States Attorney General] and William Milliken [Governor of Michigan] to "keep Williams in Illinois and have his trial in Detroit." This was followed by a number of signature-collecting movements outside of the United States. The late Mr. Bertrand Russell was also an enthusiastic supporter; he was helping not only Williams but also four other individuals who were falsely charged with kidnapping. You can argue that the issues surrounding African Americans are a domestic problem of the United States; however, it is necessary to draw ethical support from the world in order to solve these issues. In other words, we can make a difference abroad in this era of internationalization. Through the independence of nations in Asia and Africa, the world eyes the rise of the value of racial equality. Let us extend the wave to America. With your signature, let us protect the life and the fundamental human rights of Williams, and assure a fair trial to be held for him. Your signature will encourage the conscience of America and give a warning to Mr. Mitchell and Mr. Milliken that the whole world is watching the progress of the case. With our acknowledgment of the discrimination in Japan, I would like to ask for your cooperation in this contingency so that we can continue dealing with both domestic and international human rights issues. (October 4, 1970. The Japanese Committee for the Defense of the Life and Fundamental Human Rights of Robert F. Williams.)

Contact Information

Tokyo:

Takahashi, Tohoru, 2-15, Chihaya-cho, Toyoshima-ku, Tokyo, (ph.) 81-3-957-1752
Nakajima, Yoriko, 5-1 2-301, Yamasaki-danchi, Machida-shi, Tokyo, (ph.) 81-427-92-5953

Nagoya:

Miyasaka, Ei-ichi, 14, Gokenya-cho, Showa-ku, Nagoya, Aichi (ph.) 81-52-82-1998

Kyoto:

Morikawa, Masamichi, 9, Tanaka-haruna-cho, Sakyo-ku, Kyoto-shi (c/o Ebina) (ph.) 81-75-711-3001

Osaka:

Fujimoto, Masanori, 514 Yada-oudo, Higashi Sumiyoshi-ku, Osaka-shi (c/o Sorin-ji Temple) (ph.) 81-6-703-5656

Kobe:

Bando, Junkou, 1-6-9, Yahata-cho, Nada-ku, Kobe-shi (c/o Nakamoto, Minister of Kobe Kumouchi Church) (ph.) 81-78-841-0038

2. Letter to the Column, "Voice" in *The Asahi Newspaper*

Call for Your Participation in the Movement to Abolish Racial Discrimination:

Yoriko Nakajima, Machida-shi [a city in Tokyo] (Professor of Obirin University, Age 42)

I read the articles about an African American student, who was upset with racial discrimination by Japanese people and returned to America, and the readers' response to the story. This time, I would like to inform readers that a civic movement has been started in Japan, to support the effort among African Americans to abolish racial discrimination. We started this movement by reading a letter of appeal from Robert F. Williams, an African American in the American South. Through this campaign, in the last year, more than 4,000 signature petitions to ask for a fair trial on Williams's case were collected and sent to the officials in the United States. We feel the issue of racial discrimination in the United States is our business—because Japan has the very same problem. For instance, before and in the last war, many Japanese discriminated against Korean and Chinese people as whites presently do against Blacks. Those issues have not yet been resolved, as well as the deeply rooted discrimination against "brake-min [the outcast in Japan]. We believe that with our own experience, we Japanese are not only able to understand the racial discrimination in other countries, but we must cooperate in order to abolish the discrimination." On the other words, seeing the discrimination in

Japan as one of many problems in the world, we will continue our support for Williams. We would truly appreciate your participation. (June 18, 1971)

Material IV
Call for Support for the William's Case

1. A petition attached to the list of signatures:

PETITION TO
Mr. Richard M. Nixon, President of the United States
Mr. John M. Mitchell, United States Attorney General
Mr. William G. Milliken, Governor of the State of Michigan.
February 1, 1972
Dear President Nixon, U.S. Attorney General and Governor Milliken:

We, the undersigned, represent a wide range of 10,000 Japanese citizens who, as the following statistics clearly show, differ from each other in their worldview, ideology, political faith, and religion. In spite of these differences, however, we are unanimously convinced the protection of fundamental human rights is basic to modern societies and that any social progress, in its true meaning of the term, can hardly be made without substantial security of these rights. Secondly, we are firmly convinced that we are now living in a time of international interdependence and that the development of one nation depends upon those of other nations. This close relationship penetrates not only into the field of politics, economics, and international relations but also into the way of life of the people of the world, providing a common basis for human rights and needs. These are the reasons that moved us to stand together, bridging national boundaries, to aid a citizen of your country, Robert F. Williams, whose life and fundamental human rights are threatened, as if he were one of our people. We, because of our international concern for human rights and a desire for world peace, request that the case of Robert F. Williams receives your utmost attention to ensure that his legal and human rights will be fully protected, and also request that you will take emergency measures to free Robert F. Williams from a kidnapping frame-up and to drop a charge of contempt of Congress. We strongly hope that you who are in a position to represent the conscience and wisdom of the United States will understand our true intent. We further hope you will make efforts to realize the following demands* which we firmly endorsed, by mobilizing all possible and workable solutions from a democratic tradition whose creative wisdom has inspired the rest of the world.

Sincerely Yours,
Takahashi, Tohoru [Signature]
Professor Tohoru Takahashi, The Japanese Committee for the Defense of the Life and Fundamental Human Rights of Robert F. Williams
*This refers to two petitions by support groups in the United States

2. Petitions by the Committee to Aid the Defense of Robert F. Williams in Detroit, which the Japanese Committee supported

a.) Petition by the Committee in Detroit:
PETITION I
TO GOVERNOR MILLIKEN AND UNITED STATES ATTORNEY GENERAL MITCHELL
WE, THE UNDERSIGNED, FULLY AGREE THAT THE DECISION TO EXTRADITE ROBERT F. WILLIAMS WAS A TOTALLY UNJUST, CRUEL, VICIOUS, AND IN FACT, CRIMINAL ACT. ALSO REALIZING BLACK PEOPLE HISTORICALLY AS WELL AS PRESENTLY, HAVE BEEN VICTIMS OF SOUTHERN RACISTS AND THEIR SO-CALLED "FAIR AND JUST COURTS," WE CANNOT ALLOW ROBERT F. WILLIAMS TO BE SENT BACK TO FACE A LYNCH MOB IN MONROE, NORTH CAROLINA. FINALLY, UNDERSTANDING AS WELL AS REMEMBERING WHAT HAPPENED TO MEDGER EVERS, JAMES CHANEY, MACK PARKER, LEMUEL PENN, MARTIN LUTHER KING JR. AND THE FOUR LITTLE BLACK GIRLS IN BIRMINGHAM, ALABAMA AND COUNTLESS OTHER INSENE ACTS DONE TO BLACK PEOPLE BY SOUTHERN RACISTS, WE CAN NOT ALLOW ROBERT F. WILLIAMS TO SUFFER THE SAME FATE. WE DEMAND THAT THE DECISION TO EXTRADITE ROBERT F. WILLIAMS BE REVERSED IMMEDIATELY.

(This petition was made by the Committee to Aid the Defense of Robert F. Williams in Detroit)

b.) Petition by Robert F. Williams Legal Defense Fund in the University of Michigan
PETITION II
TO GOVERNOR WILLIKEN AND UNITED STATES ATTORNEY GENERAL MITCHELL
WE, THE UNDERSIGNED STUDENTS, FACULTY AND STAFF MEMBERS OF THE UNIVERSITY OF MICHIGAN, AND OTHER RESIDENTS OF THE ANN ARBOR AREA, DECLARE OUR STRONG PROTEST OF GOVERNOR MILLIKEN'S DECISION TO EXTRADITE ROBERT F. WILLIAMS TO THE STATE OF NORTH CAROLINA. WE STRONGLY DOUBT THE LIKELIHOOD OF PERSONAL SAFETY FOR MR. WILLIAMS IN NORTH CAROLINA OR THE LIKELIHOOD OF A FAIR TRIAL THERE SINCE HE IS HATED AND FEARED AS A BLACK MAN WHO STOOD UP FOR THE RIGHTS OF HIS PEOPLE AND SUFFERED ASSASSINATION ATTEMPTS AND THREATS BECAUSE OF WHAT HE BELIEVED IN. WE CALL ON GOVERNOR MILLIKEN TO REVERSE HIS DECISION IN ACCORDANCE WITH MICHIGAN'S TRADITION OF NONEXTRADITION OF POLITICALLY INVOLVED FUGITIVES. BOTH ROBERT F. WILLIAMS'S LIFE AND HUMAN JUSTICE ARE AT STAKE IN GOVERNOR MILLIKEN'S DECISION.

(This petition was made by the Robert F. Williams Legal Defense Fund at the University of Michigan)

3. Telegraph to protest the charge [against Williams] of contempt of congress December 20, 1971

To President Nixon, the Senate and the House of Representatives:

PRESIDENT RICHARD M. NIXON OF THE UNITED STATES OF AMERICA: WE JAPANESE CITIZENS CANNOT KEEP SILENCE ABOUT UNJUST TTIALS THREATENING LIFA AND FUNDAMENTAL HUMAN RIGHTS OF ROBERT F. WILLIAMS, US NEGRO LEADER STOP ABOUT 10000 JAPANESE CITIZENS INCLUDING NATIONAL DIETMEN, GOVERNORS, PROFESSORS ALREADY JOINED SIGNATURE PETITIONS TO EXPRESS THEIR PROTEST AGAINST CRUEL OPPRESSION UPON WILLIAMS STOP SITUATIONS EXTREMELY URGENT STOP WE REQUEST YOU TO TAKE EMERGENCY MEASURES TO FREE WILLIAMS FROM KIDNAPPING FRAME-UP AND TO DROP CHARGE OF CONTEMPT OF CONGRESS STOP HOPING YOU WILL SHOW THE CONSCIENCE OF UNITED STATES TO THE WORLD WITH YOUR PROMPT DETERMINATION STOP JAPANESE COMMITTEE FOR DEFENSE OF LIFE AND FUNDAMENTAL HUMAN RIGHTS OF ROBERT F. WILLIAMS STOP SECRETARY PROFESSOR TOHORU TAKAHASHI 2-15 CHIYAYACHO TOSHIMAKU TOKYO

4. Telegraph of request to cooperate with the Japanese Committee for Defense of Life and Fundamental Human Rights of Robert F. Williams, December 20, 1971

To Chou En-Lai, Prime Minister:

PREMIER CHOU EN-LAI OF THE PEOPLES REPUBLIC OF CHINA: ROBERT F. WILLIAMS, US BLACK LEADER ONCE, EXILED IN YOUR COUNTRY IS FACING THE DEPRIVATION OF HIS LIFE AND FUNDAMENTAL HUMAN RIGHTS BY FRAMEUP AND JUNJUST TRIALS TROP SITUATIONS EXTREMELY URGENT STOP WE SINCERELY HOPE THE CHINESE PEOPLE AND GOVERNMENT TAKE EMERGENCY MEASURES TO RESCUE HIM STOP WE FURTHER ENTREAT YOU TO REQUEST US PRESIDENT NIXON TO CALL AN IMMEDIATE HALT TO CRUEL OPPRESSION UPON WILLIAMS STOP WE ARE DETERMINED IF POSSIBLE TO SEND OUT DELEGATE TO PEKING TO PRESENT SIGNATURE PETITIONS MADE BY WIDE RANGE OF JAPANESE PEOPLE STOP LETTER FOLLOWING STOP JAPANESE COMMITTEE FOR DEFENSE OF THE LIFE AND FUNDAMENTAL HUMAN RIGHTS OF ROBERT F. WILLIAMS STOP SECRETARY PROFESSOR TOHORU TAKAHASHI 2-15 CHIYAYACHO TOSHIMAKU TOKYO

Material V
Correspondence from Robert F. Williams
1. Column "Voice," in *The Asahi Newspaper*

(1) Many thanks for the support for the African-American leader: Nakajima, Yoriko

We, The Japanese Committee for the Defense of the Life and Fundamental Human Rights of Robert F. Williams, thank more than 10,000 people who signed up for the African-American leader, in response to our letter last June in this column. We sent the signature petition for a fair trial for him to U.S. government officials, including the president. In spite of petitions from in and outside of the United States, the Michigan Supreme Court decided against the defendant's favor—to extradite Williams to the South. During the visit this summer, I realized that more than 2,000 African-American political leaders were striving in today's America, while many leaders, like Williams, whose lives and human rights were constantly threatened. Through the signature petition campaign, I realized the limit of the influence we can have from Japan. In addition, the campaign allowed its members to reconsider the issue of racial discrimination in Japan as one of many problems all over the world. Remember, the reciprocal support across the borders is one of the true aims of our activities. We truly appreciate your lasting cooperation.

(2) Encouraged by the signature-petition campaign:
R. F. Williams
Dear Readers of *The Asahi Newspaper*:

I truly appreciate all of your support on humanitarian grounds, for an African American who has been striving against racial discrimination. The signature petition campaign in Japan encouraged many leaders in America and boosted the support activities here. The Michigan Supreme Court made a decision to extradite me, an innocent, to the South where racial discrimination is deeply rooted. Although I see my future in a dark raging storm, your support reminds me that there is hope. By winning this case, I would like to contribute to founding a new world of equality and justice. Thank you so very much for your lasting cooperation.

October 24, 1972

2. Column "From Readers," in *The Asahi Journal*
Dear Editor and Readers:

I am an African American striving against being extradited to the American South. Here I would like to extend my sincere appreciation to Japanese people, especially the editor and the readers, for all the humanitarian support to me. This summer, Ms. Yoriko Nagajima, the organizer of my support group, visited the United States. Her precise report about the signature petition campaign in Japan deeply moved not only the media but also many charitable leaders striving for social justice—racial equality. Through the report, they determined to start a proactive support to me against a violent White group, the KKK that controls the court in the South and tortures African

Americans by its power. If I had committed a crime against an African American like myself, I might have had a better hope to expect humanitarian and equal consideration by this nation's legal system holding a strong sense of racial prejudice. I am no criminal. However, under this oppressive Americanism, being an African American, and protesting against racial oppression, makes me far more feared than being a criminal.

According to the chain of policies to imprison and destroy Black freedom fighters striving for quality and justice, the Michigan Supreme Court decided to extradite me, an innocent to the South for trial. In fact, not only the law is used to keep the status quo—racial discrimination by vengeful white supremacists, but also the Federal Government tries to threaten and ruin the rescue operation for me. Although I see my future in a dark raging storm, I feel encouraged by many Japanese people who stood up for the petition movement on humanitarian grounds against oppressors in this country. By winning this case, I would like to contribute to founding a new world of internationalism and fraternal love, as well as equality and justice, hand in hand with my friends all over the world. For this purpose, I would like to ask you to continue the proactive and widespread petition campaign.

November 24, 1972
Robert F. Williams

3. Telegraph to report the winning of the case from Williams (January 23, 1976)

BECAUSE OF SUPPORT FROM MANY PEOPLE INCLUDING OUR DEAR FRIENDS IN JAPAN, THE RACIST OFFICIALS HAVE BEEN FORCED TO DROP THE 14-YEAR-OLD CHARGES AND CAMPAIGN OF HARASSMENT. THERE IS CONTINUING HEED FOR STRUGGLE IN SIMILAR CASES. I WILL ALWAYS BE GRATEFUL FOR THE SUPPORT GIVEN TO ME BY OUR DEAR JAPANESE FRIENDS. HOPE I AM ABLE TO VISIT JAPAN IN THE FUTURE TO MEET AND THANK ALL OF YOU PERSONALLY. LETTER FOLLOWS ROBERT F. WILLIAMS

THE BLACK SCHOLAR INTERVIEWS ROBERT F. WILLIAMS[30]

Nathan Hare, one of the founders of The Black Scholar magazine journal interviews Robert F. Williams, author of *Negroes with Guns*, who is known internationally for the Black liberation struggle. In 1961, trumped-up charges of kidnapping were brought against Williams, who received political asylum with his wife and two sons, first in Cuba, then China and Tanzania. During his exile, Williams continued his revolutionary activities with broadcasts and as publisher of *The Crusader*, a monthly newsletter. Williams returned to the United States a few months ago. The Committee to Aid in the Defense of Robert Williams, box 666, Detroit, Michigan, 48206, has been formed for his legal defense. **BLACK SCHOLAR:** You were away in exile for quite a long time. Though we were always aware of your presence and impact on the Black liberation movement. And your persistent promise to return to this country, it still must have taken more than ordinary courage to come back. Why did you come back to the United States? **WILLIAMS:** Well, you see, the problem is that I didn't leave on my own. I was forced out of the country. I would still have been in the South because we had quite a movement going there. But the most positive aspect of my return to a racist America could probably be called an opportunity to demonstrate the extent of the Black man's commitment to our ever-widening struggle for liberation. I hope to set an example that will serve notice that in the face of white supremacy, terror, unjust, and cruel imprisonment and threats of cold-blooded and savaged death, the Black man can no longer be intimidated. I hope to bring home the point that the day has gone forever when bullying white men can frighten the Black man out of existence. He has the power to assassinate but not to intimidate. **BLACK SCHOLAR:** So, you did not come back expecting justice in American courts. We remember your appeal in 1969 on behalf of Afro-American militants who refused to sell out and who cannot be intimidated and in opposition to the "vicious campaign to destroy effective and potential ghetto leaders" such as Max Stanford, Huey Newton, Rap Brown, LeRoi Jones, Martin Sostre, Herman Ferguson, Cleveland Sellars, John Kenyatta, and Lee Otis Johnson. You urged that Black Americans must be inspired to display the same determination in safeguarding the human and civil rights of our oppressed people as white racists are to legally lynch us. You knew about the legalist repression of Black leaders. **WILLIAMS:** Yes, I did. I knew that a mad dog can always be expected to act like a mad dog. So, it is time to cast away illusions about peace, justice, democracy, and the redemptive potential of the savage racists. Actions speak louder than words. The Black and the weak are always victims of the white and the strong. Thus, John Bull's (England's) sterile words of censure against a minority of white squatters and poaches on the Black man's soil of Africa are quite in contrast to his "law and order" enforced by bullet and bayonet in, say, tiny and independence-loving Anguilla. But then, the contrast hinges on the difference between Black and white and the tyrannical nature of white power. Like father, like son. That's the way it is with John Bull and Uncle Sam, as far as the Black man is concerned, he has no legal or human rights that white terror is bound to respect. So, what we have is a living lesson in Black-and-white contrast! It is excessive asininity for Black people to expect justice in a hostile white jungle society. In the first place, I am not now a criminal, I have never been a criminal, and the only times that I have ever been in jail were because of my fight for justice. It's a matter of justice. The false charges against me were not motivated by criminal activity on my part but stemmed from political and racial persecution. I have as much right, or more, to live in America as Nixon, and no amount of intimidation can force me to abdicate this inalienable right. So, it's not a matter of justice. It's a matter of trying to lynch a Black man and trying to whitewash it and make it look good. And I don't know of any appeal to reason that's ever been able to really save a Black man when the white mob has been really set on lynching him. Occasionally, a Black man might be justly set free, or justly not prosecuted. But that's just occasionally, and it's an exception rather than a rule. It's something like gambling, and justice should be constant and expected, and not a thing of chance. In fact, in my chance, my case, even if they turned me loose, it wouldn't be justice. Not only am I not guilty of any crime; I've already gone through all of this harassment, and I've been handicapped in many ways, and had my life disrupted. They can't give me justice now for what they've already done. **BLACK SCHOLAR:** Before we on with all the things they did to you, and your long hard struggle to return—as well as what changes you have noticed now that you are back—would you tell us about the movement you had in North Carolina that upset the power structure so? **WILLIAMS:** Well, by now I have one charge for trying to get integration and another charge for trying to get separation. But at that time, I was fighting for integration. I was the local president of the NAACP down in Union County, North Carolina. We had a long series of struggles with white power structure for the six years I was president. You see all the while I had advocated a policy of armed self-defense. Also, I had been a candidate for mayor. Now, that is not considered very much now, but in those days they didn't even do that in Northern towns. Besides, we had our own militia. **BLACK SCHOLAR:** When was that? **WILLIAMS:** As far back as 1957, when we spent the summer in foxholes behind sandbags. We had steel helmets. We had obtained gas masks. And we had a better communication system than they have now. In fact, we had better organized self-defense forces than they have now. This was too much for the white power structure. They felt they had to make an example of me. **BLACK SCHOLAR:** Still, we remember you saying once that "violence and turmoil without strategy and meaningful goals and objectives amount to fruitless energy" since the oppressor is organized and knows what he wants. What were you and your forces fighting for in 1957 and around the time of the Montgomery bus boycott? **WILLIAMS:** First, we started to fight for an end to all forms of racial discrimination. But we came out with a ten-point program which included all of what the passive resistance movement was asking for, such as access to food facilities, buses and public toilets. We asked that the white racists abolish all discrimination in the educational system. We asked for fair employment. We asked for equal rights to receive welfare aid from the Welfare Department, and equal Aid to Dependent Child. This also is not considered as anything outstanding now, but in much of the South then, they didn't give aid to Black people; it was reserved for whites only. We fought for the right of Black people to have this. We had to fight for the right of women to have support for their children, even when their husbands were in prison. We also fought against brutality, and we tried to raise the standard of living for Black people. Also, we tried to eradicate racial discrimination in medical facilities. This antagonized the power structure to no end, and it went all the way to Washington. **BLACK SCHOLAR:** Could you tell us about one of the cases that went to Washington? **WILLIAMS:** Well, on one occasion we stopped an urban renewal program. **BLACK SCHOLAR:** That far back? **WILLIAMS:** Yes, we got a dose of urban renewal early, when it first came out. They came through the community where we lived, part of the Black community, the section where 90 percent of the Black people or more owned their own homes. Some had homes worth as much as $35,000 in terms of what money meant there then. On the other hand, there was another section of the Black community where they didn't even have indoor toilets. The urban renewal bypassed the houses that didn't have indoor toilets and went through the community with the $35,000 homes. These they condemned for urban renewal. You see, this also was where the political strength of the Black community and the militancy and the voters were and where they could afford and had the guns. Well, it so happens that about this time, when President Eisenhower was visiting India as the guest of Nehru, he made a big pronouncement there that he and the United States wanted all of the people of Asia to have decent housing and food. We saw this as an opportunity to send a telegram to Prime Minister Nehru (who had been a guest of NAACP and knew what it meant) and asked him to please convey the message to Mr. Eisenhower. We signed it as the NAACP. We expected, somewhat apprehensively, that Mr. Eisenhower would go into his theories to call it a fraud. And we expected him to really jump us when he got back. But a strange thing happened. When Eisenhower came back to this country, he personally called an Afro-American named Dr. Snowden, who was working in housing, and asked him to contact me and to assure us that he was just as interested in our homes as in the people of Asia, and to rest assured that there wouldn't be any urban renewal in that community until the law had been fully complied with. He said to let him know if I had any problems. Actually, it was carried in the press, the Afro-American. He had made a special call from the White House. That stopped the urban renewal program dead in its tracks. **BLACK SCHOLAR:** Whatever happened to it? **WILLIAMS:** That's been over ten years ago, and it just bogged down and was finished in its tracks. But the local officials have never forgiven me for that. We were always embarrassing them. We had invited students, exchange students from Japan and Britain, and correspondence journalists from overseas. We invited them into the community and gave them tours, taking them into the homes of the poverty-stricken people so that they could see how the Black people live in America. This also became a source of embarrassment to the United States that they never forgot. Plus, we had armed people, and we had a lot of clashes. **BLACK SCHOLAR:** That was prior to the college student nonviolent sit-in movement, which most people know to have originated in your state, North Carolina. But most don't know that you anticipated the sit-in movement. **WILLIAMS:** The sit-ins started across the country with the students in 1960, and we had started as far back as 1957. Then, too, we were demanding more than the breakdown of barriers to Jim Crow public facilities, as we said earlier. **BLACK SCHOLAR:** It's apparent why they would try to frame and lynch you. But who did you manage to get away? **WILLIAMS:** Well, at that time I went through Canada; from the United States to Canada; and through Mexico into Cuba. Add to that the fact that not only left North Carolina; they had an all-points alarm issued by the FBI. And they had told the local people. In fact, they had them waiting at the courthouse, a mob waiting for me, thinking it would be a matter of hours before the great FBI would catch me and return me to that town. Of course, if they had been waiting there at the courthouse until now, they would have been dead. It was also a source of embarrassment to the FBI. Not only that, but they were also running all over the country searching for homes, contacting people I knew all over the country. They had assigned 500 FBI men. I had been in Cuba for quite a while. In fact, the reason why I decided to let them know I was in Cuba was that a lot of my friends were saying that I should tell them I was in Cuba so that they would stop coming to their homes and hounding them. **BLACK SCHOLAR:** You were in Cuba for about five years, then left for China. Why did you leave Cuba? **WILLIAMS:** Well, I had some political differences with the party. And as a result, I left and went to China. There wasn't hostility or any personal feelings. The whole thing had to do with Black nationalism. We had differences in the race problem in the United States. The Party maintained that it was strictly a class issue and that once the class problem had been solved through a socialist administration, racism would be abolished. I think racism encompasses more than just class struggle. I believe now that it is a part of the American way of life. It's a part of American psychology and the mentality of America and a change in the system will not abolish racism. As a result, I was told that they couldn't support Black nationalism. But they always treated me quite well, even up to the time I left. As an individual, everything possible was done to make my life comfortable. Still, I couldn't see any need to be in exile if I couldn't conduct some type of struggle. So, I left Cuba and went to China. **BLACK SCHOLAR:** But even when you were in Cuba, you were trying to return to the United States to conduct that struggle. **WILLIAMS:** Yes; I had told the Cuban officials when I first went to Cuba that I would return as soon as I possibly could. Actually, I made an effort to return to the States in 1965. But the State Department refused to give me a travel document. And at that time, they had just issued passports to all of the Communist Party leaders who were under indictment, including Gus Hall. The Supreme Court had handed down a decision that no American citizen can be denied a passport. I discovered that there was a difference in their attitude toward Communists and Black nationalists. I was a Black nationalist, so it was impossible at the time for me to get any kind of travel document from the United States. **BLACK SCHOLAR:** How did you finally make it back? **WILLIAMS:** I lived in China for three years after that. Anyway, I left China on the way to the United States and stopped in Africa, so that from Tanzania I would be able to obtain a travel document. I had some difficulty there, in getting permission from the U.S. Treasury Department to bring my personal effects into the country. I was told by the U.S. Embassy that they might not want me in the United States. When I asked them why, they said that I was too hot. I told them that was their problem. In the beginning, they didn't want me in Tanzania and had put pressure on the Tanzanian government to force me out. But I stayed there for six months, and when they discovered that I didn't want to stay in Tanzania but was on my way to the United States, they said that I could stay in Tanzania as long as I wanted to. So, I got to England on the way back to the United States and was pulled out of the line by Customs and Immigration at the airport in London. First, these two men came up and flashed their identification. Said they were policemen and that they wanted to talk. We went into the Immigration room, where they said they were going to search me and my luggage. I asked them why was this necessary, and they said it was because of my FBI, "because your FBI has informed us that you're carrying firearms and ammunition to the United States." I asked them how many firearms and how much ammunition they can carry in a suitcase. So they started to search for me. They took out my fountain pen held it to my face and said they were going to open it and that if it exploded, I would be the first one to be killed. They were rather nervous about it, and evidently believed what they had been told. Then they went through all of my luggage. Since they didn't find anything, they called the Immigration Airport Police. After they finished another group came in the Metropolitan Police and went through the same procedure. When they finished another group came, and said it was the Criminal Investigation Department. Through all of that, I was asking them what they had to do with it, in as much as I was on the flight to another country. Also, the British Embassy in Tanzania had told me I wouldn't a visa in transit. Still, they kept me there for three hours, late in the afternoon, with different ones searching for me and trying to decide what they were going to do. **BLACK SCHOLAR:** What did they decide to do? **WILLIAMS:** Finally, they said they didn't have any place for me to stay that night (my flight wasn't due out until 10 O'clock the next day). That was the only flight daily from London to Detroit. Then they said that because they didn't have any place for me to stay, I would have to go to Pentonville. When we arrived at this place, about 14-miles across London, I told the man, (looks like a prison). He said that it was. I asked him: "What about my leaving on the plane tomorrow?" He said: "You stand about as much chance missing that plane as the Queen of England." (Meaning that he wanted me out of England). But the next day when the time came for me to leave nobody at all came to pick me up. I lay in this prison incommunicado for three days. **BLACK SCHOLAR:** How did you finally get word out? **WILLIAMS:** It happened that a young African was in there. He was being released one day when I was waiting in the reception room in hopes that somebody would come and get me. But they never did show. Anyway, this young man was coming out of prison, and the warden asked him if he had all of his personal belongings he had checked in, and he said no. What was he missing? "A Mao book" (talking about a little red book of quotations from Chairman Mao). The man became indignant and reached under the desk got the book and threw it up on the counter. Then he pointed to me and said: "There is one of your buddies from China. He's Maoist, too." Of course, he meant this in a sarcastic way. But he didn't know that that let me know that this was a reliable brother. So, I turned to the African and asked him if he was going out. He said yes. I asked him if he would tell the people in the Black community that I had been taken off a plane to the United States and was being held incommunicado. He said he would. So, I told him my name and where I was going. At this point, they tried to push him out of the room passed me and closed the door. I put my foot in the door. Then the warden told the guards to take him back. He said saying as they were taking him away: "Don't worry, brother; I'm going to tell it as soon as I get out." **BLACK SCHOLAR:** How long did they keep him in? **WILLIAMS:** I really don't know. But the next day the news had gotten out. That was when a group came to see me in prison-a sister and two young brothers. They came in and said they represented The Black Panthers of England. Then they turned to the warden, who was standing with them, and said: "Where're going to free our brother, either peacefully or with force. It's up to you to decide." This shook the man, and I myself was a bit surprised, because I didn't know they had a Black Panther organization in Britain. Least of all, that they were so militant and outspoken. It turned out that they had also contacted other Black groups and the outspoken faction of the Asian population, also the British Civil Liberties Union and some other white liberals. All of these groups started demonstrations. But in the meantime, I had gone on a hunger strike, which I maintained for five days. Because I didn't announce that I was on a hunger strike, they didn't take the first two days seriously. They merely brought in the food, and I didn't eat it. I didn't eat and I didn't drink any water. So, on the third day, they got worried because I hadn't taken any fluid. They moved me out of the prison into the hospital and brought in two doctors to examine me. The doctors said, well, a person could make it without food for many days, but not without water. **BLACK SCHOLAR:** Most persons who go on hunger strikes take some kind of fluids. Why did you decide to drink no water? **WILLIAMS:** Well, I never believed in this passive idea of a hunger strike. I have always assumed that if a person went on a hunger strike, that meant everything. Later, I found out from the British officials that that was why they became so alarmed. **BLACK SCHOLAR**: What did they do when they became alarmed? **WILLIAMS:** First, they sent a prison chaplain to see me, and he asked if my refusal to eat was due to religious beliefs. I told him, no, it was due to principle. I also told him that I remembered reading about how they had taken Black people into captivity as slaves-how his forefathers took my forefathers into captivity. And they feed them. They feed them just enough to keep them alive. And also, they subjugated them. But I couldn't understand how a man could stay alive in captivity. So, I told him that he and the rulers of Britain might be the same as their forefathers, but I am not the same as my forefathers. I told them that they couldn't take me into captivity like a beast in a cage. That they would either have to kill me or set me free. They would eventually have a dead body on their hands in any case, because I wasn't going to submit to their captivity. **BLACK SCHOLAR:** What charges had they lodged against you to justify or rationalize imprisonment? **WILLIAMS:** They had openly admitted that they didn't have any charges against me, therefore no reason to confine me. I told them and the chaplain that I didn't see anything humane about taking away a man's freedom, without reason for deprivation, and then pretending to be merciful to the point of bringing him food. If your opinion of him is such as to cause you to deprive him of his liberty, then you should be willing to deprive him of his life-without cause. This had them a little shaken up. So, I told the chaplain that I didn't want anything from England, that England didn't owe me a thing, but my freedom. And they couldn't take my freedom away and give me something else. **BLACK SCHOLAR:** Aside from your hunger strike, what finally made them give in, or give up, on keeping you in captivity? **WILLIAMS:** Well, the Blacks (West Indians, Blacks who were born in Britain, and the Africans) were demonstrating around the jail and at TWA, with whom I had a ticket to Detroit. Also, with them were Asians and white liberals. The demonstrations were very big and they started each night. You could hear them through the walls, over the walls and into the jail. So, the warden came in and said the reason they were holding me in prison was because TWA had refused to fly me out of Britain. I replied that I had already paid for the ticket and that they could have denied me the right to fly at the point of origin but could not stop me in mid-flight and dump me in a foreign land unless I had done something to warrant it. They didn't have any charges against me, and when they sold me the ticket that was a contract. So, I told him that he had better get in touch with TWA and tell them that it's going to cost them a million dollars. Finally, that afternoon two representatives came from TWA. I told them the same thing and demanded that they read that section of the code relating to the protection of the passenger since they had read one protecting the carrier. They became rather nervous and left. Then, on the fourth day, they came in the late afternoon about five O'clock and said that I was leaving. I asked them how could be leaving when the plane left at ten in the morning. At the airport, they finally told me I was being sent on a flight to Cairo. I said Cairo, where? They said Cairo, Egypt. I told them I had just passed through Cairo and had no need to go back; that my ticket was paid for and called for the three facts that I was being transported to Detroit, Michigan. They repeated that TWA was afraid to carry me out. I asked why, and they said that TWA was afraid I would hijack the plane and endanger their passengers. I told them I had already been to every place that people hijack planes to. **BLACK SCHOLAR:** As a matter of fact, you once issued a statement from China to Black Americans, stating that "aircraft hijacking should be discontinued among Black militants." **WILLIAMS:** I remember. Plus, where I wanted to go, I already had a ticket; so, it wouldn't make sense for me to hijack a plane to Detroit. Anyway, I asked them if they weren't afraid, I would hijack the plane to Cairo, since didn't want to go there, to get to Detroit, where I wanted to go. While they were debating it, one of the service trucks rammed the airplane out on the field and the airplane was delayed. So, they took me back to prison. The following day, the fifth day, they brought me back again to the airport. I asked them where I was going, and they said Cairo. I then asked them if they had brought the undertaker. They wanted to know what the undertaker had to do with it, and I said because he was the only one who would be able to put me on that plane to Cairo. He informed me that he was under orders from the Ministry of Foreign Affairs to use force if necessary. I explained that force could get my body on the plane but not me. They had lined up about fourteen policemen along the hall, while the man came over to repeat his orders to use force, and asked if he was ready to start. He looked at me and he looked at the other men, and I told him once more that he would have to kill me in London to get me on that plane. So, they went out into the corridor for a caucus. Then he made a phone call and came back and said they wouldn't have to use force if I agreed to go back to prison. I said I had been in prison all during my stay in England, so they took me back. Then the doctor and the priest came back again and asked me if I would please accept some juice. They even suggested that the church could supply the juice and my food, so I wouldn't have to accept it from the prison. I replied that the church couldn't feed me in a British prison. Finally, on the sixth day, they came and told me: "You are leaving." I asked them where to and they said to Detroit. I asked them how, and they said they would take me on a ship. The shipping line had agreed to take me. I told them I had an aircraft ticket and wasn't going on a ship. So, then they said, well if you agree to let the CIA escort you (some man in the Embassy from the CIA in London). I told them, no, I would not submit to any American arrest on foreign soil; Americans didn't have any jurisdiction over me there. So, finally, they said that TWA had agreed to provide a private plane which would fly me to Detroit with my lawyer. By now, people were demonstrating at the U.S. Embassy as well, and some of the Black Panthers of England had broken into the Embassy grounds and threatened the American officials. Well, the next morning because the people were planning a big demonstration at the airport at the time, I was to leave, they drove me straight up to the plane, skirting around the airport. They had my lawyer waiting there, and another Black man unknown to me in African dress. He started shaking my hand as I came up and introduced himself and followed me on the plane. Later, he said he was a vice president of TWA and began to explain that TWA was the most liberal airline, with more Blacks working for them including Black stewardesses and one or two Black pilots, a record he called progressive. He said he hoped I would be considerate of TWA, and I replied that I didn't see where their policy was considerate of me. With nobody on the plane (it flew a special route across the North Pole), they said the trip (with full regular staff on the plane) was costing them 20,000 dollars' worth of services for a 500 dollar ticket. I said that was their hard luck. But they brought us on it. **BLACK SCHOLAR:** What happened when you got back to the United States? **WILLIAMS:** I was met at the airport in Detroit by the FBI, arrested and taken to the Federal Building for fingerprinting. While the FBI man was fingerprinting my right hand, another man came up and slipped a subpoena into my left. He said he was a U.S. Marshal, and this was a subpoena from the Eastland Committee, the Internal Security Committee. After I left court, I had to go and set bond and then I got subpoenaed to Washington. It took three of them before I was forced to go down there. It wasn't a federal offense but the FBI had gotten into it because they were trying to help North Carolina officials. They said I was a fugitive from justice-a fugitive from injustice. **BLACK SCHOLAR:** Yes, we noticed in the Detroit Free Press this morning that so many college students at the Earth Day protest here at Michigan State yesterday called Governor Milliken a "racist pig" because he agreed to extradite you to face kidnapping charges in North Carolina. **WILLIAMS:** You see, like the rest of the power structure, it was more than they can digest the fact that I not only left the United States, but went from Canada, Mexico, and Cuba to China and also Vietnam, through the Soviet Union. Their idea, their feeling, is that a nigger not only was able to escape, but he went abroad. And abroad I was treated like I might have been the head of state, the head of the United States. In fact, I was able to go places their people couldn't go. As a result of this, all of the reactionaries in the government developed an intense hatred for me. Everything that happened in this country while I was aboard, they blamed on me. They claimed I was involved somehow in Watts, the incident there, in Detroit, and in Harlem; in most of the uprising in this country, according to J. Edgar Hoover. **BLACK SCHOLAR:** How do you suppose that the uprisings in Watts, Harlem, Detroit, Newark and the like began? **WILLIAMS:** These things came out of the community. I think they were spontaneous. I learned about them through the newspapers. Also, they had many conspiracies going the so-called "Stature of Liberty plot," the so-called "plot" on Roy Wilkins and all of these people. I learned about it through the newspapers like other people. But they still always kept this up, because of their hatred, and because they wanted to try to tie the Black movement up with the Communist movement abroad. This is another reason I wanted to come home; it knocked the blocks out from under J. Edgar Hoover and much of his efforts to link the Black movements in this country with the international Communist movement. So, now they don't have me as a link to try to push this further. **BLACK SCHOLAR:** We remember reading a copy of a so-called "secret FBI report" about two years ago (which generally didn't seem very current at the time or accurate before that) where there appeared to be a kind of fixation on you as an "extremist." **WILLIAMS:** It is traditional Americanism for the white racist power structure to brand all who work uncompromisingly for Black liberation and social justice as extremists. There can be no such thing as "extreme" methods implored against a beastly oppressor in a noble enterprise, undertaken on behave of social justice and the liberation of wretched slaves.

America was founded on the extreme belief that cut-throats, prostitutes, criminals, and social scum from Europe had a right to slaughter and massacre an indigenous people in a white crusade of extending "Christian civilization." America even dares to piously refer to these original land grabbers and thug killers as "bluebloods." This is really the extreme of extremism. **BLACK SCHOLAR:** Right on. Many of the things you were doing in the 1950s-then regarded as extreme have now grown popular, among Blacks at least. Since you've returned, what changes have you noticed? **WILLIAMS:** There have been some changes, but they are mixed, like a chart with ups and downs, zigs and zags, some things slightly better, some worse. At best, it is a patchwork progress if you can call it progress at all. I don't think anything has really helped the great masses of Black people. The greatest change has been in the attitudes of Blacks, particularly the so-called "Black bourgeoise." Many of them have become more conscious of what's going on they've been forced to and are more willing to identify with our people. More race pride is especially apparent among our youth, more cooperation and more militancy. When I left, there was a big nonviolent, pacifist movement. I was just the opposite of that. Of course, I believe in pacifist and passive tactics win these things can be fruitful; I believe in any method that will work. But I don't believe that a man should subject himself passively to the violence of oppressors and tyrants without a violent response in an effort to defend himself. Most people believed that way or so they said but they merely whispered and cowered under, they said, for fear of losing white liberal funds. So, in those days they condemned me; including, to my surprise, a lot of today's most outspoken advocates of self-defense. Back then the going thing was what the white man had told them: to turn the other cheek and appeal to the conscious of the white oppressor. I knew that you couldn't do that; you can't appeal to the conscious of a beast when you're dealing with savages and brutes and tyrants. So, this is one major thing that I see. And it is a change that has influenced the Black bourgeoisie and the power structure, though the power structure lately has become even more repressive. But in some ways the fact that the Black man was no longer passive and would fight caused the power structure to give more attention to the Black man. **BLACK SCHOLAR:** What has been the outcome of this new Black awakening set against increased white oppression, for the Black liberation movement? **WILLIAMS:** Well, in the wake of the uprisings, the Black man had the power structure pretty much on the run had he been well enough organized and persistent in his goals (really understood what he wanted and pressed hard for it), but I think that we lost the initiative. As a result, we are entering dangerous times when the government is seizing the initiative, planning apparently to use repression rather than eliminate the social ills causing the conflict. More and more rights are being taken away and more and more rights are given to the police. This is leading to a police state in which a Black man is going to be on the bottom rung of the ladder. This is all in the name of "law and order" for the sake of "peace in the streets." These are very difficult and crucial times that we are facing, as the repression is going to grow sharper.

 BLACK SCHOLAR: What can Black people do to prepare for and offset this increasing repression? **WILLIAMS:** One thing, I've noticed too much bittering, too much conflict, among our people. I think this is an outgrowth of the new militancy which too often condemns the so-called "Uncle Tom" without trying to win him over.

The Uncle Tom today may be the militant tomorrow. This is no time for superficial divisions among us. The cause of our survival dictates that we unite all of our people and ask aid from wherever we can get it. Those who rap themselves in the raiment of self-righteous political sages and arrogantly proclaim themselves the true believers and saints of purity are the antithesis of social progress and transformation. There are many sheds in the spectrum of color. To limit one's scope of perception simply to Black and white is to become a victim of stupidity. We must also guard against being erroneously swayed by the Fabian histrionics of put-up Black Marxist whose political line just so happens to coincide with the politics of the CIA. At this historic juncture in our struggle for survival, human rights and self-determination, progressive Black nationalism offers the greatest hope for unity of purpose. Progressive Black nationalism is anti-imperialist, anti-monopoly capitalist, and anti-racist. It stresses deliverance from both the white man's tyranny and his paternalism, and it can be a powerful cohesive factor that motivates our people in a common cause toward a common goal. **BLACK SCHOLAR:** Is it possible to have any form of cooperative struggle with other oppressed groups? **WILLIAMS:** Yes, it is essential for us to cooperate with and solicit support from other sectors of the deprived, but to relinquish our right to act in our own best interest for survival and well-being is a criminal default on our part. We must collectively be ourselves. We collectively must lead ourselves. We collectively advance ourselves. We must collectively preserve ourselves and must collectively and love ourselves. Without concerted action, our cause is lost. **BLACK SCHOLAR:** You mentioned that progressive Black nationalism is, among other things, anti-monopoly capitalism. What do you think about so-called "Black capitalism"? **WILLIAMS:** It's one of the things creating disunity and is a part of the establishments effort to recognize the leader of certain groups. No doubt, Black capitalism and minority enterprise will grease the potbellies of a selected few tokens, but the vast majority of our people will remain the victims of vicious and cruel Americanism. In fact, beginning with the Reconstruction Era, there was ushered in a new hope for the so-called "emancipated Black slaves of America." Infantile Black capitalism was encouraged. The power structure promised equality before the law, Black suffrage and equitable participation in American society. The brevity of that new mood of democracy should be a tragic lesson of history. The American record speaks for itself. Is it any more righteous now than it was then when those celebrated, "liberty-loving" racist gentlemen hypocritically fashioned the Declaration of Independence and the Constitution? Capitalism is ruthless, cunning, swash-buckling, murderous, and cutthroat. To expect Black capitalism and minority enterprise to be dished out on a gold-plated serving platter is tantamount to hoping to lay claim to the mythological pot of gold at the end of a rainbow. **BLACK SCHOLAR:** After that, it would be superfluous to ask you about Nixon's new policy of "Benign Neglect." But let's go back to the matter of unification for a moment. What can we do toward achieving unification? **WILLIAMS:** Well, the first thing is that people who have a common destiny must develop a common outlook and common solutions to problems. We hear a lot of talk about "Black revolutionaries"; but as Black revolutionaries, our first task must be to revolutionize ourselves, and transport ourselves. That is the most difficult task of a revolutionary because, otherwise, a revolutionary can't bring about change. Revolution means change. But no change can be brought about by a person until he has changed himself and is transformed inwardly. Also, the change in others can have some influence on ours. So, the biggest thing I see is selfishness. We got to fight selfishness and ego. And we've got to fight it to the point that we'll stop feeling that we've got to have the final word; that if we don't have the final word, then let everything go down the drain and be destroyed. We also have got to stop feeling that we've just got to be the leader, that if I am not the leader, then we don't need one. **BLACK SCHOLAR:** This seems to be the problem in Africa, too. **WILLIAMS:** Yes, there are far too many states in Africa-little vest pockets. Africa has been Balkanized. The African people are fond of each other and can get along, but the leaders are the ones who, in conjunction with the imperialists, are responsible for the condition. All of them will say that they want African unity and to create a united Africa. Then each one feels that he should be the leader of a united Africa. That's also how I see our movement in the United States. Instead of devoting ourselves to our salvation, everybody talks about unity and wants unity, but the leaders do not want unity, or a united front, unless it's under their direction. That's also one of the reasons why I have come back to this country. I don't feel like it's necessary for me to be a leader or to lead somebody. And I've made no effort. In fact, I've tried to get out of as much leadership as possible. I think we have to start some place. So, if all of us start setting that example, the sooner we can get down to what needs to be done. We also need to have more communication and more exchanges, to talk and discuss our problems. Forget about who the leader is and get down to the problem. The idea is that we must be willing to fit in wherever we can, wherever we will, wherever we're needed, wherever the situation dictates. If we don't reach that stage, we'll never make it. The situation will work out the leadership. I think we need collective leadership, anyway. **BLACK SCHOLAR:** Speaking of the need to have more communication and the parallel problems of egoism in Africa and Afro-America, what about the problem of communication between Blacks on the two continents? **WILLIAMS:** We remember your 1,000-mile-plus motorcycle ride across some of the most rugged terrain in Africa. Afro-Americans must make a determined and conscious effort to counteract the imperialist white man's propaganda in Africa. Our people must strive for closer relations with the African people and their devoted leaders. We must exert special effort to spread the truth about Americanism as it relates to Black people. More of our people must endeavor to visit Africa and contact the youth. We must stir ourselves on behalf of counteracting the man's well-planned and financed effort to alienate our people. While we concentrate great effort on improving our relations with our African brothers, we should not neglect other sympathizers and potential allies in other countries. We must strive to offset the racist power structure's distorted image of our people and our predicament in savage America. We must become more conscious of the relativity of the Black man's problems in America. To those of the deprived peoples of the world who are our natural allies. We must give more attention to foreign relations and the winning of friends on our side. **BLACK SCHOLAR:** Further, in that connection, there was something you said a while back about accepting aid wherever we can. But today the Black movement appears to be in a quandary or dilemma over whether to accept money from white sources or even on occasion, whether to work for a white institution. What is your view on this matter? **WILLIAMS:** When we can get aid without strings attached, we should accept aid when and wherever we can find it. I don't think we should become so belligerent and hostile that we say we can't accept aid from whitey, or honky, or whatever they want to call him. I don't think that's a good strategy, and I don't think it's a revolutionary one. If you're trying to win a battle, you must concentrate everything on that battle. **BLACK SCHOLAR:** What about the problem of white allies? That's a much-debated issue. **WILLIAMS:** Well, you have to realize that there are all kinds of allies-temporary allies and permanent allies. Some are only going to go so far, and you have to know that. On the other hand, you can neutralize a potential enemy, making him an enemy you won't have to fight. I think we must adopt that attitude and start longing at our problems from there. We've got to brace ourselves for some hard days ahead. **BLACK SCHOLAR:** You failed to comment upon the contention among brothers over whether, when they are employed by a white firm, let alone a government agency, they are "working for the man." **WILLIAMS:** It is erroneous to think that one can isolate oneself completely from institutions of a social and political system that exercises power over the environment in which he resides. Self-imposed and premature isolation, initiated by the oppressed against the organs of a tyrannical establishment, militates against revolutionary movements dedicated to radical change. It is a grave error for militant and just-minded youth to reject struggle-serving opportunities to join the man's government services, police forces, peace Corps and vital organs of the power structure. Militants should become acquainted with the methods of the oppressor. Meaningful change can be more thoroughly effectuated by militant pressure from within as well as without. We can obtain valuable know-how from the oppressor. Struggle is not all violence. Effective struggle requires tactics, plans, analysis and a highly sophisticated application of mental aptness. The forces of oppression and tyranny have perfected a highly articulate system of infiltration for undermining and frustrating the efforts of the oppressed in trying to upset the unjust status quo. To a great extent, the power structure keeps itself informed as to the revolutionary activity of freedom fighters. With the threat of extermination looming menacingly before Black Americans, it is pressingly imperative that our people enter the vital organs of the establishment. Infiltrate the man's institutions. **BLACK SCHOLAR:** You frequently refer to youth, and you have long been an idiot to many of them on college campuses. For instance, as early as 1967, students at Howard University demanded and got your film, "Robert Williams in Red China," and your book, *Negroes with Guns*, placed in the university library against the administration's will. What is your advice to Black youth? **WILLIAMS:** There is so much. But aside from what I have been saying-which generally would apply to all age groups-it is imperative that revolutionary youth undergo personal and moral transformation. There is a need for a stringent revolutionary code of moral ethics. Revolutionaries are instruments of righteousness. Violence applied in the pursuit of justice is what distinguishes revolutionary violence from that which is committed by tyrants and villainous thugs. Clean up the ghetto. Strong fratricidal warfare and conflict. Discourage the agent's provocateurs, Judases, and criminal elements. Prepare for a struggle for survival. **BLACK SCHOLAR:** Speaking of youth, now that Black studies have been largely co-opted and corrupted, some have claimed that it is no longer a revolutionary goal. Do we need Black studies? **WILLIAMS:** Black studies, yes; but what Black studies? Some Black studies are no improvement over white studies when racist slanderers of Blacks are allowed to select new material that will have the same effect and serve the same purpose as the old. It must be borne in mind that a great portion of material produced by Black intellectuals under the aegis of the white power structure is anti-Black and pro-white. White publishers are the most forceful advocates of Americanism. Black studies, yes, but they should be inspiring and uplifting. Such studies should encourage wholesome family ties, morality, dignity, courage, devotion to freedom, and high ideas. They should serve to raise the intellectual level of all who participate and should eulogize the good attributes of our people rather than serve as a surreptitious method of propagating intellectual pornography. It is a first-magnitude shame that at this late date of our poignant and turbulent sojourn in oppressive America, even some Black nationalists still permit white racists to define what constitutes Black history, Black leadership, Black morality, classical Black literature, art, music, politics, aspirations, alienation, and Black capitalism. I think we have had enough of the white man's version of white studies. Why accept his version of Black studies? Also, we've got to do more than talk about what is not relevant in Black studies and in academic life. We've got to start talking and thinking about what is relevant and what is not relevant in the Movement, particularly insofar as what we discuss and what we plan, what our ambitions are as a people. Also, we have to start thinking along the lines of survival, because the white man is going to be very desperate. **BLACK SCHOLAR:** On survival and the white man, what is your conclusion about the future of this country? **WILLIAMS:** I think the situation is going to get much worse, starting this summer. Sand I think that somewhere in 1970, the United States will undergo a drastic change. It will never be the same again. It may not be completely destroyed. It may not fall. But it's going to be obvious to everybody by the end of this year that it's on its way out and that something else is going to have to be substituted.

Robert F. Williams Interviewed by U.S. Students for the Marxist Leninist Quarterly, 1972

Editor's Note:

The following exclusive interview was given by Robert F. Williams, exiled American Negro leader, to a number of students who traveled to Cuba during the summer of 1963. The interview was held in Havana in mid-August. The following is an uncut verbatim transcription of the tape recording of Robert Williams's remarks.

Q. What is the present trend of the Black movement in the South? Which organizations can lead to a solution of the racial situation in America?

A. The oppressed Black people are becoming more militant. The major organizations that now operate in the South claim to follow a pacifist nonviolent line. The struggle in the South shows that this philosophy is not sufficient.

It is very difficult at this state to say what organization will have the proper line to lead the Afro-American to freedom. New mass organizations may rise out of the ruins of the organizations we see today. The Afro-American masses will have the final say.

Q. What ultimate political program do you envisage for the U.S.?

A. I see in the future a militant organization able to rally many people, broad in scope, serving many purposes, above all working to improve the standard of living of all the people in the U.S. and in the South.

We must concern ourselves at this point with the struggle at hand: to abolish the oppression, the brutality, and the injustices, which now exist, by means of the courts and the system. We know there must be drastic changes in the system. This will take place as a form of evolution as well as revolution. We should not go off on a political line at this stage of the struggle.

People rally to the cause of injustice. Most modern revolutions have been started by people resisting tyranny.

Political positions have frightened a good many of our people away from struggle in the South. We have had some bad deals with politicians in the past. Our people suffer and seek redress. They want relief. They know that political promises are no good. I don't think that a political line will be adequate to motivate our people in this freedom fight.

Q. How does your program take into account sections of the white masses who might favor it?

A. If white workers feel that they should hate us, I feel that they should hate us on a basis of equality.

We know of exploitation. We know that racism sprang from exploitation itself. Racism is an outgrowth of a need to justify racial exploitation.

We must concentrate on the people who suffer most. The Black people are the lowest strata, the lowest class, economically, politically.

A lot of people speak of a working class movement: as if we were not workers, as though Black people were just Black people; as if our struggle were not a struggle of the working classes; as if it were not a class struggle. Even while many of the white workers are oppressed, they have certain petty privileges in comparison to the Black workers. It happens that most of the oppressed are white, while the most oppressed are Black. We did not create these conditions, but we must correct them. My program to try to eliminate these conditions is thus directed primarily at Black workers.

Many white people, the great majority, are not our allies. They are just a few in comparison with the mass. We should cooperate with these people as freedom fighters. We should be willing to accept help from any place we can get it. I don't think we should exclude them. I don't think they should be in a position to dominate our movement. This is not because they are white people, but because we have had certain experiences as Black people. We know what it is to be Black, to be discriminated against, to be turned away. A man can study medicine for seven or eight years and become an expert on medicine. A man can become an expert in education in six, seven, or eight years, but a Black man can be a Black man for 75 years and he's still not considered an expert on being Black. White people come along with two to three years' experience in a human relations organization, and, suddenly, they become experts and they think that they should have a dominant position in our organizations. This is what I oppose.

We are not opposed to them. We think that they should join the fight. But they shouldn't join this fight to make some contribution to charity. They are responsible for this society in which they live. So this becomes their duty. When they perform this duty, we should accept them into our organization.

Q. What do you think of King's statement that he cannot control the demonstrations and the masses in the South?

A. I think the statement is typical of a leader caught up in the web of circumstance. Time has moved beyond his narrow scope and beyond his philosophy. I think Martin Luther King is sincere. I think he has made a contribution but I think he has made vital mistakes. He says that self-defense, which he calls violence, is immoral. To call self-defense immoral is to oppose one of the strongest human traits. Self-defense means self-preservation. When Rev. King says he cannot find any case of violence that he can justify, this means that Martin Luther King rejects the American Revolution and rejects the Civil War of the United States.

Rev. King says he is a religious man. He says his doctrine is based upon the Christian religion. He is a minister himself, and ministers, especially Baptist ministers, like Rev. King, have a tendency to preach from the Old Testament. There is a contradiction between what Dr. King is preaching and the teaching of the Old Testament. The Old Testament says—some say that this is a myth, but that is beside the point. Christians are supposed to believe it and Martin Luther King says he is a Christian—that once the Devil was in Heaven and the Devil started making Heaven miserable. The Devil felt that he could subvert God. He didn't see any reason why he should be a secondary figure when he could be God. So, he thought he could seize the power of Heaven. He started a conspiracy to take over Heaven. When God discovered that this man was making trouble, making life miserable for the angels, the Old Testament says that God ordered the angels to use force to remove the Devil from Heaven. The angels used such force until they threw the Devil out of Heaven so hard that he descended all the way into Hell. And what is more violent than that? What is more violent than throwing a man into Hell? If Martin Luther King tells us that we are not to resist violence with force, he is asking us to be better than his God. I don't see how this can possibly come to be on this earth.

The United States was born in violence. Many men have died to preserve the "American Way of Life." I wonder what the world would be like today if men did not take up arms against Hitler in the Second World War. I wonder how Martin Luther King would have stopped Hitler. I wonder if he would tell us that Hitler could have been stopped with the power of nonviolence and love.

If nonviolence and love are so powerful, I am sure that the U.S. government would use it in South Vietnam, and in other countries, even against Cuba. If nonviolence and love are so powerful, why don't the racist use nonviolence and love in the South?

I can't understand why hundreds of thousands of dollars are being contributed by "liberals," and even by some people who consider themselves socialists, for propaganda among our people in the South. We are the victims; why should the victims be taught nonviolence and love? The oppressors are responsible for the violence, but I don't know of a single workshop that these liberals and Martin Luther King have held for the racists of the South: for the Minutemen, for the John Birchers, for the police, or for the KKK. This looks a little one-sided. I'm sure that if nonviolence had been so powerful, somebody would have utilized this power in Birmingham against those vicious two-legged and four-legged dogs.

Q. Is or can armed resistance in America be of a political nature?

A. It can be of a political nature. This is one of the reasons that the nation's officials and the local officials in Dixie are so afraid of the idea of armed resistance. When they are armed, people have a tendency to resist all evil. People may decide there are many things wrong with the system, not just from the racial point of view. They would be willing to resist any injustice that they encounter. Pretty soon this would move in the unions. This would go into all phases of American life.

The Constitution of the United States guarantees American citizens the right to bear arms. Many people get excited and take the attitude that when you speak of arms you must be some kind of a thug. Yet, men are bearing arms every day; men are being drafted every day.

Look at the policemen on the beat. Look at his gun. Look at his club. This is a method of violent intimidation against citizens.

Men are being drafted into the Army. I don't hear the liberals complaining about that.

The liberals are all worked up about the possibility of self-defense guards, of Americans fighting back; they say it is against principle, it will bring retaliation; they say we are outnumbered and we don't have a chance. As revolutionaries we must resist from a basis of principle, but it is not the duty of freedom fighters to consider arms. A revolutionary is successful when he overcomes great odds. There was never a time in the history of the world when the oppressed people had an advantage. If we had the advantage there'd be no need to resist, because we'd already be in a position to bring about the conditions we desire.

In civilized society, the law is supposed to be a deterrent to protect the weak from the strong. Our society is not civilized. There is a breakdown of law. It is a social jungle and there is no deterrent. We must create a deterrent so that the racists will know that they cannot attack us, they cannot attack our women and children, they cannot invade our homes with impunity. They are no longer going to have immunity.

This immunity that the racists have enjoyed has caused more violence than we would otherwise have had.

We know that the racist is basically a coward, because he depends upon the supremacy of his violence, the supremacy of his numbers. He depends on the supremacy of his law to back him up in the evil he does. The only way to counteract this effectively is by maintaining our power to resist, and by creating our own deterrent. This may lead to some political repercussions, but we are not now concerned with politics. We are concerned with survival and where this leads is not our fault. Our need for defense grows out of the failure of constitutional law to protect our rights. This failure is responsible for whatever consequences may follow upon it, especially armed resistance.

Q. What do you think of Kennedy's position on the racial question in America?

A. Kennedy is caught between a crossfire. Kennedy must be loyal to the international capitalists, not the petty capitalist in the South who owns a cotton mill or some small sweatshop. He must think in terms of the raw materials, the people to be exploited in the underdeveloped countries. It so happens that most of these people are colored. The U.S. is trying to create an image of the government as a government of justice and equality, to show that the racism, the brutal oppression against the Black people is not sponsored by the government. To convince the colored people of the world that the government of the United States is not a segregationist government, it is necessary for Kennedy to make moves such as sending troops into the South, dispatching troops to the University of Mississippi. But this is no contribution of the Kennedy administration to the race problem.

Kennedy is the commander-in-chief of the armed forces. Kennedy appointed his cabinet. There is police brutality in the South and in the North and in the West. Muslims were gunned down in the streets of Los Angeles. Under the XIVth Amendment to the Constitution, Kennedy's own brother, attorney general of the United States, has the authority to move into any case where police brutality shows itself, to prosecute these brutal racist policemen. But, we don't know of any case where they have punished the police. We don't know of any case where the police have been indicted. We've just seen Birmingham. How many of the racist cops in Birmingham who beat Negroes were punished?

The U.S. government is one of the largest housing agencies in the U.S. The Federal Housing Administration, owned and operated by the Kennedy administration, is segregating housing. Although Kennedy has made a proclamation declaring segregated housing illegal, these conditions still exist. Kennedy's proclamation was hypocritical. He has not done what he could do. He has not used the power and the authority of his high office.

Kennedy says that we need a civil rights bill. We've long had a bill of rights in the U.S.; the XIVth Amendment gives all the authority that is needed. Why should Kennedy, instead of enforcing the XIVth Amendment, ask for new legislation? Because he wants to give the appearance to the world that he is waging a great battle for the human rights of the Black people.

But we know that this is not true. The U.S. government contributes a great portion of the funds of the welfare agencies of the South. Southern agencies are denying Black Americans the right to feral aid. Local agencies in the South are denying Black children the right of Aid to Dependent Children. The Kennedy administration is not doing anything about this. In Washington, Black Americans are not given their right of promotion on federal jobs.

People who look at the facts, people who carefully consider Kennedy proclamations will see right away that they're not genuine, that he is not a believer in Afro-American rights, that he is not a believer in human rights.

In Monroe, when we had the frame-up cases, when we had the violent clash with the KKK, we asked, appealed to the Justice Department, appealed to the Kennedy administration for a month, to enforce the XIVth Amendment. We had many people across the nation write, wire, and telephone the White House asking for an investigation of the Monroe Police Department. The Kennedy administration's answer was always that this was a local matter to be taken up with the local officials.

Four attempts were made on my life. Two attempts were made in the presence of and were aided by the local police. Yet the Justice Department, under the administration of John F. Kennedy, said that this was not a matter for the FBI. But when the racist police said that there was a kidnapping in Monroe, the Kennedy administration entered the picture right away. They started looking and searching across the country for the people that had been framed.

Right now, one of Kennedy's top aides is a racist from Monroe, North Carolina. This racist is Henry Hall Wilson Jr. who is a White House Aide and an advisor to Kennedy. He has also been a legal advisor to the KKK of Union County, North Carolina.

With all of the brilliant men, qualified men, throughout the whole of the U.S., Kennedy went into a town of 12,000 people and found a man who had been active in defending the KKK as a lawyer, who had been active in the racist legal system of Union County. He took this man to the White House. Wilson was part of the Democratic Party and in the pay-off of the part. He was the man who interested Kennedy in the prosecution of the Monroe defendants. Now we must ask: If Kennedy is sincere about civil rights, why did he bring a racist from a small southern town into the White House to advise him?

The Kennedy administration is now appointing many southern judges with long records as racists, as avowed segregationists, as members of the White Citizens Councils. Yet Kennedy is appointing these men to met out justice to the so-called Black Americans.

In the United Nations at this time one of the greatest supporters of South Africa and Portugal is the U.S., the Kennedy administration. This administration is defending the right of South Africa and Portugal to sit in the council of civilized nations. Why? Because the U.S. is in sympathy with these racist nations. The U.S. is afraid of any precedent against racism which might someday boomerang against the U.S.

The U.S. has been the chief advocate of denying the people of China, the People's Republic of China, the right to sit in the UN. But this same nation defends racist, savage South Africa and Portugal in the UN. How can we have confidence in the Kennedy administration when it says it is for human rights, for civil rights, for the Afro-American?

Q. What do you think the effects of Mao Tse-tung's statement about the situation of the Black man in America will be on the American public? What about the rally to protest the situation of the Black man in America, that the Chinese have planned for the 12th of this month (August)?

A. The effect depends on whether or not the American people are given information about the statement and the rally. One of the greatest news blackouts in the world is taking place in the U.S. now. We hear people boasting of freedom of speech and freedom of the press. Yes, freedom to print what is favorable to Washington; Freedom of speech means freedom to praise the present system in Washington. Freedom of speech means freedom to praise the present system in its evil undertaking.

Mao's is a great statement that is sure to have a lot of effect, especially on the colored peoples of the world. I think it will serve to give some spirit of solidarity between the Chinese and the Afro-American people. This is one of the longest and clearest statements yet made by the head of a country condemning racial persecution in the U.S.

The rally that is to take place in support of our fight for liberty, in support of the march on Washington the 28th of this month (August) is a great act of solidarity. This is one of the first major acts of its type in the world.

We have had a rally here in Cuba. It was carried out by the North Americans who live here and by people from other countries. This was in solidarity with the freedom struggle and especially in protest against Birmingham.

But, this will be the first time that such a mass rally is held, the first time that the government of a country has taken such a stand, that the people are coming into the streets to back this up. This should boost the spirit and the courage of our oppressed Afro-Americans. Our people should know that this is a demonstration of sympathy, of the feeling of brotherhood of other peoples throughout the world who understand our problem.

It is significant that Mao also made an appeal to all of the peoples of the world to support the Afro-American in his struggle for freedom. He made it clear that the liberation of the Afro-American will also mean the end of world imperialism. It means that this is not just a national problem. U.S. racism is an international problem; U.S. racism is very closely tied in with U.S. imperialism. We must start thinking; our people in the U.S. must start thinking from an international point of view.

The world has changed. This is one reason why I consider it a great mistake for the liberals, the Uncle Toms, the pacifists, as well as the fighting Negroes, to take the position that any resistance to the racist oppressor will bring about the extermination of our race. This is not true. The U.S. cannot exterminate 20 million people without committing suicide. Conditions are not the same now as they were when Hitler exterminated 6 million Jews in Germany. The African countries are coming into being; the Africans are coming into power; the African countries are participating in the UN; and we know that all these people are sympathetic to our cause.

The world is beginning to see that we are in the front line, in the vanguard, against the oppressive, racist, imperialist forces, against the brutal tyranny practiced by the U.S. at home and around the world. The enemy that is the oppressor of the Black people in Birmingham; the enemy that would unleash vicious police dogs on little girls, 6 to 8 years old; the vicious officials and police who would beat a woman to the ground with a club; the police in Albany, Georgia, who would beat a pregnant woman to the ground and kick her in the stomach; this is the same enemy that would gas women and babies in South Vietnam. This is the same enemy that would destroy the people of Korea. This is the same enemy that would like to move into and dominate Africa, that would like to introduce racism into Africa.

A few weeks ago there was an editorial in the *Toronto Globe and Mail* about a U.S. Air Force base in Newfoundland. These military people moved in and established racial segregation in the nightclubs in Canada. The Canadian people are protesting this racial segregation introduced into Canada by Americans, by the Yankees. Wherever the U.S. flag flies in the world, racism moves in its wake. It is a bearer not of democracy, not of Christian brotherhood, but of ill-will, racial discrimination, of race hatred, of racial oppression, of exploitation, of brutality. U.S. racism is a menace to the security, to the peace, to the well-being of the entire world.

Now that other countries are beginning to demonstrate on our behalf, now that the leaders of other countries are beginning to speak out on our behalf, the race problem is making the U.S. the laughing stock of the whole world. We can be sure that unless the U.S. makes some changes, it is going to be rejected as the "leader of the free world."

Q. What effect does the anti-communistic attitude in the U.S. have on the movement in the U.S.?

A. I've had some experience in this area myself. The KKK reactionaries, the fascists, the John Birchers, the racists, and sometimes even officials have called me communist; have said that I was following the communist line, and being used by the communists. Now I find that the U.S. Communist Party is saying that I'm a reactionary. They are opposed to my policy. They have attacked me on a number of occasions. So, we can't get involved in worrying about labels. On one side they are going to call us one thing and on the other side they are going to call us another. The fox is going to think we are a dog, and the dog is going to think we are a fox. We are not concerned with what they think. We had better be concerned with liberating ourselves.

It is very important that we not be used by these different groups, by these people who are fighting their own personal battles. But we shouldn't be concerned with witch-hunts. We should be looking for allies. Wherever we find allies we should be willing to work with them as long as they don't dictate our policy or try to force certain political lines upon us. I don't think we should get into debates about whether a person is communist or not. We are not a detective agency, not an agency of intelligence, not police agents, and we shouldn't get involved in that type of thing. We are not going to be able to satisfy all factions. We must decide what line we are going to follow, stick to that line, and come hell or high water, not allow ourselves to be diverted.

Q. If any organization is accused of being communistic, what action should it take?

A. It should work harder in its field, keeping its objective in view. Always concentrate on the objectives. To get into the name-calling struggle means to divert energy away from the main struggle. The racists have discovered that this is a tactic that can be used effectively to divide us, to slow us down. They are going to use this tactic. We are going to be called different names.

Personally, I would feel very inadequate if I didn't arouse the anger of some faction. The mere fact that you can arouse some people to anger means that you are accomplishing something.

Q. Concerning the back-to-Africa [...]

A. If people want to go back to Africa, they are not going to be able to go back without a fight. Self-determination is not granted by imperialist countries, racist countries, just on the basis that the exploited would like to leave. Puerto Ricans would like to leave. Are they allowed to leave?

We are a colony in the U.S. How can we expect them to grant us self-determination and freedom just because we would like to leave? The back-to-Africa movement is part of our struggle. No matter what it is we would like to do, we will have to fight for the right to do it. Some people may want to go to Africa and some people may want a separate nation within the U.S., and some people may want integration, but none of these things will be given without a struggle. So, we are going to have to be united in battle, whether we are together after the battle or not.

Even though we are on the bottom scale of the economic ladder in the U.S., the purchasing power of Afro-Americans is bigger than that of the nation of Canada. The countries of the world are already engaged in a struggle for world markets and no country is willing to give away world markets.

We have the case of Cuba. Cuba has declared itself independent. But do you think that they will leave Cuba alone? Do you think that Cuba is left to live in peace? If 6 million people cannot have self-determination in peace, how can 20 million people leave from the heart of the U.S., from the colony within the U.S., in peace?

I hope that the Nationalists will soon understand that there is more to going back to Africa than packing a suitcase. It's more than just going to get a ticket. It may be necessary to shoot their way out. I'm certainly not against the back-to-Africa movement. I see it as a healthy sign. It means that these oppressed Black Americans are fed up with the system. They see the U.S. as corrupt and they won't have anything more to do with it. When people reach that stage they are preparing for action.

I believe that the time is coming when these groups will be united under the proper leadership and direction. They are going to make a great contribution to our freedom struggle.

Q. Concerning the Muslims [...]

A. The Muslims are a fast-growing group and a good group, because of their militancy. There's a great deal of misunderstanding and misinformation, some deliberate, about the Muslims. Many people get upset over the Muslim movement, especially the so-called liberals. Some people are more worked up over the Muslim movement than they are over the racists, and the brutal savage police of the South. Some people talk about the Muslims teaching hatred, but they've said the same thing about me. This criticism has also come from the U.S. Communist Party. They have said that I'm as bad as the Muslims and the same as Malcolm X. Whatever that means, I consider it a compliment.

I wonder what they mean by "teaching hate." I can't speak for the Muslims, but, yes, I teach and advocate hate. I teach and advocate hatred for all forms of oppression, tyranny, and exploitation. I teach and advocate hatred of the haters. Why should we be required to love our enemy? Are we the only people on earth who are going to be required to love our enemies? We don't find the people who criticize the Muslims advocating that the racist of the South love their enemies. When the U.S. is at war or preparing war, preparing the conquest of other peoples, we don't find a love campaign in the U.S.

Our mission is liberation. Our mission is to fight, and I don't think people can be psychologically prepared to fight unless they have some emotional feeling, some hatred, for what they are going to fight. Racial oppression is brutal, savage, barbaric. Why shouldn't normal people hate savage things? I feel, personally, that hatred is an emotion as much as love. It is abnormal to expect people who are oppressed to love their enemies. If dogs are to be released on children, if babies are to be arrested and beaten by brutal policemen, if it is teaching hatred for me to advocate contempt for people who would do this, for people who are not human beings, not even fit to belong to the human race, then I plead guilty of teaching hatred.

Q. I hear you're trying to get back into the States. What program have you implemented to do so? What program can we as students inaugurate to help you do so?

A. There's no formal program yet. This is just being discussed at this stage. I have received letters from many people who say that I should be on the scene in the U.S. at this time. I feel that this is a very important time for our struggle for the liberation of our people.

The Cuban people are very good to me. If I want an easy life, this would be the place for me, but I feel committed, indebted to the struggle and to those who have supported me and fought together with me in the U.S., especially in the South. I feel that we have a duty to perform there.

I resent being driven from my homeland by racists. I resent being framed. I resent the law in a country that calls itself "Leader of the Free World" that allows people who are fighting for freedom to be driven from their homeland. I won't rest until I'm free to go back.

Now we are considering ways of bringing about pressure, ways of getting a lot of people together. It means, perhaps, starting a mass movement. The object would be to petition the government in such a way that the government will have to intervene in this case, and in such a way that one of the governors in the U.S. will be as humane as the Cuban people and the Cuban government and will grant me asylum so that I will be able to be on the home-front.

The students can be very helpful because the students are from many different sections and communities. They will be able to work in their communities, arouse people, get people interested in the movement. They can pass petitions; distribute literature presenting our plan to the people on a mass scale. The students will be able to speak to student groups, campus groups. The only way my return will be possible is through the force of great numbers, through the desire of great numbers of people to see justice for those who have been fighting in the South.

I think that people should consider that I was a leader in the NAACP, a branch president. I think they should consider the fact that Medgar Evers was also a leader of the NAACP. Medgar Evers is dead and I'm in Cuba because the Cuban people rescued me from the same vicious people who killed Medgar Evers.

I'm exiled in Cuba; I still live in Cuba. I feel that I should be able to make a contribution to the struggle to make the U.S. a fit nation to live in, to make the U.S. a responsible nation that will be a land of people able to stand up before the world and say that it is a land of democracy. We will need many people to do this, to arouse the conscience of those in the U.S. who still have a conscience. The students can play a very important role in this. We expect each student to form his own committee and think in terms of what he can do in his own community to serve the cause of justice.

The Muslims are very polite people. They are never arrogant. They are never overbearing. They always think of their fellow men as brothers. The Muslims are gaining many members. Many people who are not Muslims are sympathizers of the Muslims.

Some people say that they don't have the proper direction. They say that the Muslims are not following a true revolutionary path. I don't think we should be concerned with that. The Muslims are dissatisfied with the brutality visited upon our people. The Muslims are dissatisfied with the corruption of the system. This in itself is good.

Let's look at the object of their hatred. It is hatred of oppression and the oppressor. I think the Muslims represent a normal life. I can foresee a day when the Muslims will evolve to a different stage. Recently, the Muslims have decided to enter the political field, to organize, run candidates, and support candidates who fight for equality and justice. This is a step forward. The Muslims are beginning to evolve the same as our militant organization. Among the Muslims, our people are being inspired to have initiative and backbone. This is good training. It prepares our people for the battle that is sure to come.

The most significant thing that the phony progressives and former liberals don't like is that the Muslims say that the U.S. government is doomed. If this is not revolutionary, I would like to know what it is. This is more than a lot of so-called progressives have dared to publish in the States. The Muslims say that by 1970 there will be no more U.S. government; they also say that the system is so corrupt that the oppressor is the Devil himself. The Muslims take the position that they must come out from among such people, that they must not have anything to do with such people. I don't see how anyone can argue against people who take this position.

It's not the Muslims—the white man rejected the Black man before he ever became a Muslim and this is why he is becoming a Muslim. It is a matter of a scapegoat to blame for something that is brought on by the attitude of the white supremacist himself. I don't know what the "liberals" and Uncle Tom Negroes expect from the Muslims. Do they want the Muslims to announce to the world that they love everybody, that they love the oppressor, that they love Uncle Toms, that they love sell-out artists, they are going to be good little boys, that they are going to act like followers of Daddy Grace and Father Divine, that they are going to stick to their religion and not harm the good white folks?

The so-called progressives who constantly bemoan the misinformation about the progressive movement spread by the capitalist press, who ask the general public not to believe the lies of the capitalist press, turn to the same press that they ask us not to believe when it speaks against the progressive movements. They ask us to believe the slanders, the smears, the lies against the Muslims. They ask us to take the misinformation of the same capitalist press that they have accused of being habitually lying and corrupt.

Ask the liberals where they obtain their information about the Muslims—they will tell you: not from a Muslim, but from some magazine articles, or from some newspaper, or from some interview that they heard. I'm pretty sure that many of the so-called liberals and progressives are not even interested to really find out what the Muslims stand for. The Muslims are not for domination by the white supremacists, by those paternal big daddies who would like to direct the path of the Afro-American struggle. They resent the Muslims on this ground. They resent the Muslims because the Muslims have retaliated against their rejection of the Black man by rejecting them.

Many Afro-Americans who are not members of the Muslim Mosque are Muslims at heart. This is not the fault of the Black American who has been rejected by white society; it is the fault of the white society that has rejected the Black American and has left him no place to go. Today we find a reaction to this rejection. This reaction takes the form of the Muslim movement and the African nationalist movement, all of the other nationalist movements. This is a healthy sign.

I don't know what topple who have rejected and abused people, denied people the right to live as human beings, expect our people to do. A master can kick a dog, and can drive a dog away from home, can leave a dog to sleep on the cold ground, but the dog comes back each time and laps at the very foot of the master that bused him. We are not dogs. We are not going to maintain dog's loyalty. That is why you are going to find more and more people in sympathy with the Muslim movement. I'm not Muslim, but I'm in sympathy with them because I see good in their organization. I see that they are preparing our people for a possible struggle in the future, and, most of all, because they see the end of the oppressive government of the U.S.

I have confidence in the masses of the people. With the conditions that we're undergoing now, our people are not going to allow our leaders to become more conservative. Our leaders are being pushed along now, being forced to become more radical.

They may establish some businesses, but not of the caliber that can bring prosperity to our people. That would require many years. You must remember, the Muslims themselves admit that the present government will not last longer than 1970. They're certainly not going to be able to raise the standard of living of our people to an extent that will allow them to become conservatives. If they do, they'll lose their mass following, the sympathy of our people. I don't think that is going to come about.

DEPARTMENT OF JUSTICE FEDERAL BUREAU OF INVESTIGATION SUMMARY

ROBERT FRANKLIN WILLIAMS

The files of the Passport Office, Department of State, reviewed by a Special Agent of the FBI on November 12, 1969, disclose that Robert Franklin Williams applied for a new passport in Detroit, Michigan, November 6, 1969, for proposed travel to Sweden for three weeks to lecture. He stated his intention to depart by air in the Spring (1970) and stated that he expected to take another trip abroad within five years. No passport has as yet been issued on the basis of this application. The subject, born on February 26, 1925, in Monroe, North Carolina, gave his permanent residence and mailing address as 18640 Justine, Detroit, Michigan. He indicated that his marriage to [**Mabel Williams**] had not been terminated. In the event of death or accident, he requested that [_____], himself with driver's license W 452-745-261-148. He listed his occupation as Writer and gave his Social Security Number as [_____].

APPENDIX: REPUBLIC OF NEW AFRICA (RNA) (-6*-)

A source advised in May 1969, that the Republic of New Africa (RNA) is an all-Negro organization founded in Detroit, Michigan, in March 1968. ROBERT F. WILLIAMS, who was then residing in Peking, China, was named as its President-Exile. After fleeing the United States in 1961 following the issuance of a local warrant in North Carolina on a charge of kidnapping growing out of a racial incident, Williams published and broadcast hate-type material in Cuba and China prior to his return to the United States in September 1969. A [_____] has advised that the purpose of the RNA is to establish an independent Black nation within the United States, demanding the States of Alabama, Georgia, Louisiana, Mississippi, and South Carolina in addition to $10,000 per Black citizen as payment for 400 years of ancestral slave labor. A [_____] advised on March 14, 1969, that an army of the RNA, known as the Black Legion members, dedicated to Black freedom and committed to the concept of systematic armed revolution, has been established. Black Legion members are expected to participate in military training and engage in firearm practice. The RNA plans to establish an underground Black Legion in addition to an aboveground Black Legion in order to avoid detection by the police. According to this source, Black Legion members acting as bodyguards at a session of the Second National Convention of the RNA in Detroit, Michigan, on March 29, 1969, were involved in a shoot-out with members of the Detroit Police Department which resulted in the killing of one policeman and the critical wounding of another.

LEGACY OF RESISTANCE: TRIBUTES TO ROBERT AND MABEL WILLIAMS[31]

October 25, 1996

Words are inadequate to express my love, admiration, and appreciation for my parents. Their commitment to each other, family, community and our people has been exemplary. On July 19, 1996, my parents celebrated their 49th Wedding Anniversary. For all these years they imparted to my brothers and me life-giving values with eternal consequences. I am grateful to God for blessing me with my parents, Robert Franklin Williams and Mabel Robinson Williams, who have lovingly equipped me to fulfill his divine purpose for my life.

Mom and Dad, you are my heroes.

John C. Williams, Detroit

Robert F. Williams, who championed the cause of justice for African Americans in Monroe, North Carolina, in the 1950s, whose flaming pen raged against American racism from his exile in Cuba and China during the 1960s where he globalized the African American struggle as a part of the worldwide movement for human rights; whose tireless voice thundered from Baldwin, Michigan, with the call to liberate America's oppressed during the 1970s and 1980s, died on October 15 in Grand Rapids, Michigan, at the age of 71. The Baldwin, Michigan, resident had contracted pneumonia as a result of Hodgkin's disease. "Rob's" courageous leadership and his uncompromising commitment to self-defense and the international solidarity of oppressed peoples from the agonizing years of the McCarthy era to the present have inspired the works of many individuals and organizations in the United States and abroad, including such groups as the Freedom Riders, the Revolutionary Action Movement (RAM), the League of Revolutionary Black Workers, the Republic of New Africa, the Black Panther Party, and the Student National Coordinating Committee. His comrade in arms, Malcolm X, held Rob in the highest regard. The NAACP, which previously stripped Williams of his Monroe Chapter leadership because he was "too militant," last year restored his membership. Robert Williams's counsel was invited by such renowned world leaders as Ho Chi Minh, Fidel Castro, Ernestro "Che" Guevara, as well as numerous rank-and-file activists in the liberation and decolonization movements in Africa and Asia. When China's Mao Zedong heard Rob describe the plight of Black America, the veteran of Asia's Long March for Freedom issued a call to world citizens and leaders to elevate the struggle of Black America above that of a domestic battle for civil rights to a place of equal status with that of all revolutionary movements around the world. Following the U.S. bombing of Hanoi, when Vietnam's "Uncle Ho" said he would release the first downed U.S. fighter pilot through Robert Williams, the State Department maintained a profound silence when Williams contacted Washington. The Williams's family returned to the United States in 1970 and settled in Detroit, then in Baldwin, Michigan, where Robert and Mabel continued to raise their tireless voices on behalf of the elderly, environmental justice, to uplift our dispossessed young, and to fight for human rights anywhere on this embattled planet.

Charles. E. Simmons, Detroit

I remember your quiet confidence, your persistent passion and your unerring vision and wisdom for the realization of the new society.

Ron Scott, Detroit,

From Japan-

We, representing more than 13,000 Japanese people who sent their signatures for the sake of Robert F. Williams for his fair trial in 1970–1972, express our deepest condolences and sorrows on his death. It's in our vivid memories that he proposed that we join in solidarity to fight for world peace in 1977 when he and Mabel visited Japan. He was a son of intelligence and powerful action with which he protected the life and civil rights of local Blacks. We believe that his contribution toward social justice and racial equality will be recorded in human history and his great love for the discriminated against people will live on in the hearts of those people forever. With our warmest encouragement and love to the bereaved family

Yoriko NaKAJIMA
Shigemi TAKAHASHI
Jun EGAWA
Ken-ichiron SENBON
Aiki YAJIMA
P. S. Three large newspapers in Japan reported his death.

Rob Williams: The Crusader

Rob Williams became a hero because he was willing to assume responsibility for grappling with the contradictions of his community and his generation. In the 1950s and 1960s, the main contradiction faced by southern Blacks was that NAACP leaders, mainly preachers and members of the middle class, were unable to stand up to the KKK violence, which was terrorizing their communities. Rob Williams, the offspring of a working-class family and an ex-Marine, refused to accept that Blacks who were being sent all over the world to terrorize people should be terrorized at home. So, coming out of obscurity (as Fanon put it), he organized the grassroots members of his community to stand up against the KKK. As a result, he became a national leader who was admired and respected all over the world. We honor Rob Williams best by doing for our generation and our communities what he did for his.

Grace Lee Boggs, Detroit

As a youth I respected and admired Martin Luther King, but Robert Williams was my hero. It was his words and actions that moved my young spirit. I admired his determination and was awed at his strength in the face of all criticism and oppression. As a young adult in 1971, on my very first meaningful job, I had the good fortune to meet Mabel Williams and I realized the source of Rob's enduring strength. Although I knew and admired Mabel for several years, I did not meet Robert in person, until 1975. I was bothered by his very ordinary manner. He was so like everyone else, funny, and opinionated. Coming to know Robert and Mabel taught me what makes a hero. It is ordinary

people with courage, commitment, and compassion, who taking a stand when others run away, out of fear for their own best interest. Robert listened and advised the community during the years 1977 through 1983 when police abuse and intimidation were directed, and unrestrained against the African-American citizens of Lake County. In 1977, Robert Williams mobilized and organized the community to come to the defense of Ruby Nelson, a victim of police brutality. Born out of that movement was the People's Association for Human Rights, an organization under Rob's guidance and wisdom that came to the aid and defense of many citizens in the years that followed. Robert Williams changed the attitude in Lake County, Michigan, and Lake County is a better place today because of Robert Williams. Lake County citizens, Black and white, owe Robert Williams recognition and appreciation for the lessons he taught us about injustice, how it manifests itself and how to fight it. Robert taught us not to judge and separate ourselves from one another. He taught that we must stand together. And that we must stand up for justice for others if we are to have justice for ourselves. Mentor, friend, and leader is what Robert and Mabel have been to us all. On behalf of the FiveCAP, Inc. Board and staff, I thank Rob for the privilege of working with him on the FiveCAP Board of which he was a member for over ten years. We love you and will miss you.
Your friend,
Mary L. Trucks, Scottsville, Michigan
Rob Lives! A Tribute to a Great African American Internationalist Freedom Fighter

Robert F. Williams, known as "Rob," was born on February 26, 1925, in Monroe, North Carolina. Rob in his teens organized a group called X-32 to throw stones at white men who drove nightly into town trying to assault Black women. He was trained as a machinist in the National Youth Administration where he organized a strike of workers at the age of 16. He moved to Michigan where he worked for a year at the Ford Motor Company as an automobile worker. In the late 1940s, he wrote a story in *The Daily Worker*, "Some Day I am Going Back South." Rob joined the U.S. Marines in 1953 before attending West Virginia State College, North Carolina, and Johnson C. Smith College in Charlotte, North Carolina. In 1955 as a husband, married to Mabel Williams, and father of two sons (Robert F. Williams, Jr. and John C. Williams), he returned home with an honorable discharge from the U.S. Marine Corps. Keenly aware of social injustice, he joined the local NAACP and eventually became its president. He was a former member of the Monroe Unitarian Fellowship and the Union County Human Relations Council. He was the first African American leader of modern times to organize and advocate armed self-defense on the part of African American victims of racist violence. In 1957, in the face of the KKK invasion of the Black community, he organized armed self-defense units. Because of his militancy, he was stripped of his presidency by the national NAACP. But the Monroe NAACP chapter grew from a membership of fifty to two hundred and fifty. Rob successfully fought and exposed racial legal injustice in the infamous "Kissing" case in which two African American boys, ages seven and nine, were charged with rape because a seven-year-old white girl had kissed the nine-year-old Black boy on the cheek. He also organized and advocated peaceful demonstrations and tactics for equality. He staged sit-ins at lunch counters, organized boycotts of department stores, desegregated the library and conducted pickets at the city-owned, whites-only swimming pool throughout 1960 and 1961. He was a candidate for Mayor of Monroe in 1960, running as an independent. Also, in 1960 he visited Cuba and became a member of the Fair Play for Cuba Committee. He was a forerunner in the movement toward Black political empowerment. Rob's physical and political stance on armed self-defense greatly impacted Malcolm X who was then a Minister of the Nation of Islam and on one occasion let Rob speak at Mosque No. 7 in New York and raise money for arms. Believing in the right of peaceful demonstrations, Rob invited "Freedom Riders" to come to Monroe in 1961 to test nonviolence. Racist whites surrounded the nonviolent demonstrators and attacked them. A racial riot broke out as shots were fired. During the race riot, a white couple wandered into the angry Black community. For their own protection, Rob allowed them to take shelter in his home. Although they left unharmed, the local authorities pressed kidnapping charges. Pursued by 500 FBI agents, Rob and his family were forced into exile. Rob's successful escape from "legal" racism was one of the early victories of the civil rights movement. He went to Cuba where he was given political asylum by Fidel Castro and welcomed by the Cuban people. He was a personal friend of Ernest Che Guevara. While living in Cuba for five years, Rob and Mabel organized and broadcast "Radio Free Dixie" bringing the message of collective armed self-defense to the African American masses who were battling the racists in America's streets. In 1962, he published *Negroes With Guns* about his experiences from 1957 to 1961. He also continued to publish *The Crusader*, which called upon Black Americans to unite with their allies in Africa, Asia and Latin America (the Third World) and with progressive whites in the United States. Appealing to all heads of state to call for support of the civil rights movement, Rob was influential in the issuance by People's Republic of China Chairman, Mao Tse-tung, of a Declaration of Support for the cause of African-American liberation. As international chairman of the Revolutionary Action Movement (RAM) Rob traveled in Asia representing the African American freedom struggle. He moved to the People's Republic of China in 1966, residing there and meeting and talking with Chinese leaders during the height of the proletarian Cultural Revolution. Visiting North Vietnam, he met with President Ho Chi Minh. His example inspired the formation in the southern United States of groups like the Deacons for Defense (1965) and a change in policy by the Student Nonviolent Coordinating Committee (SNCC) from on-violence to armed self-defense (1966). The Black Panther Party (1966) and the League of Revolutionary Black Workers considered him the godfather of armed self-defense. While in China, Rob was elected president-in-exile of the Detroit-based self-determination organization, the Republic of New Africa. He visited Africa and was imprisoned in Britain. while trying to return to this country. In 1969, he returned to the United States, living in Michigan, where he fought extradition to Monroe, finally succeeding in having all charges dropped. Rob was a Fellow at the University of Michigan Center for Chinese Studies and served as director of the Detroit East Side Citizens Abuse Clinic where, according to higher authorities, he was "too" successful in rehabilitating patients. In Baldwin, Michigan, where he settled, he was active in the People's Association for Human Rights. He traveled around the country fighting racial abuses wherever he found them. Rob was working on completing his

autobiography. At his untimely death due to Hodgkin's Disease on October 15, 1996, he was planning to further escalate his leadership activities in the African-American liberation movement even at the age of 71. His fighting spirit and leadership will be felt forever. The American press did not expose our people to Rob as they did Martin Luther King. Rob's shining example as a courageous, sincere, scientific, spiritual visionary, and honest freedom fighter will be honored. His insight and foresight will be followed by the millions of African Americans, who will never cease in the relentless struggle for self-determination, freedom, and equality until we win.
Muhammad Ahmed (Max Stanford), Philadelphia, PA

Few Americans can yet understand and appreciate the tremendous contribution which Robert F. Williams has made to our country. Few among us experienced and remember the South before a handful of courageous people like Robert F. Williams risked all to combat the ruthless, racist terror which engulfed African Americans. Robert actively organized armed self-defense when the authorities were most often actively involved in racist terror or, at best, looked the other way. Robert's vocal advocacy of the right of self-defense of African Americans during the 1950s was a crucial pillar of the Civil Rights Movement throughout the 1960s. Scholars are now only beginning to study the crucial, pre-1960s era. When the story has been thoroughly studied and told, Rob's role will tower. I only regret that he has not lived to see this change in our understanding which is only beginning to stir.
Gwendolyn Midlo Hall, East Lansing, Michigan

This is a salute to Robert F. Williams, a Black hero who defied the enemies of our people and took a courageous stand in defense of Black liberation. During the 1960s when my Comrades and I were radical students at Wayne State University, we formed Uhuru to organize ourselves to struggle against American capitalism, racism, and imperialism. We were inspired by the socialist and liberation movements around the world and the Black liberation movement in the United States. Robert Williams, as a Black liberation fighter (and his newsletter, the Crusader) had a special significance for us because he symbolized a militant, bold form of Black manhood. He dared to confront and struggle against the racist U.S. government that continues to be the principal oppressor of Black people. I, along with three of my Uhuru comrades (Charles Johnson, General Baker and Charles Simmons) met Robert Williams in Cuba in the summer of 1964. We were impressed by his dignified persona, the brotherly way he related to us, and the respect the Cuban and Chinese officials accorded him. In him, we found a sincere and dedicated brother who was committed to the highest humanitarian values. We salute you, Robert Williams, for taking a defiant stand against the U.S. government. We salute you, Robert Williams, for serving as a role model for Black freedom fighters. We salute you, Robert Williams, for publicizing our struggle abroad. We salute you, Robert Williams, for supporting revolutionary struggles around the world. We salute you, Robert Williams, for leaving a radical legacy of struggle against oppression for present and future generations. We will not forget you. History will not forget you. We shall always admire you for embodying humanitarian qualities and practicing radical leadership in the Black liberation struggle. Your comrade.
Luke Tripp, St. Cloud, MN

Notes

1. See the Robert F. Williams Papers, Bentley Historical Library, Box 2.
2. S. Abdullah Scheleifer writes Robert Williams from Carioa, February 1971
3. Robert Williams writes Marc Scheleifer from Detroit, August 11, 1971
4. "Militant Hopeful on Racial Justice-Williams Finds, U.S. Today Yield Chance for Change," *The New York Times*, September 15, 1969.
5. On the way to the United States, Williams was arrested at the London Airport, and imprisoned by London City Police for unknown reasons. In addition to Williams's hunger strike against the arrest, the London Committee for Defense of Human Rights started their protest. As a result, after negotiations with the government of England, the U.S. government ended up arranging a special flight for Williams to the United States. This incident drew a lot of attention in the United States and led to ruin the CIA's plan of hindering Williams's return by advertising him as a scoundrel of the Blackest dye.
6. "Contempt of Congress, New Williams Charges," *The Enquire-Journal*, Monroe, NC, November 19, 1971.
7. Given that telegraphs between Japanese Committee and Williams were often not delivered or the contents were altered, we faced great difficulties in communicating with Williams.
8. Robert C. Cohen, *Black Crusader: A Biography of Robert Franklin Williams* [Robert F. Williams?]. Secaucus: Lyle Stuart Inc., 1972.
9. "Japanese Group Appeals for Robert F. Williams," *The Enquire-Journal*, Monroe, NC, December 4, 1975.
10. This was an incident that African American activists were imprisoned for a false charge with arson, and an example of oppression against the civil rights activists.
11. "Robert Williams Sets Conference and Rally," *The Enquire-Journal*, Monroe, NC, January 15, 1976.
12. "Public Reaction Mixed about Williams' Return," *The Enquire Journal*, Monroe, NC, December 4, 1975.
13. "District Attorney, Will Not Prosecute Williams," *The Enquire-Journal*, Monroe, NC, January 17, 1976.
14. "Prosecutor Is Critical of Activist," *Charlotte News*, NC, January 16, 1976.
15. "Black Revolutionary to Return to Face North Carolina Charge," *The New York Times*, December 2, 1975; "Black Separatist Williams Loses His Extradition Fight," local newspaper in Michigan, December 2, 1975; "Robert Williams Loses Long Extradition Battle," *The Enquire-Journal*, Monroe, December 2, 1975; "Carolina Arrested Black Activist," *Detroit Free Press*, December 17, 1975; "FBI Murder Attempt Charged by Williams," *Detroit Free Press*, January 25, 1976.
16. See 12.
17. See 12.
18. Kirk Cheyfitz, "Robert Williams, Exile and the Long Road Home," *Detroit Free Press*, December 25, 1976.
19. The pamphlet written by the Japanese Committee to support Williams, The Japanese and the Black in the U.S.A.," Why Do 10,000 Japanese Support Robert F. Williams," 10.
20. See Material II, 2.
21. "Apology to 'Colored Brothers'," *The Asahi Newspaper*, June 12, 1972.
22. "Growing Civic Movement against Discrimination, over 5,000 Signatures to Support African American Leader," *The Asahi Newspaper*, July 4, 1971.
23. Yukiko Fukuda (180 signatures), Makio Hashizume (142 signatures), and Jun-ichi Sasaura (118 signatures).
24. Shin Iizuka in Ichihara-city.
25. Yoshio Yamagishi in Nagano-city, and Noriko Kyouseki in Yamanashi.
26. Miyuki Nagai in Fukui (105 signatures), Akemi Iwai in Kyoto (100 signatures), Masao Tanaka in Ueda-city (154 signatures), Kenji Tsuribune in Sendai-city (80 signatures), Hiroshi Matsudaira in Urawa-city (100 signatures), Akisuke Fukuhara in Tokyo (60 signatures), and Yuko Furumura in Kamakura-city (311 signatures).
27. Yoriko Nakajima, "The Presidential Elections and African Americans," *The Asahi Newspaper*, November 2, 1972.

28 Knowing the phone line was tapped; it was a bad idea making a flight reservation from the Williams in Michigan.
29 "Tokyo Prof Seeks to Free Black Activist," *The Sunday News-Detroit*, August 27, 1972.
30 *The Black Scholar* interview with Nathan Hare was recorded on April 23, 1970, and published May 1970.
31 The dedication and the publication of the pamphlet, *A Legacy of Resistance,* occurred on Friday, November 1, 1996, on Wayne State University's main campus in Detroit, Michigan. Some tributes are addressed to Rob personally while others are memorials.

Chapter 5

BALDWIN, MICHIGAN, AND THE NATION, 1973–2002

Rosa Parks Visits Baldwin Elementary School. Mabel Williams, Al Nichols (a 1961 Bug Reds graduate, former basketball all-state Detroit Free Press 1960 selection, and Baldwin Elementary School Principal from 1972 to 1998), Rosa Parks, and Elaine Steele, longtime friend of Mrs. Parks and co-founder of the Rosa and Raymond Parks Institute for Self-Development. Photographer Eugene Harmon. Courtesy of Al Nichols.

One Man Protest. Williams stages One-Man Protest of *The Lake County Star* over the editor's refusal to publish a protest letter. When the editor refused to accept a paid advertisement, Williams staged a one-man demonstration, filed a lawsuit against the paper, and won the suit. He was awarded $1500 dollars, funds he used to organize the Lake County Peoples Association of Human Rights. Protesting as the Town Crier, Williams with the help of Mabel and a local artist constructed the poster and created a sandwich of a poster that he marched back and forth down M-37 with a battery pack, cassette player, and flashing star and strikes forever lighted helmet as he paraded back and forth the office of *The Lake County Star*, playing the song, John Brown's Body. Courtesy of *The Lake County Star/Pioneering Press*.

Poster of *Lake County Star* refusal to publish news of Robert Carew's case. The poster was designed and erected by Robert Williams. Courtesy of the Lake County Historical Society.

Gwendolyn Midlo Hall and Robert Franklin Williams in 1976 in Monroe, NC, at the home of one of Mabel Williams's sister's house the evening before Rob's extradition hearing was dropped. Photographer John Williams. Courtesy of Gwendolyn Midlo Hall.

Robert F. Williams Speaking. Robert F. Williams points finger during speech at the Black Solidarity Conference at Tuffs University, Medford, MA. November 14–17, 1976. Photography courtesy of Aukram Burton, *RamImages.com*

Robert F. Williams and Queen Mother Moore. Robert F. Williams and Queen Mother (Audley) Moore at the Black Solidarity Conference at Tuffs University, Medford, MA, November 14–17, 1976. Photography courtesy of Aukram Burton, *RamImages.com*

Rear view of Robert F. Williams being introduced before speaking about U.S.-China Relations at the headquarters of the Chinese Progressive Association Northeastern University. Courtesy of Northeastern University Library, Archives and Special Collections, (M163) Box 12, Folder 38. 1978.

USA: Propensity To Self-Destruct

The ship of state is rudderless. It lists and drifts in a stormy sea wrought with disaster. It fiercely approaches. Society at large grumbles and curses almost in whispers as a once great empire enters a state of disintegration. The psycho-motor mechanism of the great colossus has seemingly become paralyzed. The will to survive has been short circuited by the ever mushrooming spirit of narcissism and nihilism.

The powerful valence of meism has become a cancerous scourge devouring the very organs essential to the survival of the American society. The once high spirited, creative and energetic American people now sit moping like immobile Buddhas as the nation crumbles and falls about them. In one of the most crucial moments in the history of the nation the American people seem incapable of any massive outcry or sustained movement with the momentum to reverse this catastrophic trend.

In this most crucial moment of first magnitude problems, great and once affluent America is saddled with third rate leadership. The government in Washington is so bankrupt that a third rate Hollywood actor has been mandated by a desperate but apathetic people to re-enact the discredited scenario of Herbert Hoover.

David Stockman, the invigorator of the neo-Hooverism has let the cat out of the bag—or what is believed to be a cat, actually a skunk. Mr. Stockman has verified what we sensed all the time. We were convinced from the very beginning that the new Gurus were merely spouting hot political air. Now Mr. Stockman has told it plain and simple that the Reagan boys do not know what they are doing. Yes, they are just "throwing out a lot of figures". They are running a scam game on the American people and all the feigned effort of

(continued on page 2)

Front Page of *The Crusader* Editorial Letter, volume XIII, number 1, Winter 1983. In the image, Williams writes "As Family Physician, I Advise War as A Cure," as commentary about unemployment and the U.S. economy with a picture of Adolph Hitler, the KKK, and the John Birch Society in the background.

Robert and Mabel Williams on September 2, 1996. The Williams couple, who were married for forty-nine years, are seen sitting in the yard outside their cottage in Pleasant Plains Township of Lake County, Michigan. This photographs was taken approximately forty-three days before Robert Williams passed. He died at the age of 71 from Hodgkin's Lymphoma on October 15, 1996. Courtesy of John Herman Williams.

LETTERS BETWEEN RICHARD T. GIBSON AND ROBERT F. WILLIAMS

June 15, 1976, Brussels, Belgium[1]

Dear Rob,

This is a hurried reply to your letter of May 17th, which just arrived today. Of course, I will look into financial problem in Luxembourg. It is ironic that you raise this problem because only a month ago, Lyle Stuart asked me if I would write a book for him on Luxembourg banks, (They have become the poor man's Switzerland, with nearly all the advantages of secrecy and without the negative interest now charged by the Swiss on most foreign deposits). Anyway, while I would hesitate to say that there is no dirty business afoot in your case, it seems to me at first glance like a typical capitalist trick. Luxembourg is three hours away by train or less. In addition, I have some friends there who may be able to provide me with information on this bankruptcy. At the moment, however, I am awaiting vistas from the Tanzanian Embassy in the Hague for a long planned and much delayed trip to Tanzania, Kenya, and Zambia. I hope to get over there by the 1st of July at the latest, once I have my visa. The biggest problem is that none of the three countries has an embassy in Brussels: Tanzania's is in Holland and Kenya and Zambia are in Bonn (another three hours by train from here). Nevertheless, I will try to get the information you want as quickly as possible and will write to you before my departure for Africa. By the way, is there anyone in Tanzania you would like me to lookup? Or in Zambia? (our friend Babu is still in jail, held without trial for years because the Zanaibaris will never give a fair trial and Julius does not want to release him for fear of arousing the ire of the island government). My regards to your wife and family. Cordially as always, Richard.

June 28, 1976, Brussels, Belgium[2]

Dear Rob,

I spoke today by phone with my friend Jean Heisbourg in Luxembourg. He has been investigating your problem there and he tells me that the firm in question is not yet in bankruptcy. It has been placed under the administration of the three people you mentioned in your letter. This means that there are assets and you have a chance of getting your money. As I am going to Tanzania and Zambia on the 30th, I have asked Jean to write directly to you with further information when he gets it. (He has a friend who is a lawyer and, in a small-pocket sized country like Luxembourg, everybody quickly learns everything!). If there is anything in Dar or Lusaka I can do for you, write to me. Wishing you and your friend all the best, Richard

August 5, 1976, Brussels, Belgium[3]

Dear Rob,

I have just returned from my African trip and must write in haste to pass this information from my friend in Luxembourg, Jean Heisbourg. (He is, by the way, Secretary of the Luxembourg-China Friendship Association) He has discovered that the assets of E. O. F. corporation are to be liquidated as soon as legal procedures are completed. The lawyers have been trying for several months to wind things up, but do not expect positive action from an incompetent court before December of this year. The good news for you is that, unlike claims from West German and Swiss lawyers, your claim (file no. 469) has been accepted as valid by the "College des Curateurs) as of 9 June 1976. However, it is not certain how much of your claim 105,010 DM will be paid out to you eventually. That is all that I can say at present. There will be no judgment or obviously payment before December if you have any precise questions, my friend is ready to try to find answers to them, but he is certain that you will have to be patient about getting all or more likely part of your money. I am sorry that I cannot tell you any more at present. I am off on Sunday, the 8th, for three weeks in Italy. I expect to be back here just before the beginning of September. With best wishes, Richard Gibson

August 20, 1976, Baldwin, Michigan[4]

Dear Richard,

Your cards and letter have been received. Did you hear any additional news about Babu while in Tanzania. I certainty appreciate your running down the situation in Luxembourg. I received a letter from the court appointees but it was in French and no person in this vicinity understands legal and banking terms in the French language. I am greatly relied on to know that I can expect returns. I hope it comes through soon. Since I won my case in North Carolina, the economic campaign against me has been stepped up. Six universities canceled my speaking engagements within ten-day period. Also, I have been informed by the IRS that they have files on me in a special category that included only 750 Americans. So, the dirty work goes on! Because of the hostility of the different agencies working under the aegis of the CIA, I feared they had staged the situation in Luxembourg in order to make sure their salvation strategy would have more immediate results. Have you heard any official re3ason as to why the E.O.F. corporation failed? It seems strange to me that experience businessmen would be as unbusinesslike as they were. Do you know why some claims are being denied? Anyway, I am more than happy to know that the court has accepted mine. Sincerely, Robert F. Williams

LAKE COUNTY PEOPLES ASSOCIATION FOR HUMAN RIGHTS LETTERS TO MICHIGAN CONGRESSMEN

June 21, 1994, Baldwin, MI[5]

The Honorable David Bonior
Dear Congressman Bonior:

The Lake County People's Association for Human Rights is requesting your support for our Enterprise Community Application to the U. W. Department of Agriculture. The Lake County (Idlewild) area proposed for designation is one of the most poverty-stricken in Michigan and the United States. The infant mortality rate for Lake County is over twice that of the states. The unemployment rate usually exceeds twice that of the state of Michigan. Despite this, Lake County has a rich history, energy and commitment. For four (4) long months we have worked to prepare the Enterprise Community Strategic Plan Application. We met and worked twenty-seven (27) times since March 1st because it offered us a real opportunity for economic development and quality of life. We are crestfallen to learn that the Michigan Democratic Delegation will not sign a letter to support our application. Lake County is unique and deserving of that support. We are a historically democratic county. We have the largest African-American population in rural western Michigan, and we've worked hard. We are told that the reasons for withholding support have nothing to do with us. Clearly, we do suffer anyway. As an important leader we ask you to please support us. It is a verifiable fact that Lake County is the only rural Michigan Enterprise Community Application to be submitted to the USDA. Thank you for your consideration.

Sincerely,
Robert F. Williams,

June 21, 1994, Baldwin, MI[6]

Dear Congressman Conyers:

We are asking you to sign the Michigan Congressional Delegation Support Letter for the Lake County (Idlewild) Enterprise Community Application to the U.S. Department of Agriculture.

Additionally, we are requesting your support and leadership to obtain the Democratic Congressional signatures on the letter. The Lake County (Idlewild area) population as you know is the largest rural population of African Americans in West Michigan. Our area suffers from conditions of pervasive poverty. The Enterprise Community designation offers us economic and quality-of-life opportunities which have not existed before. We have worked bottoms up for four long months holding twenty-seven (27) working meetings since March to develop the Enterprise Community Strategic Plan Application. The support of the Michigan Democratic Delegation is deserved and much needed. Lake County is submitting the only Michigan rural application to the USDA, this is a verifiable fact. Support is being withheld by those whom we have always looked to for support and leadership. The reasons we've heard for withholding support are not related to us but does hurt us. This letter is an appeal to you, someone who knows us, our history and circumstances. Please educate the other Democrats, so they know us and ask them to sign the letter for the Lake County's Enterprise Community application.

Sincerely,
Robert F. Williams

LAKE COUNTY STAR PROTEST LETTERS

"Williams questions Rotary's choice for award"[7]

"Williams questions Rotary's Choice for award." Once I found ample cause to respect those seemingly good fellows who called themselves Rotarians. I believe the Rotary International to be humane and socially responsible organization of business and professional men's clubs, "dedicated to support of high moral and vocational standards, community service and the furtherance of internal understanding." I hope recent local club conduct is not indicative of a new international tendency but represents an isolated aberration peculiar to our high prevalence of backwardness. Until learning of the local Club's selection of Rotarian of the Year. I labored under the misconception that those professions possessing these noblest of human qualities would be the last citizens to attempt to whitewash and glorify naked violence, brutality, and terror. Local Rotarians have compromised the internationally insulted womanhood and reduced Rotarian manhood to the level of Stone Age brutes. Naming one charged through community rumors with, among other things, breaking down the doors of a widow's home and publicly assaulting the weaker sex reflects on the moral and intellectual state of this community's business and professional elite. To help Lonnie Deur would be a good and humane gesture. The same quality of assistance secured by the community for Mrs. Ruby Nelson should be extended to Sheriff Deur. But for the Rotarians to crown him as the best of manhood they have to offer surpasses the limits of morbid cynicism. Such sinister and spiteful acts drag Lake County to the brink of lunacy. It makes of Rotarian traditions while rendering such a grave disservice to this antebellum and deeply racist community.

Robert F. Williams

"Constitution more than words on scrap of paper" to the Editor[8]

With great pomp and ceremony, America has last celebrated the 400th year of our Constitution. The Constitution is the world's greatest guideline for the dispensation of justice and the regulation of our conduct toward our fellow man. To many the Constitution is just a classic document from which to pick and choose. There is a tendency for too many to reverse it in the abstract while concretely trampling it underfoot. In Lake County, we have just witnessed a ceremony wrought in splendor and befitting its glory. The prevailing hope seems to have been to endear it to the following generations, hopefully, who will cherish and defend it until the end. The point seems to have been missed that the best way to perpetuate it is to practice what it admonishes. Ceremony is good by compliance is its essence. The Constitution supposedly guarantees every American equal protection and treatment under the law. Anything less is hypocritical. Beyond the sound of the gala observance, a fellow American languished in the Baldwin jail. Robert Carew has been accused by what is generally thought to be his distraught common-law wife, of rape and kidnap. He has been imprisoned for almost a year on overstated charges that would evoke laughter in a more just-minded community. The justice system should never be used to execute personal vendettas. To do so is criminal. Robert Carew's case seems much more racially and politically motivated than the average criminal case. It is more than obvious that he is out of reach of the promise of the Constitution. He faces two possible life sentences. There have been other so-called "rape charges" in Lake County; however, none have engendered the official ire that Carew's has. Local officials seem more than anxious to place the Carew case in a first-magnitude criminal category. Can it be because antebellum minded authorities feel that Carew has compromised virtuous white womanhood? Why does Carew's case weigh so heavily on the scales of Lake County's bankrupt justice? While town criers broadcast the magnificence of Lake County, and while they move might and main to prettify a community of ugly justice, the so-called "foreign media" is spoon-fed managed and deceptive news. Certain officials are more than anxious to utilize the media in special cases, while Robert Carew is silently crucified on Lake County's cross of hypocrisy. Those who love the Constitution, those who live justice and those who claim to be Christians are derelict in their duty to God and humanity so long as they stand mute while such a travesty of justice prevails. If Lake County is too incompetent and too ungodly to properly serve as a steward of the U.S. Constitution, then it is high time for the state to fill the breach. It is time for those who believe in justice to stir themselves and here perhaps the Constitution then will be more than glowing words on a scrap of paper, signifying nothing.

Robert F. Williams, Baldwin

HAPPY HOPEFUL NEW YEAR 1995 JOIN THE RIGHT TO LIVE MOVEMENT, BUY YOURSELF A GUN

Dear Friends,

If one can truly attune heart and soul to the wavelengths of truth and reality, the thunder of a ferocious storm can be heard not very far in the distance. It is more than obvious that an ill-wind is blowing an impending crisis over the American landscape. In short, we are about to be "NEWTED" by the reactionary axis of Gingrich, Dole, Helms, and Thurman. This heartless squad of Pied Pipers is sitting on the stage for a storm as vicious as any the world has ever known. They are the new masters of deceit, dissension, and hypocrisy. The most shameful truth is that they have cloaked their wicked scheme in the phony cloak of conservatism, Christian and family values. They are more than shrill in manipulating the general public's greed and prejudices. The essence of their theme is to get the government off our backs and to put more money in our pockets by reducing tax and public spending. It is shocking to see how many seemingly intelligent people are falling for this ruse. The hue and cry are not for the salvation of the human being but for the dollar. Through sly innuendo, the weak-minded sector (which is myriad) is being led to believe that the ills of America are being heaped upon an otherwise prosperous America by Affirmative Action for minorities and handouts to the "shiftless" poverty-stricken poor American. It is stunning to see how many people have accepted this line of thought without reservation. These "Christian" hypocrites are the extreme loudmouths who pretend to champion the cause of prayer in the schools. The lack of prayer in the schools from their point of view is the cause of America's decline. They seem not to be concerned with the lack of sincere and effective prayer in their homes and the churches. They claim to be the true believers and defenders of family values while advocating the removal of certain essentials for the survival of the family. They are in the vanguard of a great cry in the land for the death penalty and the construction of more prisons. They call themselves Christian champions of God's tenets, but they reject Christ's admonition on attitude toward prisoners, widows, and the truly poor. To them, murder is ok if it is done in the collective passion of a community of killers. Even the innocent can be killed without the slightest pang of conscious so long as it is carried out under the color of the authority of the ruling mob. The so-called "law-abiding citizen" is whining against tax money being used to support the poor, but wealth fare for the rich seems a natural thing. Graft on the part of the industrialists and politicians is acceptable. There is a mean-spirited movement afoot in this nation designed to reverse all humane policies to the era preceding Franklin Roosevelt. Some scholars maintain that Roosevelt staved off an impending revolution by undermining Hooverism. If we accept this premise as a truism, then where is the new gang of heartless political buffoons leading the nation. They favor removing the safety net from beneath the poor. Have they never heard of Maria Antoinette and her proposal to "Let They Eat Cake?" They claim to believe in Christian tenets, but they don't accept the proclamation of the penalty of reaping what is sown. Not only are they endeavoring to shite the poor at home, but they are also embargoing Cuba and Iraq consequently denying suffering innocent babies and old people medicine and sustaining nutrition. They are defiantly creating inhumane conditions directed at the wretched of the earth while claiming to liberate them from oppressive leaders. These dispensers of the New World Order are boastful of the condition that there is only one superpower in the world and now that they have the power to play God, the entire world is expected to crawl in their direction. The New Year and the New World Order might be full of upheaval, turmoil, and rude awakening. But at any rate, it is commonly said that what goes around comes around. So, duck and hope for a Happy New Year. Robert F. Williams

This past year was quite an eventful one. Robert was still working with the stranger Calvin Cunningham. He recruited a lawyer for him after his death sentence was overturned. A new trial was granted in Charlotte, North Carolina. Ms. Melissa El, of Detroit volunteered to represent him, but the hateful, cantankerous white woman judge denied Cunningham the competent services of Ms. El. The poor fellow ended up pitifully attempting to defend himself in a kangaroo-type trial. Even so, he was given a life sentence instead in that trial. While in N.C. in mid-March attending the trial,

Robert's 95-year-old aunt, Addie Williams, passed away. She was the mother of 15 children, grandmother of 70, great-grandmother of 164 and great-great-grandmother to 71. Most of these offspring showed up to pay their last respects along with many church members and friends. The family was so large that one of the largest churches in town was utilized to accommodate the going-home services. Our son, John, is still working at Life Directions in Detroit as director of their Youth Leadership Project. We have spent more time with him this year. I particularly enjoyed helping him to get settled in his newly acquired home. Franklin, the youngest of Williams males, this year was graduated from Iowa State University. Rob did numerous talk radio and personal interviews and lectures this past year. Unfortunately, he missed the Black Family Conference in Louisville, Kentucky where he was scheduled to speak. Still working on his autobiography, in early August his blood pressure started to elevate out of control. We made an appointment at Mayo Clinic in Rochester, MN for a health Check-up and went out there for what was supposed to be a four-day stay. We ended up staying nineteen days, eight of which he spent in St. Mary's Hospital following lung surgery for a suspected cancer. Thankfully it turned out not to be cancer, prostate cancer was identified, however, resulting in the need for follow-up trips. John went with us on our first trip out to Minnesota, we stopped in Wisconsin where we visited Tim Tyson and his family. Tim is an ardent historian from N.C. who, while doing his doctoral thesis, came to Michigan's Bentley Historical Library where the Robert F. Williams collection is housed. He also came here to visit and interview Robert. At that time, he was a professor at Duke University in the Black Studies Department. He became deeply involved in his research, has since had his thesis published and has relocated to the University of Wisconsin. We had a most pleasant visit with them. John and a friend drove us out to Mayo for the first follow-up and we took Amtrak back through Chicago to Grand Rapids. Despite the medical nature of the trips, they were pleasant and enjoyable. My lifelong friend, Maria Williams Harris, came over from Malo Alto, California, and paid a most enjoyable visit. Numerous students and researchers have contacted us throughout the year with an interest in studying the Monroe Story. The Charlotte Observer sent a reporter and photographer for an interview in preparation for a series which is supposed to appear in January. It seems that at least some of the true history of our struggle will be told. This year for the first time in many years, we missed the Celebration of China's National Day in Chicago because of Rob's illness. We also missed the Williams Family Reunion and our Winchester Alumni Reunion. My main occupation as director of senior services for our county takes up most of my time. However, I am still involved in numerous community activities. Just before Christmas, we received the news that our county has been designated as an Economic Development Community (EZ-EC). This is one of the projects which have taken a tremendous amount of work on the part of our total community and hopefully now will help us create jobs and develop the area. Earlier this year, we hosted Professor Carl Grimes and several of his architectural students from Lawrence Tech. They studied and designed prototypes for an Historical Museum Conference Center around Idlewild's Paradise Lake area to reflect the area's rich cultural heritage. I took part in our second KWANZAA celebration working with local leaders and young people and the event was fantastic. Our social cultural club The Merrymakers purchased land this year and are hopeful of starting to build it in the future. We were fortunate enough to have a very mild winter until after Christmas. As the New Year came in though, it was snowing like mad. Robert is still counting down to my expected retirement date so he can escape the cold and snow. I am looking forward to spending more time with my grands. "Robbie" and "Ben" and to dedicate more time to the development of an Idlewild Historical Museum. Love, blessings, and best wishes for a glorious New Year!

Mabel R. Williams

LETTERS FROM ROBERT F. WILLIAMS AND CALVIN C. CUNNINGHAM

February 12, 1994, Baldwin, MI[9]

Dear Calvin:

Your letter Was Received some time ago. I'm sorry the court will not help in getting attorney El to represent you. We are still trying on this end. I'm going to keep trying. We may make it yet.

Sincerely,
Robert F. Williams

P.S. As soon as the weather breaks on this end, I will be down there.

June 27, 1995, Baldwin, MI[10]

Dear Calvin:

Thanks for your prayers and your card. I finally made it back home after a second month at the Mayo Clinic. I'll be able to drive by August and I hope to visit Monroe by then. Make sure you register me on the visitor's list. Have you heard anything from your appeal yet?

Sincerely,
Robert F. Williams

August 8, 1995, Baldwin, MI[11]

Dear Calvin:

Your letter was received some time ago. If my health holds up, I may see you later this month. What are the visiting days and times there? You informed me that I am on your visitors list, but you didn't tell me the days when you may have visitors. Have you heard anything from the appeal yet?

Sincerely,
Robert F. Williams

HAPPY HOPEFUL NEW YEAR JOIN THE RIGHT TO LIBE MOVEMENT BUY YOURSELF A GUN[12]

LETTERS FROM CALVIN C. CUNNINGHAM AND RONALD J. STEPHENS

January 1, 2015, Salisbury, N.C.[13]

Dear Professor,
God's Love,

All I ever got from Mr. Robert F. Williams was notes. He would let me know when he was coming to see me. I have been railroaded by the courts and gave a death sentence. Mr. Williams has seen the evidence I had and got me a lawyer. The court took the lawyer away from me because they didn't want the truth to come out about what they had done to an innocent Black man. I'm sending you some things that Mr. Williams wrote. I'm also sending you some of what was done to me. I'm innocent and have the evidence to prove it. Can you help me?

PS I'm sending you two letters.

March 28, 2015, Salisbury, N.C.[14]

To Professor Stephens,

God's Love,

Thanks for the cases you sent me and the other information but what I need is a lawyer. The Das in my case said that there was no evidence in my case. They said that there was only scientific and circumstantial evidence. They lied because I have all the evidence, plus they lied to Melissa El. One judge gave me Melissa as my lawyer. Two lawyers had railroaded me and had me moved out of the courtroom that I was getting help in and put me in another courtroom. There, they did everything they could to keep Melissa from being my lawyer. That had nothing to do with my case because I had fired them two months ago. They didn't want the world to find out what they had done to me. They knew that there was no evidence against me, so they hid the evidence, then told that lie with the Das that there was no evidence. I need Melissa El to handle this for me. I have everything she needs to prove my case. Over the years, I got everything that they said didn't exist, plus my case was false. It's a lot of money in my case, just about 2 million dollars. Mr. Williams told me that I could trust Melissa El. He never told me anything wrong, so I trust her. I need her to look at this evidence that I have. She will be well paid to prove this case. There's no evidence and no witnesses against me. Professor, get Melissa to come see me. When she gets here tell these people that she is my lawyer and tell them to tell me to bring my paperwork with me. Okay.

April 3, 2015, West Lafayette, IN[15]

Dear Calvin,

This is to let you know I made telephone contact with Attorney Melissa El on your behalf this morning. We talked for about 20 minutes. I read your letter to Attorney El and scanned it and sent it to her attention as she requested via email. Based on the conversation with Melissa you may be getting a visit from her sometime during the month of May 2015. Attorney El also mentioned the Innocent Project, documents about them I sent to your attention in my last communications. She indicated that when she visits you in May she will be taking notes and documents about your case, and most likely working closely with members of the Innocent Project. That's all I must report for now. I wish you well, and please do keep in touch regarding updates pertaining to your case.

Sincerely,
Ronald J. Stephens, Professor

DEDICATION OF THE ROBERT F. WILLIAMS COMMUNITY DEVELOPMENT AND FAMILY CENTER PUBLISHED IN THE *LAKE COUNTY STAR* [16]

Get the Facts Straight, May 22, 2000

To the Editor:

This letter is sent in response to last week's *My View* column, entitled "Bucky's List of Top Twenty Outrages of the Year." While I respect your right to express your opinions regarding your likes and dislikes regarding the political and community activities of Lake County, I now take the time to ask you to become a responsible journalist. When one makes accusations, and innuendo about the integrity of individuals, the writer ought to follow one basic principle. "Get the facts right!" I'm sure that many of the individuals named in that article will take issue with your accusations because of misplaced facts. I will not take the time to go through all 20 "outrages," however, I will say that I am outraged that you would take journalistic license to malign the history and name of Robert Williams. You have the right to dislike and to state your dislikes; however, to state unequivocally, that Robert Williams's name *should not be placed on a public building* such as the new FiveCAP facility, is indeed outrageous. And to say that Williams is not an appropriate role model is itself an insult to the community of Lake County. You ought to take another look at the facts of the cause for which Robert Williams took his stand. His legacy to Black boys and girls and humankind is that if you are not willing to stand for that which you believe, then you will fall for anything. More than that, he was an outstanding community member who gave counsel to many. I have no idea what purpose your list of outrages was to serve, but I will tell you that continued articles of this kind will only add to the polarization of the members of this community and diminish your credibility in this community.

Sincerely,
Stanley U. Sims, Pastor, Tabernacle African Methodist Episcopal Church Idlewild

Robert Williams is a Role Model, May 22, 2000

To the Editor:

Having crossed over into the new millennium and having survived Y2K, I am counting my blessings and taking a stand for tolerance. With this renewed spirit of idealism in mind, I am compelled to respond to your "20 outrages" and particularly, your outrage number three on the naming of the new FiveCAP center after Robert F. Williams. As an African American mother and grandmother, I am proud to say that I have known an African American man who had the courage to stand up in the face of danger and protect his family, his beliefs, and my rights with his life. Not only do I feel that he is a superb role model for Lake County children, but I feel if we had more African American men who had Robert Franklin Williams' courage, we would have fewer needs for places, such as the Michigan Youth Correctional Facility, that graces our fair community. Furthermore, I take exception to your statement, "Although a hero to a small collection of Idlewild supporters," Robert F. Williams was more than a hero to anyone, he was a leader who was not afraid to lead in the face of danger. He led a cross section of the nation and as the *North Carolina News and Observer* pointed out in its article on the *100 Strong, the Visionaries of the Century* (August 22, 1999) "The visionaries who shaped 20th century North Carolina were ruthless industrial buccaneers and high-minded intellectuals, fearless political leaders and … The one thing they had in common was a vision of North Carolina—an ability to see what others could not—and enough drive to be trailblazers." Williams contributed to the America we know today and that alone is enough to make him a role model for all youth, not only Lake County youth. I commend the FiveCAP Board and executive director for their progressiveness in naming this building after him. I hope you and others will take time to know more about him than the FBI textbook definition you presented in your outrage.

Sincerely,
Audrey Kathryn Bullett

"Misinformation and Omissions," May 22, 2000

To the Editor:

Your December 23, 1999, issue—Opinion Page, *My View*, by Buck VanderMeer. The subject was *Bucky's List of Twenty Outrages of the Year*, Outrage Number Three, relates to Mr. VanderMeer's objections to the naming of the FiveCAP Center after African-American Robert F. Williams. Your Outrage No. 3, Mr. VanderMeer, was outrageous in its misinformation and omissions on the life of Robert F. Williams. Mr. Williams was an outspoken representative of the Black community in Monroe County, North Carolina, and president of the County National Association for the Advancement of Colored People (NAACP). He was a militant because the pleas of the Black community for justice and protection from the KKK and the White Citizen's Council went unheeded. The Monroe County Black community desperately needed racial abuse, KKK night rides and transgressions against Blacks to cease. When the brutal suppression of minority rights continued, the Black community was advised to follow an old American tradition of self-defense. Indeed, Mr. Williams did not advocate violence; he advised self-defense. Defending oneself is an act in response to external physical provocations: in the case of Robert Williams, the KKK. In the absence of justice and protection from local law enforcement officials, Mr. Williams fled the United States. He returned to this country with a clear record by the U.S. Department of State with all the rights and privileges of a U.S. citizen. He has no blemish on his record as a good citizen. Your comments on Mr. Williams regarding the naming of FiveCAP Development Family Center is not applicable to his life and are inflammatory. Mr. Williams was a freedom fighter against injustice in the United States. When Robert F. Williams passed away, he was a member in good standing with the national and local chapters of the NAACP. His passion for truth, justice, and equality makes him an appropriate role model for youths and adults.

Sincerely,
Robert L. Watkins, President, Lake/Newaygo County NAACP

May 22, 2000
Dear Mrs. Trucks,

Thank you for inviting our church to be a part of this glorious celebration of the dedication and official opening of this beautiful service facility for the community and families of Lake County.

We further congratulate you on selecting Robert F. Williams's name to place on this facility. His contributions to this community and his dedication to basic human rights for all people will long be remembered and hopefully emulated by the youth who receive educational services in this facility. And, to the Lake County Enterprise Community Board of Directors, we express a sincere appreciation for the contributions you have made to the improvement of the "Quality of Life" in the enterprise community. As we look around at the improvements made over the last eight years in our community, we can take pride in the leadership and hard work that has taken place. Once again, thank you for having included our church in this glorious celebration.

Sincerely yours,
The Reverend John E. Simpson, Pastor, First Baptist Church of Idlewild

LETTERS ABOUT ROBERT WILLIAMS FROM RICHARD T. GIBSON TO RONALD J. STEPHENS

November 19, 2001, London[17]

Dear Ron Stephens,

You were right to give Mabel my email address, and I do hope to hear from her one of these days. We unfortunately have never had any correspondence, and I must confess that I hardly know her in her own right, although I am certain she was one of the pillars of the struggle led by her late husband. I saw her last with Rob in Dar es Salaam many years ago. Of course, Rob was indeed one of the first members of the Fair Play for Cuba Committee, of which I was a founder and the first president of the New York Chapter. I later handed that post over to LeRoi Jones, now better known as Amiri Baraka, who remains to this day a friend and comrade. Robert Taber and I created FPCC when we were working as news writers for CBS News in New York. I had congratulated Rob on the stand he had taken on Black self-defense that led to his suspension from the NAACP, and I drew Taber's attention to him and his far-sighted resistance to white racism in Monroe NC, which he saw as more a local issue but a global one and that prompted his immediate positive response to the victory of the Cuban Revolution. He viewed revolutionary Cuba as a valuable ally in the struggle of African Americans against American racism and the remnants of white racist imperialism clinging to power around the world. When Taber had to leave the States for Cuba, I took over as the Committee's Acting Executive Secretary and relinquished the post when I left the United States and Africa in 1962 to V T (Ted) Lee. FPCC was dissolved immediately after JFK's assassination when it was announced by the U.S. government that Lee Harvey Oswald had been a member and indeed had organized a chapter in New Orleans because moving to Dallas where he frequented anti-Castro Cubans and other right-wingers. Whether Oswald was the patsy or a double agent, I cannot tell you, but I doubt if he was the real or the only assassin. That brings me to your problem of the chronology of Rob's struggle. I knew little then of the details of Rob's activities, although I believe that some of the accounts given by Robert Carl Cohen in his *Black Crusader* are incorrect. Surely, Mabel and the two sons would be the best and most accurate sources for you? Because of the pressure of my voluntary work here, I have not yet had time to take down some boxes of correspondence and papers that I have been able to save in order to see if there is anything in them that might be of use to you. As I said in my previous message, Milton Henry would also be a good source, even though he was very bitter about the rupture between Rob and the Republic of New Africa. Try to get him to talk, and please give him my greetings and very best wishes. Regardless of their political differences, I assure you Milton worked as hard as possible in London to make sure that Rob got out of the British prison and was not sent to Cairo, but rather was able to continue his return journey safely to Detroit and, most important of all, that the deal he had arranged with the U.S. Department of Justice was honored. Another possible source for you would be Suleiman Abdullah Schleifer, an American Jewish writer and journalist converted to Islam, who as far as I know, is still living in Cairo. When he was still known as Mark David Schleifer, he taped in

Havana Rob's account of his struggle, producing a book for Rob entitled *Negroes with Guns*. Schleifer and I later worked together briefly in the Middle East for "Jeune Afrique" and "Race Today" magazines, hoping to write a book on the Palestinian struggle, which was totally blocked by the Zionist lobby in the United States and United Kingdom. Unfortunately, I have neither heard from nor seen Schleifer for many years. When I last heard from him, he was director of the Adnan Center for Television Journalism at the American University in Cairo and was very much involved in research on Muslim history. When the Israelis captured East Jerusalem, where he was working as an editor of an Arab newspaper, he was taken prisoner, imprisoned and maltreated, but apparently released because of the intercession of prominent Jewish relatives and allowed to move to Egypt. He wrote a book on the fall of Arab Jerusalem, whose exact title I have forgotten. I cannot think now of anything else but will come back to you if I do find something that might be of interest to you. Please transmit my warmest greetings to Mabel and her sons whom I never met. Best wishes for your success,

Richard Gibson

February 18, 2002, London[18]

Dear Ronald Stephens,

This is the letter that Rob Williams sent me in 1967 when he learned I was going again to Sweden. He had hoped I could decide on his planned visit, but, as you probably know, many of the Swedish Left that had supposedly wanted him to come had changed their minds and did not protest when the Swedish government refused him a visa. This was at the height of the Sino-Soviet conflict over the international line of the world Communist movement and the arguments about "Soviet revisionism." For various reasons, Cuba lined up solidly with the Soviets and the Cuban ambassador in Stockholm, whose name I cannot recall except that his wife was Olga Finlay, worked to bring about the Swedish refusal, aided ironically by Olga's father, Enrique Finlay, who was then living with his daughter and her husband in Stockholm. I knew him well from when he had lived in New York before returning to Cuba to live; nevertheless, our meeting in Stockholm was tense as Finlay voiced allegations against an "ungrateful Williams" who was allegedly a Chinese now and was trying to sow dissension in the Swedish Left. He hinted that I, Rob Williams, and the Chinese Communist Party were now all working with the CIA to disrupt support for the Vietnamese in their struggle against the United States. This may sound far-fetched now, but it wasn't then too many gullible people on the Left over all the world. Did you receive my email yesterday? I need that information about formats for the photos as soon as possible. I will get back to you with more contextual information about the letters. Incidentally, I presume you have a copy of Rob's letter to Fidel of August 28, 1966? I also have two letters Rob me from Dar es Salaam in July 1969 before he set off for home via London. More about that later. Best wishes,

Richard Gibson

February 28, 2002, London[19]

Rob was a very controversial figure, and you can tell from Betita Martinez's reaction to my reminder to her of how she had condemned Rob's open letter to Fidel. Cedric Belfrage and Betita were at least open about their objections. Most of the Old Left weren't. It is obvious that Moscow and Washington as well as Havana were all fearful of Rob, although for different reasons, and it is next to impossible to determine exactly who was conducting the campaign of denigration against him and setting up the roadblocks to his free movement around the globe to return home and clear his name. But the biggest insinuation made by them, never proven by anyone, was that Rob was an unprincipled maverick rebel who failed to understand the priorities of the world revolutionary movement—as seen by Moscow at least—and eventually became an agent of influence of the U.S. government in the building of diplomatic links between Washington and Beijing during the Nixon administration.

April 8, 2002, London[20]

Regarding Stokely, what could Rob have said against him, except that he was a very unstable young man with charisma? However, I can see clearly that there was a contradiction between Rob and the Black nationalist groups. Rob never yearned for martyrdom. As for the plot to destroy "national shrines," the only plot that I knew of was that involving my friend from Camden NJ Walter Bowe, who was entrapped into what must have been a Contelpro scheme to blow up the Statute of Liberty with explosives provided by the FLQ in Quebec and the NYPD. I met him, a very decent young man, when I was in high school in Philadelphia through a white classmate who was a juzz buff, and I attended Walter's marriage to Sylvia Boone, who I know died tragically young, but what happened to Walter? From your account of RAM's stated objectives, no wonder Max did not want to talk. The idea of an armed defense of a minority is not insane, but that of the takeover of a country by a minority without at least passive acceptance by the majority is madness.

April 9, 2002, London[21]

When Rob was stopped in London by the British authorities en route to Detroit, there was already a deal. Milton Henry, as well as Rob, made it abundantly clear to all those arrangements for Rob's return had been agreed previously with the U.S. Department of Justice. Only Milton could, if he would, tell you with whom he had made that deal. Remember, there was no U.S. Embassy in Peking in those days and American officials that Rob could have approached, but Rob did possess a valid U.S. passport for his return trip home and an arrangement had been made for his immediate release on bail for the kidnapping charges by the Federal Commissioner in Detroit upon his arrival. Was it perhaps used on his first visit to Tanzania. In any case, can you find out where he got that passport? Milton Henry felt that somebody in the U.S. government was unhappy about the decision to allow Rob to return home. You recall the abortive effort to send Rob back to Cairo, which was just thwarted by an airport vehicle smashing the tip of the Egyptian aircraft's wing. Was that really an accident or perhaps somebody making sure that Rob's deal went through? Milton went alone to the Embassy in London to speak with people there, about which I know nothing, but the deal was eventually confirmed and made clear to the British. Evidence exists proving that the CIA had taken an interest in Rob, and it would have had the assets on the ground to arrange such a curious if provident accident. There were demonstrations in London against Rob's detention by British Black activists and much critical attention in the British press that embarrassed the British government. It is almost incredible that the U.S. Embassy in London should claim that although Rob was a wanted fugitive in the United States, they had received no warrant to have him arrested and extradited for trial to the United States, which have been the normal procedure. They maintained that it was up to the British to decide whether they could permit Rob to fly on to Detroit on TWA if they felt it was safe—because he was a dangerous character who might even hijack the plane—or try again to deport him back to Cairo airport, which he had merely passed through when his Egyptian plane from Dar es Salaam touched down there briefly before flying on to London with a new flight number. Rob was very fearful of being sent to Cairo, a city in a country where he knew no one, and he began a hunger strike in protest. To sum up, it seems obvious to me that various agencies of the U.S. government were fighting among themselves about Rob's fate. Not everyone accepted the deal, which I doubt if Whiting had initiated, but may have approved of in view of the hint of the possibility of establishing vital relations with the government of China during the Vietnam War. How did the State Department know that Rob would be willing to help? I don't know, but you might investigate this aspect of the deal. The other aspect that needs to be investigated is whether Rob made any engagements about his future role in the struggle for Black freedom in the United States.

Notes

1 Richard Gibson writes Robert Williams, June 15, 1976, in the Richard Gibson Papers, Box 13, Folder 6.
2 Ibid, June 28, 1976
3 Ibid, August 5, 1976
4 Ibid, August 20, 1976
5 Williams writes Congressman David Bonior, June 21, 1994
6 Williams writes Congressman John Conyers, June 21, 1994
7 Williams questions Rotary's choice for award, *Lake County Star,* June 8, 1978, 4.
8 Constitution more than words on scrap of paper, September 25, 1987, 5. This letter to the editor was published in The Lake County Star.
9 Robert Williams writes Calvin Cunningham, February 12, 1994, in the Robert F. Williams Papers, Bentley Historical Library, Box 12
10 Ibid, June 27, 1995
11 Ibid, August 8, 1995
12 Robert and Mabel Williams Newsletter, 1995, in the Robert F. Williams Papers, Bentley Historical Library, Box
13 Calvin Cunningham writes Ronald Stephens, January 1, 2015, author's personal collection.
14 Ibid, March 28, 2015
15 Ronald Stephens writes Calvin Cunningham, April 3, 2015, author's personal collection
16 *Lake County Star, Letters-to-the-Editor,* May 20, 2000.
17 ,
18 Richard Gibson writes Ronald Stephens, November 19, 2001, in the Richard Gibson Papers, Box 13, Folder 5,
19 Richard Gibson writes Ronald Stephens, February 18, 2001, in the Richard Gibson Papers, Box 13, Folder 5,
20 Richard Gibson writes Ronald Stephens, February 28, 2001, in the Richard Gibson Papers, Box 13, Folder 5,
21 Richard Gibson writes Ronald Stephens, April 9, 2001, in the Richard Gibson Papers, Box 13, Folder 5,

EPILOGUE

There are a plethora of unresolved issues and realities raised surrounding the activism of Robert and Mabel Williams, and their interactions with Castroism, Maoism, and Robert's relationship with Richard Gibson (a CIA informant) who stayed in contact with him in exile in Cuba, China and after his return to the United States from 1971 to 1976. My analysis of Robert Williams not only foregrounds the importance of a multifaceted representation of him but also focuses on dual themes of racial oppression and the victimization of black men and women within the overarching structure of American white patriarchy. Robert Williams' defiance with Mabel's support against racism, advocacy for armed self-defense, moral character and conviction, and pragmatic decisions during the Cold War/Civil Rights era were executed strategically and with accountability. Williams offered a progressive vision that influenced emerging as well as future generations of activists who would insist on changes and reforms in American society and worldwide. Williams stood out as a centrally important yet often misunderstood and complex figure in twentieth- and twenty-first-century American history. Williams writings and voice were unsettling and offered disturbing criticisms about the inactions of the American government and the broader racist white voting population which continues to resonate today. The observations he made domestically and abroad about white America demonstrate a consistent pattern of resistance to and against white supremacy, racial injustice, and discrimination. This stance not only spurned a backlash among white American leaders but also caused a resurgent "new civil rights movement" with grievances among middle and working-class Black and white Americans against racism. Relevant today are Black Lives Matter movement activists dominating the scene and making visible the extent of white supremacy in America, particularly the complicity of white Americans and those ethnic groups (peoples of color) that are benefiting from the oppressive forces of racism and the denial of rights guaranteed to African Americans. Williams becomes important today since armed militias are patrolling U.S. southern borders and claiming fourteenth amendment rights since the government is not providing protection and security for its citizens. They are claiming the right to protect themselves when their justifications are unwarranted. With the rise of hate speech among white Americans who continue to dismiss and ignore the rights of African American families, the hypocrisy does not end there when it comes to voter suppression laws in a number of states. By centralizing the resistance of Robert Williams and his domestic and international activism and ideals about democracy and American patriotism, his story as presented in this volume introduced him as a defender of justice, equality, and the civil and human rights of African Americans. The isolationism and counterattacks of some white Americans in the United States seem rooted in false claims about a replacement theory. Williams' messages of resistance involving racial injustice were not only timely but also relevant then and now. He was an important figure who was grounded in a humanity-based as opposed to a materialist-based society. Williams was an advocate for social and economic equality, equity, and inclusion. The lessons Americans can learn from the experiences of Robert and Mabel Williams, and their neighbors in the Newtown community of Monroe, North Carolina, when considering the accusations and denials of the racial injustices they received without government protections speaks volumes about the threats of racial violence in white America. What was happening to Black families and community members in Newtown during the 1950s and 60s is quite different from the revisionist history we are witnessing today through the efforts of armed militias who support former president Donald Trump's misguided advocacy and evocations by using Nazi rhetoric at a political rally in New Hampshire a few months ago. The story of Robert and Mabel Williams not only exemplifies the importance of self-preservation and human dignity but also serves as a vehicle for social and political changes and reforms that are urgently needed to come from American politicians and not only from leaders and activists from the bottom-up. At the center of the racist white threats of a race war, Robert and Mabel Williams, their allies, fans, and supporters responded responsibly by taking an unprecedented action that challenged and inserted social justice into the national and international spotlight. The stance that the Williamses embraced and attempted to enact nationally, regionally, and internationally brings to the forefront a set of core issues surrounding human and civil rights. The uninformed opinions of privileged white Americans and other ethnic groups in Cuba and China were conveyed in *The Crusader* newsletter and Radio Free Dixie broadcasts gave voice to the reality that there "is no justice for the Afro-American in racist [white] America." Recognizing the efforts and influences of white supremacy and powerbrokers worldwide, even among Marxist-Leninist philosophers, reveals the contradictions and hypocrisy. Williams had recognized how some Marxist-Leninist leaders and members "participated in the human rights struggles" for Afro-Americans and was clear in Cuba [and China] that Afro-Americans "need not be told by any philosophy or by any political party that racial oppression is wrong." Racial discrimination, white oppression, and violence, from Williams perspective itself, will inspire African Americans "to rebellion, and it is on this ground that the people in Monroe [and elsewhere] " protested and "refused to conform to the standard of Jim Crow lies in a Jim Crow society. It is on this basis that they have struck out against the inhumanity of racial prejudice." However, what he stood for as a patriot and military veteran about white racists, integrationists, Black nationalists, and Marxist-Leninists of the period and today was not acceptable or appreciated. The pragmatic solutions Rob Williams offered and raised need addressing when it comes to equality and the Black race. In this edited volume, I have illustrated using Robert and Mabel Williams's words what they understood and fought for, which remains the human rights guaranteed African Americans. Their grievances to white American politicians, judges, business leaders, and citizens continue to insist on practicing a better democracy against all forms of racial discrimination, racial violence, white oppression, violence, and terrorism. Different from the resentment of white racists and the limited visions of Black nationalists, Robert Williams's contacts abroad in Cuba and China put him on another level from the nationalist and Marxist-Leninist supporters of the period who had never seen, experienced, or witnessed what he accomplished on the ground firsthand. Robert Williams' perceptions, pragmatism, and flexible actions as a Black internationalist were about presenting solutions to a contagious race problem and crisis in America. This flexible, independent-minded citizen, visionary, and civil rights leader successfully agitated against white supremacy and navigated Castroism, Maoism, and an assassination in America. Robert Williams remains an important Black international and transnational figure who helped (next to Malcolm X) to shape the development of the Black Power Movement. The Robert and Mabel Williams spousal team understood that in white America, African Americans and their right to bear arms to protect themselves and their communities represents an expression of their freedom of speech rights, and rights to protest against any form of injustice without fear of repercussions. Together, the couple proudly instigated and agitated for effective changes and reforms against racist thinking and practices in America and worldwide. The Williamses focused on God-given rights through a platform in support of African Americans, Asians, Latino/as citizens of the world, by demanding that white politicians cast off the shackles of the old traditions and focus on change. Neither Robert nor Mabel Williams accepted, embraced, or internalized under any terms of second-class citizenship. Their articulations, strategies, and formative aspects of forging a human rights war and revolution helped to facilitate the coordination of Black, Asian, Latin American, and white rebellions during the 1960s and beyond. As Americans they understood that children everywhere on the planet deserve to face a future with confidence, good health, and trust in the political and religious institutions that shape their lives. The story about Robert and Mabel Williams is about responsibility, and a testament to their determination, and resilience, despite the economic, political, and social forces that worked against them.

In We Are the Leaders We Have Been Looking For, Eddie S. Glaude Jr. reflects on how ordinary people can be the heroes of our democracy. The story of Robert and Mabel Williams is a testament to the ethical power of courage and passion in defense of racial justice and what ordinary citizens can do to create and sustain a just and democratic society. This approach not only highlights the plight and resilience of the couple but also encourages a honest and reflective dialogue about the rights of black men and women in America and around the globe, which appears to be influenced by pervasive racial ideologies and hierarchies. Through this lens, there has never been such an urgent time than to actualize lessons learned from the activism of Robert and Mabel Williams.

Part III

Part III includes a selected bibliography of published works written by and about Williams. This selected bibliography consists of important institutional papers in archival collections, including the papers of Robert F. Williams, Gwendolyn Midlo Hall, Mae Mallory, Conrad Lynn, Richard T. Gibson, and others, as well as a list of primary and secondary sources, including books, government documents, as well as a list of secondary sources, including books, book chapters, dissertations, peer-reviewed journal articles, pamphlets, and the online newspaper articles I discovered that were useful in my scholarship.

SELECTED BIBLIOGRAPHY

Manuscript Collections by Repository

Bentley Historical Library

Robert Franklin Williams Papers, 1925-96. 10 boxes
Gwendolyn Midlo Hall Papers, 1939-1998, 5.5 linear feet

Amistad Research Center

Gwendolyn Midlo Hall Papers, 5.40 linear feet

George Washington University Special Collections

Richard T. Gibson Papers, 1948-2004, 11.5 linear feet, consisting of 23 document boxes

State Historical Society of Wisconsin

Robert Carl Cohen Papers, 1963-1978, 5 archives boxes and 9 tape interviews
Committee to Combat Racial Injustice Records, 1957-1965, 2 archives boxes and 1 reel of microfilm (35mm)

University of Minnesota

Robert Carl Cohen Papers, 1969, 3 folders

Wayne State University Walter Reuther Archives

The Detroit Revolutionary Movement Records are now available online
George L. Weissman Papers, 1935-1985, 3 linear feet
Mae Mallory Papers, 1961-1967, 1 linear foot
Republic of New Afrika Robert F. Williams, Sr. Papers, 3 photographs
Robert W. Dunn Papers, 1919-1937, 2 linear feet

Library of Congress

National Association for the Advancement of Colored Peoples Papers, Manuscript Division

Interviews

David Cecelski (1999 August 20). Interview with Mabel Williams. Interview K-0266. *Southern Oral History Program Collection* (#4007). Oral History Interview with Mabel Williams, August 20, 1999. Interview K-0266. Southern Oral History Program Collection (#4007): Electronic Edition. "He Would Not Be Disarmed": Robert Williams, Armed Self-Defense, and Civil Rights in Monroe, North Carolina (unc.edu)

Robert Carl Cohen (1962) Havana Interviews with Robert F. Williams, Tape 885A, No. 1-3. The interview was recorded at the Hotel Capri in Havana for WBAI-FM (New York)

Robert Carl Cohen (1968). *Let It Burn: The Coming Destruction of the USA?* Robert Franklin Williams Interview in Tanzania, East Africa.

Interview with Mabel Williams (9 November 1999) Lincoln, Nebraska.

Interview with Jeff Davenport (11 August 2014) Idlewild, Michigan.

Interview with Mary L. Trucks (14 August 2014) Idlewild, Michigan

Interview with John Chamber Williams (3 January 2015) Detroit, Michigan

Interview with Robert F. Williams (21 July 1993) Baldwin, Michigan.

Interview with Ahmad Muhammad (18 July 2015) Philadelphia, PA.

Interview with Gwendolyn Midlo Hall (11 September 2022) by email.

Government Documents

Williams, Robert F. Federal Bureau of Investigation Subject Files, University of North Carolina Charlotte, J. Murrey Atkins Library (file no. 100-HQ-387728), 1 linear foot.

Williams, Robert Franklin. Federal Bureau of Investigation Subject File. Manuscript Collections, J. Murrey Atkins Library Special Collections and University Archives, University of North Carolina Charlotte, 2000. 1 Linear Feet. Ms0329.

Testimony of Robert F. Williams, Hearings before the Subcommittee to Investigate the Administration of the Internal Security Act and Other Internal Security Laws of the Committee on the on Judiciary United States Senate Committee Ninety-First Congress, February 16, 1970, and March 24-25, 1970.

Testimony of Robert F. Williams. United States Committee on the Judiciary United States Senate. (1971). Washington, D.C.: US Government Printing Office.

Transcript of Court Ruling on Ruby Nelson in Lake County, MI

State of Michigan, Circuit Court for the County of Lake. The People of the State of Michigan -v- Ruby Nelson aka Ruby Nelson Chatman aka Ruby Chatman Fuller. Transcript of Record of the Court's Opinion Following Non-Jury Trial. Filed June 5, 1978.

Pamphlets

Why 10,000 Japanese Support Robert F. Williams, a pamphlet written by the Japanese Committee to support Williams and urging a reversal of his extradition in Charlotte, North Carolina, Japan, 1-21. Information about the pamphlet was cited and referenced in Yuichiro Onishi's article, "Yoriko Nakajima and Robert F. Williams: Reasoning with the Long Movement Thesis." Transpacific Correspondence: Dispatches from Japan's Black Studies, 2019, 183-202.

Nelson, Truman (1963). *People with Strength in Monroe.* New Ork: Committee to Aid the Monroe Defendants.

Williams, Robert F. (1968). *Listen Brother.* New York: Worldview Publishers

Documentaries

Cohen, Robert Carl (1968). *Let It Burn: The Coming Destruction of the USA? Robert F. Williams Interviews*. Boulder, CO.

WBTV Documentary (1966). "Robert Williams: The Violent Crusader." Monroe, North Carolina.

Dickers Carmichael, Sandra and Churchill L. Roberts (2005). "Negroes with Guns: Rob Williams and Black Power." The Documentary Institute of the University of Florida at Gainesville, Florida. California Newsreel.

People Republic of China (1964). "Robert Williams in China." University of Michigan, Bentley Historical Library, Ann Arbor, Michigan.

Books

Cohen, Robert C. (1972). *Black Crusader: A Biography of Robert Franklin Williams*. Secaucus: Lyle Stuart.

Cruse, Harold (1967). *The Crisis of the Negro Intellectual: A Historical Analysis of the Failure of Black Leadership*. New York: Quill.

Foreman, James (1972). *The Making of Black Revolutionaries*. Seattle: University of Washington Press.

Frazier, Robeson Taj (2015). *The East Is Black: Cold War China in the Black Radical Imagination*. Durham: Duke University Press.

Hall, Gwendolyn Midlo (2021). *Haunted by Slavery: A Southern White Woman in the Freedom Struggle*. Chicago: Haymarket Books.

Henderson, Errol A. (2019). *The Revolution Will Not Be Theorized: Cultural Revolution in the Black Power Era*. New York: SUNY.

Jeffries, Lance L. (2006). *Black Power in the Belly of the Beast*. Urbana: University of Illinois Press.

Moore, Carlos (1988). *Castro, The Blacks, and Africa*. Los Angeles: Center for Afro-American Studies, University of California.

Moore, Carlos (2008). *Pichon, A Memoir: Race and Revolution in Castro's Cuba*. Chicago: Lawrence Hill Books.

Nakajima, Yoriko (1989). *Kokujin no Seiji Sanka to Daisanseiki America Shuppatsu*. Tokyo: Chuou University Press.

Obadele, Imari Abubakari (2013). *Foundations of the Black Nation*. Baton Rouge: The House of Songhay.

Ogbar, Jeffrey O. G. (2004). *Black Power: Radical Politics and African American Identity*. Baltimore: The John Hopkins University Press.

Onaci, Edward (2020). *Free the Land: The Republic of New Afrika and the Pursuit of a Black Nation*. Chapel Hill: The University of North Carolina Press.

Plummer, Brenda Gayle (2013). *In Search of Power: African Americans in the Era of Decolonization, 1956–1974*. New York: Cambridge University Press.

Rasmussen, David (2021). *American Uprising: The Untold Story of America's Largest Slave Revolt*. New York: An Imprint of HarperCollins Publishers.

Reitan, Ruth (1999). *The Rise and Decline of an Alliance: Cuba and African American Leaders in the 1960s*. East Lansing: Michigan State University Press.

Seniors, Paula Marie (2024). *Mae Mallory, The Monroe Defense Committee and World Revolution: African American Women Radical Activists 1958–1987*. Athens: Georgia: University of Georgia Press.

Smith, Arthur (1969). *Rhetoric of Black Revolution*. Boston: Allyn and Bacon.

Sugrue, Thomas (2009). *Sweet Land of Liberty: The Forgotten Struggle for Civil Rights in the North*. New York: Random House.

Sutherland, Bill and Matt Meyer (2000). *Guns and Gandhi in Africa: Pan African Insights on Nonviolence, Armed Struggle and Liberation in Africa*, 224–39. Trenton: Africa World Press.

Sweig, Julie (2002). *Inside the Cuban Revolution: Fidel Castro and the Urban Underground*. Cambridge, MA: Harvard University Press.
Theoharris, Jeanne (2013). *The Rebellious Life of Rosa Parks*. Boston: Beacon Press.
Ture, Kwame (2003). *Ready for the Revolution: The Life and Struggles of Stokely Carmichael [Kwame Ture]*. New York: Scribner.
Tyson, Timothy B. (1999). *Radio Free Dixie: Robert F. Williams and the Roots of Black Power*. Chapel Hill: The University of North Carolina Press.
Ward, Stephen M. (2016). *In Love and Struggle: The Revolutionary Lives of James and Grace Boggs*. Chapel Hill: University of North Carolina.
Wilkins, Roy with Tom Mathews (1982). *Standing Fast: The Autobiography of Roy Wilkins*. New York: Penguin Books.
Williams, Robert F. (1962). *Negroes with Guns*. New York: Marzani and Munsell.
Williams, Robert F. (1998). *Negroes with Guns*. Detroit: Wayne State University Press.
Yoriko, N. (1989). *African Americans: Their Political Participation in the Third Century*. Tokyo, Japan: Chuo University Press.

Book Chapters

Mullen, Bill V. (2004). "Transnational Correspondence: Robert F. Williams, Detroit, and the Bandung Era." In *Afro-Orientalism*, 73–112. Minneapolis: University of Minnesota Press
Tyson, Timothy (2006). "Robert F. Williams: 'Black Power' and the Roots of the African American Freedom Struggle." In *The Human Tradition in the Civil Rights Movement*, edited by Susan M. Glisson, 227–52. Lanham: Rowman and Littlefield.

Journal Articles

Barksdale, M. C. (1984). "Robert F. Williams and the Indigenous Civil Rights Movement in Monroe, North Carolina." *Journal of Negro History*, 69: 73–89.
Brock, Lisa and Ottis Cunningham (1991). "Race and the Cuban Revolution: A Critique of Carlos Moore. Castro, the Blacks, and Africa." *Cuban Studies*, 21: 171–85.
Bush, Larson (1999). "Am I a Man? A Literature Review Engaging the Socio-historical Dynamics of Black Manhood in the United States." *The Western Journal of Black Studies*, 23: 49–57.
Dagbovie, Pero Gagio (2013). "God Has Spared Me to Tell My Story: Mabel Robinson Williams and the Civil Rights-Black Power Movement." *The Black Scholar*, 43, no. 1–2: 69–88.
Frazier, Robinson Taj P. (2011, December). "Thunder in the East: China, Exiled Crusaders, and the Unevenness of Black Internationalism." *American Quarterly* 63, no. 4: 929–53.
Gotfried, Eugene (2001). "Reflections on Race and the Status of People of African Descent in Revolutionary Cuba." *AfroCubaWeb*.
Kelly, Robin D.G. and Betsy Esch (1999). "Black Like Mao: Red China and Black Revolution." *Souls*, 1, no. 4: 6–41. Reprinted in *Afro Asia: Revolutionary Political and Cultural Connections Between African Americans and Asian Americans,* edited by Fred Ho and Bill V. Mullen. North Carolina: Duke University Press, 97-154.
Mares, Richard (2019). "Catching Hell: Robert F. Williams's Life as a Black Radical in Exile, 1961–1966." *Journal for the Study of Radicalism*, 13, no. 2: 121–58.
Onishi', Yuichiro. (2019). "Yoriko Nakajima and Robert F. Williams: Reasoning with the Long Movement Thesis." *Transpacific Correspondence: Dispatches from Japan's Black Studies*, 183–202.
Perez, Pedro (2004). "An Open Letter to Carlos Moore by Pedro Perez Sarduy in Cuba Update, Summer 1990." *AfroCubaWeb*. http://www.afrocubaweb.com/lettertocarlos.htm
Rucker, Walter (2006). "Crusader in Exile': Robert F. Williams and the Internationalized Struggle for Black Freedom in America." *Black Scholar*, 36: 19–34.

Sout, David. 1996, October 19. "Robert F. Williams, 71, Civil Rights Leader and Revolutionary." *New York Times*, 52.

Stephens, Ronald J. (2003). "Narrating Acts of Resistance: Explorations of Untold Heroic and Horrific Battle Stories Surrounding Robert Franklin Williams's Residence in Lake County, Michigan." *Journal of Black Studies*, 33, no. 5: 675–703.

Stephens, Ronald J. (2010). "Praise the Lord and Pass the Ammunition: Robert F. Williams' Crusade for Justice on Behalf of 22 million African Americans as a Cuban Exile." *Black Diaspora Review*, 2, no. 1: 14–26.

Umoja, Akinyele (2013). "From One Generation to the Next: Armed Self-Defense, Revolutionary Nationalism, and the Southern Black Freedom Struggle." *Soul: A Critical Journal of Black Politics, Culture, and Society*, 15, no. 3: 218–40.

Wendt, Simon (2007). "They Finally Found Out that We Really Are Men: Violence, Non-Violence and Black Manhood in the Civil Rights Era." *History & Gender*, 19: 543–64.

Williams, Robert F. "Denounces Fidel Castro, Charges Forgery." *Carolinian*, June 17, 1967, FOIAAb3b. Sanitized-Approved for release: CIA-RDP75-00149R000800070010-9.

Dissertations

Dwight, Meyer (2010). "Employing Masculinity as an Agent of Social Change: An Examination of the Writings and Tactics of Robert F. Williams." Dissertation. Kent State University.

Hill, Denise (2016). "Public Relations, Racial Injustice, and the 1958 North Carolina Kissing Case." Dissertation. University of North Carolina, Chapel Hill.

Mares, Richard (2017). "Too Western in My Approach to Tyranny: Black Internationalism and Robert F. Williams' Activist Network in the Cold War, 1950–1976." Dissertation. Michigan State University, East Lansing, MI.

Meyers, Dwight (2010). "Employing Masculinity as an Agent of Social Change: An Examination of the Writings and Tactics of Robert F. Williams." Dissertation. Kent State University.

Printed and Online Newspaper Articles

Bill, William Raymond (1983, July 12). "Letter to the Editor: Must Solve Problem without Violence." *Lake County Star*, 5.

Blackstock, Nelson. (1988). *COINTELPRO: The FBI's Secret War on Political Freedom*, with an introduction by Noam Chomsky. New York: Pathfinder Book.

Blevins, Sheriff (1982, October 7). "Much ado about Nothing: Suit Events never Happened." *Lake County Star*, 4.

Blevins, Sheriff (1983, September 13). "Sheriff Urges 'pro' Citizens to Write." *Lake County Star*, 4.

Blevins, Sheriff (1983, September 27). "Don't Believe All The Trash You Read." *Lake County Star*, 4.

Brogan, Michael (1969, December 3). "Williams Quits as New Africa President." *The Detroit News*, 3, Section A.

Bullett, Audrey K. (2000, January 6). "Robert Williams is a Role Model." *Lake County Star*, 5.

Civil Rights Complaint Settled (1989, April 20). *Lake County Star*, 1.

Burden-Stelly, Charissa (2018, September 13). "Stoolpigeons and Treacherous Terrain of Freedom Fighting." *Black Perspectives*, 1–6.

"Cuba Radio Blasts Miss. Riots in Program Beamed to Dixie." (1962, October 10). *Chicago Defender*, 5.

Day, Ada Mae (1980, May 1). "Letter to the Editor: Water Tower Marks Breed Ill Feelings." *Lake County Star*, 4.

Dechow, George F. (1987, October 19). "The View from the Back Desk." *Lake County Star*, 4.

Duan, Ruodi (2017, March 8). "Black Power in China: Mao's Support for African American 'Racial Struggle as Class Struggle'." https://medium.com/fairbank-center/black-power-in-china-maos-support-for-african-american-racial-struggle-as-class-struggle-767312a66abb

Glazier, Douglas (1969, December 4). "Milton Henry Takes Command of RNA." *The Detroit News*, 15-C.

Gunter, Anthony (2020, March 3). "Rosa Parks and Rob Williams Sparked a Revolution Against Racism—But Has the US Squandered Their Legacy?" *Independent*, 1–10.

Hanson, Joseph (1967, October 2). "Cuban Rally Hails Black Struggle." *The Militant*, 4.

Harkness, Holly (1996, November 18). "Robert F. Williams Memorial Honors Life of Struggle." *The Militant*.

Hawkins, John (1969, December 12). "Detroiters Protest against Moves to Extradite Williams." *The Militant*, 3.

Hawkins, John (1970, February 6). "The Attempt to Extradite Williams." *The Militant*, 11.

Hudson, Frederick B. (2005, November 15). "Miss Rosa Parks and Robert Williams: Rosa's Wealth." https://www.laits.utexas,edu/africa/ads/1339.html

Johnson, Ethel A. (1978, June 8). "Letter to the Editor: Deur Needs Help." *Lake County Star*, 4.

Karasienski, Donna L. (1978, January 5). "Miles Angered by Questioning: Goodman Faces Contempt of Court Charges." *Lake County Star*, 5.

Karasienski, Donna L. (1978, January 5). "Nelson to Appear in Circuit Court: New Information Surfaces in Prelim." *Lake County Star*, 1.

Kelley, Gregory P. (1978). "Justice Over Racism: Lake County Woman Released." *The Lansing Star, Week Ending July 5, 1978*, 1.

Kelsey, Arthur T. (1978, November 23). "Letter to the Editor: Story did Injustice." *Lake County Star*, 4.

Lavan, George (1964, February 24). "Framed-Up Kidnap Trial Opens in Monroe, N.C." *The Militant*, 1–2.

Lavan, George (1965, February 8). "Monroe Kidnap Verdict Upset." *The Militant*, 8.

Leppek, Kyle (1978, October 11). "Photo Documenting Rosa Parks Baldwin Visit Given to BCS." *The Lake County Star*. lakecountystar.com

McCellan, Kelly (1979). "Letter to the Editor: Deputy's Wife Questions Aikens' Letter." Lake County Star, March 22, 5.

McCellan, Mark (1982). "Letter to the Editor: Former Deputy Calls Sheriff's Resignation." *Lake County Star*, September 16, 6.

"Williams Rebuffed in Extradition Bid." (1970, January 30). *New York Times*, 90.

Morley, Jefferson (2018, May 15). "CIA Reveals Name of Former Spy in JFK Files—And He's Still Alive." *Newsweek Magazine*.

Morley, Jefferson (2018, May 17). "What The Curious Case of Richard Gibson Tells Us About Lee Harvey Oswald." *Assassination, News: JFK Facts*, 1–5.

Morrison, Derrick (1969, December 5). "Robert Williams Ordered Extradited." *The Militant*, 12.

Morrison, Derrick (1970, April 24). "N.Y. Black Militants Framed, Chicano Victories in Texas." *The Militant*, 12.

Murray, Colin. (1965, February 15). "The Militant Master-Mind." *The Telegram*, Toronto, 10.

Nakajima, Yoriko (1971, May 25). "Kokujin Sabetsu, Nihon demo Atsui Kabe." *Asahi Journal*.

Nakajima, Yoriko (1971, June 4). "Futatabi Williams no Tameni." *Asahi Journal*.

Nakajima, Yoriko (1971, June 12). "Sabetsu, Hon no Ichibu." *Ashahi Journal*.

Nakajima, Yoriko (1971, June 18). "Jinshu Sabetsu Teppai Undou ni Sanka wo." *Ashahi Shinbun*.

Nakajima, Yoriko (1971, July 4). "Sabetsu e Hirogaru Shimin Undou." *Asahi Shinbun*.

NewsBreak: Target pulls Black History Month book. https://share.newsbreak.com/623j60eo

O'Connor, Mike (1982, May 27). "FBI Investigation Complete Inmate Program Dumped." Lake County Star, 2.

O'Connor, Mike (1982, July 8). "Shooting Victim in Fair Condition." *Lake County Star*, 1.

O'Connor, Mike (1982, July 15). "Scott Arraigned; Sheriff and Court Officials Meet." *Lake County Star*, 1.
O'Connor, Mike (1983, February 23). "Blacks Alleged Police Infringed on Rights." *Big Rapids Pioneer*, 1.
O'Connor, Mike (1983, March 1). "Blacks, Police Make Some Progress." *Lake County Star*, 1.
O'Connor, Mike (1983, July 5). "The Sheriff Asks for Restraint." *Lake County Star*, 1.
O'Connor, Mike (1983, July 12). "Sheriff Says Shooting not Racial." *Lake County Star*, 1.
O'Connor, Mike (1983, July 26). "Prosecutor Says Deputy Justified." *Lake County Star*, 3.
O'Connor, Mike (1983, September 20). "Issues Far from being Resolved." *Lake County Star*, 1.
People's Association for Human Rights (1983, October 4) "Letter to the Editor: Association Calls for Sheriff's Resignation." *Lake County Star, 3*.
Peterson, Curtis (1971, November 1). "Black to Black Day." *The South End*, 1.
Ping, Shirley (1983, September 20) "Letter to the Editor: Disappointed in Sheriff." *Lake County Star*, 6.
Ricke, Tom (1969, December 4). "President of RNA Resigns." *Detroit Free Press*, 15-B.
Ring, Harry (1966, April 18). "The Tricontinental Conference." *The Militant*, 5.
Ring, Harry (1967, 23 January). "Cuba since the Tricontinental Conference." *The Militant*, 10.
"Rosa Parks and Rob Williams Sparked a Revolution against Racism—But has the US. Squandered their Legacy?" (2017, November 29). *The Conversation*. https://theconversation.com/rosaparks-and-rob-williams-sparked-a-revolution-against-racism-but-has-the-us-squandered-their-legacy.
Serrin, William (1969, November 2). "A Meet Revolutionary: The 2 Worlds of Robert Williams." *Detroit Free Press*, 1A, 6A.
Sharp, Eric (1980, May 5). "Baldwin was Irritated by Racial Insults on the Town Water Tank." *Detroit Free Press*, 3B.
Simpich, Bill (2019, July 14). "Fair Play for Cuba and the Cuban Revolution: How American Antiwar and Solidarity Movements in 60s Impeded an Effective Invasion of Cuba." *Socialist Viewpoint*.
Sims, Stanley U. (2000, January 6). "Letter to the Editor: Must Get to Base of Problem Now." *Lake County Star*, 5.
Sitton, Clade (1961, August 29). "Leader of Carolina Pickets Flees Home—Freedom Riders in Monroe Vow to Continue Fight on Segregation." *The New York Times*, L+.
Smith, Denise (1979, March 22). "Deur Ends Silence-responds to Charges." *Lake County Star*, 1.
Smith, Denise (1979, May 17). "Deur Acquitted of Assault Charge." *Lake County Star*, 3.
Smith, Denise (1979, August 9). "Deur Ousted." *Lake County Star*, 1.
Smith, Denise (1979, August 9). "Deur Recalled Vote Aug. 7." *Lake County Star*, 1.
Smith, Denise (1979, October 4). "Blevins Wins Sheriff's Seat." *Lake County Star*, 1.
Smith, Denise (1980, May 8). "Out of Proportion." *Lake County Star*, 4.
Smith, Denise (1980, August 7). "Letter from the Editor." *Lake County Star*, 4.
Smith, Denise (1980, September 11). "Pray for Peace." *Lake County Star*, 4.
Stout, David (1996, October 19). *The New York Times*, 11.
Toles, Irshaad (1982, May 12). "Personal Letter to Robert F. Williams, Jackson, Michigan."
Trucks, Mary L. (1980, May 22). "Letter to the Editor: Reader Says Editorial Out of Proportion." *Lake County Star*, 4.
Waters, Mary Alice (1969, May 30). "PLP Discovers Cuba Is Bourgeois." *The Militant*.
Watkins, Robert L. (2000, January 6). "Letters: Misinformation and Omission." *Lake County Star*, 5.
Weissman, Constance (1963, December 16). "Racist Harassment Drives Negro Victim to Breakdown." *The Militant*, 8.
Williams, Mabel R. (1997, March). "The Story of Robert F. Williams." *Lake County Enterprising Newsletter*, 4.

"Williams Rebuffed in Extradition Bid." (1970, January 30). *The New York Times*, 80.

Williams, Robert F. (1964, June 5). "Mao Interview Historic First." *Muhammad Speaks*, 11–13.

Williams, Robert F. (1970, February 15). "Williams' 8-year Odyssey." *Detroit News*, 1E, 4E.

Williams, Robert F. (1978, June 8). "Letter to the Editor: Williams Questions Rotary's Choice for Award." *Lake County Star*, 4.

Williams, Robert F. (1989, April 20). "Letter to the Editor: Constitution more than Words on Scrap of Paper." *Lake County Star*, 5.

Wittenberg, Henri E. (1972, August 27). "Tokyo Prof Seeks Free Black Activist." *The Detroit Free Press*, 10-B.

"U.S. Negro who fled to Cuba Now Assails Castro from Haven in Peking." (1966, November 14). *The New York Times*, 27.

VandelMeer, Buck (1999, December 2). "Lake County Receives Renaissance Zone Designation." *Lake County Star*, 1: 13.

VandelMeer, Buck (1999, December 23). "Bucky's List of Top Twenty Outrages of the Year." *Lake County Star*, 4.

VandelMeer, Buck (2000, May 4). "Lake County Prepares to Celebrate Robert F. Williams Day." *Lake County Star*, 1.

VandelMeer, Buck (2000, May 11). "Community Turns Out for Dedication of Robert F. Williams Center." *Lake County Star*, 3.

Part IV

Part IV, the appendices, consists of transcripts of interviews with Jeffrey Lee Davenport, Mary L. Trucks, and John Chambers Williams (Robert and Mabel's youngest son). It also includes an anthology of poems written by Williams. The interview with Davenport who first became acquainted with Williams after an event that happened nearly forty years ago when more than a dozen Michigan State Police (MSP) officers, Lake County Sheriff Department (LCSD) deputies, and FBI agents surrounded his residency in Pleasant Plains Township. A police report had been filed by the Birmingham Police Department (BPD) by Davenport's employer regarding a bomb threat he made during a heated telephone conversation with his supervisor. Davenport threatened to blow buildings up in the city of Birmingham after being frustrated as a result of the racist conduct, behavior, and treatment he received from coworkers in the city's maintenance department. The BPD in turn informed the MSP and LCSD to advise them of Davenport's Lake County residence while he was on leave from work. The BPD requested the LCSD to conduct surveillance on Davenport but not to confront or arrest him. More than thirty law enforcement officers representing the three agencies were on the scene and had surrounded his cottage while on the lookout for him. Davenport was not identified or located in the area. Davenport's cottage was searched and officers confiscated two handguns and other firearms from the premises. The interviews with Trucks and John Williams focused on Williams's activism and circumstances surrounding his poetic aspirations, which span over the course of his travels and life in Lake County. Many of the poems need literary analysis. Robeson Taj Frazier illustrates how in "each issue(s) of the *Crusader*, Williams included at least one poem that creatively drew connections between black liberation struggles in the United States and anticolonial movements in Asia, Africa, and Latin America. *An Ocean Roar of Peace* is one such example. In it, Williams articulates a politics of solidarity that proposes that oppressed groups of color become one great voice and speak in unison as they reshape world affairs … , a unified roar that would de-mythicize and demystify the power of the West—their puppeteers—and construct a new world order of peace and international friendship."[1]

Note

1 Robeson Taj P. Frazier, "Thunder in the East," 929.

APPENDICES

POEMS WRITTEN BY ROBERT F. WILLIAMS

Pearly Teeth at the White House, April 1963

Now the darkies came from miles around.
To the white folks' White House to dance and clown
There was dark laughter and frolic in the old staid hall.
As Kennedy went slumming at this White House Ball.
Now Hamp played jazz and sounded blue.
While the House slow-dragged and twisted too,
Oh, what a ball, good times on "Slick John" and Lyndon B.
And comic books entitled, "Freedom for the Free."
Said a racist: "We served the Nigras no brew nor wine.
For fear of brickbats and razors flying—"
Old two-faced Lyndon was full of cheer.
He gloated: "Now ain't y'all glad to be here!"
Oh, how the cats jumped, both black and white
To celebrate emancipation night.
And so, went this glorious night of nights.
Where frolicking fools drank punch in lieu of Civil Rights.
And when the climaxed, this great event.
The darkies tucked their tails and went:
Back to their dark ghetto to dwell
Back to their chains and racist hell.

Birmingham, USA, June 1963

Hear the painful groaning and the tolling of the bells.
The world looks with horror where the great white father dwells,
Hear the sound of jury in the land of the racist knave.
As thug cowards attack babies in the "home of the brave."
Hear the brave songs of babies, martyrs eternally.
The slave tugs against his chins in the "land of the free"
The lion of freedom leaps from the bosom of a lamb
Where violence is the law in racist Birmingham.
See the pious Christian in his God damned racist world,

And the priests who bless a cop who beats a baby girl,
Oh, this I the "land of freedom" where racist Christian's dwell
The Klan will ride again tonight, and God can go to hell!
Like Pontius Pilate, the Christian denies the blame.
He roams his racist jungle devoid of human shame-
Oh, little black girl of courage, weeping child of sorrow
Joy will come to you, for you'll be queen tomorrow.

Black Madonna of Harlem Square, July 1967

Oh, lovely Madonna of Harlem Square
Mournful of the trials and tribulations you bear.
Timeless are the soulful songs you sing.
Through the eternal wintery night where never dawns the spring.
Your life is a confrontation with cupboards bare.
And death is borne like a vapor on the wintery air.
In rat infested tenements where starving babies cry
And the poignant blues becomes an infant's lullaby.
Oh, lovely Madonna dispels the sorrow from your face.
Your sturdy ebony hands can mold a mighty race.
Oh, lovely lady of the ghetto, throw your despair to the wind.
For yours is the charge to raise up a race of mighty men.
What your hands mold is what the race shall be
So, take care of the twig to nurture a mighty tree.
Oh Madonna, forsake the dream of mink and pearls and silk.
In a ghetto dungeon where babies starve for care and milk.
Oh sister of travail seize the fleeting hour
Our fate is in the hand that dares to grasp the power.
Exhort the infant slave to dare to rebel.
And like a mighty Sampson to bring down the roof of hell.
Oh, lovely lady, give us men to do and dare.
A Toussaint from your ghetto dungeon down in Harlem Square.

America the Bruteful, Summer 1969

Oh, how ill-gotten her mighty wealth
From whence she dopes and drinks herself to death—
Frantically she dances to a sordid tune.
Swears and curses that age has flown too soon.
Oh, what a despicable species of the human race
Drunken and lewd with yet a haughty smirk upon her face—
Self-proclaimed saint with Bible in her hand
Oh, thanks to her that God is a mighty man.
Blasphemous woman full of vanity and disgrace

How artful the veil that hides her demonic face—
Scarlet Mother of brutes and spiteful knaves
Who ghoulishly consume the blood of paupers and of slaves.
Oh, how decadent and given to savage rage.
Gaudily painted, drunken and clinging to a moribund age—
Bruteful America painting with death and laughing hysterically.
Cursing the God, she made for his impotence of eternity.

The Hangman

Into our town, the hangman came,
Smelling of gold and blood and flame.
And he paced our bricks with a diffident air,
And built his frame on the courthouse square.
The scaffold stood by the courthouse side,
Only as wide as the door was wide.
A frame as tall, or little more,
Then the capping sill of the courthouse door.
And we wondered, whenever we had the time,
Who the criminal, what the crime.
The Hangman judged with the yellow twist,
Of knotted hemp in his busy fist.
And innocent though we were, with dread,
We passed those eyes of buckshot lead.
Till one cried: Hangman, who is he,
For whom you raise the gallows tree?
Then a twinkle grew in the buckshot eye,
And he gave us a riddle instead of reply.
"He who serves me best," said he,
"Shall earn the rope on the gallows tree."
And he stepped down, and laid his hand,
On a man who came from another land.
And we breathed again, for another's grief,
At the Hangman's hand was our relief.
And the gallows-frame on the courthouse lawn,
By tomorrow's sun would be struck and gone.
So, we gave him way, and no one spoke,
Out of respect for his Hangman's cloak.
The next day's sun looked mildly down,
On roof and street in our quiet town.
And, stark and black in the morning air,
The gallows tree on the courthouse square.
And the Hangman stood at his usual stand,
With the yellow hemp in his busy hand.

With his buckshot eye and his jaw like a pike,
And his air so knowing and businesslike.
And we cried: "Hangman, have you not done,
Yesterday, with the alien one?"
Then we fell silent, and stood amazed:
"Oh, not for him was the gallows raised . . ."
He laughed a laugh as he looked at us:
". . .Did you think I'd gone to all this fuss.
To hang one man? That's a thing I do,
To stretch the rope when the rope is new."
Then one cried "Murderer!" One cried "Shame!"
And into our midst the Hangman came
To that man's place. "Do you hold," said he,
"With him that was meat for the gallows tree?"
And he laid his hand on that one's arm,
And we shrank back in quick alarm.
And we gave him way, and no man spoke,
Out of the fear of his Hangman's cloak.
That night we saw with dread surprise,
The Hangman's scaffold had grown in size.
Fed by the blood beneath the chute,
The gallows tree had taken root.
Now as wide, or a little more,
Then the steps that led to the courthouse door.
As tall as the writing, or nearly as tall,
Halfway up on the courthouse wall.
The third he took - - we had all heard tell –
Was a usurer and infidel,
And: "What," said the Hangman, "Have you to do
With the gallows-bound, and he a Jew?"
And we cried out: "Is this one he
Who has served you well and faithfully?"
The Hangman smiled: "It's a clever scheme.
To try the strength of the gallows-beam."
The fourth was a man of a darker hue.
Then the rest of us, by a shade or two.
And "What concern," he gave us back,
"Have you for the doomed - - the doomed and black?"
The fifth, the sixth, and we cried again:
"Hangman, Hangman, is this the man?"
"It's a trick," he said, "that we hangmen know,
For easing the trap when the trap springs slow."
And so, we ceased, and asked no more,

As the Hangman tallied his bloody score.
And sun by sun, and night by night,
The gallows grew to monstrous height.
The wings of the scaffold opened wide,
Till they covered the square from side to side.
And the monster crossbeam, looking down,
Cast its shadow across the town.
Then through the town the Hangman came,
And called in the empty streets my name –
And I looked at the gallows soaring tall,
And thought: "There is no one left at all.
For hanging, and so he calls to me.
To help pull down the gallows tree."
And I went out with the right good hope.
To the Hangman's tree and the Hangman's rope.
He smiled at me as I came down.
To the courthouse square through the silent town.
And supple and stretched in his busy hand,
Was the yellow twist of the hempen strand.
And he whistled his tune as he tried the trap,
And it sprang down with a ready snap –
and then with a smile of awful command,
He laid his hand upon my hand.
"You tricked me, Hangman!" I shouted then,
"That your scaffold was built for other men . . .
And I no henchman of yours," I cried,
"You lied to me, Hangman, foully lied!"
Then a twinkle grew in the buckshot eye:
"Lied to you? Tricked you?" he said, "Not I.
For I answered straight, and I told you true.
The scaffold was raised for none but you."
"For who has served more faithfully.
Then you with your coward's hope?" said he,
"And where are the others that might have stood.
Side by your side in the common good?"
"Dead," I answered, and amiably,
"Murdered," the Hangman corrected me:
"First the alien, then the Jew . . .
I did no more than you let me do."
Beneath the beam that blocked the sky,
None had stood so alone as I –
And the Hangman strapped me, and no voice there,
Cried "Stay!" for me in the empty square.

Pusher Man, ca. 1970

A pusher man came to our town.
With a bag of death and a phony crown
He spoke of magic and what he could do
Of joy so thrilling and so new
He spoke of flight beyond the earth
With pain unknown and all was mirth.
His was a promise sure to convince.
Of a Heaven on earth with one recompense.
Lo, a bad man come to our town.
And soon down was up and up was down.
"Just a little snort and a happy too"
An angel-elect became a prostitute.
A young boy enrolled in his criminal plan.
And sold his soul to the Devil man.
A bad man came with a crown of death upon his head.
And led a flock where only devil tread.
Behold the plague upon our town.
That fills the cocaine burial ground.
Doom and misery everywhere
As Zombies roam with no love or care
O' the town was cursed with crime and shame.
When goodness fled and the pusher man came.
He spread his bags of powdered gold.
South, he spent five years of his life in exile.
in Cuba, and three years in China. He now resides.
in Michigan, where he is working on assembling the
Robert F. Williams Collection for the U. of Michigan.
And collected life for the product he sold.
A slave master came and brought his auction block.
As he plied his trade in human stock.
Pusher man came from the depths of hell.
Proclaiming joy as his victims fell.
He rode the fast lane in his gaudy style.
As a weeping mother lost her precious child
Legions of vultures laid siege to a hallowed ground.
As spineless elders surrendered our town.
The slave master boldly staking his claim.
With a writ from hell to kill and maim.
Once law and order did abound
Before the pusher man brought evil magic to our town.
Now, very home is a forbidding jail.
Where locks, guns and restraining bars prevail.
O' when will there comes a Minute Man

With a call to arms to liberate our land?
Send the pusher man back to hell.
And build a temple where all his victims fell.

Tomorrow, Past

Once there was love and laughter in the streets
And each soul took in stride triumphs and defeats,
Patient contentment from every face,
Life then did not move at such a savage pace.
Chivalry passed unobstructed through the city gate,
And vogue did not lend itself to malice nor to hate,
There were foul brigades, yes, to be sure,
But contained by great multitudes of the innocent and the pure.
But what brutal curse has befallen this place,
Home to the soulless heart and the enemy face?
Where now is the folksy culture grand?
Of music and laughter that once warmed our land.
Once she wore a golden crown of diamonds on her head,
But now in sadness and longing, she quests for simple bread.
In the wake of squander, the city prays a prayer of need,
While the gods exact their penalty for corruption and for greed.
The land is a jungle and every house a jail,
Where once was love and laughter is now a grizzly hell.
Lost! Lost! The devil's vultures in tone,
Her glory was yesterday and tomorrow has come and gone.

The Freedom Man, 1980

I heard the brazen Yankee boast—
Proposing to himself a toast
Lord, he called himself, of all the universe,
As he bucked his chest and quenched his thirst.
Oh, Yankee drunk and Yankee grand,
Loudly proclaim himself the Freedom Man.
Jingoist flag waver, stars and stripes unfurled,
Self-appointed policeman to all the world.
Yankee brazen in hypocrisy.
Calls himself custodian of democracy. Hater of human flesh that's black
Leader of the free world pack,
Yankee braxen and ridden with hate
Speaks of freedom too little, too late
Yamkee, Yankee, with all his boastful gall,
Too dumb to read the handwriting on the wall.

Re-Run, 1980

Gonna sit right down and write ole Uncle a letter.
Gonna let him know hard times ain't getting' no better.
Food's so high, I can't eat.
You can see hard times walking the streets.
Hey brother, what's the word?
The morning grapevine, I ain't heard.
Hey somebody, what's going down?
Looks like ole Boss Hardtime's back in town.
Want a gig but ain't got a prayer
I'm down on my luck, my wallet's bare—
Tuned in on the tube to get the word
A.B.S. commercial is all I heard.
Got the morning paper, read it through and through
Good time's coming in another year or two.
Brothers' re all groaning, mumbling kinda low—
Streets full of people with no place to go.
Trouble, trouble, troubles on my mind
Don't want no re-run from 1929.
Too many people don't know what to do
Gonna be a hell of a rumble if Uncle don't come through!

A Cross of Cocaine, 1981

Now Mama didn't want me to shoot no crap,
To drop myself out like a soulless sap—
She wanted me to be all nice and sweet
To shun the pitfalls of a dead-end street.
Please don't tell her how I lost my way—
And that I'm just a wretched slave in the devil's den
With a soul consecrated to grief and sin.
Oh, I've got no lover, I've got no home,
Misery is my companion in the allies where I roam.
I'm too weak to get up and go—Too sick to stay.
Panic's brought a price I can't afford to pay.
My weary bones are aching—my soul's up tight.
I'll die a thousand times in the shadows of this night.
A cold world mocks me in my eternal pain.
And I know I'll never be myself again.
Someone called a friend turned me on
Curse the friend though he's dead and gone.
Oh please, don't tell my Momma, my life is vain.
That the pushers have nailed me to a cross of cocaine.

Homeward Journey, 1981

The road is wide and long.
And dark with nights unheard song;
There is an anxiety throbbing in my breast.
And my heart is driven by an ardent quest.
A magnetic force about my feet.
Turns them to my native street,
And I have lost the will to roam.
The road that was never home.

China: The Future Revisited, December 16, 1986

A land as vast and as restless as the sea
Dehumanized, yet daring to dream a future yet to be,
A land with its humanity spread over all the earth.
Motherland of untold wealth yet plagued with painful death.
Plagued with all vicissitudes known to man.
Earthquake, famine, flood and salvation, ever threatening the land-
Coveted, invaded, plundered from every quarter compromised.
Yet dreaming and struggling against every plot devised.
With liberty furiously aflame within her mighty breast,
Rose, in anger, took up the sword to affect her quest.
I saw her young and heavy laden, dauntless in her sorry
With a heart of steel building a bridge to reach tomorrow.
Behold! I saw her then, I see her now
Tall in the sun with her mighty hammer and shining plow.
Broadly smiling and proud, she stretched out her hand to me
In warm and kindly welcome only, a returning friend could see.
Great China, a shining hope and tribute to humanity
China revisited; I saw the future blowing from her face.
Let all the world take notice and cynics pause to see
And awesome giant awakening whose glory is yet to be.

A Spark of Reconciliation, December 1988

Hold fast to hope my fellowman.
In a world disheveled and dark.
Look to a great new dawning.
Behold a flicker of a spark.
Let the rhetoric of hatred be muffled.
With no madness to enflame
O' let there be a new day dawning.
World without greed, no ego to defame.

O' raise a hymn of peace across the world.
And jointly fight the plague of man
Cage the beast of war.
And confer to understand.
A dove of peace wings from the East,
A hopeful tide of circumstance
Let all the world fan the spark.
That peace may have its chance.
Faint, but yet a spark perhaps of reconciliation
East, West, North, South in the Heavens and the sea
Let the trumpets sound in ceaseless peace.
From here to eternity.
Hold fast to hope my fellowman.
Though the world is now a dark and ghastly place
Once before all was dark.
Before the rising sun bore its beaming face.

A Poem of Comfort for Calvin Cunningham: S and L Blues, 1995

Once my heart hung loose and free.
Oh where, of where can good times be?
Hard times bounding over the hill.
Lost the dream I thought I had.
Dreamed a million, a million I spent.
Woke up this morning didn't have a cent.
Made the big times where heavies play.
Woke up a pauper at the break of day.
Can't remember Sally, or was it, Sue.
Hard times was waiting to take its due.
Down on my luck, poor luckless me
Some cat stole a billion and got of
F Scot free.
Aint got a gig, ain't got a cent.
Wish I had what S and L Intendent.
Maybe another dream will come my way.
If hard times will let me make the day.
Hard times will lewt mew make the day.
Hard times bounding over the hill.
Misery can crush—it can kill.

Interview Transcripts with Two Lake County Associates and John C. Williams about RFW

Jeffrey Lee Davenport
Idlewild, MI
August 11, 2014
Approx. 60 minutes
Ronald Stephens=RS
Jeff Davenport=JD

RS: It's Monday, August the 11th, and I'm interviewing Jeff Davenport, longtime Yates Township resident, and we're going to talk about Jeff's experiences in Idlewild, his experiences and encounters with Robert Franklin Williams, who was a resident in Pleasant Plains and very active in the Yates Township and entire, all of Michigan, and Lowell County, Michigan, basically—after Robert William's return to the United States. Now, Jeff Davenport is, in this interview, his willingness to have this interview is of adult age. He'll talk about his age, his experiences, and his agreement to this interview which we will also have a release form signed following the interview. There's no danger or threat to anyone in the interview and if there is any information that may be threatening to Jeff, he has the opportunity to ask that that not be mentioned or documented without his explicit consent for a second time. So, at this point, I'm going to open it up to Jeff, who will give us a little background about himself, his entry into Yates Township, the Idlewild community and his involvement with Robert Williams.

JD: Well, my family-owned property in the Yates Township, Idlewild area, since the early 50s and 60s. I started coming to this area at the age of 10 years old. My father brought me here and wanted me to experience the Idlewild area.

RS: May I ask a question? Did you know the approximate date that your family purchased the property and began coming here? When you were ten years old, what year was that?

JD: When I was ten years old ... now you gotta make me do some math.

RS: Well, how old are you now?

JD: I'm 51 years old now, so it would have been 31 years ago.

RS: Thirty-one years from 2014.

JD: Now hold on, is that 31? No, it's been longer. I would have been 10, it would have been 41 years.

RS: 41?

JD: Yes.

RS: So, it would have been approximately in the early 70s.

RS: Yep.

RS: Okay.

JD: That's a rough guess, but so, at that point, I was coming here every summer and spending the summers here. Several years grew up here during the summer, went home, went back to school.

RS: Where did you go back to school at?

JD: Well, I was going to school at, at that time, I was in, I think, the eighth grade so it was probably Kennedy Junior High School.
RS: Where, in Pontiac?
JD: Yeah, in Pontiac, Michigan. That's where I grew up, predominately. And you know we spent our summers here. My young adult years, drinking age years, you know we did a lot of that back in the day when we turned 21.
RS: That would have been in the 80s?
JD: Yes, that would have been in the late 80s. And then I became employed with the city of Birmingham in the Department of Public Works, and that's basically where my story with Robert Williams begins because I was going through a lawsuit with the city of Birmingham. And that year I was young, distracted, and they were doing things to me in the lawsuit that I felt was unfair. So, some threats were made, law enforcement got involved, and essentially …
RS: For the sake of clarity, what kind of things were they doing that you felt was unfair, unjust?
JD: They were threatening me, trying to force me into dropping my lawsuit through threats and things of that nature.
RS: Okay, so it was about your employment?
JD: About the lawsuit. It was discrimination lawsuit, I was the first Black, well actually the second black to be hired with the city of Birmingham. The first Black didn't get his 90 days in, they terminated him on his 89th day. But fortunately, I worked for them as a temp for three years prior to getting the position. And then I worked with them ten years, and over ten years I was discriminated against, you know racially discriminated against, which led up to some issues I had with, mental issues, depression, things of that nature. And I started seeing a doctor who was, he had two PhDs. He was, he had just finished his second PhD in forensic psychology, so I was a case study.
RS: What was his name?
JD: Dr. John Paul Jones.
RS: And he had finished his second PhD or both PhDs form what school?
JD: I don't know where he went to school, but anyway, he was my doctor for several years and anyway, I was getting heavily depressed behind the lawsuit, you know, and I was under doctor's care extensively, through the lawsuit and after the lawsuit. But anyway, some threats were made to me, I made some threats back to them, and essentially, they called in law enforcement.
RS: What kind of threats, can I ask, did you make to them?
JD: Well, they made death threats to me, and I made death threats back to them.
RS: Okay. What kind of threats if you don't mind sharing?
JD: What do you mean?
RS: Like, what did you say? "I'll blow your house up"? Or …
JD: Basically, that's exactly what I told them. I told them I'd blow the damn building up, and them with it, all of them in it. Basically, at this time, so—But I never made that threat directly to them. I spoke to my doctor, and my doctor then released that information based upon his experience with handling patients on that level.
RS: Got it.

JD: So, he released that information to them, I came back home. When I got back—
RS: What year was this?
JD: Oh, I don't—'92 maybe? I think, '92, '93, around in that year. I'm not for sure, it's been quite a few years. Memories that I often think, and rethink: Well, how could I have done it a little differently? But it was what it was at that time.
RS: Okay.
JD: So, I had threatened to blow them up, basically, is what I said to the doctor: I'd blow their asses up. And he repeated that to law enforcement. At that time, I had been living downstate, and then I chose to move up north because I felt it was a lot safer for me. You know, living up north in the area that I knew, that I knew those individuals down there threatening me didn't know, so I felt more comfortable living here. So, it took the police quite a long time—
RS: And when you say living here, you mean …
JD: Idlewild, yes.
RS: Okay.
JD: I moved back to this area and found a safe haven basically. It was my safe haven. I knew every time I went down to you know, the Detroit, Bloomfield area to see my doctor, I was at risk. So, I knew that once I was in Idlewild, you know, it's a small community and everybody knows everybody, so a stranger in town is a stranger in town.
RS: Right.
JD: So, it was very conducive for me to stay here. So, once they found out where I was living, then they made the report of the threat to my employer and my doctor. Then they felt as though I had reached a state of mind that I could carry out such attacks.
RS: And when you say, your employer, you mean the city of Birmingham?
JD: Yes, that was my employer.
RS: OKAY
JD: And they thought at that point, that I could carry out a threat because my mental status had gotten to that point.
RS: Okay. So, what was your position working for the city of Birmingham?
JD: I worked in the Sewer and Water Department.
RS: Okay, all right.
JD: I was an equipment operator, which is the next level up—No, I'm sorry, I was a pipe-tapper. I was at the third level.
RS: Got it.
JD: And their whole take on the thing with me being there: I was hired at such a young age, that I had the potential to work there 45, 50 years. And there was another guy who got hired as a young adult that I would always make the statement; I'm going to be here longer than you. So anyway, I went through a lot of discrimination, being called racial slurs like "Nigger," "Nigger for the day," things of that nature, on a consistent basis. And of course, over the years, it wore down on me. And I started seeing the doctor and I was seeing him while I was still working, and then it got to the point that they had to remove me from the job, because my mental status had dilapidated considerably. So, at that point, you know, I was still living down there but, you know, the threats were coming in a little bit heavier, things was happening to me, and I felt it necessary that I needed to go someplace where I could be safe.

RS: So, you relocated to Idlewild?

JD: I basically I relocated to Idlewild. Once I got to Idlewild, I lived very low key, but I was still seeing the doctor, still experiencing threats of that nature, and finally I made a big threat. Once I made the really big threat, that's when the state police became involved and very concerned.

RS: Okay, so when you were living here in—where were the threats, I mean they knew where you lived at this point?

JD: No, they didn't know where I lived. You know, I would receive mail, phone calls, things of that nature.

RS: And the mail would be forwarded?

JD: No, I would pick it up when I went down there.

RS: Okay, got it.

JD: I didn't, no one knew that I was living here. No one. Okay, this was my safe haven. No one knew where I was living. I didn't want anyone to know where I was living. The immediate family didn't know where I was living because they could accidentally or inadvertently tell someone where I was living and then it would no longer be a safe haven.

RS: Right.

JD: So, I basically—I basically just stayed here, and then went down there and saw my doctor once a week.

RS: Right.

JD: And then finally, like I said, I made the threat, and state police located me.

RS: And the threat was in the company of your doctor?

JD: Yes.

RS: Got it.

JD: So, the state police located—first of all, the detective that was assigned to the case wrote out the warrant, the search warrant to come up here and search my cabin where I was living. At this time the Unabomber was blowing up, you know, sending bombs through the mail and basically, we were profiled the same. I lived in a one-room cabin with no running water and no electricity. He lived in a one-room cabin with no running water, no electricity. He read books, but I didn't read the type of books he read, you know what I mean? But still we were profiled the same, so. The detective wrote out a search warrant, and this was told to me by Detective Sergeant Pratt of the Michigan State Police.

RS: Formerly—he's retired now?

JD: Yes, he's retired now. But he told me that the profile that they put on me when the state police raided my house, if I had been there, they probably would have killed me. Okay? That's what he told me. And he said that in front of another state police officer. Anyway, they had, I counted myself: 17 state police cars, 2 tactical units, and the bomb squad, okay? There were four snipers, you know, but when they served the warrant on the house, I wasn't there, okay. I was not there. Fortunately, I was not there. So, at that point, going back to the beginning, I was driving around the lake, and this gentleman told me, "Hey, man you got 1,000 police at your house, they're getting ready to kill your dog." His name was Mike Leetman, and you know, Mike used to drink a lot.

RS: Was he related to the Leetman's?

JD: Yes, yes, he was.

RS: The storeowners? Near the island?

JD: Yes, yes, he was one of the original family members. Okay, he told me, so then I'm driving around the lake, and I see Deedee Carter, they call her "Ms. Baywatch." She knows everything about everybody in Idlewild. She stopped and she told me, her exact words were, "I don't know what you did, but you got 100 police at your house."

RS: So, this is roughly 1990 …

JD: '1994, '95?

RS: 1995.

JD: 1996, in that area.

RS: Couldn't have been '96, that's the year Robert Williams died. So, it was probably '94 or '95. But we'll verify the date when this all happened.

JD: Yeah, you can get a copy of the police report. You would have to get it from the state police.

RS: I know how to do that.

JD: You would have to get a copy from the state police, um, to find out the dates. I mean any information that's in the report, share it with me, I'd like to see it.

RS: Okay, keep talking.

JD: So, I headed back to the house. And uh, as I was driving down Baldwin Road, I noticed that there was caution tape, multiple state police vehicles all over the place, uniformed state police officers everywhere, and basically, I pulled up, and they had already finished searching my house. They took all the weapons I had in there, which I had a considerable amount of hunting weapons and handguns, because I hunt and fish and all those kinds of things. So, they took all my weapons and shortly after that, because they couldn't find any evidence of explosives, they couldn't take me into custody. The only thing they could do is take my weapons, which they did.

RS: Okay.

JD: That they found, I should say. Anyway, after that incident because it was a big, big incident because they had the roads cornered off, there were police everywhere. I believe that was the largest influx of state police officers that the county has ever seen. And so, after they all left, you know, probably a half an hour after they all left, I was inside my apartment, thinking, what the, you know, I

RS: Your apartment or your cabin?

JD: Well, you know my little cabin. I called it an apartment, but it was a little cabin. And Robert Williams knocked on the door.

RS: Oh. Can I ask where your cabin was located?

JD: On Baldwin Road.

RS: Baldwin and Forman Road?

JD: Yeah.

RS: In which direction? Directly across from Road Runners?

JD: No, it was kitty-corner, it would have been the Southwest corner of Baldwin and Forman.

RS: Got it.

JD: So, he knocked on the door and he introduced himself, said his name was Doc, you know. No, wait a minute, what did he say his name was? Hold on.

RS Doc Blue?

JD: Yeah, that's what he said. His name was Doc Blue. And he was in a burgundy Cadillac. And he basically asked me, what was going on? And then he shared some things with me about who he was, and he might have thought that it was something related to him or something, and I just basically told him—

RS: So, so when you say he told you who he was, what did he tell you?

JD: He said his name was Doc Blue.

RS: Doc Blue, that's his name, but what did he tell you to make you—you said that he thought that it had perhaps to do with him. What did he tell you about himself?

JD: Well, he didn't go into any explanation, or extensive detail about himself at that time. You know, he was just more concerned about what, what had transpired, and what was I involved in to have that amount of law enforcement cornered off and executing such a large scale of law enforcement on one person.

RS: Okay, and so, as best as you can recall, what exactly did he say?

JD: He said, "My name is Doc Blue," and he said, "Man, I'd just like to know what's going on with you and what happened." And I told him I had some discrimination issues, some threats were made, and that you know, the police took my threats real serious and came to see me. And then he told me that you know, he wanted to make sure that it wasn't like a ploy to get close to him, and something else, I can't remember exactly; I wasn't really paying attention at that time, because you know, I had just gone through this horrific, you know, interview with the state police, you know, they were questioning me about bombs—

RS: Okay, so, basically, he thought maybe there was a connection, that maybe you had been an agent or something and this was just a plot so that you all would get closer. He suggested that.

JD: In time, after, you know, a few days, you know, he would stop back by, and he would talk to me further. You know, this was the first time I ever met this man, this is the first time this man has ever met me.

RS: Right.

JD: You know, so I didn't know he was, and he didn't know who I was. I didn't know what he was capable of, he didn't know what I was capable of. We didn't know each other.

RS: All he knew was that there were a lot of police.

JD: All he knew was that it was an exorbitant amount of state police officers that had the whole neighborhood blocked off in all four directions, and uh, he lived right around the corner, you know?

RS: Okay, got it.

JD: He could see, not directly into my cabin, because there was a house there blocking it, but he you know, I could walk out my front door, and step a couple feet east and I could see his house. So …

RS: And his house is on Esther Road.

JD: Right. So, at that time, he might have thought they were coming for him the way they came down there.
RS: Right. Because he could obviously see from his house the flashing.
JD: Well, they weren't flashing. They didn't have to flash, there were a lot of them.
RS: Okay, but he could see them you know, pulling up and all that.
JD: Oh yeah. I wasn't there when they came.
RS: Right, but you can imagine, given the proximity between his place and yours, at that time, and the streets, the way the roads are—
JD: And where the law enforcement cars were parked.
RS: Right.
JD: And where the tactical units were parked. I mean, there were 17 patrol cars. Two tactical units and a bomb disposal unit, okay, so it was a lot. So, you look at it, and it was one person per car, and then I think there was something there from the ATF—Alcohol, Tobacco and Firearms—I think there was someone there representing the FBI, you know, and of course there were only two people from the Lake County sheriff's department. The sheriff and the undersheriff because the state police did not want the county involved. Period. But I was told that the sheriff, they thought I was in the house because I had my dog where he could come around to the front door and he could come close enough to the front door, where it would look like if he went to the front door he could bite you, but he couldn't, you know, but it looked like he could. And they wanted in, they wanted in bad, so they were talking about killing the dog. And the sheriff said, "No, we better not do that." You know, if they had killed the dog, it would have escalated what was a minor situation into an explosion.
RS: Right.
JD: Okay, you know, you just don't go and start killing people's animals, especially, that was the only friend I had at the time.
RS: So, this invasion of your space comes in your absence but everybody, major people in the community are telling you what's going on, and you encounter Robert Williams for the first time, but there were several times after, next few days, later, he came by again.
JD: Right, and he just came by, basically at that time, I was still new in the community, and I had locks. You know, and the locks were down past my waist. So, they automatically thought I was scary or whatever, I don't know what they thought.
RS: Do you have any pictures of your locks? I remember when I first met you, you had locks. This is around the same time.
JD: It was after.
RS: But I meant, kind of, it was in the 90s.
JD: Yeah, you, I met you a couple years after that.
RS: Right. Okay, so just a side note, if you have any pictures of how you looked with the locks, that would be …
JD: Yeah, I'd have to find them.
RS: Okay, so continue your story and your relationship with Robert Williams.
JD: So, he, you know basically after our first initial conversation, he stated to me that, "You know, hey man, I'd like to come back by and talk to you every now and then." I

was like, "You know, hey, no problem." But I didn't know who he was, I didn't really learn about him and his past until after he had passed away.

RS: Okay.

JD: So, our relationship, we developed—he was the only person in the whole community that would come even to talk to me after that incident. I was like the plague. Which I didn't care because I didn't want to be bothered by anybody.

RS: Right.

JD: But he was the only person that would come around and talk to me. And he would mostly talk about what had happened and you know, he did mention that um, he had issues with law enforcement and things of that nature, but he never told me that he was a militant, or you know, a person who was you know, straight Black Power type thing.

RS: So, he came off as, what? Like a concerned citizen in the community?

JD: He came off, to me, as seeing a young brother in a situation that he might have needed some guidance—because I was all alone. I truly was. And he just came, and he would talk to me about, you know, different things, but he never really got into his personal, you know.

RS: He didn't try to influence you based on his personal—

JD: No, he didn't influence me about anything. I was un-influenceable at that time.

RS: Right.

JD: He basically was just telling me about, you know, how he was kind of worried that that was a ploy to get closer to him and then you know, I told him what had happened, I ran my story down, and he did more listening than he did talking, really.

RS: So now, in a situation like that, would you say, would you stretch it and say, because there were times when he was characterized by law enforcement as being paranoid—

JD: Right.

RS: —Would you say that he behaved like he was paranoid, schizophrenia? Or would you say he was—he was basically concerned, but still willing to engage you out of concern for your welfare?

JD: Right, he came by with the intent to find out why all of those state police cars were there, all those tactical units, and the bomb disposal unit. Obviously when he saw that kind of activity, he recognized that I was somebody and he wanted to find out who I was. Because, at that time, you-you wouldn't have seen that magnitude of law enforcement for one person.

RS: Okay.

JD: When I say it was a lot, it was a lot.

RS: And especially in a small community.

JD: Right, in a small community. Everybody in the whole community knew something was going on because they had the roads blocked in four different directions. You couldn't come and you couldn't go—they had to go all the way around.

RS: Well, let me ask you another question. Were there any newspaper articles in the Lake County Star or anything about this??

JD: No. There was uh, everything to do with the lawsuit and the activities that transpired during and after were, they were under disclosure, so um, that's the reason why I don't want to get too deep into the lawsuit because there is still a disclosure.

RS: Got it. Right.

JD: But I can tell you about my experience with Robert Williams, which is not covered under this disclosure.

RS: Right.

JD: But he mostly wanted to know what I was doing, and how I was doing, and you know. His general concern was about him. After he found out that this was all about me, and not involving him, then he was just basically concerned about my general welfare and how I had handled and conducted myself.

[RS takes quick phone call, "Hi, I'm here, but I'm conducting an interview. Talk to you later."]

JD: Now, so, his, he was more concerned about, you know, what had happened to me, and how I was feeling. You know? And basically, he would talk to me, you know, about different things, about actions and reactions that I was having, you know. So—

RS: He was trying to be an elder.

JD: Right. And he was trying to make sure that whatever happened, I had a past. Because when you have that magnitude of law enforcement to get one person, and all the police leave, and that one person is still standing there, obviously, there was something—

RS: Right, but at the same time, he was also, he was, somewhere in the mix, it seems, that he was concerned as an elder and wanted to make sure that you were going to be safe through this.

JD: Sure, well, after the fact, he was more concerned about what I was doing and how I was reacting, but you know, like I said, all this happened before I met him. If they hadn't come the way they came, we probably would have never met.

RS: Right.

JD: So, but his general attitude was more concerned about my personal well-being, because, like I said the magnitude of law enforcement—they just fluctuated in, you know. That's why I can explain it. All our conversations from thereafter were just in, in consulting. I don't know if you want to call it mentoring, because at that time, I wasn't looking for a mentor, I was looking for a way to get even, you know what I'm saying?

RS: Right.

JD: So, he basically curbed my attitude towards the power of the pen, you know what I'm saying, versus violent acts.

RS: Right.

JD: You know, so a lot of things that he said to me caused me to go back and…

RS: Reevaluate.

JD: Well, re-evaluate, but more to start to document and get involved and pay attention and not act on impulse, you know. "Know your enemy better than you know yourself, because he is your enemy."

RS: Right.

JD: So, I had to go back and reevaluate and that's when I started to study my enemy and began to use the same tactics that they used against me, I used against them.

RS: So rather than him being your mentor, he was acting in a mentoring way.

JD: Right, he was acting in a mentoring way, but like I said, he was the only person that was truly concerned about my personal well-being at that point in time.
RS: Now can you give an example of how he helped to curb your attitude, get you to reassess something. Document, like, a specific example?
JD: Um, well we talked about a lot of stuff, I mean …
RS: Anything that you're at privilege to say.
JD: I'm trying to remember, it was quite a long time ago.
RS: If it comes back to you, you can just add it in.
JD: Right, but we mostly just talked about you know not acting on impulse, you know, things like that, you know, things that, you know, he wasn't recruiting me or anything like that.
RS: He was looking out like a big brother, big sister.
JD: Yeah, he was definitely looking out because—
RS: Was he like a big brother?
JD: Well, he was a tall man.
RS: I know he was taller than you, but—
JD: Not really, because he didn't come across to me as a big brother. He came across as a concerned man that was concerned about his neighbor and his neighbor's activity.
RS: Okay.
JD: You don't see bomb disposal units in Idlewild, Michigan. You don't see ATF units in Idlewild, Michigan. and like I said, the overabundance of law enforcement that was there was a concern of his. And he was the only person you know, like I said, I didn't know who he was at the time. So …
RS: So, tell me, I suppose now, the question is, about your impressions of Robert Williams as you reflect back on this individual, who is concerned when these things have happened, and you don't really know his past. And then you learned about him after his passing away. What impressions now, as you reflect back, about him?
JD: I utilized a lot of things that he showed me and talked to me about in the way I live today. You know, know your enemy. Well in order for me to know my enemy, I have to be around my enemy. So, you know, I was involved in the fire department. I got heavily involved in local government.
RS: And when you say involved in the fire department and heavily involved in local government, what do you mean by that?
JD: Um, I became a fireman, I went back to school and got every certification available to a firefighter.
RS: And how long were you a firefighter?
JD: Um, I was terminated in 1998.
RS: Okay.
JD: Because, I was, they said I was trying to make the fire department a big city fire department.
RS: Now the termination happened under Norman Burns?
JD: Yes, Norman Burns.
RS: His second term, or? That would have been, '98 would have been his second term.
JD: Yeah, well he terminated me.

RS: When did your employment with the fire department begin?

JD: Right when I first moved back up here in '92.

RS: Okay, so you worked with the fire department approximately six, seven years.

JD: Right, before I was terminated. Yep. And basically, at that point, I refused to allow someone to tell me differently, you know. If it's written in the book, and the book says this is the law, this is the way it's supposed to be done.

RS: The problem was with the township government and also the fire department.

JD: Right, well this was, this was when I was studying, and these are some of the things that he had instilled, like know your enemy, you know what I mean?

RS: Right.

JD: Well, if I'm going to do this, I'm going to go all the way. Basically, if you go do something, go all the way. Don't stop, don't go two steps when you got eight more to go and it's just right there. Continue to follow it. And you know, that's just what I did. And to this day I'm considered a rebel in the community, very boisterous, very outspoken, about all types of issues.

RS: And is that because you are doing radical or rebellious things, or that you are an active resident in the community, and you speak up based on your reading of the law?

JD: I speak up based upon fact, okay. I don't hearsay. When I take it to them, I take facts to them. Because if you take hearsay, it doesn't mean anything. But when you drive the facts right down their throats they have to respond. And those are some of the things that he talked about with me, you know, being able to get in there and make a point. Not all your points that you have to make have to be violent points, but when you become a strong, boisterous black man, in a predominately ran white community, now they would call you a racist, they want to call you radical, okay? Now, I'm a radical, but he's not a racist, but in fact, all the damage that has been done to me has been done to me by white people. I'm not a racist, I'm a radical, but if a white man continuously tries to enslave me, or empower me, and I stand up for my own rights—

RS: Oppress you, oppress you.

JD: Yeah, oppress me. And I stand up for my own rights, then they will put me on the level as Robert Williams was.

RS: Right. Troublemaker.

JD: Yeah, troublemaker, black eye to the community. And all we're doing was we [were] standing up for what we believe in.

RS: Right.

JD: You know, I'm only three generations—two generations away from slavery. I can still feel the whips on my back, even though I was never hit with a whip. I can still feel it, and I can still see the racism and I feel the racism. And these are some of the things that he touched on lightly, but he didn't force anything upon me, you know what I mean.

RS: Right.

JD: It was just guidance.

RS: Right.

JD: You know, at that point, I needed guidance, but I wasn't, I didn't know him. And you know, you don't open up to a person that you don't know the first time you meet.

RS: Right.

JD: So, he had to gain my trust, and I had to gain his trust.

RS: Right.

JD: And then, shortly after that, I mean, I don't know what happened to him you know what I mean? He just stopped coming around. Next thing I know, he was sick and passed away, you know. And then years later, sounds like FiveCAP named a building after him, okay.

RS: Right.

JD: And that point I still didn't know who he was, okay? And then I met Mabel Williams.

RS: Right.

JD: Mabel Williams was always very soft-spoken and very calm, always listened to what I said.

RS: This is his wife.

JD: At that point, I did not know that was his wife. Okay. I didn't know any of this, but that's what, you know, she would always talk to me, and you know, always, even when I would be wired up she would always talk to me in a calm, very smooth way. And you know, after becoming more involved in the community, I started to learn a little bit more about Mabel Williams and then I learned a little bit more about Robert Williams. Not associating husband and wife, okay, because I met him independently and I met her independently, but I never knew that they were husband and wife.

RS: Right.

JD: I didn't know that until several, several years later. I knew they were husband and wife when they made the dedication of the FiveCAP building in his name. That's when I found out they were married. And pretty much at that point, I had another friend who would talk about him and would tell me what he did and the things that he did, you know, and that's how I learned more about him. And I was outdone because I'm like, "WOW," you know what I mean? Two birds of a feather flock together, you know what I mean?

RS: Right.

JD: So, it was meant for me to pass the knowledge on. But, after learning about his background, you know, I still to this day say that he was a very strong black man, and he was very heavily involved into black civil rights. And as far as violence and things of that nature, I never saw that. I saw a well-educated black man and I almost want to say he was self-educated in what he did, because the type of things that he was saying were things that you can't get out of a book, you know what I mean? These are things that the human eyes and the ears and the mouth, you sense it. These are things that you gathered from being there and seeing it.

RS: Right. Experience.

JD: The experience. Just like I went through a racial discrimination lawsuit. I experienced racism like no other. I can imagine what he experienced in his age. But I wish I could have got to know him a little bit more, but I think in our short time that we got to talk, I was given a message and a task, you know? My task wasn't to follow his path, but it was to follow my own path. And he just basically set, you know, set the tone of, you know, how radical is radical? I'm not radical. I'm just saying what I want to say, when I want to say it. You're saying I'm radical. So, that was the take that the community put

on him. And it wasn't the black community, it was always the white community. As me right now, they consider me right now to be an inspired nigger and they're scared of me. Why? Because I read books, okay, I pay attention, I make sure when people say things to me that I write it down, so I can revisit it again when I decide to question them why they made that statement, or why they did that. So, our paths were quite a bit different, but we still lived in a slave mentality community. The white people think that the blacks are still beneath them. And Robert exposed that on a local level, and they didn't like it.
RS: And some of the other examples, I mean, you were around when the ruby nelson situation happened, right?
JD: I might have been around, but I'm not familiar with that.
RS: Okay, and you were around when—were you around when he staged a protest down at the Lake County Star?
JD: I don't recall.
RS: Okay.
JD: At that time frame, I was very much alone. I didn't trust anybody, okay. If you had knocked on my door, I would ask you what you want. And you would have stated what you wanted, and I would have said, "I'm not interested," and closed the door. And I would have let the dog out, because he could come all the way around to the front door. Then you would have left. I wasn't interested in trying to meet anybody, I wasn't interested in trying to meet newspapers. I was trying to get my head on straight enough to focus on this upcoming lawsuit trial, because I was very messed up, you know, I had some, I was diagnosed as homicidal and then the doctors threw a suicide on that. I didn't feel as though I was suicidal, but I was definitely homicidal.
RS: Right. Would you say this was a reaction to the treatment you had.
JD: Yeah, it was a reaction. When I was explaining to him how I felt about the white man at that time, that's when he, like I said, he revisited, or we'll revisit that conversation where he went back to know your enemy. Okay, to learn your enemy don't act upon impulse, okay, you don't have to be violent to get your point across. But protect your own ass. And that was his—that was my take on what he was saying to me. But he never once ever to me said to me he was a militant, he was black power or anything like that. His general concern was my general welfare and how I was going to act. Basically, we lived in the same neighborhood and it's like, if you got a neighbor that can draw that kind of law enforcement and you have a background such as his, he would rather be my friend than to be my enemy. And we lived in the same neighborhood.
RS: Or ignore you.
JD: Right, yeah, at that time frame, in his situation and his past, he could not ignore that situation. It was too powerful. It was, it's hard, it's hard to explain, you know what I mean? It's hard to explain. But I do understand how it was a general concern. Just like your neighborhood, you gotta protect your neighborhood. A new guy moves in there, been there three or four months, suddenly, you have an exorbitant amount of law enforcement. What's going on with that brother?
RS: Right.
JD: Let's go over here and let's meet him, let's see where he is, who he is. I wouldn't do it, you know what I mean, because my thing is I'm not nosy. But I see why he did it.

RS: Okay, so I'm going to ask you two questions, and that is, are there any closing remarks that you have about him? But also, the question I have is about anything you said that you think is a threat, threatening or dangerous, or you don't feel comfortable. Or have I forced you to say anything you don't want to say? So, could you talk about those things?

JD: I feel comfortable talking to you. I don't know you as, like, you know. I have met you on several occasions. I understand that you, yourself want to do another project, and I agree 100% to share my experience about Robert Williams with you. Even though we didn't get an opportunity to spend a lot of time together, and as they say, tear up some shit, but I did get an opportunity to meet the man and he did instill a lot of values and morals into my situation. And, when I look back, a lot of his influence made me who I am today, as far as a person of color that took the lead and to go from where I was to where I am today. Because most people who have that kind of experience with the Michigan state police don't make it to the Michigan state police homeland security division as an instructor.

RS: Which is what you did?

JD: Which is what I did. And to go and be teaching curriculums and running into law enforcement officers that kicked in my door, and now, I'm standing before them as an instructor. So going back to learning your enemy.

RS: Well—

JD: Over the years I found out they weren't really my enemies; they were just doing their job.

RS: Right.

JD: So, I took all that information that I gained, and I took it to a different level. As a matter of fact, today is August the 11th, 2014. I officially, officially renounced my certifications. I had the opportunity to recertify but I have tried so hard in this community to utilize my credentialing and my experience to help them, and they treat me like I'm a rebel.

RS: And when you say your certification, what do you mean?

JD: Well, I was certified to teach incident management. And every so often you must recertify your credentials. And what I did was choose not to recertify my credentials.

RS: Got it.

JD: And by me not recertifying my credentials, I that means I am giving up my status to teach the program with the Michigan state police through the Homeland Security Division.

RS: Got it.

JD: But I can revisit it if I choose. But as long as I don't have the current certification, they can't call me to come and teach a class.

RS: Got it. So, is there anything else you want to say?

JD: No, It's just that I like to revisit one important thing: I never ever heard him say he was a militant or a racist or you know, I never heard him mention anything like that to me. And I can't say that he was, or he wasn't, but I can say that what I learned from him in that short experience helped me to be where I am today.

RS: Thank you very much. This was a wonderful interview, and I'm glad you were able to give me the time to share this information with me about your experiences with Robert Williams. Thank you very much.
JD: You're welcome.

Mary Trucks
Idlewild, MI
August 14, 2014
Approx. 135 minutes

RS: …Executive director of FiveCAP Incorporated, and the conversation is about Mary L. Trucks' interactions, relations, and observations of Robert Williams, prior to his arrival, to Lake County. But also, her observations and experiences with him, while living in Lake County.
MT: From the beginning to the end?
RS: Yes, from the beginning to the end.
MT: We've been talking a long time about my impressions of Rob's personality and how he interacted with people. I did not know Robert and Mabel Williams before they moved to Lake County. Of course, I knew who he was, and I admired his courage. Rob gave the impression of a humble, patient man. He would listen and let people speak their minds. He took it all in and asked questions to draw out more information. And if he did not agree with their position, Rob had a way of moving his head up and down, and then he would say, "Well, we'll see about that." Once, the Editor of the Lake County Star refused to print a letter Rob wrote. He did not agree with Rob's statements. Rob offered to pay but the Editor still refused to print it until Rob marched in front of the newspaper and threatened to sue. He was very knowledgeable about the laws and matters of the constitution. Clearly the local establishment felt the pressure of his presence. He knew how to bring a spotlight on behaviors that shouldn't be occurring. The average person in the community, especially a black person, did not command the attention that Robert Williams did, he made them nervous. I have witnessed the authorities treat him with such disrespect that I was uncomfortable. One time in a meeting, Rob would ask a question and the person would answer but address it to me, as if Rob was not in the room. This did not seem to faze him at all. He always made sure that he accomplished what he went there to do. If he was there to deliver a message, the message was delivered. If we were there to get information, he got that information. Never did I see Rob respond to that kind of behavior. And I saw people who felt threatened by him more than once respond negatively toward him. I think Rob understood his effect on them and their behavior.
RS: Just so that we get context, in what context did you know Rob Williams, before we turn the table on him? Explain what you knew about him before his arrival to Lake County, where you were living and working. So what's the context of you knowing him?
MT: I first knew who Robert F. Williams was from the media. I was a teenager in high school in Detroit. The Republic of New Africa and Robert were in the news because they were a target of the Detroit Police Department. Some of their members were killed

in the New Bethel Church where they were holding a meeting. This was the church of Reverend Franklin, Aretha Franklin's father. Rob was in exile at the time, but his statements made the news. I knew that he was a person who stood up for human rights and justice at a time when it was not easy to stand up. And as a young person, I connected with his words and his actions more than I connected with the non-violence approach. Being from the Mississippi Delta, I never saw a black adult fight back, including my parents. No one could give me an answer to why we had to be lynched, why we had to run home when the white man pushed my brother off the sidewalk because he didn't step off the sidewalk, why we did not have the right to speak up for ourselves. So, when I learned of Rob, he and Malcolm X were my heroes.

RS: Right, so having this information, this background, before meeting him, and you talked about people that you knew, close friends or relatives who informed you about the arrival of his wife in the area, or the desire to move here. You were telling me some things about when you first laid eyes on him, this person that you knew something about already.

MT: I knew who Robert Williams was because he was willing to take a stand and fight to protect his family and community. Ethel Johnson, FiveCAP Board member, was a close family friend of the Williams from North Carolina. She was very active with Rob in his work in Monroe, North Carolina. And when the family went into exile, Ethel was part of the local group that turned Rob and Mabel's home into a community center. Ethel retired and moved to Idlewild in Michigan to be near her sister. She was very involved in community affairs and joined the FiveCAP board. This is when I met Ethel. Rob and Mabel returned to the United States. They lived in Detroit and Ann Arbor before settling in Lake County. Although I had seen Rob and Mabel at functions in the community, we were never formally introduced until she went to work for the MSU Extension. The Lake County MSU Extension Director brought Mabel to my Office in the Webber Township Hall and introduced me. Soon, I was working on community issues with Robert and Mabel.

When Nettie Kato, the director of the Lake County Extension Office, introduced Mabel, we talked for about six hours. She told me her story. We talked about the need to work for change, and my frustration and impatience. She told me a story that day. It was a Chinese proverb about a man who was trying to grow a garden, but his house sat near sort of a mountain. And the mountain was so high that for most of the year, it blocked the sun from his house. One day, he got the idea that he would go and move the mountain. So, he took a pail and a shovel, and he went up and day after day, year after year, he went up there and he shoveled and he shoveled. This caught the eye of the village people, and they were very curious about what he was doing. And one day, a villager, he said, "I'm going to go up and see." He went up and stood and watched the man for a long time, and saw all the man was doing was digging, filling the pail, walking to the edge, and dumping it over. He repeated this over and over. So, after observing, the villager asked, "What are you doing? And the man answered, very patiently, you see that's my house, and this mountain is shielding the sun so I can't grow anything." So, the villager is just incredulous and looks at that man, looks at him and his age and says, "You gonna die before you move this mountain." And the man said, "Yes, but then my son will shovel, and his son will shovel, and his son will shovel, and his son will shovel and eventually we will move this mountain." Mabel told me , "Change is about being a part of working for a change in values, the shoveling." The story framed my perspective on my job, and my life. After that, things happened, and Mabel came to leave the Extension and applied for a job with FiveCAP as Directors of Senior Nutrition for four counties.

RS: Right.

MT: Before I met Robert, I received at least three requests from out-of-area people who heard he was in Lake County and wanted to meet him. They asked if I would call him for them. I did call him and asked if he would see these people. Rob never refused to meet with anyone. I do recall that the first time I saw Rob and Mabel in Lake County was at a political function.

RS: What function was this?

MT: It was a Lake County Democratic function held in the cafeteria of Baldwin High School. And at that function, I saw this gorgeous woman with this beautiful African attire and headdress, and her signature smile that just drew you in. I remember Rob that evening was wearing a shirt with no collar.

RS: And before you transition into that, when you say that, revelation, a new revelation about him, and your impressions of him, that he was an ordinary person, what is the evidence, as you reflect on that experience, that he was just ordinary? I mean, in a sense, you have him on this pedestal, but you learned that he was a human being just like you, and he made you laugh or whatever. So, what were the sources of evidence to say that he was just an ordinary person?

MT: I read that what makes the hero is what you do at the moment that you are confronted with a threat or choice. Rob was complex and ordinary. He put on his shoes the same way as everyone. He was raised as a southern black person. Yes, he reacted differently that any black person I had known. He would not accept the status given to Black people. I was certainly analyzing him when I met him the first time, because I wanted to know what makes that person different. The Rob we knew wasn't the Robert Williams that the media had made him out to be. Rob was generous with his time. He tutored and mentored many of us.

RS: And what was the approximate time period? What year? Was this in the 70s?

MT: It would have been in the 70s, the early 70s, looking in the early to mid-70s, '75, '76…I will need to look at my records to get dates of certain events.

RS: Okay, I'll step out…

MT: So where were we?

RS: Okay, so then, take me back now to the time when you first met him and you're verbally interacting and exchanging information, and what happened after that.

MT: Okay, our first meeting was in a social context, and so it was just general conversation and jokes. The fact that my hero was just a funny guy too was interesting. From that, started conversations about things going on in the community. So anytime something happened, we would keep each other up to date. "Did you hear about this? Did you hear about that?" We talked about community events, and the book he was writing. Looking back, I think he was preparing me for a leadership role in the community response to acts of injustice. He was a good community organizer. He definitely knew how to connect with people so that when issues that were significant occurred in the community, people could come together and talk about them in terms of their shared interests. And things started to happen that involved individuals. The one that jumped out to me was the Ruby Nelson incident. And when Mrs. Nelson, the mother of young children? I can't remember. Three children, I think. She was arrested. I saw her on television, on the evening news, and she shot the Sheriff. Rob called and said, "We have got to find out what's happened. I'm going down to the jail and talk to her."

RS: And what was the condition in the media? How was she portrayed?

MT: She was portrayed as a crazy person. When they brought her out before the cameras, her hair was in disarray, she was totally unkempt. Mrs. Nelson suffered from an illness, it turned out she had epileptic seizures, and she was in a physical condition. One of her eyes tended to sort of wander a bit.

RS: Right.

MT: And so she definitely looked like a person who was not in her right mind. They wanted her to look that way so people would not feel sympathy and a connection. Rob said, "We don't know what happened and we needed to find out what's going on there. And I will be going to the police department now, and we need to meet." So that is when the story started to come out. It was not what any of us in the community expected it to be. The police provoked the situation. The Sheriff and his staff had a practice of retaliating against individuals, particularly black people, who they felt had been disrespectful to them. They would use their position to set them up or go after them. In Mrs. Nelson's case, they had used a complaint that had been made by a former boyfriend about a dog, a month earlier, as a pretense to go to her house. First, they went to the Lake County Community Mental Health Director and obtained an order to take her to the Mental Institution in Traverse City. The order was to have her committed for observation.

It was over the Ruby Nelson incident and people from all segments of the black community came together. People who would have not ordinarily identified with Mrs. Nelson because she was not of their group, their friends, or relatives. And he helped people to understand that what happened to Mrs. Nelson was wrong, it was all our concern, and it could happen to any of us.

RS: Right, and there's a lot of detail and in that article there's a good deal of coverage on Mrs. Nelson. Her daughter works for Dial-A-Ride. Okay, so, can we kind of chronologically, because when we were talking off-tape, you were giving me some information chronologically that is important context about the different reactions—his reactions to things that were happening, and his attempt to seek answers and seek help to solve some of these issues down in Lansing, etc. So, could you take me back to that?

MT: Rob firmly believed that one should always work within the system. This I'm sure will come as a surprise to those who only have a certain image of him. He truly believed in working within the system—the due process must be allowed to work. He advised allowing whatever provisions had been made within the system to work. In the case of negative police actions against the black community, Rob took many steps. He had gone to the county commissioners, to the Sheriff himself. Then he went to the media because the problem was not being addressed by the local authorities. He contacted Governor

Blanchard. And the Governor's liaison on racial relations, Terrence Duvernay, who was also the new director of the Michigan State Housing Development Authority (MSHDA). We didn't know Terrence Duvernay, but we came to know and respect his intelligence and abilities. Rob suggested that we take a road trip and we went to Lansing and met with members of the black caucus in the Legislature. We felt that they would care about the police attack on black people in Lake County. A State Representative by the name of Ethel Terrell chaired the Legislative Civil Rights Committee. Representative Terrell agreed to convene a meeting in Lake County to investigate racial discrimination and police abuse of power. The Governor's Legal Advisor, Conrad Mallett, called several community representatives, including myself, to say that Governor Blanchard was convening a Task Force to investigate the police and Black community issues. Since Robert was not called, it was felt that Robert's role in leading the community protest was being ignored or played down. We learned later that each of us had called Robert immediately after hanging up. The events that followed were covered extensively by the Detroit Free Press. The Sheriff testified before the Governor's Task Force, and he was allowed to sit on the Task Force. The Sheriff was allowed to respond to each victim's testimony. But when he testified, he faced the audience with guns strapped to his ankles which was very visible to the audience. People felt his actions were threatening and intentional.

RS: Nonverbal communication.

MT: Rob suggested that we demonstrate a silent protest against the Sheriff and also our dissatisfaction with this Governor's Task Force. When the Sheriff was talking, we all at once stood up and turned our chairs to face away from him and the Task Force.

RS: Before you go on, can you recall what were any specific cases involving residents that caused you all to travel down to Lansing?

MT: Between 1977 and 1983, there was escalating police abuse directed toward members of the Black community. It started with the Ruby Nelson case. The Sheriff went out to her house when her small children were home. They rushed to the house using a bullhorn to tell her to come out of the house. At the same time, the Sheriff was kicking in her door. She did not understand what was happening and responded like any mother. She acted to protect her children. She got a gun and when the Sheriff kicked in the door and entered, she shot him.

RS: Right.

MT: After that, it was an all-out attack on the Black community by the Sheriff's Department. There was the killing of Mr. Wilson, a gentleman that everyone knew as a gentle soul. Mr. Wilson was killed by a Deputy with who he had a run-in previously. And this Deputy appeared to stop Mr. Wilson for no reason. Mr. Wilson was coming back from Grand Rapids and was shot. Witnesses said they could hear Mr. Wilson screaming, "He's going to kill me, he's going to kill me."

RS: So, this deputy retaliated against him.

MT: It was incident after an incident. Any type of negative interaction with the Sheriff, the deputies, their relatives, their girlfriends, or wives, could make you a target. Black women were not off-limits for this abuse either. And they were physically aggressive toward Black women. When they were stopped for alleged traffic reasons, they worried

… it had come to a point that none of us felt safe. You didn't feel safe when you crossed the Lake County line.

RS: So, what was Mr. Wilson's name, where was he originally from before he arrived here, and what was the sheriff's name at the time?

MT: James N. Wilson. I do not know where Mr. Wilson may have lived before. Bob Blevins was the Sheriff's name—he came from somewhere around Grand Rapids. He made a public statement that he was doing what he was brought to Lake County to do. He had a record of being aggressive and violating people's civil rights. The white authorities recruited and hired him, and knew his history. They knew what he would do when they brought him to Lake County. They were still angry that Mrs. Nelson was found not guilty of shooting the Sheriff.

RS: Okay, you'll have a chance to edit. So, okay, so Mr. Wilson, what happened to him, what else? The black women?

MT: There were traffic stops for no reason. Once Lake County residents attending Ferris State College were stopped returning to Lake County. They were pulled over and harassed. If you were driving Black, they would pull you over.

RS: Right.

MT: There was a noticeable increase in the frequency of incidents that were racially motivated where many people monitored the police with scanners. There was an incident at Trout-a-rama called the Beer Tent Incident. Black women were harassed by the police and held and questioned. White persons involved were not subjected to this treatment. We were all afraid. Because it was happening to all of us. It happened to me. I was coming home from work one night. It was just about evening when I turned onto 76th Street. That's when I saw the Sheriff Deputy car trailing me. I didn't know how long, but as I turned onto 76th Street, he turned on his flasher. I knew that I was not speeding, so I kept driving. I did not speed, I did not stop. I drove purposefully toward my driveway, which was on a long two-track road. I knew when I got home that my husband would be there, and there would be a witness to whatever transpired. But I was not going to stop on a road without witnesses because of what I had heard of the police conduct toward Black women.

RS: Right.

MT: So, I looked back and saw a car trailing the police car. It was my husband. I stopped. And he came to my car and asked, "Why didn't you stop?" I said, "Because I'm not going to stop on this isolated road without a witness to what happens." I learned later, from Helen Curry and others that they heard him on the scanner say that he was trailing me, and he was told to let me go. He never gave me a reason for stopping me either. He didn't say I was speeding, or that there was anything wrong with my car.

RS: Right, okay. Any other incidents? I mean how did the alliance come up with the booklet of the reporting of cases? And as a result of the Ruby Nelson case, Robert Williams staged a one-man protest in front of the Lake County Star?

MT: You mean the Peoples Association for Human Rights. This was Robert's idea to organize, raise, and use money to help defend Black people wrongly arrested in Lake County.

RS: And what was the name of the local editor?

MT: Denise Smith was the editor when Mrs. Nelson was on trial. George Dechow was the editor when Robert held his one-man protest of the Lake County Star.
RS: Okay. What was her interaction with Rob? Was she—
MT: Clearly, from reading her articles, she did not like Rob. I'm not aware of any personal interaction she had with Rob. I knew her, because she was a tenant, and rented a house from us, before she was married.
RS: Okay, so, but take me back and tell me, revisit so I can picture in my mind the actual protest.
MT: Rob's protest?
RS: Yes.
MT: Rob's protest was, oh my goodness, he built himself a billboard. He wrote his protest on the front and the back, and he wore it. And he would just walk every day, up and down on Main Street in front of the Lake County Star office.
RS: A helmet with a light?
MT: Yes, he also made a helmet with a light on it, that's right. And he would just walk up and down, up and down, and come back the next day.
RS: Do you know approximately how many days?
MT: No, I do not recall now. I just remember that it got everybody's attention. Rob was always one step ahead of the opposition. He knew the strength of his position. So, he would go into a meeting humble and respectful. And he could respectfully disagree.
RS: Okay.
RS: "We'll see about that" was a popular line.
MT: That is what he would say when he disagreed, "We'll see about that." Because that means, "You're gonna be hearing from me again, this isn't the end of this."
RS: Right.
MT: People in positions of authority never wanted to see him coming through their door if they were on the opposite side of the issue from him. He had the confidence and the ability to control himself in situations where a less disciplined person would lose control. When he was disrespected, he did not respond kindly. He stayed humble, but he was humble without his head bowed.
RS: Right.
MT: He wasn't shuffling and looking at his feet.
RS: He wasn't submissive.
MT: He wasn't submissive.
RS: Okay. So, continue the chronology. And wasn't he involved with issues in other places too? Like in Muskegon, and I think there was something with some PCB with farmers.
MT: Yes. With the issue involving the cattle farmers, Robert came to the FiveCAP Board of Directors and said, "You know, we have farmers being affected by PCB in our community." FiveCAP applied for money, and we got funds to help farmers apply for relief. And so that was really the result of Rob's connection with the organization and his concern for that issue. He would say, "You know, as a Community Action Agency, this is about helping people out of poverty, but you have to think broader."
RS: Okay. Where were the places with the farmers that he…

MT: Mason, Manistee, and Osceola counties. The Chase farm in Osceola County was really devastated. It lost everything. It was a time when people were seeing something that they had never seen before, when hundreds of cows were being put down because they were contaminated. They had received the PCB.
RS: One of them, I'll, we'll check.
MT: The cattle were tainted beef. PCB was found in the feed, and they had to be killed. So overnight, farmers were—
RS: Devastated.
MT: Into poverty, yes.
RS: Around what time period was that? The 80s?
MT: That would have been in the 80s, yes.
RS: Okay. What were some other, I mean, at the same time these things were happening, he was traveling around the country.
MT: He was traveling, he was going out of the country as well. He was traveling around the country—people would call Rob from all over and he always had time for them.
RS: Right
MT: He always had time for everyone. There were no big people or little people, as far as Rob was concerned. If you reached out to him, he took the time to give. And if he could be of help to you, he would. And he would bring other people to help you too.
RS: Okay, so he was like a librarian community person.
MT: He was the people's legal adviser, he was their educator on social issues, he was a mentor, sometimes he was that stern person. Rob was a person who was about people helping themselves. He would help you but was not about enabling people to be dependent. He would show people how to help themselves and he would be there to offer support.
RS: Right.
MT: He was not going to, unsolicited, start to tell you anything.
RS: Right. So, he was on the FiveCAP board too, right?
MT: Yes.
RS: So how did he—at what point did he begin to be a board member? And what were—clearly the Ruby Nelson was a big case, the farmers issue was big case, the—[is there more about the Farmers case?]
MT: Mr. Wilson's case.
RS: Mr. Wilson's case was a big case…
MT: Yes, and there was the [Delbert] Dotson case, the Dotson case. Mr. Dotson had been a former Idlewild policeman in Yates Township. He was involved in a killing, it was a domestic matter, he was charged with murder. Every indication was it was in self-defense. Even the mother of the young man killed said that it was self-defense. He was still charged with murder. So, there was a rallying of the community around him. Every day, the courtroom was full as a show of support.
RS: He was also helpful to inmates in the prison.
MT: Yes. There was a time when a young lady in jail claimed a deputy had raped her. And it was being pushed under the rug. I remember Rob telling the Sheriff it was against the law for a prisoner to have sex. They tried to make it out to sound as if it was

consensual sex. Rob informed them that inmates can't give consent, it was against the law for them to have sex.

RS: Right, right.

MT: They acted as if it was like news to them, and as a result there was some action taken. And it began to shine another light on the kinds of things happening to Black prisoners in that court jail.

RS: Right. Um, what were some other things about him? Before we turn the tape on you. It's the Williams family that you have a relationship with. So, you worked with both Rob and Mabel, over the years on many different projects. Could you talk about some of that? What was it like? How these two worked together, lived together, loved together, you know.

MT: Well, what immediately comes to mind is something Mabel said about their decision to stand up as a family against injustice. It was always as a family, they stood as a unit. When they trumped up the charges in Monroe, North Carolina and the FBI was looking for Rob, he took his family. They were equally involved and committed. It was always a family matter. Mabel shared with me that it was important to them to be recognized as a black family in the struggle against injustice.

RS: So, what kind of board member was he?

MT: Thoughtful and wise. When he disagreed with my recommendations, he would simply say, "I'm not here to be a 'yes' board member." It was disagreement that brought a point of view and broadened the discussion. But Rob would see a different point of view.

RS: Okay, I want us to talk a little bit about Mabel, because she lived a little longer and did some other things with you. But before doing that, I want to go back to something about Rob and the Ruby Nelson case. And I had did some reading on labor politics in Detroit, and one Ernest Goodman, he was able to get him here. And at Mabel's memorial in Detroit that we both were at, there was a young black woman who was a lawyer—

MT: Melissa El.

RS: Yes. So, could you talk about these two people and how, and his relationship with him and how they got involved with the case, etc.?

MT: Well, Rob brought people into our lives that worked with him in the human rights movement. And one of those people was Attorney Ernie Goodman. It was Ernie Goodman and Rob who decided that I would be the community spokesperson before the Governor's Task Force. Mr. Goodman was an interesting man and a very good lawyer. He also introduced Melissa El to Rob and Lake County.

RS: Right.

MT: I remember the first time I met Ernie Goodman at Rob and Mabel's home. I walked into a room of black people and there was this one white man with white, curly hair. They were singing, "I shot the sheriff, but I did not shoot the deputy." They clearly had been drinking a little. He was having a grand old time. And I thought, "Oh my goodness, Mrs. Nelson is going up the river."

RS: Right, right, right.

MT: Anyway, that evening I was late, and I missed the formal strategizing session. So, the next day, I got a call from Rob that "We're gonna need a community spokesperson to address the Governor's Task Force and it's gonna be you. Come over and we will work on the speech with you." I went over and we worked on the speech, while Mabel prepared dinner. We ate dinner and she typed my speech.

RS: Right.

MT: But I didn't know who Ernie Goodman was because in those days, you couldn't Google. I had no idea that I was in the presence of a legal giant. A person who was cut from the same cloth as Robert Williams.

RS: Had a lot of battle wounds.

MT: Yes. So, I got to know Ernie and I would drop into the office to see him occasionally if I was in Detroit. Ernie gave us the slogan for the Lake County Enterprise Community. The first day of the trial of Ruby Nelson, Ernie came into the courtroom. The Judge and the Prosecutor were both kind of rude towards Ernie, but he was calm. So, when it was over, we walked out feeling a little bit beaten up with everything that had happened in court. Ernie was in high spirits. He walked out, standing on the courthouse steps, and he looked around. And he said, "Lake County is the right size to make a good example for justice." I had a front-row seat to see that same judge, that same prosecutor apologizes to Mrs. Nelson for the police mistreatment toward her and dismisses the Contempt of Court against Ernie. Ernie Goodman brought them to their knees. We were all in tears.

RS: The way it's supposed to be.

MT: Yes. Ernie knew the law and the court system. They were visibly intimidated. And they resented Ernie's presence.

RS: Get away with.

MT: Rob threatened the status quo.

RS: And where did Melissa fit in?

MT: Melissa El was recommended by Ernie Goodman. As was Roger Wotila, the attorney that represented Delbert Dodson. He was a young attorney from Cadillac. More and more cases came to the Peoples Association for Human Rights. Our job was to raise money to pay for the legal defense of people.

RS: Any better.

MT: It was later when Ernie Goodman approached Melissa El, a young Black female attorney. He saw and respected her talent in Detroit and asked her if she would come to Lake County and help. And she came up and met with Rob and Mabel. I don't know what she knew of them before, I know she did not know them personally. I remember Melissa. One of her first cases up here was a rape case. The longtime girlfriend (white) accused her Black live-in boyfriend of rape. Rob investigated it and felt that it warranted the support of the Association for Human Rights. So, Melissa was retained as the attorney. That was the first case Melissa tried in Lake County. Melissa was pretty and petite. I believe that she had belonged to the Church of the Black Madonna in Detroit.

RS: Mmhmm.

MT: I recall one day in the trial, I still see it: Melissa was cross-examining a witness about the specifics of the charges, which was the alleged rape. "Well, she does this move like she's tiptoeing to the bathroom, in the courtroom."

RS: Right, right.

MT: And we were laughing, but it was a nervous, embarrassing kind of laugh. He was found not guilty.

RS: Right, okay. Another issue is, when FiveCAP decided to build the new daycare, child center, it had been announced that the naming of it would be in honor of Robert Williams and there was a local—another editor of the Lake County Star who had some unflattering language or words to say about that. And there was a response by the community. I would like you to talk a little bit about that and FiveCAP's decision to dedicate it to Robert Williams.

MT: The Robert F. Williams Family Center. I don't remember that. I probably don't remember it because I gave so little importance to what the newspaper said. The board is made up of elected officials, community organization reps, and low-income people from four counties who sat with Rob and knew him over the years and had nothing but respect for him. They felt honored to have known him. We wanted future generations to say, "Who is Robert F. Williams?"

RS: Okay, that's fair. Before we turn to Mabel, any other observations, reflections about Robert Williams you'd like to add?

MT: So, what I'll leave you with is Rob was a good person whose beliefs were unshakable. It was never a question of, is this the right thing to do? It was about how can I do it?

RS: Okay, transitioning to Mabel, because I've witnessed some of your work with her, including development and everything of the Historical and Cultural Center, and trips that y'all made to go to other places and make observations, and other things, and recently, I was out of town and moving from Ohio to Indiana, so I wasn't able to make it to the memorial for her. And I knew it would be a special occasion, and so there was a dedication in her honor. And I would like for you to talk about her and her—

MT: —Genuine—

RS: Strong.

MT: Strong doesn't seem enough to even be the right word to describe...

RS: Tough?

MT: She was beyond all that. Mabel was very nice and always gracious. I'm sure marrying Robert made her think about things differently. In the South, Rob was considered crazy at best.

RS: A crazy nigger. Right.

MT: In the South, white people treated "crazy Black people" with the distance, because these people had nothing to lose. And Rob was a man with everything to lose and stood up anyway. So that was a different kind of—

RS: Configuration.

MT: He had everything to lose—loved life, loved everything, and loved America. Mabel explained their relationship to me. When she fell in love with Rob, her life was going to change. Because to love Robert Williams, to be Robert Williams's wife required her to be by his side. She was going to have to withstand what he withstood. She talked about how it came to be her cause. Mabel was equally committed. She'd tell me with tears in her eyes that when her mother died, she couldn't come to the funeral. One day, she listed for me all the things that happened in her life when she was in exile, times that we would all have wanted there. She needed her family; her family needed her. Tough times in her life—but as an exile, she was alone, amongst friendly strangers.

She never regretted it, I never once heard her say, "I wish it had been different, I wish we had not done that." I'll tell you another little side story: Rob and Mabel were invited to a literary group in Cadillac to speak. The members had all read *Negroes with Guns*, and they invited Rob over to talk about his life experiences. Rob tells his story of the police coming to the house and trying to get the jump on Rob. Mabel came and put the gun on the police officer to save Rob. Rob did the talking, Mabel sat quietly and smiled. Later, I asked one of the people present what the reaction of the group was. And he said it was strange. "Everyone liked Rob, everyone had good things to say, but one person said that Mabel scared them more than Rob." Mabel had a way of being comfortable, letting Rob speak and she would be in that supporting role, so some may not have understood they were equal partners. But what this person said was they were really impressed with how warm and friendly Rob was but scared the hell of her ... but they saw something else.

RS: They saw her comfortable in her own skin, comfortable with Rob telling the story. That's what they saw.

MS: They saw the strength.

RS: Right!

MT: They saw that she was capable of all of that.

RS: Right. Interesting. So, in your experiences in traveling, she worked with you as FiveCAP built all of this. Talk about that. Kind of worker she was, y'all traveled together...

MT: Um, Mabel worked hard. She was a good friend who would laugh with you, cry with you, and genuinely cared. One time when we were in Bitely looking at a building, the locals didn't want FiveCAP to put a meal program there. Their reason was because the Black people from Woodland Park came up to that meal site. And we went there one night to talk to the local objectors. Mabel said she felt more of a threat to our personal safety that night than she had felt since she left Monroe, North Carolina.

RS: Interesting.

MT: Rob used to tease Mabel and say, "Oh sweet Mabel." And I would tease him by saying, "Rob, Mabel wants to get rid of you." And he would say, "No, Mabel can't get rid of me, I'm never going to leave Mabel, I love Mabel, she's so sweet."

RS: Yeah, yeah, yeah, okay.

MT: And Mabel would just laugh at his teasing with her. There was always something to laugh about and she had a beautiful laugh.

RS: Were there other specific projects that you and Mabel worked on that are memorable?

MT: The senior meals sites in northern Newaygo [County], and the Idlewild Historic & Cultural Center, and the Idlewild Music Fest. We worked to conceptualize what the Idlewild Historic & Cultural Center would be, and Mabel was part of a group called The Merrymakers. I wanted that organization to be that local group that would oversee the Idlewild Historic & Cultural Center operations.

The Idlewild Historic & Cultural Center was created to tell the story of Idlewild; and to be a tourist attraction to bring people to Idlewild. We also wanted it to be a place to accommodate local outside groups coming into the community.

RS: It would be professional.

MT: Well, I'll ask you a question. How did you perceive the relationship?

RS: Oh, I thought it was interesting and there were times when I asked her the same questions.

MT: Oh.

RS: Especially when it involves festivals. So, I asked her questions about that, and so my impression was that despite whatever differences, I still saw you and Mabel working together. So, it was like you two had an understanding, but I don't know what other people's conception of that was. So that was how I read it.

MT: We—

RS: And I'll add this: I didn't see them—I didn't see them in Detroit. You know, I know who I saw in Detroit—I came all the way from Ohio, right? So, I knew what it meant to me. So that kind of impression that I had. And I knew that more than anybody up here, that you knew more about the Williams' than I could—I can't think of anybody else that lives here that has as much information as you. So that was…

MT: I think it is because we are all Southerners.

RS: Right. Yeah, I never imagined that. Um, so, recently you dedicated, is it like a space in here, or is it the museum, I mean the cultural center itself, you dedicated that in honor—

MT: Yes. This room particularly, it's the Mabel R. Williams Conference Room.

RS: Mmhmm, mhmm.

MT: I thought "R" stood for Ruth as her middle name. I didn't know it was the initial of a family name. Her middle name was Ola. If she ever told me, I don't remember. It sounds like something we would have enjoyed and laugh about. Because being from the South, we all know that Ola is Yoruba. The slaves would take a European name and add "Ola" on the end of it.

RS: Right.

MT: My sister's name is Quincola.

RS: Right.

RS: What was the—what was it like, that day? The dedication day?

MT: It was a Memorial, and a Roast. It was an event that was intimate, very intimate. It was educational, people were in tears, and laughing through the tears when one member of the Merrymakers stood up and reminded us of something Mabel would often say. Mabel would say, "I need you to help because I'm a poor widowed woman living on a fixed income." [Laughs.]

RS: Right.

MT: We watched *Negroes with Guns*, the video. For some it was taking them back in time, they were remembering times that they lived through. For everyone, it was a renewed appreciation, and gratitude for what they both had done for all of us, Black and white. And it was an interesting day. Mabel's son is a Baptist minister, and whenever you talk about Mabel, there's a couple of Catholic Priests in the mix and they all spoke of her work and kind spirit.

RS: Right, right, that's a good one. What was Rob's religion?

MT: I do not know. Rob attended the Unitarian church in Big Rapids. I think Rob was a spiritual person and he felt a connection to a higher being, but he was not a religious person. He felt he had that personal relationship; he didn't need to filter it though anybody. His Unitarian connection was because of their activism that he connected.

RS: The other title of that essay I wrote, I got that phrase when General Baker and Charles Simmons and a few others when to Cuba while Rob was in Cuba. And Charles Simmons had been wondering, and he said, "Well, what's the role of religion? And Rob's response was, "Praise the Lord and pass the ammunition." [Laughs.]

RS: That's why I titled the essay that.

MT: He said that his mother always said, "Let the Lord take care of it." That's why his book is titled, "While God Lies Sleeping." When she would say, "Let the Lord take care of that," Robert's uncle would reply, "He must be sleeping." She would say this when his uncle would express his feelings about the injustices against Blacks by whites in North Carolina.

RS: Right, interesting, I didn't know that. You talk about a number of incidents, and, in your estimation, who else in Michigan should I be speaking to? I'm gonna talk to Melissa, I got her information. I'm wondering about, you said Conrad, wasn't he a Michigan Supreme Court justice? I'm wondering if I should reach out and speak to him.

MT: Yeah, why not? Conrad helped me personally. Rob had nothing but respect for Conrad's father. They were colleagues in the Civil Rights movement in Detroit. He understood that Conrad was an agent of the governor and that they wanted this to be handled with as little notoriety as possible. Rob's involvement would bring publicity.

RS: It wouldn't get squashed like that.

MT: No. And I don't know if Conrad has ever spoken about his recollection or thoughts on the matter.

RS: Is there anybody else?

MT: You might want to talk to Elaine Steele. She heads up the Rosa Parks [Institute]. Whenever Elaine and Mrs. Parks came to visit, Mabel would let me know so I could come over if I wanted to. I think I did it only once.

RS: She's down in Detroit?

MT: Yes.

RS: And where's Conrad these days?

MT: Detroit. I saw an article some time ago in the Detroit Free Press. He is the Administrator of some hospital, I think.

RS: Okay, and then the last question is about documents. I looked through the *Negroes with Guns* collection, the Robert Williams papers, there are a few things that I haven't seen, but are there any like, Michigan state police reports I should try to get my hands on, or any other important documents that you think will add to the credibility about some of the stories? I'm thinking about the last 20-something years of his life, here in Lake County.

MT: Sometimes, Robert's presence created a roar. But when you were focused on all the things that Robert did, most were done quietly. The most important was the change in community attitudes, especially among Black people towards one another. He was the glue ... our conscience. His neighbor was spying on him. They would report when Mabel went to the mailbox, when Mabel left, and when Rob got into his car and went into town. This was in the FBI files that Rob got through the FOI. I don't know whether his son still has those records. He got boxes of them. I remember going over and reading through some of them with him.

January 3, 2015
Detroit, Michigan
Approximately 140 minutes
Ronald Stephens=RS
John Williams=JW

RS: So, John, just to get us started, I want to go back to a talk you gave when I was at Ohio University, I didn't record it at that time, but I'd like to go back and finish up there.
JW: Okay, well first, I'd like to just say, Welcome to Detroit. [Laughs.]
RS: Thank you. [Laughs.]
JW: Welcome back.
RS: So, you know, that was a very fascinating talk and the insight that came out of that is most scholars tend to singly focus on your dad as an international activist and civil rights veteran. And [they] do not consider the role that others played, particularly family members, your whole family, basically. And so, I'd like you to take me back and recap some of the experiences, beginning in Monroe, and Cuba in the short time you were there, and even in China, that you recall of your involvement as a family member working with your dad in the causes that he and your mom championed.
JW: All right, wow, that's a lot. That's a lot, so let's take one bite at a time, starting with Monroe. You know, I was blessed to have parents who loved their people. Had a relationship with God, both of my parents were, came from a local church that both families were involved in—my dad's family was, my mom's family was. Before they even got married, the families knew each other through relationships in the same church. They both had a spiritual foundation...and then he obviously went off to the service, came back. So, you had a military kind of background, and as a result of that, I think that played a major role in all our lives—coming back as a military person and being interested in the civil rights movements. You know the early 50s to the mid-50s, the NAACP was active in a lot of the things that were happening, and Dad was interested in contributing to that. And I guess, even in the military, he learned about how the military wasn't free of racism and challenges that black people had, and so upon returning to North Carolina he was gung-ho about wanting to have an impact. And he had experienced a lot of things that were negative, coming up in that Southern environment, that racist Southern environment. And so, when he assumed the position of the president of the NAACP and began to, organized in the local community, around the area's

race-related issues, he allowed my brother and I to be involved as well. So, when we did demonstrations, we picketed. Say, the swimming pool that was tax supported, my brother and I were involved in that, my mom, my brother and me. Other people who were from the local community got involved in the civil rights movement at that time. And so, I had a unique kind of experience growing up, where, as a child, you know, 7–8 years old, I as actively involved. I can remember one of the few times my father was ever arrested, I was witness to it—my brother and I were witness to it—it was over a picketing, a demonstration where we sat down at a lunch counter in our hometown that we were trying to de-segregate. This was during the time that the students were part of that movement in North Carolina as well, so we were kind of doing a similar thing but doing it locally in terms of sit-ins. And that was the first time that I ever witnessed my father being arrested. And up until that time also my experience with white people was very limited. I had very little experience with white folk, living in a segregated community, there was no real need for interaction as a child with white people. And, but, through the involvement in the civil rights movement and witnessing my dad being arrested and having heard about Emmett Till, having learned some things about our history in the South and what was happening to people throughout the South, it was a frightful thing to see your father arrested all because we were trying to integrated the swimming pool and trying to get the right for black folk to be treated fairly in terms of not having to be segregated in public accommodation, basically. So that was kind of my early exposure, and later, obviously, when things got much more complicated, much more involved in terms of the civil rights movement, up to the point of us having to leave North Carolina at the threat that we were going to be lynched. And the white establishment looked the other way. Let me rephrase that in other terms: the white establishment, at the state level, and the federal level looked the other way while the local folk were very active just trying to intimidate, terrorize us and the black community. And that's one of those things, again, where we see repeatedly, from the 50s on and much earlier than that, where lack people have looked to the federal government and the state government, expecting that they would intervene when constitutional rights were being violated but they weren't doing it. So, it created a real atmosphere of terror for us and a whole lot of black people throughout the South. But growing up, it was an interesting time. One of the things that we saw a lot of was my dad was fearless, you know? There was fear from a standpoint, personal standpoint, usually that fear had to do with us being concerned with what would happen to him, what would happen to my mom, my brother? And there were times when the local racists would also target kids, young people, thinking they were my brother and me. So, we had to live a different kind of life because of that, simply because we couldn't just go out like the average kid in the neighborhood because we were being targeted at that time by the racists.

RS: Okay, now I want to go back before we proceed. You were talking about both parents being involved in the local churches. Were they involved in different denominations?

JW: No, they were both Baptists. Elizabeth Baptist Church was the church that both families were involved with. So that was the one they both were involved with over the years. Later, though, my mom became involved with the Catholic Church and my dad was a Unitarian. And a lot of that is always interesting to me how that happened as well, because a lot of folks start off, you know, with the family, the church of the family tradition. A lot of black folks, Baptist was that tradition, but depending on the politics … One of the interesting things was the politics at the time in the 50s was Black Catholics, or Catholics as a whole, was kind of frowned on in the South. But if you were a progressive Catholic and were involved in any integrated movement of any kind, you were REALLY frowned on, you know. We were fortunate to have several priests in our community who were very progressive, they were progressive priests, and because of that, they understood that the members, the local people, were supportive of the struggle that we were waging. It was because they were pure people, in the sense of having that sensitivity to the Black community, I think my dad didn't have a problem with us going kind of from Baptist to Catholic. And especially because some of the Baptist pastors were really falling short of the mark in terms of integrity, morality, and other issues, so you know, and they weren't supportive oftentimes of the Civil Rights Movement because they were scared. So, it was almost like they were working constantly against us rather than being with us, whereas I guess the white priests had a structural support system, as well as some of them just had that progressive outlook. Eventually we kind of got with the local Black Catholic Church because we got a bad priest—well, the priests were white but [there were] two that were positive. And one was very anti-community, anti-anything progressive and didn't want to mediate. So, we just didn't want to be there for his little sermons either. So, we kind of drifted away from that and Dad was kind of a Unitarian. A Unitarian, obviously, they have their own style and oftentimes they are not pushing a religious demonization per say, they offer a different denomination to come together and share whatever it is. And they were very much into contemporary issues and how to bring resolution of contemporary contexts, how to bring to bear your spirituality? So that was a good fit for Dad. [Laughs.]

RS: You mentioned something else about your involvement as a child, 7–8 years old, the first time you, the time you saw your father arrested, and you said it was a demonstration at a local lunch counter. Do you remember the name of the store?

JW: It was one of the local drug stores uptown. You know, I'm not sure, there were a couple, there were like two drug stores in uptown Monroe that we would consistently try to hit. One was secret, but I'm not sure that's the one. In that case, we ended up going to the Supreme Court and we won that case. So, there's legal documentation on that case. So, obviously I'm saying that, to say that that can be found. My memory doesn't, I don't remember if it was Secret's or the other drug store.

RS: Okay, and I take it when you said that this was in sync as the other, you're talking about the Greensboro sit-ins?

JW: Yeah, exactly.

RS: Okay, and then, you mentioned something else about your participation in the public swimming pool demonstration?

JW: Yeah, we were consistently going there, trying to integrate. At that time, or a little bit later, pretty much during the same time period. '59, '60ish.

RS: Okay, and then—

JW: It was in between that time period too, the sit-ins and the attempts to integrate the swimming pool, that several attempts were made on my father's life. One, being with my mom was home and was able to fend off the cops who were trying to arrest him. They came to our home without a warrant to arrest him and my mom met them at the door with a shotgun and that's why they ended up not arresting him. And the thinking was that they weren't legitimate in the sense of wanting to take him in. There was some doubt in our minds whether they wanted to take him because he had been doing so many high-profile things and that confronted and didn't have a problem with reacting to negative confrontation from white clansmen as well as police officers. So, at that point, the tension was so high, you know there was doubt about what their intentions were. So, mom wasn't about to just let them come and take him without a warrant and everything, so she met them at the door with the shotgun. Of course, after that, they went away and didn't come back.

RS: There's something that I was reading some time ago, your Uncle John said about your dad, an observation he made that he noticed a change, something different about him, after he was discharged from the Korean War…?

JW: Well, he didn't go to the War. During that time period of—and that's a lot of misconception there. My dad really did not go overseas. He was in the service at the time, but I think, because he was kind of known and had already developed a reputation of being an activist or—a lot of times they were not too gung-ho about I guess sending him overseas. And then there was also a period where I guess some kind of way, when his unit was ready to be shipped and out and was in fact, shipped out, he wasn't there.

RS: Right, right.

JW: In my mind, going overseas to fight the Chinese at that early stage, just wasn't a priority.

RS: There were some other things in Ohio that you mentioned you did as a youngster. I think it was you and your brother delivering the newsletter.

JW: The Crusader. Not only did we deliver it, but we were blessed to be around when many of the articles were being edited. My mom usually would help with the editing and do the typing the final draft of it. My dad would type his own stuff and write it. As a family all the time we'd sit down, Mom would read it and we would critique it and he would get input from us. Mrs. Ethel Johnson, who was another activist who lived down the street from us, a close family friend and activist, would be a part of that process many times as well.

RS: Is that Ethel Johnson?

JW: Yes. And then after we would get the content, you know, and retype it and all that and put it on stencil back in the day. A mimeograph machine was one of my tasks. So many times, I was doing that, my brother was doing that, then we'd have to staple it together. So, we had an assembly line going into the wee hours of the night. We'd usually do it on Friday and Saturday, we'd get out and sell it. So again, as kids, we were actively involved in that process.

RS: Okay, so that was in the U.S. before leaving Monroe. Were there any other memories that you had? Did you have any in Cuba?

JW: Yeah, well you know, Cuba was a very good experience in the sense that, as I said earlier in Monroe, my first real encounters with white folk on a direct level kind of were negative because of the police and how they interacted with my father, and the fact that I understood some things that were happening around the civil rights movement. But we were blessed to also have some progressive white people like, some from the Unitarian church, and others who were socialists and had a connection with them. So those interactions were very positive interactions. So as a child I didn't grow up with the fear and hatred for white people even though there was the police and that whole thing that was negative, we still had quality white people that we interacted with who were supportive of the movement and what was happening. So, I had a pretty, fairly, I guess, good perspective on, or at least, a balanced perspective and understood that not all white people were bad, even though we were experiencing a lot of negativity in that time period. But going to Cuba was a powerful experience because we had been, for a couple of summers, demonstrating, trying to integrate a local swimming pool that was paid for by tax dollars. And when we first got to Cuba, my brother and I got off the plane, and it was sunny and bright, you know, kind of like, got off the plane and were met by a Cuban host and they put us in a car, and they drove us to meet our parents. And on the way, we passed all of these public facilities, swimming pools, and it was just a rainbow of kids, and it was loud, and they were having fun, yelling and screaming, jumping off diving boards, playing, and they were every color of the rainbow, basically. And it was just such a stark contrast because, you know, even though I had some positive interactions with white people, most of the interactions never happened because I was in a segregated community, and I knew that there was a lot about this issue to integration and fairness and justice and freedom for black folk. So just kind of leaving that kind of environment, being involved in that experience, to integrate with the hope that it would mean equality, and improvement of life for black people, and to see the negative reaction of the system and how violently people responded in the South and then to end up in a place like Cuba, it was just amazing. The initial contrast was just like, Wow. And from there on it kind of took off, and it was a wonderful 3 years I had living there. My brother and I went to boarding school with other Cuban students our age, and so we re-patriated Cubans, so there were bilingual folk. It was a good experience, and it took me a while, and my brother a while, to get the language thing. He was much better at it than I was but took me a while to get comfortable enough with the language to feel good about academics, because everything was happening in Spanish, you know, and by the time I got it down, it was time to go. I didn't really know that it was going, that I was going to be leaving Cuba on a permanent level. We ended up going to China for a visit, a celebration of one of the major— '69, that would have been—

RS: '64.

JW: Yeah, thank you. That would have been one of the anniversaries, one of the major anniversaries of the revolution there. So, we went there to participate in the celebrations of that and we got there and that was a real positive experience but in that time period, all the socialist nations were sending students to the Soviet Union or China because those were the big brothers in the communist camp. So, people from Czechoslovakia and people from Poland, people from Albania, especially Latin America that had socialist leanings. So top students went out, left the country to get educated. So, we were there, in China, at the time, and there were happening in Cuba that I had no sense about because I wasn't involved in the political side there, but my dad, being the strategic person that he was, was already looking for an escape route if there was a need for one. When we got to China, you know, he ended up kind of saying, what do you think about staying over here? And we were like, WHAT? No, we just got comfortable, and we have friends, the classic response of a teenager. No! Man, no. But that turned out to be a positive experience as well. Bought into it. And, we didn't have a lot of traditions. Dad, again being the strategic, as well as military-disciplined, person that he was, it didn't matter where we were really. It was, what's the alternative? You're living in exile. If the Cubans try to kill you, what are you going to do? So, we got that message.

RS: So, before I ask you to say something about your experience in China, now, I want to go back to the exile, because this is another point that is unclear. How your family got to Cuba, and I just heard vague recollection about that, that the family was split up. So, could you go back to that? You said you and your brother, so neither your mom nor your dad was with you when you were riding to Cuba?

JW: Exactly. Matter of fact, everybody—my mom and dad weren't even together, didn't arrive in Cuba together. My dad, I believe, arrived first, and my mom arrived, and then months later, my brother and I arrived in Cuba. And so, there were three different ways, and to this day, I'm not totally sure about the route that they took.

RS: I'm aware of the route your dad took. He left Canada and went to California, San Diego, and then crossed the border into Mexico, and from Mexico to Cuba. So, he was first. And then your mom arrived, but so, where were you and your brother?

JW: We were in New York, we spent a significant amount of time in New York, just kind of with the relatives, not relatives, but adopted family. But the folk that didn't know a whole lot about us other than that we were people from down South that the authorities were after and it behooved us not to be caught by the authorities, so there was like an underground railroad scenario where people stepped up and said, you know, we'll take the boys and so my brother and I were able to stay together for those months in between the time we arrived in Cuba and the time we saw our parents. For those months, we never saw either one of our parents.

RS: So, you and your brother were in New York that entire time?

JW: No. We stayed in New York, we were with two families in New York, and then we left New York and then we did end up in Canada after New York. Canada to Cuba. And then in Canada, we were with one, two, we lived with two different families there as well.

RS: You don't remember the names of those families?

JW: One of the things I can say, one of the families was a white family, and one was a black family.

RS: One of the things your mom told me in the early 2000s, must have been 2002, she came to visit our campus in Nebraska, and she said that there were people that were supportive of the cause, subscribing to The Crusader, and they were willing to be of help because they were aware of what was going on.

JW: Absolutely. Progressive folk that we stayed with in Canada were white progressives, then we stayed with a black family that was a little bit less conspicuous, obviously. Blended in a little bit better. But that was a really interesting time period for us, a real challenge, as kids, you know, we didn't know really what was happening with our parents.

RS: As a historian, dates are important. So, if you have this, if you have the date, you left Canada for Cuba in a passport or something, if you could share that date, that would really be helpful, chronologically.

JW: Boy, that would really be tough. Probably it would narrow it down some based on some of the events that were happening in Cuba. Because again, as a child, we were not just—weeks and days and weeks and months, it doesn't matter what went by, you just didn't have a sense of how much of it.

RS: I do have a chronology of your dad, and I have the date that he arrived. Maybe that will be helpful? I could share that chronology with you.

JW: I figure that with the dates I do have, that would narrow it down some.

RS: Okay, so now you're in China, and I recall, I recall during the time you spoke at Ohio University, you talked about some of those experiences that you had in China that you had with some of the, the general cultural issues that you learned, the language, and then you talked about your engagement with some of the children who, in a sense, you were separated from, since your family was in political exile. Could you talk about some of that?

JW: Well, a couple of things. When my brother and I ended up in China, my parents returned to Cuba, so we had, we ended up in a boarding school there, as well. And we had a guardian over in China, the Chinese identified the guardian for us. And that was obviously someone that could, from the Chinese perspective, they wanted someone who could speak English, who kind of knew something about American culture, so we had a man who lived there who was American but who was married to a Chinese woman and was a party member. So, I guess they felt comfortable with him being our guardian, but for all intents and purposes, most of the time we were at school anyway. We were under the auspices and the authority of the school people, who were all Chinese. We went to a regular high school and middle school, which was Peking University extension middle school and that was kind of like a middle and high school combined. And by that, and because of that, it was considered one of the better schools in Beijing ... We, so there was a small enclave of Americans who lived in what they called the Friendship Community, and the Friendship Community housed a lot of, like a compound, it housed a lot of foreign guests who were guests of the Chinese government who were helping with different kinds of endeavors that the Chinese were involved with—radio, producing programs with English and other languages, so you had people from all over the world living in these complexes. But we didn't live in the complex, that was another reason why we had the adopted kind of like family, our host family. And so, when we left school on the weekends we would go to our host family, instead of the complex. My dad was adverse with us being involved with a lot of American/British and other European countries that had people there because they felt that, and rightfully so, that a lot of them were involved in CIA activity, and so that was the last thing he wanted us involved in. And being in China, it just made sense in his mind, for us to be involved in the Chinese culture and absorb as much of the Chinese thinking, as opposed to being contaminated by, you know, European thinking about Chinese and even about what was happening here at home, and other people's perspectives. Clearly my parents had all the time been involved with the struggle in different ways, from radio broadcasts to putting out

The Crusader, continuing that whole process. And speaking and interacting with people, sharing the experience, and soliciting support for people who were involved in the struggle on this end…So that was kind of a part of that issue, and so, I was living, we spent most of the time with our Chinese classmates in the Chinese school, interaction with non-Chinese students, but there were times that we did, because of the school we were in. There were probably about 15-20 foreign students there as well other than ourselves, and that was always an interesting experience, and again you just got a little bit of what that was like when we first went there, because there were kids from Thailand, Indonesia, Africa, couple of British guys, Japanese students, 3 or 4 Americans other than my brother and I at that school. And the Chinese said, we're going to set up a special cafeteria for you guys, so you don't have to eat the same kind of food as—because the diet, especially back in the day, was very different. It's not like Chinese food you get out here. You're talking about the hard-core student diet, and when you're a student back in the day, you're living off the blood, sweat, and tears of the peasants, who made it possible for you to go to school. And so, their thing was, you're going to school to get it, you're not going to play, you're not going to be comfortable. You're going to get an education and get out of here to go and contribute to your people who are in desperate need. So, it's an awesome thing when you think about that and see where the Chinese are today, in comparison to then, and the systematic programming of their kids, you know? I mean, the young people were programmed to think, selfishness was frowned upon. If what you were doing was about you, and not about the community way of being, then it's frowned upon. And so then, doing what you're doing academically and being serious about it was a very real thing for them. It was a totally different type of environment, so when they came up with this idea of separate dining facility, some of the kids did want it and some of us didn't, so half of the Americans obviously jumped on it, because of meat and better-quality food; you're not going to do that in front of the Chinese students. So, they set up a little room on the side that you could go in and of course the Chinese students sooner or later found out that you're eating better than they were, but still you wanted to act like you were doing what they were doing. My brother and I stayed with our classmates, and so did a couple of the Japanese. Some of the people had special dietary needs because they were Muslim, like the Indonesians, but some honestly did have health issues and so they probably really needed a more nutritional diet but for the rest of us, you just go on and do what your classmates are doing. So that was a wonderful experience there, as well. We ended up, so a lot of the things that the classmates did we didn't have to do. Like going to the countryside and working, helping the farmers harvest wheat, helping them harvest rice, do physical manual labor. That was always a part of what they believed in, it's good for you to work. Like the old folk say: We don't care if you are going to become a scientist, or a doctor, or an intellectual, you get out there and work and mingle with the peasants, so when you come back, you'll appreciate it a bit more, what you have. That was a powerful pleasant experience in that way. And though some of the everyday quality of life was challenging, different, it was acceptable, and it wasn't like—you know, it also depends on what you come from, what you bring from the table. Coming from the South and coming from a situation where there are economic blockades constantly, faced against my dad, and my mom sometimes having to work menial jobs to put food on the table. Having the delicacies and certain kinds of food wasn't a major concern. Same thing with Cuba, because of the blockades. Remember we were there during the height of the economic blockade, they were literally trying to starve the Cubans out, the CIA, you know, destroying the sugar cane crop and trying to kill off the pig, the source of food. So, hard times, hard times weren't anything new for the brother. We knew about hard times, but we also knew about love and the spirit of the people. And Cuba was a high spirit, too, it was like, we aren't going to let the bastards choke us out. Whatever kind of sacrifice we must make; we're not backing down. David and Goliath. That's amazing that it's taken this long for this country to acknowledge how stupid the policy has been for 50 years. They've kissed with the Chinese, they've kissed with the Soviet Union, they've kissed with all the people that they were so anti-, but with Cuba, in this hemisphere, they're still trying to bow them. But of course, because of money, there's money to be made, the corporate people are kind of saying, hey, you know what? Forget all of this. Let's get down there and get some money, y'all holding up the money. So, the politicians are having to fall in line now because it's about the money.

RS: Back to, you stayed with a family, now there's two memoirs of people who were in Cuba, now I'm drawing a blank on the woman's name, it seems like Bonita, Bita something? And then there was Sidney ... they had written memoirs and they mentioned your family there. I'm trying to remember; it seems like the woman's memoir who said that you all stayed with her family. I cannot remember her name.

JW: In Cuba? Or in China?

RS: In China.

JW: Okay. Uh, only woman's family we really stayed with, the only family we spent significant time with was the Rittenberg's. But there were, in the summer, there were some summer experiences that we had. We went to a farm, kind of a government farm, it was a dairy farm and there was an American couple who had, for all intensive purpose, lived in China were living as Chinese citizens and had no intention of coming back. We kind of spent some time with them, so I don't know if it was them. I can't—Hinton. Does Hinton ring a bell with you?

RS: Sort of.

JW: They had kind of like, been in China before pre-revolution time, and one of the Hinton's wrote, he was a historian, who wrote very well about China in the revolution, I can't even think of his first name.

RS: That's who it is.

JW: He wrote, quite a very good book on the liberation of China, and pre-liberation time and post-liberation time. Red Star of China, that's what it is. He's the author of that. But then he had a sister who was there, and we spent time with his sister. JoAnn Hinton. That may have been who they were talking about. That's really the only people we stayed with, that was weekends primarily—the Rittenberg's.

RS: I can send you the title.

JW: Yeah, I'd love to see it. Rittenberg was a real interesting guy himself, real interesting. Sidney ended up doing prison time in China, he ended up doing prison time in China, because the Chinese, during the cultural revolution, they suspected him as being an

American agent, so he ended up doing time. And it was interesting because Sidney was probably one of the most, how do I put it, like a cat with nine lives, you know? He's a guy that lands on his feet all the time, doesn't matter what side, he always lands on his feet. He's a Rittenberg, so he's Jewish, and obviously, you know, he's white. And he was there in China before the revolution. But fluent in Chinese, you'd hear him speak and think he was Chinese. Was a member of the Party, of course, that became controversial whether he truly was or wasn't, especially when he started establishing relationships back here, it got to be hairy, trying to look at him and figure it out. At the end of the day, because of the Israel connection, down there on the international level, don't mess with him. So, he came back and established a business where he was doing, refurbishing computers and shipping them over. So, he's still on good terms with both. He's fine. A lot of that, is what people don't understand about that period, that I think would be important, is that survival in an international scene in the 1960s, the late 60s, was no joke, okay? People were being assassinated, people were being killed all over the world, in that period you lose [Kwame Nkrumah], period before that you lose Lumumba, you got people on the international level, and China was kind of like a hotbed of support, and you have people coming and going revolutionaries. So of course, the antirevolutionary forces are going to be, counter-revolutionary forces are there too. Like when dad was in Cuba for a season, he has a bodyguard, but he also packed. He had to. We may not be around, so you know, you must do what you must do, brother. Counter revolutionaries, what you do call them? Based out of Miami, infiltrating and trying to do it. But people just don't have an appreciation of that, on this side of the conversation. And it is important for our people to understand that. It's almost like, Well you're over there in a cakewalk. And it's like, no, it wasn't a cakewalk, and it required a lot of strategic-ness, a lot of diplomacy, it required a lot of shrewdness to maneuver and survive. If you went there with the wrong folk, it would cost you. And same thing with going later to Africa, and back to Detroit. And so, Detroit Syndrome, it's the same thing. You must understand that we, just of recent years, people have come to understand COINTELPRO, if you understand that, that was going on the same time we hid here, how the FBI, CIA had identified and had labeled Robert Williams, then you understand that even surviving that required a lot of thought and shrewdness on his part. But a lot of those people don't have an appreciation of, really.

RS: Okay, this is great, perfect. Before that, because you, your mom and your brother arrived in the US beforehand, but before that, there was a false issue of *The Crusader*. What do you recall about that? Because in Let it Burn, the documentary your dad with Robert Cohen.

JW: *The Crusader*, by the way, Robert Cohen, or you're saying the video?

RS: Right, in that, he mentioned something about CIA forces, but he also mentioned there were certain officials in the Cuban government. And I went to a conference at UMass Amherst, and there was a brother that recently published an article, and he was under the impression that it was the CIA, and I asked if he had any evidence of that. And of course, he didn't have any concrete evidence. Because I was working under the assumption that it was these Communist officials working within the Cuban government and some US Cuban people that were responsible. What is your take on that whole scenario?

JW: Interesting. I think basically that there was, what was clear, they were anti-folk. Whoever published it, they were folk who had an interest that was very different than ours. If you consider the sensitivity of living in Cuba under the circumstances under which we were living there, there were forces obviously that didn't want us there. Obviously, the United States interests that didn't want us there because of some things that were happening, mainly The Crusader, as well as the Radio Free Dixie that was happening, and it was having an influence in people over here. But they had a legitimate reason why they wouldn't want that. And there was another group of folks who just wanted to disrupt and had always been working to disrupt Cuba. So, all of them are candidates you know the counter-revolutionary crew, the anti-Cuba crew, as well as the CIA and the FBI being anti-black liberation. The other side of that that would, that I think for me, if you want to talk about the forged copies of that season, you must talk about the fact that the ban by the US government, by the US postal service, of *The Crusader*, which, you know gives it a little bit more weight, as well. If it's not effective, why would you ban it? If it's not having an impact, what's the point of banning it, okay? So, forgery and banning kind of go hand in hand, so for the people who would tend to think CIA, it would make sense. For the folk who think antirevolution people, like Cuba, that would make sense, because in the forged copies, I can remember, we felt bad about the fact that there was a negative portrayal of the Cubans, so we believed that that was designed to create friction between the Cuban supporters of the movement and the African American people who were involved in the liberation struggle.

RS: Can it be linked also to the Cold War? Because out of communism, you had the two forces, the Cubans following the Soviets, and China, on the other hand, not. So, it was also to create friction between your dad's relationships with both Cuba and China.

JW: You know, both scenarios are possible, you know? On the one hand if you look at it, when you look at how the US has spoken about Cuba even to this very day, you can see where they would also have a very vested interest in trying to ensure that African Americans never really develop a sense of true solidarity with the Cuban Revolution. So, I think that was a real angle as well. Obviously, with Assata Shakur being in Cuba, on some levels, you know, I think it's helped some, in terms of that whole controversy of people feeling like there's this great gulf between African American liberation struggle and the Cuban revolution, so again, it just shows you the complexity of dealing on that international level. It's not as simple as it appears, it's just complicated and dangerous.

RS: Speaking of that you said something about people not understanding the international dimension. Now in the US, there's a domestic, nationalist agenda. Would you say that the nationalists were aware of what was going on with your dad?

JW: Not really, except for those who were willing to take the time to read *The Crusader*. If they really read *The Crusader*, they would have understood a lot more when he returned. The truth be told, he didn't need to say another word. He summarizes the experience, the revolutionary experience of Cuba, of China. He synthesizes it and he puts it in writing for you, but you want him to come home and execute it like he's a foot soldier? What's wrong with that thinking?

RS: Very interesting. Now, speaking—

JW: And they're trying to kill this man? They've been trying to kill him from day one, from the 50s on. And you want him to come and be involved in skirmishes with the police on a local level, on a local scene? What's wrong with that? And you want to believe that you're mature? Now, what better position could the CIA come up with to eliminate someone who they have already told you is one of the most dangerous men in the country. Not because he can shoot better than anyone else—but he probably could, because he was an excellent marksman—but because of what he had in terms of intellect. But you wanted him to be a foot soldier. And you have the goal to question his dedication and commitment? Oh, you know, I ain't got time for the bullshit, really. Because if you're serious about our people contributing, see, I mean…he could have been doing a whole lot of other stuff. He wanted to be an agent. He would have put his life on the line over and repeatedly and given you a formula to help you and our people survive. And even in doing that, it'll cost because it's one of those things that to this day, the truth still stand

RS: He wrote a piece in *The Crusader* about the cultural revolution in the U.S.? Is that one of them?

JW: When you say the piece, help me out. Say it again.

RS: You said that if one was seriously reading *The Crusader* the answers were in *The Crusader*, and one of the pieces, there were many, but one of them, I'm drawing a blank on the title of it, but it's about the cultural revolution and the black community or something like that. And in that piece, he not only connects the black revolutionary movement to the movement in Cuba, but also the Chinese Cultural Revolution. And he puts it in a US based context for Black America.

JW: And if you think about the time, and I want to say it about this without editorializing on the other part, if you think about what was going on with us and the Black Panthers and look at the same time frame as *The Crusaders* of that time period, of what was being said. You know, we shouldn't get caught up in cultural nationalism to the point that it disintegrates and becomes nothing more than just, you know, when in fact, our people are in dire need of some solid, real, revolutionary thinking. Let's address the needs of the people, let's become, not exploited, not adopting old cultural processes that are not going to advance the cause of our people. Just because something is cultural or traditional doesn't mean that it's revolutionary. Revolutionaries need to look at how it's going to impact the lives of people today, so if it's not going to impact the lives of people in a positive way, then you don't want to embrace that stuff. Every culture in the world, when revolutions come along, they assess, which past cultural events are positive, and which are negative. But when you have the Chinese, you have Mao Zedong talk about how culture, there's no such thing as culture for culture's sake, that all culture serves a purpose. And all we must do is look at them, at what the black exploit films of the 60s, and we look at the mess we see on TV today. There's some that has some redeeming value but a lot of it that involves black people is nonsense, is buffoonery, things that involve, that don't serve our posterity well. It just won't. So, all of that is kind of like, analytical stuff that you need people who have analytical ability to put it forth. And you know, there are people I think in every generation that God blesses you with that have analytical ability, but people don't always recognize it. That's why Jesus says that a prophet is recognized in everywhere but his home. So, the Vietnamese who are fighting a war against the vote can appreciate intellectual, analytical ability of a person's writings. Revolutions all around the world can appreciate it but at home, in a limited way, want you to be a foot soldier, you go anywhere in the world where true revolutionaries are, and they take their hats off to you. To respect you, to thank you, for your analytical ability and giving us a sense of the nature of what we are up against here. And now, that looks so deep. That is like, truth, and it's kind of like what Malcolm said about, well, Brother Williams was decades before his time in his thinking, you know…Deep thing, brother.

RS: This is…without snitching too many names, this raises some other issues because at the same time, the Black Panther party, and us, were infiltrated by FBI agents. So, one of my readings is that your dad understood that. That was one of the things he understood when he returned—

JW: He understood the concept that revolution is not a tea party. That's a direct quote from Mao Zedong. But it's the violent overthrow of one system of another. And just like Frederick Douglass would say, and they ain't just giving it up, y'all. If you're afraid of the struggle, then you shouldn't be trying to do this, because you know, if you want the rain, you gotta take the thunder with it. So, a lot of times, philosophical revolutionaries act on the mission, and that's okay, because there's a need for that, but you understand that, by itself, at the end of the day, the real deal is, are you going to put it on the line? And are you going to do what needs to be done, to advance the cause? And you do it based on your gift and calling and talents. You don't expect everyone to do what you do the way you do it. And that's a major issue our people struggle with even to this day. It's like somebody being crazy coming to you and saying, why isn't he in the community? He could be taking all that he does and running a community somewhere. Why is he up in the university? Why doesn't he go up in the hood? I mean, some people that's their thinking—not understanding that, wait a minute, this man can help with greater contribution and impact, touch so many more people by doing what he's doing. Why would you want him to, you know, be—there are people that can do that, plenty of people who can run a community center. So, and people I believe, again, spiritually, are gifted a called and talented to do different things, and you have to allow people to do it. Some people are politicians and wouldn't do anything but be a politician. I wouldn't want to be a politician, it's not my thing. So, you know, you let people do what they do, and are equipped to do, and you appreciate it. When they all come together with a common goal, and that is to advance the cause of our people, then you don't have all of this back fighting and undercutting and folk trying to outdo other folk, and it becomes counterproductive. And we got too much of that, even to this day. If a brother wants to be a politician, let him be a politician. If he's a genius in music, let him be a musical genius, putting out stuff that's going to benefit the masses, and the people in the cause. Same thing, you know, I ain't trying to get in nobody's bedroom—if they're gay, that's fine. We've had gay people around from the beginning of time, you know, it ain't my thing, but it's like, if they're doing what they're supposed to be doing, who cares who they're sleeping with? It's not my business, as a pastor and as a believer in the Bible, I might say, well, hey, brother, if you ask me, I'm going to give you a scriptural interpretation about the matter, but I'm not going to try to convince you that you've got to give it up because God gives you free will and I understand and I'll pray for you. In due season, in due time, you'll get the revelation.

RS: That answers a lot. The other thing I've noticed in my research, is when your dad finally returned with all of the hardship that he had to endure, before returning, was he had to testify because, in front of what was one of the house committees, and he had a major extradition case that he was fighting. And he was also on tour, through the U.S., speaking to African Americans, speaking to Chinese American groups, discussing the—

JW: And prison groups.

RS: And, some academics. And several conversations, several themes are coming out of these different talks. One is about, particularly for the African Americans and to the broader—the important role that China will play in the future, and what we can learn from that. That was one of the major themes. But in the academic arena, at Wayne State University, the University of Michigan, University of Massachusetts—Amherst, he was on panels, and one of the persistent things, he was greatly disappointed with the condition of the black community when he returned. He thought that we had gone backwards, and that we needed to do something about the problems in the black community. Could you speak to some of that?

JW: And again, especially during the period of China, and some of those crusaders that came there, because you understand that that was in anticipation of returning to the US because it was always his intentions to come back to the US, so the idea is that certain thoughts and certain kinds of information need to be disseminated before then because he understood that once you get back into the States there's no guarantee that you'll be able to disseminate anything because they might lock you up and throw the key away. They may, you know, drug you and your mind will be ruined, so some things, you say while you have the opportunity and do while you can do that. But, one of the themes in The Crusader in that time period that you hear the same themes echo in that academic community, the talks that you're concerned about, was the need for what I tend to think of as revolutionary—how do I put it?—the need for revolutionaries to be very pragmatic, to understand that there's a need for integrity, that there's a need for morality, and that was a big one, morality, and that included and dealt with the issue, how do we treat children? Uh, you know, there's poetry that he, as well as articles that he wrote about, that there is no such thing as illegitimate children, because there was a lot of sentiment in it at the time, in the social, the social political scientists and the social workers and the system was talking a lot about illegitimate children, how do you support them and do we have an obligation to support them, you know, all that was going on in that time period of the 60s. And so, the idea that hey, the people in our community, we have a responsibility. We take care of people in our community. If we have a drug problem, we have a responsibility to take care of the drug problem in our community. If we've got thieves in our community who are preying on senior citizens in our community, we need to take care of that. So, a lot of that, what was happening in that time period that was spoken to in The Crusader, basically, was brothers, revolutionary men, you know, clean up the ghetto. Don't be thinking that your adversaries are going to do it for you. You need to organize and doing what you need to do. Don't let people just come in, abuse the women, abuse the children, meaning even my own people, meaning proletariat folk, folk who are selfish and self-centered who will destroy the fiber of a community that we got to raise children in. That we, the intellectual folk and as even the black intellectuals had a responsibility, rather than running away and leaving folk, where's the leadership, right? So, those were real kinds of issues that dad believed were critical. Because, remember this, and you see it, you know what, and it's a deep thing, because you see it all around the world. What you see all around the world is people who start off powerful revolutionaries, but for somewhere along the line, they get messed up in their thinking, and no longer are pro-people, but end up abusing the people. And they started off trying to get external forces that were oppressing their people off of the people's backs, but then some kind of way they get corrupted by the power, and prestige, and then they become just as bad as the oppressors, all right? So, we could see that then, in the 60s, early 60s. So it's like, as we progress in our movement, we need to make sure that we have good solid people who love—First rule, you have to love the people. If you don't love people, you are prone to do anything. Money becomes your issue, personal pleasure becomes your issue, so you'll exploit the sisters, you'll exploit anybody for personal pleasure, destroying the opportunity for true unity. Destroying the opportunity for, destroying the potential for being effective in creating a quality environment for your own people and if it's a revolution, and that's what you're trying to do, what are you trying to do? At the end of the day, it's not just about philosophy. Embracing somebody's philosophy, you know, you can learn from Maoism, you can learn from Marxism, you can learn from some of the best black nationalists of the past, but at the end of the day, if it's not going to advance the cause of the people, if that's not your motivation, then it won't. What are you doing? So a lot of that stuff was spoken to, again, so yeah, naturally—when he comes back and sees the drug pandemic, and with some understanding of a lot of folk locked up, okay, understanding that yes, there's a criminal justice system that has been set up and designed to lock your butt up, to get you off the streets, and weaken the communities that they're scared of, black manpower in the neighborhoods. They can't control the neighborhood as long as they have brothers out there that are serious about defending and caring for the family, what's happening in the community and taking responsibility for that. So, you know, jail 'em, drug 'em, and kill 'em. Three ways. If you can't sell 'em, if you can't get them to sell out, drug 'em out, kill 'em out. So, the plan was being executed and oftentimes, you know, folk didn't see it. And then the criticism, there has to be a combination, even in looking at diagnosing the problem, you know, it's not all one way. Yeah, the system itself is against you, but sometimes you know, we contribute to our own demise by virtue of, again, not having the right kind of morality. So, you trying to do a little something-something on the side that's illegal, that has nothing to do with advancing the cause of the people, but maybe is lining your own pockets for whatever reason sand what you're trying to do, and in the process, you're hurting your own people, and you're making yourself vulnerable to get caught in the system. It's a trap, so you end up ten fifteen years locked up, okay? So, again, having a sense of you know if you—the fundamental, the army. Where's your army? In this world, at the end of the day, if you don't have an army, you ain't got nothing. Because—like Frederick understood, you know, power concedes to nothing but greater power. So, if you can't bring nothing, you know, and the boys say, Richard Pryor say, Money talks and B.S. walks, well, you can take that money thing and you can also talk about who got the gun at the end of the day, who has the power, really? So.

RS: I want to ask a specific question about RNA, whose agenda was on reparations. What I see, the five most racist southern estates that we see dominating the political world in the US right now, and what was your dad's feelings about reparations?

JW: Very much. Philosophically, my dad had very little if any that I know of, conflict with you know, the philosophy and the theory behind the NRA, uh—the RNA. Reparations, yes, as a people, we're entitled to that, you know, other people got that. Other people ended up, and that was one of the learning experiences overseas, where you have in almost all of the socialist nations where they had different nationalities, many times they would set up autonomous regions, where these people could have their own government, basically, similar to the Native Americans in this country, where on the reservation, you set up your own government, you run that thing, you know. So, from those five states that you talked about, the thing to also remember, something they had in common was that they had some of the largest black populations in all states. That becomes another major issue, because see, again, where the masses of people are, that's where our activity needs to be if you're talking about establishing a base. You don't go where you don't have people, because as a revolutionary, you know, you flow better among the masses of the people, it's like fish and water. You can be a fish out of the water, but you're not going to survive and bring forth the energy that's needed. And you're not going to be putting out and doing the things you need to be doing to advance the cause of the people if you're not, you know, concentrating on a base. And so, the whole idea of having that kind of base just makes sense, especially in those states. The other thing is that it was a very strategic plan, in the sense that if you think about it, almost all those states also have water access. So, for international trade connections—so you're not totally dependent on and landlocked in America. The other thing was that for those who really kind of studied the philosophy, and the reparations would be the means to start a lot of institutions that initially you would need and all that. But also, there was never an advocacy of people in the north moving in mass numbers to space. That was never the plan, and it was never the advocacy, because it was clearly understood that you know, there was a strategic advantage to having your people all over the country. And if the base is intact and the people have been trained properly, you attack the base, you know, you're not going to survive. It's just that simple. And that's where you already got a majority, or a large percentage of our population is living still there. So, you know, a lot of times folk think they smart, but because they have been conditioned to think inside of the box, it's almost inconceivable to them that it's even possible for something like that to work. But you have models of how, all over the world. Even to this day, the UN and even in this country they're talking about all the hot spots, where you have all the ethnic tensions, how do they eventually solve them? They give them some land. That's how they solve it. Heck, Palestine, to this very day, right now, right? How are they talking about solving it? Well, the Jews have their party and give the Palestinians their part. So, it's not that farfetched, but then you know, for us, we love master, so we don't believe we have the capacity to even, oftentimes, do something on our own, separate from that. And we love it, so, we figure like, you know—and you know, again, the world is changing, the world is changing, and you reap what you sow. And for a season, as an imperial, capitalist season, we are able to have the benefit of taking natural resources from other people and doing pretty much what we wanted to do and what not, and now, you know, we're coming into an era where we are dependent on a lot of folk—and when I say we, I am talking about this government, this system, American—you know, are now dependent on some of the very people that they've dogged for decades. And the folk aren't stupid, they don't understand your true colors. Chickens do come home to roost sooner or later, you know? Even this whole manufacturing—I mean what do you manufacture now, or are you just mean to consume? Sooner or later, you know, that stuff runs out, it really does. And so, in an interesting kind way, as far back as we can go, Marcus Garvey, Elijah Muhammad, same thing, you know, understand, you gotta separate out from this joker, because if you don't, when he has to pay up, if you're locked up with him, you gonna pay up, too. Same thing as a divided house cannot stand, but just taking it from a more positive, that was more of a reactive standpoint, and then you got the positive, affirmative standpoint, well, you know, we need to be, everybody needs to work together because this bad boy is not going to stand unless it does because eternal strife will destroy you. So, basically, reparations, yeah, he was all for reparations.

RS: The philosophy and theory behind it. But what about the pragmatics?

JW: The pragmatic side of it? Obviously, that need to be worked out, he knew that wasn't—you know, dad was kind of—of the persuasion that we had to struggle on multiple fronts, you know, we do the civil rights thing, we do the economics thing, and we do the reparations thing at the same time. And it was important, and is important, to this day, it remains—I think it remains—important. I mean other people have gotten reparations, how you do it now, obviously is a major kind of concern. Yeah.

RS: So, then, what was the conflict—I talked to you know Max Stanford and Mohammed Ahmed, and also talked to somebody else and these were like just really informal, private conversations, and the best that they remember is that there was some name calling by certain individuals, claiming that your dad was no longer a revolutionary, blah, blah, blah. So, what was his concern about needing to resign as president? Well, I guess he was president because he was president-in-exile and when he returned, he was president. So, what was his, in your observation, what was his concern that he needed to resign then?

JW: Well, a host of things, and your kind of alluded to some of them, in terms of the many tasks that he had on him, that he was steal dealing with. The extradition thing, that had all the, from a legal standpoint, was just—

RS: A nightmare.

JW: Yeah, a continuous issue there. You know. And he had still all of the weight of having been identified as one of the most dangerous black men in the country that was constantly under surveillance and there was always a threat of annihilation that was on him. He still had the responsibility of a family, okay, and I think, philosophically, he didn't have a problem with the RNA; I think part of the pragmatism and lack of thought through posturing, was problematic for him. Having seen and having understood what he understood from being out there in the real world, where the adversary oftentimes wasn't as nice, simply because they didn't have the legal constraints that they had in this country and so they had to kind of pretended like they were going to do the legal thing with you. He understood that when the legal thing didn't work and they didn't have any other means of dealing with you, they'd kill you, it's just that simple, you know. And understanding that if you want to have an impact on the most fundamental level, you have to survive, because dead, you're not going to be able to do anything. All that's going to happen is that other people are going to talk about you. And they're going to spin it and put it the way they want to put it, and you're not going to be making any contribution beyond what you already made. So, you got to live. To be able to analyze a situation and give some input, you've got to survive. And so, we understood, and again, you can go back to The Crusader, and it's like, Alright fellows, you can't be out here, woofing, selling woof tickets, can't be out here parading in a certain way and think that this man's not serious about his survival, because he's real serious and he sees you as a real threat, and therefore, you know how you present yourself and what you do and what you do publicly vs. non-publicly makes all the difference in the world. And what you even do when you think you're doing it in, in a nonpublic way, you always understand, you know, that the enemy's sleeping with you.

RS: That's a good answer.

JW: So, think through what you're doing. What organizations other than the RNA at that time period, and a few others, were like the focus of the government for crying out loud. And so, being here in the city, okay, which was the headquarters again, and with a lot of the things that were happening here in the city, the drug epidemic going as well, you become vulnerable. And when you come into a situation where you remember now, okay, organizationally, my dad was strong in putting together organizations, grassroots organizations. Because of his love for his people and his commitment to his people, he's able to look people in the eye and say, I understand your struggle and your family and what you need and I'm willing to walk with you. I'm walking to walk with you and help you to the point that people see that he's genuine and so now the people that join up with you are people who will put their life on the line with you. But when you come into a situation where you didn't walk with the folk somebody else trained, walked with and attracted the folk, you really don't know what you're dealing with. And their loyalty, there's no guarantee that their loyalty is to you, right? So, I mean, there were some very pragmatic people, kinds of situations that you know, that caused that. And you know one of the things again, adventurism is something that you learn also in true revolutionaries, you learn that adventurism is crazy. And there's plenty of work and writings from Mao Zedong on adventurism. Adventurism will get you killed and will not advance your cause, so there's a distinct differentiation between being strategic and doing what you gotta do to advance your cause and being an adventurist. If you want to go on the 5 o'clock news and make threats and talk about what you're planning and what you're going to do, fine, but you know, if you're trying to really work an agenda here, and trying to advance a cause for your people, that's not the approach. So, anybody who's doing that is not the approach. It's dangerous, it's adventurist. It's not a long-term commitment to a protracted struggle that needs to be waged. And always it must be about the love of the people, and really, that whole thing of who gravitates to you? It matters, you know what I'm saying? I mean, Jesus had 12 out of a hundred and some people, he had 12 disciples. And out of 12 disciples, he had an inner circle of 3. You figure.

RS: And one of them was a traitor.

JW: And he knew it. And you think about Judas factor, and what he was, was the traitor. They knew he was putting his hand in the cookie jar constantly. Selfish, the selfish one, the one who you know, so, it's a heavy piece. So, philosophically, he didn't have a philosophical issue with it. I think you'll find; it wasn't just my dad in terms of seeing the need to kind of shift that gear and do some things differently. Milton Henry did the same thing if you look at the situation. He didn't remain on the same level, and he had been kind of in the very outset of you know, creating some of the framework, some of the philosophical framework and what not. Brilliant brother. There's a brother, that you know, masterful stuff, but there were other people involved who weren't quite as masterful and weren't quite as mature, and you know, hadn't developed. Not to say that it's like everything else. In the Bible there's John, [and] Mark, who becomes really, great writer of the Bible. Mark, the Gospel of Mark and a few other parts of the Bible. But he was somebody that Apostle Paul said, this boy, when we really need him, he got flaky on us and went, left when the thing got rough, he left. But then in the latter years, you hear Paul say, you know, John, Mark was all right. But it took time for him to mature and grow into, you know, becoming what he needed to be. And it's the same way with people; all people have seasons and processes that they must go through. Even you know, people will oftentimes talk about Malcolm, talking about what Malcolm could have been if Malcolm had lived, you know, what Dr. King could have accomplished had he lived, you know. And it's true, with maturity you change, you grow, you learn from experience, so many of those who were involved in that whole piece, it was a stepping-stone and a learning experience for them. And have done great things since that time.

RS: This is great. I have only a few more questions, but could we take a five-minute break?

JW: Absolutely.

RS: Okay, one of, there's a professor at Michigan State University in the Department of History, Pero Dagbovie. He wrote, he's been the first intellectual to write about, I think in any sincere way, about your mother and your father's involvement. The night that I first met your dad, in private, was in his cottage in Pleasant Plain, down the street from Idlewild, or a couple of blocks, right? And it was an interesting, eye-awakening experience to me, and I'm saying this because that's the first time I've lived in a rural area, and I lived over in Ludington, and I drove over to Lake County at about 6 o'clock but I didn't leave until about 4 in the morning, because we sat up talking, right? And one of the conversations while we were talking, because your mom sat up a little bit, she was in the kitchen doing something, and she came in the room, and she was sitting down listening. And he said, "Well, you don't have to be here, and she said, I been here all this time." So right then I understood, that—one of the things about Pero's article is that he brings that to bear, but there's a lot missing. So, in one of my recent interviews, I'll say this without mentioning the person's name because of confidentiality issues, right, one of the comments made was how dedicated your mom was to her marriage with your dad. And so, the question that I asked about a question that I had always floated in my head about your brother, really, is drilling from back. So when I asked about the question about your brother, I really want to get a good context, not to snoop too much into that, but to highlight that as an example of the commitment and the kind of loving relationship that you and your mom had, and the importance of that you and your brother by birth of your mother and father, being aware of your brother by blood of only one of your parents, right? And so that's the context of my wanting to know that information, and so my question is about your brother, Franklin—I guess the first question is, is he older than you?

JW: He's my younger brother, he's my younger brother. And from my mother's perspective, he was a stepson ... throughout his life, he has had a relationship with my mother, okay, so he was part of our extended family, a stepson to my mom, and to me, he's, my brother. And again, because of my dad's relationship with his mother, I respect not only him as my brother, but I respect his mother. One of the things that has always been and has been consistent in terms of my dad is caring for his family, and so I do not divulge intentionally certain information, that's personal, as it relates to my brother, as it relates to his mother. My dad believed firmly in the idea of struggle. We struggled because we wanted to make life better for our posterity, right? And so, one of the things that he was always concerned about was how the decisions that he made politically, how the ripple effect would affect my brother and I, that had to be a legitimate concern, as well as my mother, okay. And that same concern extended to my other brother, younger brother, and his mom. So, I respect that and continue in that vein of thinking in terms of his well-being and her well-being. The whole struggle was about justice, fairness, equality and opportunity, and we don't want to saddle them with all the mess that we had to endure because of affiliation on one level, and in my instance, not just affiliation but also embracing of certain kind of struggle. And at some point, in life you choose to accept on a personal level that this is just, that this is fair, and that you know you're in because you're in, not because of affiliation. And I am one to choose to believe as a Christian, especially as a Christian minister, that truth and fairness and justice and, you know, those things are foundational. And so, I'm in the movement because I choose to be, but yes, there is a ripple effect also that impacts all who have been involved in that, and so but yeah, it was a, my brother's mother and my mother have had a civil and a decent relationship over the years, and so it's an extended family situation.

RS: Right, I know exactly what you mean and how to frame that. Your older brother, his name was Robert.

JW: Robert F. Williams, Jr.

RS: Your younger brother, what was his name?

JW: Franklin Williams.

RS: And Franklin spoke at the memorial at Wayne State. So that pamphlet, *Legacy of Resistance: Tributes to Robert and Mabel Williams*, I think is the title of it? He spoke there and I think his speech was printed also, but yeah, that's what I needed, that's it. No more on that. All right, so, we're wrapping up now, and while we're wrapping up, you made some statements about speaking truth to power. And I mentioned that one scholar discusses

your father in a very surface-level way by saying that when he returned to the US in 1969, that he spent a few years in the Detroit area and then he and your mom migrated to Baldwin, Michigan, he says, to retire. And my research suggests that he remained active for the last 20-plus years of his life. [Laughs.] And so, I want to talk about some of those activities that he was involved with that you and I have had a chance to talk about, and of course, I have published already about some of it. So, let's talk about that.
JW: Okay, you got one to start with?
RS: Well, I think the main case, probably the biggest case that happened was the Ruby Nelson case. And out of that came the development of the Lake County Association for Human Rights—or the Lake County People's Association for Human Rights.
JW: And again, you know, and it's always interesting to note and see how grassroots work happens, and you look at even the format of the People's Association for Human Rights and it was, as a nonprofit corporation, but it was a membership nonprofit corporation, which speaks of the commitment to the notion of mass involvement, getting the people involved. We embraced the philosophy that said basically, the people are the motivating force behind history, the moving of history, and the making of history. That's why it's significant and you know, to follow a quick detour, it's significant that when you have these demonstrations around police brutality and it becomes a mass movement, that's again, that's people. When the people get out there and the people get sick and tired of being sick and tired, that's when change happens. You know, you can always have individuals who are ahead of their time, who can see things, who are in leadership, and can point out things; but ultimately, until the people are aware, the conscious level is raised, and conditions, many times, economic, social conditions are ripe, you don't really have the kind of movement that you envision, that your visionaries may already see and know and understand needs to happen for positive change to happen. For Dad, it was always, so he was dealing in the People's Association as you probably know, a lot of individual cases, situations where blacks that were having negative encounters with the police and criminal justice system up north, negative encounters with the school system, negative encounters with systems, institutions, that were not doing right by our people. And as a result of that you know, again, you deal with it, you encounter that kind of mess and then when you're driven by the spirit, okay, and you have a commitment, a true commitment to your people and you see people being abused or taken advantage of, then you don't just sit idly by, you speak out and you do what you need to do, even at a cost to yourself. And so, it was in this period, during that period, when all of this was happening, especially right after the Ruby Nelson case, I'd been kind of in Indiana. I'd been in Indiana going to law school and I had kind of finished up there and I was working in Indiana and talking to my dad, just becoming aware, kind of like, well, here we go again. Like, we got people, police force, well sheriff, people in the sheriff's department basically making noise and threats because of his political activity in a small community up north where in my mind, he doesn't have the kind of network that he had developed in North Carolina, you know. Again, people that he had had eye-to-eye contact that had been brought up in the trenches, he could depend on who would die for him, and he would die for them. He didn't have those kinds of relationships initially there, in Baldwin, so my thought was, hey dad, I'm going to come home. You want me to come

on up to Baldwin, you know, I'll have your back. His thing was, nah, nah, I can handle this, I got this. But he was constantly still both developing the rapport with the people, and so, even to this day, there's a respect for Robert Williams in Baldwin, in Idlewild. People's stuff gets vandalized, destroyed, but folks like, that's Rob's stuff and because he dealt with the caliber of people. That's always the interesting thing, you know, the black bourgeoisie always has a perspective about things, but Dad dealt with all kinds of folk. He dealt with the NAACP there, with some of the people running for political office in the black community, the "upper" crust. But he also dealt with the brother in the street, the brother who was getting his butt whipped for no good reason other than they thought they could get away with it and no one would be concerned about the average brother who's on the street getting beat up by the police. But dad was a caliber of person that you know, recognized the value of each individual and the importance of individuals. He developed rapport, so guys on the street loved him more than , much more than a lot of the people in the upper echelon because of where he had been and who he had been associated with, gave him a little respect, but it wasn't like they didn't understand the depth that came from him just caring about people and loving people.

RS: Do you see any parallels or any similarities/differences between his activism in Monroe versus his activism in later years in Baldwin?

JW: Not really. I think it's all the same motivation, you know. The same motivation and the same times of fundamentals, that's the critical issue. If you are who you are, you know, your value system, what you believe in, and what you've been brought up with, it comes through. It doesn't matter what environment you're in, you're pretty much still committed to that value system. Sometimes it requires strategic responses to different stimuli, you know, that you may encounter, different forms of racism, different forms of negative influences, you know, you must respond to them different based on the practical needs. But by and large, it all comes out, your response comes out of love and commitment to your people and to the principles of justice and fairness and fair play, and you know, a lot of those foundational, fundamental principles that you supposedly are entitled to under the US constitution. Everyone loves and goes around the world telling everybody how great we are and promulgating those things, supposedly, but denying black people those things here at home. That was the other side of the complexity of international peace. On the one hand, the US was trying in the 60s to sell "democracy" to all these people in the world and they're supposed to be better than communism, better than socialism, but dogging black people. Literally putting the dogs and water hoses and jailing and assassinating and killing black folk, for wanting to exercise, you know, their constitutional rights. So then you have a man out there on an international level who is calling attention to that and you know, that just created a whole other dynamic of hatred against him. But it was an important part of the struggle that someone needed to carry. Malcolm, in later years in his life, was developing in that way as well and that, through the UN and reassigning human rights issues struggle. But you know, my dad was out there, already doing that, and we were like ambassadors to the movement in those third-world arenas. And so, back to the issue of the parallels. There were parallels in the kinds of struggles and that's one, one level, from a historical perspective, looking at it, it's a disappointment, it's a disappointment in the sense that you expect more. You figure, like, 20 years later, 30 years, 40 years later you're having to right the same old thing, the same old kinds of issues. So, some things have changed, and I think it speaks to a greater principle, a more important principle, even you can have a change of laws. You can change that, but to really deal with the reality, the de facto, that's a whole other issue and most of the time you're talking about people embracing spirit, having the right kind of spiritual orientation where they accept the fact that all human beings are made in the image and likeness of God, and they are creatures created by God. So, you can't say you respect God and not respect people made in his image and likeness, and for so long, that's been the issues that black folk, have not wanted to give us that basic due, that we are made in the image and likeness of God and should be respected or no other reason than that.

RS: I want to tease at this a little more. In Monroe, he worked with a shrewd attorney, Conrad Lynn, and they had a committee—I'm drawing a blank on the exact name, the committee against racism or something in Monroe in North Carolina. He was a younger, strategic civil rights activist and leader, but one who had military training and a desire to become a propagandist for the U.S. government. And it appears that through that role, he used those tools of propaganda and had the benefit of using the law and understanding the U.S. Constitution. A younger Robert Williams. In Baldwin, he worked with a shrewd labor activist and attorney, Ernest Goodman, and later a younger, up-and-coming attorney, who, Melissa El, who talked about the amazing learning experience that she gained from working with him and understanding of how to win a case, not just in the court but outside the courts, too. And sort of as an elder, veteran Civil Rights leader, activist, internationalist, and so, I'm seeing a few differences. And kind of the differences that I'm seeing is, here is someone who's been around the block a few times, by the time he hits Baldwin, Michigan, and in a broader sense, and can seriously make an impact that he is, to this day, seen as an important historic figure in that whole area. And so, when I ask the question, I'm seeing some different things. And I'm not sure if there were consumer law issues that he was fighting in Monroe like he was fighting in Baldwin. And so, when I asked the question about the parallels, am I imagining things or are you seeing this as you reflect on this question, a more veteran Robert Williams during those last 20 years?

JW: Well, no doubt his life experience and experience in the social, political movement gave him a lot more tools, and his tools were more advanced, obviously. Just like me thinking, I need to go home and help you out here, and he's like, nah, I got this, you don't have to worry about this. I got this, I'm all right, you know. And really totally and on some levels just running circles around some of the adversaries and frustrating them totally because they were not really equipped, they didn't have a reason to be equipped to handle a person of this caliber. And that is kind of a similar experience for a lot of folks, like Chuck Wayne and the legal thing, it's the same thing. You hear people talk about how brilliant he was, and the judges sometimes sit there, trying to figure out how to handle him and what to do with him. It's a similar kind of deal when you are mature, and you know what you're fighting and you know how to fight it, so, yeah on that level, the maturity and the experience level was very different there. And having the tools to bear. The other thing is interesting parallel if you want to draw another parallel,

Conrad Lynn was a communist. He was a black communist; though my dad was not a communist and never has embraced or put out the position that he was a communist. He had enough understood though to understand that many of the issues that were concerned about and that we were fighting for, many of the people who were communists would appreciate the same struggle. And when you think of in terms of Ernie Goodman being here, he was part of a collective—Coleman Alexander Young, Ernie Goodman, and several other well-known historical figures in Detroit were part of a collective, and Paul Roberson was part of the same collective, and that collective had strong, I can't say, I won't say, but it had strong socialist leaning and during the McCarthy era they went through hell, you know, because they were being labeled Communists. Whether they were or not—I—history, some of them clearly were, make no bones about it. So, there's that parallel that's here again, as well, but also, Dad just because he embraced the whole idea of constitutionality and constitutional law, he was also able to deal with people like Kunstler, okay, fighting extradition, you know. Kunstler was one of his attorneys down in North Carolina. Karen Galloway, a young black woman attorney down in NC, when Kunstler, because he wasn't a local attorney, Karen Galloway later became a judge down there, was the person who represented, who was the local lawyer that represented my dad. And so played a similar role as Melissa El here, and neither one of them was communists but both understood constitutional law and the importance of constitutional law and had an abhorrence of people violating peoples' fundamental rights, black people in particular. So, you know, there are those parallels that are there, clearly. That kind of speaks to the whole idea of the united front, which is something that was very important, that was gleaned from that whole process, you know, from North Carolina to Cuba to China and back, again that, you know, you have to be able to unite with people on certain principles and certain realms and certain issues of struggle. You don't have to agree on every point, you don't have to agree on every strategy. But if their principles and objectives that are important to achieve and are going to benefit your people, yeah, you unite with folk and you work with folk towards that end. And also, you understand that on an international level, in Tanzania, the president of Tanzania, made a statement a long time ago that there's no such thing as a permanent ally when you're dealing with international affairs, people looking out for their interests. It's nations or groups of people and they may be an ally today but that doesn't mean they're going to be an ally tomorrow, and you just understand that, and work on that and look out for your own best interests and what you have identified—when I say own best interest, I say group or collective group in this, so black people—and black people can't expect other people to carry water for them if they're not going to get nothing out of it.

RS: What did you say to the attorney, I'm not aware of her, Gwendolyn Midlo Hall? In Detroit? Fighting extradition charges?

JW: Oh, no. William Kunstler. Bill Kunstler, he's dead now, but he was real, William Kunstler, white guy, out of New York. William Kunstler just, you Google him, he represented a whole lot of just radicals in the country from whites to black side, based on the constitution. I can't think of some of the people offhand, but I mean if you just Google him.

RS: How's his last name spelled?

JW: K-u-n-s-t-l-e-r, something like that, Kunstler, yeah, Jewish guy. But, uh, a real dynamic guy. Who were some of the people? I can't think of them. But just a brilliant constitutional—

RS: I'll look him up ... Okay, and then, okay, well we are basically at the end, this is kind of getting at, I think this is an important perspective here. Do you see any parallels with the community activism of the 1950s and 60s in Monroe and the community association in the 1980s and 90s in Baldwin, and, of your dad, and some of the more contemporary issues that have been unfolding, especially centered around police community-black community relations, and if so, what parallels do you see, and what lessons possibly could be learned from that?

JW: Well, we've kind of touched on some of that already, but basically, unfortunately, the unfortunate side of that whole thing is that we are having to repeat some of the same challenges, or we're having to address some of the same challenges that we shouldn't be having to address at this stage, I think of the history of the nation. That we should be much further than where we are, that as a corporate, form a corporate standpoint, let me rephrase that, from a United States, we the people, perspective, we should be further ahead than where we are, in terms of race relations, and a sadness that at this day and time we're having to fight some of the same kind of battles that we fought 40, 50 years ago. And the other side of that—is that oftentimes, we must be mindful of that history, and it is important to know that history. And there's an African proverb that goes, if you don't know the history, you're doomed to repeat it, sometimes you must look back to understand and appreciate where you need to go forward. And so there's that need for our people to understand the history of the struggle and some of the intricate, strategic aspects of it, not just a broad just cursory review of and paint it just as it was one-dimensional which was really—

RS: You were saying...it does that when I first turn it on.

JW: There's a disservice in not painting a full and accurate picture of our history in the civil rights movement, especially as it relates to some of the struggle that was going on that would oftentimes be classified as the militant aspect of the struggle. Starting from SNCC on up, looking at it, not just from Robert Williams' perspective, but looking at it from the SNCC Movement, the radical youth that came out of that movement and even the strategies that they implemented are important. And we must give more attention to some of the strategic aspects of the struggle that our young people are able to appreciate not only the sacrifice as well as the techniques and of course, the young people today are doing some awesome things in their own right because of the technology, in particular. They're using it on some levels, a lot of time they come under criticism, but they are just stronger and better, those who are wanting to bring about change, when they also understand the history and some of the strategies that were used in the past that served them well. And in some instances, unfortunately, some of the starts that are essential, that for survival, you know, and so, it's ... I kind of lost my thought on that, but that was just one piece of the question, I don't remember the other part right now, so you'll have to refocus me on the other part.

RS: Okay, I think the other part was about, you know, the specific issues and strategies for addressing those issues in the 1950s and 60s and again in the 80s and 90s and as we look at some of the more recent or cont. issues in the African American community involving, particularly, law enforcement, whether you saw any parallels. I guess the other part of it was, was there any, you know, somebody said your dad was a man ahead of his time. When you say a man is a person ahead of his times—are there any issues, concerns, strategies that he employed that if we look back and studied him, that we could, and if we had addressed that, not just in the black community, but as you said, a nation, would we be farther ahead?

JW: Absolutely. And you know a lot of that hinges on commitment and doing more than paying lip service to some fundamental principles. There's a lot of lip service to the Constitution and fundamental principles but when it comes time for government to implement policies and laws, it depends on the people. And that's just the reality, you know, institutions are made up of people and the institutions are no better than the people that make them up. So, to have uneducated folk, to have folk who don't know the history, to have folk who are not committed to whatever position that they're holding, and not being committed to the fundamental principles of the constitution, is problematic. And that's always been problematic and will continue to be problematic and very specifically, if you have people on the police force, in the police force, in the sheriff's department, people in state government, people in national guard, people in the army that are not people who embrace the concept of justice, who embrace the concept of equality for all people, who do not embrace fundamental rights and understand that everybody is entitled—black people in particular and brown people in particular and red people—are just as much entitled to those rights as they are, then we'll always have conflict and that has to be addressed. And people who are concerned about their survival, we don't have a choice but to address it, and so that's why, again, a divided house can't stand. And it just stands to reason that the power structure knows that they have, and do indeed, to intervene at a certain time but they wait until there's a crisis and then they want to intervene, and they want to tweak it and they want to spin it and turn it into something that it's really not. And then everyone wants you to come and sing Kumbaya, all is well, when all is not well. All is well for you because you're not being impacted in a negative way, but you want us to line up with you one time you feel a little pinch or a little threat from someone externally, well, you gotta make up your mind, you know, are we a part of the family or are we not? And if we're a part of the family, then we need to be treated like we are a part of the family rather than treating us like we're not a part of the family but when you need us, then you want us right there, you know. So those kinds of issues continue, and it's said that they continue but it's a reality. One of the things that we said about my dad, yeah, he was a nationalist and was very much concerned with the wellbeing of our people, that was his primary concern, but he was also one that believed in the constitution, he believed in fundamental rights and fairness and this country has great potential and he wanted to see the country live up to that potential and that's part of the challenge. And that's part of, I guess, also being a leader who had the ability to understand that, you know, that there are a lot of good things worth preserving but there was need for some radical change, as well. And you know, a lot of that comes out of the spiritual base as well as the social, political evolvement/involvement in the movement. But it starts off with the spiritual base, the fundamental principles.

RS: This is the last question. This question is really hijacking off the one I just asked, and that really is getting at the role of technology. And I'm thinking about how African Americans have addressed injustices in their communities. Like, are there lessons that can be learned from that. So let me give you an example from what I'm seeing, this is just preliminary: I see your dad using communication mediums, writing letters to the editor in Monroe, creating his own newsletter to get his message out, in Cuba, creating his own reading program to get his message out, in Baldwin, doing some similar activities, writing letters—

JW: And continuing The Crusader.

RS: That's correct. And staging a one-man protest, and the—one thing, just off the top that I see different about, you spoke to the current younger generation, and that is the use of social media, a lot of what we initially learned from Ferguson was because somebody, through their cell phone was videotaping what was going on, and it was broadcast through Tweeter, Facebook, all of it. And so in a way, your dad understood the importance of technology in combatting these issues and in some senses, that's sort of like, that use of technology is on some kind of continuum as we look at time periods. So that's kind of what I'm trying to get at.

JW: Well, you summarized it. Like I said, young people are creative. And that's the good thing, they've come under criticism about a lot of things, but young people are creative, and the idea is the thinking. If the thinking and the philosophy—you know, philosophy is nothing more than thought. And if the right thinking is there, then you don't worry about the methods and the methodology because it will happen. People are creative in that way, they will look and assess the particular situation, they're pragmatic, and they'll come up with ways and means to address what they have to address and confront what they have to confront. But what I think Dad, one of the things that he really understood, and I can think from a personal perspective, not always understanding it myself as a young man, you know, was the idea that how you think is important. And what you expose your mind to, and how you develop your mind and not to be manipulated and controlled, but to be an independent thinker, enough to recognize when you're in danger and recognize when you're being had, and recognize when people are not being honest and truthful, that all of that is fundamental and when you lay a good foundation, then you don't sit up and worry, will people make the right choices and decisions in terms of their strategies. So, again, and it kind of goes back to The Crusader, okay, give the folk what they need foundationally, and if you lay a proper foundation, folk are smart—who are serious—are smart enough to take it and build on the foundation and run with it, and deal with the particularities, the peculiarity of the struggle that they may be confronted with in the season. And so, you know, I would anticipate that yeah, young people will continue, the strategies will evolve. But some of them are fundamental, some things that gotta happen just gotta happen, that they have come up with some ways to communicate and getting that word out fast. Back in the '60s even, because of the cultural thing came in, there were a lot of things like drums, like in Detroit, and they talk about the movement and there was also the play about the grapevine and the drum. And there were brothers who were saying that, in Africa, they got talking drums, and it used to freak the white folk out, because they didn't know what the brothers were communicating up in the wood, but the brothers were reading the drums. So, it's the same kind of idea.

RS: You can even take that back to slavery

JW: Yeah.

RS: The prohibiting of slaves using the drums.

JW: So, what we're talking about is folk being able to communicate and right away, a brother on the hilltop, tapping out them drums, and the brother's way over in the next village knowing what's going on, and the Haitian rebellion, it's the same thing. You know, the tradition stuck, the drums. So powerful. And so, it's kind of that yolk, but it's the same thing in Christianity. It says, train up a child in the way that they should go and when they grow old, they will not depart. So foundational, laying the proper foundation is important. And that's why good historians are important. That's why I appreciate your work as well, seriously, because on one level, it's just basic information that our folks just need to understand. They don't have to like it all, they don't have to embrace it all, but they just have to at least understand it. And if they have access to it, and right now, heretofore, a lot of access has been denied. Just a lot of different levels but that's beginning to change and that's important.

RS: Okay, I lied, I'll frame this as your concluding remarks. But one thing that I think is important that we didn't talk about is one that no one talks about, is, and this kind of relates to communication, but Robert Williams was a poet, too. And there is a lot that can be learned from reading and studying poetry. I was hoping that you could speak to your dad as a poet.

JW: Well, you know, he wrote a lot of poetry. And almost all his Crusaders, there was poetry in them, you know. Most of the Crusaders had at least one or two poems, in each Crusader, especially in the latter years, and a lot of poetry that he wrote that has not been published that I intend to publish one day, hopefully sooner than later. Yeah, he did a lot of poetry writing, pretty much on a myriad issue, from international issues, all the way down to local community issues, observing some of the things that he was observing and expressing them in poetic form. It's interesting because even in North Carolina, you know, they put out a book every so often with some of the great poetry out of the state of North Carolina, they've included some of his works. So yeah, he was a pretty accomplished in his own wright, in terms of poetry.

RS: Any favorite poem?

JW: Yeah, there's one that kind of is so profound when you look at the time it was written. It's called "Pusherman." It was, it's kind of a heartbreaking piece, but it's a real kind of piece that depicts the devastation before people could really appreciate the full devastation of crack cocaine and heroin. And people in our community, you know, pushing, and willing to sacrifice our people just for individual profit. And it kind of speaks to that. That's one that I, you know, tend to remember. It's interesting because so many of the poems, you know, I heard them immediately after he wrote them because that's the way our family operated and I think that's an important piece as well, you know. I say my mom was so fundamental and critical in the stage of the struggle, being in the United States, Cuba, China, Africa, and back here, that she was not only privy to, but actively was involved in presenting whatever it was that was presented to the public, from The

Crusaders to a host of things. There were times when my dad was sick overseas and wasn't able to actually speak but my mom would go in his stead and do things and sort of speak for him, so she was very active and as a family, we all oftentimes at around and say, what you got, and he'd come up with it, and we'd read it together as a family…have a little input and have things that we enjoyed, didn't enjoy, or whatever. That also was a person who enjoyed music. He understood the power of music. Jazz, folk music, soul, rhythm and blues, and you see that, it comes through in Radio Free Dixie. The selection of the music, the Addie Lincolns and Nina Simone's and people of that caliber, you know, and their kind of movement music. Some of the folk music, you know, Judy Collins and antiwar people and you know, a lot of that kind of stuff was utilized in Radio Free Dixie in the 60s. He had a great appreciation of how that could impact people. So, you talked about propaganda, so when you talk about being a good propagandist and that tradition even continues today because we have young brothers and sisters who are operating in the similar tradition of appreciating music and how to incorporate music and discuss contemporary issues that are important to our people. Satellite radio has become another avenue that is just a wonderful avenue for folk to get out the word and keep people aware, you know, make people aware of some of the things today that are happening.

RS: Okay, so I'll just ask if you have any concluding remarks and I will also say that when campus resumes on Monday, at the end of next week, I'll be meeting with the transcriptionist and when the transcriptionist has completed the transcript, I'll be sending it to you. If there are any questions, this will be your opportunity to clarify questions or you want to add into questions, because it's your voice, it's your interview—

JW: Right.

RS: You'll be free to do that, so.

JW: That's great and I look forward to that. In addition to that, I am more concerned about what you get ready before you publish what you publish. That's more of my concern. You know, the raw interview, you know what I'm saying, the actual final stuff that's going to go out, that's more of my concern, making sure that I'm not misquoted.

RS: In fact, I'll be happy to share—

JW: Or stated in a way that's not quite how I meant it. I don't want to be in that position, and I think that insures us maintaining the kind of relationship we want and taking it to the next level.

RS: I would be happy to do that. As a matter of fact, I would be honored if you would take time to read it and give me suggestions and feedback.

JW: Absolutely.

RS: Because I'm interested in accuracy.

JW: I understand. And like I said to you before, we may need to revisit what we had talked about with our arrangement with this whole thing, but I want to see it successful too. So, in order to make that happen, you know, I'm willing to work in whatever capacity with you to make that happen. Continuing with the terms that we talked about, as well as … So the finished product more so is what I'm concerned with. Not about other people's perspective, they, whatever they say, that's fine to the degree that there's another position to what they said to you, that's what I'd like to be able to at least input to you, in your commentary you might want to frame.

RS: That would be more than welcome.

JW: And I understand even in terms of your perspective, you have a perspective, we may believe in a lot of the same things but that doesn't mean that your voice is my voice and vice versa. I'm aware of that.

RS: As a matter of fact, I would be honored if you would write the foreword to the book, which means that you would have the opportunity to read it and give your take on it, too.

JW: And let's do this, we'll stay strategic on that. I accept the suggestion and the thought, but let's see down the road, we don't have to lock in today, because if it's not strategically feasible, then we won't do it. There are other ways of still accomplishing that end, right?

RS: Or a blurb! You know on the back of books how you see blurbs from different people? Anything like that. Things to consider.

JW: Want to be strategic and make sure it gets out there.

RS: Not only that, make sure it gets out there and gets the attention that I'm seeking it to get. That I'm bringing an analysis and historical information that has been overlooked or ignored and I'm accurate as best as possible.

Female Voice: Is this still being recorded?

RS: Yes. At this point, if you don't' have anything else we can say this is the end of the interview, and I'll be sending you a copy of the transcript.

JW: That's fine.

RS: Thank you.

INDEX

Africa 14, 18, 26n7, 56, 57, 80–81, 83–84, 90, 96–99, 104–5, 110–11, 114, 116–17, 123, 130–31, 136–37, 142, 146, 149, 158, 163–68, 181, 215, 222, 225, 232, 241, 242, 247, 262, 275
Afro-American 13, 16, 19, 35, 50, 52, 54–55, 71–72, 75, 77, 80–84, 86–89, 91–94, 97, 104, 110–15, 118, 120–24, 126–33, 135, 137, 139, 143–45, 152–58, 160–61, 222, 224, 232, 235, 239–40, 242, 245, 280
Afro-Asian Journalist Association in Djakarta 94
Afro-Cuban 14–17, 95, 143
Ahmad, Akbar Muhammad 12; *see also* Stanford, Maxwell
Alabama 42, 44–45, 71, 91–93, 161, 166
Algiers 95, 97, 105
Allende, Salvador 15, 73
American Quarterly 28n59
anticolonialism 20
armed resistance 128, 134, 163, 237, 238
armed self defense xxii, 1, 3–5, 7, 11, 13, 83, 112, 123, 128, 134, 165, 223, 249–51, 279
The Asahi Journal 180, 183, 189–92, 197, 205, 211, 212, 220–21
Asia 24, 26n7, 80, 83–85, 90, 95, 103–5, 110, 112, 123, 124, 130, 136, 142, 149, 215, 224, 247, 250, 293

Baldwin, James 142, 151
Baldwin, Michigan xxi, xxii, 25, 34–35, 247, 250, 255–78, 353–55, 357, 359
Baraka, Amiri 15, 274; *see also* Jones, LeRoi
Barnett, Ross (Governor) 131, 137
Batista 142
Bay of Pigs 15
Beijing, China 188, 195, 276, 339
Belgium 97, 149
Bertrand, Russell 132, 138, 146, 215
Bertrand Russell Peace Foundation in London 146
Birmingham, Alabama 42, 44–45, 71, 91–93, 161, 166, 218, 246
Birmingham, Michigan 22–25, 34–35, 76, 171–251, 255–78, 305–6, 308, 314, 318, 320, 323, 332–33, 351, 353, 355

Birmingham Police Department (Michigan) 293
Black armed self defense 11
Black men 71, 128, 132, 134, 138, 162, 349
Black nationalism 4, 12, 16–17, 62, 131, 137, 156, 225, 231
Black Panther Party (BPP) 12, 158, 181–82, 226, 228, 344
Black Panther Party for Self Defense 7, 12, 247, 250, 345
Black Power 4, 11, 18, 25, 84, 128–29, 134–35, 139, 147, 158, 163, 181, 312, 317
Black resistance 5, 32
The Black Scholar 26n5, 27n35, 28n66, 34, 221–34, 253n30
blow up the building 277
Boas, Franz 43
Boggs, Grace Lee 248
Boy Scout league 95
Bracey, John 12
British Civil Liberties Union 23, 226
Brown, H. Rap 12, 163, 181, 222
Brown, John 41, 128–29, 134, 256
Brown v. Board of Education 5, 8
Brussels, Beligum 262–63
Bullett, Audrey Kathryn 273

Cadillac Motor Company 310, 328, 330
Camus, Albert (French essayist) 95
Canada 11, 96–97, 111, 112, 144, 224, 229, 241–42, 338–39
capitalism 79, 231, 234, 251
Carmichael, Stokely (aka Kwame Ture) 12, 18, 163, 181
Carolina Times 46
Castro, Fidel 4, 11–15, 17–18, 22, 28n63, 32–33, 73, 79, 105, 110–22, 141–43, 145, 168n1, 247, 250
Castro, Raul 152
Center for Chinese Studies 25, 34, 173, 250
Central Intelligence Agency (CIA) 105–6, 141–45
Chairman Mao Tse-tung 19, 76, 80, 82–84, 123–24, 127–29, 133, 135, 139, 142, 239, 250
Charlotte, N.C. 58, 249, 267

Charlotte News 252n14
Charlotte Observer 268
China (Peking) xxi, 1, 4–5, 12–25, 28n52, 32–34, 74, 76, 80–84, 89–90, 97, 103, 107–69, 174, 176, 180, 183, 194, 198–99, 204, 211, 215, 221, 224–26, 228–29, 233, 239, 246–47, 250, 268, 278–80, 337–39, 341–43, 346, 356, 360
China and Black America 129, 228, 344
Christianity 360
Civil Rights Act of 1964 251
civil rights movement xxii, 4, 7, 163, 164, 182, 206, 250–51, 332–35, 337, 357
Clarke, John Henrik 15
Cleveland 222
Cohen, Robert Carl xxii, 17, 19, 26n8, 28n64, 275, 342
COINTELPRO 342
Cold War 4–5, 12, 25, 26n7, 43, 343
Cole, James (Catfish) 6
colonialism 14, 21, 84, 124, 130, 136
colonization 29n88
Committee to Aid in Defense of Robert F. Williams 24, 210, 218, 221
Committee to Combat Racial Injustice (CCRI) 9–10, 37, 48–49
communism 24, 86–87, 126, 343, 354
Communist Party 16, 33, 42, 65–66, 105, 119, 144, 182, 187, 195, 198, 225, 276
Communist Party, United States of America (CPUSA) 12, 16, 18, 105, 112, 114, 142, 144, 151, 241–42
communists 11, 13–14, 16, 18, 19, 24, 32, 45, 65–66, 97, 105, 196, 229, 241, 337, 356
Congress 25, 28n62, 92, 153, 211, 217
Congress of Racial Equality 28n62
Conyers, John 181, 195, 197
counterrevolutionary 95, 97, 121, 122, 131, 137, 145
Crowder, Richard 67–68
Crusader 72, 360
The Crusader (*The Crusader-in-Exile*) xiv, xv, xvii, xxii, 10–12, 16, 18–21, 24, 29n75, 29n77, 32–33, 54, 72, 74–75, 95, 104, 108–9, 112, 140, 142, 144, 147, 148, 157, 221, 248, 250–51, 260, 280, 293, 336, 338, 340, 342–44, 346, 350, 359–60
Crusader-in-Exile 13, 16, 18–21, 29n75, 32, 34, 74–75, 104, 108–9
Cruse, Harold 11, 15, 26n8
Cuba xxi, 4–5, 11–22, 24–25, 26n1, 27n42, 28n63, 32–34, 54, 65–66, 71, 73–106, 108, 110–22, 124, 127, 141–45, 149, 152–53, 163, 167, 168n1, 180, 194, 198–99, 215, 221, 224–25, 229, 234, 236, 240, 242, 244, 246–47, 250–51, 267, 274–76, 279–80, 332–33, 336–39, 341–44, 356, 359–60

Cuban Embassy 143, 148, 168n1
Cuban Foreign Ministry 144
Cuban Revolution 12–16, 18–19, 65–66, 79, 88, 110, 118–19, 121–22, 142–43, 145, 152–53, 155–56, 275, 343
Cunningham, Calvin 35, 267, 270–72
Current, Gloster 49
Curry, Tommy 4, 26n9

daily worker 193
Dallas, Texas 194, 275
Dares Salaam 23, 28n64, 116, 118, 119, 163, 167, 274, 276–77
Davenport, Jeffrey L. xx, 293, 305
Davis, Angela 12
Davis, Ossie 151
Deacons for Defense and Justice 11
death threats 6, 306
Democratic Party 156, 239
desegregation 26n7, 42–43, 67, 80
Detroit 23–24, 34–35, 43, 57, 60, 161–62, 171–253, 267–68, 275, 277, 307, 319–20, 323, 327–28, 331–33, 342, 353, 356, 359
Detroit Free Press 173, 195, 252n15, 255, 323, 332
Detroit News 29n84, 172
Detroit race riot 60
Djakarta 94, 96
Douglass, Frederick xxii, 4, 8, 345
Du Bois, Shirley Graham xxii, 4
Du Bois, W. E. B. xxii, 4

Eastland, James O. 42, 181
ebony 296
Eisenhower, Dwight D. 9, 224
English School of the Air, Havana 77, 79
Europe 28n56, 80, 95, 97–100, 102, 104, 108, 122, 147, 154, 157, 161, 230
Evers, Medgar 244
exile xxi, 5, 8, 11–13, 15–18, 26n1, 27n42, 32, 104, 110, 112, 144–46, 160–61, 163, 180, 194, 199, 221, 225, 247, 250, 279, 320, 329–30, 338–39

Fair Play For Cuba Committee (FPCC) 12–13, 15–16, 32, 33, 71, 73, 105–6, 142, 250, 274, 275
Farmer, James 209
Federal Bureau of Investigation (FBI) xxii, 11, 15–18, 24, 26n12, 33–35, 78, 80, 95, 105–6, 141, 173, 181, 184, 187, 224, 225, 229, 239, 246, 250, 273, 293, 311, 327, 333, 342–43, 345
Fever, Constance 11
Fifth Amendment 198
FiveCAP, Inc 35, 36n5, 249, 272–73, 316, 319–21, 325–26, 329–30
Ford Motor Company 249

INDEX

Foreman, James 11, 26n8
Fourteenth Amendment 7, 9, 46, 65, 279
France 16, 99–101, 103, 108, 145–46, 149, 153–54, 168
Franck, Hans Goran 153, 155–56, 158
freedom 3–4, 8, 12–14, 21, 45, 53, 55, 81–85, 87–89, 91, 93, 103, 112, 118–19, 121–25, 127, 129, 133, 135, 139–41, 143, 145–46, 149, 160, 161, 168, 175, 221, 227, 233–35, 237, 240, 242–43, 246, 250–51, 274, 278, 281, 337
Freedom Riders 11, 53, 68–69, 247, 250

Galloway, Karen 356
Garuda Airport 94
Garvey, Amy Jacques 4
Garvey, Marcus M. xxii, 349
General Baker 251, 332
Ghana 96
Gibson, Richard T. (Acting Executive Secretary of Fair Play for Cuba Committee) 15–17, 22–23, 28n56, 28n57, 29n79, 29n81, 29n82, 32–33, 71, 73, 94–106, 122, 145–58, 161–62, 262–63, 274–79
Glaude, Eddie, Jr. 281
Gosse, Van 15
Graham, Shirley xxii, 4; *see also* Du Bois, Shirley Graham
Grand Rapids, Michigan 247, 268, 323–24
Great Cultural Revolution 103
Green, Bertha 71
Greensboro, N.C. 54, 161, 335
Grimes, Carl 268
Guevara, Ernesto "Che" 18, 28n63, 105, 113, 144, 247, 250
Guinea 72

Hall, Gus 225
Hall, Gwendolyn Midlo 3, 24, 29n85, 34, 251, 258, 287, 356
Hanoi 19, 84–88, 92, 95, 124–27, 160, 247
Harlem 51–52, 57, 87, 106n3, 127, 156, 160, 229
Havana 15, 19, 73–106, 108, 112–15, 117–18, 120, 142–44, 147–49, 156, 175, 234, 276
Henderson, Errol A. 29n88
Henry, Milton Robinson 23–24, 110, 161–62, 171–72, 275, 277, 351; *see also* Obadele, Gaidi
Henry, Patrick 3–5
Henry, Richard (aka Obadele, Imari) 12, 18, 23, 162–63, 172
Hill, Denise 27n20
Hitler, Adolf 80, 87, 93, 126, 132, 138, 236, 240, 260
Ho Chi Minh 21, 33, 247, 250
Hodgkin's disease 247, 251
Hokason, Tore 94–104

Hoover, J. Edgar 15, 32, 181, 229
House, Gloria 26n1, 72n3
Howard, Charles P. 94, 162
Howard University 233
human rights 13, 22–25, 33, 35, 36n4, 41, 53, 75, 81, 83, 86, 93, 123, 125, 130, 132, 136, 138, 160, 161, 164, 174, 180, 185, 187, 190, 193–201, 203–5, 207–8, 215, 217, 219–34, 238–39, 247, 264–65, 274, 279–81, 320, 327, 354
hypocrisy 31, 85, 88, 90, 124, 140, 161, 266, 279, 280
hypocrites 44, 89, 130, 136, 267

Idlewild, Michigan xxi, 25, 35, 36n3, 268, 273, 305, 307–9, 314, 320, 326, 331, 354
imperialism 15, 21, 54, 80, 82–83, 85–88, 95, 102–4, 110, 112, 121–28, 130–34, 136–40, 145–46, 148, 160, 240, 251, 275
Indians 9, 44
integration 11, 43, 62, 165, 223, 242, 337; *see also* desegregation

Jackson, Kellie Carter 8, 27n26, 27n28, 42
Jackson, Mississippi 87, 127
Japanese Committee for the Defense of Robert F. Williams 182, 195, 198, 200, 203, 207–8, 210, 215, 217, 219–20
jazz 17, 147, 361
Jim Crow 31, 41–45, 67, 89, 224, 280
John Birch Society 237, 241, 260
Johnson C. Smith College 249
Johnson, Charles 251
Johnson, Ethel 6, 7, 10, 17, 35, 36n3, 320, 336
Johnson, Lyndon Blaine (U.S. President) 82–83, 86–87, 91, 125–27, 129, 135, 137–38, 160–61
Jones, LeRoi 15, 184, 222, 274; *see also* Baraka, Amiri
Jones, R. Ray, III 153
The Journal of Black Studies 29n86, 36n4
Justice Department 11, 53, 99, 239

Kagan, Richard 188, 194, 206, 212
Karenga, Ron 22
Kelleher, Max 4, 26n9
Kelly, Frances 146
Kennedy, John F. (U. S. President) 15–16, 21, 78, 80–81, 89–90, 130–31, 164, 194, 201, 238–39
Kennedy, Robert F. (U. S. Attorney General) 33, 50, 54, 55
Kenya 262
King, Martin Luther, Jr. xxii, 6, 56, 63, 97, 112, 113, 144, 156, 161, 164, 166, 168, 181, 205, 215, 236–37, 248, 251
King of Prussia 103

Kissing Case 8–10, 32, 249
Kissinger, Henry 25, 34
Ku Klux Klan (KKK) 6–7, 11, 13, 41, 52–55, 61, 80–81, 87, 104, 126, 129, 131–32, 135, 137–38, 142, 163, 182, 220, 237, 239, 241, 248–49, 273

labor 4, 29n76, 44, 83, 90, 123, 130, 136, 166, 246, 327, 340, 355
Lake County, Michigan xxii, 22–25, 35, 36n4, 249, 261, 264
Lake County Enterprise Board 35, 274
Lake County Enterprise Zone 328
Lake County Sheriff Department 293, 311
Lake County Star 25, 35, 36n3, 36n5, 256, 265–66, 272–74
Latin America 15, 26n7, 79, 81, 84–85, 90, 103, 105, 110–12, 121, 123–24, 130, 136, 142, 250, 293, 337
Left 156, 161, 276
Lewis, John 71
liberation xxii, 1, 4, 16, 20–21, 29, 29n88, 53, 59, 62–67, , 79–81, 84–85, 87, 91–93, 102–3, 120–21, 123–25, 127, 129, 131–32, 135, 137, 143, 151, 155, 160–62, 221–22, 229, 230, 240, 243, 247, 250–51, 293, 341, 343
life 8, 12, 17, 18, 22, 32, 36, 54, 56, 65, 78, 89–91, 104, 118, 160, 165, 175, 180, 184, 187, 190, 192, 194–97, 200–201, 203, 207, 215, 217, 225, 227, 234, 239, 243–44, 247–48, 264, 266, 267, 273–74, 293, 329–30, 334, 337, 344, 350, 352–55
London News-Chronicle 9
Louis, Joe 13, 89
Lumumba, Patrice 52
Luxembourg 262–63
lynching 10, 31–32, 45, 48, 56, 59–60, 70, 222
Lynn, Conrad 9, 46–47, 174, 355–56

McCarthyism 103
McDuffie's, Erik 20, 22, 29n80
McGrath, Tom 96
McLean, Charles A. 49
Madrid 101
Malcolm X xxii, 3–4, 12, 21, 95, 106n3, 142, 163, 242, 247, 250, 281, 320
Mallory, Willie Mae 3, 17–18, 28n60, 28n62, 32, 51, 67–69, 110, 283
Manchanda, Gerrade A. (Secretary British Vietnam Solidarity Front) 95, 104, 156, 158
manhood 160, 251, 265
Mao Zedong 14, 74, 247, 344–45, 350
march on Washington 240
Marine Corps xxii, 5, 7, 27n12, 31, 39, 78, 249

Marines 5
Martinez, Betita 276
Marxist Leninist Quarterly 234–35
Marxist-Leninist 15, 22, 94–104, 131, 137, 145–46, 151, 154, 281
Marxist-Leninist Communist Party of Belgium 103
Maryland University 41
Marzani and Munsell 26n1
Mayfield, Julian 28n56, 96, 142
Medford, Massachusetts 258, 259
Mexican 83, 123, 130, 136
Michigan xxi, xxii, 22–25, 34–35, 36n4, 76, 171–253, 255–81, 305–6, 308, 314, 318, 320, 323, 332–33, 346, 353, 355
Michigan State Police (Reed City) 293, 308, 318, 332
Michigan State University 351
Michigan Supreme Court 176, 184, 220–21, 332
middle class 5, 7, 154, 248
migration 166
Milliken, William 24, 215, 217, 229
Minken, Helen 46
minority 12, 15, 63, 75, 83, 86, 126, 129–30, 134–36, 187–88, 222, 231, 273, 277
Mississippi 21, 31, 42–43, 80, 86–87, 94, 126–27, 130–31, 136–37, 143, 163, 166, 181, 199, 238, 246
Mitchell, John 215, 217
Monroe, NC xxi, 3–13, 31–32, 37–73, 81, 105, 130, 141, 163, 173, 180, 183–85, 194–98, 210–11, 213, 215, 239, 246–47, 249–50, 258, 273–74, 280, 327, 330, 355
Monroe Defense Committee 17, 32, 50–51, 55, 105
Monroe Enquirer 10
Monroe Police Department 239
Monroe-Union County Civic League 47–48, 53, 249
Montgomery, Alabama 44–45, 61, 64, 223
Montgomery Bus Boycott 6, 31, 61, 223
Montgomery Improvement Association 6
Montreal, Canada 97
Moore, Audley "Queen Mother" 172, 259
Moore, Carlos and Crisis of the Negro Intellectual 16–17, 28n65, 143, 158
Morley, Jefferson 16
Morrison, Lionel 22, 94
Morrison Training School for Negroes 9
Murray, Pauli 46
music 17, 20, 111, 147, 234, 301, 330, 345, 361

Nakajima, Yorkio 34, 194, 200–206, 209–10, 216, 220
Nation xvi, 8, 13–14, 28n63, 29n88, 34–36, 41, 44–45, 49–50, 55, 66, 81, 86, 89–91, 130–31,

136–37, 161, 166, 182, 217, 239, 242, 244, 246, 250, 255–69, 273, 275, 277, 357–58
Nation of Islam 250
National Association for the Advancement of Colored Peoples (NAACP) xxi, 3, 5–7, 9–12, 28n54, 31–32, 35, 37, 42–43, 46–49, 51–52, 56, 61–64, 70, 89, 141, 184, 223–24, 244, 247–49, 273–74, 333, 354
National Rifle Association (NRA) 6, 348
The Nationalist 52, 116, 242, 280, 343
Negroes with Guns xiv, 7, 13, 16–17, 22, 26n1, 27n13, 27n19, 32, 72n3, 77, 97–98, 100, 101, 104, 122, 146, 148, 150, 152–53, 221, 233, 250, 275, 330–32
Nelson, Ruby 25, 35, 36nn4–5, 249, 265, 317, 322–28, 353
Nelson, Truman 37
New Year 35, 266–70
New York City 142
New York Times 58, 175, 184, 195, 212, 252n4, 252n14
News and Observer (Raleigh, N.C.) 47, 273
Newton, Huey P. xix, xxii, xxiiin2, 12, 22, 25, 27n39, 222
Nichols, Al 255
Nichols, Kenneth xx
Nixon, E. D. 24, 35, 156, 181, 183, 194–95, 211, 217, 219, 222, 231, 276
Nixon, Richard 24, 156, 181, 183, 194–95, 217, 219, 222, 231, 276
Nkrumah, Kwame 121, 342
North Carolina xxi, 3, 10, 11, 23–25, 26n8, 27n20, 27n34, 34–35, 37–73, 79, 105, 140–41, 154, 163, 167, 173, 176, 180, 184–85, 215, 223–24, 229, 239, 246–47, 249, 252n14, 263, 267, 273, 280, 320, 327, 330, 332–34, 353, 355–56, 360
Northeastern University 259
Nyerere, Julius 116–18

Obadele, Gaidi xv, 12, 22, 162–63, 171–72
O'Brien, Lawrence (Postmaster General of the U.S.) 140
Oriente, Edizioni 147, 155
Oswald, Lee 15–16, 33, 201, 275

Pablo 96
Pacifism 52
Pamphlet in Support of Robert F. Williams 212, 252n19, 286
Pan Africanist 22–23, 103, 158
Pan-Africanism *see* Black nationalism
Parks, Rosa 3, 5–7, 27n15, 31, 38–39, 255, 332
Peking, China 107–70, 246
The Peking Review 168
Pentonville Prison 226

People's Republic of China (PRC) 19–20, 84, 124, 133, 139, 239, 250
Perry, Albert 3, 5–7, 9, 50, 53
Petit, Andy 18
Plinton, James 23
Plummer, Brenda Gayle 7, 27n23
police brutality 25, 35, 86, 125, 131, 137, 238, 249, 353
Progressive Party 8
Puerto Ricans 83, 123, 130, 136, 144, 242

race riots 60, 250
racial violence 10, 12, 280
Radio Free Dixie xxii, 13, 16–17, 19, 26n8, 27n38, 27n46, 28n61, 32, 91, 93, 110–12, 142, 146–47, 150, 250, 280, 343, 361
Radio Havana Cuba 15, 104, 110, 116, 118, 143
Ragsdale, George R. 140–41
rape 10, 130, 136, 199, 249, 266, 328
Reape, Harold 32, 67–68
reconstruction 8, 231
red flags 95
Reed, Mary Ruth 10
Regis, Signora 101, 155
Reitan, Ruth 14, 27n49
reparations 167, 348–49
Republic of New Africa (RNA) 7, 12, 22, 24–25, 33–34, 162–63, 165–66, 173–74, 246–47, 250, 275, 319, 348–50
resistance xxii, 1, 3, 5–12, 29n86, 31–32, 34, 36n4, 43–44, 60–61, 64–65, 82, 85, 91–92, 124, 128, 133–34, 139–40, 163, 223, 237–38, 240, 247–51, 274, 279, 352
revolution 7, 12–16, 18–19, 44, 70, 71, 75–77, 79, 81, 83–85, 88, 92–93, 103, 105–6, 110, 113, 116, 118, 121–25, 127, 133, 137, 142–43, 145, 150, 152–53, 155–56, 163, 201, 232, 235–36, 246, 250, 267, 275, 281, 337, 341–45, 347
Revolutionary Action Movement (RAM) 7, 12, 19, 22, 25, 33, 75, 84, 87, 92, 102, 104, 124, 127, 141–45, 247, 250, 277
Revolutionary Patriots of Cuba 88
Rittenberg, Sidney 341–42
Robert F. Williams Defense Committee 34
Robeson, Paul xxii, xxiiin2
Robinson, Mabel Ola xxii; *see also* Williams, Mabel R.
Roosevelt, Franklin D. 267
Royal Canadian Mounted Police 11
Ruby Nelson Legal Defense Fund 36n4, 212, 218; *see also* Nelson, Ruby
Rucker, Walter xix, 26n5, 27n22, 27n50
rumors 18, 32, 199, 265
Rushing, George 50
Russell Foundation 146

San Francisco 15, 197
Sanchez, Celia 120
Santiago De Cuba 13
Scandinavia 98–99, 104, 146, 149
Schliefer, Marc "Mark," David 26n1, 146
Schultz, John 32, 56–67
Scott, Ron 248
Seale, Bobby 12
segregation 10, 41, 42, 48, 81, 241
self-defense 1, 3–5, 7–8, 11–13, 26n6, 26n9, 46, 55, 60–61, 81, 83, 85, 87, 103, 112–13, 124, 127–28, 134, 165, 180, 223, 230, 236–37, 247, 249–51, 270, 273–74, 279; *see also* armed resistance
Senior, Paula Marie xix, 28n60
sexual violence *see* rape
sexuality 9
Shanghai 20, 90
Shrine of the Black Madonna
Sibeko, David xv, 110, 162
Simmons, Charles E. xix, 248, 251, 332
Simpson, David Ezell "Fuzzy" 8
Sims, Stanley U. (Reverend) 272
sit-ins 61, 66, 224, 249, 334–35
slavery 8, 15, 43, 59, 86, 126, 130, 136, 166–67, 360
socialist party 66
socialist worker's party 7, 9, 37, 105
spirituals 15, 251, 332–33, 335, 345, 355, 358
Stanford, Maxwell 12, 22, 145, 222, 251, 349; *see also* Ahmad, Akbar Muhammad
State Department 16, 24, 33, 54, 78–79, 141–45, 171, 174, 225, 247, 278
Stockholm 101, 154–56, 158, 161, 276
Student Nonviolent Coordinating Committee (SNCC) xiv, 75, 155, 184, 250, 357
SUNY 29n88
Supreme Court, U. S. 5, 8, 61, 164
Surge, Thomas 4
Shrine of the Black Madonna 296, 328
Sutherland, Bill 23
Sutton, Sissy 9
Sweden 16, 97, 98, 100–101, 104, 120, 144, 146, 149–50, 153–56, 161, 168, 246, 276
Swedish 22, 32, 97, 100, 104–5, 146, 150, 153–56, 158, 161, 276
Switzerland 95, 97, 99, 101, 262

Taber, Robert 15, 35, 105, 272, 274–75
Tanzanian government 119, 162, 225
Theoharris, Jeanne xix, 6
Thomas Fortune, T. 4
Thompson, Hanover 8
Three Continents Conference 98
Thurman, Strom 174, 266
Till, Emmett 31, 80, 334

time 5, 9, 13, 15, 17–18, 21–24, 33–34, 42, 44, 46, 49, 51–52, 54, 56–59, 61, 62, 64, 66, 68, 69, 71, 76, 78, 88–89, 92–94, 96–97, 100, 103, 105, 112–14, 120–22, 129, 132–33, 135, 139, 141, 145–48, 150, 152–53, 160, 162–64, 166–68, 174, 176, 180–82, 184–87, 189–93, 195–97, 199–200, 202–5, 207, 216–17, 221–26, 228–29, 231, 236–37, 239–40, 242–43, 245, 266–70, 272, 275, 305–8, 310–27, 330–46, 349–51, 353, 355–61
Toronto, Canada 96
Toronto University 96
Trans World Airline (TWA) xv, 23–24, 29n82, 171, 227–29, 277
Tripp, Luke xix, 251
Trotskyite 65, 103, 146, 156
Trucks, Mary L. 249, 274, 293, 319; *see also* FiveCAP, Inc.
Truman, Harry S. xiii
Tubman, Harriet 4
Tuffs University xvi, 258–59
Tyson, Timothy B. xix, xxii, 6, 9, 25, 26n1, 27n38, 27n46, 28n61, 72n3, 268

Uhuru 114, 251
U.S.-China Peoples' Friendship Association 263
U.S.-China Relations xvii, 35, 259
Underground Railroad 338
Union County, N.C. xiv, xvi, 3, 5, 9–10, 18, 31, 46–49, 52–54, 70, 72n3, 73, 140–41, 173, 223, 239, 249
Unitarian Fellowship 31, 36n1, 41–45, 249
United Nations 13, 57, 59, 66, 72, 81, 86, 105, 110–11, 115, 117, 125, 137, 239
United States (U.S.) 1, 4–6, 10, 12–14, 16–19, 21–25, 28n54, 34–35, 41, 44–45, 61, 64–65, 77–82, 85–93, 99, 102
United States Embassy 167, 225, 228, 277
University of Alabama 44
University of Massachusetts-Amherst 346
University of Michigan 25, 3372n2, 173, 175, 188, 197, 199, 212, 218, 250, 346
University of North Carolina 26n8, 27n20, 41

VanderMeer, Buck 273
Verges, Jacques 96, 101, 103, 105–6
Veteran xxii, 4–7, 31, 78, 247, 280, 333, 355
Vietnam 19, 21, 24, 28n62, 33–35, 82, 84–88, 91–93, 96, 106n3, 123–28, 130–32, 134, 136–38, 146, 153–54, 156, 160–61, 166, 192, 229, 236, 240, 250, 278
Vietnam Solidarity Conference 146
Vietnam War 19, 21, 146, 192, 196, 278
Vietnamese 85, 87, 124, 127, 131, 137, 146, 160, 180, 276, 345
violence 4, 8, 10–12, 16–17, 32, 46, 48, 51, 53, 59–65, 67, 70, 80–82, 85–87,

125–35, 145, 161, 164, 180, 181, 223, 230, 233, 236–37, 248, 249, 265, 273, 280, 316
voter registration 43, 48
Voting Rights Act of 1965 8

Washington, Booker T. xxii
Watts, Daniel 156
Wayne State University 26n1, 34, 72n3, 172, 251, 253n31, 346
Weissman, George 9
Wells, Ida Barnett 4, 8, 131
West Indian Standing Conference 162
West Virginia State College 249
White Citizens' Council 43, 48, 52, 239, 273
White, Georgia 10
White Supremacy 16, 21, 82, 86–87, 91, 93, 126
white womanhood 266
Whiting, Allen 34
Wilkins, Roy 32, 46–47, 52, 71, 229
Williams, Edward "Pete" 39, 96

Williams, Franklin xiv
Williams, John Chambers 14, 20, 28n52, 32, 293
Williams, John Herman xix, 261
Williams, Mabel R. 3, 26n6, 172, 247
Williams, Robert, Jr. 11, 14, 33, 249, 352
Wilson, Woodrow III xix, 6–7, 9, 17, 50, 53, 323–24, 326
womanhood 265–66
World War II xxii, 5–6
Worthy, Bill 95–96

X, Malcolm xxii, 3, 4, 12, 95, 106n3, 142, 163, 242, 247, 250, 281, 320; *see also* Malcolm X

Yankee oppressors 88
Yankees 83, 88, 97, 149, 241
Yawen, Yang xx

Zambia 262

Milton Keynes UK
Ingram Content Group UK Ltd.
UKHW012353190624
444195UK00007B/46